# Pathology of Neck Injury

*Pathology of Neck Injury, Second Edition* is a practical guide and reference to all pathological aspects of neck injury. It covers a broad spectrum of trauma to the neck region, reflecting the experiences of many distinguished pathologists and those of author, Peter Vanezis, who has more than 50 years of expertise in the field.

This highly illustrated text begins by explaining the anatomy of the neck region as it relates to trauma investigation and the various techniques required for its examination. Coverage goes on to describe penetrating injuries, comprising mainly sharp force trauma and firearm injuries. Asphyxial and related deaths are subsequently discussed in a series of chapters, before the focus turns to the examination of blunt impact, non-compressive injuries. Here special reference is made to their common occurrence in road traffic accidents. Finally, this book concludes with environmental, toxic, and iatrogenic causes of injury. Where appropriate, and especially with regard to penetrating and compressive modes of trauma, the interpretation of injuries and their differentiation into various categories such as homicide, suicide, or accident has been addressed.

*Pathology of Neck Injury, Second Edition* is an essential guide for all those involved in the relevant specialties of pathology, surgery, and forensic medicine – particularly pathologists, both qualified and in training, but also to clinical forensic practitioners, trauma specialists, ENT surgeons, and general surgeons.

# Pathology of Neck Injury

## Second Edition

Peter Vanezis

CRC Press
Taylor & Francis Group
Boca Raton London New York

CRC Press is an imprint of the
Taylor & Francis Group, an **informa** business

Designed cover image: Peter Vanezis

Second edition published 2026

by CRC Press

2385 NW Executive Center Drive, Suite 320, Boca Raton FL 33431
and by CRC Press

4 Park Square, Milton Park, Abingdon, Oxon, OX14 4RN

*CRC Press is an imprint of Taylor & Francis Group, LLC*



First edition published by Butterworth 1989



ISBN: 9781041111443 (hbk)
ISBN: 9781041111436 (pbk)
ISBN: 9781003658467 (ebk)

DOI: 10.4324/9781003658467

Typeset in Berling LT Std
by codeMantra

# CONTENTS

# ABOUT THE AUTHOR

**Peter Vanezis,** OBE, M.B., Ch.B., M.D., Ph.D., F.R.C.Path., F.R.C.P. (Glasg.), F.F.F.L.M., F.C.S.F.S., F.R.S.M., F.A.F.M.S. (UK), D.M.J. (Path) is Professor Emeritus of Forensic Medical Sciences at the University of London. After qualifying in Medicine at the University of Bristol Medical School in 1972, the author began his career in Forensic Medicine in 1974 at the London Hospital specialising in pathology, and then as a Regius Professor at the University of Glasgow, before returning to Queen Mary University of London. In 2010, he established the Academy of Forensic Medical Sciences and became an Emeritus Professor at the University of London in 2018. The author has been involved in many high-profile cases and participated and led teams in aircraft accidents and other mass disasters. He was made an OBE in 2001 for Forensic Pathology Services in Kosovo. Whilst in Glasgow, he established the first Human Identification Centre and the Centre for International Forensic Assistance. He was a member of the Forensic Advisory Board of the International Committee of the Red Cross for many years and had arranged numerous courses on human rights abuses locally and abroad. He has authored over 160 publications in peer-reviewed journals, authored four textbooks, and contributed numerous chapters in textbooks. He has also been a past president of the British Academy of Forensic Sciences and a past editor-in-chief of *Medicine, Science and the Law* (currently Emeritus EC). He is currently Vice-Chairman of Digital Autopsy UK and Honorary President of the Balkan Academy of Forensic Sciences. His research interests include various aspects of forensic pathology, identification, and developing educational needs. He has received three awards for his research from the British Medical Association (BMA) as well as a number of other substantial grants.

# CONTRIBUTORS

**Michael Freeman,** PhD, MedDRA, MSc, MPH
Associate Professor of Forensic Medicine and Epidemiology,
University of Maastricht
(Contributed to Chapter 1 'Introduction' on matters dealing with epidemiology)

**Christopher Paul Johnson,** OBE, BSc, MBChB, MD, FRCPath, DMJ
Formerly Senior Lecturer, Sub-Department of Forensic Pathology,
Royal Liverpool University Hospital
(Contributed to sections on investigative techniques in Chapter 3 and general aspects vertebral artery trauma in Chapter 11)

**Curtis Offiah** BSc, MBChB, FRCS, FRCR
Consultant Neuroradiologist and Head and Neck Radiologist at St Bartholomew's and The Royal London Hospitals
(Contributed to sections in relation to imaging of neck trauma in Chapters 2–4, 6, and 11)

**Andrew Peter Vanezis,** PhD, MB ChB, MRCP(UK), BSc
Consultant Cardiologist, Trent Cardiac Centre,
Nottingham City Hospital, Nottingham, UK
(Contributed to Chapter 13 on injuries caused during therapeutic and investigative techniques)

# PREFACE TO THE SECOND EDITION

This second edition is long overdue, and its production has been driven by the encouragement of colleagues who continue to find the first edition, published 35 years ago, valuable as a practical adjunct to case investigation and use in court.

In addition to fatalities seen at autopsy by the pathologist, I have included a number of cases relevant to clinicians dealing with patient management. It is hoped, that by doing so, such a clinico-pathological approach will enhance the understanding of neck injury from all perspectives.

I have maintained the same order of chapter titles, with very few modifications. The content of each section has been thoroughly updated, with the assistance of my contributors, to account for the many advances in the investigation of such injuries. Older references from the first edition have been retained where still relevant to current practice.

It will also be evident to those who have read the first edition that all the figures are in black and white. In this edition, they are now all in colour. The original black and white images, where no colour versions were available, have been colourised with the assistance of *PhotoPad Professional v13.19 © NCH Software.*

Clinicians and pathologists need to be mindful that the extent of neck injury, particularly when combined with trauma elsewhere, may not be fully appreciated during clinical management or indeed, at autopsy. With this in mind, I have attempted, in this edition, to highlight the challenges that may be encountered during the investigation of such injuries by practitioners and the need for their thorough investigation.

# ACKNOWLEDGEMENTS

Undertaking the task of producing a second edition of this text has been a challenge, considering the first edition was published over 35 years ago. I would firstly wish to thank my four contributors for their invaluable advice on the necessary updates in the field. Professor Michael Freeman made valuable suggestions for the introductory chapter with respect to epidemiological aspects. Dr Curtis Offiah assisted in updating aspects of neck trauma imaging, which has been radically changed by the introduction of modern imaging techniques, including computerised tomography and magnetic resonance imaging. Dr Paul Johnson contributed to the section on modern techniques in the investigation of trauma, particularly involving the vertebral arteries. Dr Andrew Vanezis made a significant contribution to the final chapter, which deals with investigative and therapeutic techniques that may result in neck injury; I am truly grateful to them.

I would also like to acknowledge the help of my personal assistant Adam Konstanciak for his assistance with administration and accessing research engines. Thanks are also extended to my wife, Maria, for her the general support and for proofreading the text.

Finally, I express my gratitude to all mortuary staff and coroners across various regions of the United Kingdom for their assistance in facilitating the inclusion of cases in this book.

# CHAPTER 1

## INTRODUCTION

*Peter Vanezis*
*(with contributions from Michael Freeman)*



Many vital structures are crammed into the neck, which acts as a conduit carrying blood, nerve impulses, and air in both directions as well as food, usually downwards, to the rest of the gastrointestinal tract. Such a region is, therefore unsurprisingly, vulnerable to severe injury, the incidence and extent of which may not be readily appreciated, especially in blunt impact trauma. In cases where there are multiple injuries not confined to the neck, there may be a tendency for the inexperienced observer to concentrate on the more obvious lesions, thus overlooking or delaying the diagnosis of significant injuries to this region.

Indeed, describing the frequency and distribution of neck injuries from various causes in the general population is a complicated task, more so when the injuries of the greatest interest are those with the highest risk of death. This is largely due to the fact that, by far, the majority of neck injuries described from an epidemiological perspective are survivable musculoskeletal injuries, secondary to indirect (*i.e.*, whiplash) or blunt direct trauma. For penetrating trauma, strangulation, and other neck injury mechanisms that carry a substantial risk of death, the frequency and distribution of injuries vary greatly, depending on the country of study.

It has been estimated that neck injuries represent 5–10% of all severe trauma cases. In particular, such injuries related to motor vehicle crashes, suicide, and homicide accounted for 3500 deaths annually from US data (Rathlev et al., 2007). Both blunt and penetrating neck injuries are associated with poor outcomes. In the United States, where firearm ownership is universal, penetrating gunshot wounds account for the majority of potentially fatal neck trauma (Glance et al., 2010), whereas knife wounds account for the majority of injuries seen at autopsy in the United Kingdom and other countries where gun ownership is highly regulated (Zakaria et al, 2022); Mahmoodie et al (2012). Self-inflicted suspension injuries have been found to be more common in Asian countries (Wu et al., 2012).

In road traffic collisions, the incidence of neck injury has, in the past, been generally underestimated, particularly with occult cervical spine lesions. Freeman and Leith (2020), from their analysis of three national databases in the USA, namely, the National Automotive Sampling System-Crashworthiness Data System (NASS-CDS), the Nationwide Emergency Department Sample (NEDS), and the Nationwide Inpatient Sample (NIS), estimated that there are approximately 869,000 traffic crash-related cervical spine injuries seen in hospitals in the US annually, including around 841,000 sprain/strain (whiplash) injuries, 2,800 spinal disk injuries, 23,500 fractures, 2,800 spinal cord injuries, and 1,500 dislocations.

DOI: 10.4324/9781003658467-1

# CATEGORIES OF NECK INJURY

Injuries to the neck fall into several broad categories, bearing in mind that one type is not mutually exclusive of another. The reader will find the different types of injuries described in detail in the chapters that follow.

***Penetrating injuries***:

*Sharp force trauma – stabbing and incised (cut-throat) injuries; firearm injury, cross bow, and other penetrating trauma*

This category includes all forms of sharp force trauma, missile and other penetrating injuries from pointed objects. Penetrating injuries may present difficulties to the clinician because of the often innocuous nature of the surface injury compared to the underlying trauma. Indeed, at autopsy, one is frequently impressed by the length of the wound track and the multiplicity of internal structures injured. Such injuries carry a high mortality risk, particularly in the case of gunshot wounds.

***Non-penetrating injuries***: *Blunt impact trauma with or without breach of the skin; compressive (strangulation and other airway obstruction); blunt trauma from blows/falls/RTC and other direct force impacts to the neck*

This category comprises all forms of blunt impact, including compression. Neck compression may occur in several ways, most commonly by ligature or manual strangulation. In hanging (suspension), as distinct from other forms of constriction, the compressive force is supplied by the victim's weight. An obstructing agent within the neck structures may also result in airway compromise, not only by blocking the larynx or trachea but also by impaction within the pharynx or oesophagus. Complications of neck trauma, such as laryngeal oedema, haemorrhage, or surgical emphysema, may also cause compression.

Non-compressive blunt impact injuries may result from direct trauma to the neck structures or from indirect impact to the head or chest, causing excessive movement of the neck beyond its physiological limits. In addition, injury may result from sudden movement of the head without any form of contact.

When describing blunt impact trauma, it is convenient to divide the neck into anterior and posterior compartments. Although blunt impact trauma is found in either one or the other area, more so than with penetrating injuries, one should nevertheless appreciate that there are no boundaries to trauma, particularly when dealing with multiple impact forces such as those seen in road traffic collisions. Most anterior compartment injuries occur as a result of direct injury, whilst the majority of posterior compartment injuries are caused by indirect trauma or rapid acceleration/deceleration movements.

***Other categories:*** *Burns/radiation and other miscellaneous causes; iatrogenic/investigative causes*

Injuries resulting from toxic and miscellaneous environmental agents are occasionally encountered. These include various types of burn, such as thermal, chemical, and electrical. Damage may also result from radiation exposure (particularly to the thyroid gland), voice misuse, and on rare occasions, there may be laryngeal oedema from wasps and bee stings.

Therapeutic, investigative, and other related actions involving the neck structures may also result in lesions causing significant morbidity. Injuries may follow airway and oesophageal instrumentation or tracheostomy, particularly in those requiring prolonged airway maintenance. Angiographic and other invasive vascular procedures may result in vessel injury. Vascular injuries may also follow chiropractic manipulation or neck traction. Additionally, various surgical procedures, as well as radiotherapy, can cause injury.

## References

Freeman MD, Leith WM. Estimating the number of traffic crash-related cervical spine injuries in the United States; An analysis and comparison of national crash and hospital data. *Accid Anal Prev*. 2020 July;142:105571. doi: 10.1016/j.aap.2020.105571. Epub 2020 May 12. PMID: 32413544.

Glance LG, Osler TM, Dick AW, Mukamel DB, Meredith W.. The survival measurement and reporting trial for trauma (SMARTT): Background and study design. *J Trauma*. 2010;68:1491–1497.

Mahmoodie M, Sanei B, Moazeni-Bistgani M, Namgar M. Penetrating neck trauma: Review of 192 cases. *Arch Trauma Res*. 2012;1(1):14–18.

Rathlev NK, Medzon R, Bracken ME. Evaluation and management of neck trauma. *Emerg Med Clin North Am*. 2007;25:679–94, viii.

Wu KC, Chen YY, Yip PS. Suicide methods in Asia: Implications in suicide prevention. *Int J Environ Res Public Health*. 2012 Apr;9(4):1135–1158.

Zakaria B, Muzaffar J, Borsetto D, Fussey J, Kumar R, Evans K, Pickering C, Reid C, Coulson C, Orr L, Pracy P, Nankivell P, Sharma N. Civilian penetrating neck trauma at a level I trauma centre: A five-year retrospective case note review. *Clin Otolaryngol*. 2022 Jan;47(1):44–51.

# CHAPTER 2

## ANATOMY

*Peter Vanezis*
*(with contributions from Curtis Offiah)*



Detailed descriptions of the structures comprising the neck are to be found in numerous textbooks of anatomy, and it is not my intention to present a comprehensive account here. It is rather to provide an overall topographical picture and selective detailed accounts relevant to the types of injuries discussed in the text.

DOI: 10.4324/9781003658467-2

# ANATOMICAL DIVISION INTO COMPARTMENTS

The anatomical landmarks of the surface of the neck viewed from the front and back are shown in Figure 2.1.

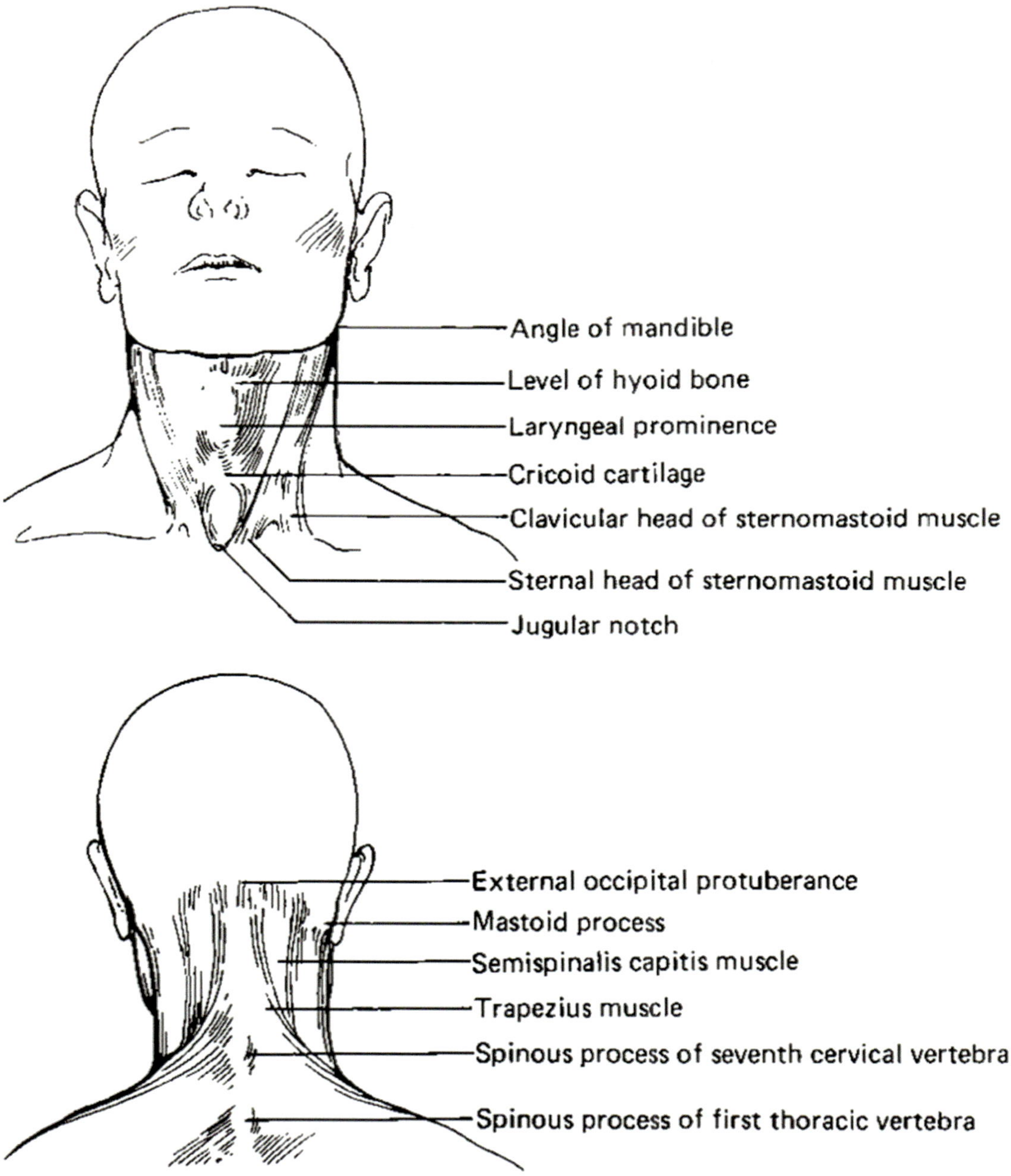


**Figure 2.1** Surface anatomy of the neck.

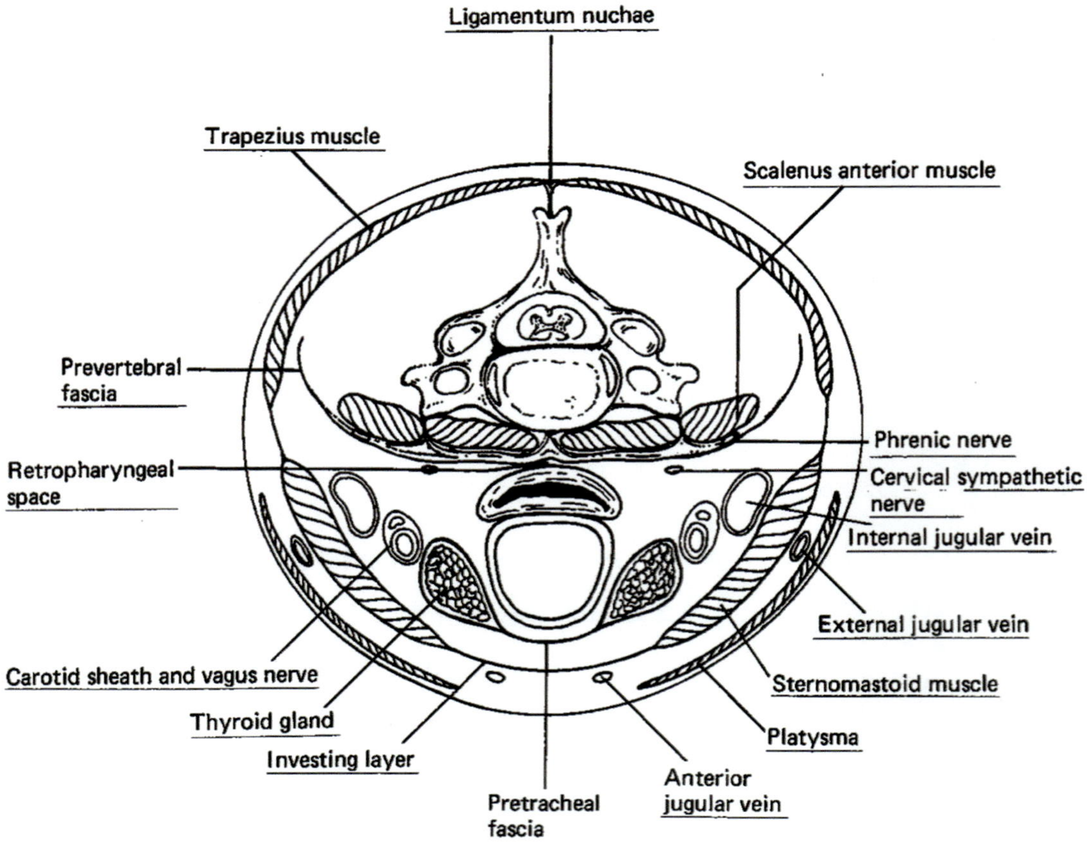


**Figure 2.2** Transverse section through the sixth cervical vertebra showing principal structures and fascial planes.

For the purposes of dissection and detailed examination, the neck may be conveniently divided into anterior and posterior compartments lying on either side of the prevertebral fascia (Figure 2.2), although it should be appreciated that neck trauma is not restricted by boundaries.

## Anterior Compartment

The anterior compartment lies in front of the sheet of prevertebral fascia. In this region of the neck lie the pharynx, oesophagus, larynx, and trachea. In front of these structures, and on either side, lie the carotid sheaths, one on each side of the pharynx. Lying above the larynx is the hyoid bone. It is connected to the mandible by the mylohyoid muscle, which forms the upper limit of the anterior part of the neck. The mylohyoid muscle separates the mouth from the neck. The hyoid bone and larynx are suspended by muscles from the skull. Inferiorly, they are connected by muscles to the sternum and scapula. Beneath these muscles, the thyroid gland, enclosed in the pretracheal fascia, lies alongside the respiratory canal (Figure 2.3).

## Posterior Compartment

The posterior compartment comprises the cervical spine and all its related structures situated behind the prevertebral fascia. The cervical spine arises from the upper border of the first thoracic vertebra, is gently convex forwards, and supports the skull. A mass of extensor musculature lies behind the vertebrae. It is supplied segmentally by the posterior primary rami and supports the cervical spine and head. A much smaller amount of prevertebral flexor musculature lies in front of

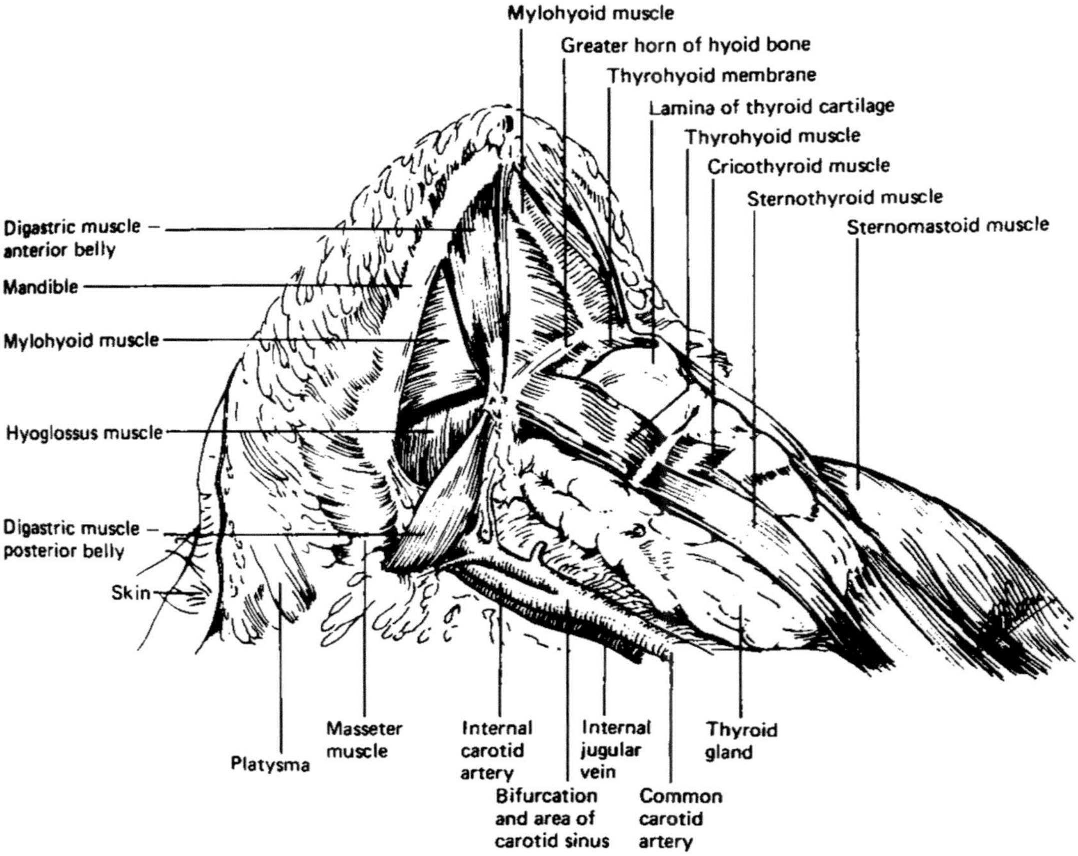


**Figure 2.3** Anterolateral view of the neck from the right side.

the vertebrae and, more laterally, is attached to the thoracic operculum and the scapula. It is supplied segmentally by the anterior primary rami. The whole mass lies flat from side to side behind the pharynx and, from here, curves away posteriorly. It is covered by the prevertebral fascia, which thus forms a vertical sheet passing laterally across the central part of the neck. The function of the prevertebral fascia is to provide a basis upon which the mobile viscera of the neck may move freely.

# DIVISION OF THE NECK EMPLOYED IN THE CLINICAL MANAGEMENT OF INJURIES

In addition to the divisions described above, from the perspective of clinical management of neck trauma, the location of injury can be classified as being either anterior or posterior to the posterior border of the sternocleidomastoid muscle. Furthermore, anterior injury may be further sub-classified into the traditional three zones of the neck first described by Monson et al. (1969) when discussing the management of penetrating trauma to the carotid and vertebral arterial systems (Figure 2.4.)

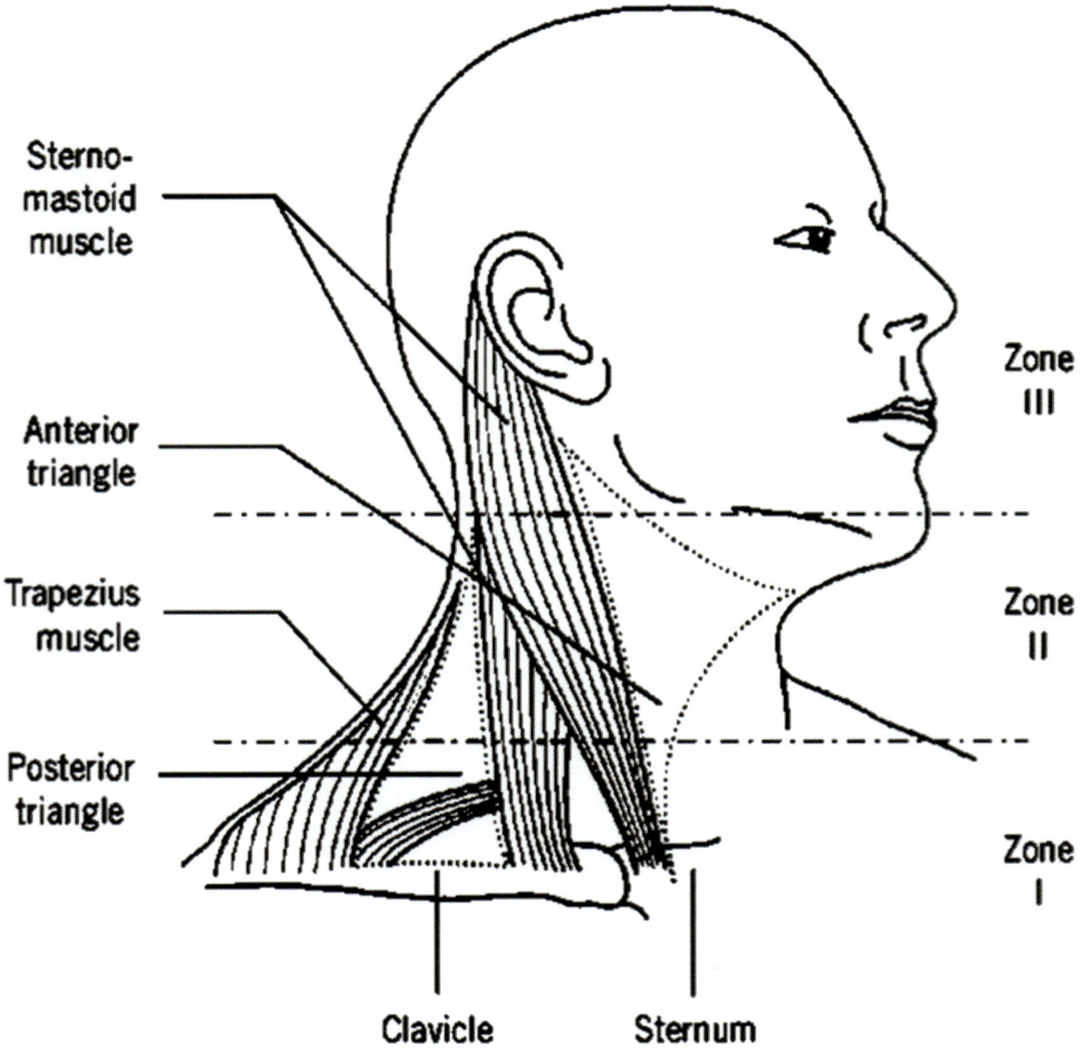


**Figure 2.4** Three zones of the neck: I: Clavicles/sternum to the cricoid cartilage. II: Cricoid cartilage to the angle of the mandible. III: Superior to the angle of the mandible to skull area. Adapted from Nowicki et al. (2018).

# THE LARYNGO-HYOID COMPLEX

In the assessment of injury, the hyoid bone and laryngeal cartilages should be examined together as a complex of associated structures that bear the brunt of trauma resulting from neck compression. A good understanding of the anatomy and the variations seen in both is essential in the analysis of injuries that might be present.

## Embryological Development of the Laryngo-Hyoid Complex

It is important for the pathologist to have a basic understanding of the embryological development of the hyoid bone and laryngeal cartilages to appreciate the variations seen in casework that are described in this chapter.

Bakker et al. (2018) reinvestigated the development of the laryngo-hyoid complex and found it to be a far less complicated process than previously thought, despite the views of most modern textbooks. The formation of the styloid process and both the lesser and greater horns of the hyoid bone derives from the second and third pharyngeal arch cartilages, whereas the body of the hyoid bone develops from the hyoid body anlage with no obvious contribution from the pharyngeal arches. The thyroid and cricoid cartilages develop from mesenchymal condensations in the neck region.

## The Hyoid Bone

The hyoid bone (Figure 2.5) lies suspended in muscle from the tips of the styloid processes of the temporal bones by the stylohyoid ligaments. Consequently, it is very mobile. The floor of the mouth and the tongue are related to it above, and the larynx below, while the epiglottis and the pharynx lie behind it. The bone also provides an adjustable pulley for the digastric muscle.

The hyoid is curved, with its convex aspect facing forward. The central portion of the bone is the body, and on either side are attached the greater horns, which are slender and project backwards. The joints connecting the body with the greater horns are cartilaginous, but after middle age, they become ossified, although there is marked individual variation.

Evans and Knight (1981), in a series of 110 excised hyoids, found complete fusion of the greater horn with the body in 39 subjects and partial fusion in 14. The youngest subject in whom fusion occurred was 18 years of age. At the other end of the age range, there were subjects in their eighth and ninth decades in whom no fusion was found.

More recently, Fisher et al. (2016) examined 136 bones (66 males, 70 females; ages 1–94) using computed tomographic images. They classified fusion into four categories based on whether it was bilateral or unilateral, and whether it was complete or partial. They also found decreasing bone density with age. When fusion has not occurred or is incomplete, allowing some degree of mobility at the joints, the bone may sometimes be mistaken for a fracture unless careful dissection is carried out.

At the junction of the body and greater horn is the lesser horn, projecting upward as a spike of bone (or hyaline cartilage), which is connected by fibrous tissue to the body and, occasionally, to the greater horn by a synovial joint. This joint usually persists throughout life but, in some instances, becomes ankylosed. The ossification of the lesser horn is extremely variable and, unusually, only one side is often found to be ossified.

The stylohyoid ligament originates at the styloid process of the temporal bone at the upper end and inserts into the lesser horn of the hyoid bone. It may be completely or partially ossified (Figure 2.6). Vougiouklakis (2006) described complete ossification of this ligament in 11 cases (0.9%) out of 1,215 forensic autopsies. Seven were males and five females. There were two cases in the second decade, five in the third, three in the fourth, and one in the sixth decade. Nine out of the eleven cases were bilateral. The two unilateral ossifications were on the left side. In one case, a

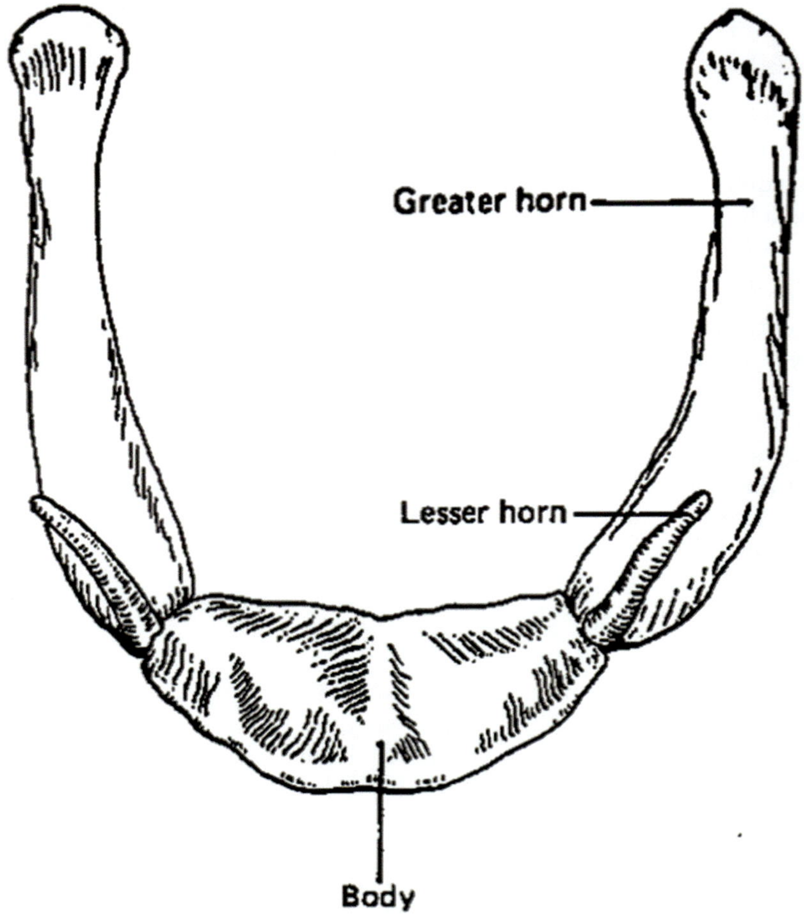


**Figure 2.5** The hyoid bone – anterosuperior view.

fractured ossified stylohyoid ligament was found. In fact, fractures of the ossified ligament are very unusual and may only be seen as an incidental finding at autopsy.

There may be various non-specific general symptoms resulting from ossified styloid ligaments, which are nearly always seen after the age of 30 years, with no predilection for either gender. Eagle's syndrome, also known as stylohyoid syndrome, is commonly characterised by severe facial and mandibular bone pain, especially when chewing, swallowing, or turning the neck. An ossified stylohyoid ligament may also cause difficulty during intubation. Particularly long ossified stylohyoid ligaments were studied in a dry male skull by Skrzat et al. (2007) (Figure 2.7).

## The Larynx

The larynx lies in the front and upper part of the neck, being placed below the tongue and hyoid bone and between the large vessels of the neck. It opens above into the pharynx and below into the trachea. In the midline, it is covered only by skin and cervical fascia. Laterally, it is overlaid by the sternohyoid, sternothyroid, and thyrohyoid muscles and the origin of the inferior constrictor muscles. It is composed of cartilages held together by ligaments and moved by muscle. Its internal surface is lined by mucous membrane. The relationship and arrangement of the cartilages of the larynx, together with the principle ligamentous attachments, are shown in Figures 2.8–2.10.

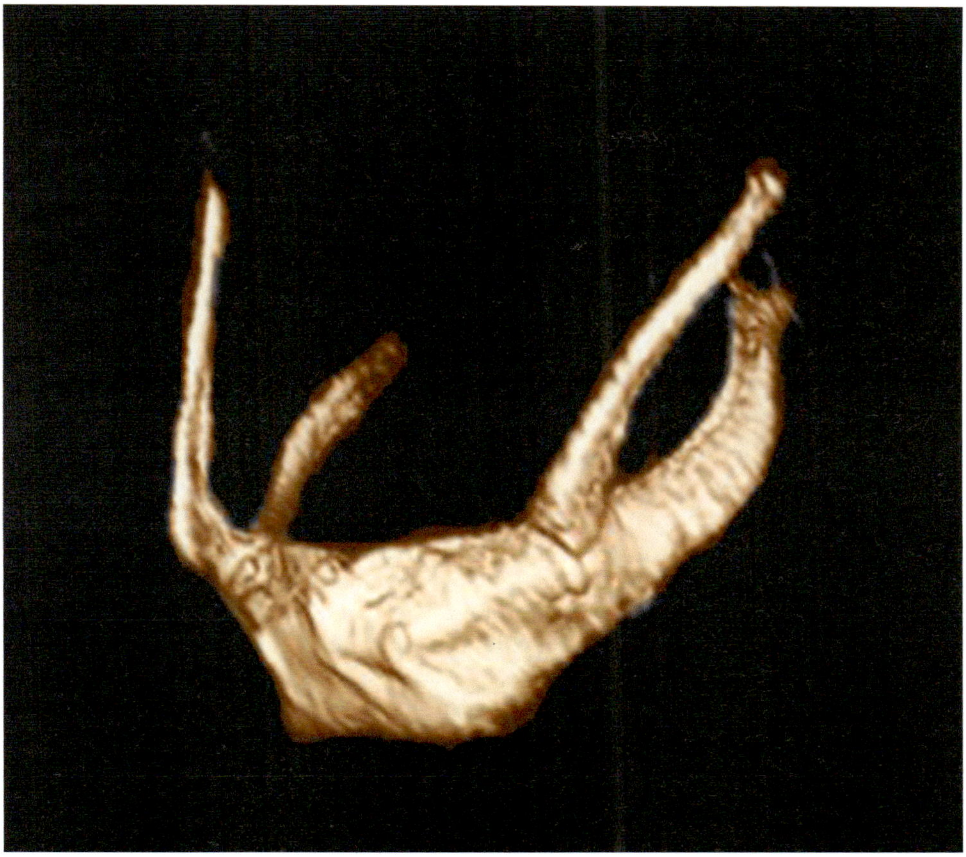

**Figure 2.6** Partially ossified thyrohyoid ligaments.

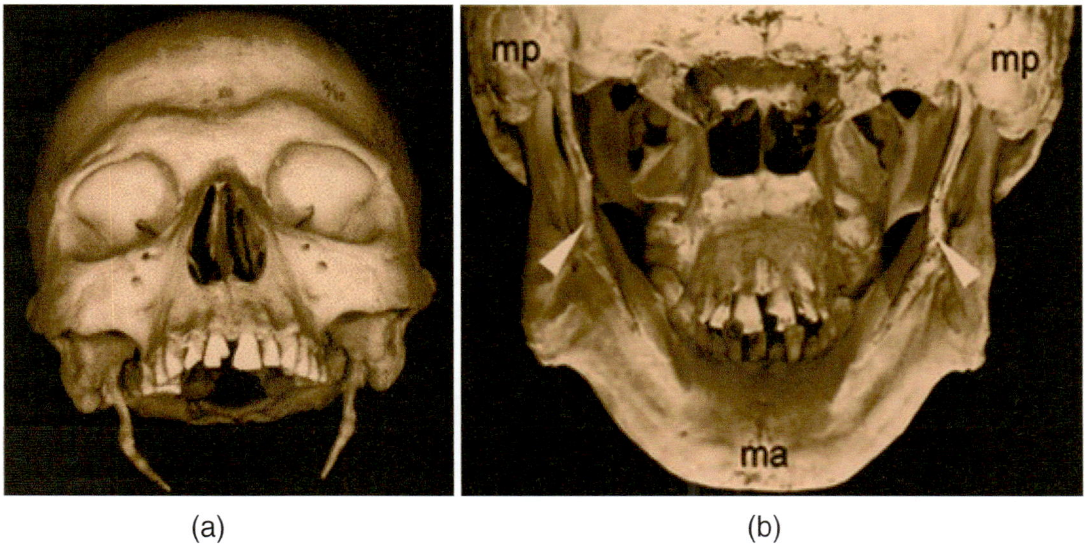


**Figure 2.7** (a) Anterior view of the skull with bilateral ossification of the stylohyoid ligaments (mandible removed). (b) Posterior view of the ossified ligaments (indicated by arrows) (ma – mandible, mp – mastoid process) adapted from Skrzat et al. (2007).

The laryngeal cartilages consist of the thyroid, cricoid, epiglottis, and the paired arytenoid, cuneiform and corniculate cartilages. The epiglottis, corniculate, cuneiform, and apices of the arytenoid cartilages consist of fibroelastic cartilage, which shows little tendency to calcify. On the other hand, the thyroid, cricoid, and the rest of the arytenoid cartilages are composed of hyaline cartilage and, with age, become ossified to a variable extent.

## Thyroid Cartilage

The thyroid is the largest cartilage of the larynx. It consists of two laminae united in front at an acute angle, forming the projection known as the laryngeal prominence (Adam's apple). The angle shows considerable variation and is said to be greater in the female (about 120 degrees), while in the male it is more acute, being about 90 degrees. Immediately above it, the laminae are separated by a V-shaped thyroid notch. Posteriorly, the laminae diverge, and the posterior border of each is prolonged into two slender processes: the superior and inferior cornua (horns).

The superior cornu is long and narrow and is directed upwards, backwards, and medially ending in a conical extremity that gives attachment to the lateral thyrohyoid ligament. Agenesis of the superior cornua is uncommon and may be mistaken for a fracture unless identified. Hejna et al. (2015) present three cases with right unilateral, left unilateral, and bilateral agenesis. One of their cases was that of a seven-year-old male child fatally injured in a motor vehicle accident. At autopsy, complete absence of the right superior cornu of the thyroid cartilage was observed, with no evidence of laryngeal trauma or haemorrhage in the cervical soft tissues. A significant finding was a large triticeous cartilage between the right thyroid lamina and the right greater cornu of the hyoid bone, which, as in this case, when elongated, may be mistaken for a fractured superior cornu.

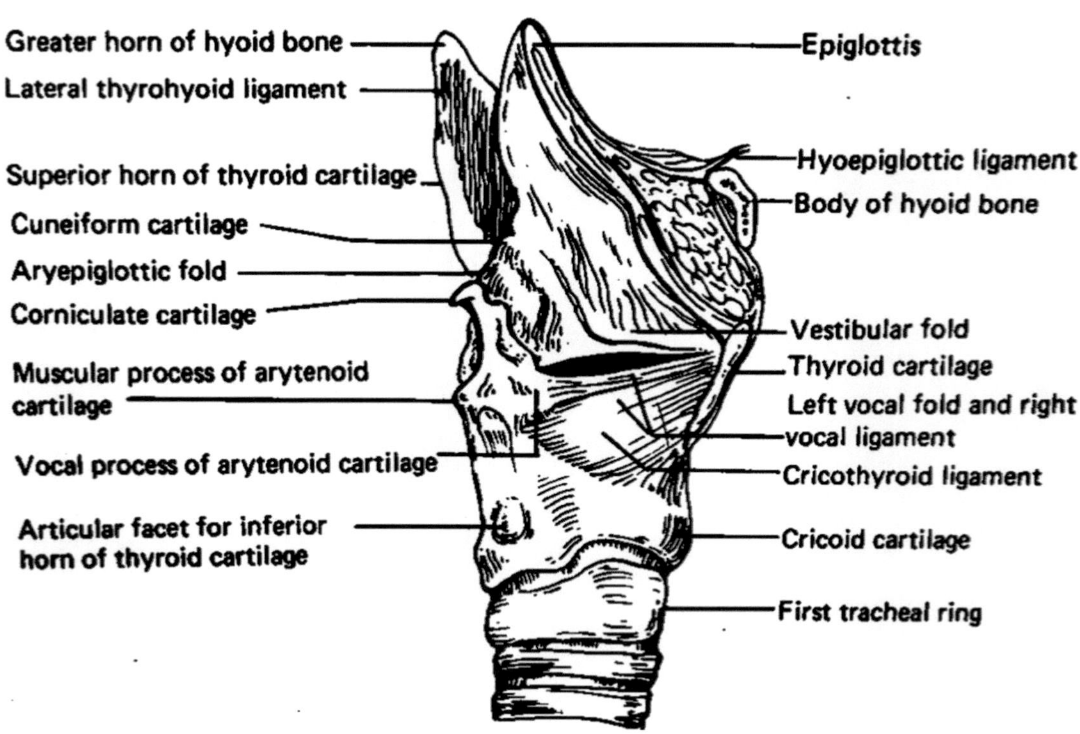


**Figure 2.8** Lateral view of the larynx from the right side. The right lamina of the thyroid cartilage and musculature have been omitted.

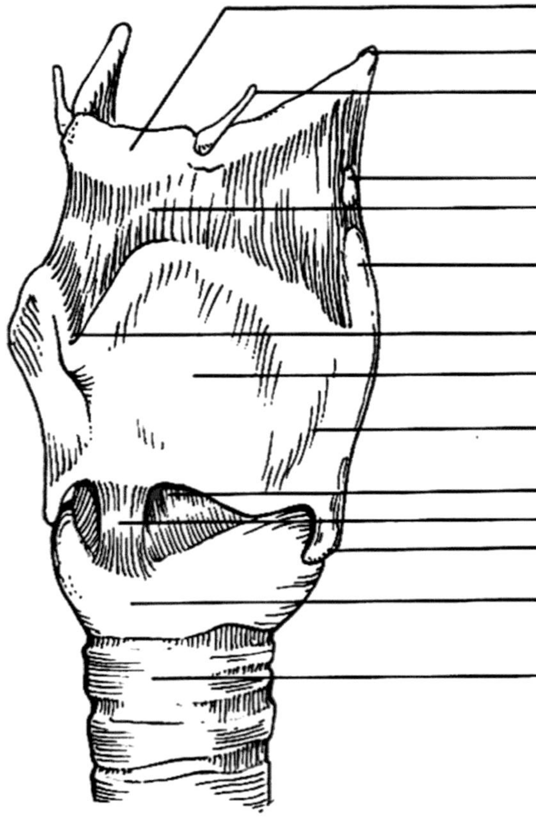


**Figure 2.9** Left anterolateral view of the larynx and hyoid bone.

Within the lateral thyrohyoid ligament, there is frequently a triticeous cartilage, which, to the unwary, may be mistaken for a fracture to the tip of the superior horn. Watanabe et al. (1982) examined 232 thyroid cartilages and noted that the triticeous cartilage was more frequently found in males and that bilateral presence was more frequent than unilateral. When this cartilage was present, the length of the superior horn was usually shortened. This is particularly noticeable when the triticeous cartilage occurs on one side only. The same authors found that the superior horns were usually straight, but in some cases over the age of 19 years, they were bent either forwards or backwards. In males, this inclination tends to be anteromedial, whereas in females, it is posterolateral.

The inferior cornu is short and thick and is directed downwards, with a slight inclination forwards and medially; on the medial surface of its lower end, there is a small oval facet for articulation with the side of the cricoid cartilage. The upper border of the thyroid cartilage in adults is at the level of the fifth cervical vertebra. Although this relationship is little changed by backwards or forwards movements of the head, its position with regard to the vertebrae is, however, altered during swallowing. In the new-born child, the upper border is level with the body of the atlas, but after 4 years, it reaches the adult position. The amount of calcification of the thyroid cartilage is variable, and although it is more common for calcification and ossification to increase with age, it is by no means unusual to find an almost completely cartilaginous thyroid cartilage in old age.

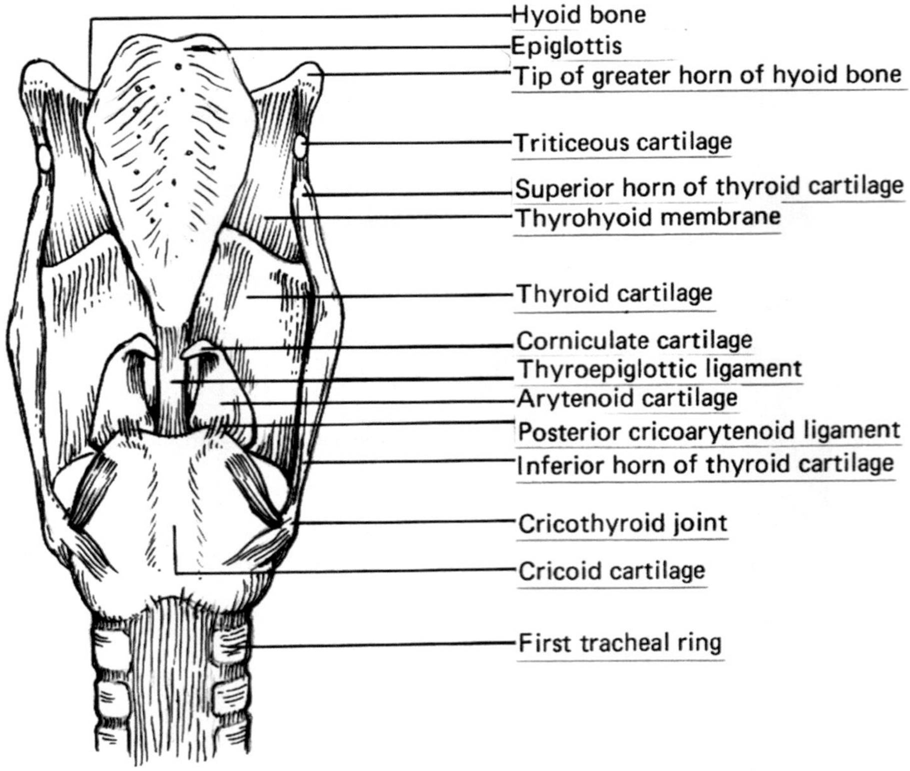


**Figure 2.10** Posterior view of the larynx and hyoid bone.

## Cricoid Cartilage

The cricoid cartilage is smaller, thicker, and stronger than the thyroid cartilage and is the only firm structure that completely encircles the air passages. It is shaped like a signet ring. Anteriorly, it is narrower and known as the arch, whereas posteriorly it forms the broad quadrate lamina.

## Arytenoid Cartilages

The arytenoid cartilages are two small cartilages articulating with the upper border of the lamina of the cricoid. They serve for the attachment of the vocal folds and of a number of muscles. They are commonly found to be calcified (Curtis et al. 1985). Each is shaped like a pyramid with a forward projection – the vocal process, which is attached to the vocal fold – and a lateral projection – the muscular process, to which are attached the posterior and lateral cricoarytenoid muscles. The superior border of the arytenoid cartilage articulates with a small cartilage, the corniculate cartilage, to which is attached the aryepiglottic fold. Within the latter is contained the cuneiform cartilage.

## Epiglottis

The epiglottis is a thin sheet of fibroelastic cartilage that projects obliquely upwards behind the tongue and body of the hyoid bone and in front of the entrance to the larynx. It is attached below to the angle formed by the two thyroid laminae by the thyroepiglottic ligament, a short distance below the thyroid notch. The sides of the epiglottis are attached to the arytenoid cartilages by the aryepiglottic folds. The posterior surface of the epiglottis, which is concave and covered with mucous membrane, has numerous small pits beneath this membrane. These pits, into which mucous glands project, are most obvious in partially decomposed cadavers and should not be mistaken, on superficial examination, for petechial haemorrhages.

## Anatomical Variation of the Laryngo-Hyoid Complex

Variation in the anatomy of the larynx and hyoid bone (as has been referred to above), as well as the marked variability of the age at which ossification may occur in the laryngeal cartilages, could present a challenge to the forensic examiner in assessing injuries to this region. This potential for misinterpretation has been highlighted by Pinhiero et al. (2018). A population-based study was carried out on a series of 207 consecutive autopsies. They found the prevalence of triticeal cartilage in their series to be 52.7% and that of agenesis of thyroid horns to be 10%. Calcification of the stylohyoid ligament accounted for 1.4%. The probability of misdiagnosis due to the presence of anatomical variations of the larynx and hyoid bone when deaths were due to pressure on the neck was high in their population (71.5%). The prevalence of triticeous cartilage in more than half of the sample

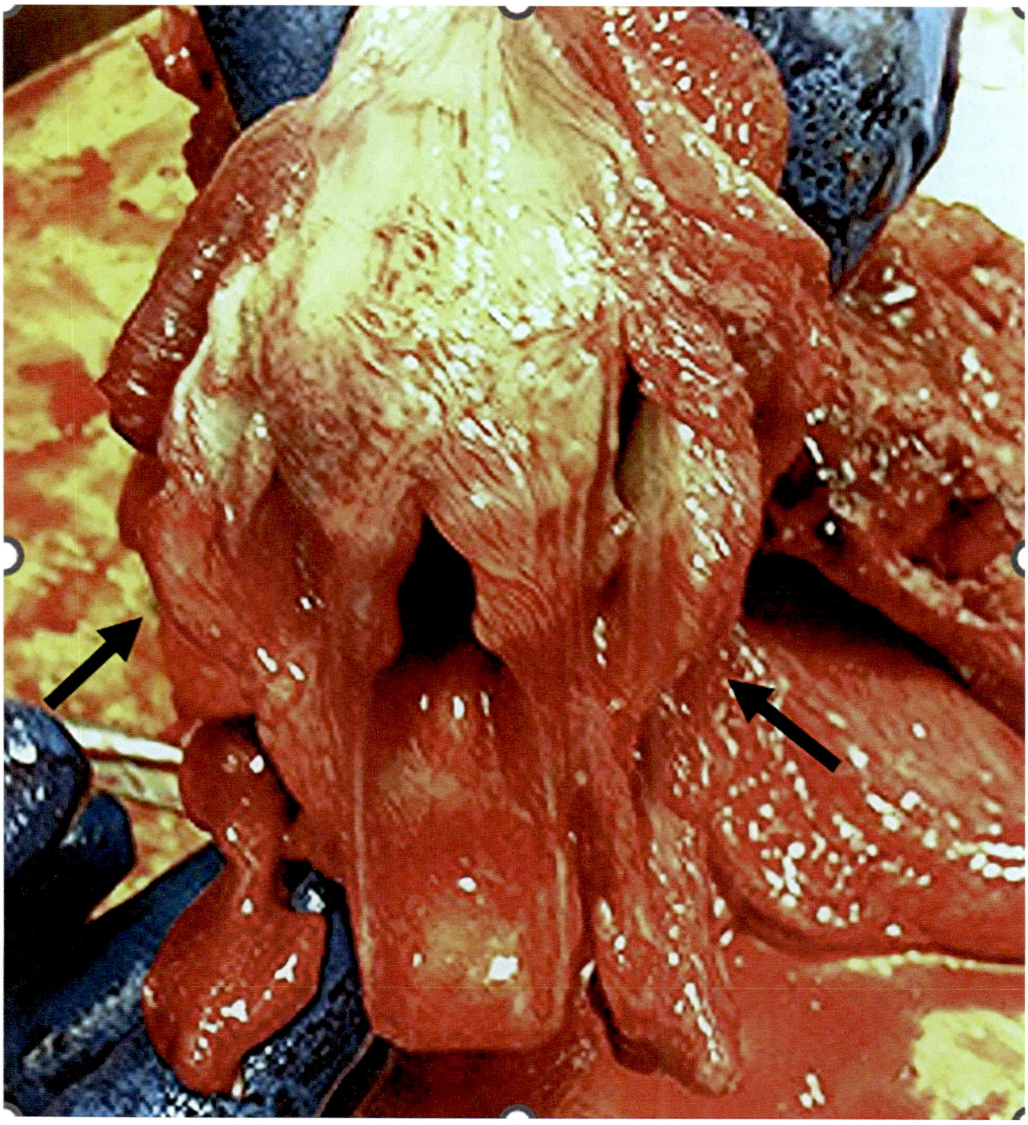

**Figure 2.11** Bilateral absence of superior thyroid cornua (arrows).

determined an important rate of potential errors (46.4%), followed by mistaken diagnoses induced by terminal segmentation of thyroid horns (7.3%) and by ectopic superior thyroid horns (6.3%). They also observed that the likelihood of a misdiagnosed laryngeal fracture, compared to the hyoid bone, was greater if the thyroid cartilage was affected, with a significantly higher proportion of false positives. The higher frequency of thyroid fractures in neck pressure, together with the prevalence and location of the triticeous cartilage on the lower third of the lateral thyrohyoid ligament, were the main reasons for these results.

Anatomical variation of the laryngo-hyoid region and its implications in the interpretation of neck trauma were also studied by Humaira and Vanezis (2021) in a prospective study of 72 consecutive cases that were not suspected to be due to neck compression. The age range was between 22 and 97 years (mean age of 63.9). The main features examined were:

- the joints between the greater horns and body of the hyoid bone,
- the triticeous cartilages for the presence or absence of one or both,
- the superior cornua of the thyroid cartilage for the presence or absence of one or both (Figure 2.11),
- the gender and age of each individual,
- any cases that displayed unique findings.

Of the 72 cadavers examined, only 6 cases (8%) displayed the normal textbook anatomy for that region, namely, the bilateral presence of the superior horns of the thyroid cartilage, triticeous cartilages, and an unfused hyoid bone. An unusual anomaly found in the series was an elongated, jointed right thyroid cornu (Figure 2.12).

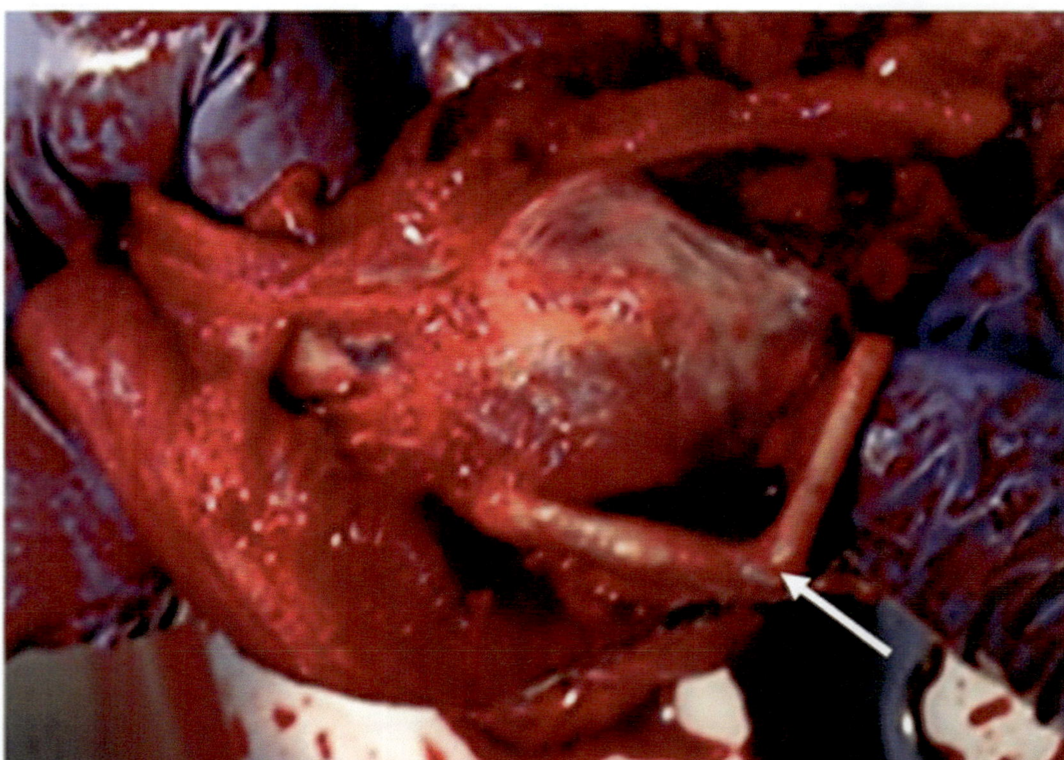

**Figure 2.12** Jointed right superior thyroid cornu (arrow).

## CERVICAL TRACHEA

The trachea serves as the conduit between the larynx and bronchial tree. It typically extends from the C6 level, just below the cricoid cartilage, to the T4–T5 level, bifurcating into the main-stem bronchi at the carina. The extrathoracic or cervical segment of the trachea is a relatively short portion, measuring approximately 2–4 cm. The average adult trachea is approximately 11 cm in length, with a range of 10–13 cm. It is composed of 18–22 incomplete cartilage rings and becomes intrathoracic at the level of the sixth ring. A segment of the cervical trachea lies superficially in the neck and is only partially covered by the infrahyoid strap muscles. As the trachea courses caudally, it tracks posteriorly and is often displaced just right of the midline at the aortic arch. The thyroid gland is just anterior and lateral to the trachea, with the thyroid isthmus typically located at the second or third tracheal ring. The oesophagus is closely apposed to the posterior wall of the cervical trachea, usually veering along the left posterior margin of the trachea as it courses inferiorly (McCullagh et al., 2022).

# PHARYNX AND OESOPHAGUS

The pharynx is an oval musculo-membranous bag that consists of a nasal, oral, and laryngeal part (Figures 2.13–2.15).

It extends from the base of the skull and is attached behind the nose, mouth, and larynx. Above, where it is part of the respiratory and alimentary tract, its wall is rigid, and it is always patent. Below the level of the laryngeal aperture, it is normally a transverse slit. The piriform fossa is a small recess on either side of the laryngeal orifice (Figure 2.12). Foreign bodies may lodge in this recess and, if the instrument employed to remove them pierces the mucous membrane, the underlying internal laryngeal nerve may be damaged. The pharynx measures some 11–13 cm in length, and its lower end is at the border of the cricoid cartilage in front and the lower border of the sixth cervical vertebra behind. Below, it is continuous with the oesophagus.

The oesophagus is a muscular tube about 25 cm long, connecting the pharynx to the stomach. It begins in the neck at the lower border of the cricoid cartilage, as noted above, and descends anterior to the vertebral column. The cervical part of the oesophagus deviates slightly to the left from the midline. The region of the lower part of the inferior constrictor muscle (cricopharyngeus muscle) at the commencement of the oesophagus is thin-walled posteriorly because of the absence of longitudinal fibres and is susceptible to injury from instrumentation.

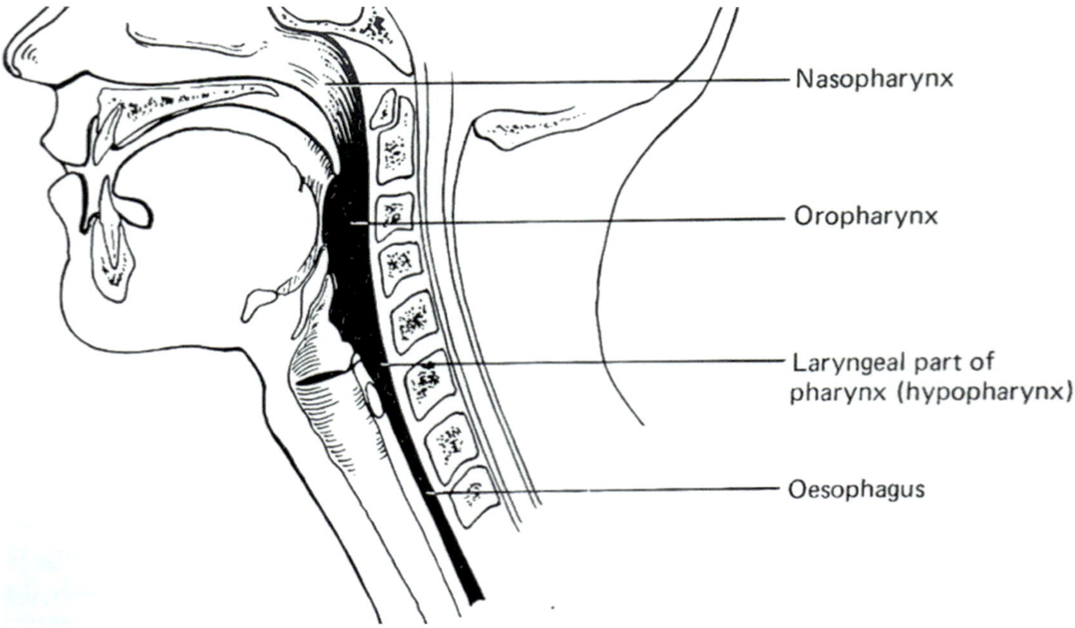


**Figure 2.13** Sagittal section of the neck and lower region of the head, showing the course of the pharynx and oesophagus.

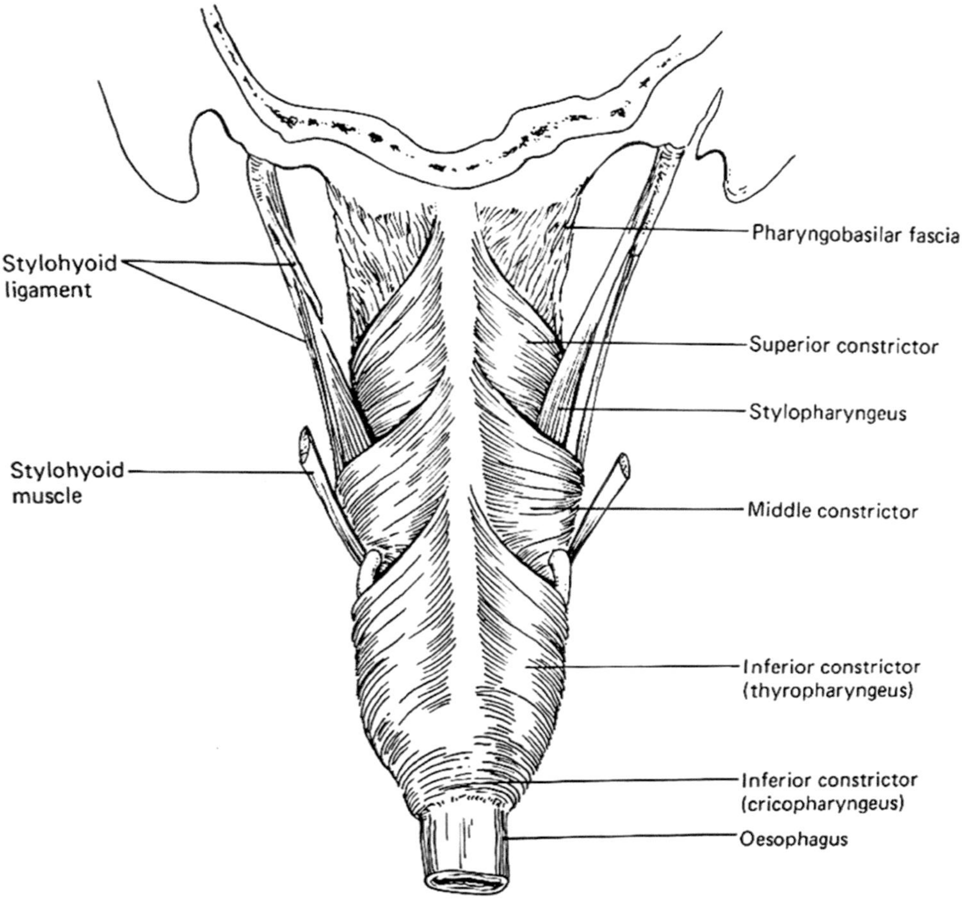


**Figure 2.14** Posterior view of the pharynx.

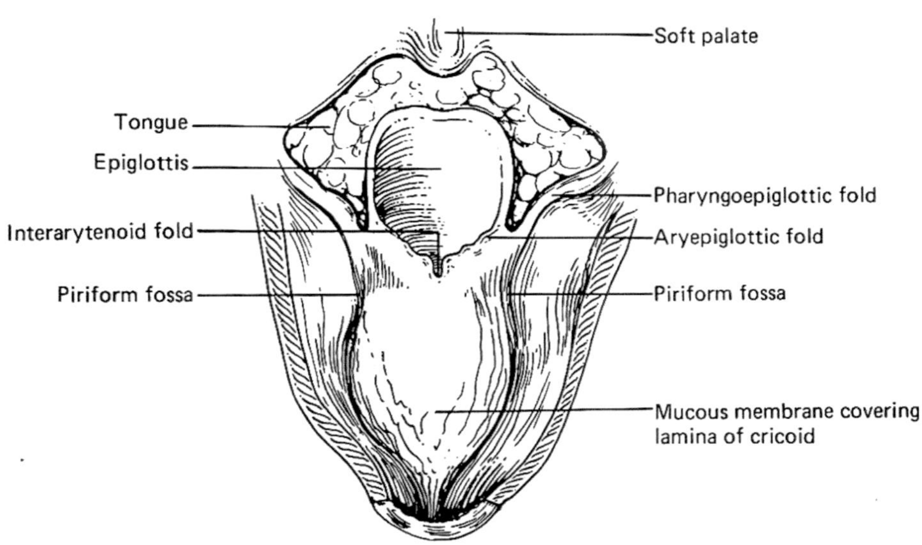


**Figure 2.15** Inlet of the larynx, showing the piriform fossa.

## THE CAROTID SHEATH

The carotid sheath (Figure 2.16) is not a fascia in the sense of a demonstrable layer but consists of a dense feltwork of areolar tissue that surrounds the carotid arteries (common and external) and invests the vagus nerve. It is thin and almost non-existent where it overlies the internal jugular vein. The carotid sheath is attached to the base of the skull at the lower border of the tympanic plate, and it is continued downwards along the vessels to the aortic arch. In front of the mastoid and along this line, the pretracheal fascia blends with it.

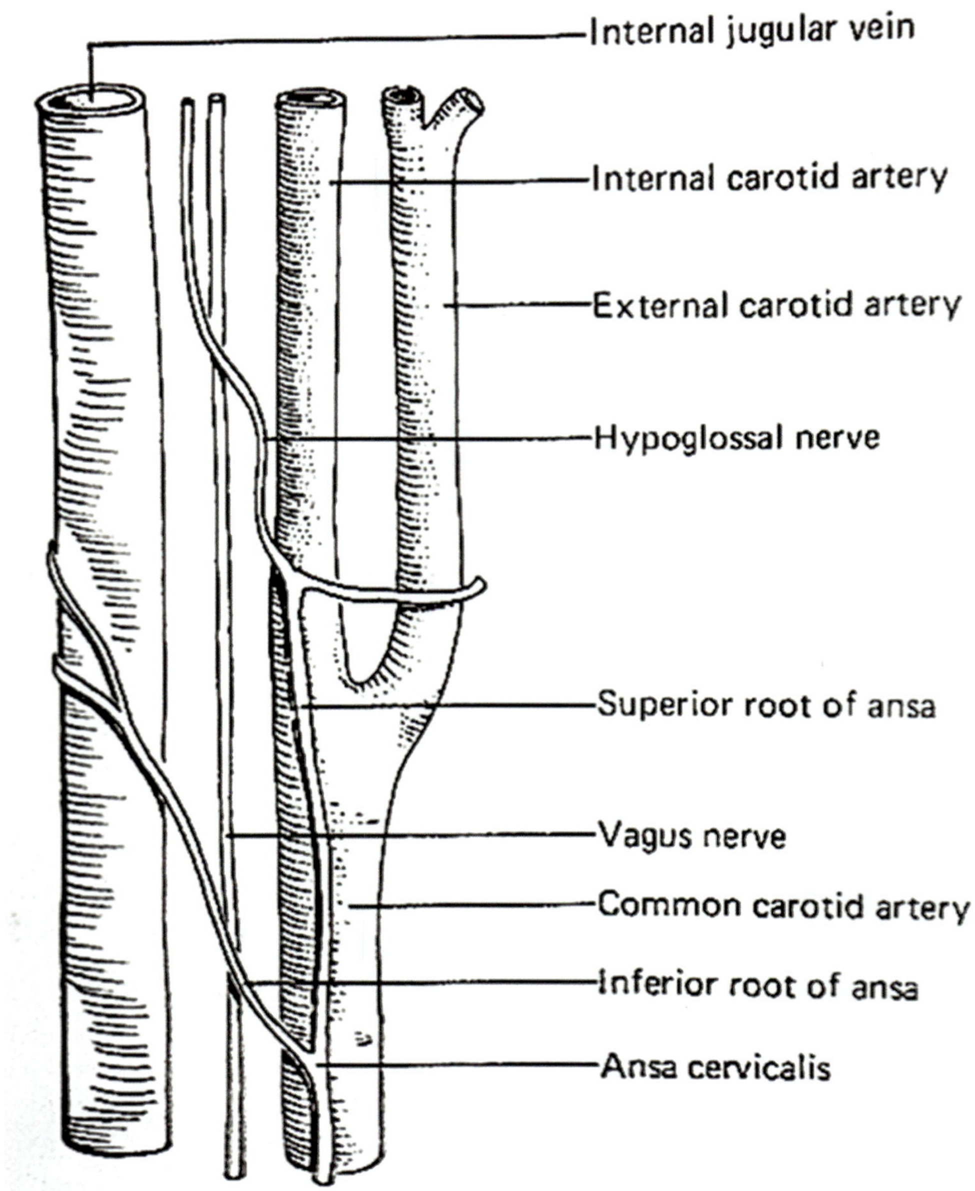


**Figure 2.16** Diagrammatic representation of the contents of the carotid sheath.

# THE CAROTID ARTERIES (FIGURES 2.17 AND 2.18)

## The Common Carotid Artery and Its Main Branches

The common carotid artery on the right side arises from the brachiocephalic artery (innominate) at its bifurcation behind the right sternoclavicular articulation. On the left side, it arises from the highest part of the aortic arch; the left is consequently longer than the right artery and is deeply placed in the thorax at its origin. It ascends obliquely in the neck. Both common carotid arteries extend from the sternoclavicular articulation to the level of the upper border of the thyroid cartilage (third cervical vertebra), there dividing into external and internal carotid arteries. Both arteries are crossed about midway by the omohyoid muscle and are enclosed in the same condensation of cervical fascia (carotid sheath) as the internal jugular vein and vagus nerve. As the common carotid artery divides, it widens; this dilatation, *the carotid sinus*, extends upwards into the internal carotid artery (Figure 2.18b). Its wall is thinner than elsewhere and has many nerve fibres from the glossopharyngeal and vagus nerves, as well as from the sympathetic trunk (superior cervical ganglion). The sinus reacts readily to changes in arterial blood pressure and, because of its position, its function as a baroreceptor mechanism allows it to exercise control over intracranial pressure.

## The External Carotid Artery and Its Main Branches

The external carotid artery extends from the bifurcation of the common carotid artery opposite the upper border of the thyroid cartilage. It is at first somewhat medial to and in front of the internal carotid artery. It then passes deep to the posterior belly of the digastric and stylohyoid muscles, above which it pierces the deep lamina of the parotid fascia and enters the gland. It divides behind the neck of the mandible into the maxillary and superficial temporal arteries. Before it enters the parotid gland, the external carotid artery gives off six branches, three in front, two from behind, and one deep (medial). The three from the front are the superior thyroid, lingual, and facial arteries, which arise below, at, and above the tip of the greater horn of the hyoid bone and diverge

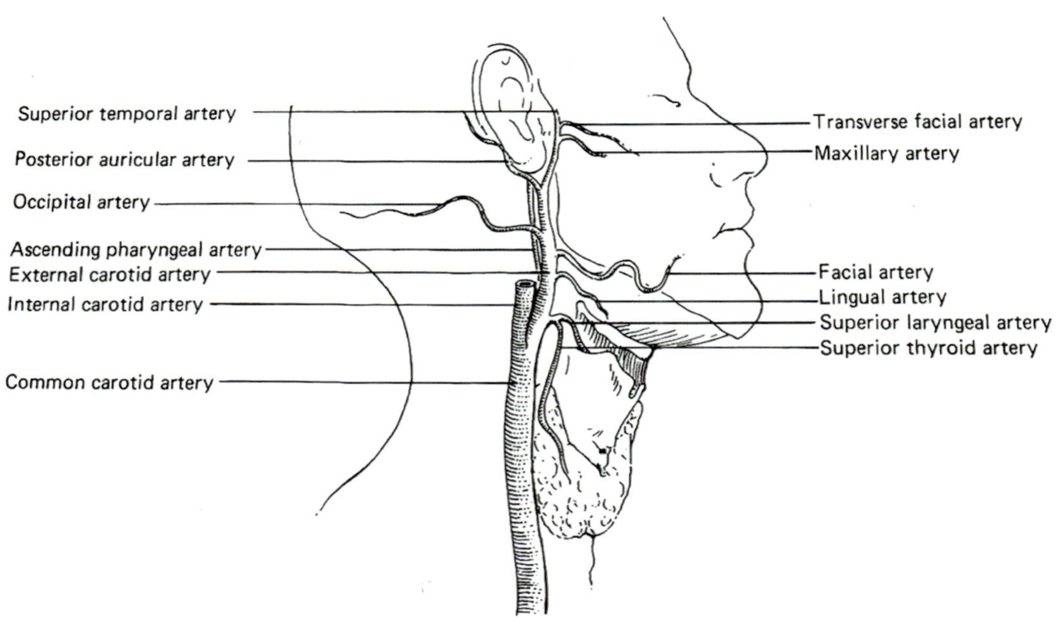


**Figure 2.17** The carotid arteries and branches of the external carotid artery (only the proximal part of the internal carotid artery is shown).

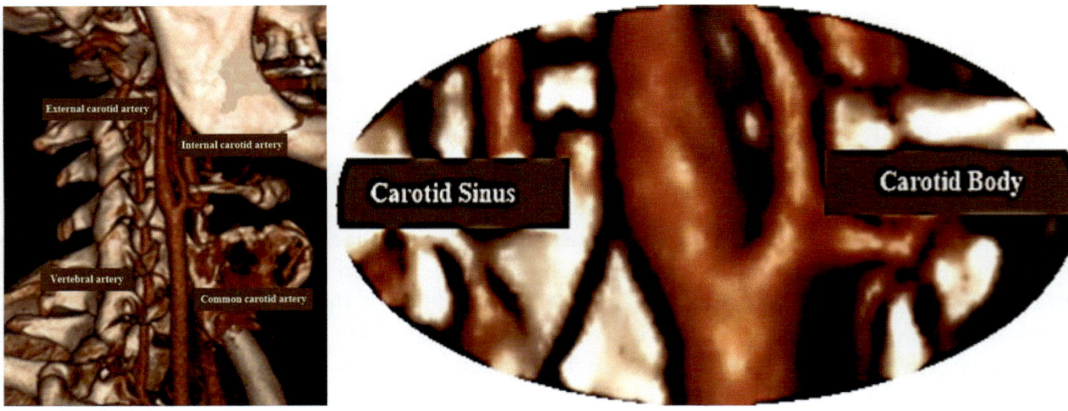


(a) (b)

**Figure 2.18** (a) Volume-rendered 3D CT angiogram showing the anatomy of the carotid and vertebral arteries in the neck. (b) Detail of carotid artery bifurcation, showing the carotid sinus and the position of the carotid body.

widely. The two from behind are the occipital and posterior auricular arteries, which pass up along the lower and upper borders of the posterior belly of the digastric muscle. The branch from the medial side is the ascending pharyngeal artery, which ascends to the base of the skull on the side wall of the pharynx, alongside the internal carotid artery.

## The Internal Carotid Artery

The internal carotid artery arises at the bifurcation of the common carotid, usually at the level of the upper border of the thyroid cartilage, level with the third cervical vertebra. At its commencement, it bulges into the carotid sinus (see above). The external carotid artery is lateral to the internal carotid at its origin but soon slopes upwards posteriorly to occupy a medial and deeper level. The cervical part of the artery has no branches and passes straight up to the carotid foramen. The artery curves forward in the petrous temporal bone and then curves upwards into the foramen lacerum in the middle cranial fossa, passes through the cavernous sinus, and ends at the anterior perforated substance where it divides into the anterior and middle cerebral arteries.

## The Carotid Body

This is a small reddish-brown, ellipsoidal structure lying behind the bifurcation of the right common carotid artery, in close relation to the carotid sinus. It may also be partially or completely wedged between the commencements of the internal and external carotid arteries and is attached to, and sometimes partially embedded in, the outer fibrous layer of these arteries. Occasionally, the organ is in the form of a number of separate nodules.

The basic histological unit of the carotid body (Figure 2.19) comprises two types of cells: the chief cell (glomus type 1 cell), which has a large round nucleus and abundant cytoplasm containing vesicles rich in biogenic amines, and the supporting, or sustentacular cell (glomus type 2 cell), which is elongated, slender, and wrapped around nerve axons. These cells are commonly arranged in clusters, with the chief cells in the centre and sustentacular cells at the periphery. Schwann cells (similar in appearance to sustentacular cells) are found in the connective tissue between the clusters, and small blood vessels are encircled by a further elongated cell, the pericyte.

The carotid body acts as a chemoreceptor, responding to changes in the chemical composition of the blood. A fall in the oxygen content or an increase in the carbon dioxide content of the blood circulating through the organ initiates reflexes through the glossopharyngeal and vagus nerves, thus

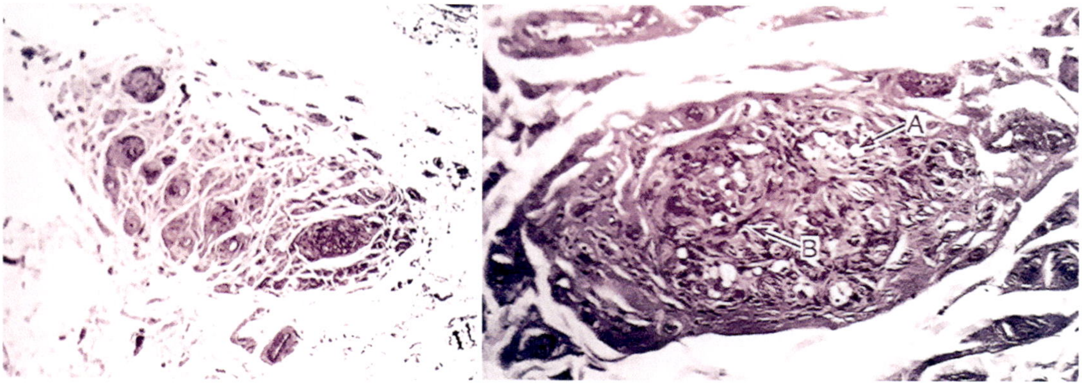


(a) (b)

**Figure 2.19** The carotid body. (a) Section showing numerous lobules of glomic tissue separated by strands of fibrous tissue, which also contain myelinated nerves and blood vessels (Haematoxylin and eosin x 60). (b) Single lobule of glomic tissue. It is arranged into clusters, and in the centre are chief cells (A), which are rounded and have abundant pale cytoplasm. These are surrounded by sustentacular cells (B), which are elongated (Haematoxylin and eosin x 420).

stimulating respiration. Chemoreceptor and baroreceptor functions in this specialised vascular area at the carotid bifurcation appear to be intimately connected, interactive, and complex; furthermore, Heath and Smith (1985) are of the view that the carotid body may also have baroreceptor properties. A comprehensive review of the pathology of the carotid body and sinus is given by the aforementioned authors in their monograph.

## THE VERTEBRAL ARTERY AND ITS MAIN BRANCHES (FIGURE 2.20)

The vertebral artery usually arises from the first part of the upper and posterior aspect of the subclavian artery and can be conveniently divided into four parts.

The first part runs upwards and backwards between the longus colli, scalenus anterior, and behind the common carotid artery. Behind it is the transverse process of the seventh cervical vertebra.

The second part ascends through the transverse foramina of the upper six cervical vertebrae, pursuing an almost vertical course as far as the transverse process of the axis, through which it runs upwards and laterally to the transverse process of the atlas.

The third part emerges from the transverse foramen of the atlas. It then curves behind its lateral mass, lies in the vertebral artery sulcus on the upper surface of the posterior arch of the atlas, and enters the vertebral canal by passing below the lower, arched border of the posterior

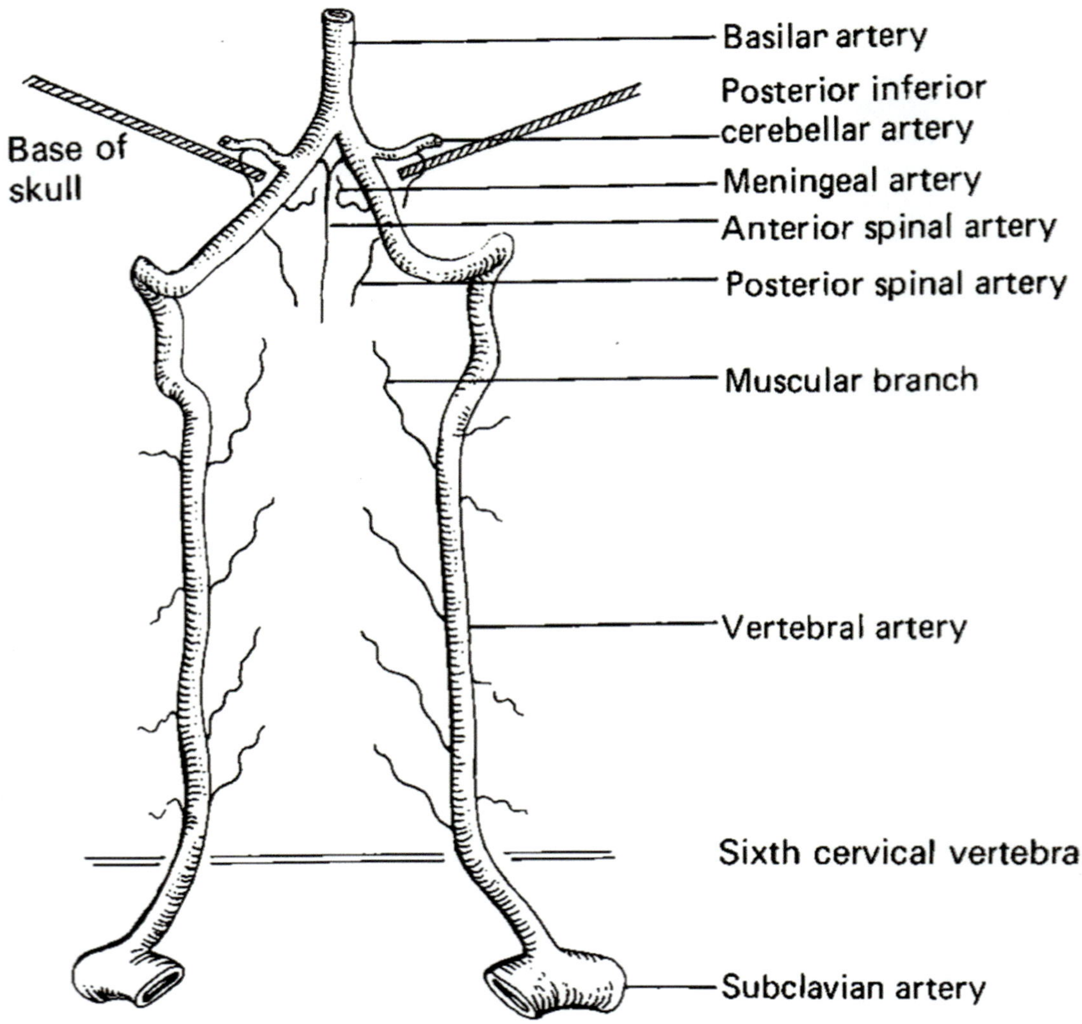


**Figure 2.20** The vertebral artery system and its main branches.

atlanto-occipital membrane. This part of the artery is covered by the semispinalis capitis muscle and is contained within the suboccipital triangle.

The fourth part pierces the dura and arachnoid mater and ascends medially to the front of the medulla oblongata, where, at the lower border of the pons, it unites with the artery of the opposite side to form the basilar artery.

The structural alteration that takes place between the third and fourth parts should be appreciated, as it is this section of the artery that appears to be more vulnerable to injury from stretching. Wilkinson (1972) examined 20 vertebral arteries from ten autopsies and observed that as the artery entered the skull, its adventitia and media underwent a significant reduction in thickness, associated with a gross diminution or total loss of elastic fibres in these two layers. The transformation was most marked in the final 0.5 cm of the cervical portion of the artery but was not complete until about 0.5 cm beyond the point of dural perforation.

Johnson et al. (1993) supported the findings of Wilkinson. They found that the vertebral arteries were, on average, larger around the origin of the vessel from the subclavian artery, and the adventitia was relatively thicker at this point, and after piercing the dura mater. The tunica media were much thinner within the intracranial segment. They also found that pronounced intimal thickening occurred with increasing age (Johnson et al. 2001).

The branches of the vertebral artery may be divided into those that have their origin in the cervical portion and those that originate inside the cranium. The cervical branches comprise the spinal, muscular, and meningeal arteries and the posterior inferior cerebellar artery.

# THE VEINS OF THE NECK

The veins of the neck (Figure 2.21) may be divided into those of the jugular system and those related to the spinal column.

## The External Jugular Vein

The external jugular vein is formed by the junction of the posterior division of the retromandibular trunk and the posterior auricular vein at the angle of the mandible in the substance of the parotid gland. It descends beneath the platysma, over the sternomastoid, and pierces the cervical fascia above the middle of the clavicle to open into the subclavian, or occasionally into the internal jugular vein. The vein receives the posterior external jugular, the suprascapular, transverse cervical, and anterior jugular veins. The latter vein reaches the suprasternal notch and communicates with the other anterior jugular via the jugular arch. It passes laterally under the sternomastoid to end in the external jugular vein.

## The Internal Jugular Vein

The internal jugular vein descends from the jugular foramen, being a continuation of the sigmoid sinus. It passes vertically down the side of the neck, lateral to the internal and common carotid arteries, uniting with the subclavian near the medial margin of the scalenus anterior to form the brachiocephalic vein. It receives the inferior petrosal sinus, veins of the tongue, pharyngeal, facial, and superior and middle thyroid veins.

## Venous Drainage of the Cervical Spine

The venous drainage of the cervical spine comprises the external and internal vertebral plexuses. The internal vertebral plexuses lie within the vertebral canal between the dura mater and vertebrae and receive tributaries from bones and the spinal cord. They are arranged into four

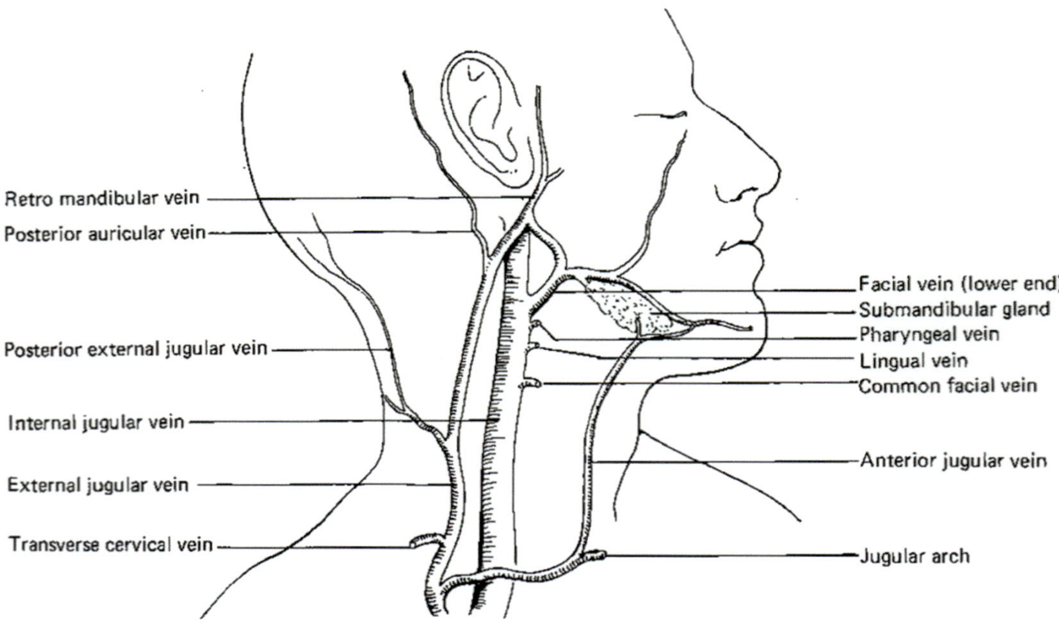


**Figure 2.21** The veins of the neck, viewed from the right side.

longitudinal veins (two anterior and two posterior). They form an intricate network around the foramen magnum, which connects with, amongst other venous channels, the vertebral veins.

The anterior external venous plexus lies in front of the vertebral bodies, and the posterior plexus lies on the posterior surfaces of the laminae, around the spines and the transverse and articular processes. Both anterior and posterior external plexuses anastomose with the internal venous plexuses.

## Venous Drainage of the Pharynx and Upper Oesophagus

The upper oesophagus is drained by three groups of veins: the intrinsic and extrinsic veins, and the venae comitantes of the vagus nerve. The intrinsic group is further subdivided into subepithelial, submucous, and perforating veins. The submucous group is the largest and drains into the pharyngolaryngeal plexus. The pharyngolaryngeal plexus is divided into two groups: the ventral group on the back of the cricoid cartilage, and the dorsal group in the posterior wall of the pharynx.

# THE CERVICAL VERTEBRAE

The seven cervical vertebrae together, with their related muscle masses, ligaments, and joints, serve to support the head, enable a large range of movements, and support and protect the upper part of the spinal cord. The upper two (atlas and axis), together with the seventh cervical vertebra, have specialised morphological characteristics which will be described separately from the remaining vertebrae (C3–C6), which increase only in size from above downwards.

Cervical vertebrae all possess transverse foramina and lack costal facets. Although there are many variations, the upper six cervical vertebral transverse foramina usually transmit the vertebral artery, venous plexus, and a sympathetic plexus of nerves. In most anatomical specimens, the vertebral artery does not pass through the transverse foramen of the seventh cervical vertebra. At times, complete or partial division of one or more transverse foramina by a bony bar may be found (Figure 2.22). This is more frequently true of the transverse foramen of C7 than at any other level.

During embryological development, all vertebrae have transverse and costal processes. In the thoracic region, the costal process gives rise to the rib. In the cervical region, however, the transverse process represents a composite of the embryonic transverse and costal processes. Overdevelopment of the costal process results in a cervical rib.

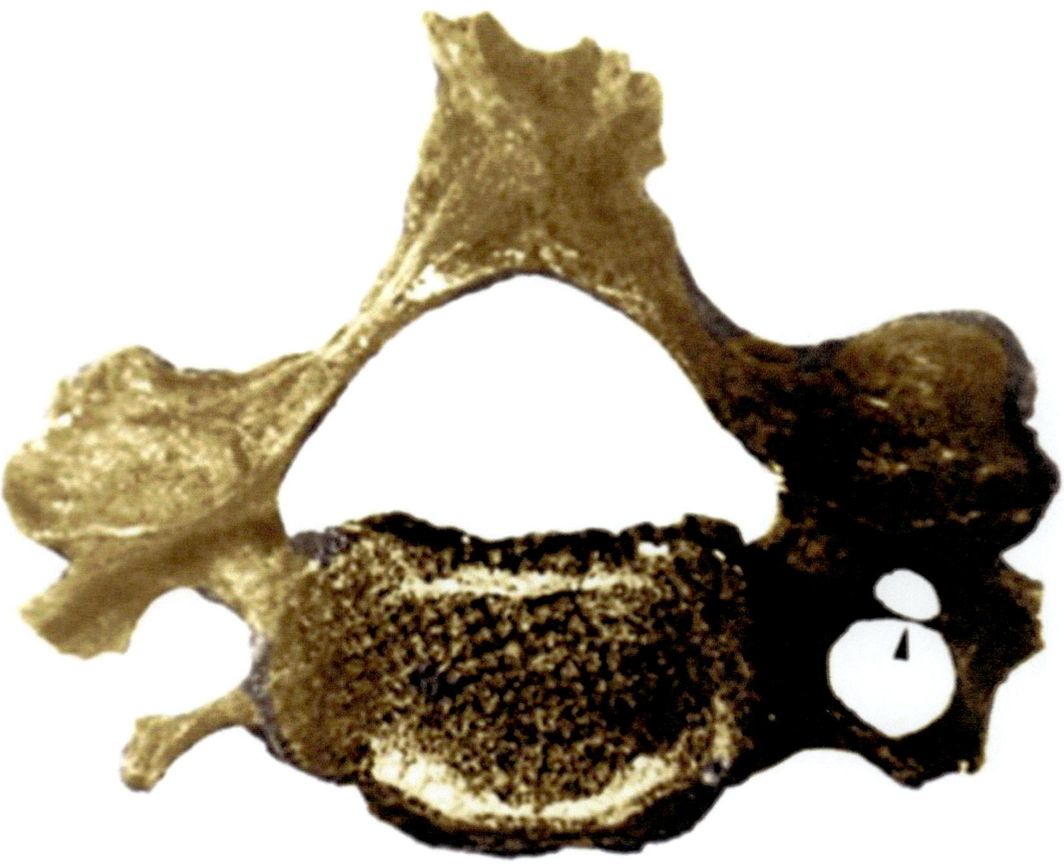

**Figure 2.22** Superior view of fourth cervical vertebra, showing division of transverse foramen by a bony bar (arrow).

## Atlas (C1)

The atlas (Figure 2.23) differs from all other cervical vertebrae in that it lacks a body and a spinous process. It comprises a posterior and anterior arch as well as a lateral mass on either side.

The anterior arch is convex on its ventral surface. Centrally, it has a tubercle to which the anterior longitudinal ligament attaches. On its posterior medial portion, there is a smooth, oval to circular facet (fovea) for articulation with the dens (odontoid process) of the axis (C2).

The curved posterior arch has a tiny, roughened tubercle, instead of a spinous process, to which the nuchal ligament and several muscles attach. Just behind the superior articular facet of the lateral mass on each side, the posterior arch is grooved, forming the vertebral artery sulcus. In this region, the first cervical spinal (suboccipital) nerve lies between the vertebral artery and the sulcus.

The lateral masses of the atlas are quite large and bear the weight of the skull. Each lateral mass carries two superior and two inferior articular facets. The superior articular facets, which are large, concave and kidney-shaped, articulate with the occipital condyles. The inferior articular facets, which are slightly concave, and circular, articulate with the superior articular surfaces of the axis and permit rotation of the head at the atlantoaxial joint. A small tubercle for the attachment of the strong transverse ligament of the atlas projects medially from each lateral mass. This ligament divides the vertebral foramen of the atlas into a smaller anterior compartment, which contains the dens, and a larger posterior compartment which provides protection for the spinal cord, its meninges, and blood vessels. Anterior and posterior to the dens are the median atlantoaxial (synovial) joints.

The strong transverse processes of the atlas are the longest in the cervical spine, and muscles assisting in rotation of the head are attached to these structures.

## Axis (C2)

The axis (Figure 2.24) is readily distinguishable from all other vertebrae by the dens (odontoid peg), which projects from the upper end of the body. Just above the junction of the dens with the body of the axis, there is a distinct constriction of the dens in the form of a neck. Anteriorly, the dens has an oval or circular facet for articulation with the corresponding facet on the innermost surface of the anterior arch of the atlas. Posteriorly and posterolaterally, the neck of the dens is grooved by the transverse ligament of the atlas. The apex of the dens is pointed, and it is here that

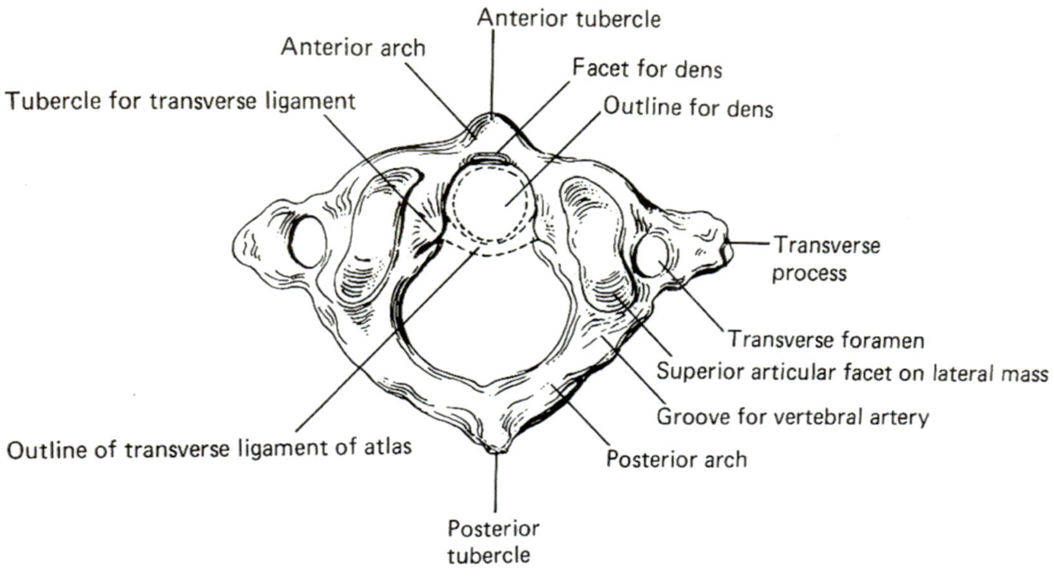


**Figure 2.23** The first cervical vertebra (atlas).

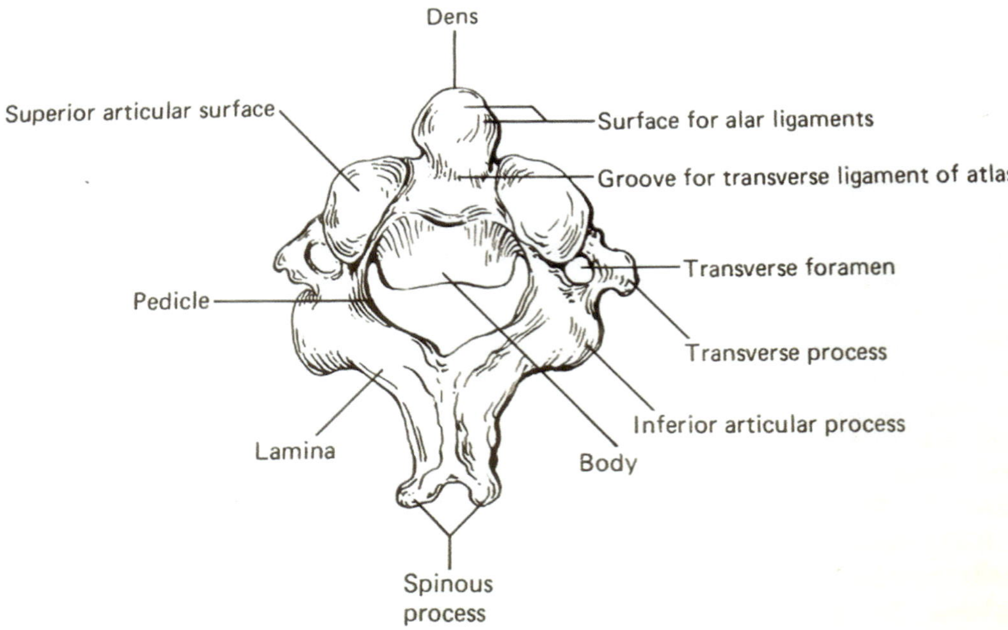


**Figure 2.24** The second cervical vertebra (axis).

the apical ligament attaches. Just below the apex of the dens, its sides are flat and roughened for the of the alar ligaments. The apical and alar ligaments join the dens to the anterior and lateral margins, respectively, of the foramen magnum.

The pedicles of the axis are broad and strong and are covered in part by the superior articular surfaces. Strong, thick laminae (thickest of all cervical vertebrae) fuse dorsally with a very broad, short, bifid spinous process. The transverse processes, which are pierced by the transverse foramina and end in a single tubercle, are much smaller than those in the other cervical vertebrae.

The large, oval, slightly convex superior articular surfaces of the axis, which are directed inferolaterally, extend laterally from the vertebral body and pedicle. Although the inferior vertebral notch is deep and accommodates the third cervical spinal nerve, there is no superior vertebral notch and, therefore, the second cervical spinal nerve passes dorsal to the superior articular surface over the lateral atlantoaxial joint. The inferior articular process, which has an articular facet, is similar to that of the more typical cervical vertebrae (C3–C6). The axis does not have an articular pillar or a lateral mass.

## Vertebrae C3–C6 (Figure 2.25)

The vertebral body is elliptical in shape, being wider from side to side than from front to back. Its ventral and dorsal surfaces are slightly concave and are usually of equal height.

The upper surface of the typical cervical vertebra appears slightly convex from front to back and concave transversely, owing to the laterally raised lips of the uncinate processes. The upper anterior surface is bevelled and in the articulated spine overlapped by the protruding rim of the anterior inferior surface of the body above. The remainder of the lower surface of the body is reciprocally concave anteroposteriorly and convex transversely. Laterally, the lower surface is bevelled to accommodate the uncinate processes of the vertebra below.

Uncinate processes are not present at birth. These structures grow and assume their full height in the adult. They are thought to function as guide rails for the vertebral bodies to prevent lateral displacement during movement of the cervical spine. The uncinate processes are half-moon-shaped

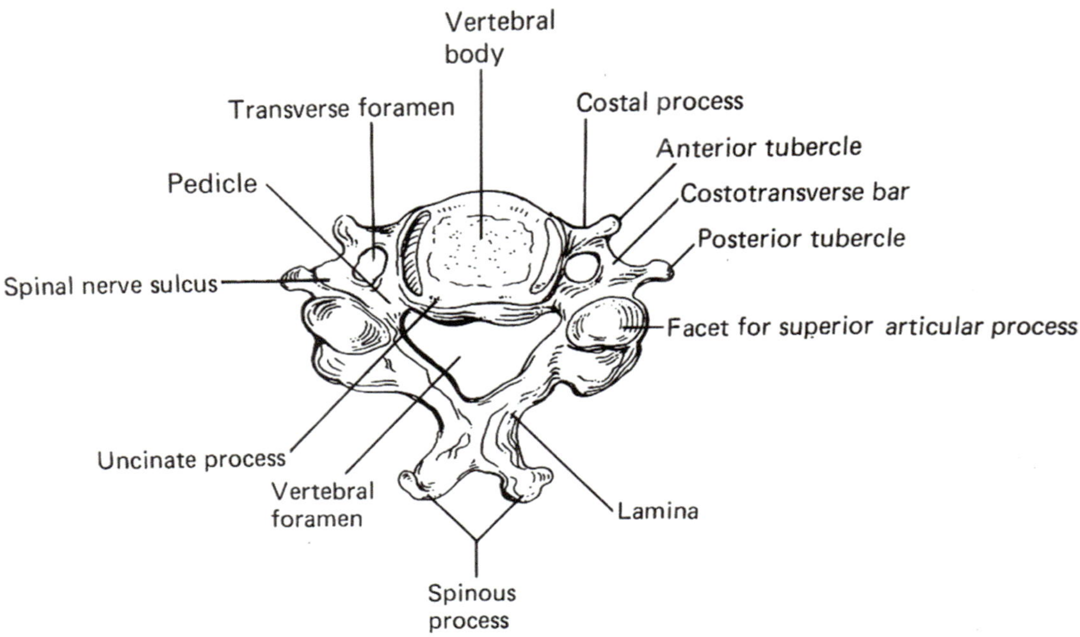


**Figure 2.25** A typical cervical vertebra (C3–C6).

lips that project cranially from the upper lateral margins of the vertebral bodies of C3–C6 and from the posterolateral upper margin of C7 and Tl. Within the substance of the intervertebral discs, between the uncinate processes and the laterally bevelled lower surface of the vertebral body above, lie the uncovertebral (uncinate) joints.

The short, stout pedicles spring from the dorsolateral aspects of the vertebral body. In a typical cervical vertebra, the pedicles are notched to an equal depth on both the superior and inferior surfaces. Cervical laminae are relatively narrow and thinned cranially but somewhat thicker caudally. The vertebral foramen is large and triangular rather than oval. The spinous processes are short and directed dorsally and caudally. They are usually bifid in Caucasians, but not in Black persons. The division of a spinous process may be of unequal size.

The superior and inferior articular processes on each side, and the bone between them, form the rhomboid-shaped articular pillars. These pillars project laterally from the junctions of the lamina and the pedicle. The articular facets are oval and flat – the superior facets face upwards and dorsally; the inferior, downwards and ventrally.

At times, the costal process of the sixth cervical vertebra is quite large and may be seen on lateral radiographs projecting ventral to the vertebrally body. This is a well-known anatomical variation. The carotid artery is situated immediately ventral to the C6 costal process. The artery may readily be compressed against the enlarged costal process, which is therefore called the carotid tubercle.

Situated between the anterior and posterior roots of the transverse process is the transverse foramen. The foramen is limited anterolaterally by a curved bar of bone, the costotransverse bar. The bar is deeply grooved on its upper surface; this sulcus is for the ventral ramus of the spinal nerve.

## Seventh Cervical Vertebra

The presence of an elongated, thick, non-bifid and nearly horizontal spinous process is the most distinctive feature of C7 (Figure 2.26). This may be easily palpated at the root of the neck. C7 is therefore often referred to as the vertebra prominens. The spinous process ends in a bulbous tubercle to which the nuchal ligament attaches.

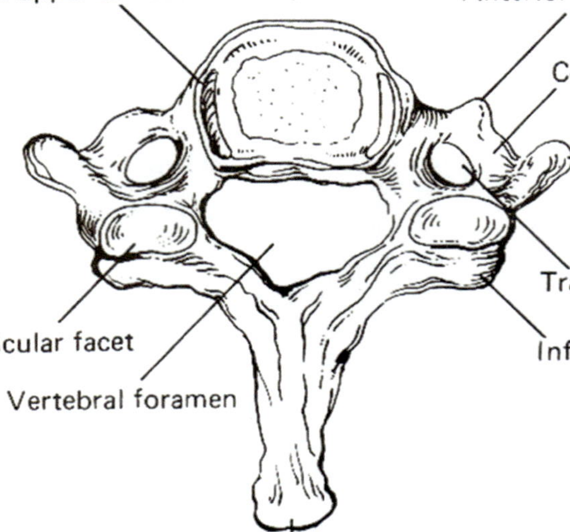


**Figure 2.26** The seventh cervical vertebra.

While its transverse process is large, it does not nearly equal that of the atlas in lateral extent. The posterior root of the transverse process is quite prominent and extends as far laterally as the first thoracic transverse process, while the anterior root is quite small or absent.

At times, the anterior root of the transverse process of C7 may develop separately to form a cervical rib. About 2% of skeletons have cervical ribs, which are more prevalent on the right than the left. Cervical ribs may be associated clinically with thoracic outlet neurovascular compression syndromes.

If the transverse process of C7 extends beyond the lateral aspect of the transverse process of Tl, then it is said to be elongated and may have similar clinical consequences to cervical ribs.

Anatomical specimens show many variations in the transverse foramina of the seventh cervical vertebra. While they may rival the size of foramina in other cervical vertebrae, they are frequently smaller, occasionally divided into two compartments by a bony spicule, as noted above, and, infrequently, they are entirely absent.

Occasionally, the left vertebral artery ascends through the left seventh transverse foramen. More commonly, the vertebral veins traverse them bilaterally. Usually, the vertebral artery passes ventral to the transverse process rather than through the transverse foramen.

## The Intervertebral Discs

The fibrocartilaginous intervertebral discs (Figures 2.27 and 2.28), comprising the outer anulus fibrosus and inner nucleus pulposus, are the major connecting bond between adjacent vertebral bodies. They are amphiarthrodial joints, being only slightly movable.

## The Apophyseal (Zygapophyseal) Joints

The vertebral arch articulations are diarthrotic synovial joints, referred to as apophyseal, zygapophyseal, or facet joints. Their articular surfaces are covered with hyaline cartilage. They are surrounded by a loose articular capsule, having a synovial lining and a synovial disc or meniscus. Viewed laterally, the apophyseal joints in the cervical region are inclined obliquely downwards from the ventral to dorsal aspect of the spine.

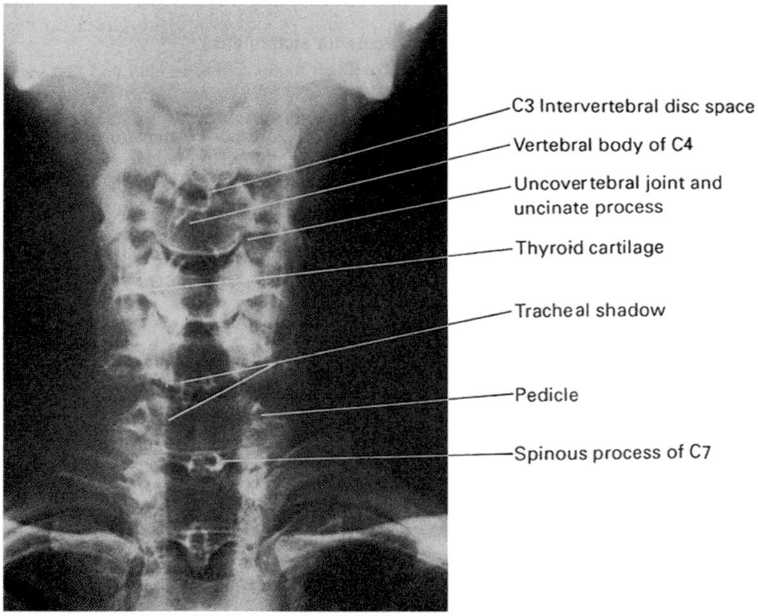


**Figure 2.27** Anteroposterior radiograph of the cervical spine.

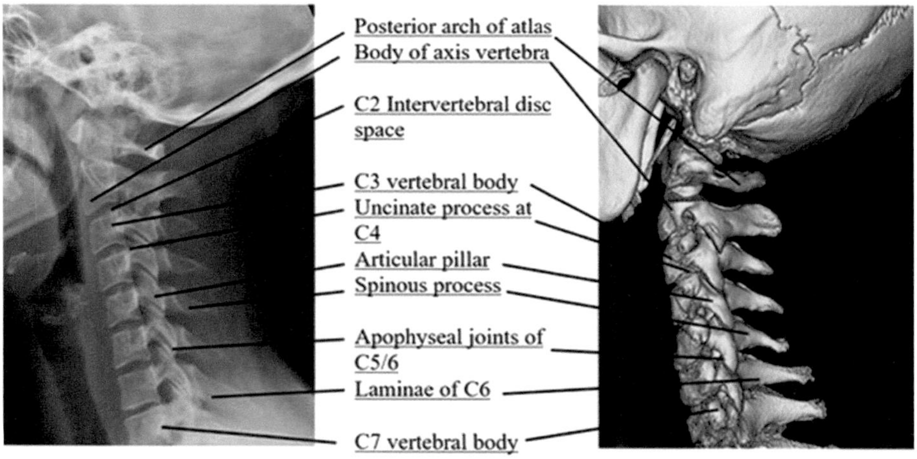


**Figure 2.28** Cervical spine: (a) left lateral radiograph and (b) volume-rendered 3D CT image.

# THE INTERVERTEBRAL FORAMINA AND COURSE OF THE CERVICAL SPINAL NERVES

Cervical intervertebral foramina are oval and increase progressively in size from C2/C3. There are eight pairs of cervical nerves, seven cervical vertebrae, but only six pairs of cervical intervertebral foramina. The presence of eight cervical nerves and only seven vertebrae is due to a rearrangement of somites during embryological development. There are no intervertebral foramina between the skull and the atlas nor between the atlas and the axis. The first cervical spinal nerve exits from the vertebral canal between the base of the skull and the atlas, on the cranial side of the posterior arch of the atlas in the sulcus of the vertebral artery. The second cervical spinal nerve leaves the vertebral canal between the posterior arch of the atlas and the pedicle of the axis. It crosses the dorsal aspect of the lateral atlantoaxial joint, ventral to the ligamenta flava. The next five succeeding cervical spinal nerves exit the vertebral canal through intervertebral foramina above the level of their corresponding vertebral foramina. The eighth cervical nerve, however, exits between C-7 and Tl.

# THE SPINAL CORD, MENINGES, AND OTHER RELATED STRUCTURES (FIGURES 2.29–2.31)

The vertebral canal, within which lies the spinal cord, is formed by successive vertebrae of the articulated spine. The boundaries are as follows: ventrally, the vertebral bodies with their intervening vertebral discs and the posterior longitudinal ligament; laterally, the pedicles and intervertebral foramina; dorsolaterally, the articulated articular processes, the laminae, and the ligamenta flava. In the cervical region, the canal is large and triangular, and the spinal cord occupies only about half of its cross-sectional space.

For the most part, the spinal cord is oval with greater lateral than anteroposterior dimensions. Ventrally, it has a deep midline groove, the anterior median fissure, and dorsally, there is a shallow sulcus, from which a posterior median septum of neuroglia extends into its substance. The posterior median septum within the spinal cord is attached to the incomplete posterior median septum in the subarachnoid space.

The structures internally consist of a central mass of grey matter in the form of a fluted column surrounding the central canal. The grey matter, in turn, is enclosed in a cylindrical mass of white matter. It is almost divided into two halves by the anterior median fissure and the posterior median septum. The latter extends forward as far as the grey matter of the grey commissure, which contains the central canal. The anterior fissure does not completely separate the white matter. A narrow white commissure lies anterior to the grey matter. In the cervical spine below C3, the anterior

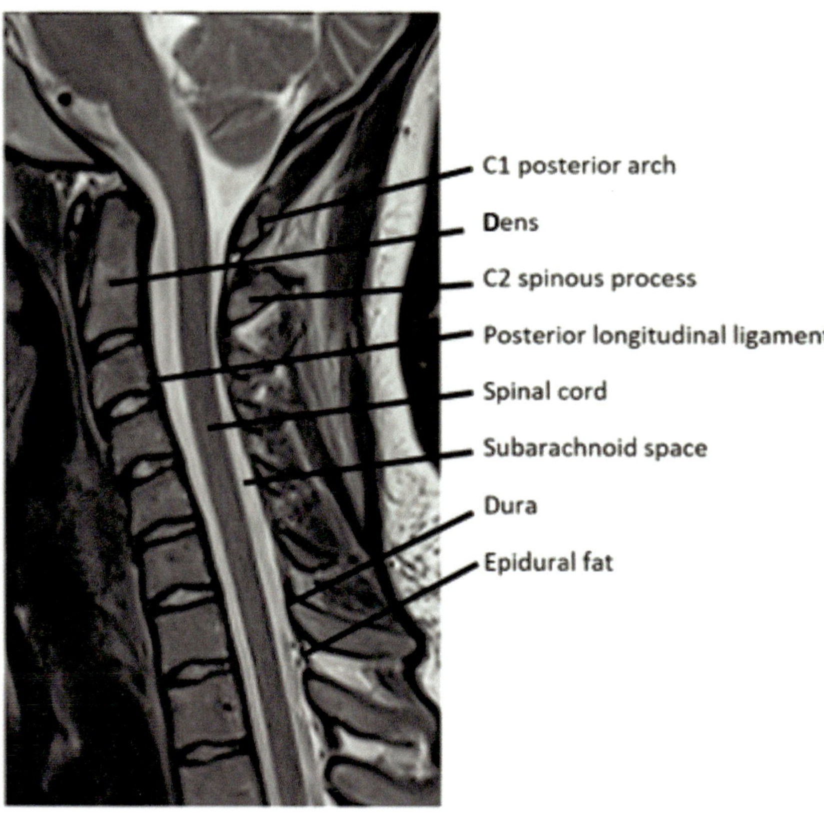


**Figure 2.29** Sagittal MR image of the craniocervical junction and the cervical spine, showing the vertebrae and cervical spinal cord.

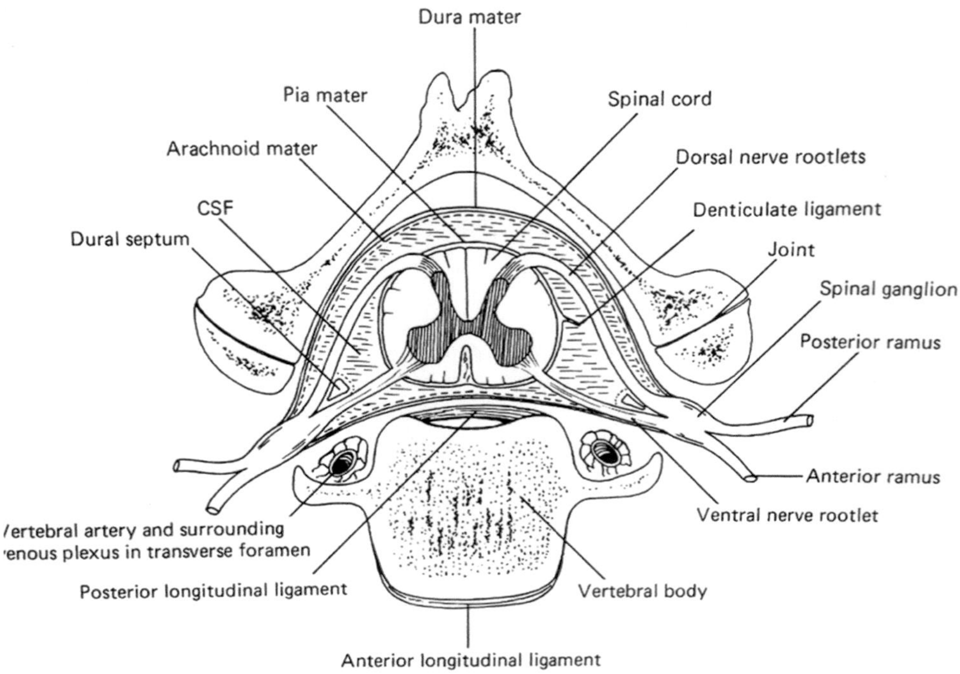


**Figure 2.30** Transverse section through a mid-cervical level, showing the arrangement and relationships of the spinal cord and surrounding structures.

grey horn extends far laterally into the white matter. At C4 lie the motor cells for the diaphragm (phrenic nerve), while below this level, the lateral extension of the anterior horn contains the motor cells for the upper limb muscles (brachial plexus). The posterior grey horns are slender, and there is a large amount of white matter.

Along the posterolateral sulcus of the spinal cord, a series of nerve filaments emerge and join to form a dorsal (posterior) sensory root of a spinal nerve. In a similar fashion, the ventral (anterior) motor roots arise from nerve filaments located anterolaterally on the cord.

The spinal cord segment is the part of the spinal cord from which the spinal nerve arises. Grossly, it is the distance between the most cranial filament of one root and the highest filament of the root below. These rather arbitrary spinal cord segments do not correspond to the similarly numbered vertebrae. Furthermore, the spinal cord segments are not of uniform length.

Within the subarachnoid space, the separate dorsal and ventral nerve roots are immersed in cerebrospinal fluid and are intimately covered by pia mater. At the intervertebral foramina, the roots turn laterally, where they are enclosed by an arachnoid-dural sheath. The dorsal (sensory) and ventral (motor) roots unite just beyond the dorsal root ganglion, forming a mixed spinal nerve trunk. Most dorsal root ganglia lie in the intervertebral foramina (the exceptions being the first and second cervical nerves).

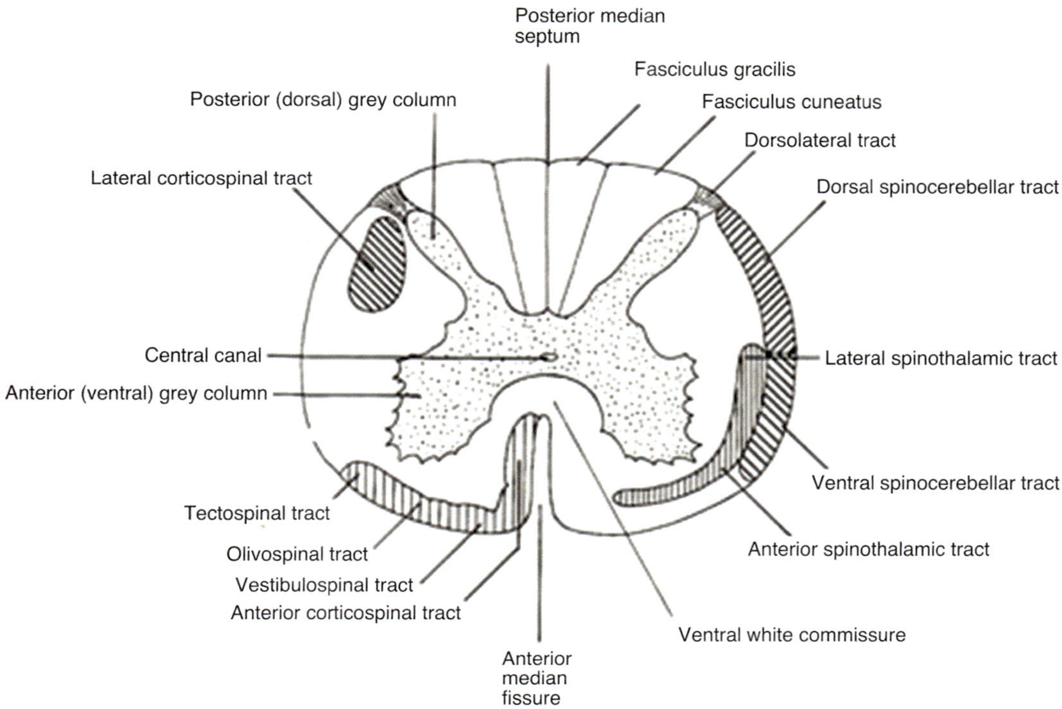


**Figure 2.31** Cervical spinal cord, showing the main structures.

## References


de Bakker BS, de Bakker HM, Soerdjbalie-Maikoe V, Dikkers FG. Variants of the hyoid-larynx complex, with implications for forensic science and consequence for the diagnosis of Eagle's syndrome. *Sci Rep*. 2019 Nov 4;9(1):15950. doi: 10.1038/s41598-019-52476-z. PMID: 31685955; PMCID: PMC6828966.

Curtis DJ, Allman RM, Brion J. Holborow GS, Brahman SL. Calcification and ossification in the arytenoid cartilage: Incidence and patterns. *J Forensic Sci*. 1985;30:1113—1118.

Evans KT, And Knight B. *Forensic Radiology*. Blackwell Scientific, Oxford, chap. 4, 1981, p. 123

Fisher E, Austin D, Werner HM, Chuang YJ, Bersu E, Vorperian HK. Hyoid bone fusion and bone density across the lifespan: Prediction of age and sex. *Forensic Sci Med Pathol*. 2016;12(2):146–157.

Heath D, Smith P. *The Pathology of the Carotid Body and Sinus*. Edward Arnold, London, 1985.

Hejna P, Janík M, Urbanová P. Agenesis of the superior cornua of the thyroid cartilage: A rare variant of medicolegal importance. *Am J Forensic Med Pathol*. 2015;36(1):10–12.

Humaira P, Vanezis P. Anatomical variation of the laryngo-hyoid region and implications in the interpretation of neck trauma – A prospective study of 72 consecutive cases. *Int J Legal Med*. 2021;135 (Suppl 1): S11–S119.

Johnson CP, Baugh R, Wilson CA, Burns J. Age related changes in the tunica media of the vertebral artery: Implications for the assessment of vessels injured by trauma. *J Clin Pathol*. 2001;54(2):139–145. https://doi.org/10.1136/jcp.54.2.139

Johnson CP, Lawler W, Burns J. Use of histomorphometry in the assessment of fatal vertebral artery dissection. *J Clin Pathol*. 1993;46(11):1000–1003. https://doi.org/10.1136/jcp.46.11.1000

McCullagh KL, Shah RN, Huang BY. Anatomy of the larynx and cervical trachea. *Neuroimaging Clin N Am*. 2022 Nov;32(4):809–829. doi: 10.1016/j.nic.2022.07.011. PMID: 36244725.

Monson DO, Saletta JD, Freeark RJ. Carotid vertebral trauma. *J Trauma*. 1969;12:987–999.

Nowicki JL, Stew B, Ooi E. Penetrating neck injuries: a guide to evaluation and management. *Ann R Coll Surg* Engl. 2018;100(1): 6–11.

Pinheiro J, Cascallana JL, Lopez de Abajo B, Otero JL, Rodriguez-Calvo MS. Laryngeal anatomical variants and their impact on the diagnosis of mechanical asphyxias by neck pressure. *Forensic Sci Int.* 2018;290:1–10.

Skrzat J, Mróz I, Walocha J, Zawiliński J, Jaworek JK. Bilateral ossification of the stylohyoid ligament. *Folia Morphol (Warsz)*. 2007;66:203–206.

Vougiouklakis T. Overview of the ossified stylohyoid ligament based in more than 1200 forensic autopsies. *J Clin Forensic Med.* 2006;13:268–270.

Watanabe H, Kurihara K, Murai T. A morphometrical study of laryngeal cartilages. *Med Sci Law.* 1982;22:255–260.

Wilkinson IMS. The vertebral artery. Extracranial and intracranial structure. *Arch. Neurol.* 1972;27:392396.

# CHAPTER 3

## TECHNIQUES OF EXAMINATION

*Peter Vanezis*
*(with contributions from Curtis Offiah, and Christopher Paul Johnson)*



DOI: 10.4324/9781003658467-3

## PRELIMINARY CONSIDERATIONS

Although examination of the neck is an integral part of the post-mortem examination, it is surprising how often significant injuries are overlooked. In this chapter, procedures in basic autopsy practice as applicable to the neck region are described, as well as more specialised techniques which may also be employed as necessary.

Prior to the autopsy, it is essential to consider the circumstances in which the person was found, as well as any previous relevant medical and social history. This information will give invaluable guidance as to what procedures and investigations may need to be carried out or recommended by the pathologist. Nevertheless, it cannot be sufficiently strongly emphasised that the pathologist should always keep an open mind and be aware of any other possible circumstances which may have led to death. In any event, one should always bear in mind the possibility that an account of events, particularly when acquired at a very early stage of an investigation, may be inaccurate or muddled, because many of the true facts may not yet be to hand or the relevant witnesses or other informants may not be reliable.

As part of the initial investigation prior to the start of the direct external examination of the body, it is a good practice to carry out radiographic imaging, and it is indeed mandatory when assessing trauma, particularly where the death is suspicious or overtly of a homicidal nature.

A thorough appraisal of injuries to all parts of the body is essential. In many fatal neck injury cases, there are injuries to other parts of the body that may help the pathologist in assessing the circumstances of death. The absence of associated trauma is equally as important an observation.

Photography is not only invaluable in providing a permanent record of injuries but is frequently of value in enabling comparisons to be made between certain injuries or other marks and possible causative agents. Whenever photographs are taken for the purpose of comparison, including superimposition, the images should be of a similar scale. If comparison is with the actual agent or impressions made from it, e.g., bite marks, then life-size images are necessary (i.e., 1:1). In all images used for comparison, it is essential to include two scales at right angles to each other, thus taking into account possible distortion from the curvature of the region in question. To this end, it is also necessary to photograph the injury at right angles to the plane of its central area. Further images may be taken, if necessary, at the edges of the injury if it is extensive or the curvature is sufficiently steep, again keeping at right angles to the subject. The use of ultraviolet reflection techniques to photograph bruises and other marks on the skin has proved extremely useful. Unlike visual rays, which penetrate the skin and are diffused by the skin when the ray is reflected, ultraviolet radiation does not penetrate the skin so deeply, and the reflected ray is not diffused to the same extent. The resulting photographs therefore show greatly enhanced skin detail (Figure 3.1) (Ruddick, 1974; Cameron et al., 1973; Hempling, 1981; Krauss and Warlen, 1985).

In addition to the reflective ultraviolet technique, Dubey et al. (2022), in their study, reported that the application of near-infrared photography would be the best of the investigative techniques for visualisation and photo-documentation of forensically relevant post-mortem findings such as trace evidence (e.g., blood spots and soil particles on dark clothing), external findings (e.g., contusion on the victim's body), and also internal findings in road traffic collisions, gunshot injuries, and drowning victims (e.g., mud particles in the trachea of a drowning victim and the location and extent of scalp contusions in road traffic accident cases).

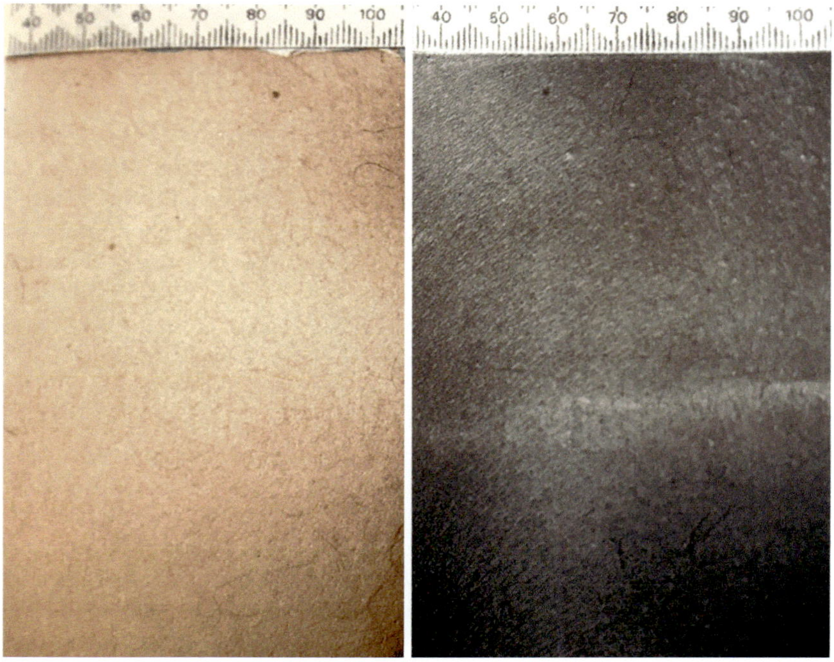

(a) (b)

**Figure 3.1** (a) Ligature mark made by sash cord on the subject's arm photographed by exposure to normal visual rays, and (b) the same ligature is greatly enhanced when photographed using reflective ultraviolet light.

# DISSECTION OF ANTERIOR NECK STRUCTURES

## Initial Incisions, Dissection of Anterior Musculature and in Situ Inspection

At this stage, it should be appreciated that great care should be taken in the handling and dissection of the neck because of the possibility of producing artefactual haemorrhage. When blunt neck trauma is suspected, the initial procedure should be removal of the brain in order to drain the blood from the neck vessels prior to any skin incision to the neck region. Further preliminary procedures, such as division of the superior vena cava (Camps and Hunt, 1959), or division of the trachea and removal of the chest organs, have also been suggested. From my own experience, however, drainage of blood from the head alone is perfectly satisfactory.

A 'Y' incision beginning from behind both ears and meeting in the midline of the chest (Figure 3.2) is the most satisfactory method, allowing adequate initial exposure of the anterior neck structures (please refer to Chapter 2 for a description of the anatomical location of the structures in this region). Once these skin incisions have been made, certain precautions should be taken, as recommended by Prinsloo and Gordon (1951). These authors advise that the neck should be inspected in situ and the prevertebral fascia exposed without incision of major blood vessels. Indeed, they demonstrated dissection artefacts, which were quite indistinguishable from antemortem bruises. Camps and Hunt (1959) also encountered such artefacts, especially after dissection of the neck shortly after death (Figure 3.3).

Excision of the carotid arteries may be carried out separately or together with the posterior neck structures. Ludwig (1979a) prefers removal after embalming so as not to interfere with this process.

The skin of the neck should be dissected back with care to enable a clear examination of the subcutaneous tissue, including the platysma muscle, to detect any bruise that might be present. Indeed, in cases of ligature or manual strangulation, it may be the only location where bruising is found. The initial dissection should be superficial to the sternomastoid muscle (invested by the

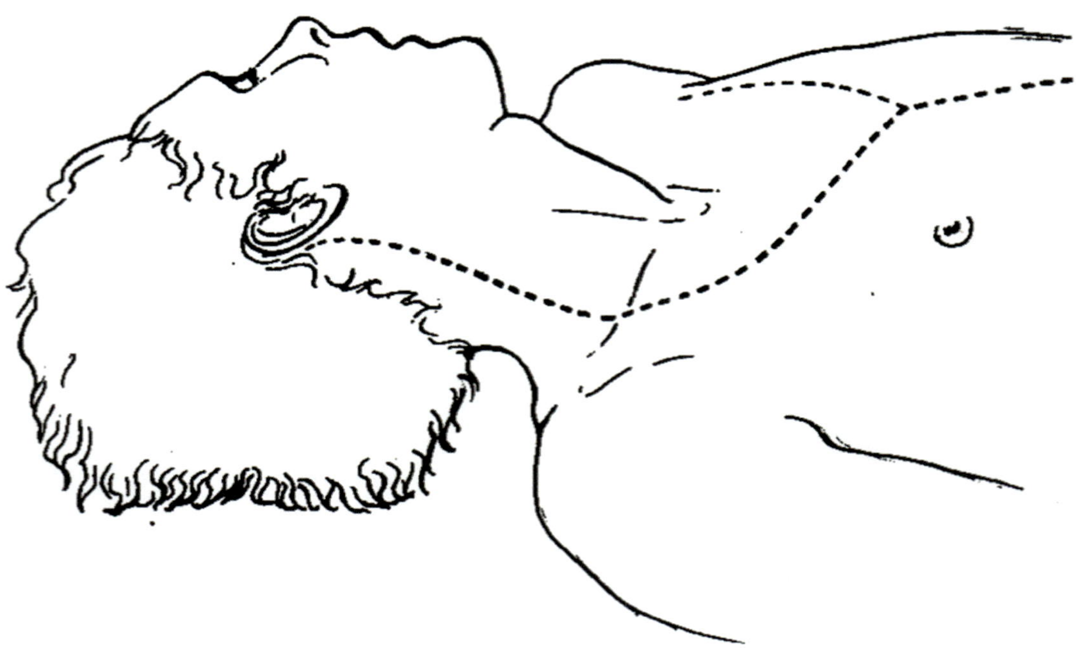

**Figure 3.2** Y-shaped incision recommended for exposure of the neck structures.

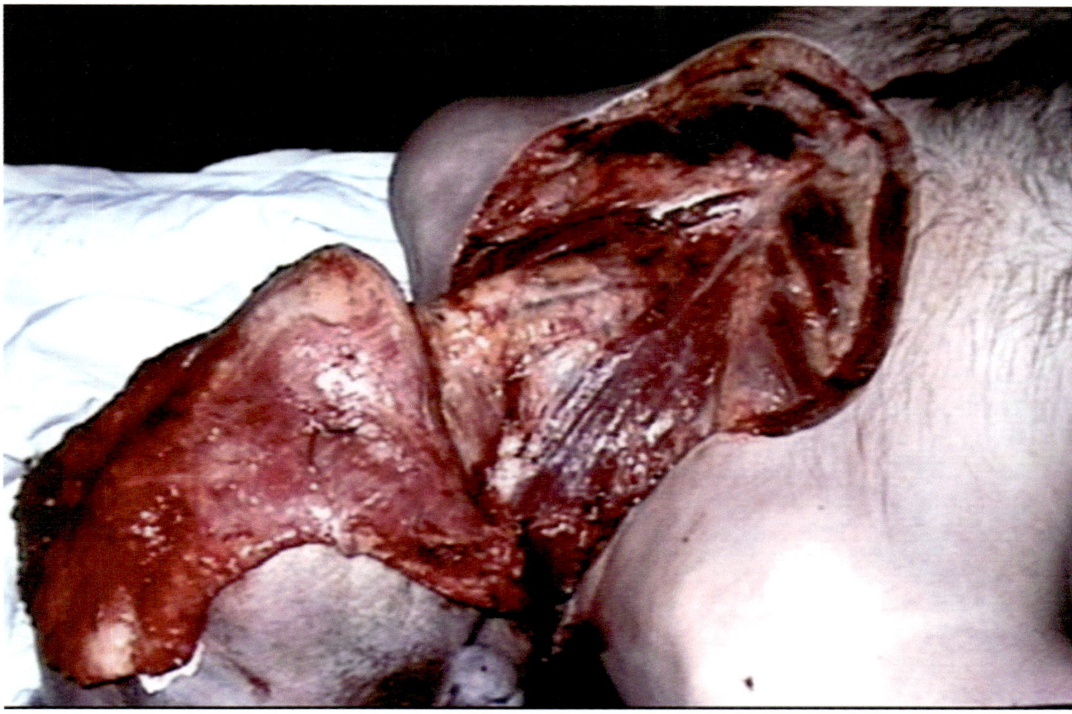

**Figure 3.3** Anterior neck structures exposed for inspection.

deep cervical fascia) to identify and inspect the external jugular vein before examination and dissection of the major muscle masses.

The anterior neck muscles should be examined layer by layer, documenting the dimensions, distribution, and character of any injuries and particularly their relation to any surface trauma. The sternal head of the sternomastoid should be identified, cut away from the manubrium, and reflected. The clavicular head can then be released. This attachment is more lateral, of variable width, and is situated along the middle third of the upper surface of the clavicle. The main belly of the sternomastoid can then be reflected off the underlying structures up towards its attachment to the mastoid process. The underlying musculature will then become more visible and accessible. Both the suprahyoid and infrahyoid muscle groups should be identified and inspected. In doing so, and in order to avoid the production of dissection artefacts, care should be taken not to cut through any major vessels until the prevertebral fascia has been inspected for bruising.

The larynx and associated structures, the hyoid bone, tongue, pharynx, and upper oesophagus, are usually examined once they have been excised. The contents of the carotid sheath, the carotid arteries, internal jugular vein, and nerves (principally the vagus), can be inspected in situ once they have been exposed anteriorly after the reflection of the sternomastoid and division and reflection of the omohyoid muscle. The vessels and nerves should be mobilised by careful dissection with a scalpel (not blunt dissection) before the laryngeal structures are removed. In cases of neck compression, it is important to identify bruises, particularly near the carotid bifurcation; before removal of the larynx, it is easy to produce haemorrhage from small vessels on dissection, which may be mistaken for antemortem bruising. It is important to remember, however, that antemortem bruising of the carotid artery is not a common finding following compression of the neck.

## Excision of the Anterior Structures

The next step is to excise the tongue, hyoid bone, larynx, and related structures. At this stage of the examination, there should be a clear view of the laryngeal strap muscles, thyrohyoid membrane, and mylohyoid muscle. A scalpel should be used to incise through the suprahyoid, lingual, and other muscles attached to the inferior surface of the mandible and its internal anterior (post-mental) surface, thus gaining access to the oral cavity and keeping as close as possible to the inferior margin of the mandible (Figure 3.4). A sweep of the scalpel blade is then made along both sides, keeping as close as possible to the mandible. In doing so, the submandibular and parotid glands should be identified and inspected. The tongue can therefore be freed and dissected away from the mouth. While gripping the tongue and pulling it forward beneath the mandible, care should be taken to divide the stylohyoid ligaments as close to the cranial end as possible. Occasionally, particularly in the elderly, these structures are calcified, and it may be difficult to free the hyoid bone from them. The tongue must also be freed from the styloglossus muscle by dividing this muscle as high as possible. With the tongue gripped in this manner and partially mobilised, a horizontal incision should be made with a scalpel in the soft palate just above the uvula and into the oropharynx. The incision is then continued through the mucosa and musculature surrounding the oropharynx down to the prevertebral fascia. The hyoid bone, laryngeal structures, pharynx, and upper oesophagus can then be carefully dissected off the prevertebral fascia and either removed with the thoracic organs or divided at the thoracic inlet. If these structures are being examined to assess a penetrating injury, it is advisable to demonstrate the direction and length of a track of such a wound with a probe before dissection. Detailed examination of sites of injury can be carried out after excision.

## Dissection of the Larynx and Hyoid Bone

Detailed dissection of the larynx should begin with inspection of the strap muscles for bruising or other injuries. Each muscle should then be reflected away from the laryngeal skeleton to expose the thyroid and cricoid cartilages. The superior cornua are best dissected posteriorly through the pharyngeal mucosa covering their posterior surface. A longitudinal incision is made on either side so that the length of each cornu may be exposed and undisplaced fractures may thus be seen (Figure 3.5).

**Figure 3.4** Diagrammatic representation of anterior neck structures. Dotted lines indicate where incisions should be made for exposure and removal of the tongue, hyoid bone, larynx, and related structures.

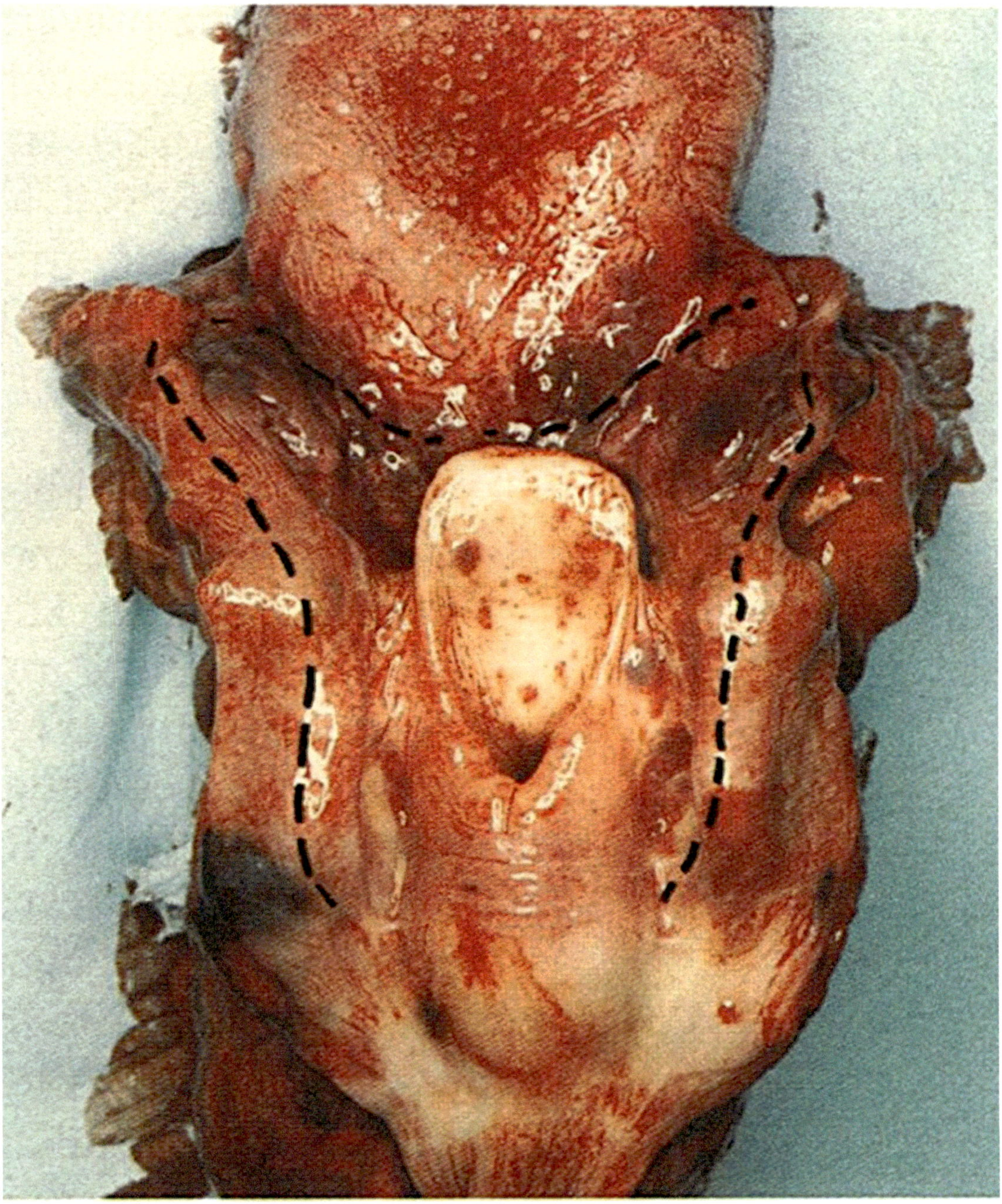

**Figure 3.5** Posterior view of laryngeal structures after excision. The dotted lines indicated where incisions should be made for exposure of the hyoid bone and both superior cornua.

When examining the laryngeal cartilages, the possibility of previous fractures of the thyroid cornua with consequent deformities of these structures should be considered. Care should also be taken not to mistake the triticeous cartilage (see Chapter 2) for a fracture of the tip of the superior cornu. This cartilage is present in the thyrohyoid ligament, beyond the tip of the cornu.

The hyoid bone is examined by a transverse incision through the pharyngeal part of the tongue, continued forward through the hyoglossus muscle, thus exposing the superior surface of the hyoid bone. Incomplete fusion of the greater horn of the hyoid bone with the body is common and variable and may sometimes be mistaken for a fracture; hence, the necessity for a careful dissection to expose the surface of the bone.

## Examination of the Fixed Laryngo-Hyoid Structures

A detailed examination of the larynx and hyoid bone can be carried out after excision and formalin fixation. A prospective forensic study of these structures involving 191 cases of homicidal strangulation from 1984 to 1997 was examined by Maxeiner (1998). The basic steps included complete resection of the thyroid cartilage, a horizontal incision through the cricoid cartilage before opening the larynx dorsally, inspection of the laryngeal joints, and incisions of the laryngeal muscles. Using this procedure allowed the author to detect several injuries, which otherwise would have been destroyed or overlooked. These included incomplete fractures restricted to the dorsal surfaces of the thyroid laminae and incomplete or non-dislocated fractures of the cricoid cartilage. Extensive laryngeal muscle haemorrhages, especially of the vocal folds, were found in almost half of all cases of manual strangulation.

# RADIOLOGICAL EXAMINATION OF THE LARYNX AND HYOID BONE

## Plain X-ray Examination

This method of imaging may be carried out either in situ to avoid allegations of post-mortem trauma caused by clumsy excision of the anterior neck structures or after removal (Figure 3.6). Anteroposterior, lateral, and oblique views should be taken. Excellent results may be obtained with the excised larynx. Good soft tissue detail will also show the airway shadow, which, in strangulation, may show marked narrowing of the supraglottic region.

## Post-mortem Computed Tomography (PMCT) with 3D Rendering

Maiese (2014) found that in cases of asphyxia-related death (with special regards to homicidal strangulation), post-mortem computed tomography (PMCT) with 3D documentation could be very helpful in revealing injuries on the small structures of the neck that can also be masked by soft tissues and surrounding small haemorrhages. This imaging technique thus provides a useful guide for the pathologist when dissecting the neck to avoid artefactual injury to delicate structures, such as the hyoid bone or thyroid cartilage.

Gascho et al. (2019), from their study, concluded that PMCT demonstrated equivalent results to the autopsy for the detection of hyoid and thyroid fractures, but (non-enhanced) computed tomography (CT) is not reliable for the detection of haemorrhages in the neck. They did, however, find that compared to the autopsy, PMCT and MRI showed advantages in the detection of pneumomediastinum and soft tissue emphysema.

In child abuse cases, the use of CT may assist in cases where there has been attempted or fatal strangulation. Bird et al. (1987) demonstrated in three infants a large cerebral infarction confined to vascular territories associated with small subdural hematomas. There was no history or visible evidence of significant head trauma. In the fatal case, the presence of a hemispheric infarct, thin subdural hematoma, and an area of subintimal haemorrhage in the carotid artery ipsilateral to the infarct was confirmed. The remaining two patients survived with residual hemiparesis.

## Use of Micro-CT

The overall principles of microcomputed tomography (micro-CT) are similar to medical CT, as it uses a stack of 2D radiographs to examine the internal structure of a sample. Micro-CT is a recent imaging technique that achieves a spatial resolution of 1 μm or less, which lends itself to the examination of small and delicate structures such as the larynx. However, there is little information to date regarding the appearance of the larynx at this scale, thus complicating the interpretation of the micro-CT images. In the study by Baier et al. (2019), micro-CT was used to examine ten larynges from strangulation deaths and to compare them to nineteen samples from donor individuals to distinguish between naturally occurring features and actual trauma. It was found that there were several features that mimicked damage in the donor group.

Fais et al. (2016) reported the case of a 45-year-old schizophrenic patient found on the floor of the bedroom of a psychiatric ward in cardiopulmonary arrest, who died after two days in a vegetative state. His roommate claimed responsibility for the killing of the victim by neck compression, but this was considered unreliable by the prosecutor. Autopsy, toxicological analyses, and multi-slice computed tomography (MSCT), micro-CT, and histology of the larynx complex were performed. Micro-CT analysis of the thyroid cartilage revealed the bilateral presence of ossified triticeous cartilages and the complete fragmentation of the right superior horn of the thyroid. Additionally, however, it also demonstrated a fracture on the left superior horn,

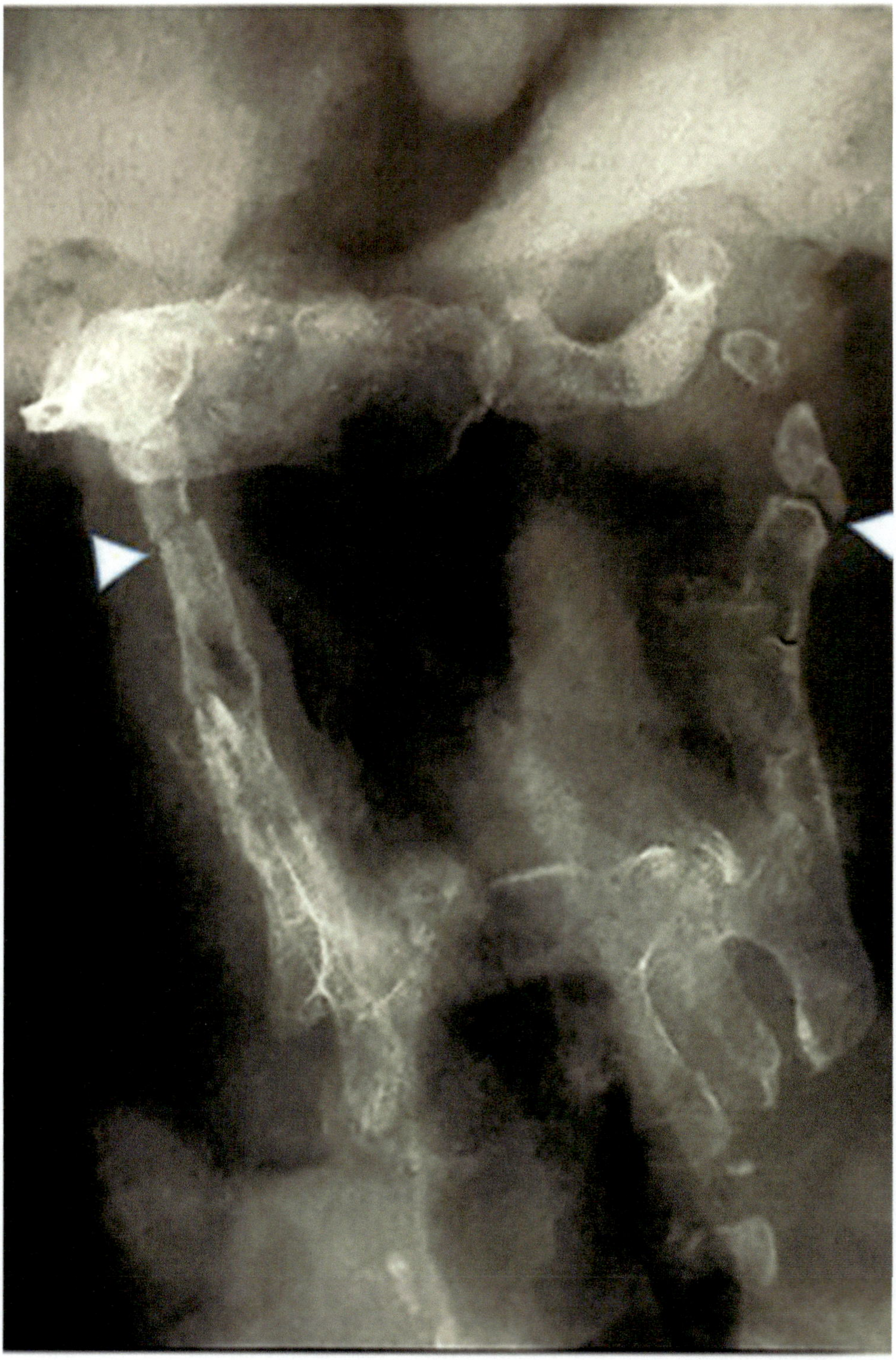

**Figure 3.6** Anteroposterior radiograph (taken as a macroradiograph) of excised larynx and hyoid bone, showing fractures to both superior cornua (arrows).

which was not clearly seen with MSCT. Based on the evidence of intra-cartilaginous laryngeal haemorrhages and bilateral microfracture at the base of the superior horns of the larynx, the death was classified as a case of asphyxia due to manual strangulation. The authors concluded that micro-CT was a useful tool in cases of subtle fatal neck compression for the detection of minute laryngeal cartilage fractures, especially in complex cases with equivocal findings on MSCT (Figures 3.7 and 3.8).

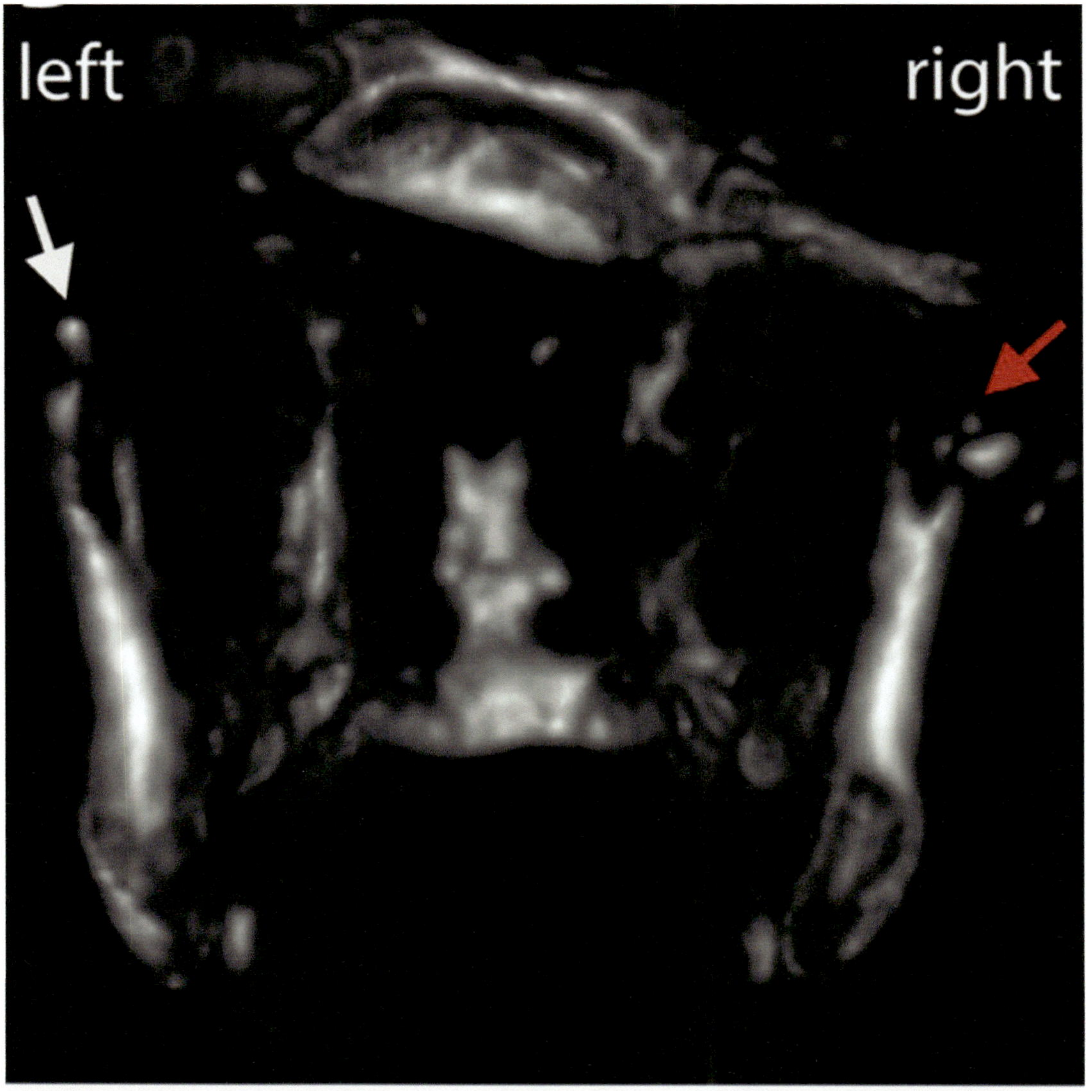


**Figure 3.7** Multi-slice computer tomography (MSTC) images of the larynx complex. 3D reconstruction of the MSCT images showing bilateral ossification of the triticeous cartilages (white arrow) and the presence of multiple displaced fragments in the right superior horn of the thyroid cartilage (red arrow) (with permission from Fais et al., 2016).

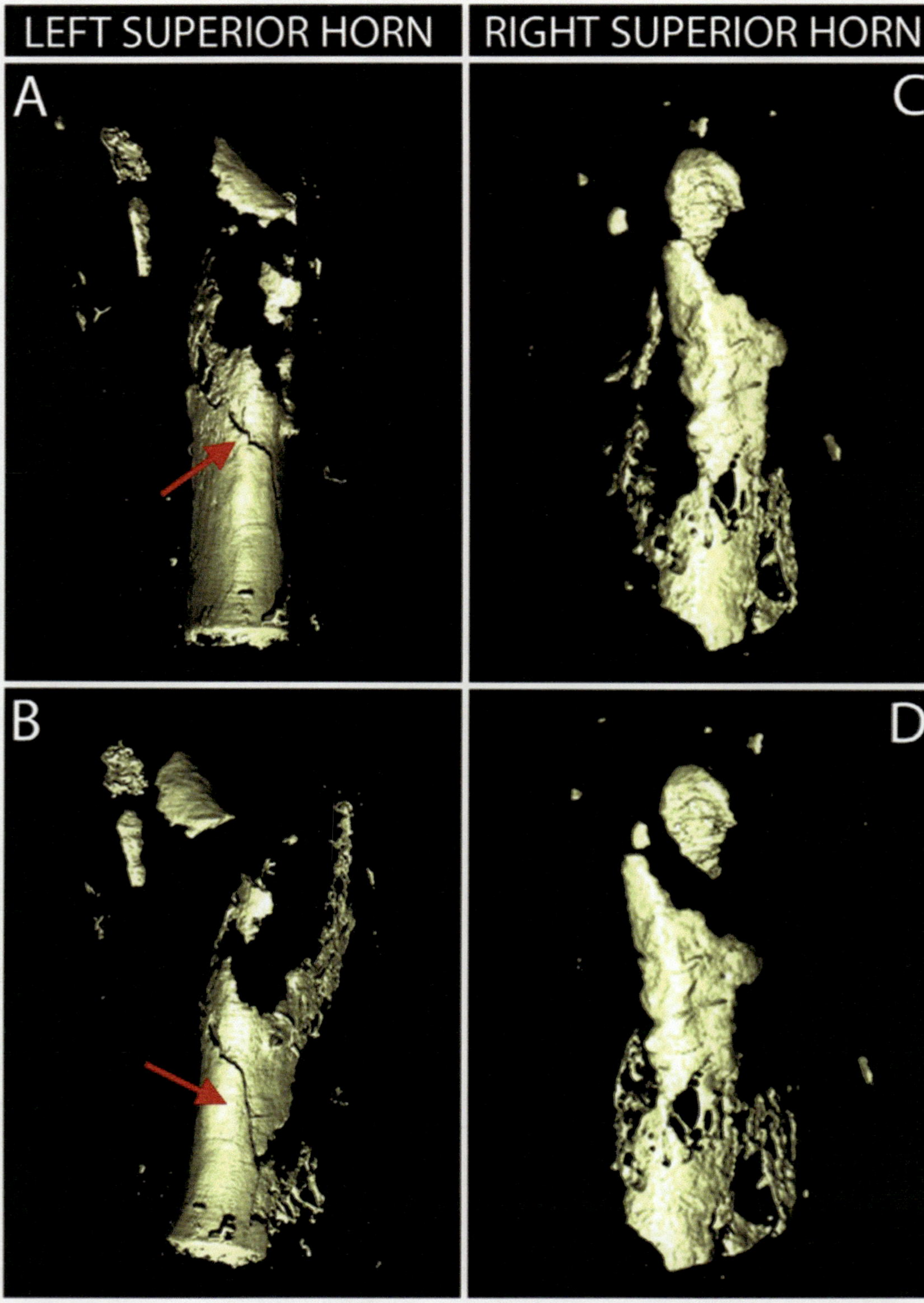


**Figure 3.8** 3D reconstructions of the micro-CT images, showing an oblique linear fracture of the left superior horn of the thyroid cartilage (A and B; red arrows) and the complete destruction of the right superior horn of the thyroid cartilage (C and D) (with permission from Fais et al., 2016).

# EXAMINATION OF THE POSTERIOR STRUCTURES

Accurate assessment of injuries in the posterior neck structures at autopsy can be difficult because of their location. To identify a number of injuries to the cervical vertebrae, cord, and vessels, it is often necessary to excise and retain the posterior neck structures for further examination. In practice, however, this can only be carried out in selected cases, particularly where injuries are in dispute. The cervical cord, of course, can only be properly assessed after excision, and a technique for its removal is described below. Furthermore, although trauma may be suspected to structures such as the vertebral arteries, quite commonly, there are other associated injuries to nearby structures that need careful evaluation.

The advent of improved imaging techniques such as PMCT and magnetic resonance imaging (MRI) has given the pathologist a useful adjunct in the examination of such injuries (Figure 3.9). In a recent study by Makino et al. (2017), the authors found a substantial number of cervical spine injuries that were detected by either PMCT or autopsy alone. PMCT was more useful in assisting in the detection of hidden bone fractures but was less effective in revealing intervertebral disc injuries; these were more readily discovered at the autopsy. Further description on the use of PMCT, MRI, and ultrasound for the detection of trauma is given at the end of this chapter.

## Procedures for Examination of the Vertebral Arteries

Because of the relative inaccessibility of the vertebral arteries, to ensure that they are examined thoroughly and with minimal artefactual damage if trauma is suspected, part of the examination, prior to dissection, should include angiography. Vanezis (1979) recommended post-mortem

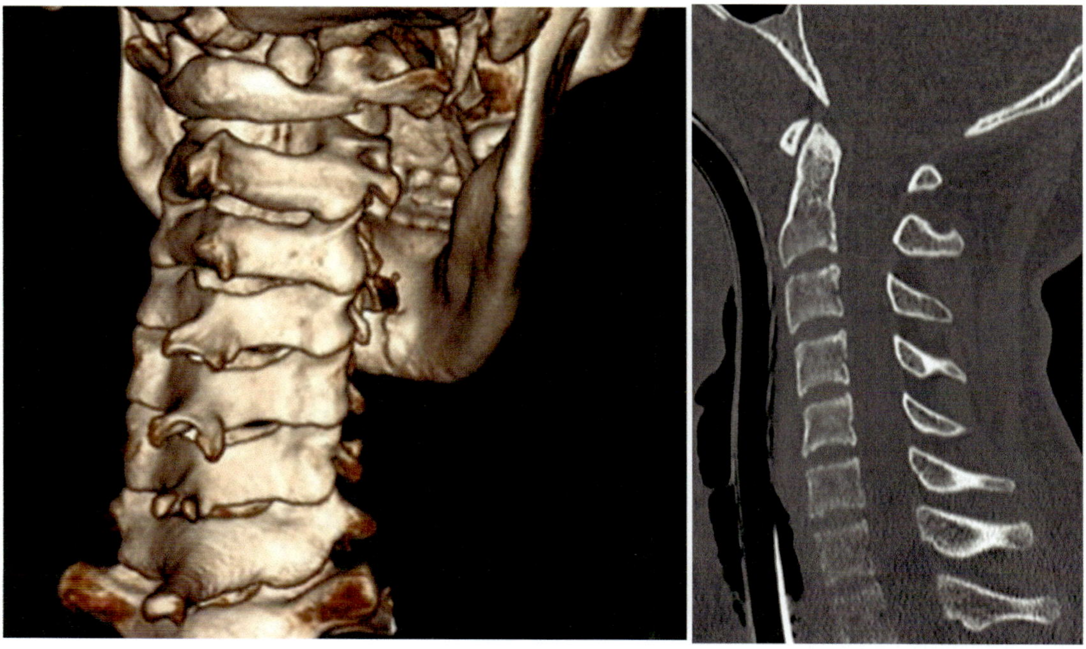

(a) (b)

**Figure 3.9** (a) Volume-rendered (3D) reconstructed CT image of the cervical spine. The post-processing results in reduced detail compared to the axial source CT dataset images, (b) but is useful for presenting images in the courtroom setting.

angiography followed by radical excision of the cervical spine and base of the skull, followed by examination of the vertebral arteries within the decalcified cervical spine. This technique has now been modified using modern imaging techniques combined with more targeted dissection.

## Angiography

Johnson et al. (2017) developed a simple and effective post-mortem angiography method using fluoroscopy and a clear modern contrast medium suitable for use in the autopsy room. The contrast medium was injected through an angiographic catheter positioned (with a water-filled balloon) in the extracranial vertebral artery (ECVA) just behind the clavicle, whilst the base of the skull and upper cervical spine area was visualised by fluoroscopy following digital subtraction of the bony images. The procedure was developed over a series of eight traumatic basal subarachnoid haemorrhage (TBSAH) cases and using unfixed cadaver specimens (Figures 3.10 and 3.11).

A clear leak point was identified in three cases and the likely site indicated in a further fatality, which were all subsequently shown to be tears on histological examination. The authors were of the view that the technique was useful in identifying the main site of vascular tearing in about 50% of cases of TBSAH and able to delineate the important anatomy of the vessels prior to dissection of the upper neck and posterior fossa, thus minimising handling artefacts and guiding the histological sampling of the vessels.

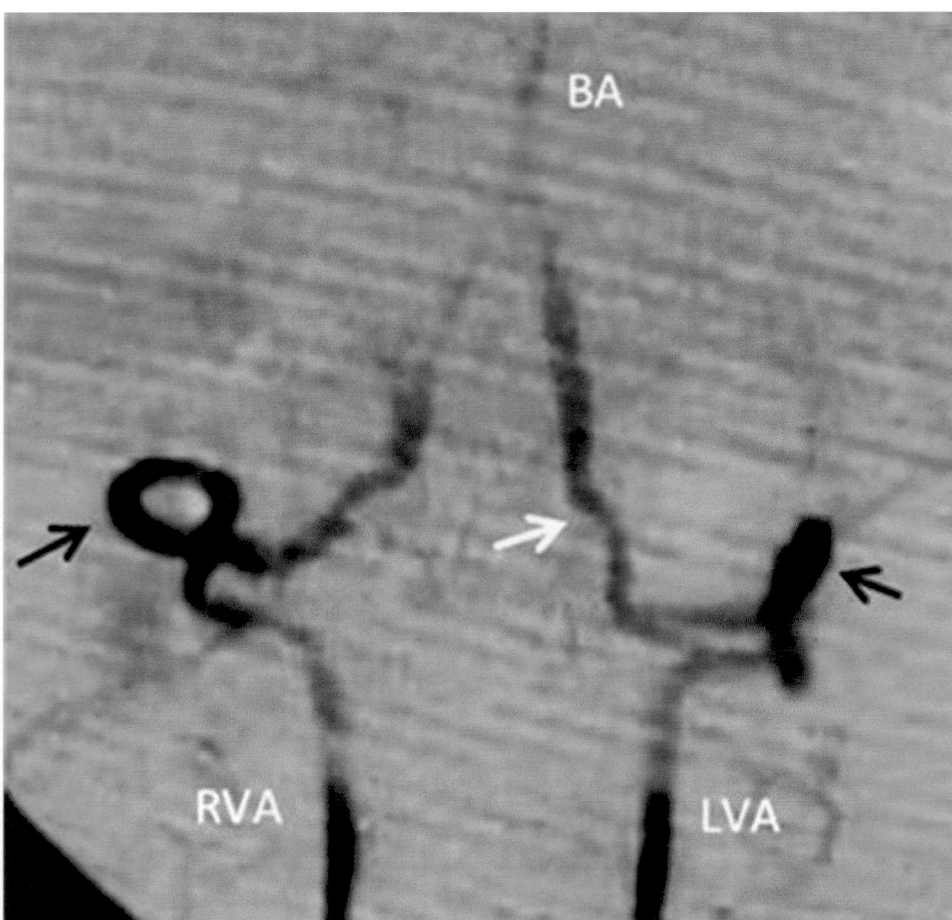


**Figure 3.10** TBSAH case with no leak of contrast. White arrow shows a small deviation of the vessel at the level of the dura. Black arrows show well-formed upper cervical loops. RVA (right vertebral artery) and LVA (left vertebral artery).

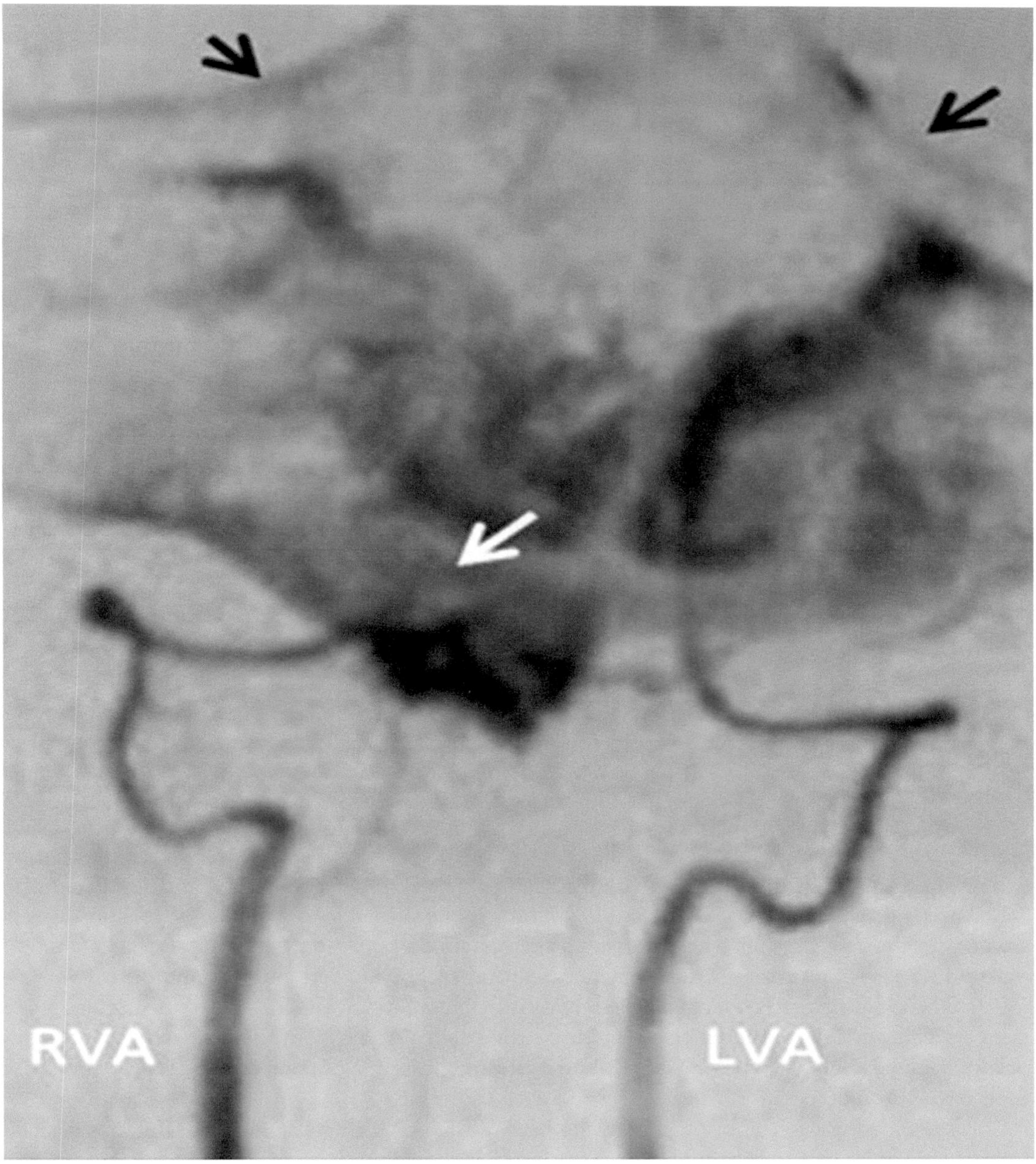


**Figure 3.11** TBSAH case. Injection of contrast via the right ECVA with left vessel open. Clear leak of contrast (white arrow) from the right intracranial vertebral artery (ICVA) with contrast outlining the intact tentorium (black arrows) and the posterior cranial fossa.

## Selective Excision of Neck Vessels

Selective excision only of the neck vessels may also be carried out, and in the United States of America, this is done in some institutions after embalming. The use of a chisel to selectively remove vertebral vessels was described by Ludwig (1979a) and more recently, by a slight modification of this method, by Bromilow and Burns (1985). The latter authors' method involved the use of a Swann Morton No. 5 scalpel handle with a No. 11 blade, a Swann Morton No. 3 scalpel with a No. 12 blade, and a pair of curved universal wire cutters. Essentially, the anterior aspect of the transverse process is cut through with the wire cutters to reveal the artery all along its course. The vessel is then mobilised, taking the usual precautions to avoid artefactual damage. The basilar artery is severed, and the vertebral vessels are mobilised, together with a cuff of dura, then pulled through and removed in their entirety. It should, however, be appreciated that removal of the vertebral arteries by local excision, whilst quick and relatively easy with a little practice, may nevertheless produce artefactual damage, which may be unacceptable, particularly when associated injuries such as transverse process fractures or venous plexus injuries are suspected.

More recently, in cases of TBSAH, Kim et al. (2015) advocated the use of posterior neck dissection to examine the intracranial vertebral arteries and the dura-penetrating region. After dissecting the muscle surrounding the cervical vertebrae, the posterior laminae of the cervical vertebrae are cut, and the spinal cord is exposed. The dura surrounding the penetrating portion of the vertebral artery is then cut, as well as the extracranial vertebral artery just below the dura. Using this method, they were able to safely examine the entire intracranial vertebral artery, including the point of dura penetration. With the cut in the vertebral artery just below this region, a 1–2 cm portion of the distal extracranial vertebral artery could be viewed. If the vertebral artery is cut between the first and second cervical vertebrae, 3–4 cm of the extracranial vessel can be examined.

A posterior neck dissection technique that enables visualisation of the entire vertebral arteries is described by Galtés et al. (2012). Their method involves dissection of the vertebral canal by posterior laminectomy of the posterior arches and cuts into the transverse foramina, allowing good exposure of the transverse part of the vertebral artery, a critical segment for the traumatic injuries that remain unobserved during the anterior neck approach. Thus, associated trauma is much better visualised using this technique.

## Dissection and Examination of the Cervical Spine, Cord and Other Posterior Neck Structures

Examination in situ of the cervical spine and its related structures cannot be carried out with ease by gross inspection alone. Furthermore, attempts to relate the degree of mobility of the less accessible higher part of the cervical spine with injury are frequently misleading. Accurate assessment of the extent of trauma frequently requires examination of the excised cervical spine and adnexa, preferably with a portion of the base of the skull. Not only is one then able to evaluate the relationship and integrity of the vertebrae and their joints, but the vertebral vessels and cord can then be examined.

To effect excision of the posterior structures, the author uses an anterior approach (Vanezis, 1979). The cervical spine is sawn through anteriorly between C7 and T1. The surrounding posterior cervical muscles are then incised to release the cervical spine from the skin and subcutaneous tissues of the back of the neck. With the spine thus mobilised, a portion of the base of the skull is then sawn through so that it can be removed with the spine.

If it is decided not to remove a part of the base of the skull, then the neck specimen is released from the skull by incising through the posterior atlanto-occipital membrane (taking great care to avoid the vertebral artery at this point), the tectorial membrane, cruciform ligament, apical or alar ligaments covering the dens, and the anterior atlanto-occipital membrane.

Once the specimens have been radiographed (with anteroposterior, lateral, and oblique views) and assessed grossly, then the next step will be to decalcify the cervical spine to facilitate a detailed evaluation of trauma.

The endpoint for adequate decalcification depends on the type and strength of the decalcifying fluid. The following method may be used. The neck structures are fixed in a 4% saline formaldehyde solution for three to five days depending on the size of the specimen. Decalcification is then carried out in 10% formic acid in 4% saline formaldehyde. The length of time necessary for decalcification is approximately four to five weeks, with frequent changes of the decalcifying fluid. To avoid tissue trauma, formic acid is preferred to nitric acid, although the period for decalcification in the former is longer.

When decalcification has been completed, or is nearing completion, slices of the specimen may be taken transversely at requisite levels and inspected grossly for any obvious trauma, if necessary, with a dissecting microscope. Sections for histological examination may then be cut at various levels of the cervical spine and accompanying excised base of skull, to include the vertebral artery and venous plexus (Figure 3.12).

In a more recent study, Matshes and Joseph (2012) demonstrated the usefulness of excision of the posterior neck structures using a posterior approach. The excised structures were then decalcified after radiography, and the cervical spine was sectioned at each level and examined grossly and histologically. With these techniques, the authors were able to facilitate the examination of complex cases, particularly where death has occurred after neurosurgical and chiropractic procedures.

## Excision of the Spinal Cord

Removal of the spinal cord when not excising the posterior neck structures en bloc may be carried out either using an anterior or posterior approach. The latter approach is described. A midline incision is made posteriorly from the occipital protuberance down to the fourth lumbar vertebra (although one is concerned here with cervical cord trauma, the cord should be removed in its entirety). The skin and underlying tissue are dissected away on either side of the spinous processes, and the laminae are exposed. To avoid artefactual damage to the cord, the laminae are divided

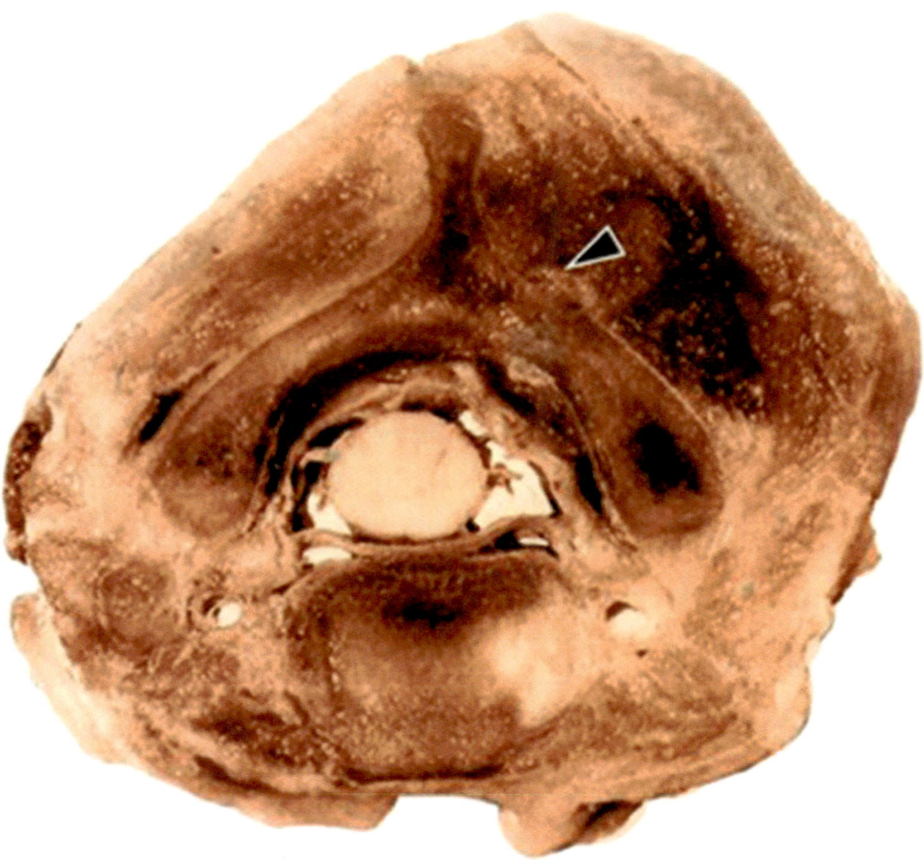

**Figure 3.12** Transverse section through decalcified cervical spine at the level of C3. A stab wound had penetrated between C2 and C3. Note the fracture of the right lamina of C3 (arrow) with substantial surrounding haemorrhage (viewed from below).

as close to the transverse processes as possible with an electric saw or bone forceps. At the lower end, a transverse incision is made so as to enable one to grasp the lumbar portion and lift the spinous process upwards in one piece. The spinal cord, surrounded by dura mater, is now exposed and inspected. The dura is gripped with forceps and drawn gently aside to expose the extradural nerves, which are then divided on either side. The dura and lower nerve roots at the distal end of the spinal canal are divided transversely. The dura is picked up with the forceps so as to raise the cord gently, allowing the remaining connections to be severed. The spinal cord and dura mater are now divided as near to the foramen magnum as possible and removed. If the posterior structures had previously been removed, then the cervical cord can be exposed by sawing through the laminae of the excised vertebrae as described above.

# EXAMINATION FOR AIR EMBOLISM

Air embolism may occur in sharp force trauma or by therapeutic procedures such as operations in the head or neck region. Cervical veins subject to penetrating trauma may take in air, which then embolises to the right ventricle of the heart and may have fatal consequences. Detection of air embolism, however, requires the prosector to be aware of the possibility prior to dissection because the introduction of gas into veins is almost invariable once major veins have been incised. Air sucked into injured veins affects the contractility of the heart and is found on the right side, pulmonary trunk, and arteries.

Older publications such as Ludwig (1979b) recommended that the thoracic cavity should be opened by lifting out the sternum and attachments, clamping the internal mammary vessels below the sternoclavicular joints, and then cutting across the sternum distal to these clamped vessels so that the sternoclavicular joint area remains intact. The pericardial sac was then carefully opened, and if a large fatal pulmonary air embolism was present, it should be readily apparent and associated with distension of the right atrium and ventricle with fine frothy bright red blood. It must be borne in mind, however, that if the victim has survived for a number of hours, air will dissolve and not be visualised. Any undue delay may result in gases due to decomposition mimicking an embolism.

A chest radiography, or if available, CT scanning, where death has occurred very soon after the embolism, will be best placed for diagnosis. In a forensic setting, the exclusion or differentiation from gas developing after death due to autolysis, which will affect veins and arteries in the same manner as stated above, remains an important challenge (du Plessis and du Toit-Prinsloo, 2017; Kauczor et al., 1995).

# GENERAL COMMENTS ON THE USE OF COMPUTERISED TOMOGRAPHY (CT), MAGNETIC RESONANCE IMAGING (MRI), AND ULTRASOUND TECHNIQUES FOR DETECTION OF NECK TRAUMA

The following techniques, although they have proven to be useful over recent years in autopsy cases as discussed above, are nevertheless more applicable in a clinical situation and are not always available for routine use in autopsy practice. Nevertheless, from the medico-legal point of view generally, knowledge of their applications and interpretation is essential.

## Computerised Tomography

CT is the mainstay and first line in the imaging assessment of traumatic injuries for clinical management and treatment of the majority of significant acute traumatic injuries of victims and secondarily for extracting forensic radiological findings relating to those injuries. There have been significant advances in CT technology (in particular, multi-detector technology) over the last decade, which makes CT scanning central to the clinical (and subsequently forensic) evaluation of various types of traumatic injuries. The technique involves volume acquisition of a stack of axial slices of the body or region of the body using X-ray tubes and an array of aligned detectors. In the live patient, intravenous contrast can be injected into the patient/victim to identify significant vascular injury (for example, in stab injuries), active haemorrhage, and identification of bone trauma and visceral injury. CT scans are particularly valuable in the demonstration of and assessment of skeletal injuries such as cervical spine fractures, as well as the hyo-laryngeal complex (in non-fatal strangulation, for example), particularly as the laryngeal cartilages begin to calcify in adulthood. Current CT imaging techniques allow post-processing of images to produce sophisticated 3D image reconstructions of regions of interest for demonstration. The inherent disadvantage of CT scanning is that it utilises ionising radiation (X-rays) with all of the potential hereditary and deterministic side effects associated with ionising radiation exposure.

In the post-mortem setting, where radiation exposure to the target is less of a consideration (although other considerations may come into play), PMCT scans are particularly useful in the evaluation of fractures, fracture-dislocations, identification and localisation of metallic foreign bodies such as bullet fragments, broken blade tips, or shrapnel (Figure 3.13).

## Magnetic Resonance Imaging (MRI)

MRI does not utilise ionising radiation as the basis of its physics but rather relies on the application of radiofrequency pulses in a strong magnetic field and, therefore, does not harbour the potential risks in imaging of the live patient. It has superior soft tissue detail to CT imaging and can demonstrate soft tissue anatomy, including the major neck vessels, well by the use of specific MRI techniques and parameters but suffers from the limitations of the length of time to perform the scans (significantly longer than CT acquisitions), which means it is not suitable in acute trauma assessment, as well as relative and absolute contraindications in patients with ferromagnetic material or foreign bodies in situ (such as some medical devices or bullets and knife blade tips) which may be subject to dysfunction or movement in the magnetic field. MRI scan images are also very susceptible to patient movement artefact during the scan acquisition, which results in significantly reduced and potentially non-diagnostic detail.

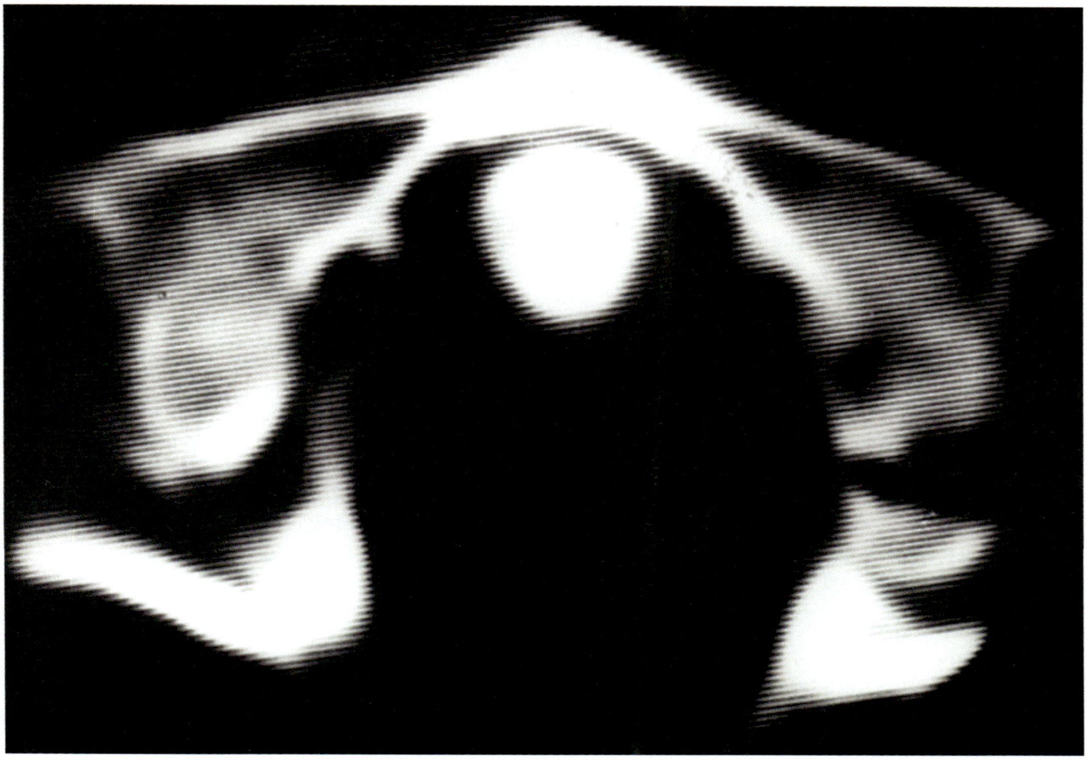

**Figure 3.13** CT scan of the cervical spine, showing a fracture of the right superior articular facet of the lateral mass of the atlas (arrow). The deceased fell from a height, landing on her head and causing asymmetrical compression of the cervical spine (Courtesy Professor J.M. Cameron).

## Ultrasound

Ultrasonography, particularly using Doppler instruments, is useful in assessing flow through blood vessels. While still used in the cold clinical setting of assessing carotid atherosclerotic disease, it has very limited value in the acute clinical setting, such as vascular injury. The assessment in penetrating trauma has been superseded by the more specific and more sensitive imaging modality of CT, specifically CT angiography. Even in relation to surgical planning for carotid atherostenotic disease, CT angiography will be the preferred form of imaging.

## References

Baier W, Burnett BA, Payne M, Warnett JM, Williams MA. Using micro-computed tomography to examine the larynx in cases of suspected strangulation-a comparison of case findings and control images. *Int J Legal Med*. 2020 July;134(4):1441–1450. doi: 10.1007/s00414-019-02194-y. Epub 2019 Nov 12. PMID: 31713681; PMCID: PMC7295822.

Bird CR, McMahan JR, Gilles FH, Senac MO, Apthorp JS. Strangulation in child abuse: CT diagnosis. *Radiology*. 1987 May;163(2):373–375. doi: 10.1148/radiology.163.2.3562816. PMID: 3562816.

Bromilow A, Burns J. Technique for removal of the vertebral arteries. *J Clin Pathol*. 1985 Dec;38(12):1400–1402. doi: 10.1136/jcp.38.12.1400. PMID: 4078022; PMCID: PMC499500.

Cameron J, Ruddick R, Grant J. Ultraviolet photography in medicine. *Forensic Photogr*. 1973;2 (3):9–12.

Camps FE, Hunt, AC. Pressure on the neck. *J Forensic Med*. 1959;6: 116–135.

Dubey A, Rupani R, Sharma V, Singh RK, Kumari S, Verma AK. Reflected near-infrared photography: Digging deeper into post-mortem examination. *J Forensic Leg Med*. 2022 Aug;90:102397. doi: 10.1016/j.jflm.2022.102397. Epub 2022 July 12. PMID: 35841695.

Fais P, Giraudo C, Viero A, Miotto D, Bortolotti F, Tagliaro F, Montisci M, Cecchetto G. Micro computed tomography features of laryngeal fractures in a case of fatal manual strangulation. *Leg Med (Tokyo)*. 2016 Jan;18:85–89. doi: 10.1016/j.legalmed.2016.01.001. Epub 2016 Jan 4. PMID: 26832384.

Galtés I, Rodríguez-Baeza A, Subirana M, Barbería E, Castellà J, Medallo J. A proposed dissection procedure for vertebral arteries in forensic pathology. *J Forensic Sci*. 2012 Jan;57(1):212–214. doi: 10.1111/j.1556-4029.2011.01904.x. Epub 2011 Aug 9. PMID: 21827482.

Gascho D, Heimer J, Tappero C, Schaerli S. Relevant findings on postmortem CT and postmortem MRI in hanging, ligature strangulation and manual strangulation and their additional value compared to autopsy - a systematic review. *Forensic Sci Med Pathol*. 2019 Mar;15(1):84–92. doi: 10.1007/s12024-018-0070-z. Epub 2019 Jan 9. PMID: 30627977.

Hempling SM. The applications of ultraviolet photography in clinical forensic medicine. *Med Sci Law*. 1981 July;21(3):215–222. doi: 10.1177/002580248102100310. PMID: 7278534.

Johnson CP, Murphy M, Johnson GA, Wills SM, Medcalf JE. A simple post mortem room angiography method for the investigation of traumatic basal subarachnoid hemorrhage. *Forensic Sci Med Pathol*. 2017 Mar;13(1):4–9. doi: 10.1007/s12024-016-9820-y. Epub 2017 Jan 17. PMID: 28093693.

Kauczor HU, Riepert T, Wolcke B, Lasczkowski G, Mildenberger P. Fatal venous air embolism: proof and volumetry by helical CT. *Eur J Radiol*. 1995 Dec 15;21(2):155–157. doi: 10.1016/0720-048x(95)00683-h. PMID: 8850515.

Kim S, Kim M, Lee BW, Kim YH, Choi YS, Seo JS. Investigation of bleeding focus in the intracranial vertebral artery with the use of posterior neck dissection method in traumatic basal subarachnoid hemorrhage. *J Forensic Leg Med*. 2015 Aug;34:151–154. doi: 10.1016/j.jflm.2015.06.008. Epub 2015 June 20. PMID: 26165675.

Krauss TC, Warlen SC. The forensic science use of reflective ultraviolet photography. *J Forensic Sci*. 1985 Jan;30(1):262–268. PMID: 3981118.

Ludwig J. Removal of the neck vessels. In *Current Methods in Autopsy Practice*, 2nd edn. Saunders, Philadelphia, 1979a, pp. 118–120.

Ludwig J. Air embolism. In *Current Methods in Autopsy Practice*, 2nd edn, Saunders, Philadelphia, 1979b, pp. 363–366.

Maiese A, Gitto L, dell'Aquila M, Bolino G. When the hidden features become evident: The usefulness of PMCT in a strangulation-related death. *Leg Med (Tokyo)*. 2014 Nov;16(6):364–366. doi: 10.1016/j.legalmed.2014.06.009. Epub 2014 July 5. PMID: 25059990.

Makino Y, Yokota H, Nakatani E, Yajima D, Inokuchi G, Motomura A, Chiba F, Torimitsu S, Uno T, Iwase H. Differences between postmortem CT and autopsy in death investigation of cervical spine injuries. *Forensic Sci Int*. 2017 Dec;281:44–51. doi: 10.1016/j.forsciint.2017.10.029. Epub 2017 Oct 28. PMID: 29101907.

Matshes EW, Joseph J. Pathologic evaluation of the cervical spine following surgical and chiropractic interventions. *J Forensic Sci*. 2012 Jan;57(1):113–119. doi: 10.1111/j.1556-4029.2011.01935.x. Epub 2011 Oct 31. PMID: 22040123.

Maxeiner H. "Hidden" laryngeal injuries in homicidal strangulation: How to detect and interpret these findings. *J Forensic Sci*. 1998 July;43(4):784–791. PMID: 9670500.

du Plessis M, du Toit-Prinsloo L. Venous air embolism: An under-recognised entity in blunt-force trauma and the importance of radiology. *Med Sci Law*. 2017 Apr;57(2):95–99. doi: 10.1177/0025802417699346. Epub 2017 Mar 14. PMID: 28438096.

Prinsloo I, Gordon I. Post-mortem dissection artifacts of the neck; their differentiation from ante-mortem bruises. *S Afr Med J*. 1951 May 26;25(21):358–361. PMID: 14855047.

Ruddick R. A technique for recording bite marks for forensic studies. *Med Biol* Illustr. 1974;24:128–129.

Vanezis P. Techniques used in the evaluation of vertebral artery trauma at post-mortem. *Forensic Sci Int*. 1979 Mar-Apr;13(2):159–165. doi: 10.1016/0379-0738(79)90280-9. PMID: 447149.

## Further Reading

Vanezis P. ACP Broadsheet no 139: June 1993. Postmortem techniques in the evaluation of neck injury. *J Clin Pathol*. 1993 June;46(6):500–506. doi: 10.1136/jcp.46.6.500. PMID: 8331170; PMCID: PMC501282.

# CHAPTER 4

## PENETRATING INJURIES

*Peter Vanezis*
*(with contributions from Curtis Offiah)*



DOI: 10.4324/9781003658467-4

# INTRODUCTION

Firearms or knives are responsible for the vast majority of penetrating injuries caused by missile or sharp force trauma. Occasionally other objects are responsible, such as glass fragments, shrapnel, and other debris resulting from explosions, arrows, and other pointed objects. Although penetrating injury to the neck represents a relatively small proportion of all trauma cases (5–10%), it results in injuries with a high degree of mortality, as well as complex clinical situations that can be challenging for healthcare providers (Vishwanatha et al., 2007).

The relative frequency between firearm and sharp force trauma varies in different countries, depending on the ease of availability of firearms. Madsen et al. (2016) carried out an audit on 510 patients with penetrating neck injury over 46 months, comparing the incidence of gunshot wounds with stab wounds to the neck in a South African metropolitan trauma service. The injuries were subdivided by manner of injury (homicide, suicide, accident). They observed that the majority of these injuries, 452 (89%) were due to stab wounds, with 58 (11%) resulting from gunshot wounds. Both groups of patients shared a similar sex and age distribution, with those sustaining gunshot wounds being more likely to have injuries to other parts of the body. Furthermore, the mean injury severity score (ISS) was higher for the gunshot wound group.

# SHARP FORCE TRAUMA

## Stabbing

The neck is the second most common region, after the chest, to suffer fatal sharp force trauma. Injury may either be homicidal, suicidal, or accidental. The author of this text, in common with a number of others (Vassalini et al. 2014; Rouse 1994; Mitton and du Toit-Prinsloo 2016; Krywanczyk and Shapiro 2015), found that stabbings to neck structures varied in incidence from around a quarter to over a third of all cases (Table 4.1). Frequently, in such cases, there are also injuries to other regions of the body.

The neck, which carries many vital structures within such a tight space and acts as a conduit between the brain and the rest of the body, when subjected to sharp force trauma, may result in devastating effects on the individual. The anterior neck structures, which are not protected by the cervical spine, are particularly vulnerable to trauma. The injuries seen are essentially penetrating, as in stab wounds, or incised (slash) wounds, which are longer rather than deeper and are produced by impacting the skin in a tangential manner.

The incidence of different types of neck injuries from stabbing and their effects is described by Demetriades et al. (1997). They demonstrated that 20% of stab wounds to the neck, in a prospective study of 223 patients, were associated with significant injuries to vital structures. The incidence of the types of structures injured is shown in Table 4.2.

Stabbing is the most common method of homicide in the United Kingdom, and as stated above, more than one-third of all cases involve the neck, including those encountered by the author. Self-inflicted or accidental stabbing is much less frequently encountered, particularly in the neck region. Occasionally, differentiating such injuries from homicidal infliction may pose difficulties. It is not unreasonable to assume that any sharp force trauma to the neck or elsewhere, from a practical point of view, should be treated as a homicide until proven otherwise.

### Type of Stabbing Agent

In most instances, the implement used is a knife (Figure 4.1), although other pointed objects are occasionally encountered, such as a screwdriver (Patel, 1998; Schulz et al., 1995).

The latter authors describe the case of a 50-year-old female victim who died of recurrent pulmonary embolism three months after having received multiple screwdriver stab wounds to the neck and upper spine. Autopsy showed that one stab had penetrated the middle part of the cervical spinal cord and thus caused an incomplete tetraplegia. In the region of the healed spinal cord and the affected meninges, a considerable amount of hair and textile fibres, surrounded by foreign body giant cells and elastic fibres of the spinal ligament, were found, all of which had been carried into the stab track by the blunt tip of the screwdriver. In addition to the primary clinical findings, this unusual transportation of matter into the depth of the stab wound allowed identification of the murder weapon.

Other examples of stabbing from different pointed implements have been reported by a number of authors. The use of the handle of a metal comb has been described by Hendry and Stalker

**Table 4.1** Neck injuries from 117 stabbing cases examined by the author during the period 1974–1986 (Vanezis, 1989). Forty-three cases (37%) involved the neck. Figures in parentheses indicate the number of cases where the neck trauma contributed to death

| | Homicide | Self-inflicted |
|---|---|---|
| Neck injured alone | 23 | 1 |
| Neck and one other region | 15 (6) | 1 (1) |
| Neck and two or more other regions | 3 (2) | |

**Table 4.2** Incidence of type of injuries from neck stab wounds (Demetriades et al., 1997)

| Injury | Stab wound (%) |
|---|---|
| Vascular | 14.6 |
| Aero-digestive | 3.4 |
| Spinal cord | 1.1 |
| Peripheral or cranial nerves or sympathetic | 4.5 |
| Haemo- or pneumothorax | 13.5 |

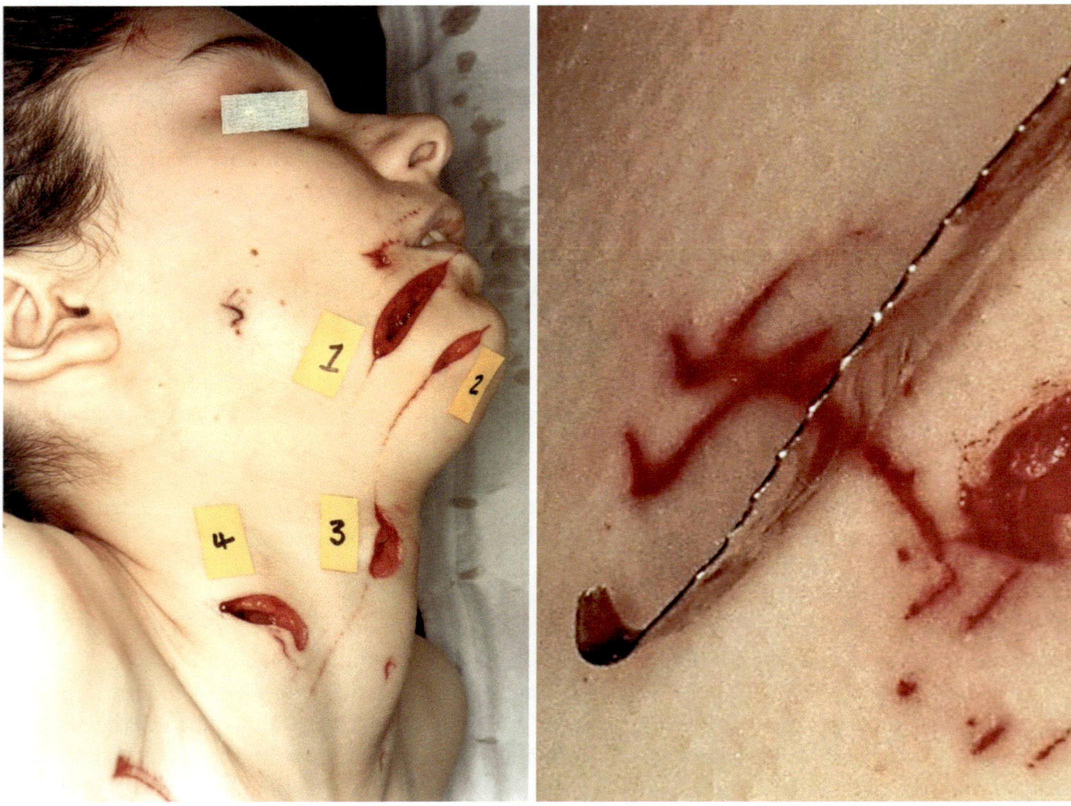


(a) (b)

**Figure 4.1** (a) Multiple stab wounds to the face and neck caused by a serrated knife, and (b) its tip had become bent during the course of stabbing, and there are accompanying "S"- or "?"-shaped superficial injuries accompanying the larger wounds.

(1967). Rothschild et al. (2001) reported the case of a 65-year-old male who, during a fall down a staircase, knocked a picture from the wall breaking the glass frame which hit him in the neck and cut through his right vertebral artery. Glass fragments were noted within the wound track. A further accidental penetrating injury was reported by Hewett and Mellick (2012), who described the case of a nine-year-old girl who, at school, fell on a sharpened pencil that penetrated the left side of her neck. The author of this text has seen a knife sharpener used as a stabbing implement. The roughened metal sides of such a tool produce a characteristic pattern of surrounding grazing (Figure 4.2).

Accidental sharp force trauma from needlefish has occasionally been reported. Barss (1985) cautioned that needlefish, which are found in Ocean, may cause severe stab wounds to swimmers.

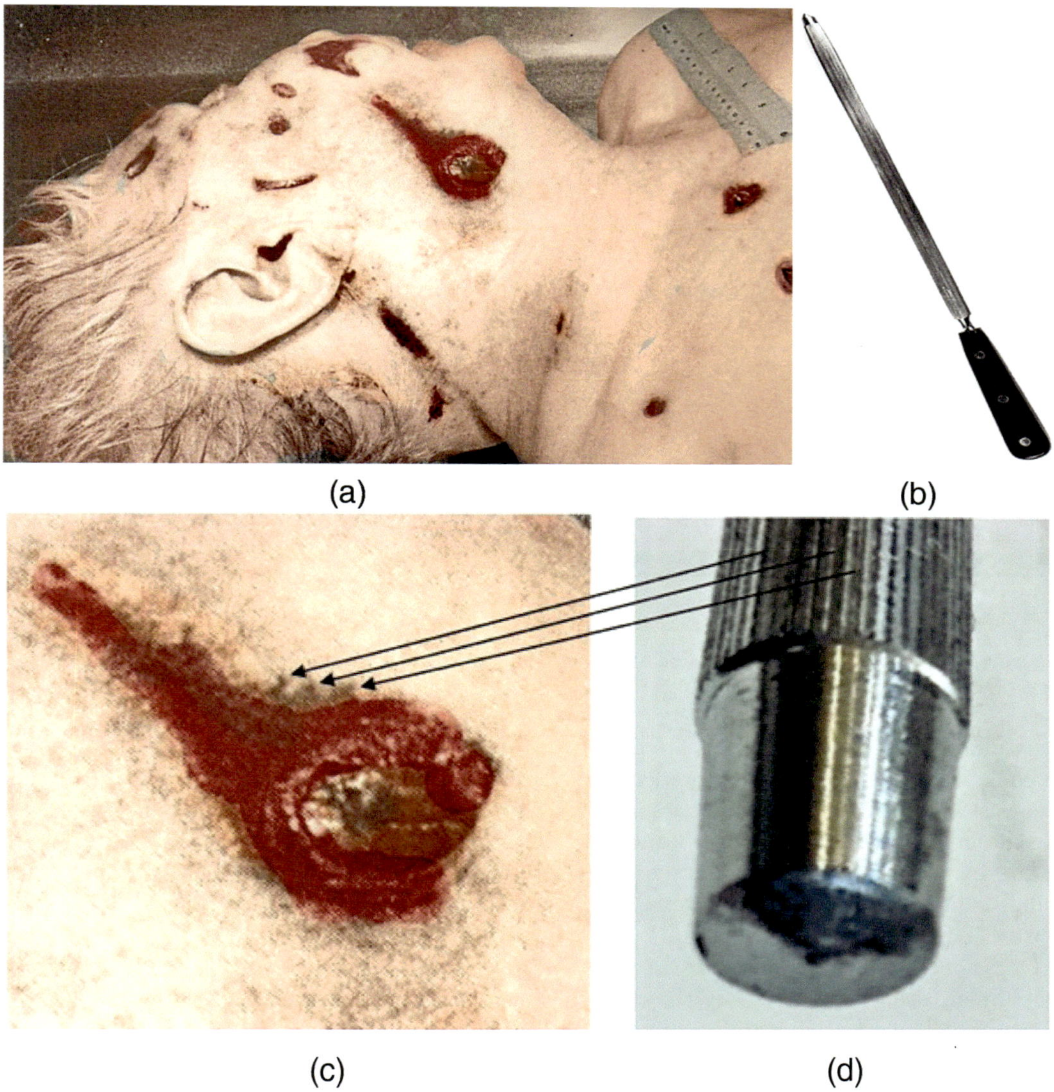


**Figure 4.2** (a) Stab wound caused by (b) knife sharpener. (c) Detail of wound showing patterned grazes (arrows). (d) Pointed end of sharpener with grooved shaft matching grazes on wound.

As their name implies, their jaws elongate into a long, narrow, rigid beak that can penetrate the body. He describes, among his cases, a 12-year-old New Zealand girl who had been injured in the neck by a needlefish. She was found to have an expanding haematoma in the right supraclavicular triangle. Exploration of the small wound (about 2 cm in diameter) revealed a wound in the sternocleidomastoid muscle. The tract went into the prevertebral fascia, and a haematoma was noted in the prevertebral muscles. The carotid sheath was intact. She did, however, shortly thereafter develop a classic picture of Brown-Sequard syndrome, suggesting hemisection at cord level C6-7.

## Site and Direction of Wounds

The question often arises as to whether an assailant is right- or left-handed. It is also often necessary to establish the relative positions of the attacker and the victim. Occasionally, it is possible to reach useful conclusions from the evidence at the site and the direction of wounds, particularly when such injuries are on the chest. Generally, however, such opinions should be guarded, and

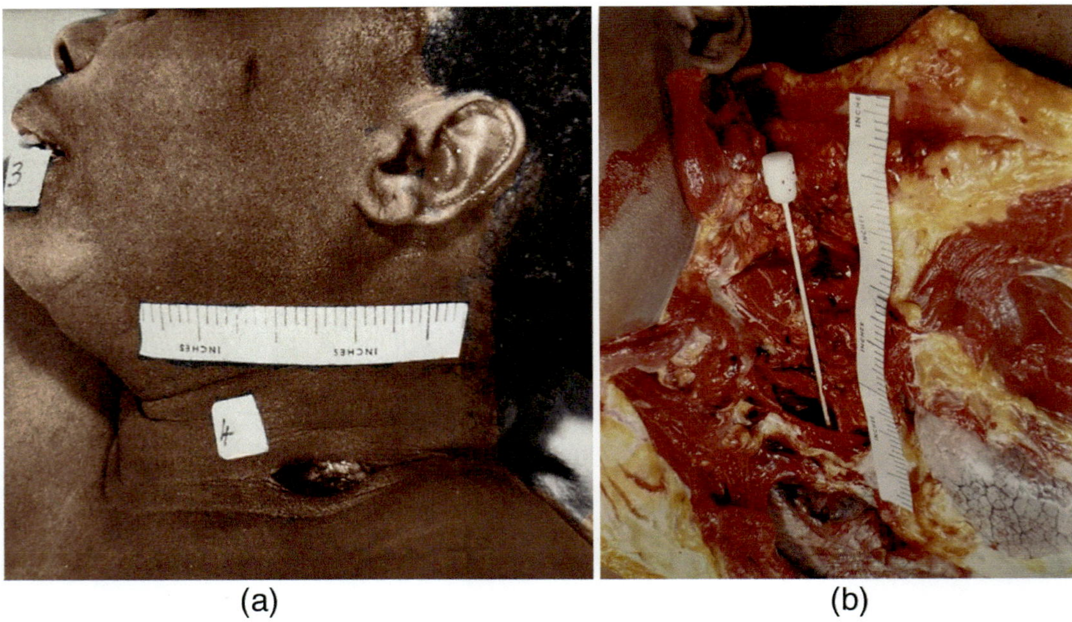


**Figure 4.3** (a) Stab wound on the left side of the neck, and (b) Its track was downward into the apex of the upper lobe of the left lung.

even more so when neck injuries are concerned, particularly if there are no injuries to any other regions. Nevertheless, there is a predominance of left-sided injuries (de Villiers and Grant, 1985). The vast majority of neck wounds track downwards or in a horizontal direction, whereas very few are directed upwards (Figures 4.3 and 4.4). Their trajectory may be apparent from the history of the incident and can be predictive of underlying neurovascular injury. For example, there is a higher incidence of subclavian vessel injury because the majority of these wounds track downwards. (Bagheri et al., 2008).

Occasionally stab wounds may also occur at the craniocervical junction. In such cases, the instrument used is deflected by the occipital squama into the atlanto-occipital or atlanto-axial interspace. The surface wound itself, which is situated in the suboccipital or retromastoid region, may appear insignificant (Figure 4.5). de Villiers and Grant (1985), in a series covering a period of eight years, found eleven patients with stab wounds at this level: seven were on the left and four on the right. Penetration of the dura mater, with cerebrospinal fluid leakage followed by meningitis, occurred in five patients, and vertebral artery injuries were seen in four.

## Self-Inflicted Versus Homicidal Stabbing

Stabbing of the neck is, from most authors' accounts, an unusual mode of suicide. In a case seen by the author of this text of self-inflicted stabbing, the tip of the knife blade had broken off and was found embedded in the neck. The knife was present and held in the deceased's right hand (Figure 4.6). Although most victims are adult males, Hasekura et al. (1985) reported such an injury in a ten-year-old child. Generally, differentiation between various categories of stabbing is not difficult. There are occasions, however, when the circumstances may not be so straightforward, or, more commonly, questions arise during a trial which may challenge the conclusions reached.

Assessment of the general conditions of the scene, e.g., forced entry, scattered and broken articles, stolen property, and widespread blood splashes and smears, are all strongly suggestive of foul play. As a rule, with self-injury, the deceased may be found in a relatively comfortable position, e.g., sitting in a chair or lying in bed, whereas homicide victims are frequently sprawled haphazardly, or may have been deliberately placed, for example, under a bed or in a wardrobe. In nearly all

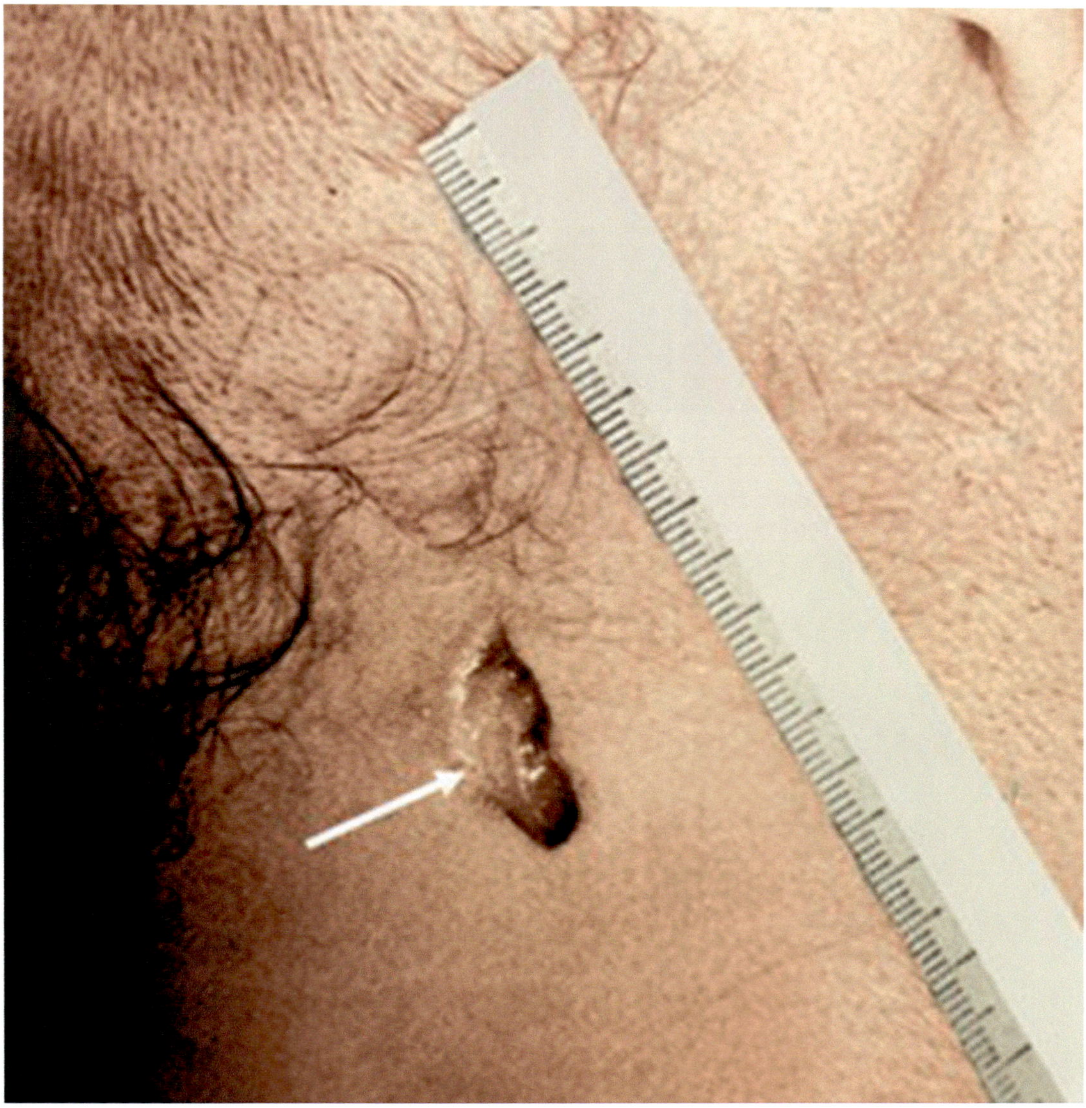

**Figure 4.4** Stab wound of the right side of the neck, which shows shelving of its posterior surface. The track of the wound, as indicated by the arrow, is slightly upwards.

self-inflicted stabbings, the offending instrument is found either still within a wound on the body, in the deceased's hand, or close by. It is possible, however, that the weapon may have been left in another room or removed from the scene by a second person to conceal the self-inflicted nature of death. Nevertheless, where the weapon is not literally close to hand, one should presume homicide until there is convincing evidence to the contrary. Other corroborative evidence of suicide, such as a note, may be found, although it ought to be borne in mind that the incidence of written evidence in suicides is less than 50% (Patel, 1971).

In homicidal stabbing, wounds are frequently multiple, usually also present on other parts of the body as well as the neck, particularly the chest, and are commonly accompanied by defence injuries to the upper limbs. Self-inflicted wounds frequently have accompanying tentative wounds (Racette et al., 2008). In one series, such injuries were found in 15 (50%) of 29 suicidal stabbing cases (Vanezis and West, 1983; Figure 4.7). Only two cases in the latter series involved the neck, and in one there were accompanying tentative wounds.

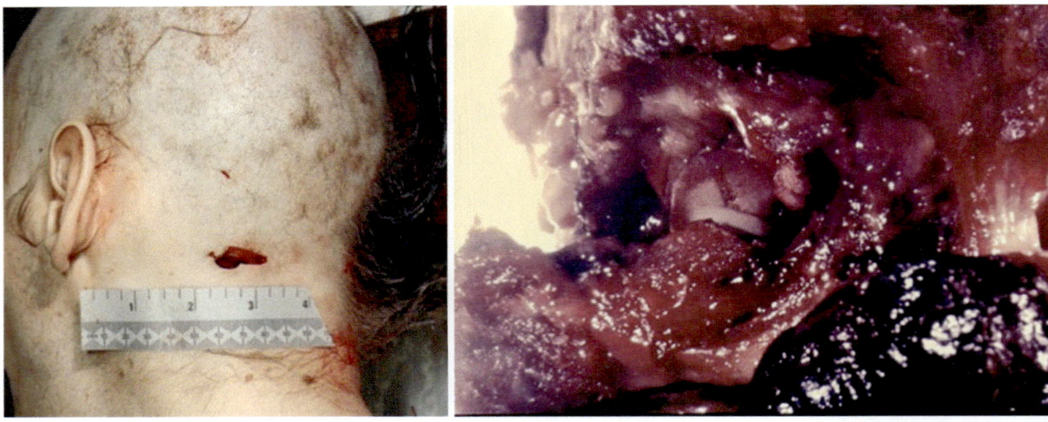

(a) (b)

**Figure 4.5** The knife which caused the surface wound (a) deflected downwards after impacting the left occipital condyle (arrow in b), resulting in severance of the vertebral artery.

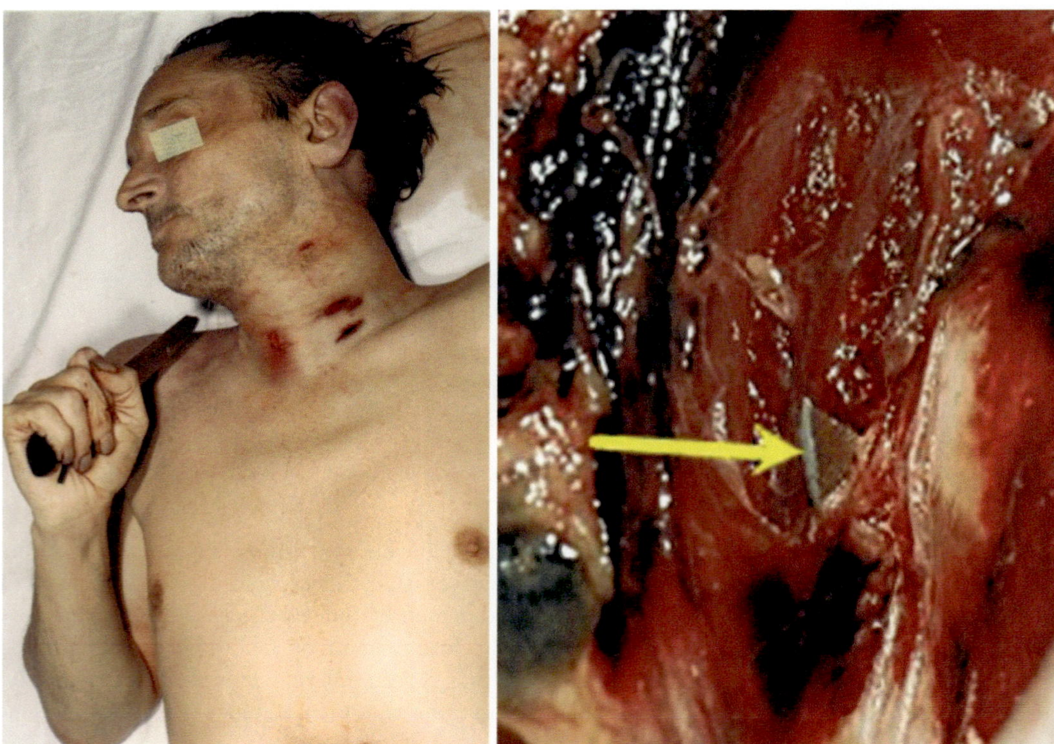

(a) (b)

**Figure 4.6** (a) Multiple self-inflicted stab wounds to the neck. There were also five on the abdomen. The knife is held firmly in the right hand and its tip is broken. (b) Anterior view of the neck after removal of the larynx. The tip of the blade is embedded in the cervical vertebral column (arrow). There is a further stab wound at C5. Substantial haemorrhage is also seen tracking along the carotid sheath.

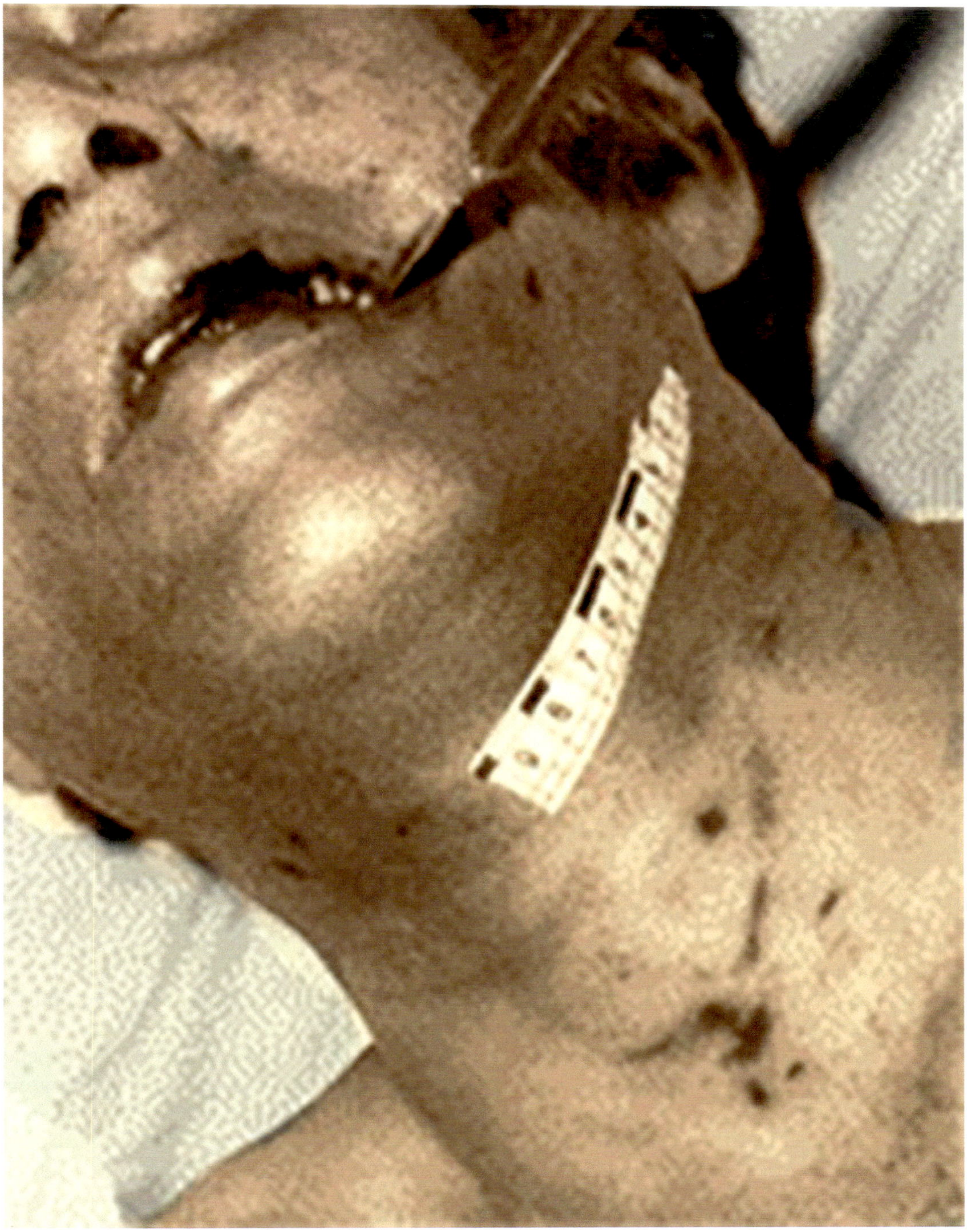

**Figure 4.7** Self-stabbing through the mouth which incised the right internal carotid artery. The knife is retained in situ. Tentative wounds are seen on the front of the neck.

There may also be superficial wounds to the wrists or arms, tending to be in an approximately parallel direction. A more recent case examined by the author revealed four stab wounds to the right side of the back of the neck, one of which entered above the atlas vertebra and up through the foramen magnum (Figure 4.8). Numerous tentative wounds were found on the right lower

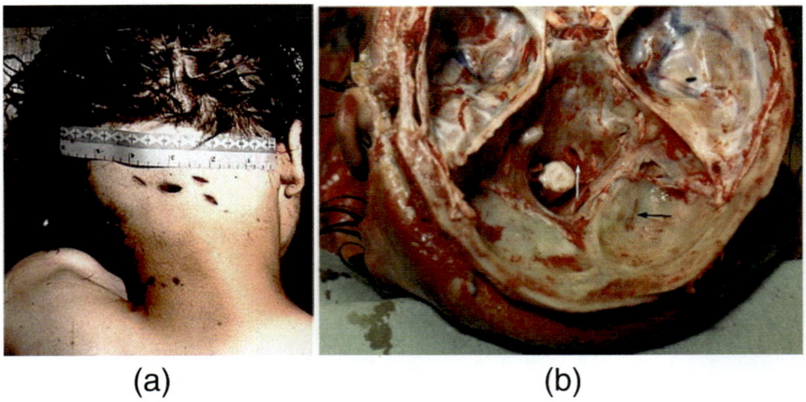

Figure 4.8 (a) Self-inflicted stab wounds to the back of the neck; all wounds were within reach of the deceased's right hand, (b) Internal view of the base of the skull showing penetration through the foramen magnum of the second wound from the left (track indicated by arrow). The third wound from the left has caused a linear fracture to the occiput (arrow).

abdomen, and there were also two deep chest wounds. The victim was right-handed and could reach the back of the neck to produce such injuries with relative ease.

A homicidal stabbing is shown for comparison in Figure 4.9. It illustrates the need to exercise extreme caution in such cases.

## Accidental Stabbing and Other Accidental Sharp Force Penetrating Trauma

Accidental stab wounds from knives are rare. King (1885) reported a case in which a knife became detached from a machine consisting of a large revolving wheel with a number of sharp knives at its circumference, which was used for shaving down the spokes of wheels. The unfortunate victim, who was standing about 10 feet away (3 metres), was struck and suffered a deep stab wound to the side of the neck.

Roll and Klintschar (1998) describe the death of a 72-year-old woman from a broken part of a rotating knife of an agricultural mower impacting on the neck. The knife had travelled approximately 100 metre through the air before hitting her while she was sitting on a balcony with her two elderly female friends. The knife cut through many vital structures at the front of the neck, including both carotids, the trachea, and the oesophagus, leading to death from exsanguination.

Road traffic collisions may occasionally include penetrating wounds to the neck due to splintered glass or, indeed, from any sharp, broken pieces of metal detached from a vehicle. Two unusual accidental causes of penetrating injury are described below:

Koehler et al. (2011) present the case of a 24-year-old driver who died when a metal pole penetrated the victim's neck, producing a through-and-through injury. He was seen driving in the wrong lane, then, after drifting back to the correct lane, he hit a stationary bus, a newspaper machine, a metal sign pole, and then came to rest in a driveway. At the scene, there was a 2-metre-long, severely twisted metal sign pole that was angular at one end. It was concluded that the driver lost control of his car, hitting a mailbox and then a signpost. The bumper of the vehicle sheared the pole, causing it to become airborne, which then penetrated the front windscreen, entered the right side of the neck, exited on the posterior side, and then exited through the back windscreen. The pole then came to rest on the pavement behind the vehicle.

In the case reported by Jothee et al. (2018), a defective airbag booster metal canister was responsible for causing penetrating injuries to the neck. A fragment of the canister was found lodged in the paravertebral muscles. The 27-year-old victim lost control of his motor vehicle and subsequently collided with a tree by the roadside. Examination of the car revealed that the metal fragment was from a defective airbag booster canister, which shattered upon deployment.

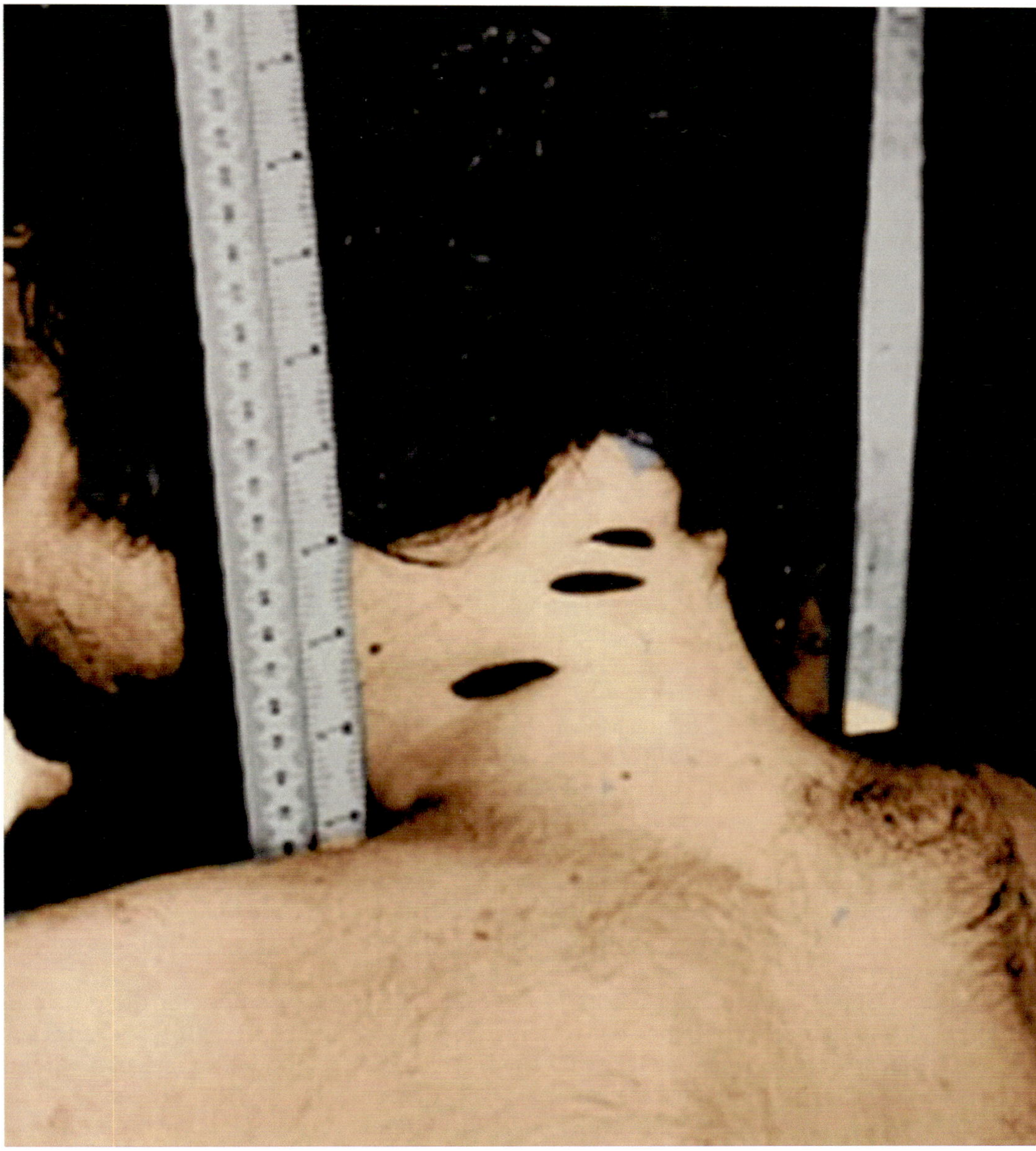

**Figure 4.9** Homicidal stabbing. There are three stab wounds to the left side of the neck (compare with Figure 4.7a). In addition, there were numerous stab wounds and defence injuries to other regions of the body.

Penetrating injuries may also occasionally be encountered in accidents involving glass, such as falling onto or through plate glass in doors, for example, or mirrors. A further such case is described by Rothschild et al. (2001) (see above). Holding and falling onto a sharp pencil, causing a fatal injury to the jugular vein in a 5-year-old girl, is described by Polson et al. (1985). A case is also reported by Abdelmasih et al. (2019) of an 11-year-old girl who fell onto a sharpened pencil, which entered the left side of her neck. The pencil was lodged in the left common carotid artery; prompt hospital intervention resulted in a full recovery.

## Incised Wounds

Although the term incised wound refers to any type of injury involving sharp force, it is generally understood to relate to wounds that are characterised by having greater length than depth of penetration into the body. With respect to the neck, most incised wounds are either homicidal or self-inflicted. On very few occasions, as with stab wounds, they may be accidental and are particularly seen in road traffic collisions where such injuries may be caused by fragments of glass.

The internal structural injury caused by cut-throat wounds was described by Rao (2015) in an autopsy study of 74 cases. He found that the external jugular veins were involved in all the cases. The larynx, trachea, carotid, and internal jugular vessels were involved in 68 cases (91.89%). The cervical vertebrae were least affected, with injury being found in 6 cases (8.12%).

### Homicidal v Suicidal

The distinction between self-inflicted and homicidal neck wounds may be difficult, if not impossible, to make from the autopsy examination alone. The circumstances surrounding the death, including assessment of the scene where the body was found and consideration of the victim's antecedent history, are essential to any examination of such cases.

A number of features in the character and distribution of such wounds, however, are frequently of value in making the distinction between self-infliction and homicide. Self-inflicted injuries, when made by right-handed persons, normally begin high on the left side of the neck and pass downwards across the front to end on the right side. They are deeper at their origin and then tail off on the right. Such wounds may also be horizontal, lying across the front of the neck. They are usually linear and clean-cut, since the skin is likely to have been held under tension (Figure 4.10).

Separate shallow wounds – 'tentative' or 'hesitation' incisions – are strongly indicative of self-infliction. There are quite often other accompanying incised wounds to the wrists or, occasionally, tentative stab wounds, particularly on the chest. Some self-inflicted incised wounds may be extremely deep, leaving multiple pronounced score marks on the cervical vertebrae. It is extremely rare for a victim to excise their own larynx, and occasionally reported in early publications (Harmer, 1912; Giles, 1956). In a case described by Schuessler (1944), the victim, using a single-edged razor, cut his throat and pulled out the hyoid bone, larynx, trachea, and part of the anterior oesophagus. With prompt treatment, he survived and his oesophagus was reconstructed.

Homicidal wounds, as a rule, do not have the regular, planned appearance of those that are self-inflicted, and they are unaccompanied by tentative injuries (Figures 4.11–4.13). Nevertheless, they are frequently accompanied by incised wounds which may be difficult to interpret without accompanying obvious self-inflicted injuries. As a rule, they are more haphazardly placed on the neck and, in some cases, have more irregular edges. In addition, such wounds tend to be deeper, although this is by no means invariably so. Accompanying stab wounds may also be present on the neck and other parts of the body, as well as defence cuts on the backs of the arms and hands. There may also be non-cutting injuries to the body which may have contributed to the cause of death.

A further important point concerns the implement which may have been used. The question needs to be asked whether the implement in question could have caused the injuries or whether it had been substituted for another. Such a problem was posed by the discovery of the body of the Earl of Essex in the Tower of London in 1683 (Taylor, 1891). The deceased was found with his throat cut and a razor lying near him. This implement was found to be 'much notched,' whereas the throat had been smoothly and evenly cut from one side to the other, down to the vertebral column. Some considered this to be an act of suicide; others, of murder. The medical witnesses who supported the view of suicide were asked to explain who it was that such an even wound could have been produced by a notched razor. They said that the deceased had probably drawn the razor backwards and forwards across the cervical spine. Taylor pointed out, however, that before this could be achieved, all the great vessels of the neck must have been divided.

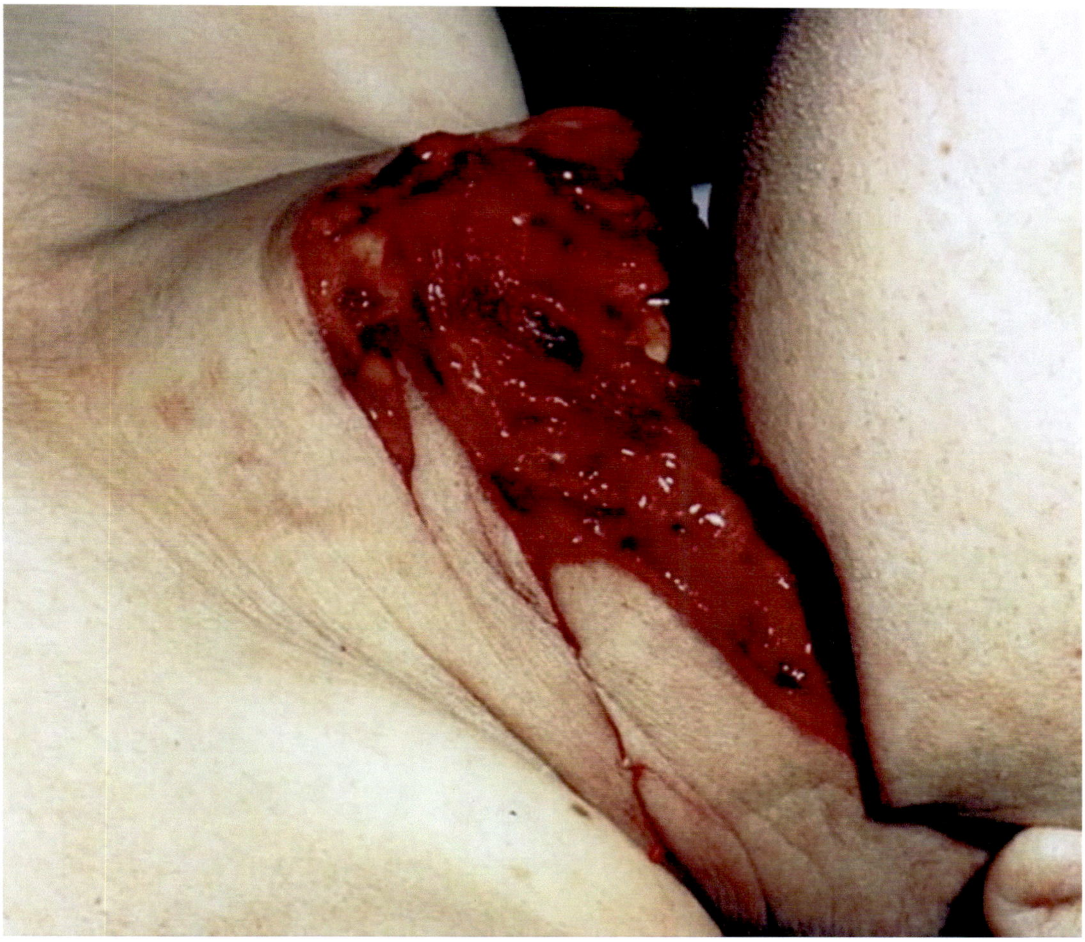

**Figure 4.10** Self-inflicted cut-throat wounds causing extensive injury to the anterior structures. Note the parallel alignment of the three deep wounds. In addition, they all slope downwards as they cross the deceased's neck, travelling from his left side.

A case of attempted murder in a middle-aged woman was seen by the author. The victim survived a number of severe incised wounds to her neck (Figure 4.14). Her larynx and pharynx were incised at the level of the false vocal cords, through the pyriform fossa, and into the prevertebral fascia. A large number of blood vessels were also cut. She required urgent medical intervention, including blood transfusions and a tracheostomy, to save her life and enable reconstruction of her larynx and pharynx. She made a full recovery.

## Accidental Incised Wounds

Incised wounds may be caused by glass in road traffic collisions, in which case the accidental nature of such injuries is obvious. Such wounds may be accompanied by numerous small abrasions from glass fragments, and particles of glass may be found in wounds if carefully searched for. Two unusual cases of cut-throat wounds in two auto-rickshaw drivers are reported by Swain et al. (2018). The shattered glass from their broken windshields was responsible for the wounds. In both cases, fatal incised wounds were present over the neck, cutting the soft tissue along with the major vessels. Death was due to exsanguination caused by neck vessel injury in one case and trachea along with neck vessel injury in the second case. Although the wounds on the neck initially suggested homicide, they were found to have occurred accidentally as a result of a road traffic accident involving a head-on collision of the two rickshaws.

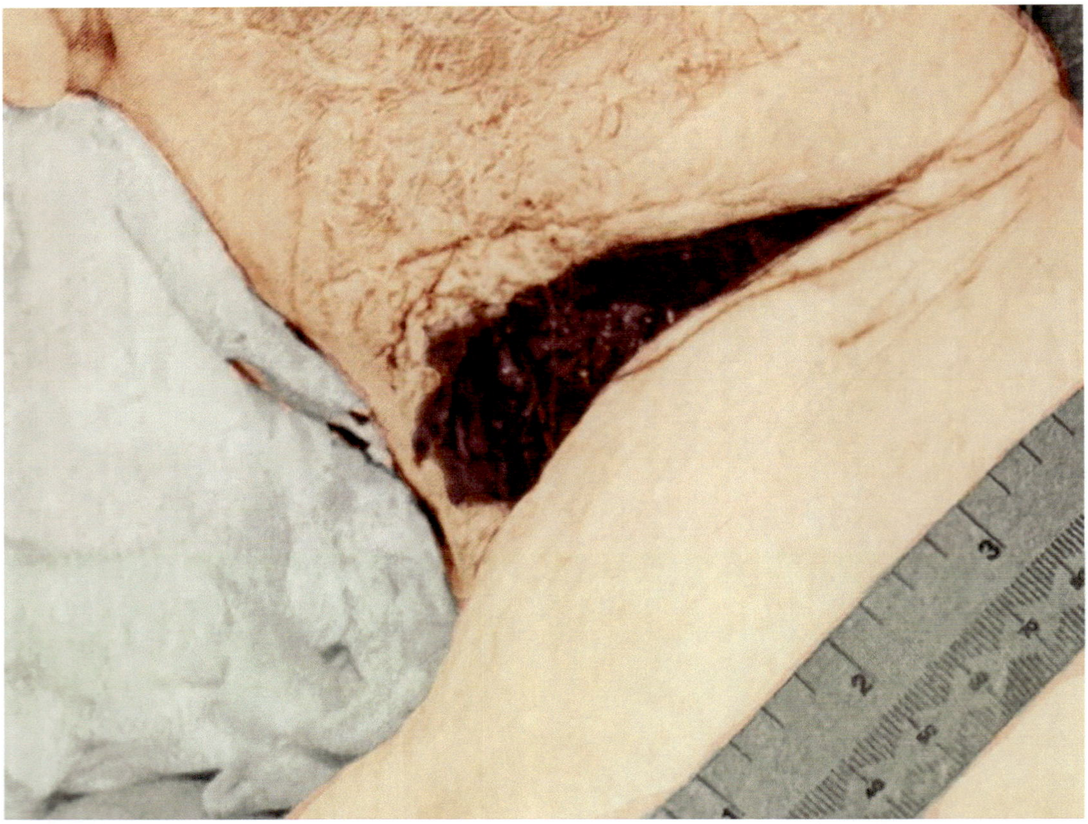

**Figure 4.11** Homicidal incised wounds to the back of the neck. The deceased had also suffered multiple stab wounds to the front of the neck and chest.

Accidental cut-throat injuries from other causes are extremely rare and usually involve a sharp-edged weapon. Cutting and tearing injuries can be produced by chain saws (Pratt, 1985) and are typically accidental in nature. Typically, injury is incurred by contact between the neck and the moving chain saw blade, which has teeth on its side and edge. This is usually in a direction from below upwards and produces multiple tears and cuts into the affected tissue. The wounds are relatively clean, in an approximately straight line, and usually consists of multiple parallel cuts with tags of tissue around the wounds. Rarely, chain saws have been used to commit suicide. Grellner and Wilske (2009) report two such cases involving young women with psychiatric disorders using electric saws. Tentative saw cuts were noted. The depth of the wound varies greatly depending on the duration and force of the saw's application to the head and neck. The width of the wound varies with the lateral motions of the saw.

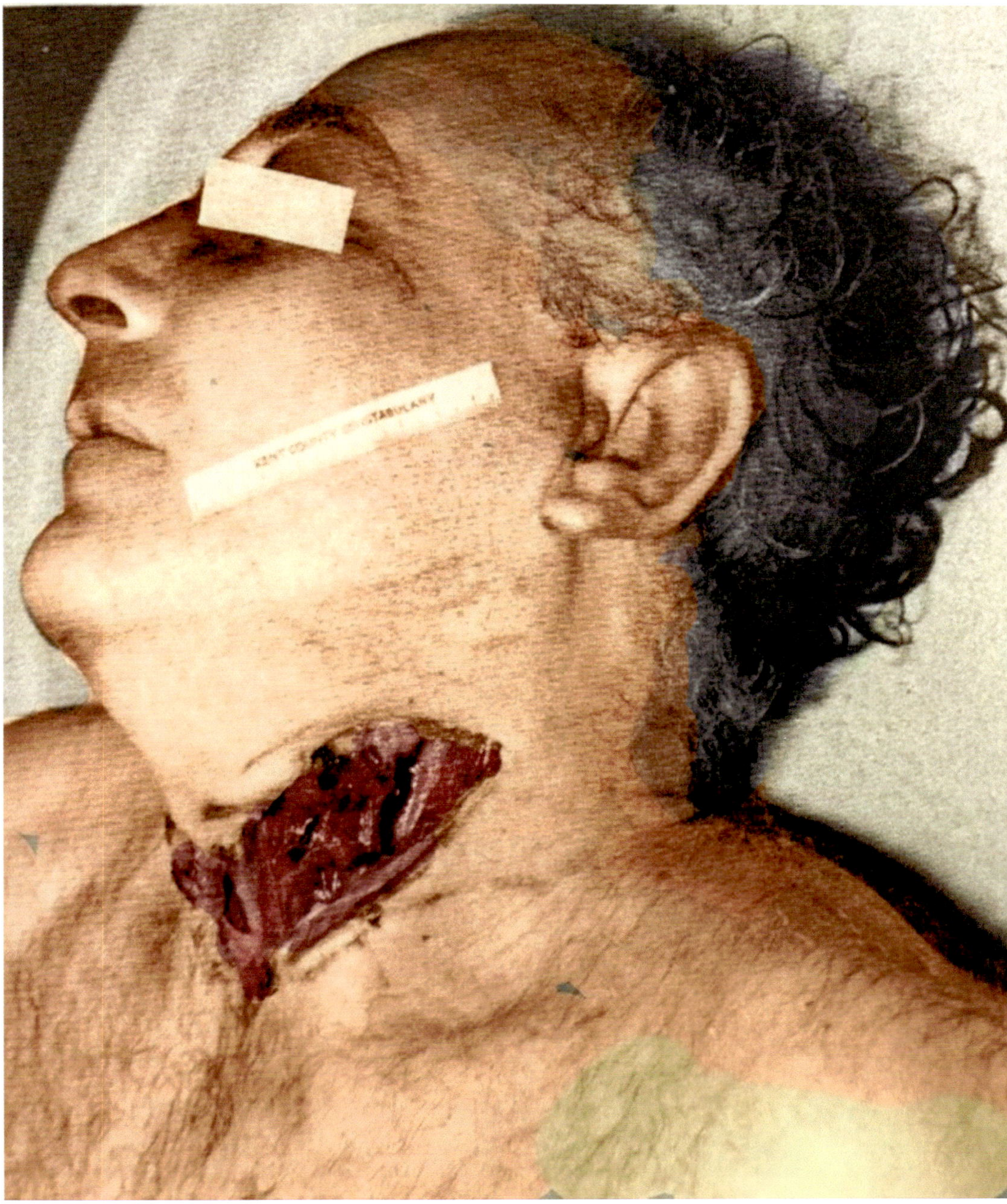

**Figure 4.12** Homicidal cut-throat wounds produced by glass from a broken bottle. Note the irregularity and depth of the fatal wounds. There are accompanying superficial incised wounds and other injuries to the face.

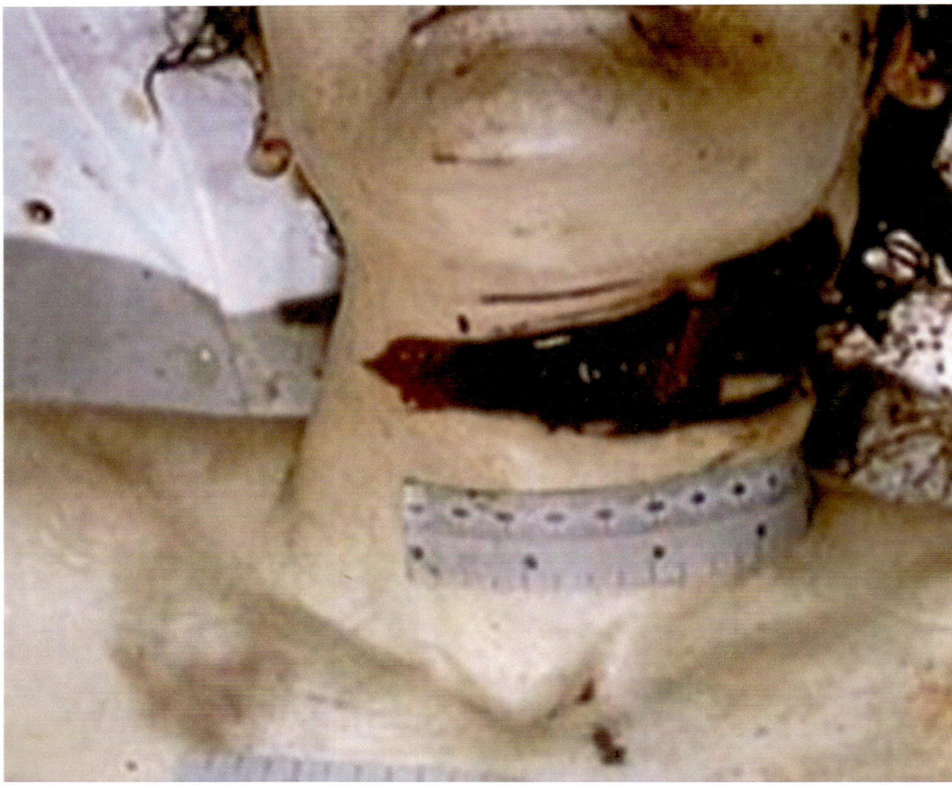

**Figure 4.13** Deep incised wounds to the front of the neck. There are fingernail grazes to the face and neck caused by the assailant holding the victim down in a supine position.

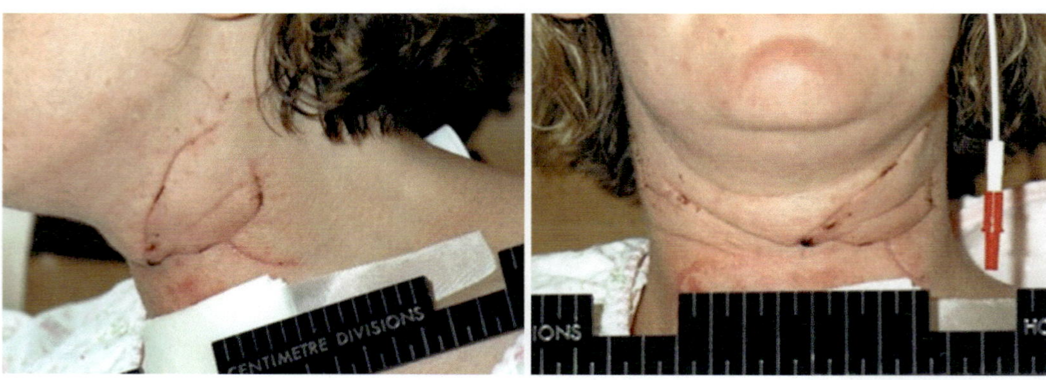


(a) (b)

**Figure 4.14** Left (a) and front (b) sides of the neck showing multiple healing scars from incised wounds.

# MISSILE WOUNDS

Firearm ammunition accounts for the vast majority of missiles causing penetrating injury. Examples of other agents less often encountered include blast fragments, arrows and bolts fired from bows, and glass fragments, particularly from road traffic collisions.

The effect of missile wounds to the neck may be catastrophic because major vessels, including the carotid, subclavian, and vertebral arteries, as well as many other critical structures are contained in such a confined space; even minimal motion of a penetrating bullet can simultaneously cause significant vascular and nerve injuries, resulting in serious, life-threatening conditions.

## Firearm Wounds

The vast majority of firearm injuries to the neck are homicidal in nature (Figure 4.15). Gunshot injuries cause profound morbidity and significant mortality, especially when they occur in the neck. These injuries occur in both military and civilian settings. In addition to homicidal wounds, one occasionally sees suicidal injuries, and rarely, accidental ones. The high density of vital structures in the neck (see below) makes injury to this region potentially devastating, with a frequently fatal outcome.

Meyer et al. (1985), in a series of 140 patients with homicidal firearm injuries, found only six to the neck region (4%). Self-inflicted wounds in this region are very unusual (Figure), with the head and chest being the most common sites (in that order). Eisle et al. (1981) analysed 226 cases of firearm suicide and found that only ten of these (4%) involved the neck. The sites of election in these cases were clustered around the midline (Figure 4.16). The types of weapons used were a rifle in eight cases, a handgun in one, and a shotgun in the other.

Pinto et al. (2009) discussed the contribution the radiologist can make to the successful treatment of patients with gunshot wound by assessing the missile path in emergency conditions using plain film and multidetector-row computed tomography, as well as evaluating the extent of wounding by determining missile fragmentation and secondary missile paths. They also emphasised that the leading cause of death from firearm injuries to the neck was vascular injury. However, they discussed the difficulty in predicting such injury because of erratic trajectories and the variable ballistic properties of missiles from different types of firearms.

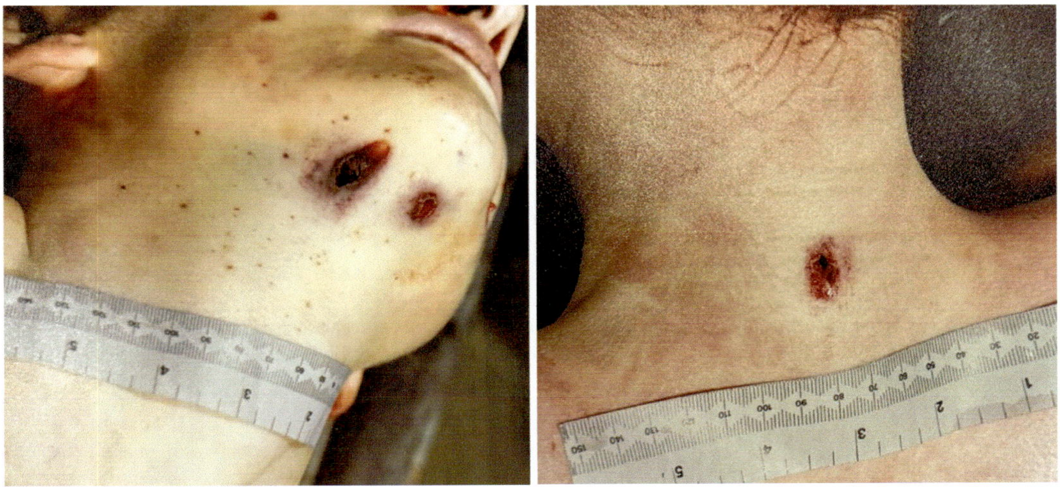

(a) (b)

**Figure 4.15** (a) Two homicidal near-contact gunshot entry wounds caused by a 0.38 revolver. The bullet that had caused the elongated wound travelled backwards, injuring the spinal cord at C3 and exiting at the nape of the neck (b). The other bullet travelled upwards and outwards, fracturing the body of the mandible and exiting at the left cheek.

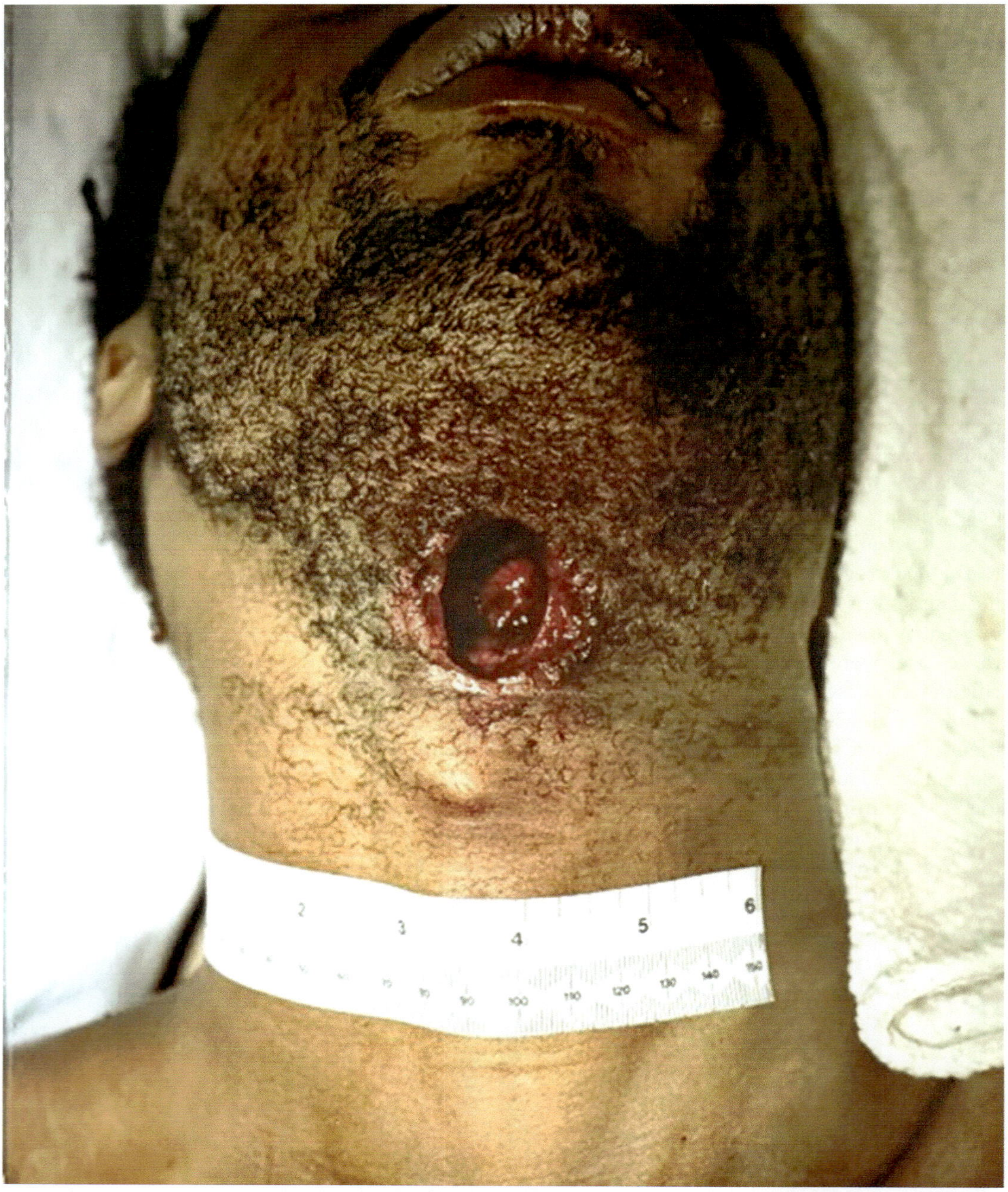


**Figure 4.16** Self-inflicted shotgun wound. The wound is centrally situated above the prominence of the thyroid cartilage and has tracked upwards and to the deceased's left, causing extensive vascular injury to the neck and comminuted fractures of the mandible.

## Blast Injuries

Breeze et al. (2012) found neck wounds in 152 of 1,528 (10%) battle-injured service personnel. Seventy-nine percent of neck wounds were caused by explosions and were associated with a mortality rate of 41%, compared with 78% from gunshot wounds.

Although current UK OSPREY neck collars can potentially protect zone I from explosive fragments, 58% of service personnel chose not to wear the collar. The most common cause of death from explosive fragments was vascular injury (85%). Zone II was the most commonly affected area overall by explosive fragments and had the highest mortality, but zone I was associated with the highest morbidity in survivors.

## Other Missile Injuries

An accidental crossbow bolt death is described by Kondo et al. (2018), in which a 60-year-old man suffered a fatal injury that entered his neck and travelled upward into his left cerebral hemisphere. He was taken to a hospital and died after approximately three days of conservative treatment. At autopsy, a penetrating wound was found between the upper part of the left anterior neck and the left fronto-parietal region. A traumatic intracerebral hematoma was observed in the left frontal lobe, along with severe traumatic subarachnoid haemorrhage throughout the brain. Cerebral contusion and hematoma without any organisation were also noted around the track. According to the authors, the deceased was probably trying to load an arrow into the crossbow by placing it on the floor, pointing upward, and made a mistake in its operation that resulted in the shooting of the arrow.

Suematsu et al. (2022) reported a case of attempted homicide from a penetrating neck injury caused by a crossbow bolt. The patient was a 49-year-old woman who presented at the hospital with the crossbow bolt in situ in the neck from right to left. Computed tomography revealed the crossbow bolt in contact with the bilateral external and internal carotid arteries and that the bolt caused dissection of the left main trunk of the external carotid artery. The bolt was removed successfully without significant bleeding, and no complications occurred during the surgery.

# INTERNAL STRUCTURAL INJURY FROM PENETRATING WOUNDS

From a number of clinical studies, the current mortality rate in civilians with penetrating neck injuries ranges from 3% to 6%. During World War II, it was 7%, and 11% in World War I. Higher mortality rates occur with injuries to large vessels, such as the carotid or subclavian arteries and veins (Alterman, 2021). Indeed, vascular trauma is present in 25% of penetrating neck injuries, with mortality rates approaching 50% in some studies. Tracheobronchial injuries may have an incidence of less than 10% to as high as 20%, with a mortality rate of as high as 20%. Injuries to the cervical oesophagus can result in devastating complications and outcomes, such as leakage of saliva, bacteria, refluxed acid, pepsin, and even bile. If undiagnosed, this can produce early suppurative infection and an intense necrotising inflammatory response in the neck, as well as a more devastating outcome if it descends to the mediastinum. An 11–17% increase in the overall mortality rate has been observed after delays of 12 hours in the diagnosis of oesophageal injuries.

Although it is outside the scope of this text to discuss the clinical evaluation of neck injuries in detail, it is nevertheless important to understand the clinical approach to the evaluation of such injuries in living patients to enable the reader to gain more insight into the pathological outcome of such trauma. Since the 1970s, clinicians have divided the neck into three anatomical zones. Zone I (base of the neck) extends from the sternal notch to the cricoid cartilage, Zone II (mid-neck) from the cricoid to the mandibular angle, and Zone III (upper neck) from the angle of the mandible to the base of the skull (see also Chapter 2). However, the evaluation and management of haemodynamically stable patients with penetrating neck injuries have evolved considerably over the previous four decades. During that time, mandatory endoscopy and angiography for Zone I and III penetrations, or mandatory neck exploration for Zone II injuries, became popular. Currently, modern sensitive imaging technology, including the use of multi-detector computed tomography angiography (CTA), is widely available, and imaging triage can now accomplish what operative or selective evaluation could not; i.e., a safe and non-invasive evaluation of critical neck structures to identify or exclude injury (Woo et al., 2005). As a result of such developments in the evaluation of the injured patient, the use of anatomical zones has recently been re-evaluated in favour of an evidence-based strategy employing a non-zonal approach to management in such cases (Shiroff et al., 2013; Low et al., 2014; Nowicki et al., 2018, Strickland et al., 2019).

## Vascular Injuries

Some 95% of injuries to the carotid, jugular, subclavian, and innominate vessels are due to gunshot or stab wounds (Livingstone, 1983). The common carotid artery has been found in most studies to be the most frequently injured part of the carotid arterial system, followed by the internal and then the external carotid (Figures 4.17 and 4.18). The highest incidence of morbidity and mortality, at 50%, is seen in internal carotid artery injuries in some series (Tisherman et al., 2008). Partial or complete disruption accounts for the majority of injuries to the carotid arteries.

Associated venous injury is frequently present and contributes significantly to the mortality of such cases. Internal jugular vein injuries represent 20% of all injuries to the neck. These injuries differ from arterial injuries, as they represent injuries to a low-pressure system that can tamponade with no major haemorrhage, and mortality has been reported to be as low as 2.6% (Stafforini and Singh, 2023).

Rarely embolisation of a bullet may occur, although most cases have been described in regions of the body other than the neck. Embolisation appears to occur more frequently with shotgun pellet wounds than with single missile gunshot wounds because of the large number of pellets, their small size, wide patterns of injury, and low velocity. Cogbill and Sullivan (1995) report the case of

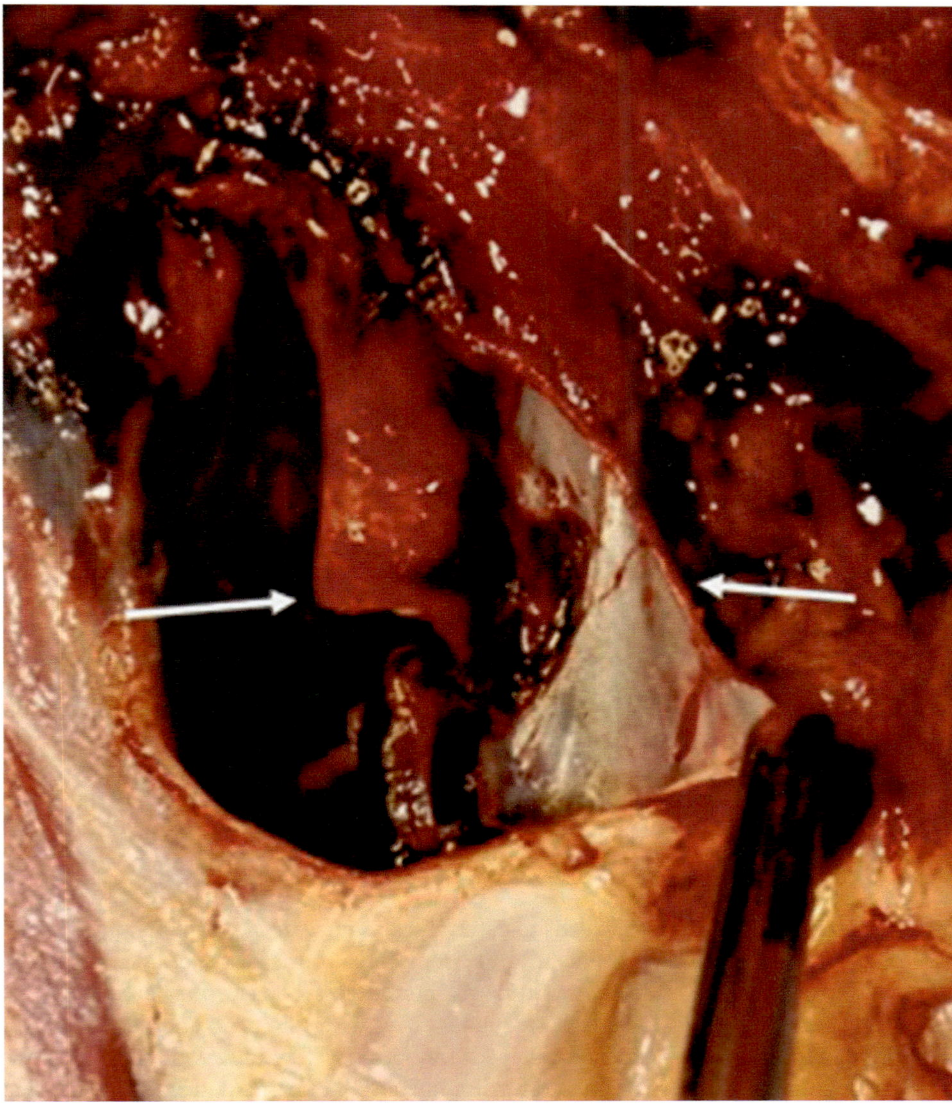

**Figure 4.17** The left common carotid artery and the left internal jugular vein (arrows) are transected as a result of a single stab wound.

a middle cerebral artery pellet embolism and delayed appearance of a carotid artery pseudoaneurysm following a shotgun wound of the neck in a 12-year-old boy who was successfully managed. Embolisation, particularly with injury to the veins, should always be specifically looked for; it is discovered more commonly than is usually suspected.

There may be ischaemic changes to internal organs due to diminished blood supply to a region from the effects of penetrating or blunt trauma. Karnecki et al. (2014) reported two cases of ischaemic stroke secondary to traumatic internal carotid artery thrombosis leading to middle cerebral artery thrombosis. One of the cases was of a 57-year-old man, a carpenter who sustained a penetrating injury to his neck from a fragment of wood. He was in his warehouse when he was struck very hard in the face, in the region of his left cheek, by an irregularly shaped wood fragment which resembled a large splinter (measuring about 26 cm in length and with the greatest cross-sectional dimensions of 3.5 × 1.5 cm) that broke off from the board

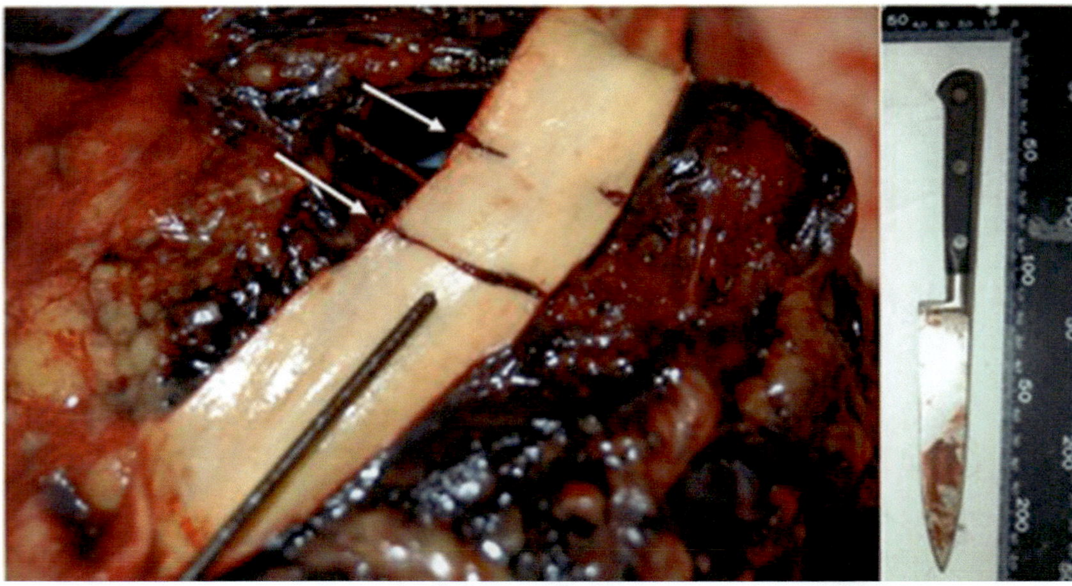

**Figure 4.18** Two cuts across the right common carotid artery at the base of the neck. The knife used is shown on the right.

being processed on his machine. The autopsy revealed a thrombus occluding the left internal carotid artery and the proximal segment of the left middle cerebral artery, a large area of infarction in the temporal lobe and adjacent parts of the frontal and occipital lobes of the left hemisphere of the brain, cerebral oedema with features of subfalcine and tentorial herniation, a comminuted fracture of the left maxilla, and an occipital bone fracture in the region of the occipital condyle with the fragment impression. There were no atherosclerotic lesions in the carotid and basal cerebral arteries.

Penetrating neck trauma frequently leads to arterial wall injury in the form of contusion or vessel wall dissection with the formation of intramural haematoma, outer arterial layer damage (adventitia), and the formation of pseudoaneurysm or segmental vessel spasm. In particular, Cox et al. (2007) found that, in the military setting, pseudoaneurysms of the head and neck were the most common vascular injuries discovered on delayed evaluation. The authors diagnosed these aneurysms in 9% of patients who were evaluated for significant penetrating injury to the face and neck.

Suppurative inflammation may also develop in the periarterial space, should the patient survive long enough after the trauma. The above-mentioned primary vessel wall injuries, associated with an injury limited to at least the endothelium and intima, predispose to the development of thrombosis with subsequent vessel occlusion and ischaemic stroke. Focal ischaemic brain injury was secondary to the thrombosis of the internal carotid artery and middle cerebral artery.

Penetrating trauma to the vertebral arteries (Figure 4.19) is much less common than blunt injury, partly due to the relatively protected position of the vessels. Penetrating wounds to the neck region frequently injure a number of structures along their track; hence, it is not difficult to overlook vertebral artery injury.

Occasionally, such lesions have been misdiagnosed as carotid artery injuries (Holmes, 1873; Sutton and Pratt, 1971). Indeed, vertebral artery lesions not initially recognised may occasionally lead to complications including fistulae and/or aneurysm formation (see Chapter 12). Matas (1893) was the first to give a comprehensive account of such lesions. Notably, many such cases have been reported in war casualties, the arterial injuries being caused by fragments of shrapnel, bullets, and other missiles (Kuttner, 1917; Makins, 1919; Seeley et al., 1952; Elkin and DeBakey, 1955).

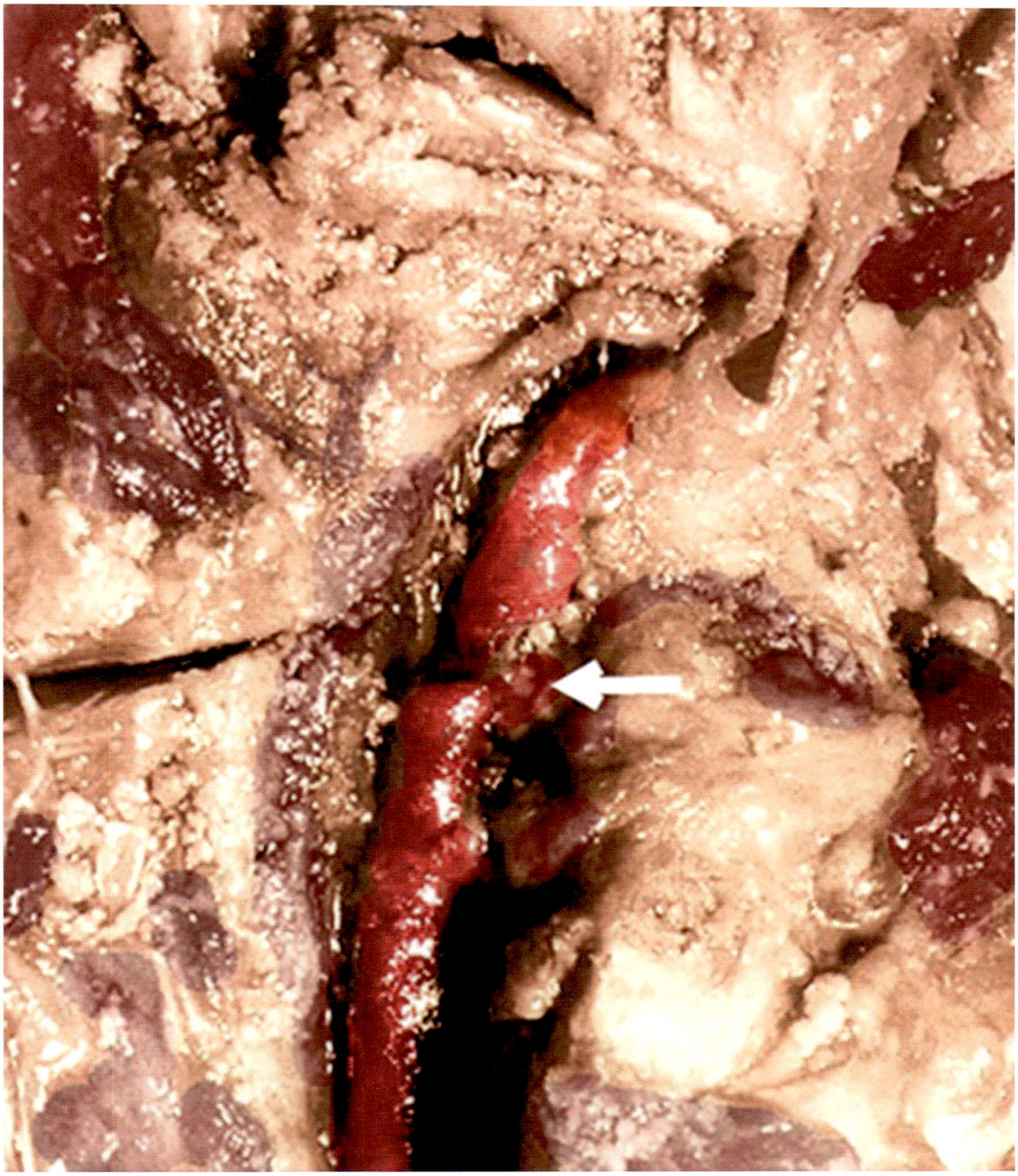

**Figure 4.19** The knife has cut through the second cervical vertebral body and completely transected the left vertebral artery (arrow).

A fatal vertebral artery injury caused by a dog bite has been described by Oshima et al. (2008). The dog bite was inflicted on an elderly woman by a Tosa dog. She died from a vertebral arterial laceration with an associated C5 vertebral fracture; the carotid artery was undamaged. Detection of the offending dog was unsuccessful with DNA analysis but was made by comparisons of the dental casts of the dog with the victim's wounds.

Park et al. (2007) relate the case of cerebellar infarction in a 50-year-old woman caused by vertebral artery injury from a stab wound that severed the vessel between the transverse processes of

C3 and C4. She had a hypoplastic contralateral vertebral artery and, as a result, ultimately suffered infarction of the cerebellum due to the lack of preservation of the posterior inferior cerebellar artery blood flow.

## Laryngo-Tracheal Injuries

Penetrating injuries of the cervical larynx and trachea are relatively infrequent. They are life-threatening either because of the immediate danger to the airway or the gravity of associated vascular, pharyngeal, oesophageal, or spinal cord trauma (Levy et al., 1997; Figures 4.20–4.22).

## Pharyngo-Oesophageal Injuries

A penetrating injury of the cervical oesophagus can be fatal if not recognised and adequately treated. Lares Dos Santos et al. (2019) reported the case of a 50-year-old man with a fatal penetrating injury to the oesophagus. The authors found a 3.5 cm wooden toothpick fragment in the upper oesophageal region, covered by a purulent substance and associated with puncture wounds. The wound had led to contamination of the peri-oesophageal space with corrosive digestive fluid and bacteria, leading to diffuse cellulitis with suppuration.

Impacted foreign objects within the oesophagus may occasionally cause perforation. Wahed et al. (2014) found, from 96 adult patients with oesophageal perforation, that four were due to the impaction of foreign bodies. The median age of their patients was 69.5 years.

Makhani et al. (2014), from their study of 327 cases of traumatic injuries of the oesophagus, found that young males sustaining a gunshot wound were the most likely to experience this injury. They also found that there was higher morbidity and mortality when the thoracic oesophagus was involved compared to the cervical oesophagus alone (44.7% vs. 17.9%). Those with injuries at both sites had a very high mortality, similar to those with isolated thoracic oesophagus injuries (42.9%). For both blunt (60.9%) and penetrating (58.8%) mechanisms of injury, the cervical oesophagus was the primary site of involvement.

Massive fatal haemorrhage may rarely occur; such a case was reported by Russo et al. (1986). The subject, an 81-year-old edentulous female, swallowed a chicken bone which perforated through the oesophageal wall at the level of the thyroid gland and lacerated the adjacent right common carotid artery.

Onat et al. (2010) treated 30 patients surgically between 1980 and 2008 for non-iatrogenic traumatic cervical oesophageal perforation. They observed emphysema in 70% of their patients. They further stated that the presence of cervical emphysema was suggestive of oesophageal perforation and warranted further diagnostic study with contrast oesophagography or contrast-enhanced computed tomography.

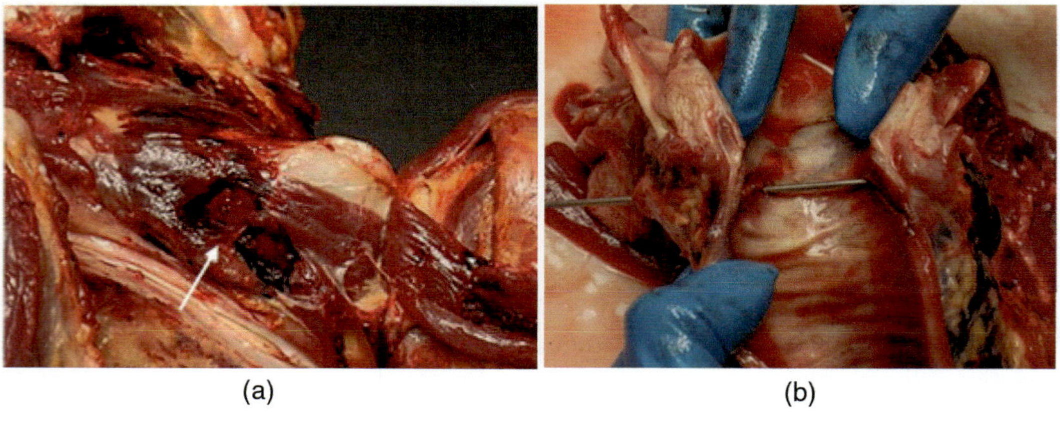

(a) (b)

**Figure 4.20** (a) Stab wound to the left side of the neck tracking through the sternocleidomastoid and cutting through the upper pole of the left thyroid gland (arrow) and base of the thyrohyoid muscle; (b) then into the cricoid cartilage and exiting on the opposite side.

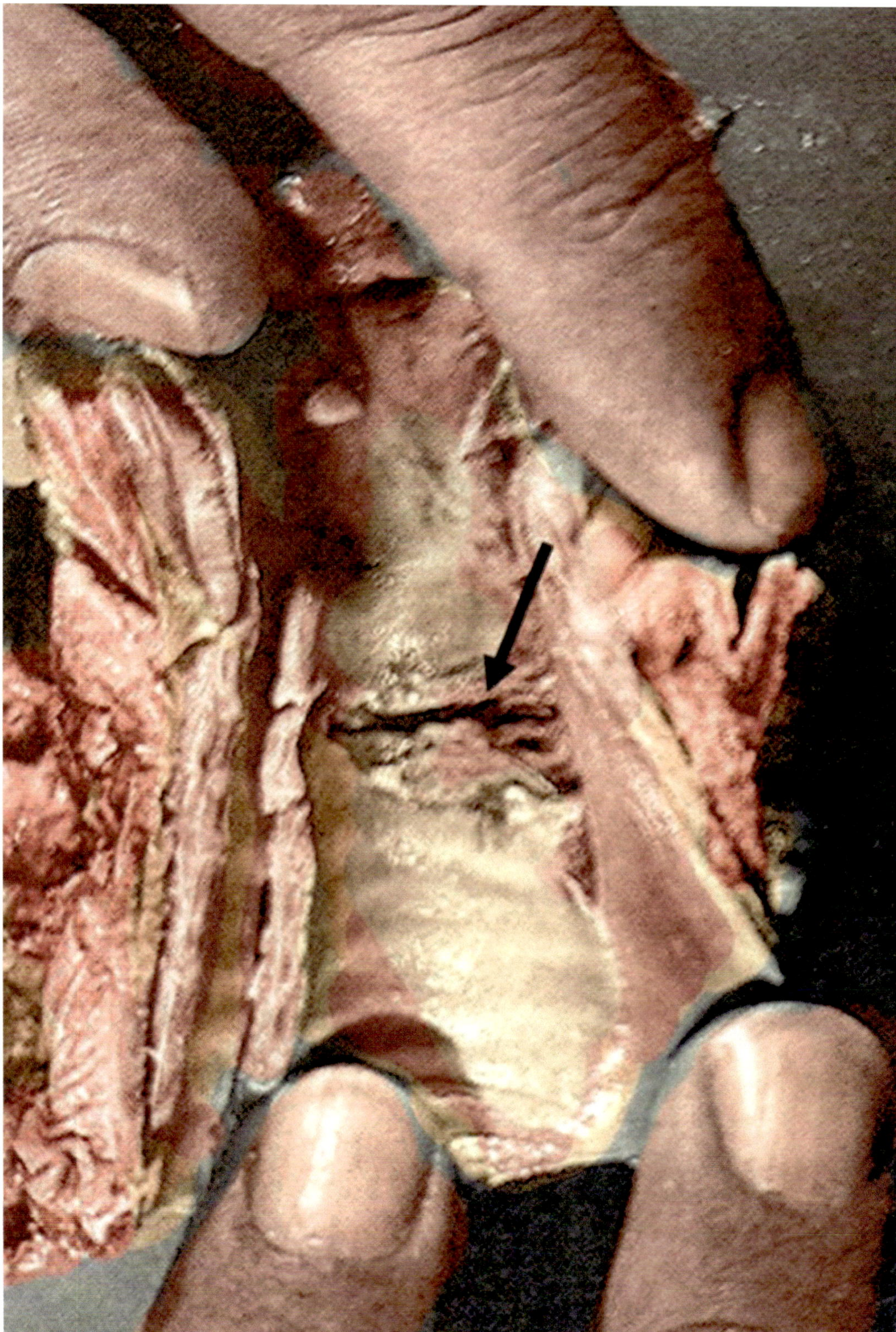

**Figure 4.21** Penetrating wound of the upper trachea caused by a pointed stick (arrow).

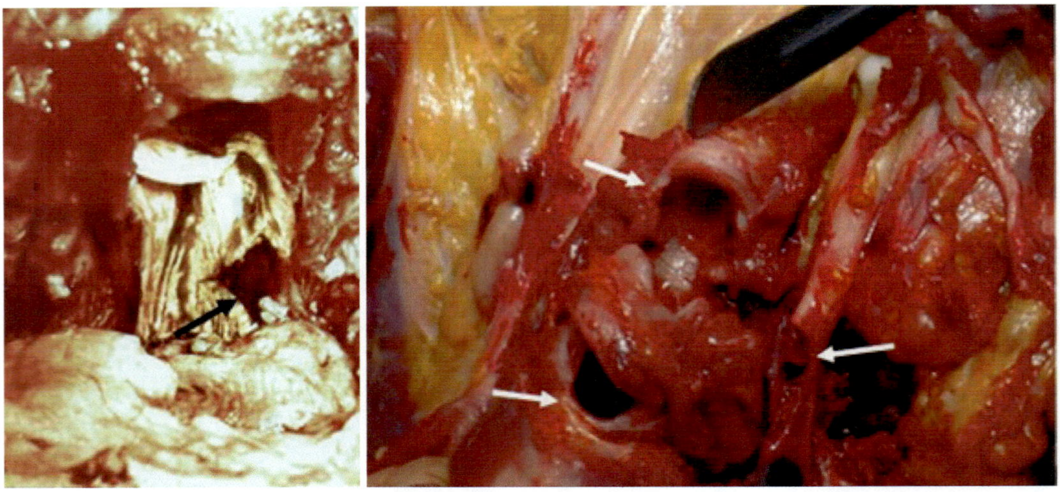

(a) (b)

**Figure 4.22** Homicidal cut-throat wounds: (a) incised wound to the cervical oesophagus and (b) injured structures including the cricoid cartilage, trachea, left common carotid artery, and internal jugular vein (arrows).

## Spinal Cord and Nerve Root Injuries

A recent systematic review and meta-analysis of penetrating spinal cord injury by Bin-Alamer et al. (2022) analysed 1,754 cases from US data. The mean age was 19.2 years (range, 16–70), and most patients were male (89.9%). Missile spinal cord injury was the most common type, affecting 1,623 patients (92.6%) (Figure 4.23), while non-missile spinal cord injury accounted for only 131 cases (7.4%).

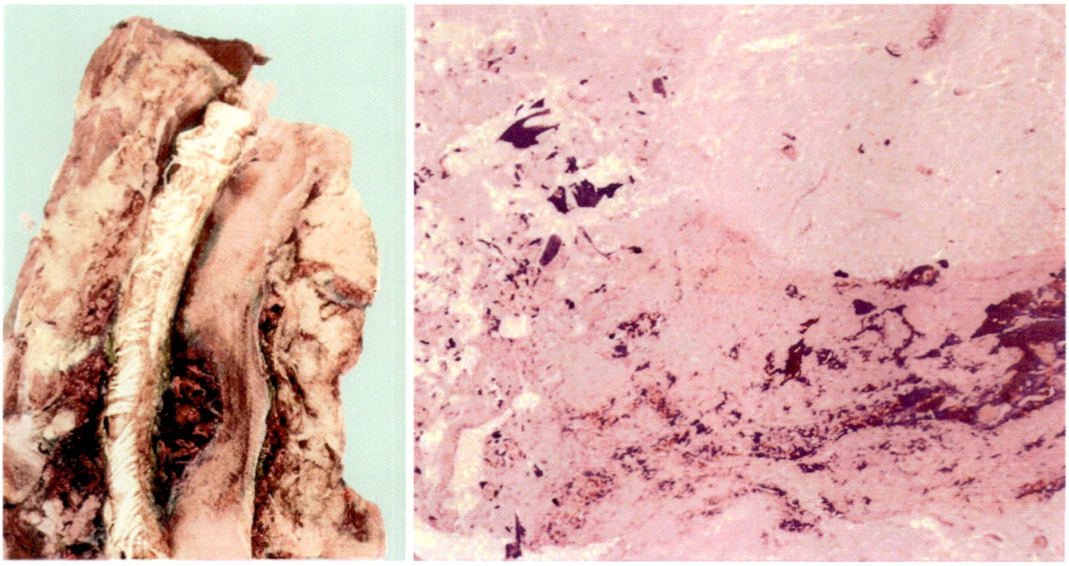

(a) (b)

**Figure 4.23** (a) Extensive tearing of the spinal dura mater from a gunshot injury at mid-cervical level. (b) Transverse section of the cervical cord from the same case. There are acute cervical cord contusions, substantial haemorrhage, and spicules of bone within the cord. The latter were driven into the cord by the missile (haematoxylin and eosin x 32).

Saeidiborojeni et al. (2013) surveyed 57 patients with spinal cord stab wounds attending a hospital emergency department between 1999 and 2011. The weapons used involved sharp objects such as a knife, dagger, whittle, and Bowie knife. The distribution of the wounds was cervical (40%), thoracic (42%), and lumbar (18%). A large study in South Africa in 1977 found that 450 of 1,600 patients admitted with stab wounds over a period of 13 years had sustained spinal cord injury (Peacock et al., 1977). It was reported that 63% of the wounds were in the thoracic region, 7% in the lumbar region, and 30% in the cervical region (21 of these cases showed complete transection of the spinal cord). Burney et al. (1993), in the United States, found that spinal cord injury comprised 2.6% of all trauma cases, with approximately 1% of those attributed to stab wounds.

Most stab wounds to the neck track in a downward or horizontal direction, whereas only around 10% travel upwards. Rubin et al. (2001), in relation to cervical spine injury, found that laterally directed horizontal stab wounds were particularly dangerous because the blade could pass between two vertebrae to transect the cord, resulting in irreversible injury. The more common stab wounds, inflicted from behind, usually produce incomplete cord damage (Figure 4.24). According to Peacock et al. (1977), this outcome is due to the protection of the spinal cord by the spinal processes, causing the blade to be deflected laterally.

Beer-Furlan et al. (2014) report the case of a 34-year-old man brought into hospital with a single stab wound from an assault with a screwdriver. Neurological examination revealed an incomplete Brown-Sequard syndrome, with grade IV motor deficit in the left leg and contralateral hemi-hypoalgesia below the T9 level. The screwdriver had been retained in the neck and was seen on radiological examination at T9 level. The authors were of the view that the incomplete deficit was a result of the Phillips screwdriver dissecting, rather than cutting through tissue, thus minimising damage. It should also be appreciated that a weapon such as a screwdriver with a rigid shaft will concentrate a large amount of force over a small area, allowing easier penetration of bone compared to a knife. Less damage will also occur when the knife blade is deflected laterally on the vertebrae, as discussed above.

Occasionally, the tip of the knife may break and be retained in the cervical spine, particularly if there is a turning motion of the victim or the knife, whilst it is within the spine. Zaldivar-Jolissaint

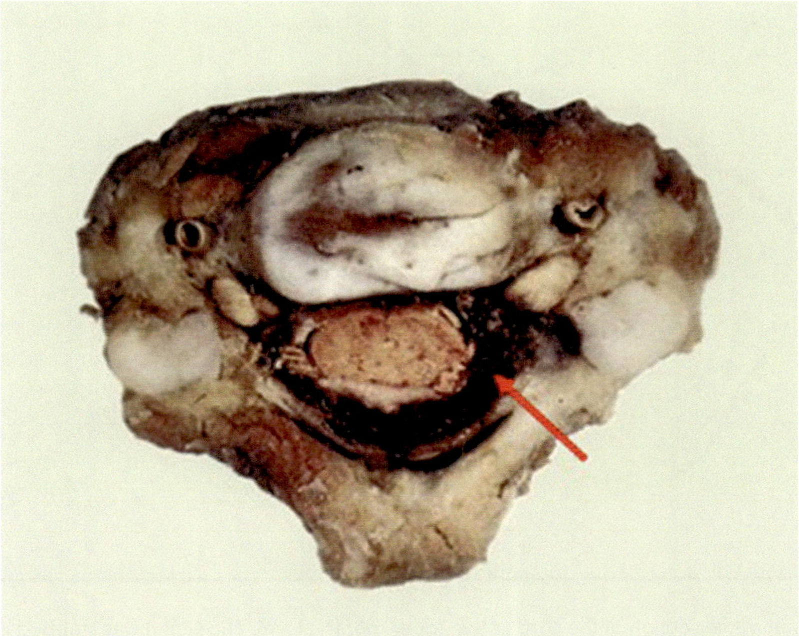

**Figure 4.24** Transverse section of the cervical spine at the C3 level showing spinal subarachnoid haemorrhage from a stab wound to the right side of the back of the neck.

et al. (2015) describe a case where a broken knife blade was retained in the cervical spine when their patient sustained a stab wound to the supraclavicular triangle from a small pocket knife (see also Figure 4.6b). It was initially managed in a local hospital by simple primary wound closure without any radiological examinations, and then the patient was discharged. He continued to have mild persistent local neck pain, and subsequent radiological investigations revealed a foreign body (the broken blade of a pocket knife) embedded in the left neural foramen between the C6 and C7 vertebrae, penetrating the disc space. The blade was lying between the left C7 nerve root and the ipsilateral vertebral artery. Initially, he was neurologically normal, but a few days later, he developed a delayed left C7 radicular deficit, and following urgent exploration, the blade was successfully removed.

In Lipschitz and Block's series (1982), the direction of the stab wound was found to be either horizontal or downward. One of their patients with a stab wound to the second cervical vertebra developed a Brown-Sequard lesion and died of antibiotic-resistant meningitis (Figure 4.25).

It is not unusual to find severe injuries due to glass from shattered windscreens in road traffic collisions. Nevertheless, injury to the spinal cord from flying glass is only occasionally reported (Isu et al., 1985). The latter authors also gave an account of spinal cord and root injuries caused by acupuncture needles.

## Intrathoracic Injuries

With stab wounds directed downwards, particularly near the thoracic inlet, it is not uncommon to find major trauma to intrathoracic organs (see Figure 4.3). Such injury may include a collapsed lung from a puncture wound near its apex, or there may be severe intrathoracic haemorrhage resulting from injury to the arch of the aorta or one of its main branches.

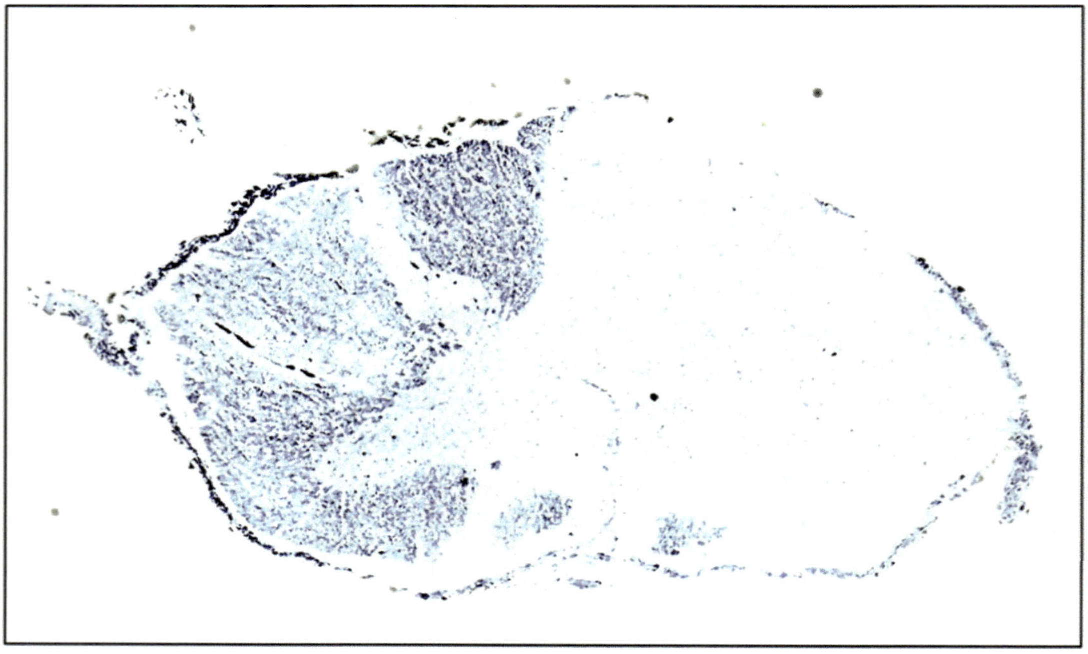

**Figure 4.25** Transverse section of the cord at the upper thoracic level. The victim was stabbed in the lower part of the neck and developed a Brown-Sequard syndrome. The signs and symptoms produced by such a lesion, which involves one-half of the spinal cord, essentially consist of loss of motor function on the side of the lesion, together with loss of sensation on the opposite side (Luxol fast blue x 8).

# ACUTE FATAL OUTCOME

Without doubt, the most common result of penetrating injury to the neck is substantial haemorrhage. In addition, with transection of the carotid arteries, the blood supply to the brain is rapidly depleted. Tracking of blood supply through tissue planes may be substantial and also has catastrophic effects, principally on the airway. In such cases, the larynx appears to be constricted by the surrounding blood, thus causing asphyxiation. There may also be secondary glottic oedema.

The author of this text reported an unusual acute complication involving a young man who developed asphyxia from airway compression following a stab wound to the neck. He had suffered a partial incision of the right common carotid artery as well as injury to other smaller vessels nearby. The blood had tracked through tissue planes of the neck and compressed his trachea, thus resulting in virtual closure of his airway (Figure 4.26).

Demetriades et al. (1996) cautioned that even with a seemingly patent airway, rapid expansion of a hematoma may cause airway obstruction. They advised early intubation, even in the absence of

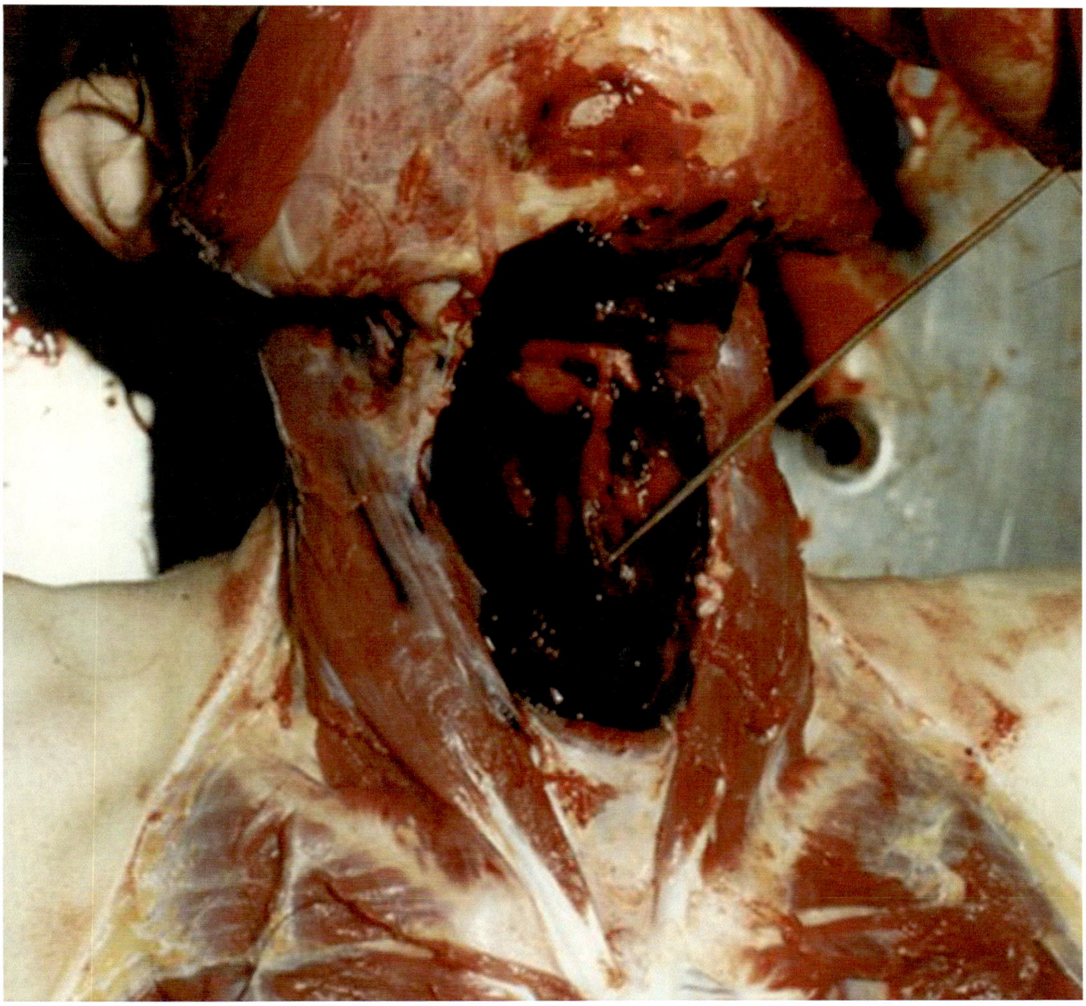

**Figure 4.26** Young male stabbed in the neck. Blood has surrounded his larynx and compressed his airway, causing asphyxia.

respiratory distress. Asphyxia is also a major mode of death in cases where blood has been inhaled and the larynx and trachea have been injured. Frequently, in such cases, substantial haemorrhage is also present, and therefore the mode of death should be regarded as a combination of events (Pate, 1989).

## References

Abdelmasih M, Kayssi A, Roche-Nagle G. Penetrating paediatric neck trauma. *BMJ Case Rep*. 2019;12(5): e226436.

Alterman DM. *Penetrating Neck Trauma in Medscape*. Chief Ed. Geibel J., 2021. https://emedicine.medscape.com/article/433306-overview#a7

Bagheri SC, Khan HA, Bell RB. Penetrating neck injuries. *Oral Maxillofac Surg Clin North Am*. 2008 Aug;20(3):393–414. doi: 10.1016/j.coms.2008.04.003. PMID: 18603199.

Barss PG. Penetrating wounds caused by needle fish in Oceania. *Med J Aust*. 1985;143: 617–622.

Beer-Furlan AL, Paiva WS, Tavares WM, de Andrade AF, Teixeira MJ. Brown-Sequard syndrome associated with unusual spinal cord injury by a screwdriver stab wound. *Int J Clin Exp Med*. 2014;7: 316–319.

Bin-Alamer O, Bhenderu LS, Stuebe C, Sagoo NS, Palmisciano P, Haider M, Aoun SG, Haider AS. Penetrating spinal cord injury: A systematic review and meta-analysis of clinical features and treatment outcomes. *Spinal Cord*. 2022 Oct;60(10):845–853. doi: 10.1038/s41393-022-00813-x. Epub 2022 May 23. PMID: 35606414.

Breeze J, Allanson-Bailey LS, Hunt NC, Delaney RS, Hepper AE, Clasper J. Mortality and morbidity from combat neck injury. *J Trauma Acute Care Surg*. 2012;72(4): 969–974.

Burney RE, Maio RF, Maynard F, Karunas R. Incidence, characteristics, and outcome of spinal cord injury at trauma centers in North America. *Arch* Surg. 1993;12: 596–599.

Cogbill TH, Sullivan HG. Carotid artery pseudoaneurysm and pellet embolism to the middle cerebral artery following a shotgun wound of the neck. *J Trauma*. 1995 Oct;39(4):763–767. doi: 10.1097/00005373-199510000-00030. PMID: 7473973.

Cox MW, Whittaker DR, Martinez C, Fox CJ, Feuerstein IM, Gillespie DL. Traumatic pseudoaneurysms of the head and neck: Early endovascular intervention. *J Vasc Surg*. 2007 Dec;46(6):1227–1233. doi: 10.1016/j.jvs.2007.08.021. PMID: 18154999.

Demetriades D, Asensio JA, Velmahos G, Thal E. Complex problems in penetrating neck trauma. *Surg Clin North Am*. 1996 Aug;76(4):661–683. doi: 10.1016/s0039-6109(05)70475-8. PMID: 8782468.

Demetriades D, Theodorou D, Cornwell EE, Berne TV, Asensio J, Belzberg H, Velmahos G, Weaver F, Yellin A. Evaluation of penetrating injuries of the neck: Prospective study of 223 patients. *World J Surg*. 1997;21:41–48.

Eisle JW, Reay DT, Cook A. Sites of suicidal gunshot wounds. *J. Forensic Sci*. 1981;26: 480–485.

Elkin DC, DeBakey ME (eds). Vascular surgery. In *Surgery in World War II. Office of the Surgeon General, Department of the Army, Government Printing Office*, Washington DC, 1955, pp. 256–263.

Giles C. Suicidal laryngectomy. *J Forensic Med*. 1956;3: 91–93.

Grellner W, Wilske J. Unusual suicides of young women with tentative cuts and fatal neck injuries by chain saw and circular saw. *Forensic Sci Int*, 2009;190(1-3): e9–e11.

Harmer D. Total laryngectomy by a suicide. *Proc R Soc Med*. 1912;5 (Laryngol Sect):133–134. PMID: 19975918; PMCID: PMC2005732

Hasekura H, Fukushima H, Yonemura I, Ota M. A rare case of a ten-year-old child stabbing himself in the throat. *J Forensic Sci*. 1985;21: 659–666.

Hendry WT, Stalker AL. Satb wound of medulla by handle of metal comb. *Med Sci Law*. 1967;7: 213–215.

Hewett KM, Mellick L. A case of penetrating neck trauma in a child. *Pediatr Emerg Care*. 2012;28: 49–51.

Holmes T. The surgical treatment of aneurism in its various forms. Lecture III. Verebral aneurism. *Lancet*. 1873;2: 105–108.

Isu T, Iwasaki Y, Sasaki H, Abe H.. Spinal cord and root injuries due to glass fragments and acupuncture needles. *Surg Neurol*. 1985;23: 255–260.

Jothee S, Shafie MS, Mohd Nor F. Fatal penetrating neck injury due to defective airbag inflator. *Forensic Sci Int*. 2018;291: e4–e7.

Karnecki K, Jankowski Z, Kaliszan, M. Direct penetrating and indirect neck trauma as a cause of internal carotid artery thrombosis and secondary ischemic stroke. *J Thromb Thrombolysis*. 2014;38(3): 409–415.

King. Wound of vertebral artery, recovery. *Lancet*. 1985;2: 993.

Koehler SA, Shakir A, Williams KE. Accidental through and through penetrating injury to the neck. *Am J Forensic Med Pathol.* 2011;32(1): 17–19.

Kondo T, Takahashi M, Kuse A, Morichika M, Nakagawa K, Tagawa Y, Taniguchi T, Taguchi Y, Fujiwara T, Tsuchiya J, Nakamura M, Sakurada M, Asano M, Ueno Y. Autopsy case of a penetrating wound to the left cerebral hemisphere caused by an accidental shooting with a crossbow. *Am J Forensic Med Pathol.* 2018;39(2): 164–168.

Krywanczyk A, Shapiro S. A retrospective study of blade wound characteristics in suicide and homicide. *Am J Forensic Med Pathol.* 2015;36: 305–310.

Kuttner H. Die verletzungen und traumatischen aneurysmen der vertebralgefasse am hales und ihre operative behandlung. *Beitrage zur Klinischen Chirurgie.* 1917;108: 1–60.

Lares Dos Santos C, Gouveia RH, Vieira DN. Unusual case of a fatal upper esophageal trauma caused by a toothpick. *J Forensic Leg Med.* 2019;62: 82–86.

Levy RD, Degiannis E, Hatzitheophilou C, Maberti P, Kantarovsky A, John KD, Saadia R. Management of penetrating injuries of the cervical trachea. *Ann R Coll Surg Engl.* 1997 May;79(3):195–197. PMID: 9196340; PMCID: PMC2502896.

Lipschitz R, Block J. Stab wounds of the spinal cord. *Lancet.* 1962;2: 169–172.

Livingstone AS. Vascular injuries of the head and neck. *Otolaryngol Clin North Am.* 1983 Aug;16(3):671–8. PMID: 6634188.

Low GM, Inaba K, Chouliaras K, Branco B, Lam L, Benjamin E,,Menaker J, Demetriades D. The use of the anatomic 'zones' of the neck in the assessment of penetrating neck injury. *Am Surg.* 2014;80: 970–974.

Madsen AS, Laing GL, Bruce JL, Clarke DL. A comparative audit of gunshot wounds and stab wounds to the neck in a South African metropolitan trauma service. *Ann R Coll Surg Engl.* 2016;98(7): 488–495.

Makhani M, Midani D, Goldberg A, Friedenberg FK. Pathogenesis and outcomes of traumatic injuries of the esophagus. *Dis Esophagus.* 2014 Sep-Oct;27(7):630–636. doi: 10.1111/dote.12132. Epub 2013 Aug 29. PMID: 24033532; PMCID: PMC3938994.

Makins G. *On Gunshot Wounds to the Blood Vessels.* John Wright, Bristol, 1919.

Matas R. Traumatisms and traumatic aneurisms of the vertebral arteryand their surgical treatment, with the problem of a cured case. *Ann Surg.* 1893;18: 477–521.

Meyer JP, Lim LT, Schuler JJ, Castronuovo JJ, Buchbinder D, Woelfel GF, Flanigan DP. Peripheral vascular trauma from from close-range shotgun injuries. *Arch Surg.* 1985;120: 1126–1131.

Mitton L, du Toit-Prinsloo L. Sharp force fatalities at the Pretoria Medico-Legal Laboratory, 2012–2013. *S Afr J Surg.* 2016;54: 21–26.

Nowicki JL, Stew B, Ooi E. Penetrating neck injuries: A guide to evaluation and management. *Ann R Coll Surg Engl.* 2018 Jan;100(1):6–11.

Onat S, Ulku R, Cigdem KM, Avci A, Ozcelik C. Factors affecting the outcome of surgically treated non-iatrogenic traumatic cervical esophageal perforation: 28 years experience at a single center. *J Cardiothorac Surg.* 2010 May 31;5:46. doi: 10.1186/1749-8090-5-46. PMID: 20509978; PMCID: PMC2907573.

Oshima T, Mimasaka S, Yonemitsu K, Kita K, Tsunenari S. Vertebral arterial injury due to fatal dog bites. *J Forensic Leg Med.* 2008;15(8): 529–532.

Park JJ, Shim HS, Jeong JH, Whang SH, Kim JP, Jeon SY, Kwon OJ. A case of cerebellar infarction caused by vertebral artery injury from a stab wound to the neck. *Auris Nasus Larynx.* 2007;34: 431–434.

Pate JW. Tracheobronchial and esophageal injuries. *Surg Clin North Am.* 1989 Feb;69(1):111–123. doi: 10.1016/s0039-6109(16)44739-0. Erratum in: *Surg Clin North Am* 1989 June;69(3):following viii. PMID: 2643176.

Patel F. Vasovagal death from screwdriver stabbing of the neck Case Report. *J Clin Forensic Med.* 1998;5: 205–206.

Patel NS. *A Study on Suicide.* PhD thesis University of London, 1971.

Peacock WJ, Shrosbree RD, Key AG. A review of 450 stab wounds of the spinal cord. *S Afr Med J.* 1977; 51:961–964.

Pinto A, Brunese L, Scaglione M, Scuderi MG, Romano L. Gunshot injuries in the neck area: ballistics elements and forensic issues. *Semin Ultrasound CT MR.* 2009 June;30(3):215–220. doi: 10.1053/j.sult.2009.02.006. PMID: 19537054

Polson CJ, Gee DJ, Knight B. *The Essentials of Forensic Medicine.* 4th edn. Pergamon Press, Oxford, 1985, pp. 179–180.

Pratt LW. Chain saw injuries of the head and neck. *Ear Nose Throat J.* 1985;64: 215–222.
Racette C, Kremer C, Desjarlais, Sauvageau A. Suicidal and homicidal sharp force injury: A 5-year retrospective comparative study of hesitation marks and defense wounds. *Forensic Sci Med Pathol.* 2008;4: 221–227.
Rao D. An autopsy study of 74 cases of cut throat injuries. *Egy J Forensic Sci.* 2015;5: 144–149.
Roll, P. Klintschar, M. Fatal missile injury from the rotating knife of an agricultural mower. *Forensic Sci Int.* 1998;94(1-2): 1–8.
Rothschild MA, Karger B, Schneider V. Puncture wounds caused by glass mistaken for with stab wounds with a knife. *Forensic Sci Int.* 2001;121: 161–165.
Rouse DA. Patterns of stab wounds: a six year study. *Med Sci Law.* 1994;34: 67–71.
Rubin G, Tallman D, Sagan L, Melgar M. An unusual stab wound of the cervical spinal cord: A case report. *Spine* 2001;26: 444–447.
Russo SS, Taff MI Ratanaproeksa O, Spitz WU. Sudden death resulting from chicken bone perforation of the oesophagus. *Am J Forensic Med Pathol.* 1986;7: 263–265.
Saeidiborojeni HR, Moradinazar M, Saeidiborojeni S, Ahmadi A. A survey on spinal cord injuries resulting from stabbings: a case series study of 12 years' experience. *J Inj Violence Res.* 2013;5: 70–74.
Schuessler WW. Self -infliction excision of the larynx and thyroid and division of the trachea and oesophagus with recovery. *JAMA.* 1944;125: 551–552.
Schulz F, Colmant HJ, Trtübner K. Penetrating spinal injury inflicted by screwdriver: unusual morphological findings. *J Clin Forensic Med.* 1995;2: 153–155.
Seeley SF, Hughes CW, Cook FN, Elkin DC. Traumatic arteriovenous fistulae and aneurysms in war wounded: Study of 101 cases. *Am J Surg.* 1952;83: 471–479.
Shiroff AM, Gale SC, Martin ND, Marchalik D, Petrov D, Ahmed HM, Rotondo MF, Gracias VH. Penetrating neck trauma: A review of management strategies and discussion of the 'No Zone' approach. *Am Surg.* 2013;79: 23–29.
Stafforini NA, Singh N. Management of vascular injuries in penetrating trauma. *Surg Clin North Am.* 2023 Aug;103(4):801–825. doi: 10.1016/j.suc.2023.04.018. Epub 2023 May 23. PMID: 37455038.
Strickland M, Roedel E, Inaba K. Penetrating cervical vascular injuries. *Curr Trauma Rep.* 2019;5: 40–47. https://doi.org/10.1007/s40719-019-0161-7
Suematsu T, Murakami T, Takamatsu J, Shimizu T, Toyota S, Taki T. Crossbow Bolt Penetrating the Neck Removed with the Assistance of an Endovascular Approach: A Case Report and Literature Review. *NMC Case Rep J.* 2022 June 15;9:157–163. doi: 10.2176/jns-nmc.2022-0035. PMID: 35836494; PMCID: PMC9239694.
Sutton D, Pratt AE. Vertebral arterio-venous fistula. *Clin Radiol.* 1971;22: 289–295.
Swain R, Dhaka S, Sharma M, Bakshi MS, Murty OP, Sikary AK. Accidental cut-throat injuries from the broken windshield of an auto rickshaw: Two unusual cases. *Med Sci Law.* 2018;58(3), 183–185.
Taylor AS. *A manual of medical jurisprudence*, 12 edn (ed. Stevenson T.), J and A Churchill, London, 1891, p. 354.
Tisherman SA, Bokhari F, Collier B, Cumming J, Ebert J, Holevar M, Kurek S, Leon S, Rhee P. Clinical practice guideline: penetrating zone II neck trauma. *J Trauma.* 2008 May;64(5):1392–1405. doi: 10.1097/TA.0b013e3181692116. PMID: 18469667.
Vanezis P, West 1 E. Tentative injuries in self stabbing. *Forensic Sci Int.* 1983;21: 65–70.
Vanezis P. *Pathology of neck injury* 1st Ed. Ch. 4, p37. Butterworths, London, 1989.
Vassalini M, Verzeletti A, De Ferrari F. Sharp force injury fatalities: A retrospective study (1982–2012) in Brescia (Italy) *J Forensic Sci.* 2014;59: 1568–1574.
de Villiers JC, Grant AR. Stab wounds at the craniocervical junction. *Neurosurgery.* 1985 Dec;17(6):930–936. doi: 10.1227/00006123-198512000-00010. PMID: 4080126.
Vishwanatha B, Sagayaraj A, Shalini G, Huddar SG, Kumar P, Datta RK. Penetrating neck injuries. *Indian J. Otolaryngol. Head Neck Surg.* 2007;59:221–224.
Wahed S, Dent B, Jones R, Griffin SM. Spectrum of oesophageal perforations and their influence on management. *Br J Surg.* 2014 Jan;101(1):e156–62. doi: 10.1002/bjs.9338. Epub 2013 Nov 22. PMID: 24272950.
Woo K, Magner DP, Wilson MT, Margulies DR. CT angiography in penetrating neck trauma reduces the need for operative neck exploration. *Am Surg.* 2005;71(9): 754–758.
Zaldivar-Jolissaint JF, Bobinski L, Van Dommelen Y, Levivier M, Simon C, Duff JM. Delayed presentation of deep penetrating trauma to the subaxial cervical spine. *Eur Spine J.* 2015 May;24 Suppl 4: S540–S543. doi: 10.1007/s00586-014-3681-4. Epub 2014 Nov 19. PMID: 25408256.

# CHAPTER 5

## COMPRESSIVE NECK INJURY I: GENERAL SIGNS ASSOCIATED WITH ASPHYXIA

*Peter Vanezis*



DOI: 10.4324/9781003658467-5

# INTRODUCTION

Compression of the neck most frequently results either from the application of a ligature or from manual means (hands, forearms, upper and lower limbs). With hanging (complete or partial suspension), as distinct from other forms of compression, the applied force is supplied by the weight of the victim, although occasionally also contributed to by the hands in applying the ligature. Most compressive neck injury cases fall into either homicidal or suicidal categories, whereas accidental deaths, although important, are less often encountered.

Neck compression may be caused in several ways, in which there is obstruction of the airways and associated structures in the neck, causing oxygen deprivation. In different types of compression, death frequently results from a combination of mechanisms involving the various structures that are compressed, i.e., airway, blood vessels, and nerve structures. The most common mechanism is a direct result of acute airway and vascular obstruction, rather than by airway, vascular, or nerve compression alone.

In relation to hanging, it should also be stated that there is good justification for including it as a subtype of ligature strangulation rather than as a separate entity (Petreca et al., 2023; Sauvageau and Boghossian, 2010). The latter authors point out that the biomechanics of ligature strangulation are identical to those in hanging, except that the tightening force is not the weight of the body. These entities are, however, highly different from each other in the circumstances surrounding the death, which accounts for the reason why hanging is distinguished from other forms of strangulation. The author of this text is in agreement with this recommendation.

# NOTE ON ASPHYXIA AND USAGE OF THE TERM 'MECHANICAL ASPHYXIA'

At this point, I ought to be clear that it is beyond the scope of this book to examine and discuss the different forms of asphyxia and, in particular, the complex nature and various forms of its presentation to the forensic practitioner. For further details regarding its classification, the reader is referred to the recent comprehensive text edited by Madea (2021), as well as the publication by Sauvageau and Boghossian (2010) and the commentary on the latter authors' article by Byard (2011).

It is necessary, however, to point out that the author of this text will use the term mechanical asphyxia in relation to physical obstruction of the airway at all levels of the neck region. This usage takes into account the fact that the word mechanical relates to 'the study of the effect of physical forces on objects and their movement', despite its use by many pathologists as being related purely to restriction of breathing from compression of the thorax or abdomen.

Furthermore, it is essential to appreciate that the circumstances and findings in asphyxia-related deaths from physical airway obstruction may be complex; occasionally, the forensic practitioner may encounter a combination of both mechanical and non-mechanical (environmental/non-physical) asphyxia, for example, in fire deaths (Fein et al., 1980).

# GENERAL SIGNS IN DEATHS RESULTING FROM NECK COMPRESSION

There are a number of signs as well as other factors, that influence and are applicable to the various types of compression described in the chapters that follow. The assessment of compression of the neck relies on the evaluation of a number of physical signs that are specific to the mode of compression, as well as general signs that have been regarded as associated with such deaths. The relevance of each of the signs with which forensic practitioners are familiar is considered below:

## Petechial Haemorrhages

Much has been written about petechial haemorrhages and their role in asphyxia deaths. Tardieu (Figure 5.1) was one of the first to describe them in the skin, eyes, and viscera, and they are still occasionally referred to eponymously as 'Tardieu's spots'.

He regarded them as pathognomonic of deaths from suffocation (1855) and strangulation (1859). An earlier description of such haemorrhages was given by Christison (1829), who found them in the conjunctivae of the last of Burke and Hare's victims. Nevertheless, he emphasised caution when examining asphyxia deaths, particularly those due to suffocation, in which such haemorrhages are frequently absent. Petechial haemorrhages are typically seen in the eyes, face, and neck (Figure 5.2) and internally in the mucous membranes of the mouth (Figures 5.3).

Other regions in which they are commonly seen include the submucosal laryngeal surface, especially the epiglottis (see Figure 5.4), the tongue, pharynx, muscle sheaths, and other viscera, particularly the subepicardial and subpleural surfaces, and the scalp.

They occur as a result of blood escaping from capillaries and may either appear on the skin as a fine rash or form larger aggregates if sufficient in number. Such coalescence of haemorrhages is seen particularly in the eyes (Figure 5.5).

Haemorrhagic 'spots' seen on examination of the cranial aponeurosis of the scalp should be assessed with caution. It is very common to tear or cut through small blood vessels supplying this region when reflecting the skin, thus causing artefactual haemorrhagic areas resembling petechiae (Figure 5.6).

Levy and Hirsch (2000) reviewed the pathogenesis of conjunctival and facial petechiae and the potential for their misinterpretation in cases where there has been obstruction of the airways. They point out that these are simply the result of increased cephalic venous pressure and, in themselves, should not be regarded as supportive evidence of asphyxia. They also state that their potential value can only be appreciated as part of a complete autopsy. The author of this book, whilst accepting the caution and need to avoid their misinterpretation, as well as the reservations of many authors in older publications, is of the view that they are useful signs of mechanical airway compression deaths when seen in the face and eyes, provided they are corroborated by injuries or other physical signs to these regions. In particular, the presence of petechiae immediately above, for example, a ligature mark and their absence below it is strong evidence that at this mark there has been compression of the neck (see Figure 5.2). This may be confirmed by vertical histological section from above down to below the line of compression to show congestion and rupture of capillaries above (Figure 5.7). This observation may be of value, particularly in cases of alleged strangulation of new-born children. A soft piece of cloth is frequently used, being the nearest material available. The marks produced are often very faint or absent, and furthermore, the skin of the baby's neck is usually creased and furrowed, making the determination of a ligature even more difficult.

In some circumstances, visceral petechiae (Tardieu spots) can appear after death, and they are such a common finding in so many different types of deaths from all causes that any interpretation of their significance is open to question. Petechiae in the brain substance are sometimes said to

**Figure 5.1** Auguste Ambrose Tardieu (1818–1879), Dean of the Faculty of Medicine and Professor of Legal Medicine at the University of Paris.

occur in asphyxia. Such findings are, however, most likely to be the cut ends of congested vessels and not petechial haemorrhages. The doubtful significance of visceral petechiae in mechanical asphyxia has been further emphasised in a study by Zaini and Knight (1982), who demonstrated that many so-called subpleural petechiae were not true haemorrhages but were 'pseudo-petechiae' due to intrapleural channels, air blisters, thickened pleural plaques, or dust pigment.

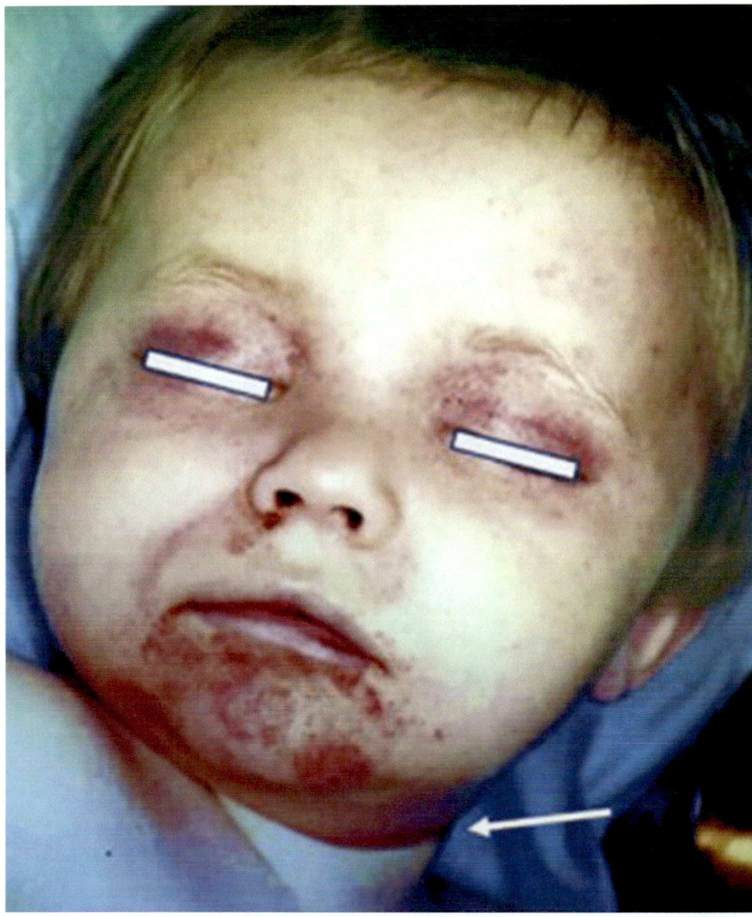

**Figure 5.2** Petechial haemorrhages on the face and neck in a young child. All petechiae are above the ligature mark (arrow).

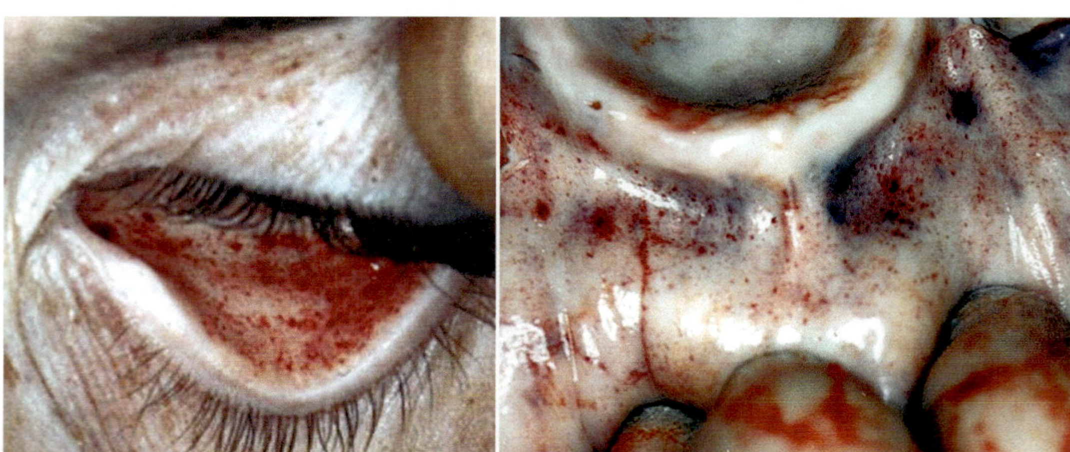

(a) (b)

**Figure 5.3** Petechial haemorrhages: (a) in the conjunctiva and eyelids and (b) in the mouth – at the inner aspect of the upper lips, gum margins, and hard palate (case of manual strangulation).

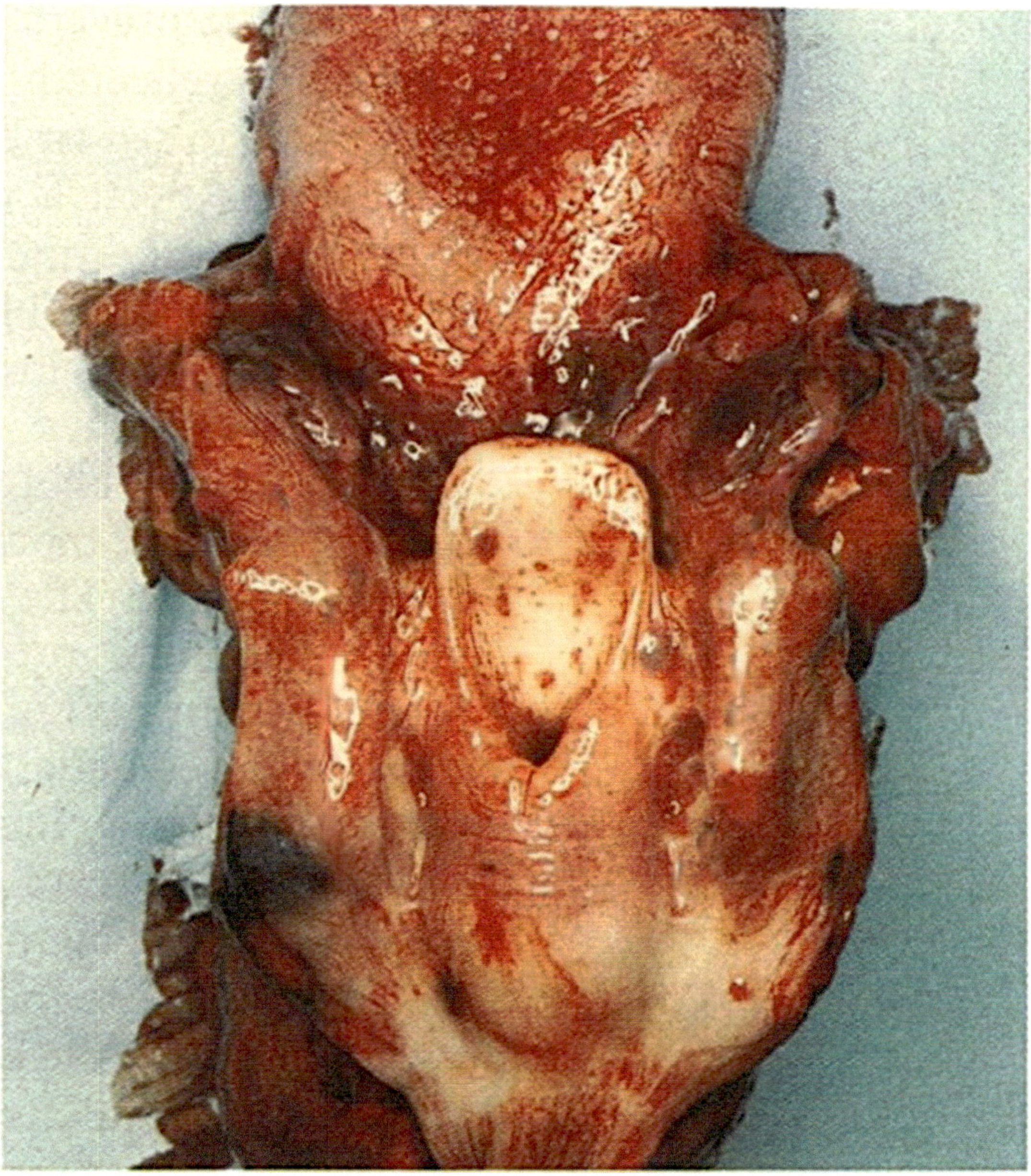

**Figure 5.4** Petechial haemorrhages on submucosal surface of epiglottis and below.

Petechial haemorrhages within hypostasis are seen in many types of death, but they are usually more pronounced in cases where there has been a degree of postural airway obstruction, such as in alcohol intoxication or status epilepticus (Figure 5.8). They have also been found to be significantly present, independent of the position of the deceased or hypostasis, in the conjunctivae and eyelids significantly in cases of alcohol and/or drug intoxication, as reported by Flaagøy et al. (2016) and Mæhle et al. (2022). Their findings are based on studies of 590 deaths and 865 deaths, respectively.

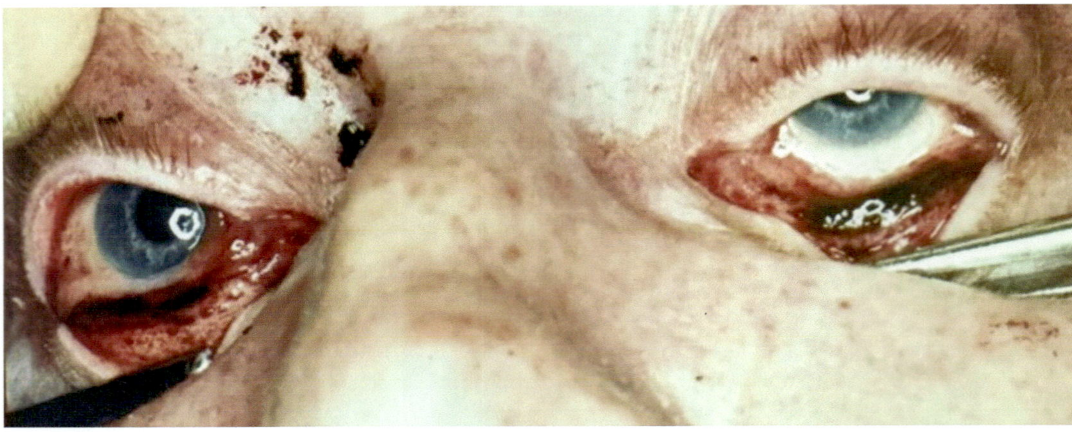

**Figure 5.5** The lower palpebral conjunctivae show coalesced petechial haemorrhages.

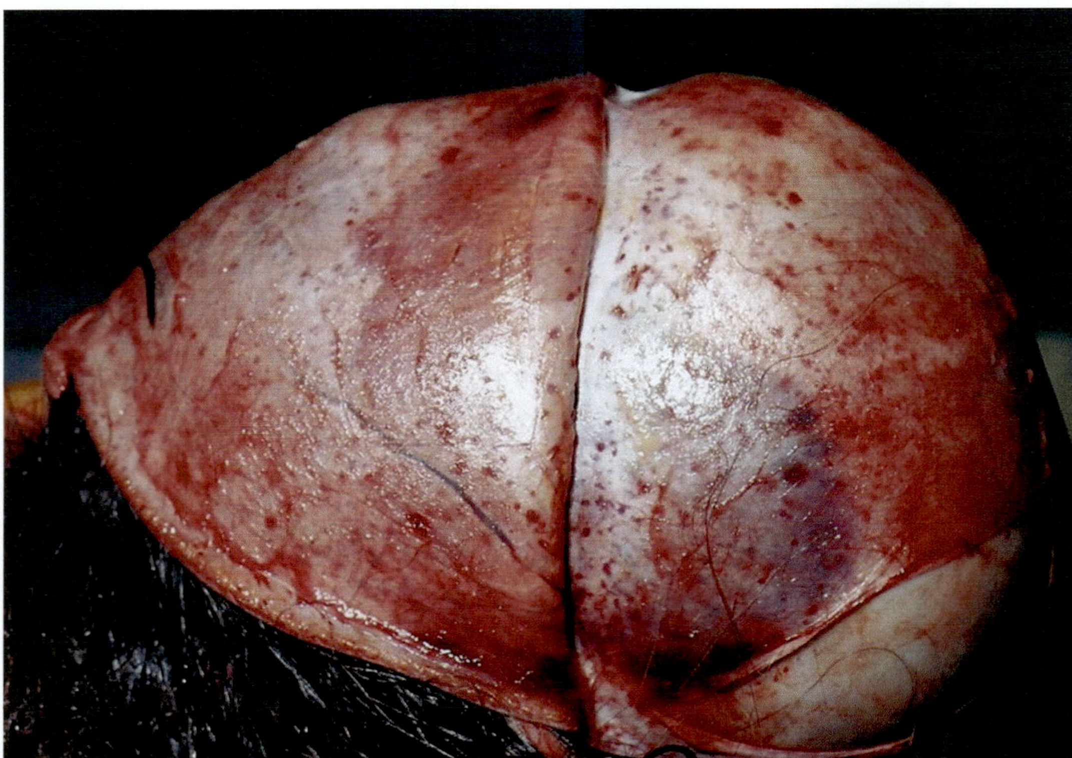

**Figure 5.6** 'Petechial haemorrhages' most likely a post-mortem artefact, produced by reflecting the scalp and cutting through the underlying blood vessels.

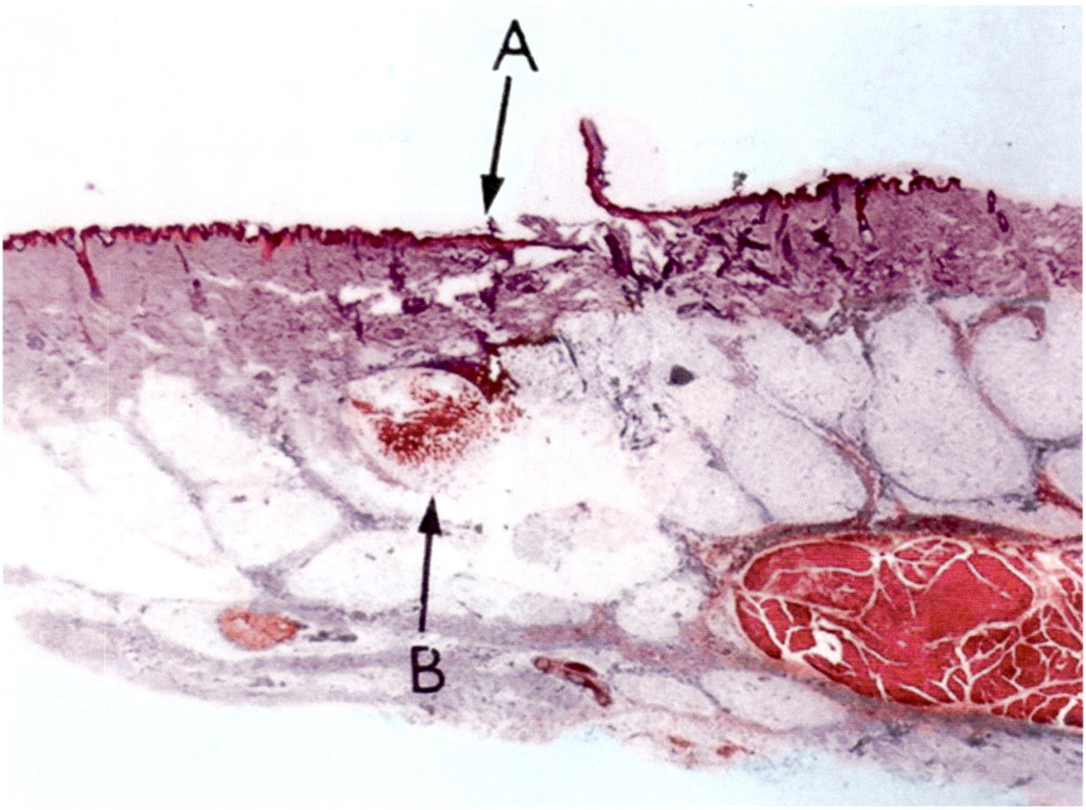


**Figure 5.7** Section of line of compression of neck with a ligature. Flattening of the epidermis seen (A) as well as a well-defined capillary haemorrhage above the mark (B). (Haematoxylin and eosin x8).

## Cyanosis

The bluish colour of the skin, referred to as cyanosis, has to be interpreted with a great degree of caution in cases of mechanical obstruction of the airways. In order to appreciate the difficulties in the interpretation of cyanosis, one must be aware of the physiological mechanisms of its causation.

Its appearance on the skin and mucous membranes is due to the presence of reduced haemoglobin in the blood of superficial capillaries. It depends on the absolute amount of reduced haemoglobin in the capillary blood, not on the relative proportions of reduced haemoglobin and oxyhaemoglobin. It has been found that a haemoglobin level of 5 g/100 ml of capillary blood, or an oxygen unsaturation of 6.7 ml/100 ml, is about the threshold at which cyanosis appears. An anaemic subject who, therefore, has a total of less than 5 g of haemoglobin, i.e., an oxygen-carrying capacity of less than 6.7 ml/100 ml, does not ordinarily become cyanotic. Thus, the presence of cyanosis means the tissues are hypoxic, although its absence does not necessarily indicate the absence of hypoxia.

In mechanical airway obstruction leading to hypoxia, there are two mechanisms of causation of cyanosis:

1. Reduction of alveolar $PO_2$: A diminished alveolar $PO_2$ may occur because of reduced respiratory minute volume when the airway is obstructed. The blood passing through the lungs will, therefore, not be oxygenated.
2. Abnormal reduction of haemoglobin in the systemic capillaries: Decreased blood flow above the level of constriction of the neck gives rise to stagnant hypoxia, with cyanosis confined to this region.

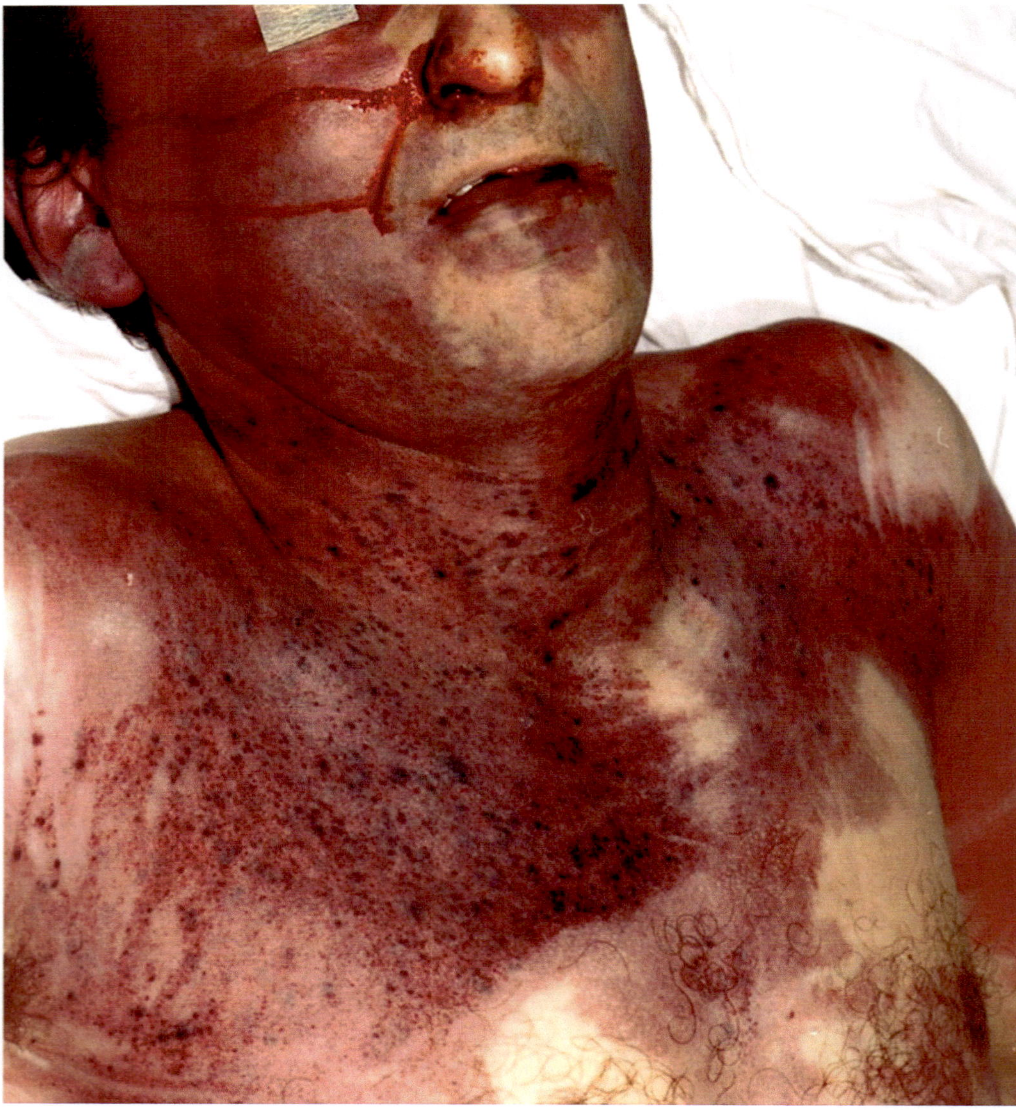

**Figure 5.8** The deceased was intoxicated with alcohol and was found in a prone position. Petechial haemorrhages are confined within areas of hypostasis.

Cyanosis detected at autopsy is frequently misleading and of no use as a sole diagnostic criterion of hypoxia caused by airway obstruction. One should examine the colouration of the cadaver critically, noting the distribution of hypostasis and bearing in mind that assessment and detection of true cyanosis within such areas are totally unreliable and quite a common finding in many cadavers, regardless of the cause of death.

Nevertheless, the face and neck may show a combination of congestion with a degree of cyanosis above the level of a constriction, with relative pallor beneath (Figure 5.9). Such an observation is useful when taken into account the circumstances of the death, provided the face has not been lying towards the ground, in which case the distinction from hypostasis may be impossible.

In addition to cyanosis, and particularly if there has been a prolonged struggle, because of the increased venous congestion, there may be tissue oedema causing swelling of the facial features, including the eyes (Figure 5.10).

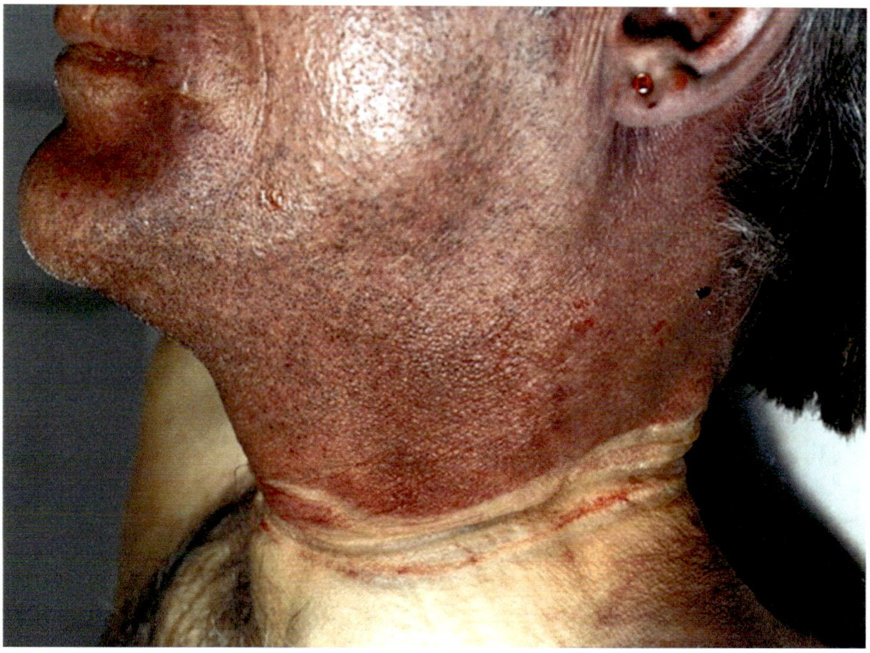

**Figure 5.9** Congestion with cyanosis of the face in a male who strangled himself. Below the ligature mark, there is pallor indicating the obstruction of the venous return to the heart and relative patency of the arterial neck vessels.

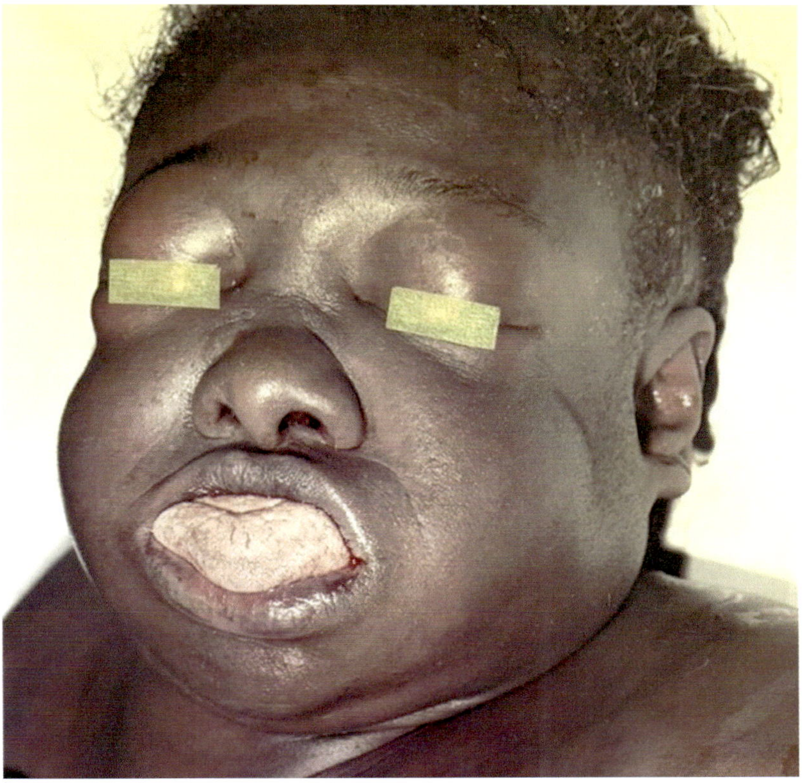

**Figure 5.10** Swelling of facial features and protrusion of the tongue resulting from ligature strangulation.

## Congestion Externally and of Internal Organs

Congestion of the surface of the body and of internal organs is such a common and non-specific finding seen in many types of deaths and cannot in any way be regarded as a reliable sign of mechanical asphyxia.

## Otorrhagia

Barranco et al. (2022) recently pointed out that otorrhagia (bleeding from the ear) is poorly described in cases of neck compression and is therefore often an underestimated finding. The middle ear is drained by two veins that flow into the internal and external jugular veins (which are superficial in the neck). Compression of the neck creates an obstruction of the jugular blood return and vascular congestion of the middle ear with haemorrhage. This is the first potential mechanism of otorrhagia in strangulation. The second mechanism is based on the hypothesis that respiratory effort against a closed glottis can cause rupture of the tympanic membrane. It has been suggested that compression of the neck simulates a closed glottis. Therefore, laryngeal or pharyngeal obstruction might cause an increase in pressure in the middle ear through the Eustachian tube. Such an increase in pressure (in a nonextensile cavity) could cause a middle ear injury and bleeding. It seems that both mechanisms could be synergistic and cause otorrhagia in cases of strangulation. Two cases of ligature strangulation with haemotympanum and otorrhagia are reported by Duband et al. (2009), and a further case is reported by Živković et al. (2021) of an elderly woman who was found partially hanging in a kneeling position.

## Pulmonary Oedema

Pulmonary oedema may be present in deaths from mechanical obstruction of the airways, but its severity is extremely variable and, indeed, it may be altogether absent. The interpretation of such a finding is questionable without other corroborative evidence of airway obstruction, as it is commonly seen in many types of death. Its pathogenesis following acute airway obstruction is thought to be due to alveolar and capillary damage induced by the negative pressure generated by attempts to inspire against the closed upper airway (Oswalt et al., 1977; Lang et al., 1990). The degree of oedema, however, is no guide to the length of time the airways are obstructed before death occurs; indeed, quite severe oedema can be seen in rapid deaths.

## Fluidity of Blood

Up until a few years ago, it was erroneously thought that blood maintained its fluidity in cases involving asphyxia associated with airway obstruction and that this was a useful diagnostic sign. Mole (1948) concluded, however, that it can occur from any sudden death associated with 'shock or collapse' during life. Animal studies (Takeichi et al., 1984, 1985, 1986) have shown that fibrinolysin activation occurs as a result of the release of plasminogen activator through the receptors on the vascular wall for various vasoactive materials that increase during the agonal period. Fibrinolysis is also activated by the leakage of plasminogen factor due to increased permeability and to degeneration or necrosis of the cell membrane as the result of excessive acidosis after death, and non-specific leakage of enzymes associated with blood coagulation may occur. Thus, the fluidity of blood results from an imbalance between clotting and fibrinolytic factors and is not specific to deaths associated with an asphyxial mode of death.

## References


Barranco R, Tettamanti C, Bonsignore A, Ventura F. Otorrhagia in strangulations: An important but often underestimated finding in forensic pathology. *J Forensic Sci.* 2022 July;67(4):1739–1742.

Byard RW. Commentary on: Sauvageau A, Boghossian E. Classification of asphyxia: The need for standardization. *J Forensic Sci.* 2010;55(5):1259–1267. *J Forensic Sci.* 56(1): 264–265.

Christison R. Case IV. Murder by suffocation. Injury of the spine after death imitating an injury during life - Experiments on the effects of blows soon after death. *Edinb Med J.*, 1829;31: 236–250.

Duband S, Timoshenko AP, Morrison AL, Prades JM, Debout M, Peoc'h M. Ear bleeding: A sign not to be underestimated in cases of strangulation. *Am J Forensic Med Pathol.* 2009 June;30(2):175–176. doi: 10.1097/PAF.0b013e3181875a8b. PMID: 19465811.

Ely SF, Hirsch CS. Asphyxial deaths and petechiae: A review. *J Forensic Sci.* 2000;45(6):1274.

Fein A, Leff A, Hopewell PC. Pathophysiology and management of the complications resulting from fire and the inhaled products of combustion: Review of the literature. *Crit Care Med.* 1980 Feb;8(2):94–98.

Flaagøy SH, Morild I, Maehle BO, Lilleng PK. Petechial hemorrhages and ethanol in deaths from intoxication. *J Forensic Sci.* 2016 Sep;61(5):1266–1269. doi: 10.1111/1556-4029.13143. Epub 2016 June 24. PMID: 27341349.

Lang SA, Duncan PG, Shephard DA, Ha HC. Pulmonary oedema associated with airway obstruction. *Can J Anaesth.* 1990 Mar;37(2):210–218. doi: 10.1007/BF03005472. PMID: 2178789.

Madea B. Ed. *Asphyxiation, Suffocation and Neck Pressure Deaths.* CRC Press Taylor and Francis Group Boca Raton, 2020.

Mæhle BO, Eide GE, Morild I, Lilleng PK. Petechial hemorrhages, ethanol, and opioids in victims from intoxication. *Forensic Sci Int.* 2022 Sep;338: 111406. doi: 10.1016/j.forsciint.2022.111406. Epub 2022 July 21. PMID: 35908337.

Mole RH. Fibrinolysin and fluidity of the blood postmortem. *J Pathol Bacteriol.* 1948;60: 413–427.

Oswalt CE, Gates GA, Holmstrom MG. Pulmonary edema as a complication of acute airway obstruction. *JAMA.* 1977 Oct 24;238(17): 1833–1835. PMID: 333133.

Petreca VG, Burgess AW, Jarvis K. Manual and instrument asphyxiation/strangulation: Examining perpetrator and victim characteristics. *J Forensic Leg Med.* 2023 Aug;98: 102575. doi: 10.1016/j.jflm.2023.102575. Epub 2023 Aug 3. PMID: 37549551.

Sauvageau A, Boghossian E. Classification of asphyxia: the need for standardization. *J Forensic Sci.* 2010;55(5): 1259–1267.

Takeichi S, Wakasugi C, Shikata I. Fluidity of cadaveric blood after sudden death: Part I. Postmortem fibrinolysis and plasma catecholamine level. *Am J Forensic Med Pathol.* 1984 Sep;5(3): 223–237. doi: 10.1097/00000433-198409000-00006. PMID: 6496435.

Takeichi S, Wakasugi C, Shikata I. Fluidity of cadaveric blood after sudden death: Part II. Mechanism of release of plasminogen activator from blood vessels. *Am J Forensic Med Pathol.* 1985 Mar;6(1):25–29. doi: 10.1097/00000433-198503000-00006. PMID: 4039106.

Takeichi S, Tokunaga I, Hayakumo K, Maeiwa M. Fluidity of cadaveric blood after sudden death: Part III. Acid-base balance and fibrinolysis. *Am J Forensic Med Pathol.* 1986 Mar;7(1):35–38. doi: 10.1097/00000433-198603000-00007. PMID: 3728418.

Tardieu A. Memoire sur la mort par suffocation. *Annales d'Hygene Publique et de Medecine Legale,* 2e serie, 1855, T. XI.

Tardieu A. Etude medico-legale sur la strangulation. *Annales d'Hygene Publique et de Medecine Legale,* 2e serie, 1859, T. XI.

Zaini MR, Knight B. Sub-pleural petechiae and pseudo petechiae. *J Forensic Sci Soc.* 1982 Apr;22(2):141–145. doi: 10.1016/s0015-7368(82)71462-8. PMID: 7097233.

Živković V, Cvetković D, Nikolić S. Otorrhagia as an intravital phenomenon in a case of incomplete atypical hanging. *J Forensic Sci.* 2021 Mar;66(2):775–778. doi: 10.1111/1556-4029.14620. Epub 2020 Nov 17. PMID: 33201512.

# CHAPTER 6

## COMPRESSIVE NECK INJURY II: MANUAL STRANGULATION

*Peter Vanezis*
*(with contributions from Curtis Offiah)*



DOI: 10.4324/9781003658467-6

# INTRODUCTION

Compression of the neck with one or both hands is one of the most common methods of homicide. Victims may include young children, elderly, and/or infirm individuals. Females, who may also show signs of sexual assault, are much more likely to be strangled than males. It is quite common to see such deaths in domestic circumstances, where, after an altercation, the woman is the victim. Sorenson et al. (2014), in a systematic review of the epidemiology of strangulation, found that women survivors were more likely than men to report that they were strangled during intimate partner violence.

One commonly finds related injuries to other regions of the body, particularly the face. There may also be other severe injuries, such as stab wounds or head injuries, that are instrumental in causing or contributing to death.

Manual strangulation should for all practical purposes, be regarded as homicidal. One must be careful to differentiate strangulation from deaths that occur instantaneously after a 'momentary' touch or slight 'unintentional' grip. Strangulation implies compression of the neck to obstruct the airways and/or blood vessels, rather than stimulation of the carotid sinus per se. In that respect, the issue of whether the cardioinhibitory reflex (vasovagal syncope) is a valid mechanism as a major cause of death in neck compression remains unresolved (Schrag et al., 2012). They surveyed pathologists in a number of countries and although widely accepted theoretically, in practice there was no uniformity of diagnostic approach at autopsy; it should therefore be used with extreme caution.

Occasionally, there have been attempts at concealing homicide, including manual strangulation, by attempting to destroy injuries, for example, by conflagration to simulate an accidental fire or, particularly in manual or ligature strangulation, by simulating hanging. A retrospective survey by Sane et al. (2024) of autopsy reports of 2,810 fire-related deaths found 13 cases (0.46%) where post-mortem burns concealed homicide. Head injury was the most common cause of death, followed by different types of strangulation. Females were reported to be more commonly involved, and the majority occurred in a domestic environment.

Other related forms of neck compression which form part of the spectrum of manual strangulation, include the use of the forearm, and may be either accidental or intentional (see section on neck holds), or, rarely, the use of the palm. Palmar strangulation, where the compression is caused directly by the palm of the hand pressing onto the neck, has been reported by Polson et al. (1985). These authors describe the case of a woman who had been strangled by an assailant who insisted that at no time had he gripped her throat. However, both horns of her thyroid cartilage had been fractured, and there was bruising of the neck muscles. He said that she had threatened to scream to attract the attention of passers-by. He had placed his right hand horizontally across her mouth and then reinforced the pressure by placing his left hand on top, at right angles to the other. In this manner, the heel of the palm would have been in front of her neck. The mechanism was tested on a cadaver of approximately the same age, who was later shown to have died of natural causes, and fractures were reproduced to both thyroid horns (Figure 6.1).

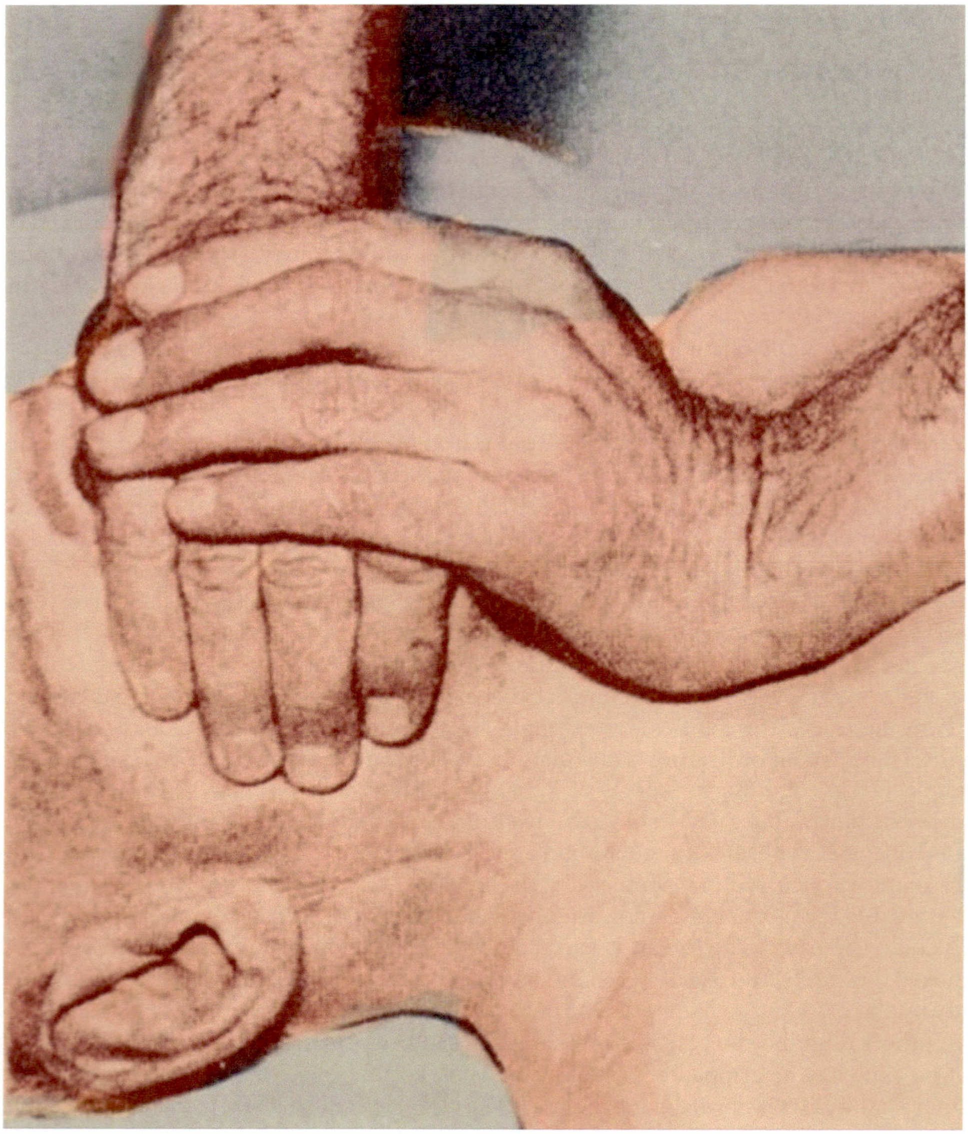

**Figure 6.1** Demonstration of the mechanism of palmar strangulation from the case described by Polson, Gee and Knight (image adapted from their illustration).

# ASSESSMENT OF VICTIMS OF MANUAL STRANGULATION

In assessing cases of manual strangulation, the following factors should be considered:

- External and internal neck trauma
- Associated injuries to other regions
- External and internal signs related to asphyxia
- Length of application, evidence of a struggle and its extent
- Force of strangulation
- Mechanism(s) causing death
- Survivability and complications

## External Neck Injuries

### Introduction

Physical signs of manual compression of the neck are variable in their appearance and can be a combination of those caused by the assailant together, with those caused by the victim attempting to remove the hands or arms from their neck.

### Bruising

One of the most common findings in manual neck compression is fingertip-type bruising (Figures 6.2–6.4). The bruises are separately placed, or they may merge more into each other, and tend to be rounded. They vary in shape and intensity, depending on how the hands are applied to the neck and the degree of force used. Bruising will be greater if the grip has been shifted, reapplied, or if the victim has struggled. Theoretically, if the pressure is maintained in one spot until the victim's circulation ceases, it is possible that no bruising will be seen because there has been no blood flowing to extravasate from the damaged vessels (Camps and Hunt, 1959).

### Fingernail Marks

Accompanying bruising or separately, one also frequently sees fingernail marks (Figures 6.5–6.9). Classically, they are crescentic skin abrasions. However, it is not unusual to see deeper lacerations caused by nails, or indeed scratch marks, which may be entirely linear. It should be borne in mind that short fingernails can also produce such marks. Nevertheless, it is essential to examine the assailant's fingernails not only to assess their length but also to note whether they have been broken or deliberately cut short after the event. One should also note that the marks could possibly have been made by the victim in a desperate attempt to remove the constricting hands or a ligature. The direction of the marks may then be of considerable significance. It should also be borne in mind that in such cases, it is unlikely that the fingernail marks will be accompanied by fingertip bruising.

Irregularities in the edges of the fingernails give characteristic marks, and there are circumstances where identification of an assailant's or victim's marks may be possible. Perper and Sobel (1981) demonstrated how they were able, in one case, to identify an assailant's fingernail marks on the neck of an 11-year-old boy. The boy in question was one of two children murdered in 1979. The other child was the male child's ten-year-old sister. They also emphasise that the matching must demonstrate individual peculiarities and not just similarity of size and curvature. In some cases, inconsistencies in the general characteristics (e.g., shape, curvature, size) permit the early exclusion of some of the suspects.

Starrs (1985) reported on the appeal to the Pennsylvania Supreme Court of the convicted killer in the two deaths described by the above authors (Commonwealth v Graves, 1983).

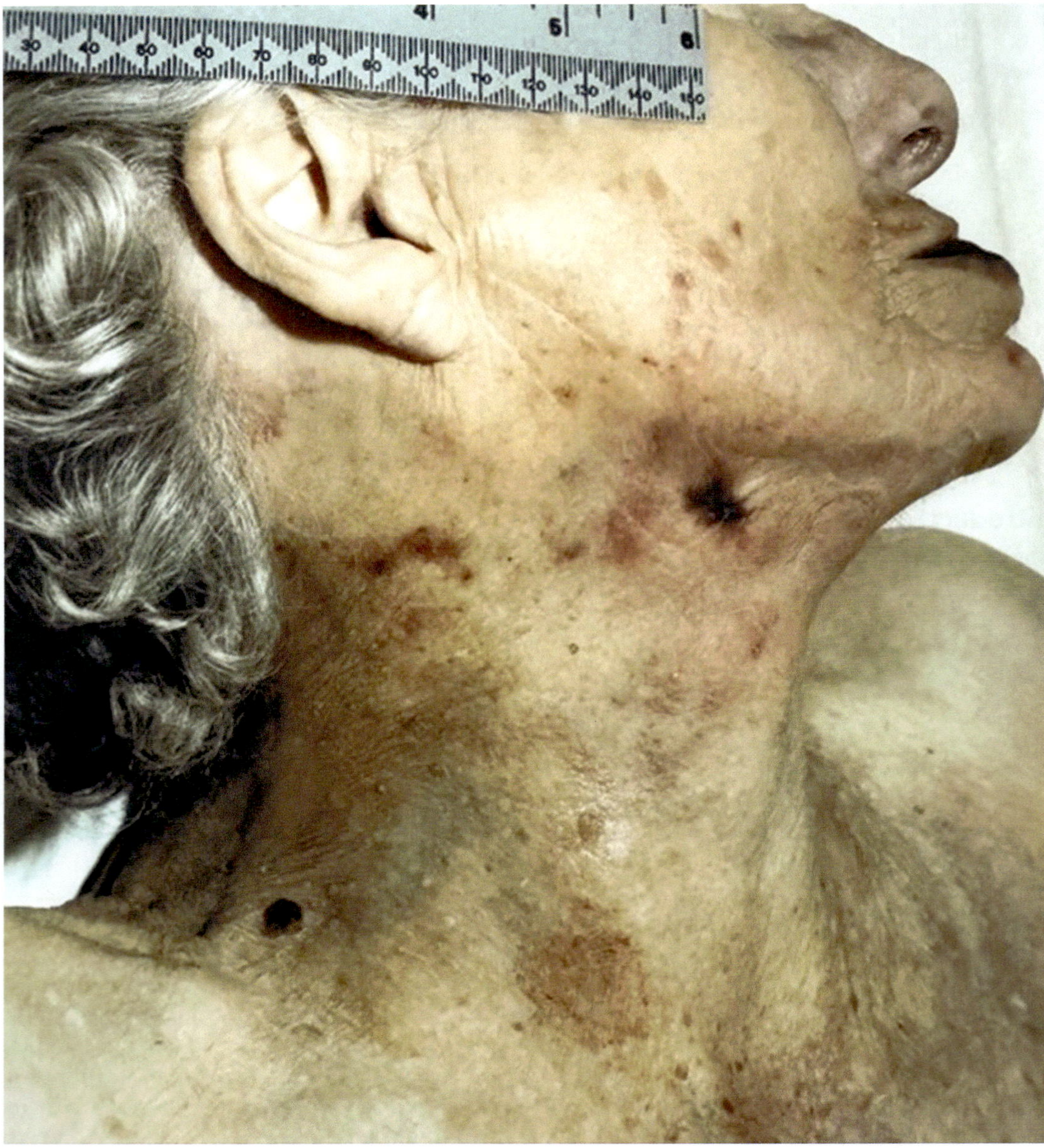


**Figure 6.2** Right side of the neck in an elderly woman, showing a line of bruises extending up to the mandible and cheek.

The court approved the trial court's admission of scientific testimony matching the accused's fingernail to the impression left on the child's neck, which apparently occurred while he was being strangled. Despite variations in some of the expert witness evidence, the court accepted that the evidence was admissible in accordance with the Frye test (Frye v United States, 1923). They further stated that

> fingernail identifications were like toolmark and bitemark comparisons and, as such the experts were found to be sufficiently skilled in those cognate disciplines to state their conclusions particularly since impressions after the fashion of bitemark cases, were taken and used for the identification in this instance.

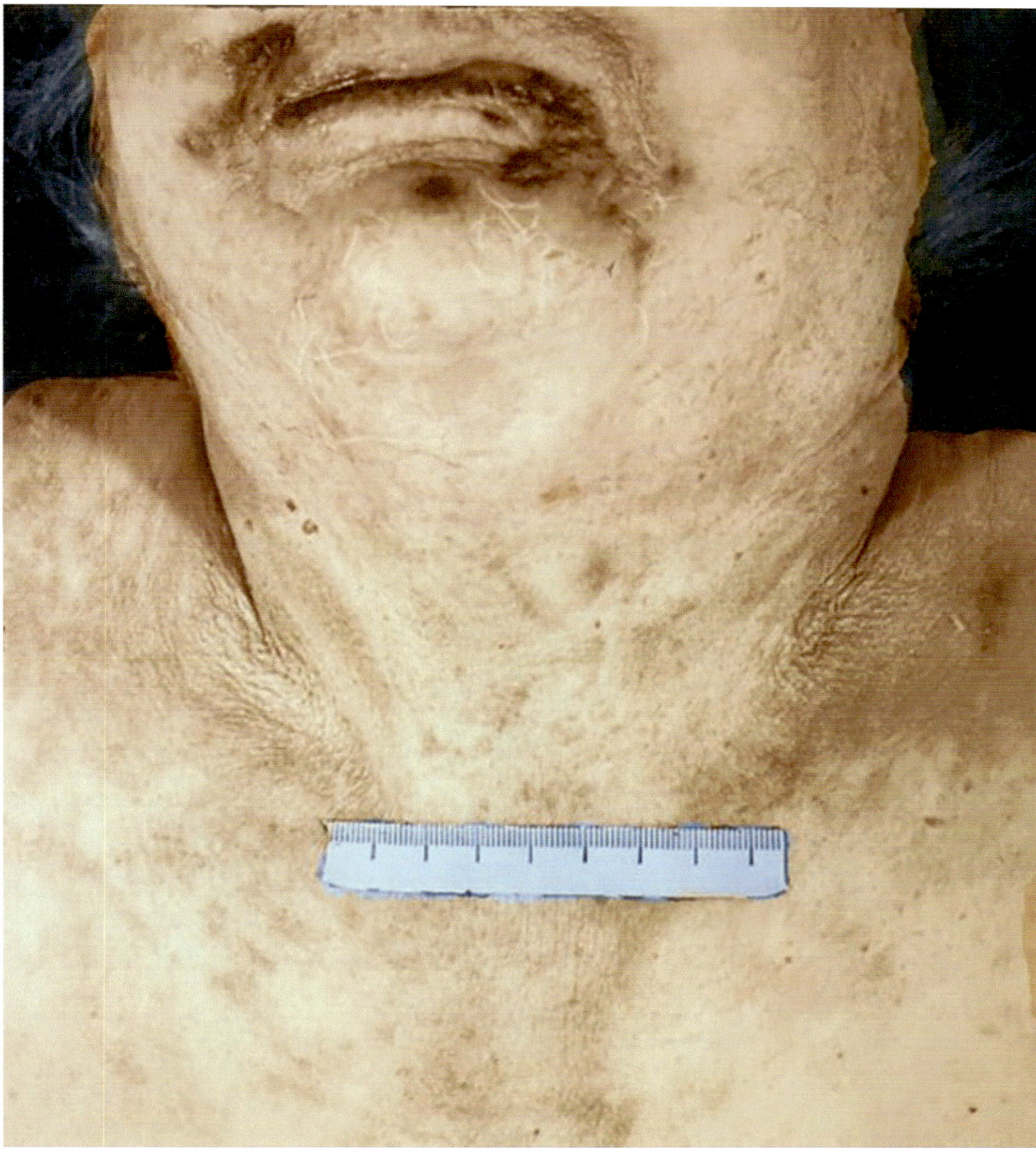

**Figure 6.3** Collection of bruises just to the left of the middle of the neck. In addition, there are several abrasions around the mouth, caused while the victim was struggling against an overlying hand.

With regard to the position on the neck of the assailant's hand(s), or, for that matter, the victim's, Shapiro et al. (1962) demonstrated in a series of simple observations that the curve of the fingernail mark was in the opposite direction to that expected when the nail was pointed centrally (commonly the case in women with longer fingernails). They concluded therefore that it was the shape of the nail which determined the direction of the curve. I have personally attempted to repeat Shapiro and his colleagues' observations but with little success. When the fingernail was pointed centrally, I observed that the curve was more likely to 'straighten out' but on no occasion did it produce a contrary curved mark.

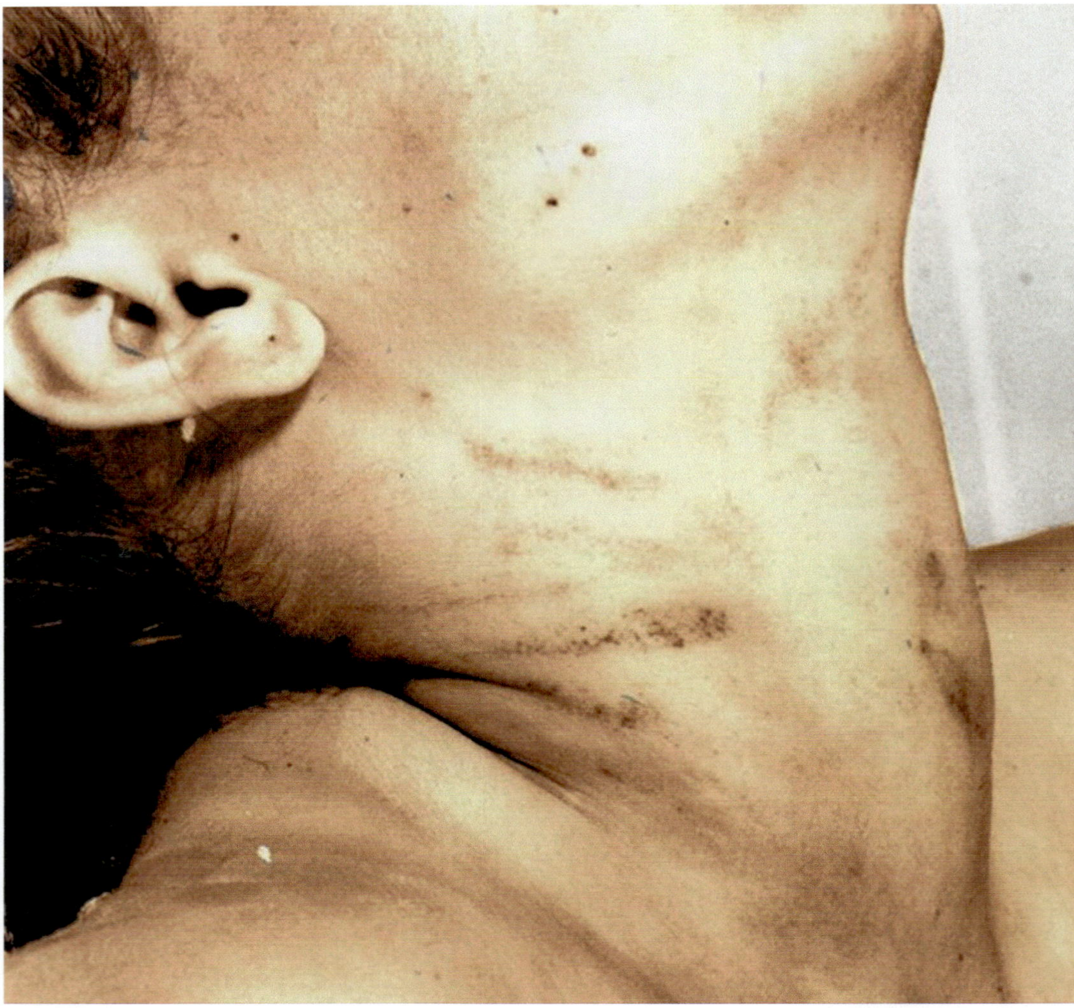

**Figure 6.4** Right side of the neck showing linear bruising resulting from forceful attempted gripping of the neck, together with shifting of the assailant's hands, probably whilst the victim was struggling.

## Internal Neck Injuries

The effect of manual compression in a person who has not died virtually instantaneously, as can occur with pressure on the carotid sinus, is to leave bruising in the underlying musculature and frequently fractures to the larynx and hyoid bone.

### Soft Tissue Trauma

In many cases, one can see appreciable bruising in the sternomastoid muscle corresponding with overlying skin injury (Figure 6.10). The muscles surrounding the larynx, both anteriorly and posteriorly, also frequently show well-marked bruising. Its distribution and occurrence at different levels serve to distinguish it from bruising seen in ligature strangulation. There is also frequently gross bruising of the laryngeal mucosa, in some cases accompanied by severe laryngeal swelling (Figure 6.11).

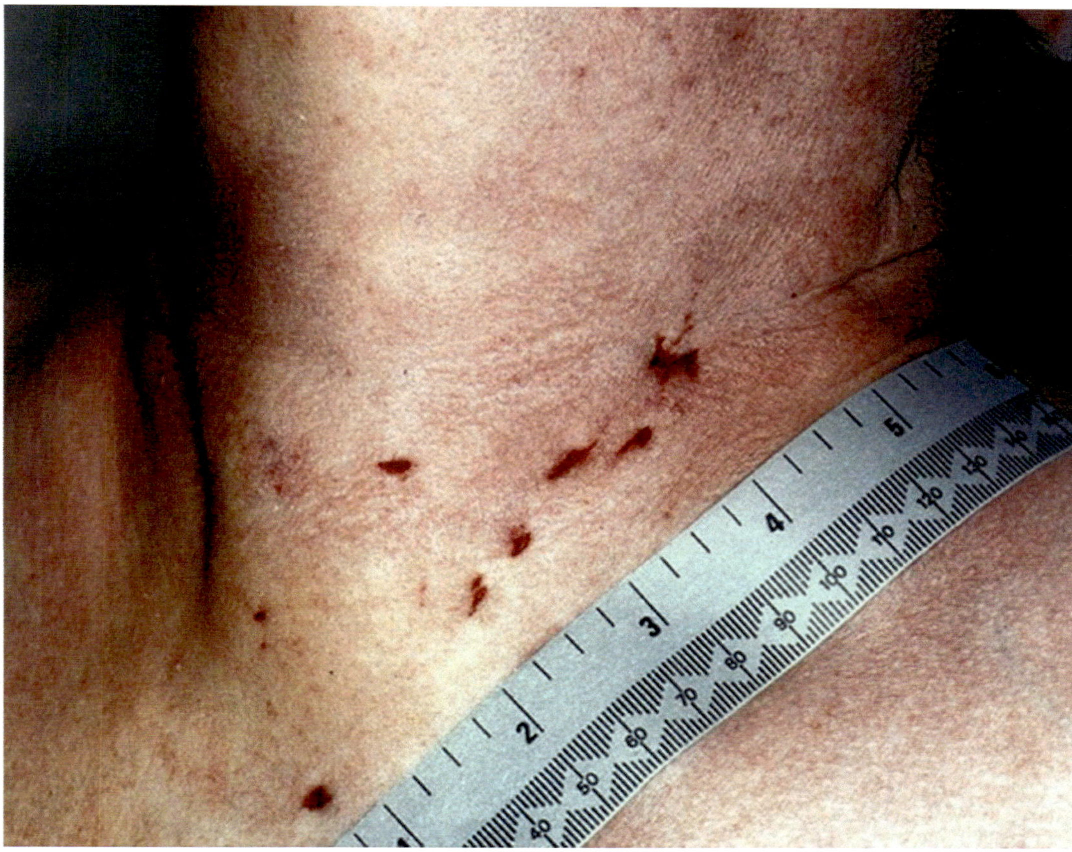


**Figure 6.5** Fingernail mark abrasions on the left side of the neck. The assailant had pressed down on the victim's neck with his right hand whilst she had been pinned on her back, and he was slightly to her right side above her.

## Cervical Vascular Lesions

Camps and Hunt (1959) thought that carotid artery tears were very rare, although Green (1973) found 11 such injuries (16%) in his series of manual and ligature strangulation. More recently, Clarot et al. (2005) reported two cases of carotid artery dissection following strangulation with delayed neurological symptoms. They emphasised that its real occurrence was probably underestimated because it was under-reported in domestic violence. They also pointed out that the internal injury may take a few hours to appear, and that the patient may be at risk of delayed death. In three further cases described by Le Blanc-Louvry et al. (2013), strangulation induced immediate stroke. Carotid artery injuries were examined using brain CT scan and Doppler ultrasonography, and then by autopsy in one of the victims. One of the two victims who survived the attempted strangulation had a unilateral carotid dissection, whereas in the other victim, no arterial dissection or thrombosis was observed. As regards the deceased victim, the autopsy confirmed the bilateral dissection shown on CT scan and Doppler ultrasonic examination and revealed that both carotid arteries were dilated up to two times the normal diameter. A carotid sheath haematoma was the only injury found at autopsy in a case of manual strangulation in an 8-year-old female victim. The presence of this injury not only helped ascertain the cause of death but also assisted in the reconstruction of the mechanism of infliction of force on the neck (Yadav et al., 2009).

Vanezis et al. (1993), reported the case of a 75-year-old female who was attacked by her husband, who attempted to strangle her. Her son, who had just arrived home, managed to pull his father off, but only after his mother lost consciousness. She was taken to the hospital, where she

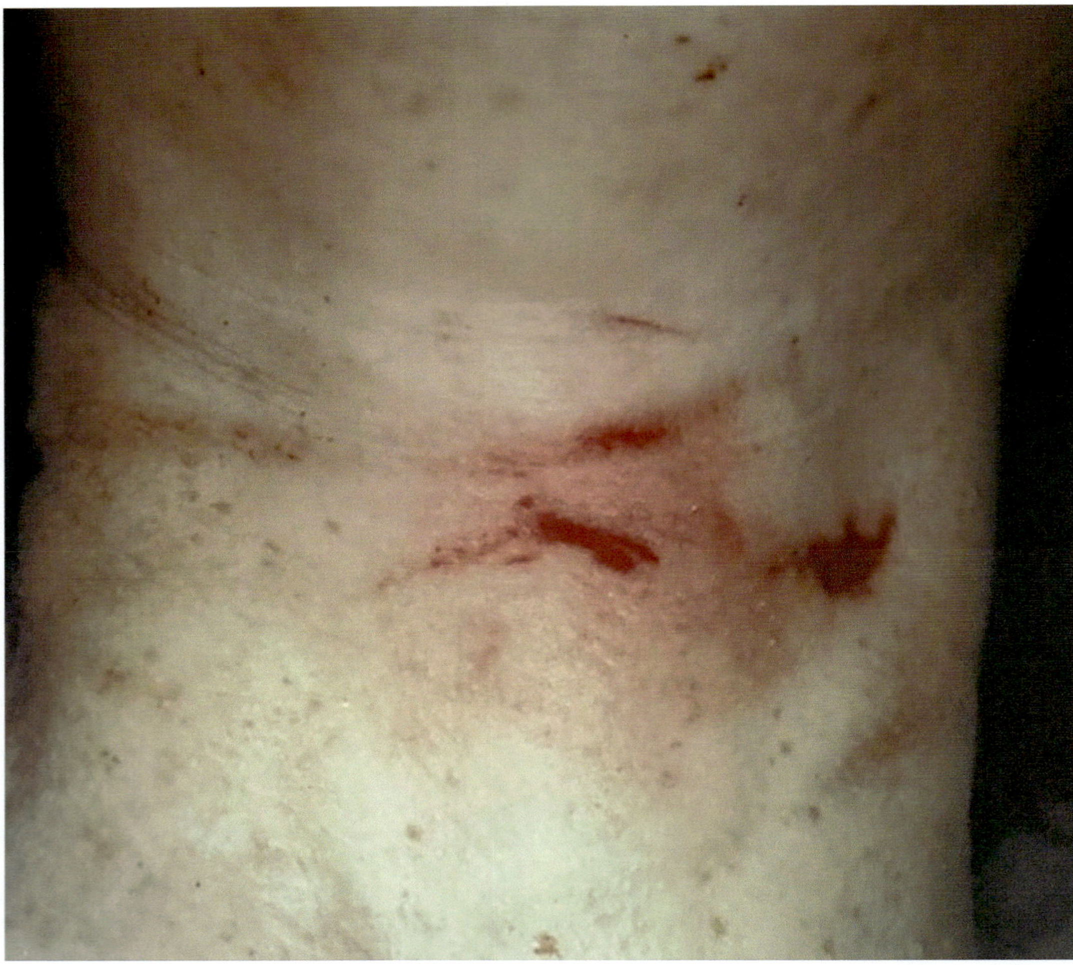

**Figure 6.6** Fingernail marks and bruising are seen in the central area of the neck, which had been gripped tightly. Note also the linear mark caused by attempted ligature strangulation.

died 48 hours later, having never regained consciousness. She was found to have a thrombus commencing at the bifurcation of the left carotid artery and extending up the internal carotid and into the cranium (Figure 6.12). The artery was free of any significant atheroma along its entire length. The right carotid artery was similarly free of atheroma. There were no bruises on the surface or underlying soft tissues of the neck and, in fact, virtually no bruises on the rest of the body. The brain showed extensive softening with haemorrhagic infarction of the left cerebral hemisphere, particularly the occipital lobe (Figure 6.13). Histological examination confirmed left parietal and occipital lobe infarction, as well as haemorrhage into the pons and midbrain. In most cases involving neck compression, a traumatic lesion is found in the arterial wall, which acts as a nidus for thrombus formation. In this case, no such injury was found. It is postulated that the probable mechanism was initial vasospasm, occluding the arterial lumen and causing neurological deficit, followed by thrombosis. This also appeared to be the mechanism in An's case (An, 1989), in which, as in the present case, no arterial injury was detected.

## Laryngeal and Hyoid Fractures

Fractures to the laryngeal cartilages and hyoid bone are more likely to occur with increasing age because the younger a person is, the less likely are the cartilages to show much calcification. Indeed,

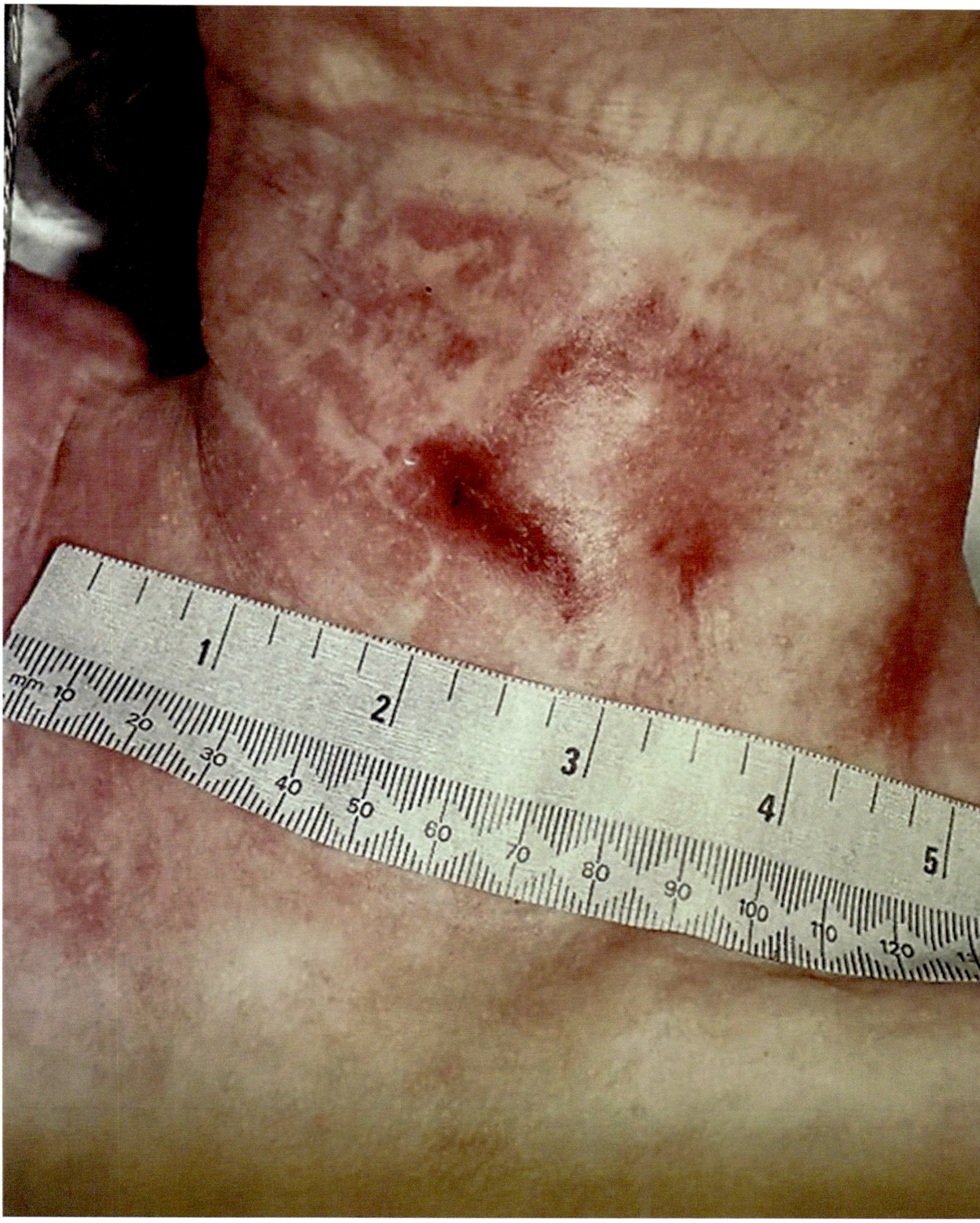


**Figure 6.7** Fingernail marks and bruising caused by gripping the central area of the neck. There is also a ribbed pattern from a tight sweater, which has formed as part of the pattern of hypostasis and did not play any part in the compression of the neck (compare with Figure 6.9).

one should not be surprised to see no fractures in a young person who has been strangled, even though there may be ample other signs of such a mode of death. Classically, fractures are seen in one or both thyroid cornua and less commonly in the hyoid bone. If there is a very substantial degree of pressure to the neck, one may occasionally see fractures to the thyroid laminae or even the cricoid cartilage. In the present author's series of 26 cases, fractures were found in 19 victims (73%).

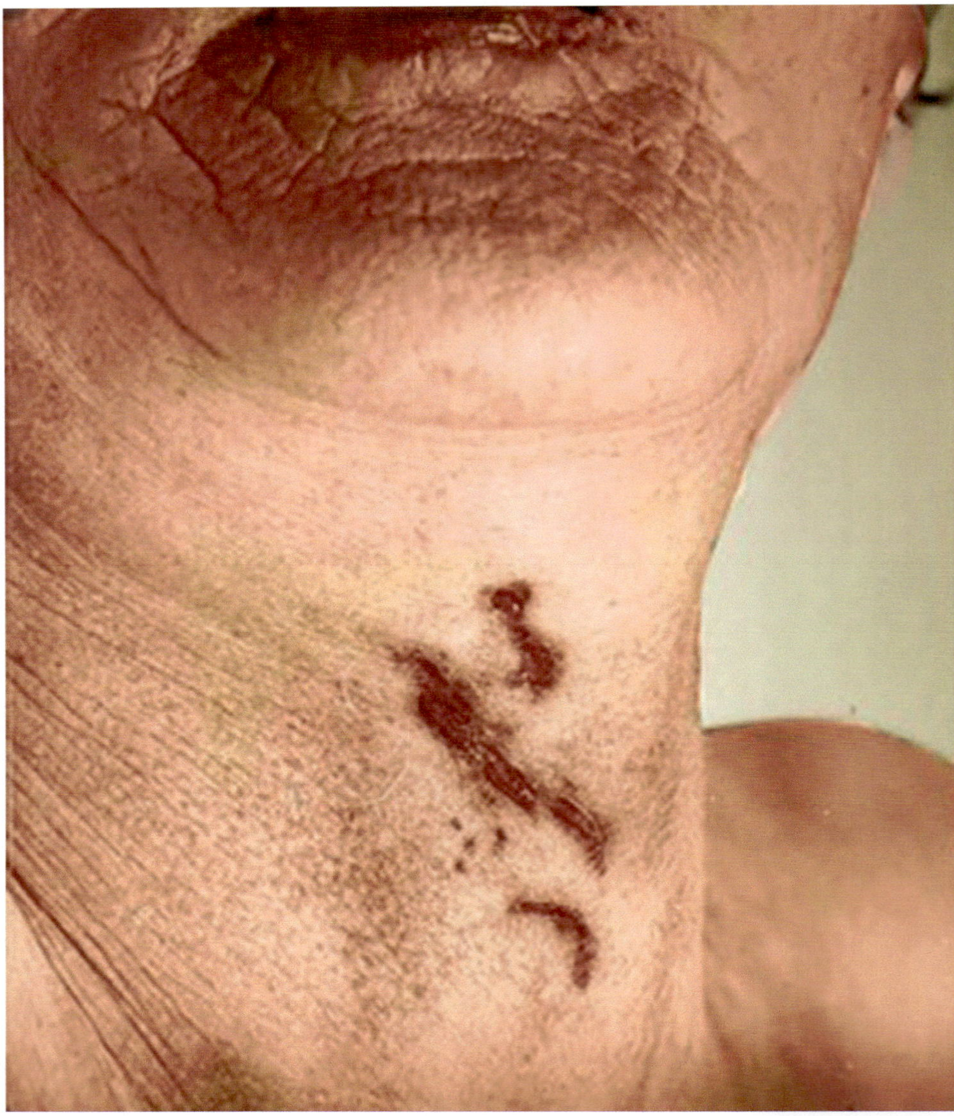

**Figure 6.8** The upper and lowermost fingernail marks in this case, also caused by gripping the central area of the neck, show an obvious curvilinear pattern.

All victims over the age of 50 years had fractures, whereas they were found in only half of those under this age. Fourteen had bilateral superior cornua fractures and five unilateral. The hyoid bone was fractured on three occasions, and all were associated with thyroid horn fractures. There was only one case with a fracture to the thyroid lamina and one cricoid cartilage fracture. The latter two were also associated with other fractures to the laryngeal cartilages and hyoid bone (Figures 6.14 and 6.15). Green (1973) found fractured thyroid cornua in half his 34 cases of manual strangulation and a substantial number of fractured hyoids (12, i.e., 35%). The number of thyroid lamina and cricoid fractures was comparatively infrequent as expected – four (12%) and two (6%), respectively. A much larger recent study of strangulation deaths in Finland (Wahlsten and Eriksson, 2020) is in broad agreement with these earlier studies. The latter authors, surveying asphyxia deaths, of which 187 were victims of manual strangulation, found laryngo-hyoid fractures involving the hyoid bone and superior thyroid cornua in almost half of the cases (more

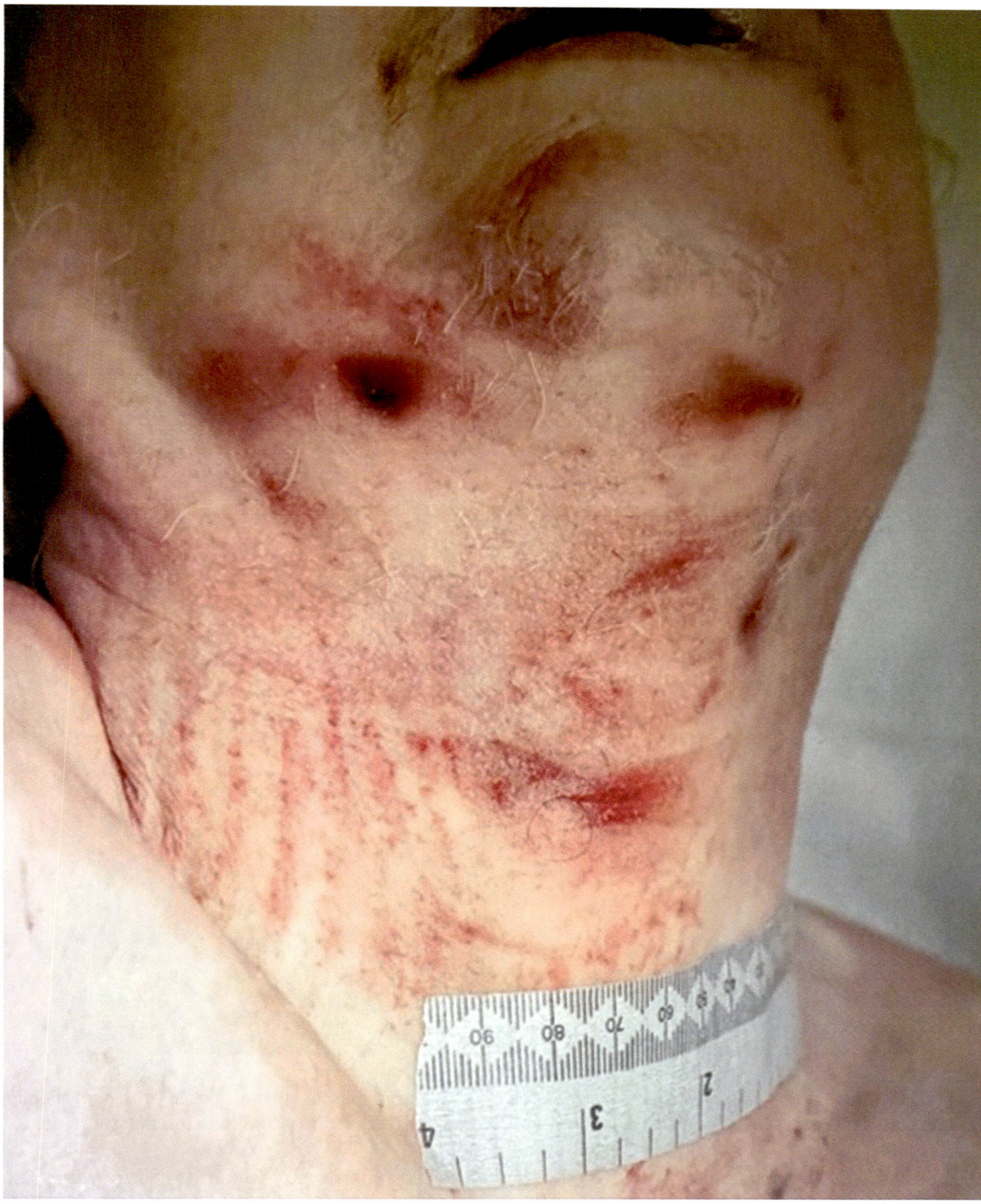

**Figure 6.9** In this case, there is a collection of fingernail marks and 'fingertip'-type bruising over the central and upper right side of the neck. Pressure has been applied at some stage through a woollen sweater, producing a ribbed pattern in the lower bruising.

frequently in older victims); fractures of thyroid laminae and cricoid cartilage, however, were rare. As expected, due to the elasticity of the larynx, no fractures in the laryngo-hyoid complex were observed in the youngest victims of strangulation.

Pollanen et al. (1998) examined the laryngeal cartilages in 12 young female victims of manual strangulation. They found intra-cartilaginous haemorrhages in 75% of cases, localised to the

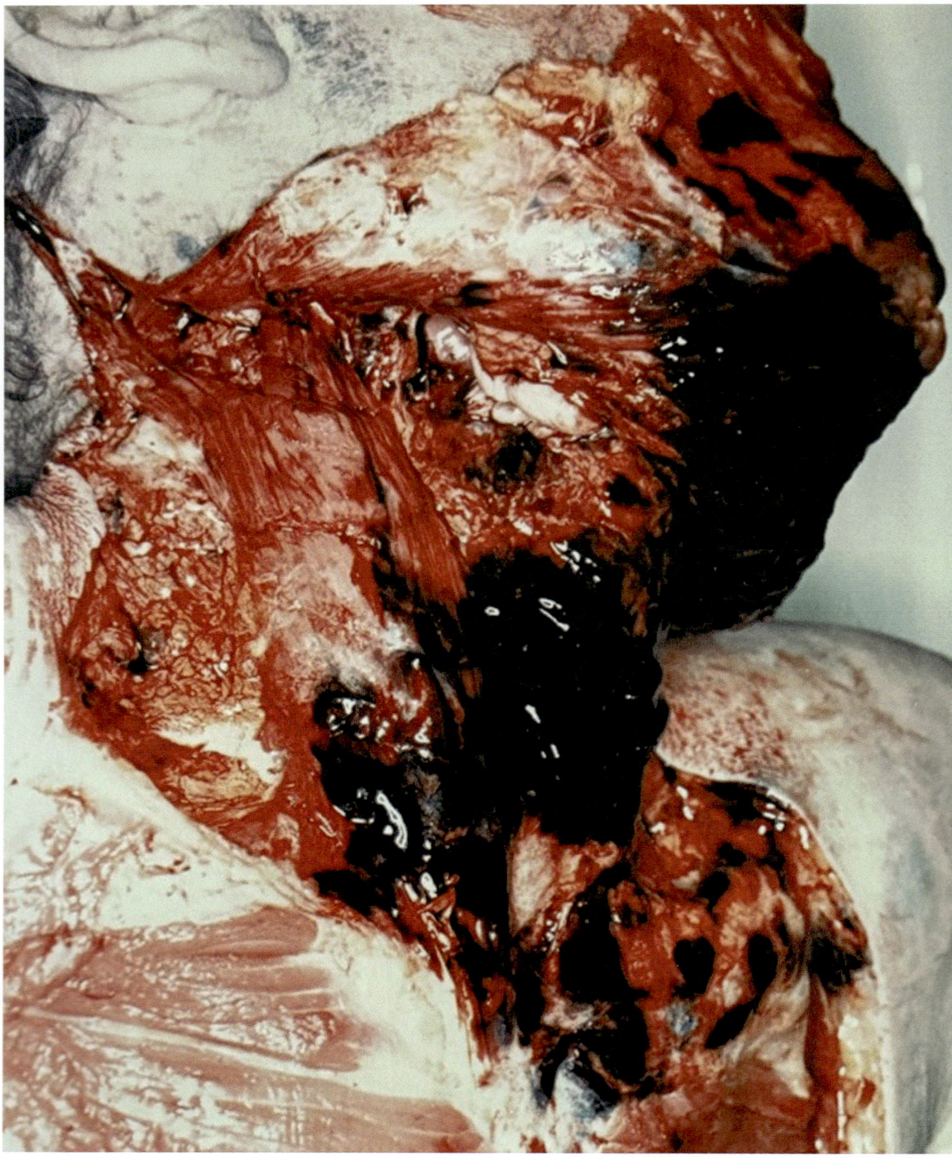

**Figure 6.10** Right side of the neck showing extensive sternomastoid muscle and soft tissue bruising, reflecting the assailant's use of prolonged forceful manual compression and the victim's struggle to free himself.

base of the superior cornua of the thyroid cartilage near the laminae. The authors' view was that such haemorrhages appeared to be a sensitive indicator of strangulation in young women (27±10 years old). These findings were not supported in a controlled study by Fieguth et al. (2003). They investigated whether laryngeal haemorrhages occurred in cases of strangulation and whether these lesions were specific to strangulation. They examined 30 larynges from victims of fatal strangulation (7 cases of manual strangulation, 12 cases of ligature strangulation, and 11 cases of combined manual and ligature strangulation). The control group comprised 40 cases of death without any neck injuries, and another group consisted of five cases of death caused by trauma with findings of non-strangulation neck injuries. In all the groups, only four solitary haemorrhages (two strangulation cases, one control, one non-strangulation neck injury) were observed that did not occur in the proximity of areas of blood accumulation. Their results suggest that histological evidence

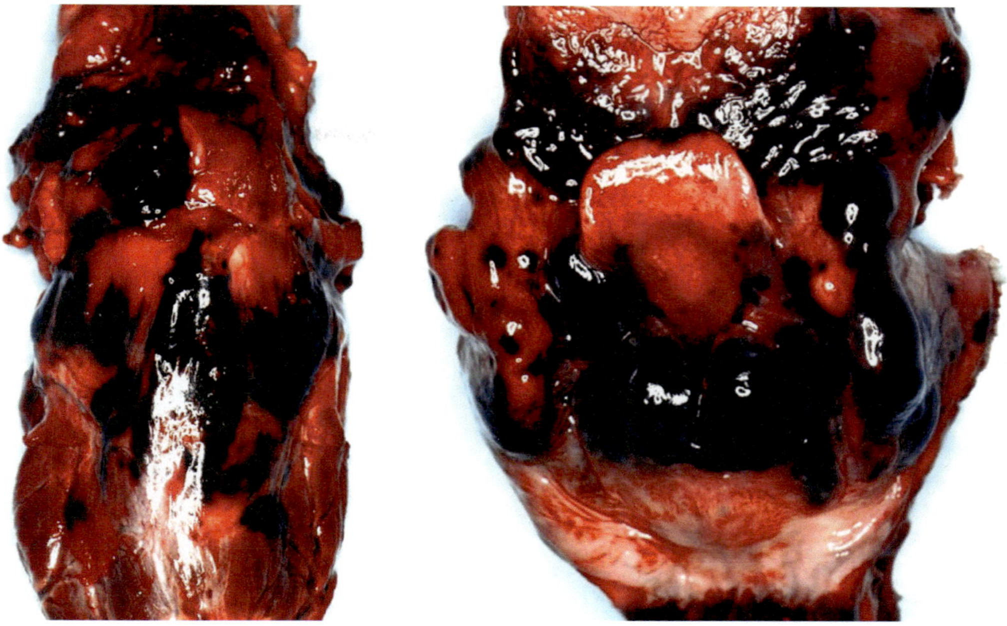

(a) (b)

**Figure 6.11** (a) Anterior view of laryngeal musculature in a case of manual strangulation. Bruising is seen at different levels (compare with Figure 7.13a), (b) Posterior view of larynx. There is severe bruising and swelling of the mucosa surrounding the epiglottis (including the epiglottic folds and below), superior thyroid horns, hyoid bone, root of the tongue, and the piriform fossa.

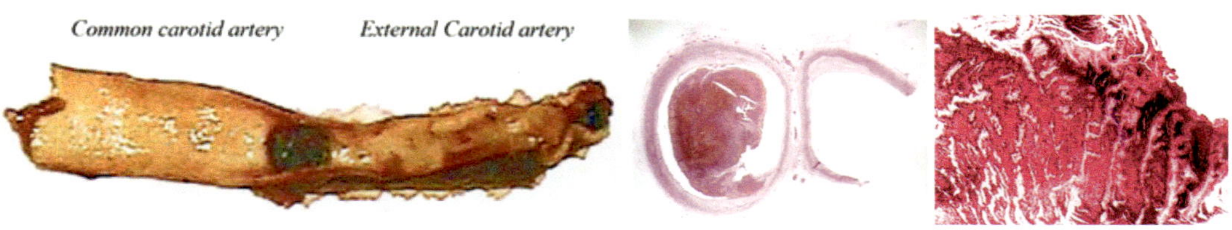


(a) (b) (c)

**Figure 6.12** (a) Thrombus at the carotid artery bifurcation, (b) Section of internal carotid artery just above the bifurcation containing thrombus partially attached to the intimal wall. Both the internal and external carotid arteries were free of significant atheroma (Haematoxylin and eosin x 7), (c) Detail of mixed thrombus showing aggregated platelets and erythrocytes with a typical pattern of stratification (Haematoxylin and eosin x 30).

of blood accumulation or of haemorrhages in thyroid cartilage is not a reliable criterion to distinguish between haemorrhagic lesions due to strangulation and other types of blood accumulation or artefacts.

## Mechanism of Compression and Effect on the Larynx

The mechanism of injury in manual strangulation, with particular reference to the larynx, usually involves lateral compression with one hand, whilst the other may be used in restraining the victim or simultaneously obstructing the mouth (see also the description of palmar strangulation earlier in this chapter). In a right-handed person gripping from the front, the thumb is placed on the right side of the neck, usually high up, and the other fingers on the left side. This would have the effect of pressing on the superior cornua of the thyroid cartilage as well as causing traction on the hyoid bone because of sudden lateral or downward movement of the thyrohyoid membrane. The hand

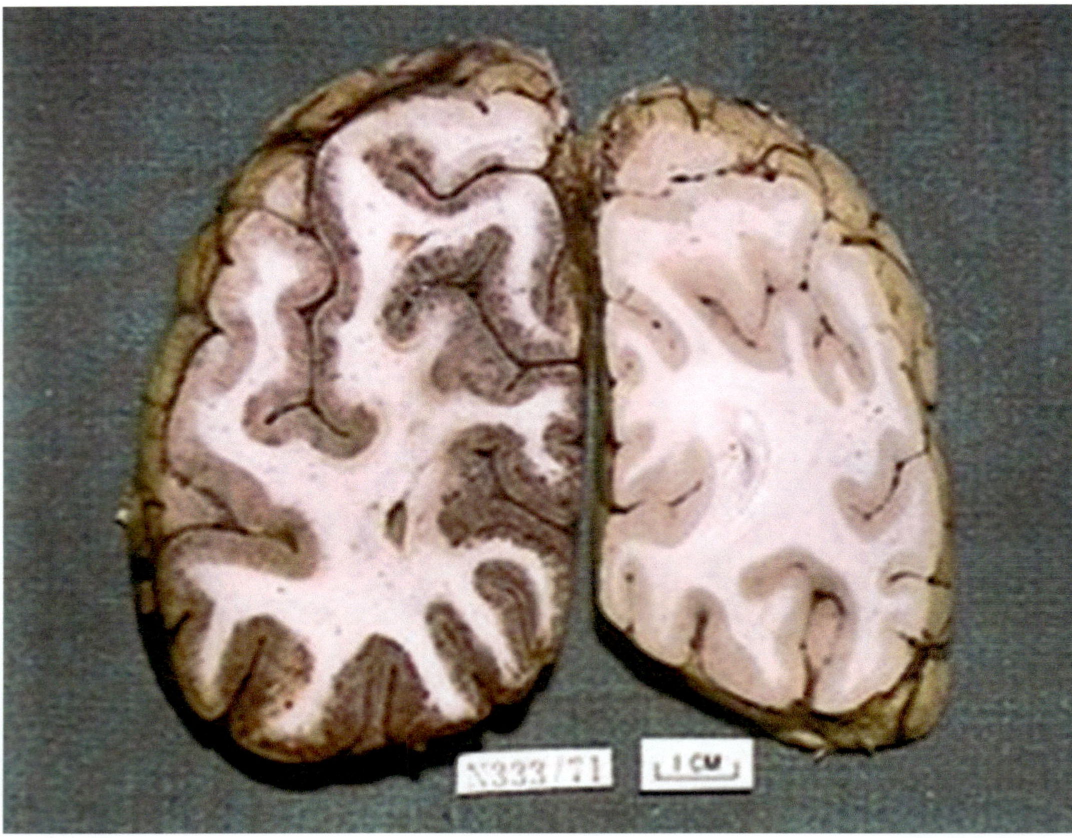


**Figure 6.13** Haemorrhagic infarction of the left cerebral hemisphere.

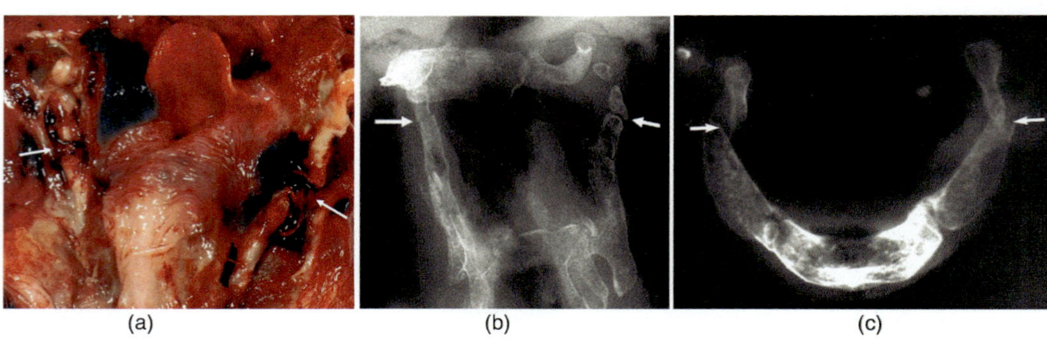


**Figure 6.14** (a) Posterior view of the larynx showing superior thyroid horn fractures (arrows). From the same person, (b) Antero-posterior view of excised larynx showing bilateral superior horn fractures of the thyroid (arrows), (c) Macroradiograph of excised hyoid bone showing fractures to both greater horns (arrows).

may indeed be high enough to produce direct injury to the hyoid bone. This occurs when the forefinger and thumb are placed under the mandible near both angles. A much less common method is to place both hands on the neck with the thumbs centrally and pressing antero-posteriorly. This would tend to compress the larynx against the cervical spine and is potentially more likely to produce injuries to the thyroid body and, occasionally, the cricoid cartilage. A similar pattern of injury may occur when strangulation takes place from behind with the thumbs at the back of the neck.

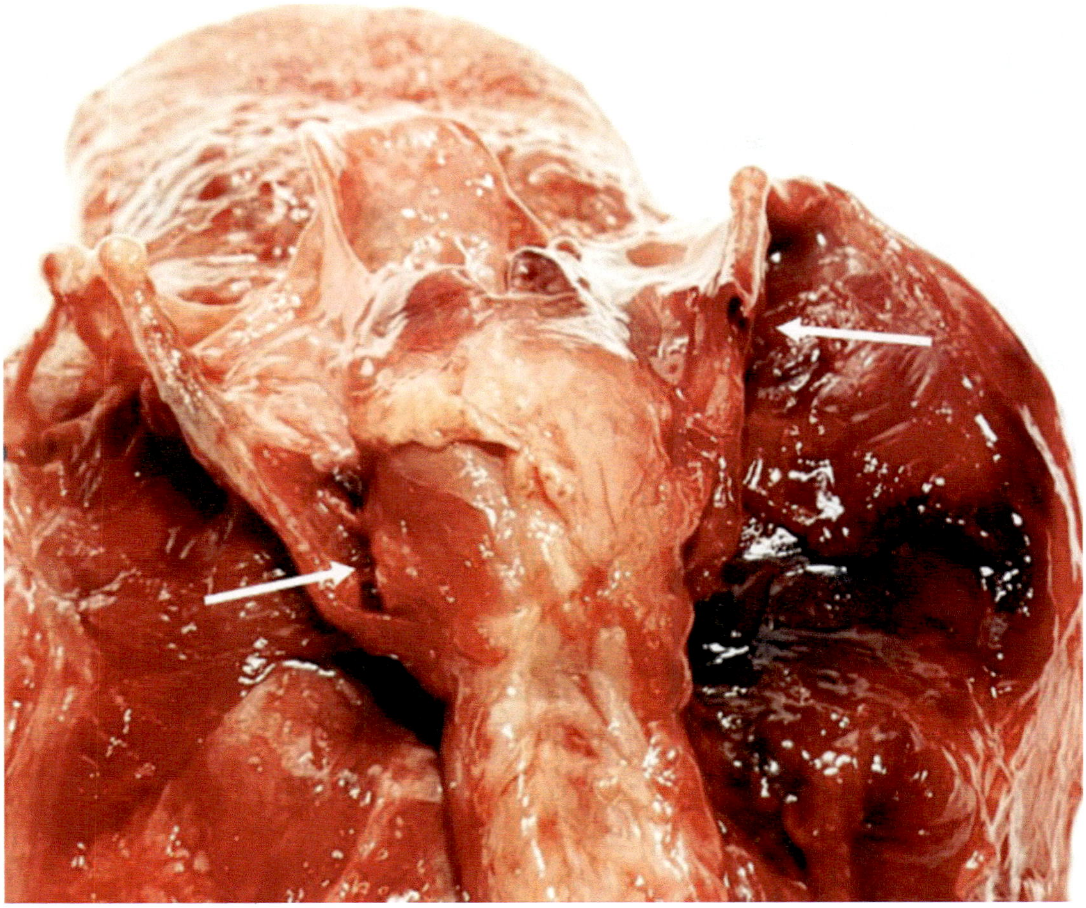

**Figure 6.15** Posterior view of larynx showing fracture to the right superior thyroid horn and fracture-dislocation of the left cricothyroid joint (arrows).

With this position, more force would be required to effect the same degree of injury because the weight of the assailant's body would not assist in causing the constriction, as with the hands used from the front.

## Associated Injuries to Other Regions

Fingernail marks and fingertip bruising on the face are quite common findings. Indeed, as well as manual strangulation, there may have been an attempt at obstructing the mouth, and bruising, abrasions, or lacerations, especially to the inner lips, are frequently seen. Such lesions indicate that the teeth and/or gums have been pressed hard against the lips by some external pressure, usually by a firm hand (Figures 6.16 and 6.17).

Head injuries are also frequently seen, and they may be caused either by blows delivered by an object, usually a fist or an open hand, or as a result of the deceased's head striking a nearby surface. The latter mode of trauma may result from the victim struggling and, at the same time, being held down against a wall or the ground and/or by the assailant pummelling the victim's head against the surface (Figure 6.18). Härm and Rajs (1981) found that 43% of surviving victims had head injuries. They also discovered that if the strangulation had been attempted in connection with rape, injuries to other regions of the body were usually not severe, although defensive injuries were seen in 73% of such cases. On the other hand, regional injuries in non-rape cases were severe, and defensive injuries

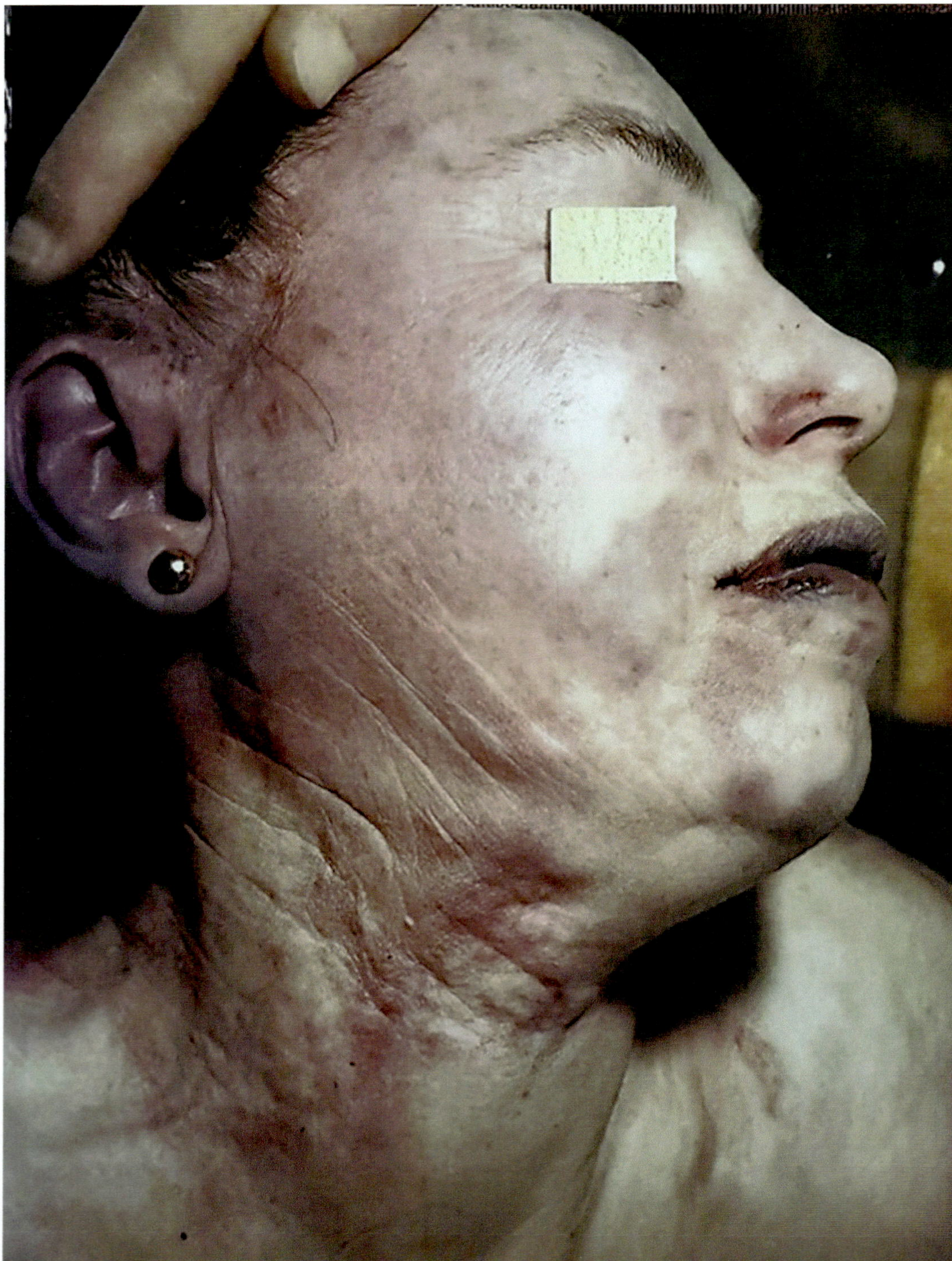

**Figure 6.16** Right side of the face showing bruising around the mouth and chin, as well as a fingernail abrasion of the right nostril.

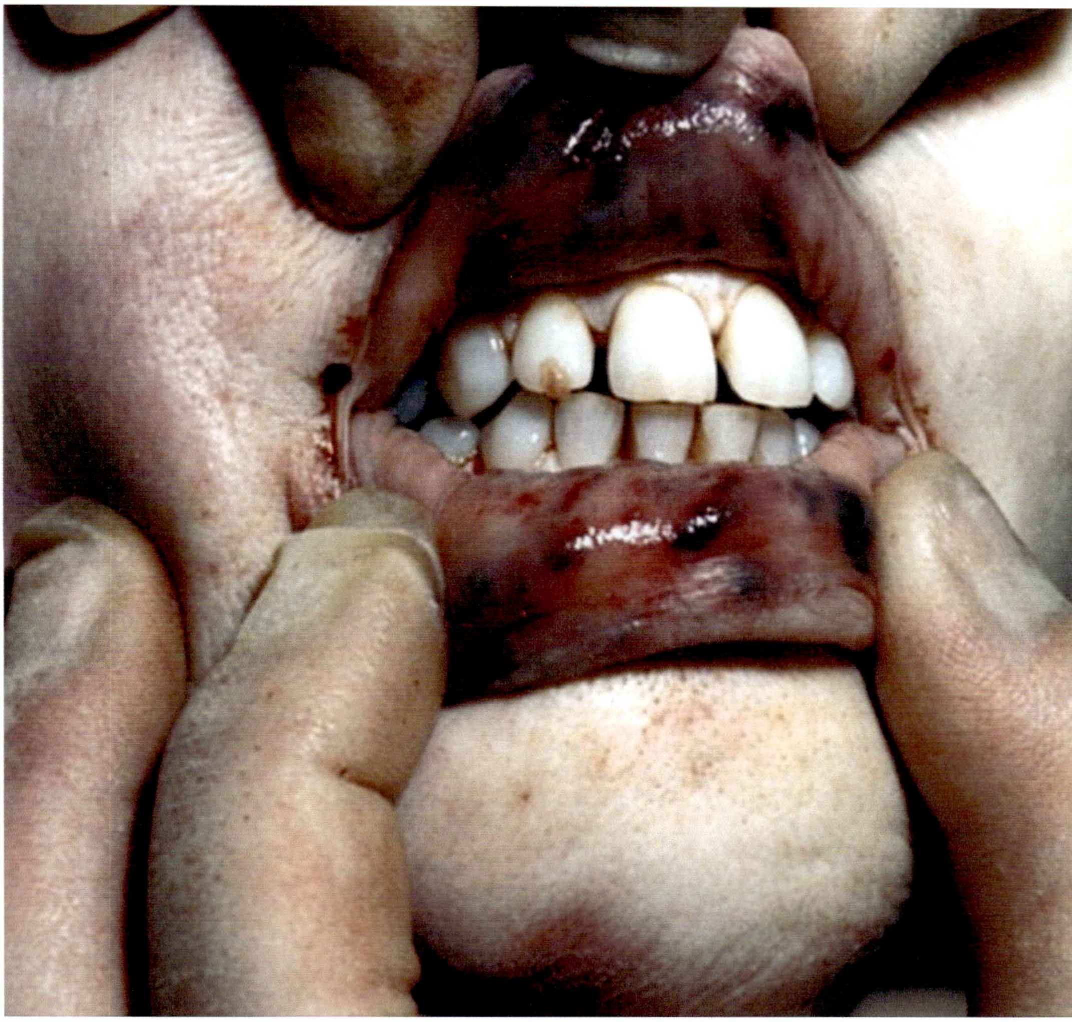

**Figure 6.17** View of the inner aspect of the lips. There are bruises and superficial lacerations caused by pressure against the victim's teeth during forceful occlusion of the mouth.

were seen in only 20% of attempted strangulations and 30% of homicides. It has become recognised more recently in a number of clinical studies of surviving victims of intimate personal violence (Gbadebo, 2024; Rajaram et al., 2021), that injuries to the head, face, and elsewhere in such assaults are common, and put survivors with head injuries at a high risk for sustaining a brain injury.

Regarding injuries to attackers, Härm and Rajs also examined 20 alleged stranglers and found injuries in 13 of them which were inflicted during the homicide. The most usual sites of such injuries were the hands, forearms, face, and neck. Nail marks were the most common findings on both assailants and their victims.

## Extent and Length of Struggle, Force of Application

Estimation of the degree of force used in manual strangulation is not possible when dealing with individual cases, although experiments, mostly of historical interest, have been carried out on cadavers to assess the degree of violence or force required to fracture the larynx. Keiller (1855–1856), in order to refute claims made by defence counsel that laryngeal fractures could be produced in an accidental manner by a simple fall from 6 feet (almost 2 metres), carried out a series of

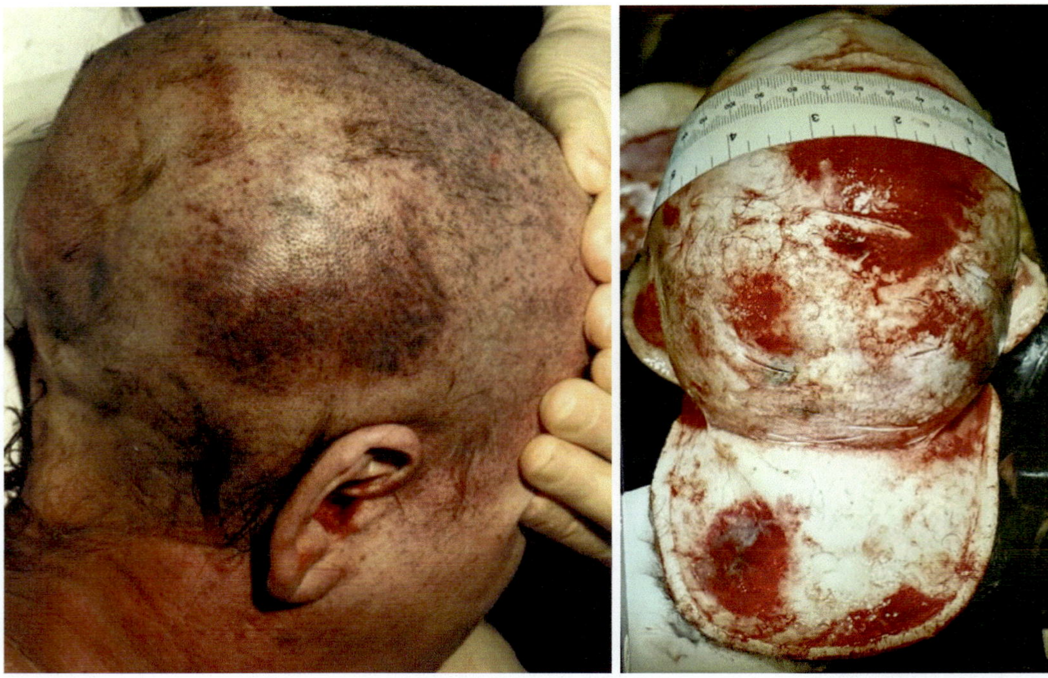

(a) (b)

**Figure 6.18** (a) Bruising of the occiput and right temporo-parietal region. Such injuries are frequently sustained by the head being forced backwards or sideways and coming into contact with a hard surface whilst the victim is struggling during the course of strangulation. They could also be caused by direct blows to the head during a violent assault which also involves strangulation, (b) Reflection of the scalp, showing soft tissue bruising corresponding to the external injuries.

ten experiments on human cadavers of varying ages using different methods to attempt to fracture the larynx. His conclusions were that laryngeal fractures from ordinary falls, as well as falls from a height of 6 feet, do not occur, and that it is a generalisation to state that extreme force is required to fracture a larynx by manual constriction, as there are many exceptions. Travis et al. (1975) investigated the force required to fracture the average adult larynx. They examined the response of fresh human larynges to static and dynamic compressive loading in 24 specimens. The mean static force values producing thyroid and cricoid cartilage fractures were 15.8 and 20.8 kg, respectively. Koops et al. (1983) carried out experiments and demonstrated that an average pressure of 8–12 kg was necessary to achieve complete airway obstruction in manual strangulation of an adult.

With respect to arterial compression, it has become generally accepted by pathologists that a minimum weight of 5 kg (carotid artery) and 35 kg (vertebral artery) is necessary for the complete compression of neck arteries (Püschel et al., 2004). The same forces can cause complete arterial compression in horizontal ligature strangulation. However, complete compression of the neck arteries does not usually occur in manual strangulation, except for where the assailant's hand is significantly bigger than the victim's neck or the pressure is aimed at the anterolateral neck region.

Measurement of force in terms of kilograms or pounds per unit area can only be a generalisation and by no means necessarily of the situation in reality. The pathologist should assess the severity of the inflicted force, taking into account the overall physical findings and circumstances, including the extent of bruising and, more importantly, the type and location of laryngeal and hyoid fractures, as well as the degree of calcification in each case. A laryngeal radiograph is useful not only for the detection of fractures but also for the assessment of the degree of calcification. It is not unusual in a young person to find severe bruising of laryngeal musculature and no fracture.

In such cases, therefore, a radiograph with little evidence of calcification is helpful. Occasionally, if death is rapid, bruising will not have time to develop, and the degree of violence may be impossible to assess, particularly if in addition, there are no laryngeal fractures. Some indication of the type of pressure and the force used is also given by the development of congestive changes, which, as a rule, are well marked if considerable force has been used.

The question of how long the assailant's grip needs to be maintained for death to occur is complex, but it is crucial from the point of view of indicating intent. There are a number of essential factors that need to be considered carefully before an opinion can be given: (i) the mechanism of death; (ii) the extent and severity of bruises, other marks, and laryngeal injuries resulting directly from compression; (iii) the extent of the physical signs attributable to asphyxia; and (iv) associated injuries to the face and other parts of the body, which indicate a combination of direct violence from the assailant as well as the extent of resistance by the victim. Occasionally one may find that, although death may have occurred very rapidly, the assailant's grip is maintained for a longer period. In one case, a man admitted squeezing his wife's throat for a period of five minutes, although the autopsy findings suggested that death had occurred when the pressure was first applied (R v Pye, Essex Assizes 1952, cited by Camps and Hunt, 1959).

With regard to the mechanism of death, Anscombe and Knight (1996) describe a case in which death occurred from hypoxic cerebral damage one week after manual strangulation and discuss the competing pathophysiological mechanisms responsible for the fatal outcome in their case, and in manual strangulation in general. They advance the view that a so-called asphyxial mode of death in manual strangulation is an unsatisfactory explanation, except where there has been continuous pressure on the neck for a period of several minutes or more. Their view, although contentious, is that reflex cardiac arrest is responsible for causing death in a proportion of such cases. They go further and propose that it is likely to be the cause of death in the majority of such cases, even in the presence of congestive/petechial changes.

## Survivability and Complications

Manual strangulation injuries are also encountered in surviving victims by clinicians, particularly otolaryngologists. Stanley and Hanson (1983) state that they only occasionally encounter the more severe cases where the forces exerted by assailants are usually sufficient to cause acute asphyxia and death. The reason for this is that most survivors, particularly in intimate partner violence (where the vast majority of the victims are women), do not suffer any complications necessitating hospital attention. Consequently, they may only consult their general practitioner, if at all, for transient hoarseness, dysphagia, and other local problems. Surviving victims usually have florid petechial haemorrhages, which may take a week or so to disappear, as well as local injuries similar to those seen in deceased victims.

Complications, however, may arise in survivors and indeed can potentially be fatal. This is especially the case where laryngeal fractures are unrecognised, particularly in strangulation cases, because they usually present with obvious mucosal disruption or submucosal haematoma formation. Delayed life-threatening airway obstruction or long-term vocal dysfunction may be the outcome (Li et al, 2016; Kuriloff and Pincus, 1989). The latter authors describe a patient who, 36 hours following manual strangulation, developed acute upper airway obstruction and a neck abscess necessitating tracheotomy, neck exploration, and drainage. Neurological complications may ensue if the carotid artery has been injured (Gbadebo, 2024; Rajaram et al., 2021).

Predicting the risk of intimate partner violence, particularly in relation to strangulation, is an important aspect of the clinical assessment of vulnerable individuals. Research carried out by Messing et al. (2022) into non-fatal strangulation examined the relationship between multiple strangulations, loss of consciousness due to strangulation, and the risk of future near-fatal violence in order to modify the 'danger assessment instrument' (developed to function as a field instrument) so as to be able to predict near-fatal and fatal violence in intimate relationships.

Survivors of strangulation resulting from cervical vessel occlusion (see also the author's case described earlier in this chapter) are described by Milligan and Anderson (1980), who encountered two female patients of reproductive age who presented with strokes one day and three days, respectively, after attempted strangulation by their husbands. Both had sustained traumatic occlusion (thought to be thrombotic, with possible distal embolisation) of the cervical internal carotid artery. Miao et al. (2009) reported the case of a 27-year-old woman, a victim of manual strangulation, who developed parkinsonism associated with selective symmetric basal ganglia lesions from hypoxic/ischaemic brain damage. Their patient was successfully treated with full recovery, following the use of hyperbaric oxygen and neuroprotective agents. Neto et al. (2014) describe a case where there was low cerebral blood flow without apparent injury to large cervical vessels as the mechanism of brain injury. They were of the view that extrinsic constriction of the cervical carotid artery due to manual strangulation may have resulted in decreased cerebral blood flow, causing ischaemia in the watershed areas of the cerebral arteries.

# COMPRESSION OF THE NECK FROM NECK HOLDS

## Overview

Neck holds have been used by law enforcement agencies for many years as a means of subduing suspects resisting arrest or controlling combative prisoners. However, following a number of high-profile deaths, particularly in the United States, such as that of George Floyd in 2020, police departments around the world have banned neck restraints or are in the process of doing so. In fact, restraint using neck holds has been a subject of controversy for years, particularly following the death of Eric Garner in 2014, after a police officer was accused of choking him (Kaur and Mack, 2020). Some departments state that they should only be employed as a last resort, when the officer believes the subject poses a threat to their own lives of others.

Two types of hold are generally recognised: the carotid sleeper and the bar arm control or choke hold (Figure 6.19), which is designed to directly obstruct the airway (Reay and Eisle, 1982). The carotid sleeper is designed to compress the common carotid arteries and produce transient cerebral ischaemia. When the person has become incapacitated in this way, the hold is released, and complete recovery is expected. Reay and Holloway (1982) assessed carotid blood flow when the neck was compressed as a result of the carotid sleeper, using ultrasound and laser-Doppler flow monitoring devices. They found that during the application of the neck hold, blood flow to the head decreased by 85% and reached its lowest point in six seconds. The objective of the 'sleeper hold' is to achieve temporary unconsciousness and subdue a person who is being restrained. The effect of neck holds, depending on how they are applied, is to restrict the vascular supply to the brain, mostly from the carotid arteries, or to obstruct the airway directly. However, the result, when restraining a person whose neck is moving whilst resisting restraint, can involve a potentially lethal combination of airway and vascular obstruction. Unsurprisingly, the aforementioned authors recommended that neck holds should only be applied as a last resort, as stated above, and only by officers who have had appropriate prior training.

## Carotid Sleeper

This hold appears to have originated from the martial art of Kung Fu, where the technique of seizing vessels of the neck is graphically described. Its purpose is to impede blood flow in the carotid arteries by pressure exerted on both sides of the neck by the upper arm and forearm acting as a pincer. The free hand is used to create the pincer pressure by gripping the wrist of the arm that is around the neck and pulling it back. With correct application, the airway should remain unimpeded during the manoeuvre. The vertebral arteries, because of their relatively protected position, are unaffected by this hold, thus continuing to supply blood to the brain. Permanent neurological damage should therefore not occur, even though cerebral ischaemia and transient unconsciousness may result, because the occluded carotid circulation is not completely compensated by the vertebral arteries.

The carotid sinus is located in the internal carotid artery just above the bifurcation of the common carotid artery and at the level of the thyroid gland, directly in the region where pressure is applied in the carotid sleeper hold. Because of its physiological and immediate effect on cardiac output, massage of the carotid sinus does not depend on vessel occlusion but only on mechanical stimulation of the neck region. It was thought to be a significant factor in producing cerebral ischaemia during vascular compression, bradycardia and sometimes cardiac arrest (Daly et al., 1979). However, more recent publications have demonstrated that the concept of compression of the carotid baroreceptors in vascular neck restraint is thought to be rare and controversial (Stellpflug et al., 2020).

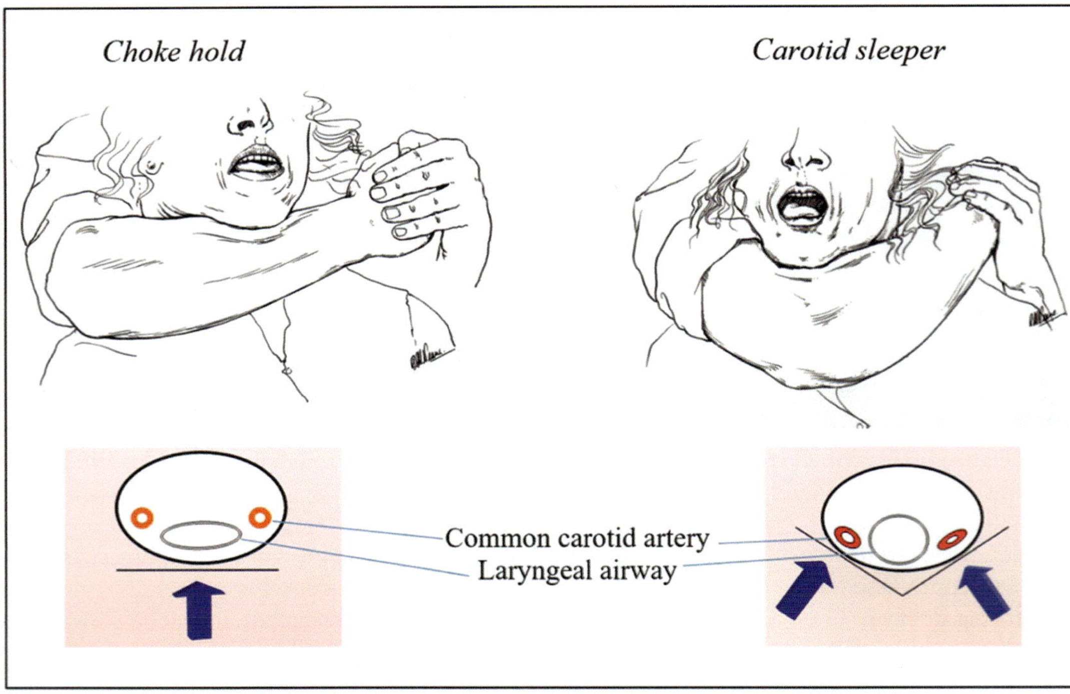


**Figure 6.19** The direction of application of pressure to the neck (arrows), with the choke hold (left), and carotid sleeper (right).

Mitchell et al. (2012) attempted to describe the mechanism behind unconsciousness or near unconsciousness during vascular neck restraint. The investigators monitored common physiological parameters, including the flow delivered through the carotid arteries to the middle cerebral arteries via ultrasound, in addition to the pressure applied to the neck using transducing balloons. They demonstrated decreased arterial cerebral blood flow due to carotid compression and concluded that this was the most important mechanism responsible for loss of consciousness.

Reay et al. (1982) conducted a similar study, and they too concluded that loss of consciousness occurred due to carotid compression. They, like Mitchell et al., used manual compression for the vascular neck restraint and ultrasound carotid monitoring. However, they monitored facial blood flow from the external carotid as their carotid surrogate. In addition to noting limited carotid flow, two out of five subjects experienced acute decrease in heart rate and mean arterial pressure, indicating some vagal stimulation via carotid body compression.

## Choke Hold (bar arm control)

The choke hold is designed to occlude the airway by forearm compression of the exposed anterior aspect of the neck. The technique is similar to the carotid sleeper, except that the forearm is placed directly over the airway. The structures that are compressed include the thyroid cartilage, which may thus be fractured. Furthermore, because of the backward motion of the forearm, the hypopharynx is also occluded by backward displacement of the tongue. The force required to move the base of the tongue, particularly to remove the hypopharynx, is not great, whereas the force required to occlude the airway is appreciable. The pressure needed to collapse the glottis is greater because of the complete cartilaginous rings, which begin to ossify in young adulthood and become more rigid with age. The situation may be worsened by the resistance of the person on whom the hold is applied. By struggling to remove the obstruction so as to improve breathing, the person inadvertently contributes to increasing the force on their neck.

## Consequences of Neck Holds

Death in such circumstances can result from hypoxia with its attendant cardiac arrest.

In this respect, the role of the carotid body is important: carotid body chemoreceptors are stimulated by a reduction in the $PaO_2$ and also by a rising $PaCO_2$ and hydrogen ion concentration. Fatal consequences of neck holds can be anticipated because of their physiological effects. Pre-existing natural disease increases the likelihood of a fatal outcome, even when a hold such as the carotid sleeper is applied correctly. Underlying cardiac disease, such as coronary artery disease and cardiac rhythm disorders, is particularly vulnerable to reflex carotid sinus stimulation and hypoxia (Cordina and Qureshi, 2009). Disease that affects the carotid arteries, most commonly atherosclerosis, can significantly narrow vessel lumina. Pressure applied to a diseased vessel can dislodge atherosclerotic plaque and produce fatal strokes. Compression of the vessel can damage the intimal lining of the vessel wall and cause an occluding thrombus to form and produce cerebral infarcts. This was the probable mechanism in Milligan and Anderson's two cases (1980).

More recently, in view of the increasing number of deaths in which neck holds have been implicated, the view voiced in many publications including that of Berkman et al. (2021), is that there is no safe way for law enforcement to restrain using carotid manipulation or traumatic manipulation of cerebral blood flow in any form. The aforementioned authors further inform us that carotid compression contributes to potential neurological complications resulting from oxygen deprivation and the risk of embolism from mechanical vessel wall trauma or arrhythmia. They also emphasise that the possibility of devastating repercussions is too high to merit the use of neck restraints in any circumstance.

In relation to neck holds in sporting activities, especially in martial arts, Koiwai (1987) stated that if the choke hold is correctly applied then fatalities should not occur. This has certainly been the case in judo, which, since its inception in 1982, has not experienced any fatalities related to such holds. In a retrospective survey of judo injuries in France over a period of 21 years (1993–2014), Frey et al. (2019) found that from 3,511 injuries, there were 47 cases (1.3%) of choking with loss of consciousness reported. No cases of death or permanent brain damage were reported after these injuries. Furthermore, there were no significant differences in the incidence rates of these injuries when compared by age, sex, or level of performance. There has been one death, however, that of a Vietnamese instructor in the related sport of 'Vo et Vat', which is a much more violent form of judo (Derobert et al., 1955).

It is not surprising that neck holds have been banned in 'serious' competitive wrestling since as far back as 1914. Their prohibition is also respected in so-called 'entertainment wrestling', although the wrestlers are somewhat adept at mimicking all kinds of potentially hazardous holds, including the stranglehold (British Amateur Wrestling Association, personal communication, 1987).

It is clear that there are no perfect conditions or justification for the use of neck holds when restraint is attempted, usually on subjects who are also at risk particularly from alcohol and drug abuse. Furthermore, even if the desired effect is to immobilise the subject by producing only temporary unconsciousness, albeit for a few seconds, the practice is a very hazardous one.

## References


An TL. Fatal thrombosis of internal carotid artery following minor blunt trauma to the neck. *J Forensic Sci*. 1989 May;34(3):699–702. PMID: 2738570.

Anscombe AM, Knight BH. Case report. Delayed death after pressure on the neck: Possible causal mechanisms and implications for mode of death in manual strangulation discussed. *Forensic Sci Int*. 1996 Apr 23;78(3):193–197.

Berkman JM, Rosenthal JA, Saadi A. Carotid physiology and neck restraints in law enforcement: Why neurologists need to make their voices heard. *JAMA Neurol*. 2021 Mar 1;78(3):267–268. doi: 10.1001/jamaneurol.2020.4669. PMID: 33369628.

Camps FE, Hunt AC. Pressure on the neck. *J Forensic Sci*. 1959;6:116–135.

Clarot F, Vaz E, Papin F, Proust B. Fatal and non-fatal bilateral delayed carotid artery dissection after manual strangulation. *Forensic Sci Int.* 2005 May 10;149(2-3):143–150. doi: 10.1016/j.forsciint.2004.06.009. PMID: 15749355.

Commonwealth v Graves, 456 A.2d 561 (Pa Super. 1983).

Cordina SM, Qureshi AI. Syncope and carotid artery stenosis. *Minerva Med.* 2009 Aug;100(4):321–327. PMID: 19749685.

Daly MD, Angell-James JE, Elsner R. Role of carotid-body chemoreceptors and their reflex interactions in bradycardia and cardiac arrest. *Lancet.* 1979 Apr 7;1(8119):764–767. doi: 10.1016/s0140-6736(79)91218-2. PMID: 86001.

Derobert L, Vacher J, Michon R. Mort au cours d'une prise de judo: strangulation [Death by strangulation in the course of judo practice]. *Ann Med Leg Criminol Police Sci Toxicol.* 1955 Jan-Feb;35(1):34–35. French. PMID: 14377007.

Fieguth A, Albrecht UV, Bertolini J, Kleemann J. Intracartilaginous haemorrhagic lesions in strangulation? *Int J Legal Med.* 2003 Feb;117(1):10–13.

Frey A, Lambert C, Vesselle B, Rousseau R, Dor F, Marquet LA, Toussaint JF, Crema MD. Epidemiology of judo-related injuries in 21 seasons of competitions in France: A prospective study of relevant traumatic injuries. *Orthop J Sports Med.* 2019 May 31;7(5):2325967119847470. doi: 10.1177/2325967119847470. PMID: 31211149; PMCID: PMC6545656.

Frye v United States, 293 F. 1013 (Ct. App. D.C. 1923).

Gbadebo A. The intersection of intimate partner violence, strangulation, and brain injury screening: A pilot project. *J Forensic Nurs.* 2024 Aug 5. doi: 10.1097/JFN.0000000000000506. Epub ahead of print. PMID: 39102334.

Green MA. Morbid anatomical findings in strangulation. *Forensic Sci.* 1973 Aug;2(3):317–23. doi: 10.1016/0300-9432(73)90046-0. PMID: 4724746.

Härm T, Rajs J. Types of injuries and interrelated conditions of victims and assailants in attempted and homicidal strangulation. *Forensic Sci Int.* 1981 Sep-Oct;18(2):101–123. doi: 10.1016/0379-0738(81)90148-1. PMID: 7297963.

Kaur H, Mack J. The cities, states and countries finally putting an end to police neck restraints. CNN, 2022.

Keiller A. Medico-legal observations on manual strangulation and death by external violence and experiments and illustrative cases. *Edinb Med J.* 1855–1856;1, 527–534, 824–829.

Koiwai EK. Deaths allegedly caused by the use of "choke holds" (shime-waza). *J Forensic Sci.* 1987 Mar;32(2):419–432. PMID: 3572335.

Koops E, Püschel K, Wischhusen F, Fechner G, Brinkmann B. Zur Obstruktion der Halsarterien und der oberen Luftwege beim Würgen [Obstruction of the neck arteries and the upper airways during strangulation]. *Beitr Gerichtl Med.* 1983;41:315–321. German. PMID: 6639601.

Kuriloff DB, Pincus RL. Delayed airway obstruction and neck abscess following manual strangulation injury. *Ann Otol Rhinol Laryngol.* 1989 Oct;98(10):824–827.

Le Blanc-Louvry I, Papin F, Vaz E, Proust B. Cervical arterial injury after strangulation--different types of arterial lesions. *J Forensic Sci.* 2013 Nov;58(6):1640–1643. doi: 10.1111/1556-4029.12197. Epub 2013 July 18. PMID: 23865759.

Li W, Liu D, Gallina K, Zhou Y. Delayed death caused by haematoma after manual strangulation: A rare case. *Br J Oral Maxillofac Surg.* 2016 Nov;54(9):1049–1050.

Messing JT, Campbell J, AbiNader MA, Bolyard R. Accounting for multiple nonfatal strangulation in intimate partner violence risk assessment. *J Interpers Violence.* 2022 June;37(11-12):NP8430–NP8453. doi: 10.1177/0886260520975854. Epub 2020 Dec 5. PMID: 33280504.

Miao J, Su C, Wang W, Lin H, Li H, Lei G, Liu Y, Liu R, Zhang W, Li Z. Delayed parkinsonism with a selective symmetric basal ganglia lesion after manual strangulation. *J Clin Neurosci.* 2009 Apr;16(4):573–575.

Milligan N, Anderson M. Conjugal disharmony: A hitherto unrecognised cause of strokes. *Br Med J.* 1980 Aug 9;281(6237):421–422. doi: 10.1136/bmj.281.6237.421. PMID: 7427300; PMCID: PMC1713281.

Mitchell JR, Roach DE, Tyberg JV, Belenkie I, Sheldon RS. Mechanism of loss of consciousness during vascular neck restraint. *J Appl Physiol.* (1985). 2012 Feb;112(3):396–402. doi: 10.1152/japplphysiol.00592.2011. Epub 2011 Nov 17. PMID: 22096121

Neto HS, Neville IS, Beer-Furlan A, Tavares WM, Teixeira MJ, Paiva WS. Hemodynamic stroke caused by strangulation. *Int J Clin Exp Med.* 2014 Sep 15;7(9):2932–2935.

Perper JA, Sobel MN. Identification of fingernail markings in manual strangulation. *Am J Forensic Med Pathol.* 1981 Mar;2(1):45–48. doi: 10.1097/00000433-198103000-00008. PMID: 7304518.

Pollanen MS, McAuliffe DN. Intra-cartilaginous laryngeal haemorrhages and strangulation. *Forensic Sci Int.* 1998 Apr 22;93(1):13–20.

Polson CJ, Gee DJ, Knight B. Palmar strangulation. In The Essentials of Forensic Medicine, 4th edn. Pergamon Press, Oxford, 1985, pp. 393–394.

Püschel K, Türk E, Lach H. Asphyxia-related deaths. *Forensic Sci Int.* 2004 Sep 10;144(2-3):211–214. doi: 10.1016/j.forsciint.2004.04.055. PMID: 15364392.

Rajaram SS, Reisher P, Garlinghouse M, Chiou KS, Higgins KD, New-Aaron M, Ojha T, Smith LM. Intimate partner violence and brain injury screening. *Violence Against Women.* 2021 Aug;27(10):1548–1565. doi: 10.1177/1077801220947164. Epub 2020 Aug 25. PMID: 32838674.

Reay DT, Eisele JW. Death from law enforcement neck holds. *Am J Forensic Med Pathol.* 1982 Sep;3(3):253–258. doi: 10.1097/00000433-198209000-00012. PMID: 7148779.

Reay DT, Holloway GA Jr. Changes in carotid blood flow produced by neck compression. *Am J Forensic Med Pathol.* 1982 Sep;3(3):199–202. doi: 10.1097/00000433-198209000-00002. PMID: 7148771.

Sane MR, Zine KU, Darandale S, Thube H. Postmortem burns to conceal homicidal deaths: An eight-year study. *Maedica (Bucur).* 2024 Mar;19(1):80–85. doi: 10.26574/maedica.2024.19.11.80. PMID: 38736924; PMCID: PMC11079746.

Schrag B, Mangin P, Vaucher P, Bollmann MD. Death caused by cardioinhibitory reflex: What experts believe. *Am J Forensic Med Pathol.* 2012 Mar;33(1):9–12. doi: 10.1097/paf.0b013e3181db7efd. PMID: 22442830.

Shapiro HA, Gluckman J, Gordon I. The significance of finger nail abrasions of the skin. *J Forensic Med.* 1962 Jan-Mar;9:17–19. PMID: 13911295.

Sorenson SB, Joshi M, Sivitz E. A systematic review of the epidemiology of nonfatal strangulation, a human rights and health concern. *Am J Public Health.* 2014 Nov;104(11):e54–e61. doi: 10.2105/AJPH.2014.302191. Epub 2014 Sep 11. PMID: 25211747; PMCID: PMC4202982.

Stanley RB Jr, Hanson DG. Manual strangulation injuries of the larynx. *Arch Otolaryngol.* 1983 May;109(5):344–347. doi: 10.1001/archotol.1983.00800190066017. PMID: 6847488.

Starrs JE. Procedure in identifying fingernail imprint in human skin survives appellate review. *Am J Forensic Med Pathol.* 1985 June;6(2):171–173. doi: 10.1097/00000433-198506000-00013. PMID: 4025271.

Stellpflug SJ, Menton TR, Corry JJ, Schneir AB. There is more to the mechanism of unconsciousness from vascular neck restraint than simply carotid compression. *Int J Neurosci.* 2020 Jan;130(1):103–106. doi: 10.1080/00207454.2019.1664520. Epub 2019 Sep 11. PMID: 31487214.

Travis LW, Olson NR, Melvin JW, Snyder RG. Static and dynamic impact trauma of the human larynx. *Trans Sect Otolaryngol Am Acad Ophthalmol Otolaryngol.* 1975 July-Aug;80(4 Pt 1):382–390.

Vanezis P, Claydon SM, Chapman RC, al-Alousi LM. Internal carotid artery thrombosis following manual strangulation. *Med Sci Law.* 1993 Jan;33(1):69–71. doi: 10.1177/002580249303300113. PMID: 8429772.

Wahlsten P, Eriksson A. Asphyxia homicides in Finland, 1983–2012. *J Forensic Sci.* 2020 Sep;65(5):1548–1556. doi: 10.1111/1556-4029.14458. Epub 2020 June 30. PMID: 32602942.

Yadav J, Badkur DS, Arora A. Carotid sheath haematoma: A case report. *J Forensic Leg Med.* 2009 Oct;16(7):411–413.

# CHAPTER 7

## COMPRESSIVE NECK INJURY III: LIGATURE STRANGULATION

*Peter Vanezis*



DOI: 10.4324/9781003658467-7

# INTRODUCTION

Ligature strangulation should be distinguished from hanging, although, as discussed earlier, they are both regarded as forms of strangulation. In the latter situation, it is the body weight that acts against a ligature around the neck and fastened to a point of suspension. Strangulation, however, with the use of a ligature, causes neck compression from force applied directly by a hand or other object applying the ligature to the neck. Generally, in ligature strangulation, the mark is positioned approximately horizontally, in contrast to hanging where in most cases the mark slopes up to the point of suspension. In homicidal ligature strangulation, it may either totally encircle the neck or be seen only at the front. The latter situation arises when the ligature is pulled tightly from behind. In addition, the position in such circumstances is usually high up beneath the mandible, at the level of the hyoid bone.

Strangulation by ligature is homicidal in most cases, with suicidal strangulation only occasionally encountered. There are also a very few accidental cases, some of which fall into the autoerotic death category (discussed in Chapter 8). The distribution of the cases encountered in two series (Vanezis, 1989; Maxeiner and Bockholdt, 2003) is shown in Table 7.1.

**Table 7.1** Manner of death in ligature strangulation cases from two series[a]

| | All cases | Homicide (all) | Suicide (all) | Homicide (by gender) | | Suicide (by gender) | |
|---|---|---|---|---|---|---|---|
| | | | | M | F | M | F |
| *Vanezis (1989)* | 17 | 14 | 3 | 2 | 12 | 2 | 1 |
| *Maxeiner and Bockholdt (2003)* | 66 | 47 | 19 | 21 | 26 | 13 | 6 |
| *Total from both series* | 83 | 61 (73.5%) | 22 (26.5%) | 23 | 38 (1:1.7) | 15 | 7 (2:1) |

[a] Accidental strangulation was not included in either series.

# EXTERNAL FINDINGS IN LIGATURE STRANGULATION

## The Ligature and Mark

In all cases in which ligatures are thought to have been involved, several basic facts need to be ascertained:

1. Whether the constricting agent found around or near the neck is responsible for the mark seen.
2. Whether, if there is no suspicious ligature as above, it is still present at the scene.
3. Whether the mark seen has been caused by a ligature.

With regard to the first two considerations, it is not uncommon to find dishevelled clothing when a struggle has taken place, and more so when there is a superadded sexual assault (Figure 7.1).

Hence, one may have to consider items of clothing such as stockings, tights, belts, torn material from a blouse, etc., as having been used to constrict the neck. If the ligature has been left tightly knotted in position, then the task is much easier; but if the ligature has been removed, then suspected materials from the scene or elsewhere require careful scrutiny.

It is not uncommon for the untrained eye, and even, on occasions, the experienced observer, to misinterpret certain post-mortem features as ligature marks. Normal skin creases, especially in infants, may be quite deep due to the generous folds of fat in young necks.

Collars and similar clothing or chains found around the neck may also leave suspicious marks, particularly on the deceased's neck when it is in a dependent position. In such circumstances, it is not unusual, for example, for the ribbing pattern from a high-neck pullover to be reproduced as part of the hypostasis. The latter should be carefully distinguished from clothing that has intentionally been pulled and tightened around the neck.

Decomposing bodies provide further difficulties. Not only are skin features obscured by putrefaction, but gaseous swelling of the neck region may accentuate crease marks or cause clothing or neck chains to press on the neck.

Close examination of a ligature mark, particularly with a hand lens, may reveal a distinctive pattern or occasionally fibres, that enable comparison with a suspected ligature, particularly if it has been removed after death. Removal of the ligature is not uncommon in homicide victims.

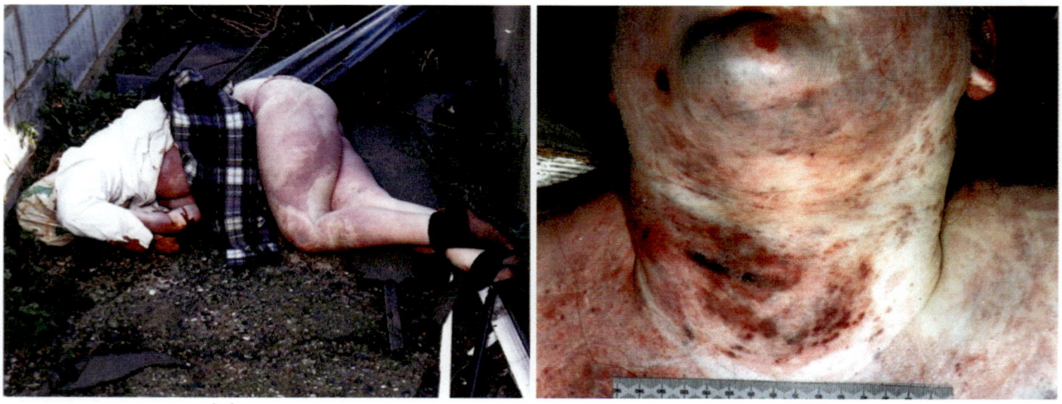

(a) (b)

**Figure 7.1** (a) The victim suffered a sexual assault prior to being strangled with a ligature and a plastic bag placed over her face. She was deposited in an alleyway after being kept in the boot of a car for two days, as indicated by the distribution of hypostasis on her legs. (b) Broad ligature marks around the neck. There is also swelling of the face and neck due to early putrefaction.

Hard, rough ligatures such as ropes frequently produce quite pronounced friction abrasions (Figure 7.2). A belt, when pulled tight and fastened with its buckle, may also leave a distinctive mark (Figure 7.3).

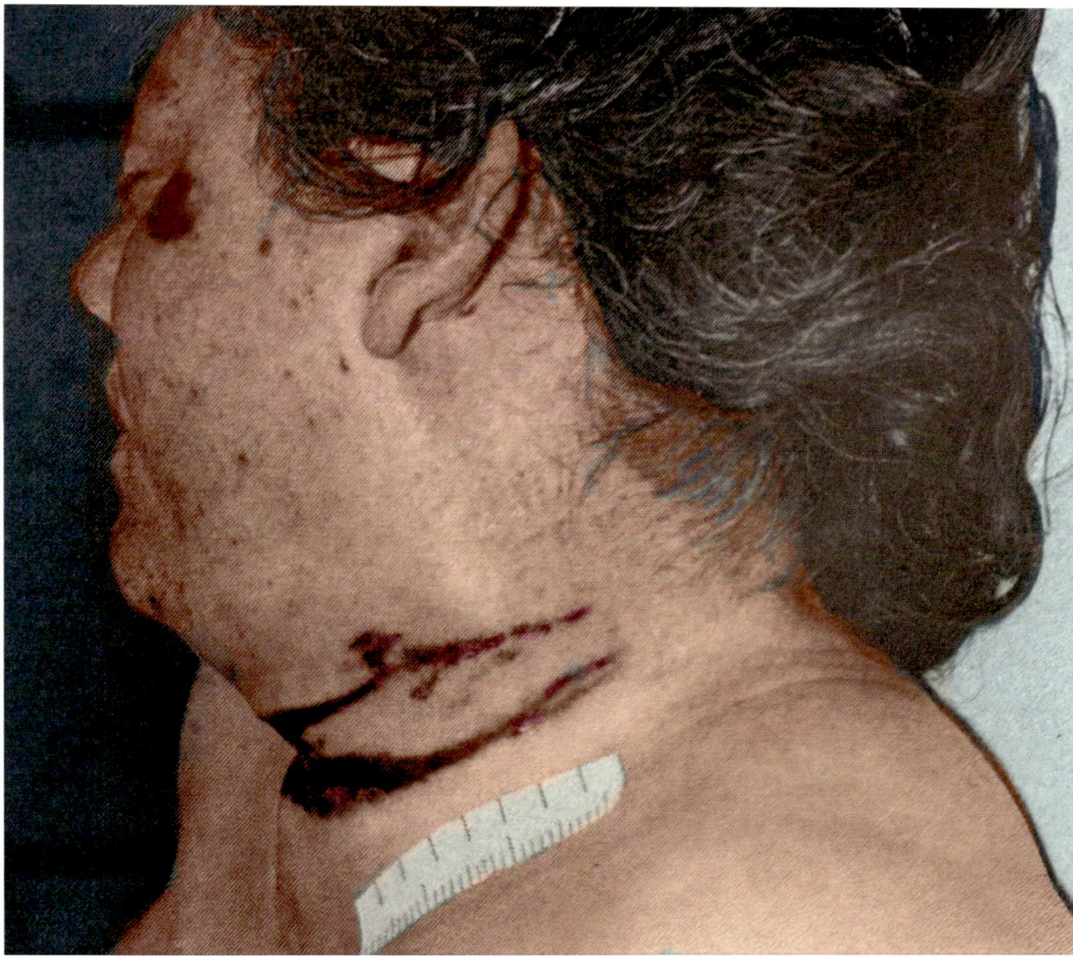

**Figure 7.2** Pronounced friction abrasions caused by a hard rope that had been used to strangle the victim.

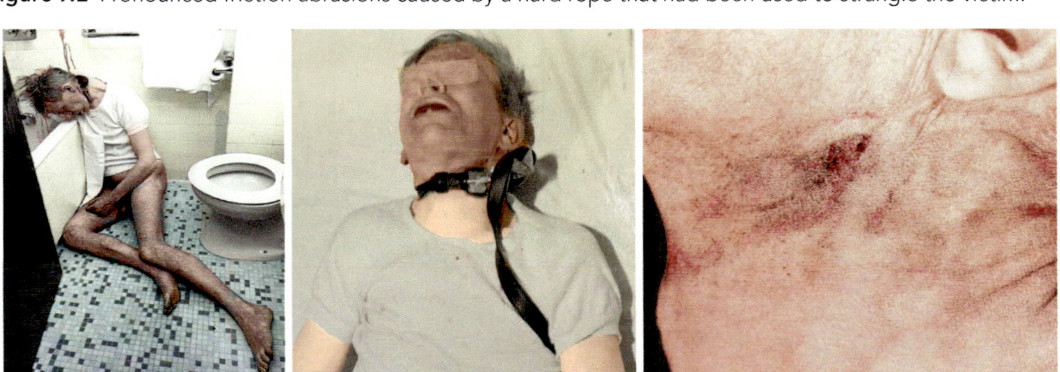

(a) (b) (c)

**Figure 7.3** (a) Suicidal strangulation in the bathroom using a belt. (b) Closer view of the belt around the neck. The buckle is on the left side, and its impression with bruising on the skin is seen on removal of the ligature (c).

The effect of smooth ligatures on the skin also depends on whether a narrow edge is presented to the skin, such as a stretched nylon stocking. In such a case, there may be a pronounced linear mark appearing to 'cut' into the skin (Figure 7.4). On the other hand, a scarf is much more likely to present a broader surface to the neck and therefore produce a much less distinctive mark (Figure 7.5). Indeed, with such soft ligatures, especially if removed shortly after application, the mark may be faint or absent. In such cases, it is worth examining the neck under ultra-violet or oblique light in order to enhance the appearance of the suspected mark (see Chapter 3).

A further observation which is applicable to self-applied ligatures, is that, not infrequently, a piece of soft material is interposed between the surface of the neck and the ligature in order to make the procedure 'more comfortable' (see Chapter 8, Figure 8.3).

If the ligature was secured around the neck with a knot, its position could be of vital importance in the reconstruction of the circumstances. The number of knots, tightness, and the method of knotting should all be carefully considered. On removal of the ligature, the impression from the knot may be visible (Figure 7.6).

The ligature should be removed by cutting the rope on the opposite side to the knot. On occasion, it may be possible to trace an assailant from the type of knot used. The reader is directed to a recent comprehensive article by Chisnall (2021) comparing knots and different methods of binding, in which he compared homicidal with suicidal methods of application in ligature strangulation and hanging. He surveyed 90 external tying cases (mainly homicides) and 56 cases involving self-tying (mainly suicides), comparing multiple knot and ligature characteristics. It was found that in suicidal cases, single knots were nearly always used, frequently in association with many turns of the ligature. A double-knotted noose, however, was used in the case described by Zecevic (1982).

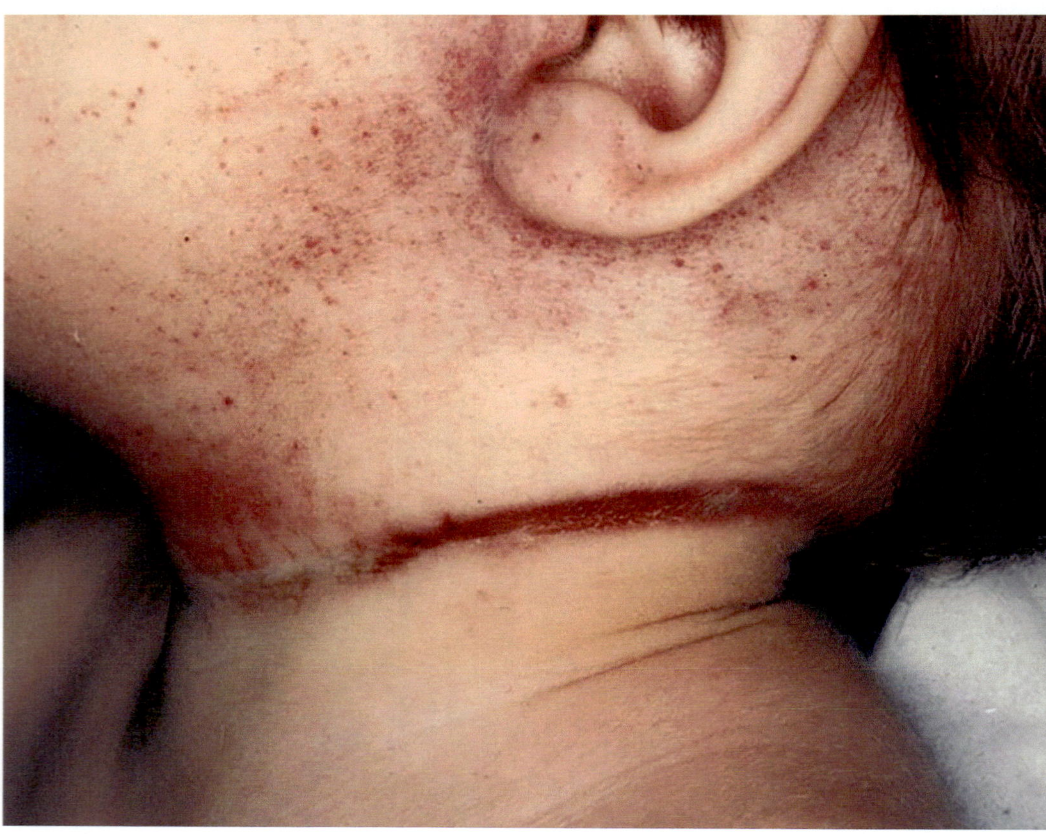

**Figure 7.4** Infant strangled with a nylon stocking. Part of the ligature mark is well delineated where most of the pressure was applied.

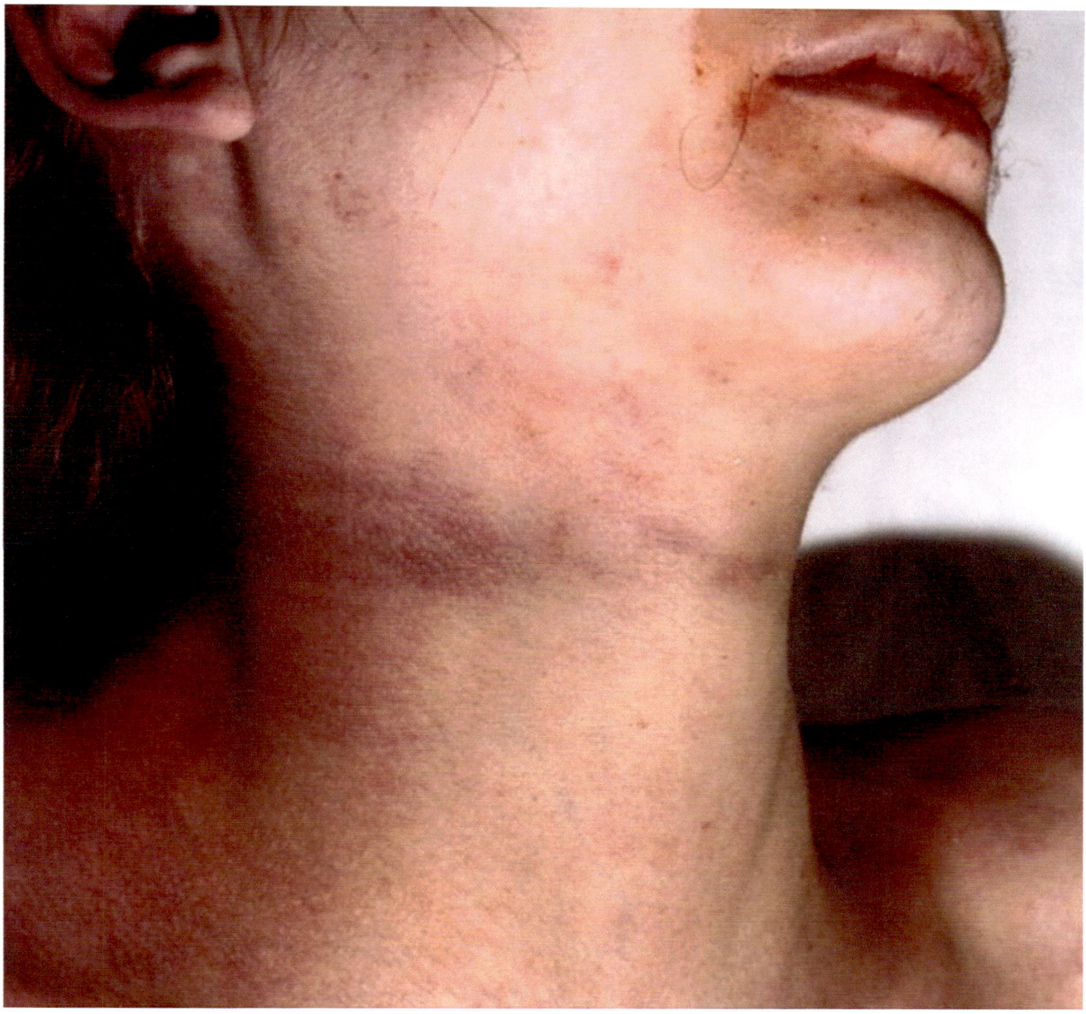

**Figure 7.5** Ligature mark made by a scarf.

Sometimes the ligature is tightened by means of a stick or similar object inserted into the ligature material and used as a tourniquet, either beneath or within the ligature. In the case shown below, a wire was used as a ligature and then twisted (Figure 7.7).

Such a method of tightening is seen in both homicide and suicide cases. The term 'garrotting' (derived from the Spanish word for cudgel) is applicable in situations where a victim is attacked from behind without warning, overpowered, and killed. A ligature is thrown around the neck and quickly tightened, resulting in rapid loss of consciousness. The assailant is then free to twist the ligature with one or more turns. In the earlier part of the nineteenth century, it was widely used in England as a form of violence, with robbery as the motive. It had become so common in the winter of 1862–1863 that an Act of Parliament was passed in 1863 imposing the penalty of flogging in addition to penal servitude for this offence (Garrotters Act 1863). The legislation had the desired effect, stopping the practice almost entirely. In Spain and Portugal, the 'garrotte' was used for executions. Initially, the procedure was to twist a cord or bandage around the condemned person's neck, but later a mechanical collar was adopted (Yitna and le Roux-Kemp, 2001; Figure 7.8).

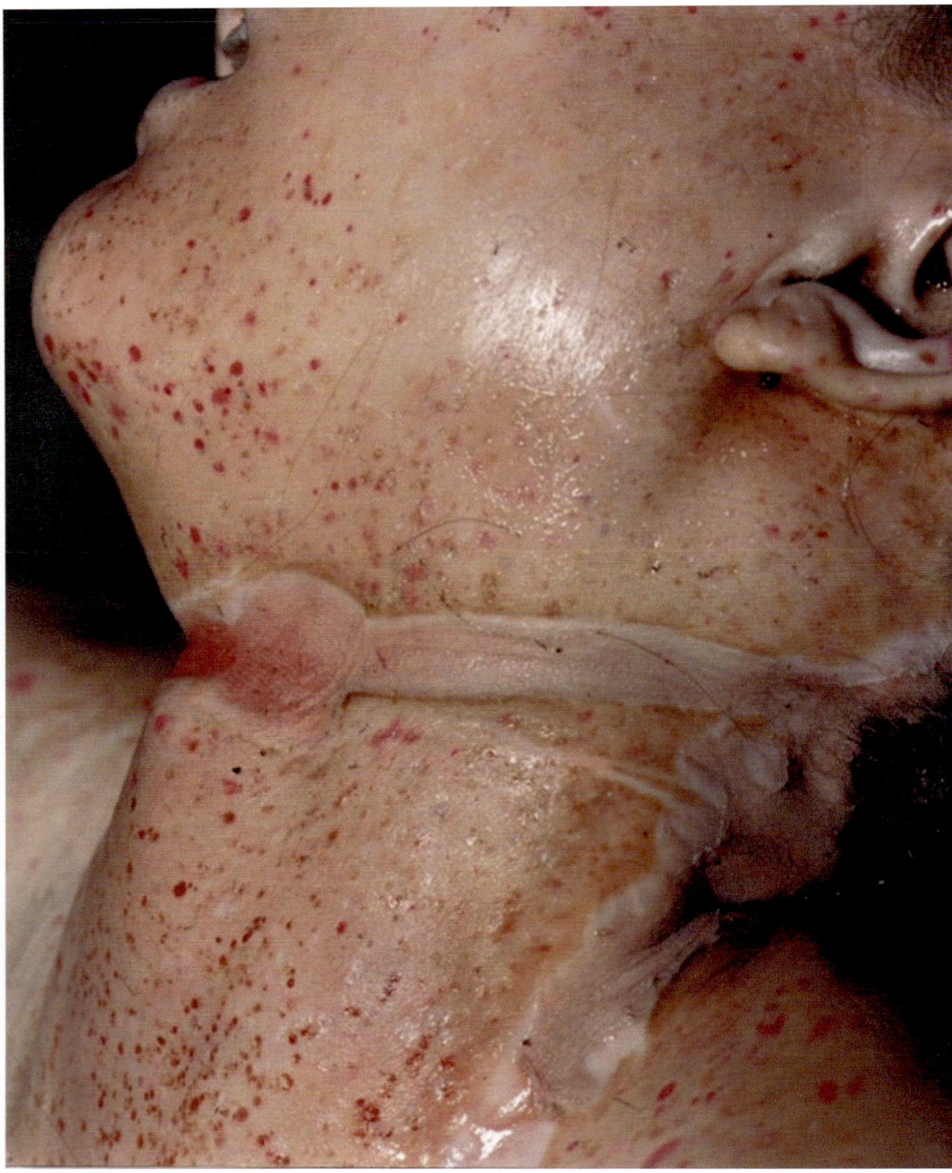

**Figure 7.6** Knot indentation into the skin showing its position at the front of the neck and on the left side, where the ligature had also been twisted (see the case study in Figure 7.10).

## Case Study – 'The Railway Killers'

The author of this text was involved in a triple murder investigation in which all deaths involved the same modus operandi, ligature strangulation following the rape of each victim (Figures 7.9–7.11). The investigation involved two murder suspects who became known as the 'Railway killers' because of the proximity of many of their victims to railway lines or stations. Prior to the three murders, the two were responsible for a series of rapes of women over a number of years (Bolland, 2002).

## Case Study – Concealment of Homicide

The use of conflagration to conceal wounds in homicide cases is not unusual, as we have also seen in one of the above cases. The case described here involves a young woman who had been strangled

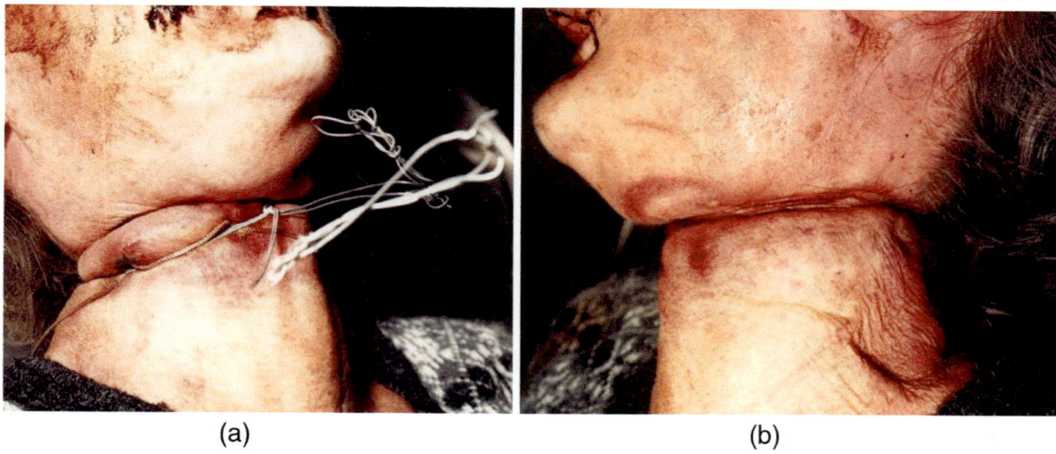

**Figure 7.7** (a) Strangulation with a wire. The ends have been twisted to tighten the ligature. (b) The depth of the ligature marks is readily appreciated after removal of the wire.

**Figure 7.8** Spanish garotte with screw and mechanical collar.

with a ligature, after which her bedroom was set on fire (Figure 7.12). It was staged to appear as though she had dropped a lit cigarette whilst falling asleep. The alarm was raised by neighbours and her young daughter. Radiographic examination was carried out prior to the autopsy. The autopsy did not show any soot deposits in the airways. Her neck, which had been flexed and partially spared from burns, revealed a ligature mark, and there were petechiae in her eyes. In addition, carboxyhaemoglobin was not present.

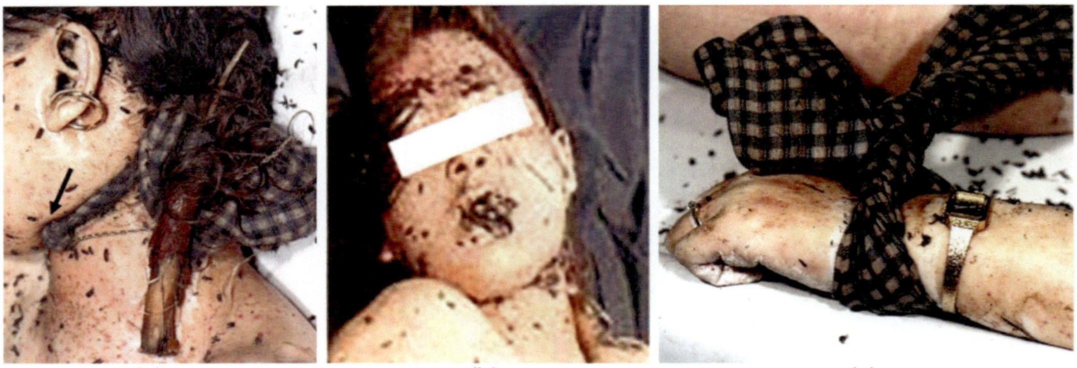

(a) (b) (c)

**Figure 7.9** First victim recovered from a local canal: (a) The left side of the neck has been constricted using part of her torn blouse. A knot had been fashioned at the front of her neck to maximise compressive force to the larynx. At the same time a broken branch was used as a tourniquet to further tighten the ligature. The latter had been wedged in the supraclavicular fossa at the lower end. (b) Part of blouse used as a gag. (c) Both hands bound with part of the blouse.

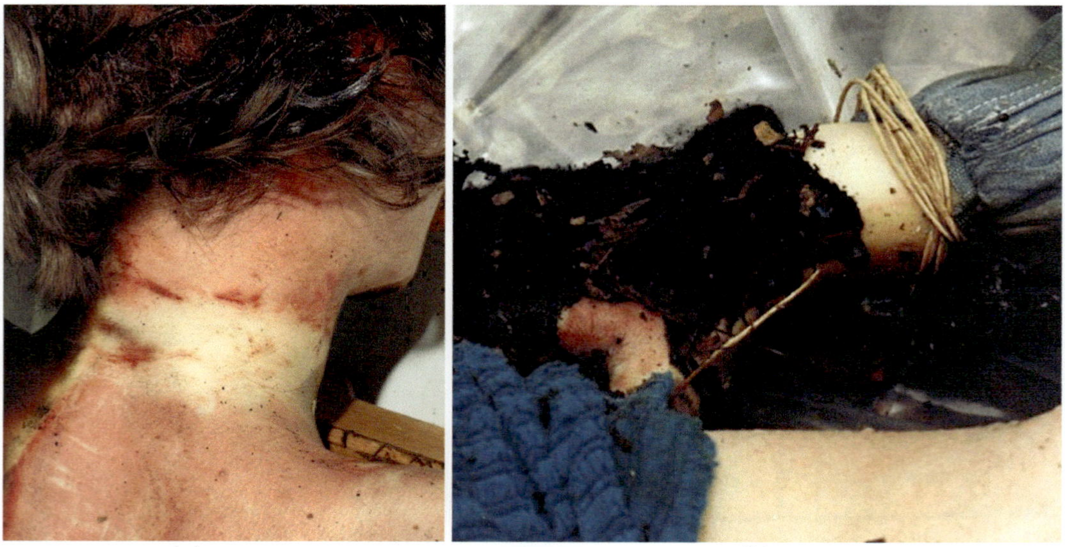

(a) (b)

**Figure 7.10** Second victim found in a wooded area: (a) Ligature mark on her neck. (b) There were attempts to burn the body to conceal the homicide. String was also found binding the victim's hands and legs. Similar string was found in the home of one of the suspects.

**Figure 7.11** Third victim found next to railway track: The deceased had been missing for a number of weeks and was found in a decomposed state. A sock can be seen in her mouth, used as a gag (arrow), and soft material fashioned into a ligature is seen loosely around her neck (arrow). Much of the cervical soft tissue had disintegrated.

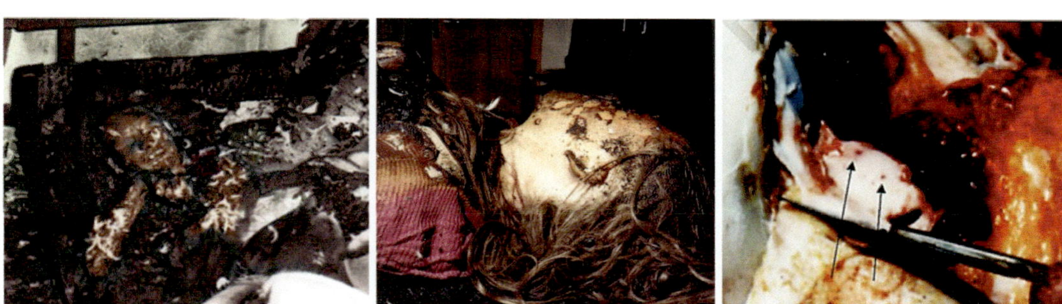

(a) (b) (c)

**Figure 7.12** (a) Victim lying on her bed. (b) Ligature mark seen when the neck is extended (arrow). (c) Petechiae in the sclera of the right eye (arrows).

# INTERNAL INJURIES

## Distribution of Bruising

Internal bruising caused by constriction with a ligature usually corresponds to the level of its application (Figure 7.13). It has been stated by Camps and Hunt (1959) that bruising is not always found from a ligature applied in life when it has been tightly secured and not removed until after the circulation has ceased. From my own experience, however, I have found that there may well be slight bruising which could be easily overlooked. On the other hand, a complete lack of soft tissue bruising is only found in vast majority of suspension deaths and not in cases of homicidal ligature strangulation.

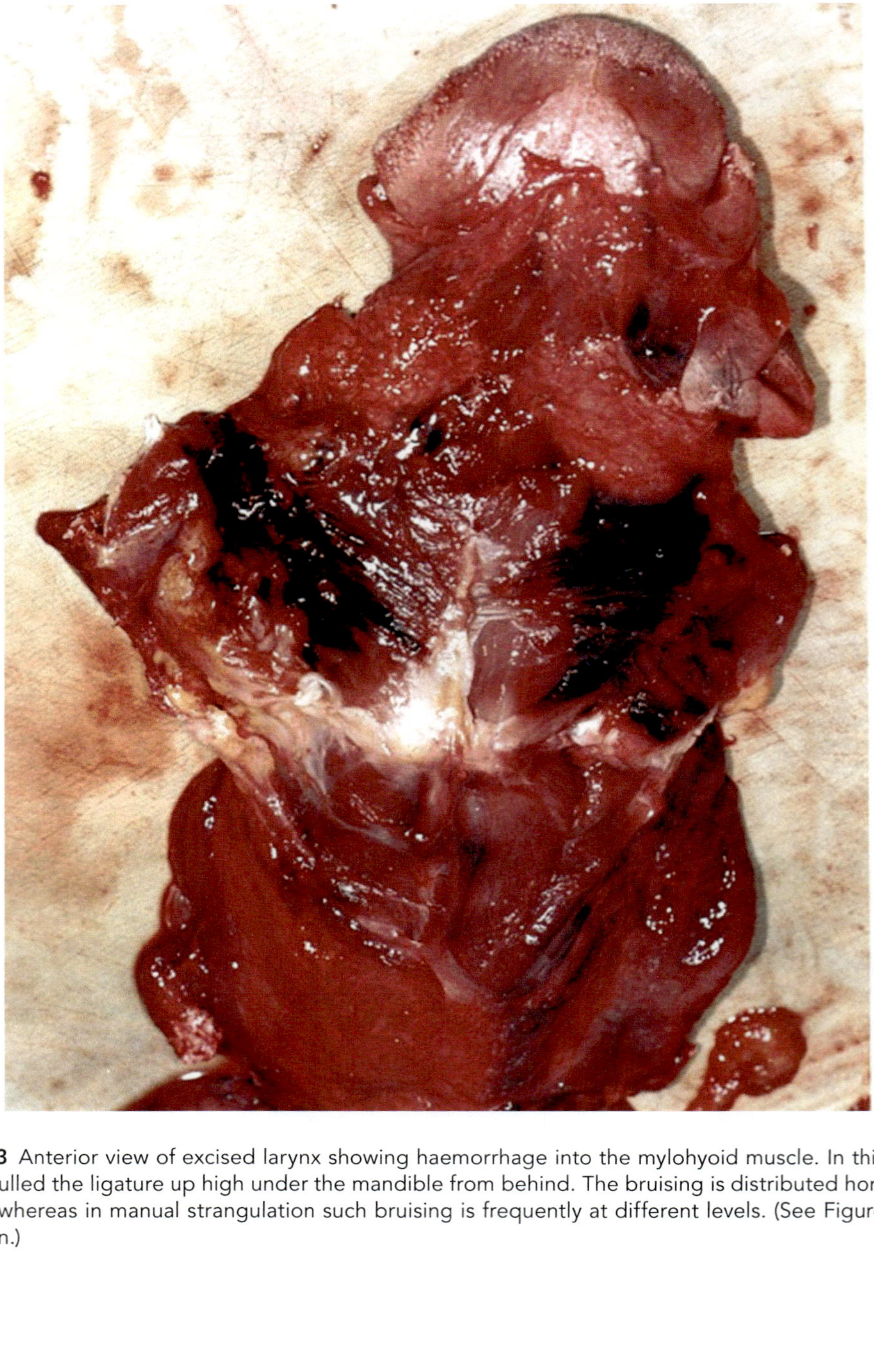

**Figure 7.13** Anterior view of excised larynx showing haemorrhage into the mylohyoid muscle. In this case, the assailant pulled the ligature up high under the mandible from behind. The bruising is distributed horizontally at one level, whereas in manual strangulation such bruising is frequently at different levels. (See Figure 6.11a. for comparison.)

## Vascular Injury

Vascular injury is rare in ligature strangulation. Claydon (1990) described haemorrhage around the carotid arteries in one of her cases. Intimal tears have been reported by Maxeiner and Bockholdt (2003). Further details on vascular neck injury can be found in the chapters on manual strangulation and hanging.

## Laryngeal and Hyoid Bone Injuries

Fractures of the thyroid cartilage and hyoid bone are seen, particularly in older victims, although the incidence is much lower than in manual strangulation.

In ligature strangulation, hyoid bone fractures are uncommon since the level of constriction is relatively low and well below the bone; traction on the thyro-hyoid membrane is also negligible. Fracture of the bone will depend on the width of the ligature, with more likelihood of compression if it is wide. It is much more usual to find fractures of the thyroid cartilage, particularly of one or both superior

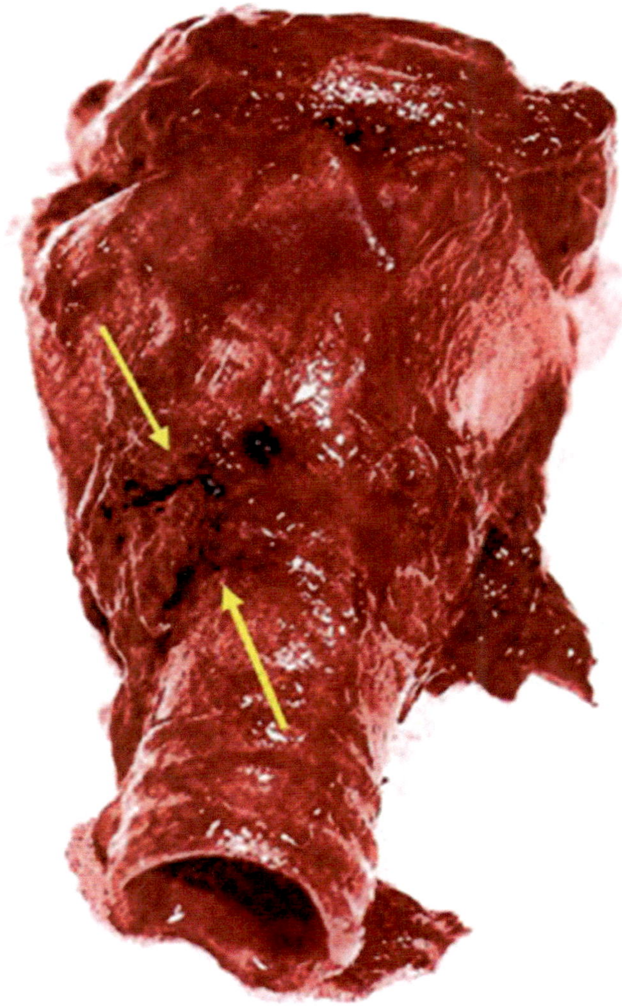

**Figure 7.14** Homicidal strangulation showing dislocation of the right thyrocricoid joint and fracture of the anterior aspect of the cricoid cartilage on the same side (arrows).

horns. Fractures of the thyroid lamina and cricoid cartilage are less common and are likely to occur only when considerable force is used (Figure 7.14). In Green's series (1973) of 31 homicide cases, 17 (54%) had fractures: 11 (64%) were of the thyroid cornua, four each (13%) of the hyoid bone and cricoid cartilage, but none involved the thyroid laminae. In my own series of cases the incidence of fractures among adults was 33%, with none found in children. The distribution is similar to Green's series.

## Intensity of Force

The degree of force used depends on the type of ligature and length of application. It should be remembered, however, that estimation of force is difficult and is better appreciated through internal examination of the neck structures. Sacco et al. (2023) pointed out that the force used in ligature strangulation is characterised by the point of application on the neck, its direction, and its intensity. They were able to quantify the intensity of force with an experimental model using a dynamometer and a mannikin. It was shown that both male and female participants in their experimental model could easily achieve a strength of 5 kg, and with a greater amount of force applied, some individuals exceeded values of 20 kg.

## Resistance of Victim and re-application of the Ligature

It is not unusual in homicidal ligature strangulation to find more than one ligature mark, each of varying intensity and crossing each other, either in parallel or at an angle to each other. Together with such an appearance, abrasions caused by the movement of a ligature across the neck are quite commonly seen, as well as associated fingernail marks, either from the victim attempting to remove the ligature or (together with fingertip bruising) from the assailant attempting to secure the ligature and/or restrain the neck from moving, or even attempting manual strangulation. Such a mixed pattern of injury is not unusual (Figures 7.15 and 7.16). The victim's clothing or necklace may also become caught in the ligature during a struggle, and marks from these require careful evaluation.

On the other hand, in suicidal ligature strangulation, although the ligature is frequently wound tightly around the neck with many turns, the marks on the neck conform quite well to the constricting agent (Figure 7.17). Occasionally, fingernail marks are seen, indicating that the victim may have unsuccessfully attempted to remove an already tightly wound ligature. Nevertheless, no cases have been reported in which the presence of physical signs indicated the complete removal and re-application of such a ligature.

## Length of Application

Accurate estimation of the duration of application of a ligature is not a realistic exercise. Such an examination can only be discussed in relative terms. Examination of the ligature mark may help if there are obvious friction abrasions caused by excessive movement of the ligature, or if there are signs of re-application and resistance, as described above. It should also be borne in mind that the ligature around a victim's neck may be kept tight by the assailant for some time after death. The intensity of the mark may thus appear quite pronounced, even though death may have occurred rapidly. Furthermore, assessment of all local injuries to the face and neck, as well as other injuries to the body, will give some indication of the extent of a struggle.

## Associated Injuries and Other Findings

In homicide cases, such injuries, in general, are similar to those seen in manual strangulation. There is, however, a tendency in some homicidal ligature strangulations to see injuries and other signs on the body that are of a more 'planned' nature. A gag may be found in the mouth, which was initially intended to silence the victim. There may also be ligatures or their marks around the limbs, particularly the wrists and ankles. These may have been placed either ante- or post-mortem,

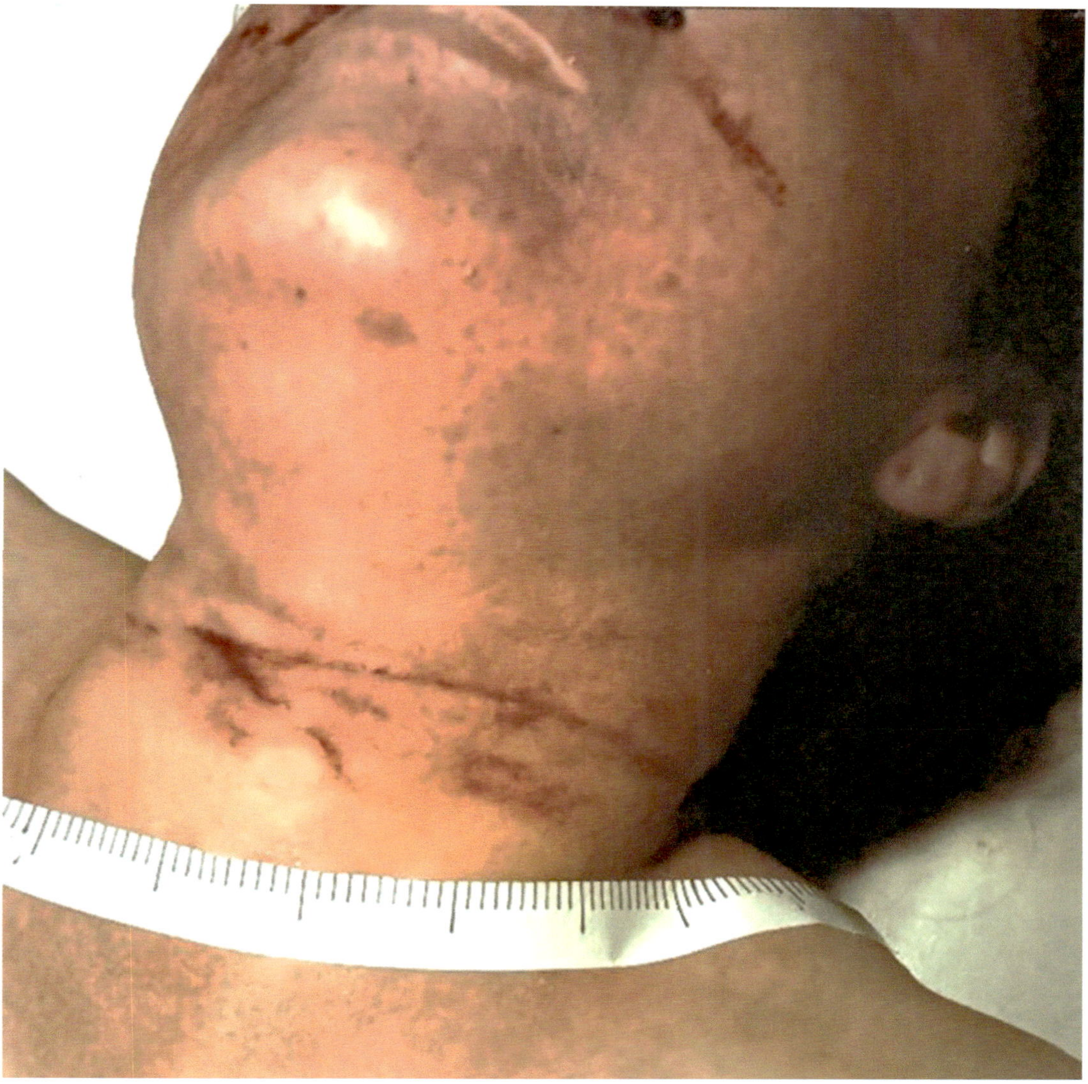

**Figure 7.15** Case of homicidal ligature strangulation in which there are several ligature marks of varying intensity. The ligature had been shifted from one position to another whilst the deceased was attempting to free herself.

and the distinction between the two types is important in determining the intention behind their use. Marks caused before death frequently present as abrasions or bruises. Their intensity will depend on the extent of struggling to loosen the bindings, as well as the characteristics of the binding material and its tightness. The manner of application of the binding is also relevant, as is the positioning of the limbs and whether there is intervening clothing. It is not unusual to see such a pattern of injuries in strangulation accompanied by sexual assault, and care must be taken to differentiate between a victim who has been surprised and overpowered by an assailant and one who may have initially been a willing party to a sado-masochistic act that has gone tragically wrong. The binding of limbs or the rest of the body after death may be used by the assailant to facilitate transportation and disposal of the victim. Such post-mortem ligature marks do not show true bruising; one sees either a grooved impression on the injured skin, or a yellow/brown dried abrasion with no sign of vital reaction.

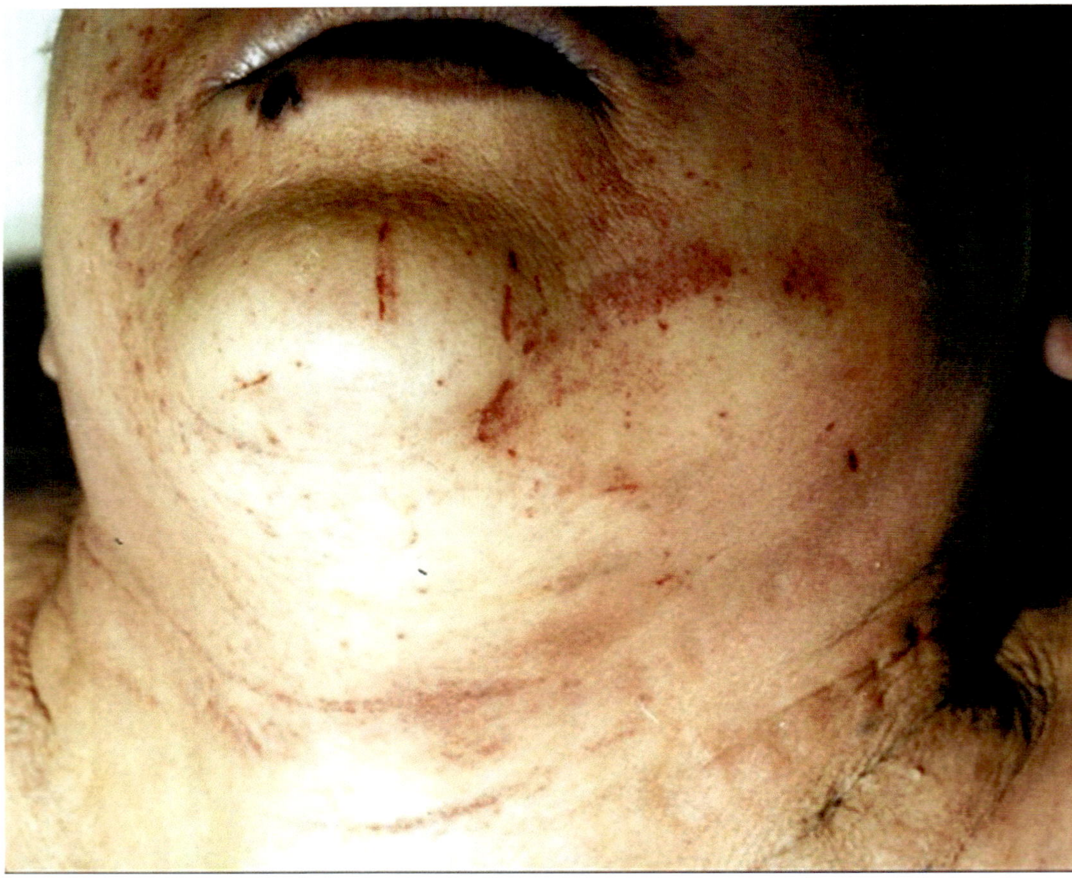

**Figure 7.16** On the neck of this victim, there are two faint ligature marks as well as associated bruises and fingernail abrasions on the neck and face.

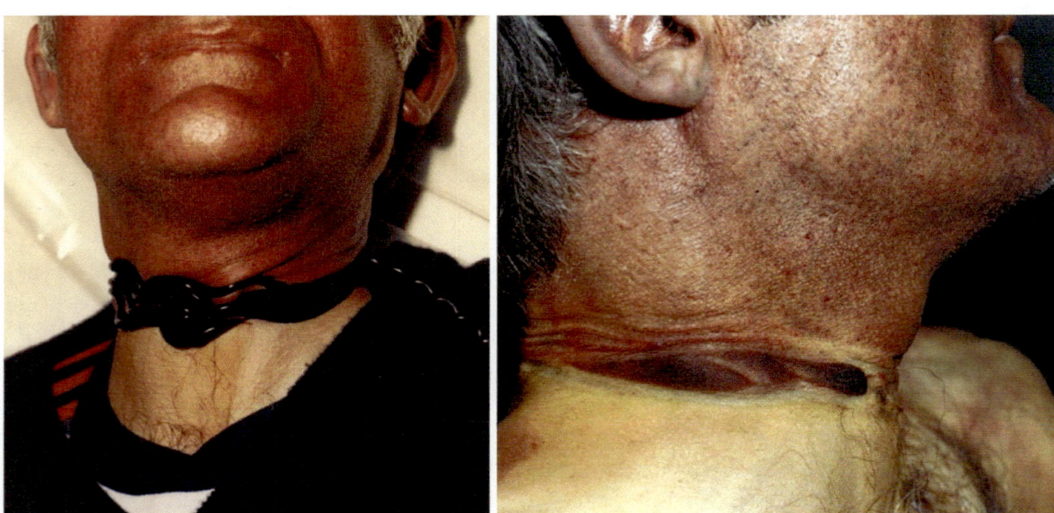

(a) (b)

**Figure 7.17** (a) Suicidal strangulation with a coiled cable from a headphone set. Note that it has been wound around the neck four times. (b) The resulting ligature mark shows a characteristic pattern and prominent bruising where the skin has been 'pinched' between each turn.

## Homicidal or Suicidal Strangulation?

It appears that the self-application of a ligature can be carried out with enough force to prevent venous drainage through the vertebral and jugular systems and produce facial congestion. Maxeiner and Bockholdt (2003), in their series, found that half the suicidal cases had prominent facial congestion, whereas similar degrees of congestion in some of the homicidal cases, were only observed where the ligature had not been removed shortly after the event.

With regard to petechial haemorrhages, Maxeiner and Bockholdt found that both groups had approximately 50% of petechiae scattered over the entire face. However, their density seemed to be higher in the majority of suicides. Unlike the suicide cases, in homicides where the ligature had been removed by the perpetrator, the petechiae were less tightly packed in the upper neck and mandible region.

A further important point of difference with homicidal ligature strangulation is that the injuries seen with self-application are usually less pronounced because less force is used. In Green's series of seven suicidal strangulations (Green, 1973), only one case was found to have injury to the underlying musculature. Furthermore, none showed laryngeal or hyoid bone fractures. The present author, however, has found one self-strangulation case with a fracture of the right superior thyroid cornu in a middle-aged male who was the sole occupant of a police cell.

More recently, in the series studied by Maxeiner and Bockholdt (2003), in which they compared 19 suicidal ligature strangulations to 47 homicidal ligature strangulations, two of the 19 suicidal victims had single fractures of the upper thyroid horns, and in one victim there was a fracture of a lower thyroid horn; other types of laryngo-hyoid injuries were not observed. In the homicidal series, the laryngo-hyoid structures were unaffected in 26 cases (12 of these victims were children or adolescents), single thyroid horn fractures were present in three cases, and more significant injuries were found in 18 cases. There were also haemorrhages in the laryngeal muscles in 12 of the homicide victims and in none of the suicide cases. They concluded that, based on their findings, laryngo-hyoid injuries could be useful in differentiating suicide from homicide if more than a single thyroid horn fracture or laryngeal soft tissue trauma is present.

# ACCIDENTAL LIGATURE STRANGULATION

## Young Children

In young children such strangulation occurs in situations in which they become entangled, such as with clothing, bedding, cords from window blinds or string from dummies (pacifiers; Figure 7.18). In such cases great care must be taken to exclude foul play, although this may sometimes be extremely difficult.

In the case reported by Milkovich et al. (2005), a low-income mother was accused of child abuse after co-sleeping with her 13-month-old daughter, whom she found entangled and strangling in her hair. The infant was initially unconscious and cyanotic but was revived by her parents before reaching the emergency department. On examination, there was a ligature mark on the neck and petechiae on the face. Although rare, the authors demonstrated that such entanglement could occur, and the mother was exonerated.

A further similar case was reported by Kindley and Todd (1978) of a 27-month-old male, sleeping with his mother, who was revived after he had become entangled and strangled by the unbraided waist-length hair of his mother.

Shepherd (1990) reported on a three-year-old child who had become entangled in a flex from a table lamp next to the bed in which the child slept. The flex, which was twin-core and approximately 2 metres in length, passed between the bed and the wall and had been unplugged. Reconstruction of the events from the scene and the post-mortem findings suggested that the child's right arm had become entangled with the flex from the lamp and then, as the child turned over, the flex had looped around the neck.

The danger posed by window blinds has been highlighted by a number of authors including Rauchschwalbe and Mann (1997). They documented the prevalence of paediatric asphyxial death from window-covering cords in the United States in children aged one month to eight years. They reported on 183 fatal window-cord strangulations between 1981 and 1995, 93% of whom were three years old or younger. Pull cords on Venetian-type horizontal window coverings accounted for 86% of documented injuries. Infant victims were more likely to become entangled while being put down for a nap, and toddlers were more likely to be suspended by the cord after falling or jumping from a height.

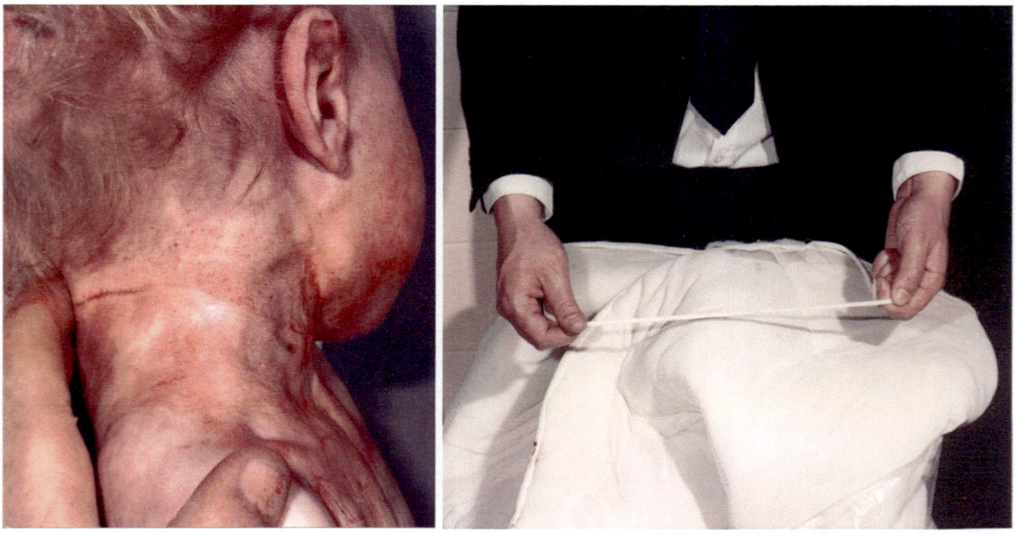

(a) (b)

**Figure 7.18** (a) Ligature mark produced accidentally in a 12-month-old infant. (b) Partially detached length of lining from a duvet in which the child became entangled.

## Adults

In adults, it has been occasionally reported in a number of different circumstances, such as in traffic collisions. Hitosugi and Takatsu (2000) reported the case of a 23-year-old man wearing a three-point seat belt who suffered a rollover traffic accident. The loose belt allowed the body to move, and subsequently, the diagonal belt applied external pressure to the neck while the car was rolling over. A number of other such cases are reported (Veenema, 1994; Agdal and Thomsen, 1978). Sharma (2015) reported a case with delayed symptoms followed by full recovery in a 22-year-old woman. She sustained accidental strangulation from a long chunni scarf wrapped around her neck while riding on a cycle rickshaw. During the journey, her chunni became entangled in the rear side wheel of the rickshaw, resulting in sudden compression of her neck. She remained symptom-free for the next three days, then collapsed. She regained consciousness on the second day of admission and remained hospitalised for the next 16 days, following which she was discharged with only some residual stiffness in the neck.

Other situations include the very unusual case reported by Mitrani (1962) of a 30-year-old woman who was apparently strangled with a cord that had accidentally wrapped around her neck and to which a cow had become tethered. It was thought that the animal made a sudden movement away from its attachment to a fence, thus tightening the cord around the woman's neck. Gill et al. (1977) reported on a further unusual method of accidental strangulation, in which two Indian women both suffered crico-tracheal disruption. In the two cases cited, the ends of their chunni scarves were caught in a power-operated rotating machine, resulting in strangulation injuries. In both, strangulation occurred from behind, and the tight cloth was pulled upwards and backwards on the thyroid and cricoid cartilages, pressing these structures against the cervical spine, which was simultaneously hyperextended. In Gordon and Shapiro's reported case (1975), an adult male had become entangled in a dog chain while under the influence of alcohol.

Accidental ligature strangulations seen in autoerotic deaths are described in the following chapter.

## References

Agdal N, Thomsen JL. Strangulation in three-point seat-belt (in Danish with English abstract). *Ugeskr Laeg.* 1978; 140: 168–169.

Bolland L. The railway murders: R v John Duffy and R v David Mulcahy. *Med Sci Law.* 2002 Jan;42(1):2–9. doi: 10.1177/002580240204200102. PMID: 11848136.

Camps FE, Hunt AC. Pressure on the neck. *J Forensic Med.* 1959;6: 116–135.

Chisnall RC. Distinguishing between homicide and suicide knots and ligatures: A comparative analysis of case and survey data. *J Forensic Sci.* 2021;66:209–228.

Claydon SM. Suicidal strangulation by ligature: Three case reports. *Med Sci Law.* 1990 July;30(3):221–224. doi: 10.1177/002580249003000310. PMID: 2398799.

Gill SS, Singh CM, Eggleston FC. Cricotracheal disruption owing to strangulation. A report of two cases with successful surgical repair. *J Thorac Cardiovasc Surg.* 1977;73: 948–950.

Gordon I, Shapiro HA. *Forensic Medicine: A Guide to Principles.* Chuchill, Livingstone, Edinburgh, 1975, p. 88.

Green MA. Morbid anatomical findings in strangulation. *Forensic Sci.* 1973;2:317–323.

Hitosugi M, Takatsu A. A case of strangulation by a vehicle seat belt. *Leg Med (Tokyo).* 2000 Mar;2(1):46–48.

Kindley AD, Todd RM. Accidental strangulation by mother's hair. *Lancet.* 1978 Mar 11;1(8063):565. doi: 10.1016/s0140-6736(78)90601-3. PMID: 76115.

Maxeiner H, Bockholdt B. Homicidal and suicidal ligature strangulation--a comparison of the post-mortem findings. *Forensic Sci Int.* 2003 Oct 14;137(1):60–66.

Milkovich SM, Owens J, Stool D, Chen X, Beran M. Accidental childhood strangulation by human hair. *Int J Pediatr Otorhinolaryngol.* 2005;69(12):1621–1628.

Mitrani I Accidental strangulation with severe laceration of the neck. *J Forensic Med.* 1962;9: 20–24.

Rauchschwalbe R, Mann NC. Pediatric window-cord strangulations in the United States, 1981–1995. *JAMA.* 1997 June 4;277(21):1696–1698.

Sacco MA, Ricci C, Fragomeni G, Bonetta CF, Cordasco F, Gualtieri S, Cavalcanti B, Ricci P, Aquila I. Reconstruction of trauma dynamics due to ligature strangulation by using a dynamometer: A technical report. *Cureus*. 2023 Nov 18;15(11):11.

Sharma A. Rickshaw scarf strangulation. *Med Leg J*. 2015 June;83(2):109–110. doi: 10.1177/0025817214563906. Epub 2015 Jan 7. PMID: 25568171.

Shepherd RT. Accidental self-strangulation in a young child--a case report and review. *Med Sci Law*. 1990 Apr;30(2):119–123. doi: 10.1177/002580249003000207. PMID: 2348764.

Vanezis P. *Pathology of Neck Injury*. Butterworths, London, 1989, p. 65.

Veenema KR. Strangulation associated with a passive restraint shoulder harness seatbelt: Case report. *J Emerg Med*. 1994; 12: 317–320.

Yitna YG, le Roux-Kemp A. A medico-legal perspective on the practice of garrotting. *Med Leg J*. 2011;79 (Pt 1):15–25.

Zecevic D. Suicidal strangulation with a double-knotted noose. *J Forensic Sci*. 1987;27: 963–967.

# CHAPTER 8

## COMPRESSIVE NECK INJURY IV: HANGING



The term hanging refers to constriction of the neck by a ligature, with the compressive force being caused by the weight of the body. Hanging can involve full suspension of the body, or be partial, if part of the body is supported in some way. The vast majority of hangings are suicides, although from time to time, one sees accidental cases, particularly in children. The so-called 'sexual asphyxias' (autoerotic deaths), many of which involve hanging, comprise a further special category. Judicial hangings are still carried out in many countries but have not been seen in Great Britain since the abolition of the death penalty for murder in 1965.

DOI: 10.4324/9781003658467-8

# PREVALENCE OF SUICIDAL HANGING

Suicide by hanging, as well as by execution, is well known throughout history. In the New Testament, we are reminded of the death of Judas Iscariot, one of the original Twelve Apostles, who betrayed Jesus to the Sanhedrin in the Garden of Gethsemane for 30 pieces of silver. According to the Gospel of St Matthew (Matthew 27:3-5), Judas felt remorse after seeing Jesus condemned; therefore, he threw the silver into the temple and hanged himself (Figure 8.1). There are also other theories regarding his death, but this explanation is the most widely recognised.

In the current society, hanging is the most common method of suicide used worldwide. A 2008 review of 56 countries based on World Health Organization mortality data found that hanging was the most common method in most countries, accounting for 53% of male and 39% of female suicides (Ajdacic-Gross et al., 2008). In England and Wales, hanging is the most commonly used method, (58.4 per 100,00 population in 2021) (Office for National Statistics, 2022). It is particularly prevalent among males aged 15–44, comprising almost half of the suicides in this age group. It is the second most common method among women, following poisoning.

**Figure 8.1** The Death of Judas (etching), c. 1634/1635, by Jacques Callot, 1592–1635. National Gallery, London.

# THE SCENE OF HANGING

Despite the fact that the great majority of hangings are suicides, such an opinion should only be proffered after careful consideration of the scene of discovery of the deceased and completion of the autopsy examination.

Most hangings occur at home (Bowen, 1982; Davison and Marshall, 1986). Other significant locations include custodial environments such as police cells, prisons, workplaces, hospitals, and secluded outdoor locations, particularly wooded areas. In a case seen by the author, a detainee in a police cell used the hatch/bolt hole in the cell door as a suspension point for hanging. He tore off part of his shirt and fashioned it into a noose for his neck (Figure 8.2). In over half such deaths (52%, 38/73), in England and Wales during the years 1990–1996, the hatch to the cell door was used as the ligature point (as in this case). All police forces have since been instructed to keep cell hatches closed when cells are occupied (Gunnell et al., 2005).

The point of attachment of the ligature chosen by the victim depends very much on what is available at the location. This is borne out by the fact that, within the home environment, many different suspension points may be chosen, including door handles and hooks, bannisters, taps, beams, rafters, etc. Although not generally appreciated by laypersons, hanging can occur from many different positions, in some cases from very low heights, with much of the body touching the ground. The essential feature of all cases is that the victim has been able to lean onto a ligature in such a way as to cause compression of the neck (Figure 8.3).

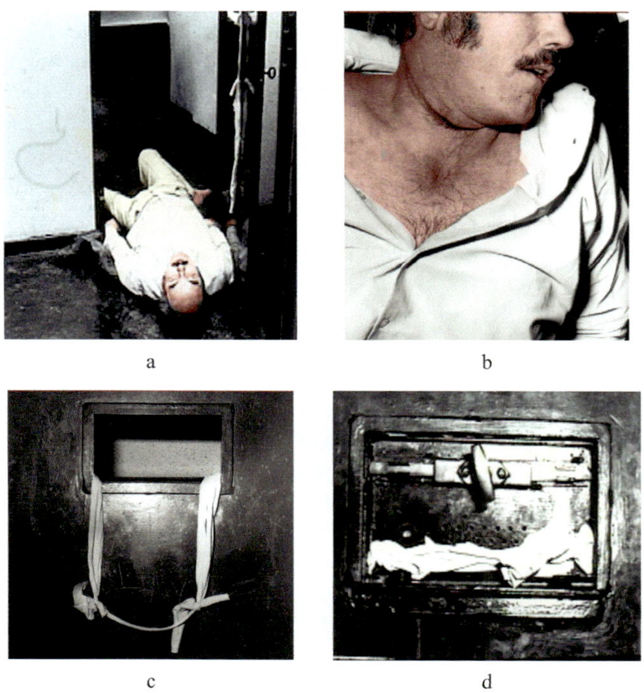


**Figure 8.2** Person found hanging in the cell of a police station. A loud thud alerted officers, who opened the cell door and found the deceased on the ground, as shown in (a). (b) Close-up of the sloping ligature mark. (c) Part of his shirt was hanging from the observation hatch on the inside and fashioned into a noose as reconstructed by officers. (d) The clothing material was fastened around the outside of the hatch whilst it was open, then the hatch was closed by the deceased prior to securing the material around his neck.

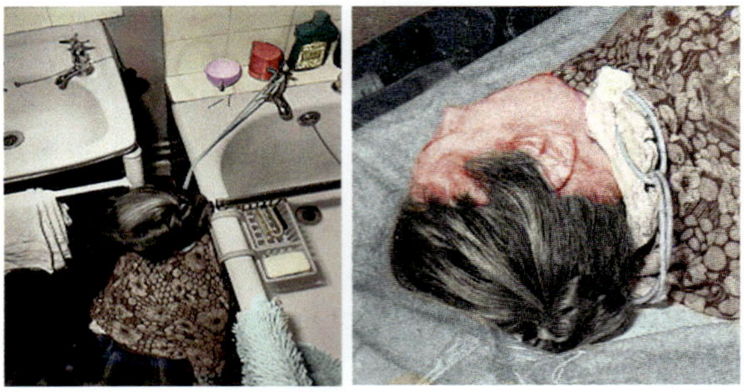

a b

**Figure 8.3** (a) In this case, the deceased is partially suspended in a very low position by the side of the bath, with the cable tied around the bath taps acting as the suspension point. (b) It is a close-up of the neck, showing soft clothing interposed the ligature and skin so as to minimise the discomfort of using the ligature alone.

In the majority of victims of suicidal hanging in two older studies found that some part of the body was touching the ground: 53.3% (Luke et al., 1985) and 59% (Davison and Marshall, 1986). However, in a later multi-centre study based on coroners' records of 149 hanging suicides, Bennewith et al. (2005) found that slightly more than half of the victims were completely suspended with both feet above the ground (78 or 52.4%). In about one-quarter (35 out of 149 or 23.5%), the subjects were partially suspended with their feet touching the ground; in 11 cases (7.4%), they were kneeling; in 13 (8.7%) cases, they were lying; and seated in 7 (4.7%). The precise position was unclear in a further 5 cases (3.4%).

At the scene, there may be a chair or some other object that the victim has used to facilitate the attachment of a ligature and to ensure suspension, achieved either by pushing away the object from beneath the feet or by jumping from it. It is also important to examine the point of attachment and the surrounding area. If the point is high, then it is likely that there will be recent disturbance of dust caused whilst the ligature was being attached. Corresponding dirt marks may also be found on the deceased's hands and possibly parts of their clothing. There may also be disturbance from dust from the attached cord or an abraded area, particularly if a beam has been used to attach the ligature.

There may occasionally be a suicide note in the vicinity, although this is by no means the usual practice. A recent study by Komar et al. (2022) revealed that of 811 hangings, 84% were male, with a male-to-female ratio of 5.1:1; 44% left a note, with females leaving notes more often (51%). However, in other studies in North America, the proportion of notes left was much lower, as cited by these authors.

A common finding at hanging scenes is that the body has been released from its suspended position and the ligature removed in order to attempt resuscitation. Reconstruction of the original position of the deceased is therefore essential in these circumstances.

## THE LIGATURE MARK AND OTHER EXTERNAL FEATURES OF HANGING

In contrast to ligature strangulation, in suspension the ligature mark usually slopes upwards (Figure 8.4) towards the back of the neck, although this may rarely be reversed (Crompton, 1986).

Furthermore, if the point of attachment of the cord is low, its course may only incline slightly upwards or be horizontal, resembling a strangulation mark. An impression from a knot may be found if the ligature is tight on the skin, usually on one side or other of the back of the neck and occasionally beneath the chin. However, quite frequently, all one sees is an interruption of the upward part of the sloping mark close to the point of suspension.

In relation to the type of knot used in suicidal hanging, either complete or partial, Chisnall (2021), in his analysis of knots and ligatures in hanging and ligature strangulation, to assess the differences between homicidal and suicidal manners of death, found that sliding or running knots appeared more frequently in suicide cases. These included pairs of half hitches or multiple half hitches, overhand slip knots or loops, nooses, and running overhand loops. He cites the findings from nine studies and assesses the weighted means for the types of knots. More than half of these different series were sliding or running knots (56.8%; Figure 8.5). Fixed knots were present in 28.9% of cases. The other 13.8% of hangings were reported as no knot found or were unknown. Most victims used a type of slip knot but appeared to show no preference for either side of the neck. When the knot is firm and tight on the neck, one may see an inverted "V"-shaped mark, with the mark sloping up to the knot and then tailing off downwards again.

The ligature mark is usually located above the prominence of the thyroid cartilage, frequently high up under the jaw. This is not surprising because the weight of the body pulls the ligature upwards until its progress is halted by the jaw. In cases where it is lower, this may be due to a running noose tightening rapidly. The position should be carefully distinguished from that of strangulation, in which the mark is usually found over the thyroid cartilage or below it. Occasionally, a double ligature mark may be seen at two levels; the lower one resulting from the initial pressure on the neck and the upper one formed by the ligature where it has pulled upwards to its final position (just below the mandible; Figure 8.6).

The typical roughened mark of a rope used for suicidal hanging, which becomes dried and brown after death and is due to friction, does not necessarily indicate a vital change. Camps (1959) produced similar marks by the suspension of a cadaver. Application of a smoother, though harder, ligature such as a plastic electrical flex leaves a characteristic rounded groove impression, sometimes with a dried brown appearance, but frequently with very little discernible abrasion to the skin (Figure 8.7).

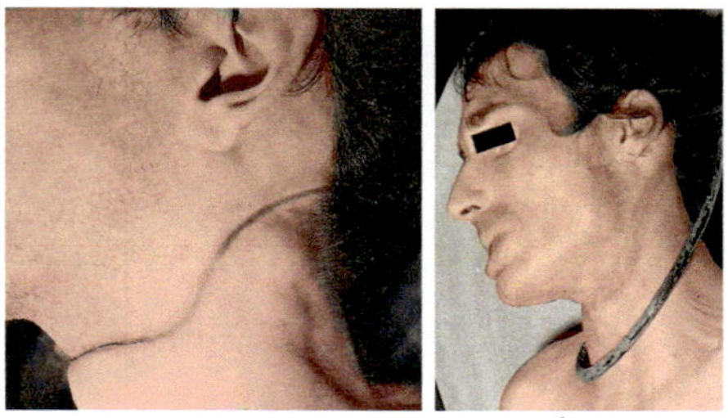

a b

**Figure 8.4** Typical sloping ligature mark in suicidal hanging. The deceased in (a) used a nylon cord, whereas the victim in (b) used a plastic cable. Note the difference in the intensity of the marks caused by the different ligatures.

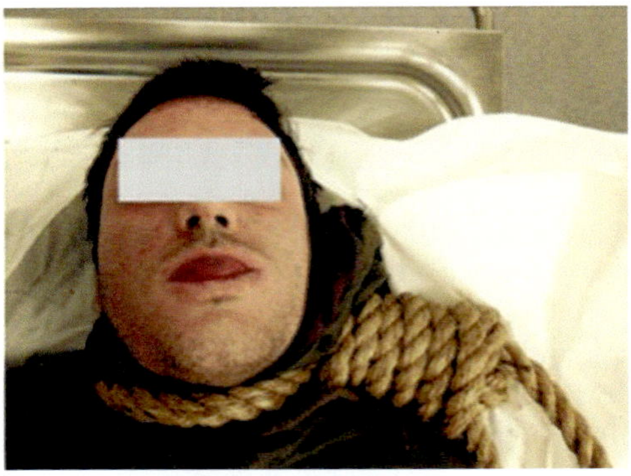

**Figure 8.5** The deceased was found hanging from a tree. The woven rope was fashioned into a 'hangman's style' noose, with multiple loops seen on the left side of his neck (suspension point). There was clothing interspersed between the rope and his neck.

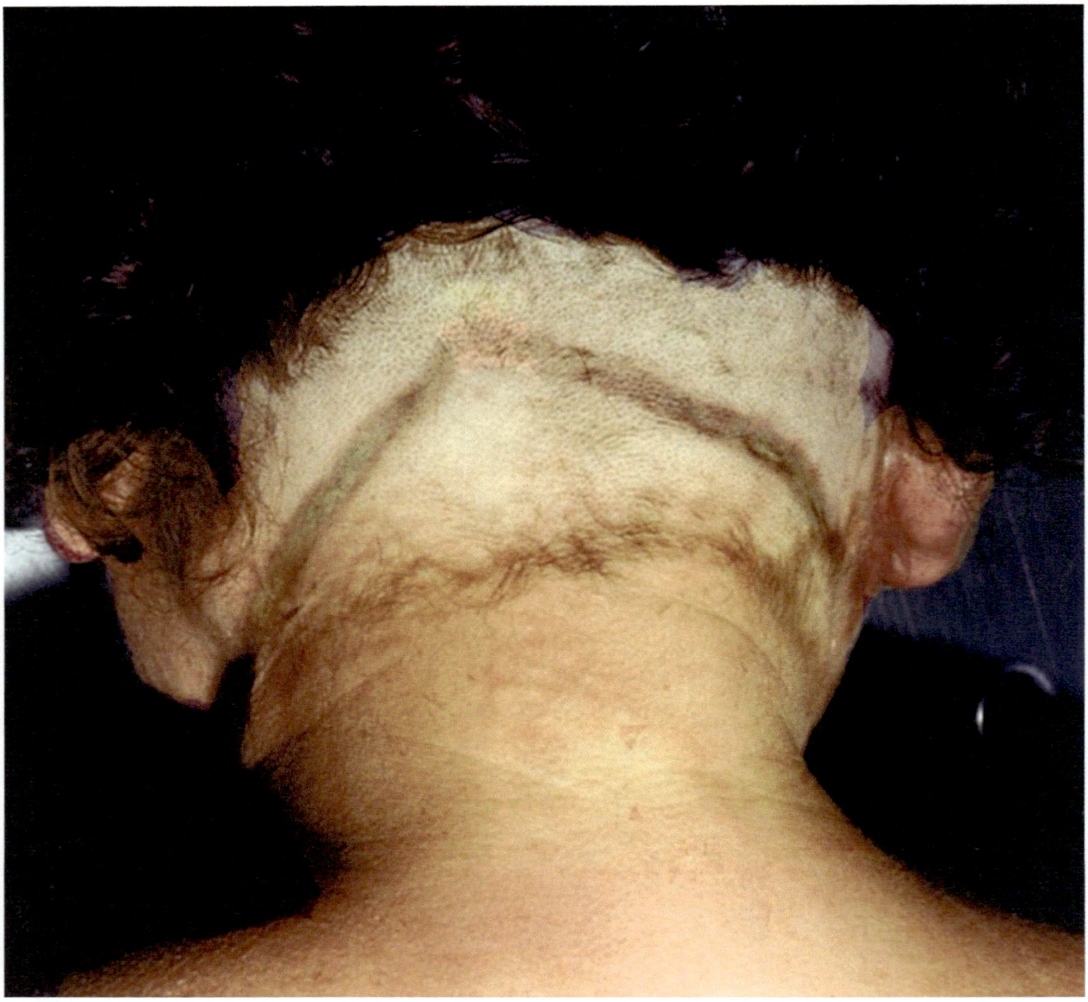

**Figure 8.6** V-shaped ligature mark with the apex of the V being the point of suspension. There is a slightly fainter horizontal mark at the back of the neck, which had formed prior to the neck slipping downwards (and therefore the ligature moving upwards) due to the weight of the body.

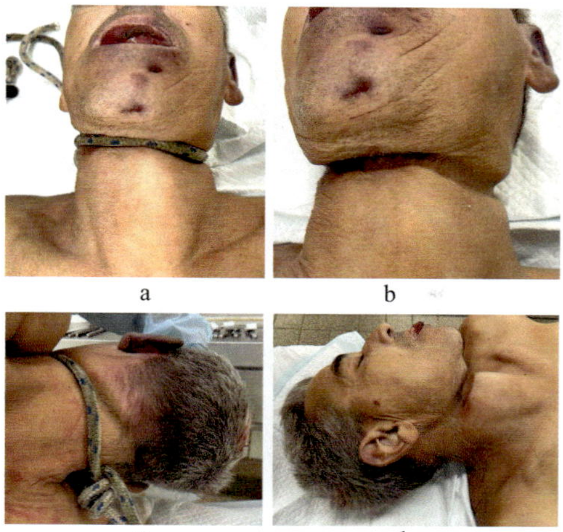


**Figure 8.7** (a) The deceased has used a strong cord as a ligature which is tight around his neck. (b) It has caused a deep furrow beneath which appears dark brown and dry. (c) It slopes up towards the point of suspension on the right side behind the ear, (d) causing a V shape, with the knot having been at its apex. The deceased also has superficial lacerations on his lower face, which relate to using another method of self-harm (see Figure 18.17).

Depending on the degree of constriction, one may see congestion, which is due to obstruction of the venous return, without occlusion of the carotid system. In such cases, one may also see petechial haemorrhages above the level of the ligature and particularly in the conjunctivae and eyelids. However, it should be appreciated that in the majority of hangings, the face appears normal or pale; the ligature mark and protrusion of the tongue are frequently the only external signs of hanging. Tongue protrusion is frequently seen in hanging (Figure 8.8) or ligature strangulation but not reported in uncomplicated manual strangulation. It is also commonly found in fire deaths and occasionally in drowning, as well as during the putrefaction stage of decomposition. Commins et al. (2024), in their series of 298 cases, found tongue protrusion in 28.24% cases of complete hanging, 23.94% of cases of partial hanging, as well as 10% of cases of ligature strangulation. None were seen in cases of manual strangulation. Protrusion of the tongue from the mouth is thought to be due to the larynx and hyoid bone being pushed backwards and upwards together with the base of the tongue resting against the posterior wall of the pharynx, thus leading to airway obstruction. This happens particularly when the ligature is positioned high, above the larynx.

Other external findings related to hanging, particularly to the limbs, are also seen in a variable proportion of deaths, up to 72% in one series (McCabe et al., 2020). It goes without saying that they should be carefully assessed by the pathologist to ascertain whether such injuries are related to hanging or occurred at an earlier time and are not associated with the death. If they did occur at the time of hanging, it is essential to assess whether the trauma seen is consistent with suicide or due to violence from the involvement of another person, in an attempt, for example, to incapacitate the victim. Although homicidal hanging is rare, one does occasionally see cases of staged hanging preceded by a homicidal manner of death.

In the above study of 82 deaths from hanging reported to the State Pathologist's Office in Ireland, the high rate of limb injury of 72% was, in all probability, because their cases had been regarded as suspicious deaths initially by the coroner. Other publications quoted below showed a much lower incidence, which is more in keeping with the full spectrum of hanging cases. Uzün et al. (2007), in addition to finding bruises of various ages, especially in women, some of which were from previous self-harm attempts, found only 56 cases out of 761 (7.4%) of suicidal hangings with superficial bruises occurring during the agonal period. A 10% rate of body bruises was observed in a study of 233 hangings by Samarasekera and Cooke (1996). The injuries seen were predominantly

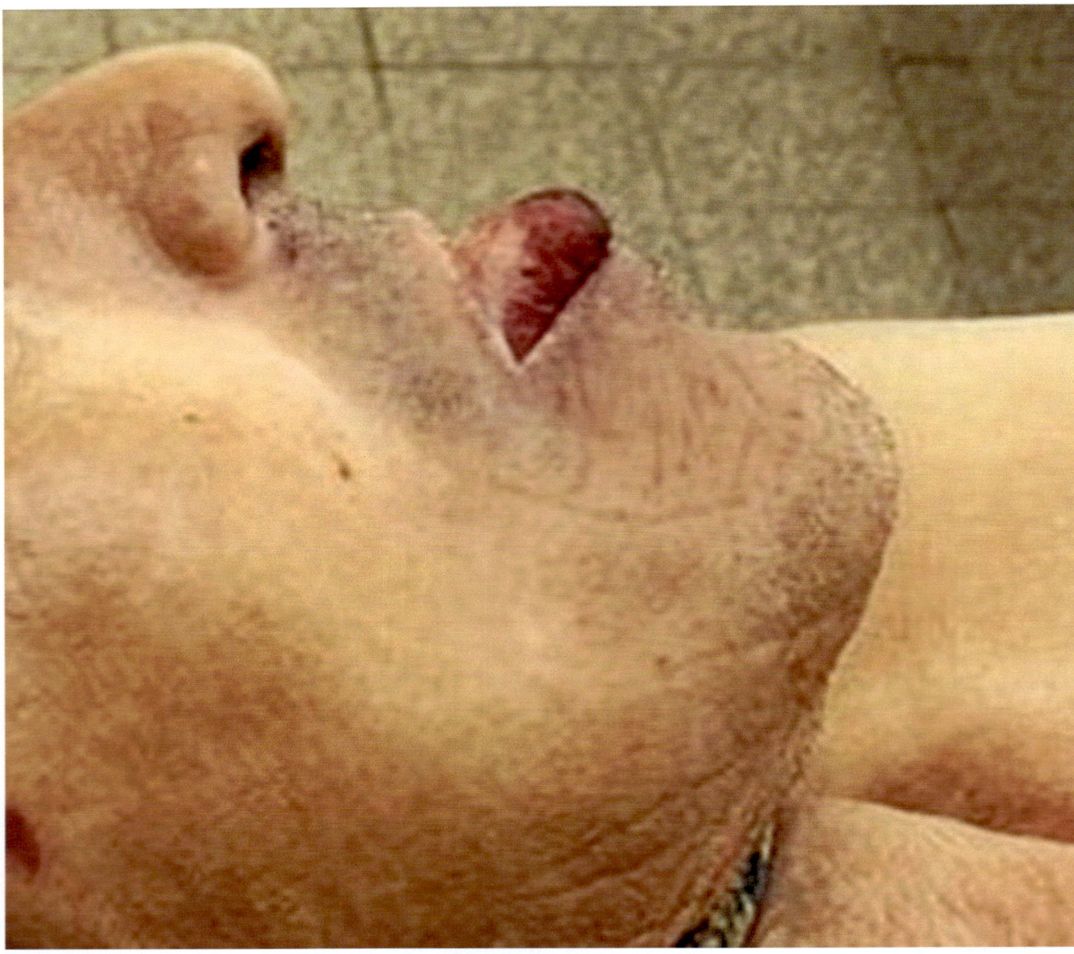

**Figure 8.8** Protrusion of the tongue in a case of partial hanging.

abrasions, followed by bruises, and only very few lacerations. In addition, as in the previous study, self-inflicted wounds were seen in a few cases. Sauvageau (2009), in a six-year retrospective study of 239 cases of suicidal hanging, reported limb abrasions in 31.9% of cases, bruises in 19.8%, and no lacerations. They found that in relation to the hanging location, the two that recorded the highest incidence of limb bruises were at staircases and in closets (66.7% and 56.3%, respectively). On the other hand, the incidence was very low for hangings in more open sites.

The production of external injuries in hanging is unsurprising. Recent studies of filmed hangings have demonstrated that asphyxia by hanging is associated with a complex pattern of body movement responses, including convulsions and alternating phases of decerebrate and decorticate rigidity (Sauvageau, 2009). These movements may lead to a pattern of bruises and abrasions, which has been described in the literature as a normal constituent of death by hanging.

# INTERNAL SIGNS OF HANGING

## Soft Tissue Injuries

Soft tissue injuries are more likely to be found when the body is fully suspended or with only the feet touching the ground (Luke et al., 1985). Nevertheless, in the majority of cases, one does not see any bruising to the strap muscles or other soft tissues. The explanation for this may be that, in most of the cases, there has been occlusion of both carotid and jugular systems, thus creating a 'bloodless' field in the vicinity of the ligature. Furthermore, once the ligature is tight around the neck, no further force is required to cause death. The incidence of such injuries has been reported in two large studies of hanging deaths, as ranging from 5.6% from 233 cases (Samarasekera and Cooke, 1996) to 9.3% from 755 cases (Tugaleva et al., 2016).

## Fracture of the Larynx and Hyoid Bone

It is surprising how often in older publications fractures of the larynx and hyoid bone were thought to be rare, or at best, uncommon. Indeed, Gordon and Shapiro (1975) stated that 'the hyoid bone is rarely, if ever, fractured in hanging, and fractures to the laryngeal cartilages are relatively uncommon'. Bowen (1982), in a retrospective study of 201 cases, did not find any fractures of laryngeal cartilages even though the highest incidence of hanging was in persons over 50 years of age. The deficiency of such retrospective studies is clear and well illustrated by Paparo and Siegel (1984). In their retrospective series of 134 hangings, they found 20 laryngeal and hyoid fractures (15%), whereas from 26 cases studied prospectively, 12 fractures were found (46%). Discrepancies between various authors may be partially explained by the ages of victims. However, I suspect that, particularly with undisplaced fractures of the laryngeal cartilages or hyoid bone, and in most cases with little accompanying haemorrhage, a large number of them remain undetected.

Later publications give a more detailed assessment of the incidence and distribution of laryngo-hyoid fractures and acknowledge the wide discrepancy seen in different studies. Wilson et al. (2023) recently reviewed by meta-analysis the frequency and pattern of laryngo-hyoid and cervical fractures in cases of suicide by hanging from 20 studies (comprising 8,523 cases). They found that the combined frequency of neck fractures in the publications they assessed was 38%, indicating that just over one-third of individuals who died from suicide by hanging had discernible fractures of the neck. The frequency from these studies showed a wide range of fractures between 6% (Meera and Singh, 2011) and 75% (Suárez-Peñaranda et al., 2008). The thyroid cartilages were more frequently fractured than the hyoid bone, occurring at frequencies of 46% and 35.5%, respectively. Fractures occurring at both the hyoid bone and thyroid cartilage in the same individual had a frequency of just under 16%. The generally low frequency of fractures may be explained by partial suspension or the lack of a long drop if fully suspended. This is in contrast to the more commonly recognised judicial form of hanging, where the long drop causes an abrupt arrest of the body and typically results in neck fractures. In suicide cases with partial suspension, the pressure and force required to cause laryngeal and cervical fractures are much less, with the cause of death in suicide hangings often attributed to the effects of cerebral hypoxia.

## Cervical Vertebral Injuries

Cervical fractures and dislocations are seen in judicial hangings (see below) but are infrequent in suicide deaths. Fractures of the cervical vertebrae had the lowest frequency, being present in only 3.78% of cases (Wilson et al., 2023) with less difference between the studies they examined. The range of eight studies that described cervical vertebral fractures had a very low frequency of such injuries, from 0% (Sharma et al., 2005) to 4% (Russo et al., 2016).

Nikolić and Živković (2014), in their retrospective study of short drop suicidal hangings, found cervical spine injuries in 25 of 766 cases (3.3%). The average age of such injuries was 71.9 ± 10.7 years (range 39–88 years). In 16 of the 25 cases, the ligature knot was in the anterior position. The most common pattern of cervical spine injury included partial or complete disruption of the anterior longitudinal ligament and widening of the lower cervical spine disc spaces, associated with the absence of hyoid–laryngeal fractures. The lower cervical spine was the most common site of injury in 22 of 25 cases, and the most common cervical spine injury pattern in the series included disruption of the anterior longitudinal ligament, widened disc space, and no vertebral body displacement (17 of 22 cases), while vertebral body fractures were less common (5 of 22 hangings). Such injuries were found to be mainly associated with an anterior knot position and may be a consequence of hypertension from loop pressure to the posterior neck and cervical spine. It should also be noted that the largest proportion of injuries was in significantly older subjects in this study, which is in keeping with the experience of the author of this text in relation to blunt force trauma to the neck (see Chapter 11). It is evident that such a comparatively high incidence in older subjects is associated with degenerative changes in the cervical spine, which are known to be predisposing factors for spine injuries.

## Vascular Injury

Transverse intimal tears just below the bifurcation of the common carotid arteries are occasionally seen in hanging, even from a short drop. In a prospective autopsy study of 178 cases of hanging, Hejna (2011), found such tears of the carotid artery, also described as Amussat's sign (Amussat, 1843), in 29 cases (16.1%). There was a significant association between the occurrence of tears in the intimal layer of carotid arteries and the older victims in the cases studied, which was very likely due to atherosclerotic, degenerative age changes in the arteries. The occurrence of such tears was independent of gender, weight, completeness of the victim's body suspension, and position of the ligature knot on the neck. The study also demonstrated that the injuries most likely resulted from a combination of direct compression of the artery by the ligature and indirect stretching because of the gravitational drag produced by the weight of the body.

Stretching causing traumatic lesions of the cervical portion of the vertebral arteries has been reported by Saternus (1984), who examined 36 cases of suicidal hanging. In a quarter of the cases, he found injury to the vessels, consisting of either rupture, intimal tear, or sub-intimal haemorrhage. When perivascular haematomas were also taken into account, the total number of injuries was more than half. There was no correlation between the type of hanging and the level of severity of injury. In none of his cases was the hanging from a prostrate position, and it was assumed that the traction to the neck in all the cases was longitudinal. Kang et al. (2015) report the case of a 54-year-old male who hanged himself by hooking an electric cord around a doorknob to hang and was sitting on the bathroom floor when he was found less than 5 min later. Initial computed tomography of the brain on admission showed a hyperdense right vertebral artery. Two days after admission, their patient remained dependent on a respirator and exhibited fully dilated and fixed pupils in addition to the complete absence of brainstem reflexes and pain response. Electroencephalography showed electrocerebral silence. Follow-up magnetic resonance imaging of the brain demonstrated a mixture of massive intraventricular haemorrhage, left basal ganglia haemorrhage, and bilateral occipital hypoxic–ischaemic lesions.

## MECHANISM OF DEATH

Leaving aside judicial hanging, which is discussed below, one should appreciate that the mode of death in suspension may be complex, with the underlying outcome being cerebral ischaemia in the vast majority of cases from asphyxia. The mechanism of death is an interplay between compression of the jugular veins, carotid arteries, respiratory tract, and vagus nerve stimulation. These four mechanisms, independently or synergistically, cause cerebral ischaemia and death. The first three mechanisms appear to be more important, as they can be related to circumstantial and physical findings, whereas vagal effects are impossible to quantify at autopsy.

The mode of death may be modified by the type of ligature used and whether a fixed or running noose is employed. Nevertheless, it is the degree of suspension that appears to play the most important role in influencing the type of mechanism involved.

When the body is either fully or partially suspended, with the most substantial weight of the body causing constriction of the ligature and with the suspension point being at the back, the main force is directed to the front and sides of the neck. This position produces an upward and backward movement of the base of the tongue to the posterior pharyngeal wall, thus obstructing the upper airway. Nevertheless, it is felt that occlusion of the vessels plays the primary role in such positions. Compromise of the cerebral circulation is severe or total, leading to rapid unconsciousness followed by death, which gradually supervenes in a few minutes. Sauvageau (2009) analysed four filmed hangings and observed rapid loss of consciousness between 13 and 18 seconds. This was closely followed by convulsions (at 14–19 seconds), a complex pattern of decerebrate rigidity (19–21 seconds in most cases), followed by decorticate rigidity between 1 minute and 1 minute 32 seconds. Loss of muscle tone was evident between 1 minute 38 seconds and 2 minute 47 seconds. Very deep respiratory attempts started between 20 and 22 seconds, and the last respiratory attempts were detected between 2 minutes and 2 minutes 4 seconds.

In cases where the body is substantially supported by a surface other than the point of attachment of the ligature, e.g., by the knees in a sitting or almost prostrate position, it is much more likely that occlusion of vessels will be incomplete. Usually, the venous circulation is obstructed, with consequent congestion of the face and neck above the ligature mark. Obstruction of the airway is more likely to occur in these cases.

Rarely, however, a suicidal hanging in which the knot is located at the front and/or has a long drop may cause cervical vertebral and cord damage. In Crompton's case (1986), the ligature passed around the back of the neck, whereas at the front, it was located over the forehead with the knot tied anteriorly. The mechanism in this case was one of hyperextension, with longitudinal distractive forces also acting on the cervical spine.

# TOXICOLOGY IN HANGING CASES

Studies of suicidal hanging in which toxicology has been carried out have shown that a large portion of deaths were found to involve ethanol or other drugs (Austin et al., 2011; Zerbini et al., 2012; Jones et al., 2013). Although pathologists are aware of the value of toxicology in such cases, it is important to reiterate that analyses of blood and urine for alcohol and other drugs provide important information that assists the examiner in having a better understanding of the events leading to the hanging, especially the state of mind of the subject and possible contribution to death. Indeed, if the deceased had been incapacitated by drugs and/or alcohol, the question would need to be asked whether the hanging could have been a homicide staged to appear as a suicide. Furthermore, it is also important to consider whether the taking of noxious substances could have influenced the subject's actions. As it is appreciated, alcohol, for example, may decrease inhibitory functions of the brain and increase impulsive and risk-taking behaviour.

San Nicolas and Lemos (2015) examined the toxicology findings in cases of hanging in the City and County of San Francisco over the three-year period from 2011 to 2013 in order to ascertain if toxicological analyses were justified when the cause of death had already been established without examination for ethanol or drugs. In their series of 102 hangings (25 females; 77 males), the manner of death in 99 of these cases was suicidal, with two accidental and one undetermined death. The average age of decedents was just under 44 years (the youngest was an 11-year-old male and the oldest was an 86-year-old female). In 33 deaths, toxicology was negative, while 69 cases had at least one positive toxicology result. Females were equally likely to have negative or positive results, but males were 37.5% more likely to have positive toxicology ($n = 56$) rather than negative toxicology ($n = 21$). For females, alcohol, mirtazapine, venlafaxine, and trazodone were the top psychoactive substances in peripheral blood. For males, alcohol, THC, cocaine, amphetamine, methamphetamine, bupropion, and diphenhydramine were the top psychoactive substances in blood.

# ACCIDENTAL HANGING

## Adults

Accidental hanging, when not related to autoerotic asphyxia in adults, is rarely reported. In the few that have been recorded, a large proportion were intoxicated with alcohol or drugs or possibly associated with some form of mental incapacity.

Cases involving entanglement in clothing causing accidental hanging were seen in a number of instances, such as the case reported by Nurhantari et al. (2002) of a 67-year-old man who was found dead in a sitting position with the collar of his sweater hanging off the brake handle of a motorcycle. The alcohol levels in his blood and urine were 284 mg/100 ml and 352 mg/100 ml, respectively. It was concluded that he had died from hanging by the sweater. The author thought that when he became inebriated, he lost consciousness and fell, with the collar of his sweater hanging from the brake handle of the motorcycle. A further unusual accidental hanging is reported by Kodikara and Alagiyawanna (2011) of a 25-year-old man, who was in a state of morphine-induced central nervous system depression, and was found dead in a sitting position with the collar of his T-shirt hanging off a jutting-out root of a tree. The hanged collar acted as a ligature compressing the neck.

Historical accounts of persons who have suspended themselves for public entertainment with tragic or near-tragic consequences are given by Taylor (1891) and Chowne (1847). Taylor describes how an American diver by the name of Scott met his untimely death – the story serves to illustrate how slight the compression of the neck may be for unconsciousness to occur. Scott publicly experimented with hanging, and on that last occasion he did so, it is probable that a slight shifting of the ligature from under the mandible caused sufficient compression of the throat between the chin and the larynx to produce rapid asphyxia. He was left on the scaffolding for 13 minutes because the spectators thought he was safe and was only prolonging the experiment, as his legs were touching the platform.

Chowne describes the case of John Hornshaw (stage name, Monsieur Gouffe), part of whose act was to

> make a loop, with a fixed knot (which could neither slip nor draw around his throat in any way) and then to place his head within the loop, putting the rope behind the lower jaw and letting the two sides of the loop pass up behind the ear.

During his act, he remained hanging for an average of 10–15 minutes. There were three occasions when Hornshaw 'mismanaged' the rope and lost consciousness, but on each occasion, there was help on hand to rescue him. Chowne reports Hornshaw's description of the sensations he experienced:

> He could hardly recollect anything that happened to him in the rope; he lost his senses all at once; the instant the rope got in the wrong place he felt as if he could not get his breath; as if some great weight was at his feet; could not move only to draw himself up; felt as if he wanted to loosen himself, but never thought of his hands.

Hornshaw added, 'you cannot move your arms or legs to save yourself; you cannot raise your arms; you cannot think.'

## Children

Many reported cases have involved accidents in infants and children. Nixon et al. (1995) examined the causes, classification, and prevention of mechanical asphyxial deaths in children under 15 years of age who had died as a result of choking, suffocation, or strangulation in England and Wales during the years 1990 and 1991 from data provided by The Office of Population Censuses and Surveys. The age distribution of the 36 hanging cases demonstrated two distinct age groups. The younger group (0–7 years) included 15 victims of accidental hanging who were killed by cords, necklaces, or clothing around the house. The group of older boys over 8 years of age were cases of self-initiated hanging. In the majority of cases, the boys were involved in play that had gone badly wrong. In three cases, there had been an emotional disturbance before the event that was possibly suicide, and in one case, there was evidence of autoerotic activity.

Sturner et al. (1976) reported 45 accidental asphyxial deaths in young children and infants, and amongst these were three hangings. One occurred when a broken cot, which had been held loosely together with rope, became partially separated, and the resulting space was responsible for the infant becoming entangled in the strands. The other two cases, previously cited by DiMaio (1973), both involved a pacifier attached around the infant's neck by a string. In one case, it became entangled with a cross-bar on the cot, and in the other, it became entangled with the corner post of the cot. Cooke et al. (1989) reported a case where a 14-month-old girl was partially suspended by her dress that was caught on an external wing nut of the crib. More recently, in relation to cribs and other objects, Dogan et al. (2010) retrospectively investigated 201 hanging deaths between 1998 and 2007 and found that 12 of 13 accidental hangings occurred in children. In seven of the cases, the accidental hanging involved a scarf that wrapped around swing-like cradles and is intended to prevent infants from falling. They concluded that accidental hanging deaths can be reduced by replacing swing-like cradles with cribs that are designed for children, as well as removing ropes in and around the house and preventing children from reaching and/or playing with rope-like objects.

# SEXUAL (AUTOEROTIC) ASPHYXIA

This form of paraphilia is recognised in all age groups, from adolescents to the elderly. It is much more common in males and is only occasionally reported in females. However, it may well be underestimated, as changes may be more subtle than in males (Byard et al., 1993; Behrendt et al., 2002; Sauvageau and Racette, 2006). The subjects may cross-dress, and frequently, pornographic material and other aids to masturbation are found nearby. The usual method of sexual gratification in these cases is to produce partial asphyxiation by the application of pressure on the neck by some form of ligature. The degree of asphyxia is intended to be controlled at will by the subject (Figures 8.9–8.11), together with some form of escape mechanism. Evidence of repeated autoerotic practice may be found, as in the case described by Eckhardt et al. (2018) of a 45-year-old man who was found unclothed on the floor of his bedroom with a belt ligature around the neck. A second rope ligature was loosely wrapped around the decedent's wrists, scrotum, and penis. At autopsy, a healed fracture of the right superior horn of the thyroid cartilage was found and confirmed with three-dimensional (3D) surface scanning and histological examination. An autoerotic death with a deformed thyroid horn caused by an old fracture from the case file of the author of this text is shown in Figure 8.12.

Other methods of sexual asphyxia include the obstruction of the mouth with a plastic bag, pillow, or similar device, including, in one case seen by the author, the use of insulating tape as part of an elaborate bondage procedure. There is also a report in the literature of an abdominal ligature being used together with suspension, resulting in asphyxia due to restriction of diaphragmatic movement (Thibault et al., 1984). In some instances, there is clear evidence of chronic indulgence in this activity.

Wesselius and Bally (1983) observed that there were two categories. The first category consisted of nearly all cases of males carrying out the act alone. The persons within this group were thought to be happy, well-adjusted, and with no suicidal tendencies. The other group consisted mainly of adult males, usually with homosexual preferences. They tended to carry out the procedure in pairs as a means of protection from accidental death. Furthermore, there also tends to be a prominent

**Figure 8.9** Case of sexual asphyxia. (a) The deceased male had been found hanging from a tree dressed in female attire. The photograph was taken after he had been lowered from the tree by cutting through the rope some distance away from the part that had been looped around his neck. Note also the binding of both wrists. (b) Position of the lower end of the rope on the tree showing the cut end. (c) The suspension point, looped and knotted at a forking branch of the trunk. The deceased's feet had slipped from where he had secured himself on the tree when a piece of the material securing his wrists was looped around the main trunk, had torn, resulting in the deceased becoming fully suspended.

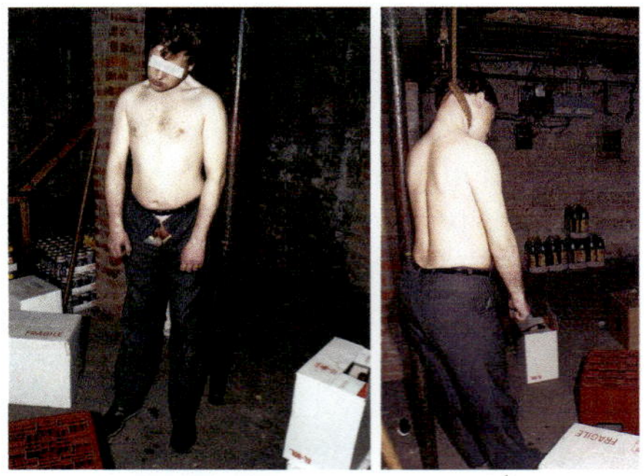

a b

**Figure 8.10** Male found hanging in a cellar of a restaurant/bar (a, anterior view; b, view from right side). He is naked from the waist up, and his trousers are unzipped, revealing his genitalia. His feet are just touching the ground. The suspension point is a beam on the ceiling, and he has fashioned a ligature comprising woven rope with a posterior slip knot.

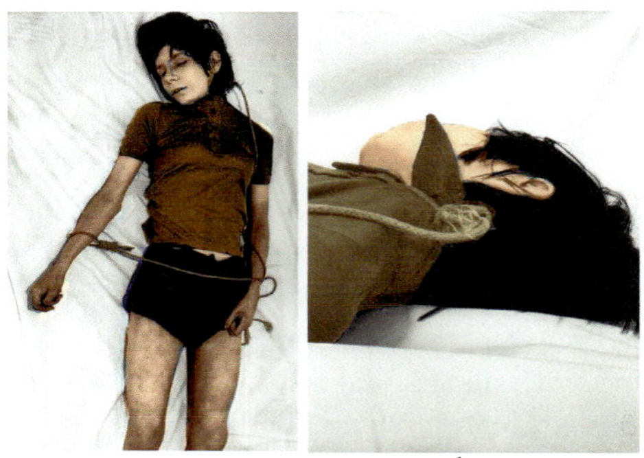

a b

**Figure 8.11** (a) Adolescent boy found at the bottom of a flight of stairs. He had looped the rope around his neck, over the bannister, then tied both wrists with one end. The wrist binding was to allow control of the amount of pressure delivered to his neck. (b) Close-up of the knot, which is below the left ear.

sadomasochistic element in this group. In such cases, one must be aware of the possibility that death may be homicidal. The death of an unwanted partner could easily be achieved by not releasing the rope around the bound partner's neck in time.

There are very few reported cases of live practitioners. Wesselius and Bally's patient, a 24-year-old Caucasian male, had been practising autoerotic asphyxia for ten years. He frequently used a towel or sheet to suspend himself or occasionally wrapped a T-shirt around his neck, crossing it once and pulling it tight to create anoxia and loss of consciousness. On occasions, he would also add bondage by tying his feet together. Immediately, seeing his feet kicking in the air, he would become unconscious and ejaculate. He stated that many times he had wished to stop the practice because he had almost died on several occasions; nevertheless, he found the impulse to repeat it irresistible.

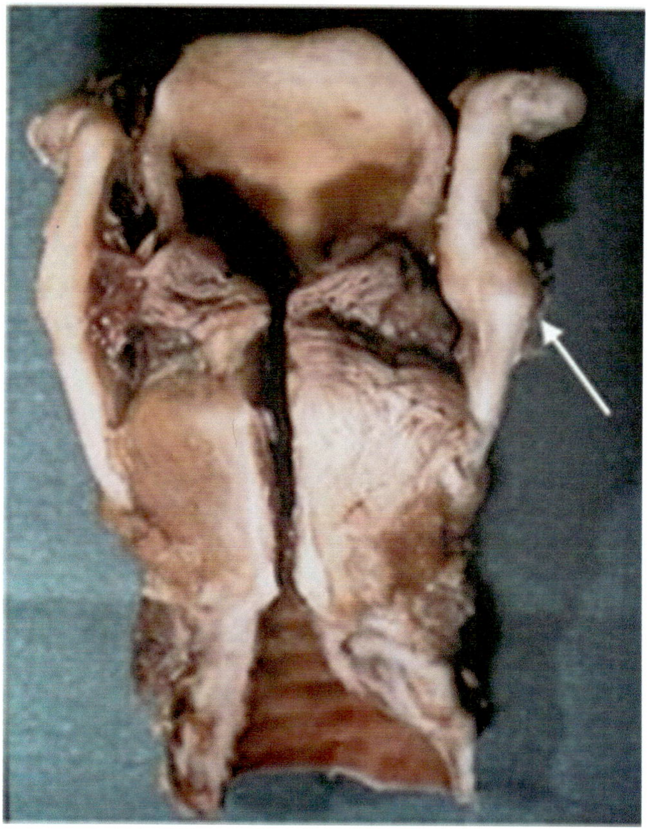

**Figure 8.12** Fixed larynx, posterior view. The right superior cornua of the thyroid cartilage is deformed as a result of an old fracture. The deceased was an autoerotic practitioner and the fracture is likely to have occurred during such activity.

## HOMICIDAL HANGING

Although homicidal hanging is extremely rare, one should always bear the possibility in mind and the importance of differentiating it from suicide. The victim may have been incapacitated in some way, either by being restrained by a number a number of persons, by drugs, or following a physical assault, and then suspended. If the victim is very young, infirm, or elderly, then the task for the assailant is easier. One may find marks of restraint and other injuries to the deceased indicative of a struggle. Seven cases are cited by Dixon Mann (1902), six of which were in children, whose ages ranged from two months to 13 years. In one case recorded by Ogston and cited by Dixon Mann, a woman tied a ligature around her husband's neck while he was asleep and then pulled him up and suspended him with it. More recently, Ruwanpura and Ariyaratne (2010) describe a homicidal hanging of a 32-year-old man who was hanged by his wife and assisted by her boyfriend. The autopsy findings appeared to be those of a suicide, apart from multiple abrasions on the lower legs and a small bruise on the inner lip. These injuries were due to the struggle before death. Furthermore, the victim was under the influence of alcohol. Other recent literature on the subject includes case reports by Vadysinghe and Sivasubramanium (2018), Sharma et al. (2011), and Doberentz et al. (2019).

# SIMULATED SUICIDAL HANGING TO CONCEAL HOMICIDE

One should always bear the possibility of a staged suicide in assessment of the scene, and particularly should take note of the following:

- Signs of dragging to the place of suspension.
- Marks at the point of suspension, which may indicate whether the rope was placed by the victim or by an assailant pulling it over a beam.
- The presence and position of a chair, stool, etc., in relation to the body and height of suspension.

Simulation of a suicidal hanging in order to conceal homicide has occasionally been reported. Srivastava et al. (1987) found three cases among 26 strangulations. I have personally encountered two cases. In one case, the deceased, a 50-year-old female, had received a fatal blow to her lower face and neck, inflicted by her husband, and was then partially suspended from the bannisters at the foot of the stairs. Her clothing was partially dishevelled from dragging, and the telephone receiver had not been replaced after the deceased's daughter, who attempted to phone the police, dropped it and then ran to her neighbour for assistance (Figure 8.13).

In the other case, the deceased, a 29-year-old female, was strangled with a ligature by her husband and then suspended from the stairs to simulate suicidal hanging. At autopsy, in addition to a double ligature mark, she was found to have petechial haemorrhages, facial congestion, bruising and scratch marks to the neck, and numerous small bruises and grazes elsewhere. It was noted that she had 'grip' type bruises to the inner aspects of both upper arms, consistent with having been lifted from behind (Figure 8.14).

In most cases, the internal signs are clearly not those of hanging, although the ligature mark in most instances is indistinguishable. The victim may have been strangled manually or by a ligature, or suffered a blow or other blunt impact to the neck. A notable example is the case of R v Emmet-Dunne, General Court Marshal at Dusseldorf, West Germany, 1953 (Camps, 1959). The killer murdered the victim by delivering a blow to the neck with the side of the hand and then suspended the body with the help of an accomplice. The deceased suffered a vertical fracture to the body of the thyroid cartilage, and there were also vertical tears to both carotid arteries. Although

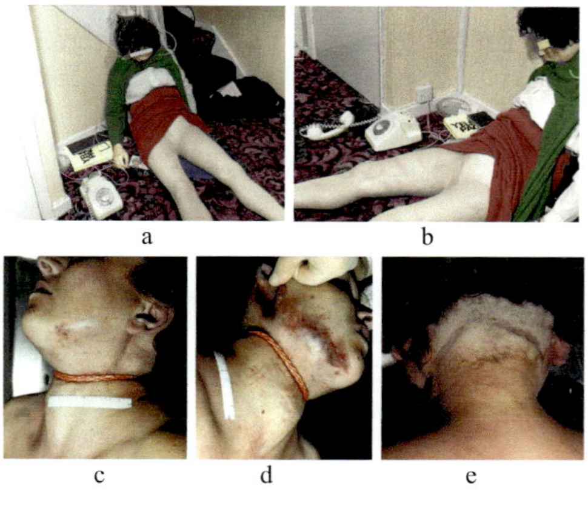

**Figure 8.13** (a) Deceased partially suspended on the staircase with telephone nearby which is off the hook (shown in b). (b) A tight ligature from a plastic flex. (c) Extensive bruising to the mandible and upper neck extending to the post aural region. (d) The back of the head with a V-shaped mark indicating that after suspension, the weight of the body had caused the tight ligature to slip upwards, leaving a fainter lower original mark (see also Chapter 7).

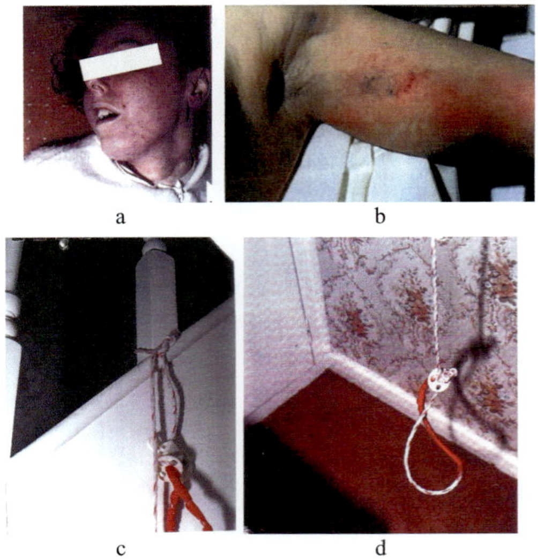

**Figure 8.14** (a) Petechial haemorrhage and congestion are seen on her face as well as a ligature mark. (b) View of left upper inner arm showing perimortem bruising from gripping the arms to lift the deceased shortly after she was strangled. (c) Suspension point looped and tied around bannister. (d) Detail of noose.

the injuries were documented at the first autopsy, their significance was not appreciated until the body was re-examined at a later date.

A challenging and controversial case involved the death of the Italian banker Roberto Calvi, who was found hanging in London on a scaffold below Blackfriars Bridge in June 1982. He was the chairman of Banco Ambrosiano, which collapsed in one of Italy's biggest political scandals. His death was ruled a murder after two coroners' inquests in London and a later independent investigation. This investigation in 1991 concluded that he could not have hanged himself because of the lack of paint and rust on his shoes, demonstrating that he had not walked on the scaffolding (Forensic Access/Cold Cases/Roberto Calvi, 2024). These findings were confirmed after Calvi's body was exhumed in December 1998, on the orders of an Italian court. Furthermore, Calvi's neck injuries were inconsistent with hanging and instead were typical of strangulation. It appears, therefore, that he was strangled and then moved to Blackfriars Bridge, where the hanging was staged. Twenty-five years after his death, five people were acquitted in Rome in June 2007 of conspiracy to murder him.

Of historical interest is the case cited by Forbes (1985). He relates the story of Richard Hunne, who in 1514 was found hanged where he had been detained at Lollard's Tower within London's old St Paul's Cathedral. Eventually, owing to the diligence of the inquest jurors who saw the body and were not convinced that Hunne had hanged himself (they were all familiar with public hangings). The Bishop of London's Chancellor, Dr Horsey, and two others, prior to hanging him, pushed a wire into the victim's nose causing lethal brain injury, fatal haemorrhage, or both, and had also broken his neck.

# UNUSUAL HANGINGS INCLUDING COMPLEX SUICIDES

Occasionally, in addition to the mechanism causing suicidal hangings, other features are seen that are designed to ensure that the suicide is successful. These include binding of the hands and/or feet, as well as placing some form of object, such as a sock or other material, including occasionally the use of a mask, to obstruct the upper airway (Figures 8.15 and 8.16).

In one study, such features were found in a quarter (23.6%) from 72 suicidal hangings (Demirci et al., 2009). Similar cases have been reported by a number of other authors, including Marsh et al. (1982), Sikary et al. (2016), Benomran et al. (2007), and Krzyzanowski (2002). In such cases, due caution is required to exclude any form of criminality. Only a thorough examination of the scene, assessment of the circumstances leading to death, social/medical history of the deceased, in addition to a full autopsy including toxicology, will allow a conclusion to be confidently reached regarding the manner of death.

Hangings, which involve one or more further significant methods of self-injury, are categorised as complex suicides. Complex suicides are rare, their incidence being reported as between 1.5% and 5.6% (Bohnert and Rothschild, 2003). They are further subcategorised into planned and unplanned. An unplanned complex suicide is defined as the use of a different suicide method after the failure of the original method (Wolf et al., 2024). The latter authors reported on three cases of suicidal hanging combined with firearm wounds and emphasised the challenging role of the pathologist in assessing both the manner and method that caused death. In a Canadian study, Racette and Sauvageau (2007) pointed out that in their experience, the combination of hanging and firearm injury was the most common type of complex suicide. In their 14 complex hanging suicides, there was use of firearms in 5 (35.7%). The author of this text examined the case of suicidal hanging in a 55-year-old adult who hanged himself attached to a fence, feet touching the ground. He had managed, prior to hanging, to amputate his right hand with an electric saw, although the fingers were not at the scene and were never found (Figure 8.17). He was also intoxicated with alcohol, the level being 157 mg/100ml. The cause of death was given as hanging, and the other findings indicate his determination to end his life.

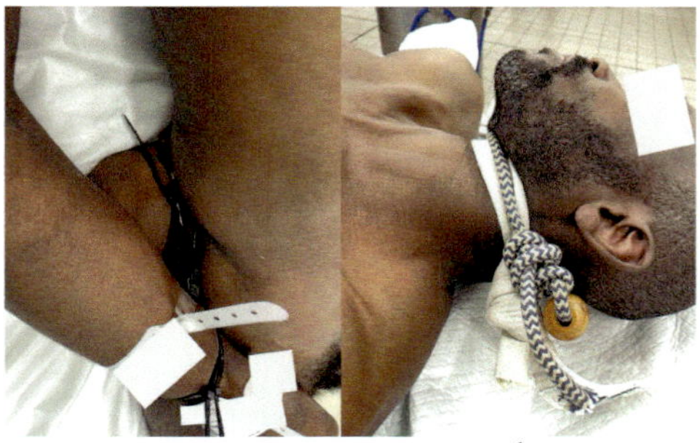

a b

**Figure 8.15** (a) Right arm of the deceased showing his wrists secured from the rear using cable ties. (b) The same subject has also used two ligatures, an outer skipping rope and an inner broader ligature. Both have knots with multiple loops.

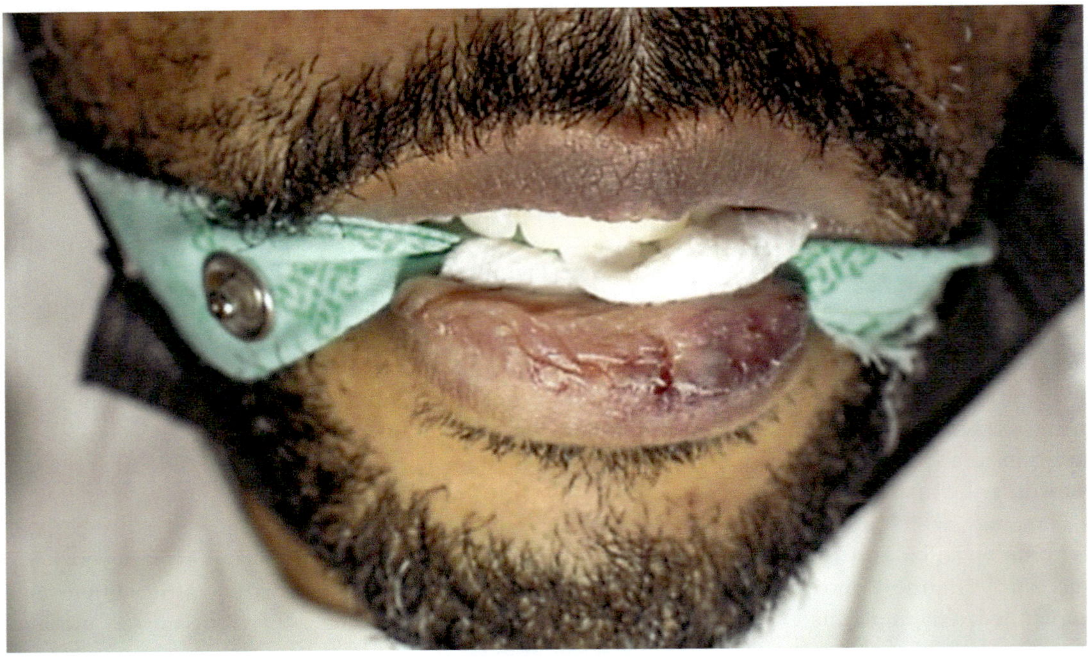

**Figure 8.16** The deceased was found hanging from a window latch. He had used a sock as gag, which he secured with a mask, and bound his hands and feet. He had also left a note indicating his intention to take his life.

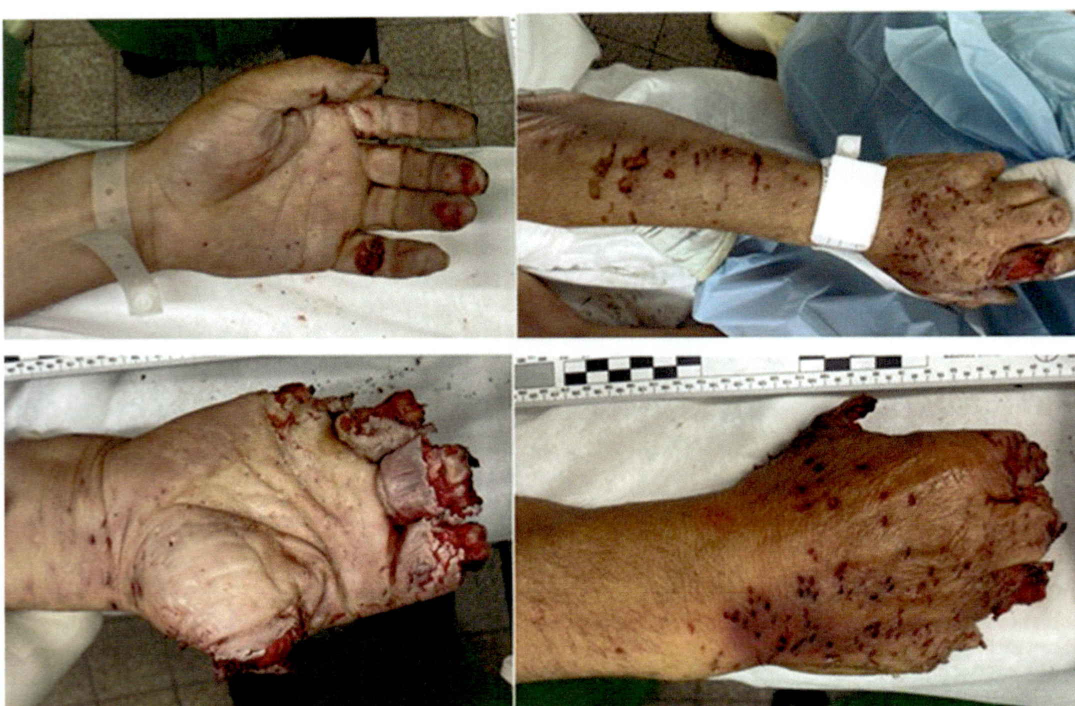

**Figure 8.17** Upper limbs of deceased: Top, left arm; bottom, right arm. The subject had used his left hand to amputate the fingers of his right hand (same case as Figure 8.7). His fingers were not present at the scene and were never found.

# JUDICIAL HANGING

Historically, judicial hangings were recorded in the British Isles in the fifth century by the Jutes, Angles, and Saxons, who derived the practices from their German ancestors. In England, hanging was established as a punishment for homicide by the time of Henry II, and in the Middle Ages, every town, abbey, and nearly all manorial lords had the right to hang. From the twelfth century, the jurisdiction of the royal courts became exclusive. Until 1868, hangings were carried out in public.

In the early days of hanging, the condemned person would be hoisted up from the ground and then allowed to dangle so that death was caused by the effects of slow strangulation. It was not uncommon for the condemned to be taken down from the gallows and successfully resuscitated. Indeed, occasionally the condemned person needed to be hanged two or three times for death to occur, as was the case with the pirate Captain (William) Kidd, who was executed in 1701. Assistance from the hangman was sometimes needed to effect the demise by pulling at the feet or hanging on the condemned person's back to provide the extra weight needed to accomplish the hanging process.

Centuries elapsed with few modifications in hanging techniques. The principal variations included rolling the condemned off a ladder or allowing the individual to tumble off a cart as it was driven away. However, these various methods still resulted in death by slow strangulation and were occasionally unsuccessful. A standardisation of hanging technique was needed to produce more uniform results.

The long drop became standard only in the late eighteenth century. It was probably first introduced in 1784 at the Newgate Prison in London. The drop length, however, could vary considerably, and its unpredictable consequences ranged from slow strangulation when the drop was a few centimetres to decapitation when it was 4 metres or more. In order to standardise the process, in 1866, Haughton published a series of tables establishing the length of drop and size of the rope in relation to the condemned person's weight.

At this time, the importance of the knot placement also became an issue among the medical and judicial professions. In 1865, when the Scottish poisoner Dr Pritchard was publicly hanged (Wood Jones, 1913), the knot of the noose was placed in a subaural position (at the angle of the mandible), and a reasonable drop was employed. The autopsy specimen revealed a fracture at the base of the skull. This fracture was produced by leverage on the temporal bone adjacent to the knot. De Zouche Marshall (1888), after witnessing several hangings, emphasised the importance of the placement of the hangman's knot. Wood carvings prior to the eighteenth century show the hangman's knots to be placed in the now less desirable suboccipital position, during the period when hoisting from the ground was popular. Following implementation of the long drop, the subaural knot was used; subsequently, with further experience, the placement of the knot beneath the chin in the submental position proved to be the most effective. De Zouche Marshall was so convinced of the importance of the submental knot position in producing an effective and reliable means of execution that he devised a chin piece through which the hangman's noose could be routed. This forced the chin into hyperextension, and the rope created a distraction-extension force with more desirable results.

Wood Jones (1913) was able to compare the subaural with the submental knot position by studying two groups of specimens housed at the Royal College of Surgeons Museum in London. The first group consisted of 100 Nubians hanged some 2000 years earlier under the Roman Empire and exhumed in the early twentieth century from the Upper Nile Valley. Wood Jones reported these in an earlier paper (1908). These individuals were thought to have been hanged with the knot in the subaural position because the locations of the fracture of the temporal bone and the fracture line extending across the base of the skull were identical to those in the lesion seen in the autopsy specimen of Dr Pritchard.

The second group of specimens was collected from the Rangoon Central Gaol by Captain CF Fraser (Wood Jones, 1913). These individuals were known to have been hanged with the knot placed in the submental position. All specimens had the characteristic features of a bipedicle fracture. Since the specimens had no soft tissue attached, Wood Jones postulated that the line of separation traversed the disc between the second and third vertebral bodies. He postulated a complete rupture of the posterior and anterior longitudinal ligaments, with severance of the spinal cord between the second and third cervical segments. Uniformly, the body of the axis, the odontoid process, and transverse ligaments were intact.

Vermooten (1921), in an independent study of four individuals similarly hanged, found lesions identical to those described by Wood Jones. It is generally agreed that death commonly occurs from a C2 fracture and a C2–C3 separation from hyperextension and severe elongation of the spine, with complete disruption of the spinal cord at C2–C3.

**Table 8.1** Judicial Hangings of 19 males from Pentonville Prison, London, from 1931 to 1959 (courtesy St Pancras Coroner's Court archive)

| Year executed | Offence | Age | Injuries |
|---|---|---|---|
| 1931 | Murder (striking the victim on the head with an instrument) | 61 | Fracture dislocation of the cervical vertebrae (level not stated) |
| 1932 | Murder (cause of victim's death not stated) | 25 | Fracture dislocation between C3 and C4 |
| 1937 | Murder (victim strangled) | 24 | Fracture dislocation between C1 and C2 with severance of the spinal cord |
| 1937 | Murder (victim strangled) | 53 | Fracture dislocation between C1 and C2 |
| 1937 | Murder (victim strangled) | 22 | Fracture dislocation between C3 and C4 |
| 1943 | Murder (victim strangled) | 19 | Brain completely torn at junction of pons and the midbrain. Dislocation between C4 and C5, spinal cord severed |
| 1944 | Murder (victim stabbed) | 37 | Spinal cord severed with dislocation between C2 and C3 |
| 1944 | Treachery | 59 | Brain torn at junction of pons and medulla. Dislocation between C4 and C5 |
| 1945 | Murder (victim shot with a revolver) | 23 | Crushing between medulla and spinal cord with dislocation between C3 and C4 |
| 1946 | Treachery | 27 | Dislocation between C2 and C3 with spinal cord rupture. Thyroid cartilage fracture |
| 1946 | Murder (victim died by asphyxiation) | 29 | Complete separation of the spinal cord at C2–C3 which was also dislocated |
| 1946 | Murder (victim died from strangulation) | 23 | Dislocation between C2 and C3 and crushing of the spinal cord at that level |
| 1946 | Murder (victim died from shooting) | 45 | Spinal cord completely severed between C3 and C4 and hyoid bone torn away from thyroid cartilage |
| 1947 | Murder (victim died from shooting) | 39 | Dislocation between C3 and C4. Injury to brain and spinal cord |
| 1947 | Murder (victim shot with a revolver) | 23 | Fracture dislocation between C2 and C3 with spinal cord laceration |
| 1950 | Murder (victim strangled) | 25 | Fracture dislocation between C3 and C4 with transection of the cord |
| 1951 | Murder (victim was stabbed) | 29 | Fracture dislocation between C2 and C3 with spinal cord injury |
| 1959 | Murder (victim's cause of death not stated) | 30 | Dislocation between C3 and C4 with separation of the cord. Fractured hyoid bone and thyroid cartilage |
| 1959 | Murder (victim's cause of death not stated) | 25 | Dislocation between C2 and C3. Fractured hyoid bone and thyroid cartilage |

The author surveyed a series of judicial hangings carried out at Pentonville Prison, London, between 1931 and 1959 (unpublished material; Table 8.1). It was found that in nearly all cases, the point of suspension was near the angle of the mandible on the left side. The injuries found were cervical dislocations in all cases, and occasionally, cervical fractures were described together with severe spinal cord and/or brain stem injury, as well as fractures to the laryngo-hyoid complex. The most common levels of cervical injury were at C2/C3 and C3/C4 (seven cases each). The other injury levels seen less frequently were at CI/C2 and C4/C5 (two cases each). In one case, the injury level was not stated. In nearly all hangings, instantaneous death was said to have occurred, although in two cases, there were signs of asphyxia.

## References


Ajdacic-Gross V, Weiss MG, Ring M, Hepp U, Bopp M, Gutzwiller F, Rössler W. Methods of suicide: International suicide patterns derived from the WHO mortality database. *Bull World Health Organ*. 2008 Sep;86(9):726–732.

Amussat JZ. *Recherches experimentales sur les blessures des artéres et des veines. Résumé des trois mémoires ens à l'Academie royale des Sciences*. Paris 1843.

Austin AE, van den Heuvel C, Byard RW. Causes of community suicides among indigenous South Australians. *J Forensic Leg Med*. 2011 Oct;18(7):299–301. doi: 10.1016/j.jflm.2011.06.002. Epub 2011 July 22. PMID: 21907931.

Behrendt N, Buhl N, Seidl S. The lethal paraphiliac syndrome: Accidental autoerotic deaths in four women and a review of the literature. *Int J Legal Med*. 2002 June;116(3):148–152.

Bennewith O, Gunnell D, Kapur N, Turnbull P, Simkin S, Sutton L, Hawton K. Suicide by hanging: Multicentre study based on coroners' records in England. *Br J Psychiatry*. 2005 Mar;186:260–261. doi: 10.1192/bjp.186.3.260. PMID: 15738509.

Benomran FA, Masood SE, Hassan AI, Mohammad AA. Masking and bondage in suicidal hanging: a case report. *Med Sci Law*. 2007 Apr;47(2):177–180. doi: 10.1258/rsmmsl.47.2.177. PMID: 17520966.

Bohnert M, Rothschild MA. Complex suicides by self-incineration. *Forensic Sci Int*. 2003 Jan 28;131(2-3):197–201. doi: 10.1016/s0379-0738(02)00449-8. PMID: 12590059.

Bowen DAL. Hanging – a review. *Forensic Sci Int*, 1982;20: 247–249.

Byard RW, Hucker SJ, Hazelwood RR. Fatal and near-fatal autoerotic asphyxial episodes in women. Characteristic features based on a review of nine cases. *Am J Forensic Med Pathol*. 1993 Mar;14(1):70–73.

Camps FE. The case of Emmett-Dunne. *Med Leg J (Cambridge)*. 1959;27:156–161.

Chisnall RC. Distinguishing between homicide and suicide knots and ligatures: A comparative analysis of case and survey data. *J Forensic Sci*. 2021 Jan;66(1):209–228. doi: 10.1111/1556-4029.14567. Epub 2020 Sep 23. PMID: 32966611.

Chowne WD. Case of accidental strangulation with recovery. *Lancet*. 1847;1:403–405.

Commins C, Bolster M, Mulligan L. To investigate the pattern of neck injuries and the role of toxicology in cases of hanging and manual/homicidal ligature strangulation in Ireland between 2016–2020: A retrospective review and analysis. *J Forensic Leg Med*. 2024 Apr;103:102686. doi: 10.1016/j.jflm.2024.102686. Epub 2024 Apr 28. PMID: 38692099.

Cooke CT, Cadden GA, Hilton JM. Hanging deaths in children. *Am J Forensic Med Pathol*. 1989 June;10(2):98–104. doi: 10.1097/00000433-198906000-00003. PMID: 2741878.

Crompton MR. Fronto-cranial suspension--an unusual form of hanging. *Med Sci Law*. 1986 July;26(3):203–206. doi: 10.1177/002580248602600306. PMID: 3747764.

Davison A, Marshall TK. Hanging in Northern Ireland -a survey. *Med Sci Law*. 1986;26:23–28.

Demirci S, Dogan KH, Erkol Z, Deniz I. Precautions taken to avoid abandoning the act of hanging and reducing pain in suicidal hanging cases. *Am J Forensic Med Pathol*. 2009 Mar;30(1):32–35. doi: 10.1097/PAF.0b013e3181873f40. PMID: 19237850.

DiMaio JM. Letter: Accidental hangings due to pacifiers. *JAMA*. 1973 Nov 12;226(7):790. doi: 10.1001/jama.1973.03230070050024. PMID: 4800639.

Dixon Mann J. *Forensic Medicine and Toxicology*, 3rd edn. Charles Griffiths, London, 1902, pp. 203–207.

Doberentz E, Markwerth P, Madea B. Differentiation of homicidal or suicidal strangulation. *Forensic Sci Int*. 2019 Aug;301: e44–e48.

Dogan KH, Demirci S, Erkol Z, Gulmen MK. Accidental hanging deaths in children in Konya, Turkey between 1998 and 2007. *J Forensic Sci*. 2010 May;55(3):637–641. doi: 10.1111/j.1556-4029.2010.01320.x. Epub 2010 Feb 25. PMID: 20202070.

Eckhardt M, Shah K, Bois M, Maleszewski J, Moore K, Lin P. Healed fracture of superior horn of thyroid cartilage in autoerotic asphyxia: An indication of prior activity? A case report utilizing 3D scanning and printing of the larynx. *Acad Forensic Pathol*. 2018 Mar;8(1):170–179. doi: 10.23907/2018.012. Epub 2018 Mar 7. PMID: 31240033; PMCID: PMC6474459.

Forbes TR. *Surgeons at the Bailey*. Yale University Press, Newhaven Conn. And London, 1985, pp. 75–82.

Forensic Casebook. www.forensic-access.co.uk/cold-cases/roberto-calvi/ (accessed February 2024).

Gordon I, Shapiro H.A. *Forensic Medicine. A Guide to Principles*. Churchill Livingstone, Edinburgh, 1975, p. 96

Gunnell D, Bennewith O, Hawton K, Simkin S, Kapur N. The epidemiology and prevention of suicide by hanging: A systematic review. *Int J Epidemiol*. 2005 Apr;34(2):433–442. doi: 10.1093/ije/dyh398. Epub 2005 Jan 19. PMID: 15659471.

Haughton S. On hanging considered from a mechanical and physiological point of view. *Phil Mag & J Sci*. 4th series, 1866;32: 23–24.

Hejna P. Amussat's sign in hanging--A prospective autopsy study. *J Forensic Sci*. 2011 Jan;56(1):132–135. doi: 10.1111/j.1556-4029.2010.01548.x. Epub 2010 Sep 14. PMID: 20840289.

Jones AW, Holmgren A, Ahlner J. Toxicology findings in suicides: concentrations of ethanol and other drugs in femoral blood in victims of hanging and poisoning in relation to age and gender of the deceased. *J Forensic Leg Med*. 2013 Oct;20(7):842–847. doi: 10.1016/j.jflm.2013.06.027. Epub 2013 Aug 8. PMID: 24112333.

Kang I, Kim JS, Lee KS. An unusual lethal cerebrovascular complication of near hanging: traumatic injury of the vertebral artery. *Acta Neurol Belg*. 2015 Dec;115(4):677–679. doi: 10.1007/s13760-015-0456-6. Epub 2015 Mar 18. PMID: 25784637.

Kodikara S, Alagiyawanna R. Accidental hanging by a T-shirt collar in a man with morphine intoxication: An unusual case. *Am J Forensic Med Pathol*. 2011 Sep;32(3):260–262. doi: 10.1097/PAF.0b013e3182186fac. PMID: 21464693.

Komar D, Denic N, Marsh B, Rumbolt N. Hangings in Newfoundland and Labrador: A 40-year retrospective analysis of medical examiner data. *J Forensic Sci*. 2022 July;67(4):1557–1564. doi: 10.1111/1556-4029.15008. Epub 2022 Feb 5. PMID: 35122244.

Krzyzanowski M, Jankowski Z, Pieśniak D, Wilmanowska A. Przypadki powieszeń ze skrepowanymi kończynami--samobójstwo, zabójstwo czy wypadek [Cases of hanging with bound limbs--suicide, homicide or accident]. *Arch Med Sadowej Kryminol*. 2002 Oct-Dec;52(4):371–379. Polish. PMID: 14669684.

Luke JL, Raey DT, Eisele JW, Bonelle HJ. Correlation of circumstances with pathological findings in asphyxia deaths by hangng: A prospective study of 61 cases from Seattle. WA. *J Forensic Sci*. 1985;30:1140–1147.

Marsh TO, Burkhardt RP, Swinehart JW. Self-inflicted hanging with bound wrists and a gag. *Am J Forensic Med Pathol*. 1982 Dec;3(4):367–369. doi: 10.1097/00000433-198212000-00017. PMID: 7165029.

McCabe M, Fyzul NN, Mulligan L, Curtis M, Cassidy M. Review of the pattern of traumatic limb lesions sustained in cases of hanging. *J Forensic Leg Med*. 2020 Jan;69:101890. doi: 10.1016/j.jflm.2019.101890. Epub 2019 Dec 23. PMID: 32056808.

Meera T, Singh M. Pattern of neck findings in suicidal hanging a study in Manipur. *J Indian Forensic Sci*. 2011;33:350–352.

Nikolić S, Živković V. Cervical spine injuries in suicidal hanging without a long-drop--patterns and possible underlying mechanisms of injury: An autopsy study. *Forensic Sci Med Pathol*. 2014 June;10(2):193–197. doi: 10.1007/s12024-014-9550-y. Epub 2014 Mar 21. PMID: 24652079.

Nixon JW, Kemp AM, Levene S, Sibert JR. Suffocation, choking, and strangulation in childhood in England and Wales: Epidemiology and prevention. *Arch Dis Child*. 1995 Jan;72(1):6–10. doi: 10.1136/adc.72.1.6. PMID: 7717743; PMCID: PMC1510983.

Nurhantari Y, Asano M, Nushida H, Nagasaki Y, Kudo R, Nakagawa K, Adachi J, Ueno Y. Accidental hanging by a sweater: An unusual case. *Am J Forensic Med Pathol*. 2002 June;23(2):199–201. doi: 10.1097/00000433-200206000-00018. PMID: 12040269.

Office for National Statistics (ONS), released 06 September 2022, ONS website, statistical bulletin, Suicides in England and Wales: 2021 registrations.

Office of Population Censuses and Surveys. OPCS Monitor PPI 93/1. London: OPCS, 1993.

Paparo GP, Siegel H. Neck markings and fractures in suicidal hangings. *Forensic Sci Int*. 1984 Jan;24(1):27–35. doi: 10.1016/0379-0738(84)90148-8. PMID: 6698449.

Racette S, Sauvageau A. Planned and unplanned complex suicides: A 5-year retrospective study. *J Forensic Sci*. 2007 Mar;52(2):449–452. doi: 10.1111/j.1556-4029.2007.00387.x. PMID: 17316249.

Russo MC, Verzeletti A, Piras M, De Ferrari F. Hanging deaths: A retrospective study regarding 260 cases. *Am J Forensic Med Pathol*. 2016 Sep;37(3):141–145. doi: 10.1097/PAF.0000000000000239. PMID: 27281442.

Ruwanpura R, Ariyaratne C. A homicide by suspension. *Med Sci Law*. 2010 Oct;50(4):224–227.

Samarasekera A, Cooke C. The pathology of hanging deaths in Western Australia. *Pathology*. 1996 Nov;28(4):334–338. doi: 10.1080/00313029600169294. PMID: 9007952.

San Nicolas AC, Lemos NP. Toxicology findings in cases of hanging in the City and County of San Francisco over the 3-year period from 2011 to 2013. *Forensic Sci Int*. 2015 Oct;255:146–155. doi: 10.1016/j.forsciint.2015.07.006. Epub 2015 July 13. PMID: 26243801.

Saternus KS. Injury of the vertebral artery in suicidal hanging. *Forensic Sci Int*. 1984;25:265–275.

Sauvageau A, Racette S. Autoerotic deaths in the literature from 1954 to 2004: A review. *J Forensic Sci*. 2006 Jan;51(1):140–146.

Sauvageau A. Agonal sequences in four filmed hangings: Analysis of respiratory and movement responses to asphyxia by hanging. *J Forensic Sci*. 2009 Jan;54(1):192–194. doi: 10.1111/j.1556-4029.2008.00910.x. Epub 2008 Nov 1. PMID: 19040672.

Sharma BR, Singh VP, Harish D. Neck structure injuries in Hanging--comparing retrospective and prospective studies. *Med Sci Law*. 2005 Oct;45(4):321–30. doi: 10.1258/rsmmsl.45.4.321. PMID: 16302378.

Sharma L, Khanagwal VP, Paliwal PK. Homicidal hanging. *Leg Med (Tokyo)*. 2011 Sep;13(5):259–261.

Sikary AK, Behera C, Murty OP, Rautji R. Hands Tied with Bag Full of Books in Suicidal Hanging. *J Forensic Sci*. 2016 Jan;61 Suppl 1:S265–S267. doi: 10.1111/1556-4029.12930. Epub 2015 Sep 9. PMID: 26352727.

Srivastava AK, Das Gupta SM, Tripathi CB. A study of fatal strangulation cases in Varanasi (India). *Am J Forensic Med Pathol*. 1987 Sep;8(3):220–224.

Sturner WQ, Spruill FG, Smith RA, Lene WJ. Accidental asphyxia involving infants and young children. *J Forensic Sci*. 1976;21:483–487.

Suárez-Peñaranda JM, Alvarez T, Miguéns X, Rodríguez-Calvo MS, de Abajo BL, Cortesão M, Cordeiro C, Vieira DN, Muñoz JI. Characterization of lesions in hanging deaths. *J Forensic Sci*. 2008 May;53(3):720–723. doi: 10.1111/j.1556-4029.2008.00700.x. PMID: 18471222.

Taylor AS. *A Manual of Medical Jurisprudence*, 12 edn (ed T. Stevenson), J and A Churchill, London, 1891, p. 413.

Thibault R, Spencer JD, Bishop JW, Hibler NS. An unusual autoerotic death: Asphyxia with an abdominal ligature. *J Forensic Sci*. 1984 Apr;29(2):679–684.

Tugaleva E, Gorassini DR, Shkrum MJ. Retrospective analysis of hanging deaths in Ontario. *J Forensic Sci*. 2016 Nov;61(6):1498–1507. doi: 10.1111/1556-4029.13179. Epub 2016 Aug 12. PMID: 27514837.

Uzün I, Büyük Y, Gürpinar K. Suicidal hanging: Fatalities in Istanbul retrospective analysis of 761 autopsy cases. *J Forensic Leg Med*. 2007 Oct;14(7):406–409. doi: 10.1016/j.jflm.2007.01.002. Epub 2007 Mar 26. PMID: 17720591.

Vadysinghe AN, Sivasubramanium M. Anesthetized by chloroform before hanging. *Forensic Sci Med Pathol*. 2018 Sep;14(3):381–385.

Vermooten W. A study of the fracture of the epistropheus due to hanging – with anote on causes of death. *Anat. Rec*. 1921;20: 305–311.

Wesselius CL, Bally R. A male with autoerotic asphyxia syndrome. *Am J Forensic Med Pathol*. 1983 Dec;4(4):341–344.

Wilson R, McFadden C, Rowbotham S. A meta-analytic review of the frequency and patterning of laryngohyoid and cervical fractures in cases of suicide by hanging. *J Forensic Sci*. 2023 May;68(3):731–742. doi: 10.1111/1556-4029.15234. Epub 2023 Mar 20. PMID: 36938845.

Wolf PM, Dettmeyer R, Holz F, Birngruber CG. Complex suicides involving the use of firearms and hanging: A retrospective study and review of the literature. *Leg Med (Tokyo)*. 2024 July;69:102337. doi: 10.1016/j.legalmed.2023.102337. Epub 2023 Oct 20. PMID: 37926655.

Wood Jones F. The examination of the bodies of 100 men executed in Nubia in Roman times. *Br Med J*. 1908;1:736–737.

Wood Jones F. The ideal lesion produced by judicial hanging. *Lancet*. 1913;1:53.

Zerbini T, Ponce Jde C, Mayumi Sinagawa D, Barbosa Cintra R, Muñoz DR, Leyton V. Blood alcohol levels in suicide by hanging cases in the state of Sao Paulo, Brazil. *J Forensic Leg Med*. 2012 July;19(5):294–296. doi: 10.1016/j.jflm.2012.02.022. Epub 2012 Mar 16. PMID: 22687772.
De Zouche Marshall JJ. Judicial hanging. *Br Med J*. 1888;2:779–782.

# CHAPTER 9

## INTERNAL AIRWAY OBSTRUCTION

*Peter Vanezis*



DOI: 10.4324/9781003658467-9

# INTRODUCTION

In this chapter, internal obstruction of the airway includes any obstruction involving any part of the airway within the neck. The term choking primarily refers to partial or complete blockage of the airway internally. Such blockage also includes external pressure from structures within the neck that are external to the air passages. Some authors also use the term smothering to include internal airway obstruction up to the level of the epiglottis (Sauvageau and Boghossian, 2010), although most authorities understand the phrase to mean obstruction of the mouth and nose externally.

# MECHANISM OF DEATH IN CHOKING

Mechanical asphyxia is the most common mechanism of death in choking. Nevertheless, death occasionally occurs very rapidly, with no visible asphyxial signs. When a full post-mortem examination is carried out and there are no physical findings to account for death, one must consider whether death has resulted from cardiac arrest following reflex vagal inhibition (see also 'café coronary' below). Such a conclusion, however, should not be arrived at lightly, and only after careful consideration of the circumstances surrounding death. It should be appreciated that where findings are negative, except for regurgitated food particles in the airways, the latter should not be assumed to be the cause of death. They should be evaluated critically, as regurgitation may have occurred as a terminal event during the process of dying.

Laryngeal spasm may be associated with choking although at autopsy, unless there is swelling or injury to the larynx, its detection is elusive. The object causing choking need not be large, but it may cause a great deal of irritation. Sudden regurgitation of acidic gastric fluid may have such an effect.

# ACCIDENTAL CHOKING

The most common manner of choking is accidental and caused by objects becoming lodged in the throat. Saccomanno et al. (2023) emphasised the need for awareness of the various risk factors that predispose individuals to choking to prevent its occurrence. Indeed, three of the most common risks for choking in general are neurological disorders, dysphagia, and dental issues (few or no teeth, unstable or unsuitable prostheses, or orthodontic appliances), particularly in the very young, elderly, psychiatric, or infirm persons, where the ability to swallow or masticate is severely impaired.

The first few years of life, when young children are learning to eat solid food and experimenting by putting all manner of objects into their mouths, are clearly the most hazardous (Sturner et al., 1976); Mittleman, 1984). The vast majority of such deaths in children occur between two months and four years of age. The size of the offending object will correspond with the level of obstruction. Foreign objects that impact in the supraglottic/glottic area are about 2.5 cm or larger, and those that lodge in the glottic region measure between 0.5 cm and 2.5 cm. The types of food that are dangerous are those that have a rounded shape, are hard, and do not break down or crumble easily.

Bamber et al. (2014) from a retrospective survey of 2165 autopsies over a 16-year period on individuals between the ages of seven days and 18 years, found ten deaths from aspiration of a foreign body. Almost half of the cases occurred before the age of two years, and the sex balance was equal. One child had an underlying medical condition, neuroaxonal dystrophy, which might have impaired swallowing and predisposed them to aspiration of a foreign body, but had been reported as being able to eat and drink normally. All but one of the cases were associated with food, four of which involved aspiration of grapes. At autopsy, the foreign body was found in only three cases. In the other infants, the offending object had been removed by the emergency services or in the emergency department.

Dunbar and Kramer (1981) emphasise that foreign bodies that lodge in the larynx are generally thin and flat. Because the laryngeal fissure is sagittal in orientation, the foreign body becomes arrested at, or just below the vocal cords in the sagittal plane and may excite an inflammatory reaction with oedema.

In adults, foreign bodies, and in particular, dental material, often become lodged in the larynx as a result of trauma. Sometimes they are revealed only at the time of endotracheal intubation. Nash (1976) reports a 19-year-old male with a head injury who inhaled a dental plate that was found 60 hours after the injury. Köse et al. (2014) reported the case of a 52-year-old male patient who had accidentally aspirated the front part of his lower dental prosthesis, which was extracted using rigid bronchoscopy.

The author of this text has seen a case of choking in a 38-year-old woman with a closed tracheostomy site, which had developed a fibrous stricture causing her to choke on food (see Chapter 13, Figure 13.1).

A further case seen by the author of this text (Figure 9.1) concerned an elderly woman in a care home who was initially investigated as a case of manual strangulation because of the fingernail abrasions to her neck and face. However, at autopsy, it was discovered that a piece of meat extended from the back of the tongue into the larynx, where it was firmly lodged. The fingernail marks were self-inflicted, caused by a frantic attempt to extract the meat.

## Laryngeal Cysts Causing Airway Obstruction

Any lesion of the larynx that produces swelling or tumours may compromise the airway. Laryngeal cysts in particular, of which there are a number of different types, may act in this manner to cause rapid death, as seen in the case encountered by the author of this text of a 55-year-old man who was found to have the upper larynx obstructed by an internal laryngo-mucocele (Figure 9.2).

Although the incidence of laryngeal cysts increases with age, peaking in the fifth to seventh decades (DeSanto et al., 1970; Newman et al., 1984), most deaths are seen in infants and young children, where any increase in the size of a cyst may cause total obstruction of a relatively very small airway. The author of this text has seen a ten-day-old infant with a thyroglossal duct cyst,

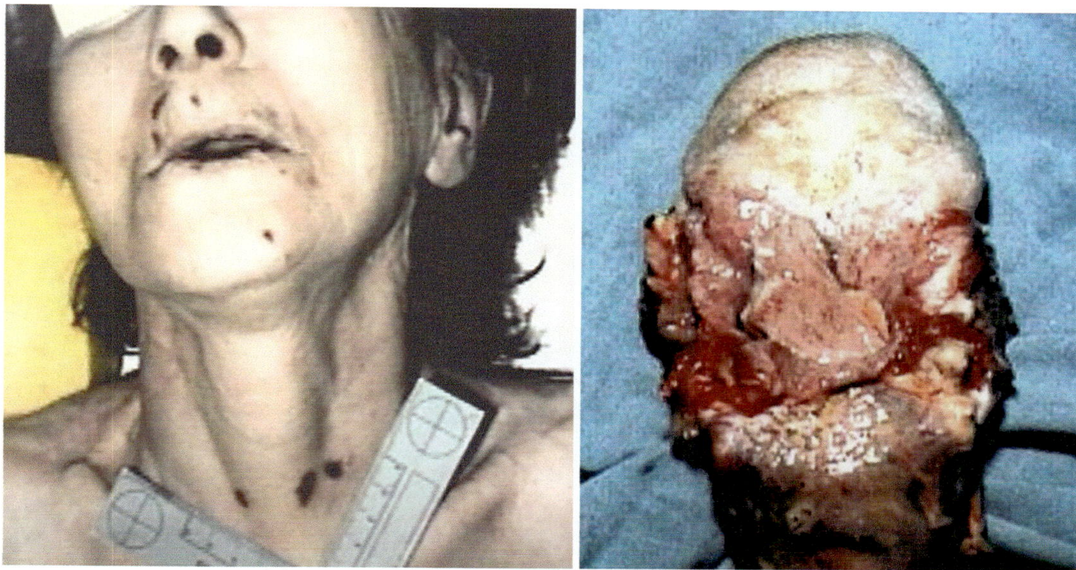

(a) (b)

**Figure 9.1** (a) Fingernail abrasions on the lower neck and face around the mouth and chin. (b) View of tongue and larynx with meat lodged in the laryngopharynx extending down from the back of the tongue.

who presented with seizures due to the anoxic effect of partial mechanical asphyxia. Death occurred suddenly two days after the onset of seizures. The cyst, which was situated at the base of the tongue in the midline, was lined by mucous-secreting cuboidal epithelium. It had caused total obstruction of the supraglottic region (Figure 9.3).

Kanawaku et al. (2006) reported the case of an 8-month-old female baby who was found collapsed in the prone position 30 min after being positioned under soft bedding. She could not be resuscitated. At autopsy, the child showed no significant pathological abnormalities, apart from a thyroglossal duct cyst of 2.0 cm diameter, which was close to the epiglottis and had caused asphyxia through airway occlusion. Being covered by the bedding may have been a contributory factor, but not the main factor in her death.

There are very few reports of fatal cases in adults. One such case was reported by Sauvageau et al. (2006) of a 55-year-old man who died from fatal asphyxia caused by a thyroglossal cyst. A further case of a laryngo-mucocele causing fatal obstruction was encountered by Töro et al. (2009). The deceased was a 55-year-old woman who presented with a feeling of discomfort and mild asphyxia. Laryngoscopy revealed a swelling near the ventricular and right aryepiglottic folds. She refused treatment and sadly died. Autopsy revealed a laryngocele filled with mucus.

## 'Café Coronary'

In adults, the term 'café coronary' has been used to describe sudden death from blockage of the upper airway by impacted food particles or, in a few cases, dentures (Figure 9.4). The phrase was coined by Haugen (1963). Although a misnomer, it graphically illustrates the sudden nature of the death and its association with consuming food. In many victims, there is also a substantially high alcohol level in body fluids, sometimes over 200 mg/100 ml of blood. The victim may be observed to slump over at the dining table or whilst walking away from the table during the middle of a meal. It is of note that there is absence of coughing, gagging, or other obvious signs of distress. These negative findings may be due in part to the drunken state of the victim.

It should also be appreciated that due to the sudden nature of collapse and absence of clear choking symptoms, café coronary syndrome may often be confused with a myocardial infarction

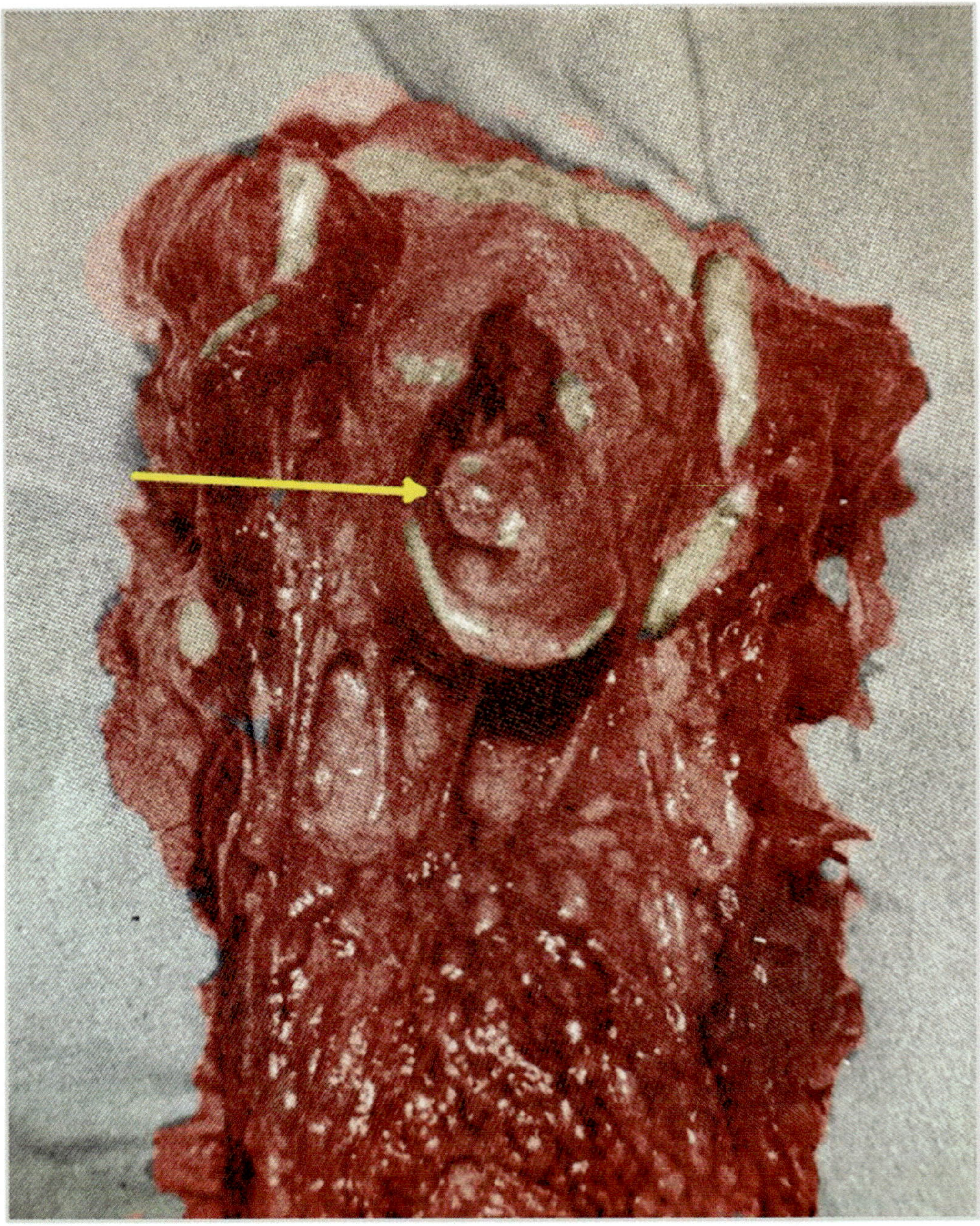

**Figure 9.2** Laryngeal cyst (arrow) in a 55-year-old man obstructing the airway and causing rapid death from asphyxia.

and, therefore, runs the risk of mismanagement, leading to a potentially fatal outcome. Batson et al. (2021) reported the case of a 75-year-old male in custody with severe atherosclerotic and hypertensive heart disease who collapsed in his cell, and his cellmate thought he had choked on food. A Heimlich manoeuvre was carried out to no avail. A physician who examined him did not see any food particles in his mouth and suspected a myocardial infarction. Resuscitation failed, and at autopsy, it was found that food, which comprised unchewed meat, was lodged in the larynx, completely blocking it and extending distally to the second tracheal ring.

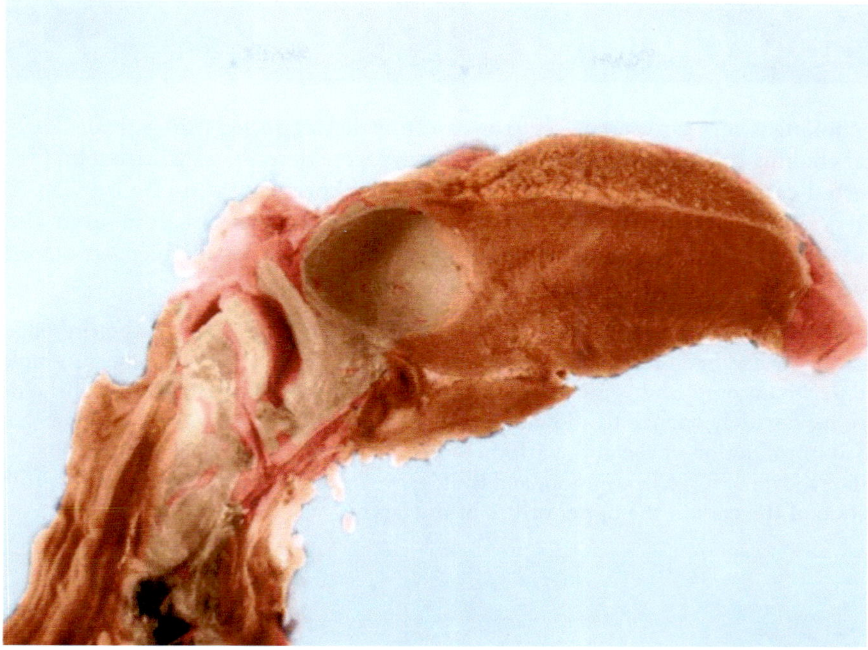

**Figure 9.3** Sagittal section of the tongue and larynx of a ten-day-old infant with a large thyroglossal duct cyst causing asphyxia from airway obstruction.

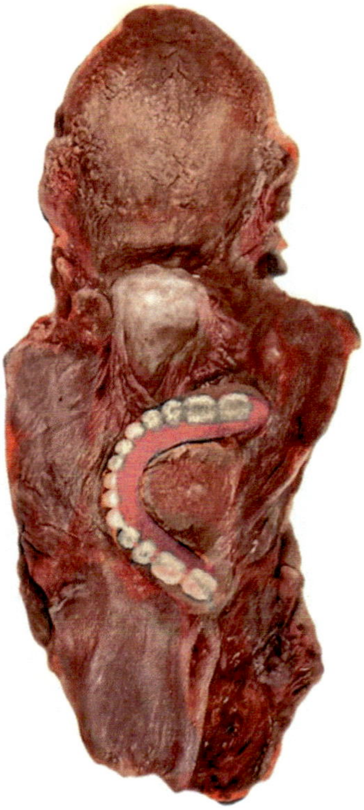

**Figure 9.4** Dentures lodged in the laryngeal pharynx.

# HOMICIDAL CHOKING

Homicidal choking is very rare and needs to be carefully distinguished from suicide. Early instances of homicidal choking by forcing objects into the larynx were described by Littlejohn (1855–1856). In one reported case of an elderly woman, a wine bottle cork was used (Figure 9.5). The author experimented with cadavers supplied by the Anatomy Department of Edinburgh University to demonstrate that it was possible for another person to forcibly thrust an object through the mouth so that it could be lodged in the larynx. Littlejohn wrote,

> The only satisfactory explanation that, in our opinion, could be given of the presence of the cork, was, that it had been forcibly placed there by another party. As to the means employed by the murderer to accomplish his purpose, our experiments show that the mouth of the deceased must have been widely opened to allow the forcible pulling out of the tongue with one hand, and the exuded introduction of the cork with the other. In doing so, the head, in all probability, was thrown into a state of forced extension, and thus, as we have shown, a greater facility afforded for the insertion of the cork in the upper orifice of the larynx.

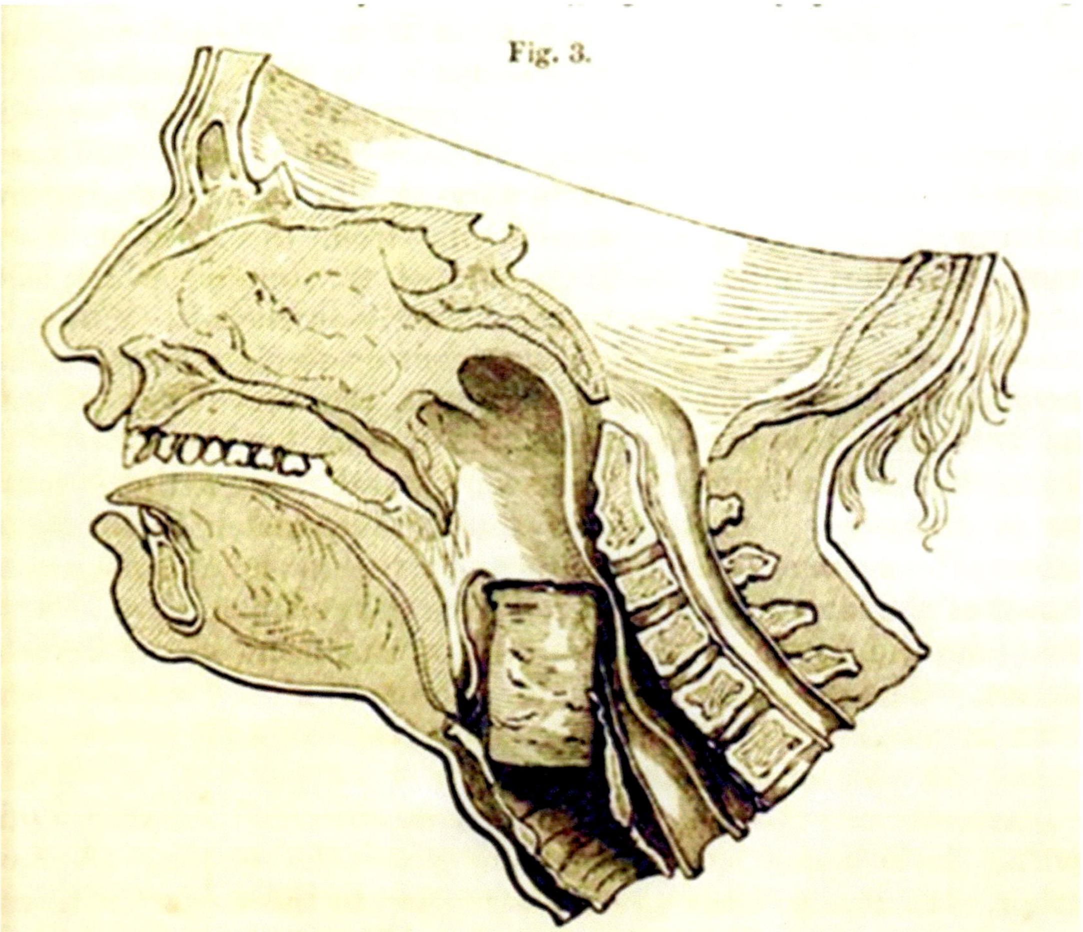


**Figure 9.5** Illustration from Littlejohn's article showing a cork from a wine bottle in the larynx of the deceased. (Royal College of Surgeons of England, Public Domain image.)

Another case described by the same author concerned a male infant who was newly born and apparently had a separate existence. The mother thrust a piece of dough into the baby's mouth, and it lodged in the larynx, causing the infant's rapid death. The offence was treated as one of infanticide.

More recently, Kurihara et al. (1992) reported a case in which a 29-year-old adult male, who was in a mental hospital, was choked to death as a result of having tissue paper thrust into his mouth by another male patient. Initially, the death was thought to be due to suicide until the death was re-examined.

A similar case is described by Saint-Martin et al. (2012) involving a 91-year-old woman in a care home suffering from Alzheimer's disease, who was killed by another elderly female resident with the same condition, by forcing toilet paper into her throat. At autopsy, pieces of toilet paper were found lodged in the buccal cavity and the laryngopharyngeal region above the epiglottis.

# SUICIDAL CHOKING

Such a mode of suicide is rare, and most reported cases have been in mental patients or persons in custody. Handyside (1842) reported the case of a 29-year-old woman who was thought to have died of apoplexy in prison. The true manner of the death only came to light in a dissecting room in Edinburgh a month after the body had been handed over to the anatomists. Handyside found a foreign body fixed to the throat. It was a tightly rolled piece of blanket, conically shaped and fastened by a pin. Its lower end lay between the arytenoid cartilages, and the pin had lacerated the throat to the left of the uvula. Renton (1908) reported on a middle-aged man who was found dead with three pieces of flannel each measuring 12 inches by 1 inch, which had been forced into the upper airway. The lowest piece had been packed firmly into the supraglottic region. More recently, Sauvageau and Yesovitch (2006) reported the case of a 58-year-old male with a longstanding history of schizophrenia who was found deceased at home with a large amount of toilet paper in his room. Post-mortem examination revealed that the victim's mouth, oropharynx, and posterior throat were filled with a significant amount of wadded toilet paper. There was no paper within the trachea, bronchi, or stomach. He had previously made an unsuccessful suicide attempt by ingesting medication and filling his mouth with toilet paper.

# OBSTRUCTION OF THE AIRWAY FROM EXTERNAL SOURCES WITHIN THE NECK

Obstruction of the airways may occur from sources external to the airways but within the neck. In relation to traumatic events to the neck structures, the author of this text encountered a case of a 48-year-old male, where there was extensive tracking of blood from a stab wound to the neck, with constriction of the larynx causing asphyxiation (see Chapter 4). In one of the cases reported by Farley et al. (1964), only a small haematoma was required to cause airway obstruction. The dangers of traumatic retropharyngeal haematoma, even with minor blunt injury, are rare but well recognised. Lin et al. (2007) presented the case of a 50-year-old man with retropharyngeal hematoma with a compromised airway due to a minor contusion of the neck. Lateral cervical radiography showed a marked prevertebral soft tissue swelling, with no cervical spinal fracture. The patient underwent emergency surgical intervention and had an uneventful recovery.

## References


Bamber AR, Pryce J, Ashworth M, Sebire NJ. Fatal aspiration of foreign bodies in infants and children. *Fetal Pediatr Pathol.* 2014;33(1):42–48. doi:10.3109/15513815.2013.846446.

Batson IS, Serinelli S, Gitto L. Café coronary syndrome - Case report and medicolegal implications. *Med Leg J.* 2021;89(4):264–269. doi:10.1177/00258172211031709.

DeSanto LW, Devine KD, Weiland LH. Cysts of the larynx--classification. *Laryngoscope.* 1970 Jan;80(1):145–176. doi: 10.1288/00005537-197001000-00013. PMID: 5411821.

Dunbar JS, Kramer SS. Radiology of trauma to the pediatric larynx. *Ear Nose Throat J.* 1981;60(8):356–365.

Farley HH, Nixon R, Peterson TA, Hitchcock CR. Penetrating wounds of the neck. *Am J Surg.* 1964;108:592–596. doi:10.1016/0002-9610(64)90162-x.

Handyside PD. Remarkable case of suicide from asphyxia by choking, from introduction of a firm plug into the fauces. *Edinb Med J.*, 1842;57:391–394.

Haugen RK. The café coronary: Sudden deaths in restaurants. *JAMA.* 1963;186(2):142–143. doi:10.1001/jama.1963.63710020011017.

Kanawaku Y, Funayama M, Sakai J, Nata M, Kanetake J. Sudden infant death: Lingual thyroglossal duct cyst versus environmental factors. *Forensic Sci Int.* 2006 Jan 27;156(2-3):158–160. doi: 10.1016/j.forsciint.2004.12.032. PMID: 16410167.

Köse A, Kostak D, Aramagan E, Durak A, Seçkin NS, Dönmez SS, Melek H. Tracheobronchial foreign body aspiration: Dental prosthesis. *Case Rep Pulmonol.* 2014;2014:465856. doi: 10.1155/2014/465856. Epub 2014 Aug 4. PMID: 25165606; PMCID: PMC4137749.

Kurihara K, Kuroda N, Murai T, Shinozuka T, Yanagida J, Matsuo Y, Nakamura T. A case of homicidal choking mistaken for suicide. *Med Sci Law.* 1992 Jan;32(1):65–67.

Lin JY, Wang CH, Huang TW. Traumatic retropharyngeal hematoma: Case report. *Auris Nasus Larynx.* 2007;34(3):423–425. doi:10.1016/j.anl.2006.10.003.

Littlejohn HD. Cases of homicidal and accidental suffocation with remarks. *Edinb Med J.* 1855–1856;1:511–524.

Mittleman RE. Fatal choking in infants and children. *Am J Forensic Med Pathol.* 1984;5(3):201–210. doi:10.1097/00000433-198409000-00003.

Nash PJ. A foreign body in the larynx. A case report. *Br J Anaesth.* 1976;48(4):371–372. doi:10.1093/bja/48.4.371.

Newman BH, Taxy JB, Laker HI. Laryngeal cysts in adults: A clinicopathologic study of 20 cases. *Am J Clin Pathol.* 1984;81(6):715–720. doi:10.1093/ajcp/81.6.715.

Renton JM. An unusual case of suicide by suffocation. *Br Med J.* 1908;1:493.

Saccomanno S, Saran S, Coceani Paskay L, De Luca M, Tricerri A, Mafucci Orlandini S, Greco F, Messina G. Risk factors and prevention of choking. *Eur J Transl Myol.* 2023 Oct 27;33(4):11471.

Saint-Martin P, Lefrancq T, Sauvageau A. Homicidal smothering on toilet paper: A case report. *J Forensic Leg Med.* 2012 May;19(4):234–235.

Sauvageau A, Belley-Côté EP, Racette S. Fatal asphyxia by a thyroglossal duct cyst in an adult. *J Clin Forensic Med.* 2006 Aug-Nov;13(6–8):349–352. doi: 10.1016/j.jcfm.2006.06.023. Epub 2006 Oct 5. PMID: 17027318.

Sauvageau A, Boghossian E. Classification of asphyxia: the need for standardization. *J Forensic Sci.* 2010 Sep;55(5):1259–1267.

Sauvageau A, Yesovitch R. Choking on toilet paper: an unusual case of suicide and a review of the literature on suicide by smothering, strangulation, and choking. *Am J Forensic Med Pathol.* 2006 Jun;27(2):173–4. doi: 10.1097/01.paf.0000203269.97907.a7. PMID: 16738440.

Sturner WQ, Spruill FG, Smith RA, Lene WJ. Accidental asphyxial deaths involving infants and young children. *J Forensic Sci.* 1976;21(3):483–487.

Töro K, Kardos M, Dunay G. Fatal asphyxia due to laryngomucocele. *Forensic Sci Int.* 2009 Sep 10;190(1-3):e1–e4. doi: 10.1016/j.forsciint.2009.05.002. Epub 2009 June 4. PMID: 19500925.

# CHAPTER 10

## NON-COMPRESSIVE BLUNT IMPACT INJURIES TO ANTERIOR COMPARTMENT

*Peter Vanezis*



DOI: 10.4324/9781003658467-10

# INTRODUCTION

It should be appreciated that, although I have divided the description of blunt force trauma to the neck into those injuries affecting predominantly anterior and posterior compartments (see Chapter 2), this is only for the sake of clarity. It should be appreciated, of course, that trauma to the neck frequently involves both compartments, particularly in road traffic collisions, which is the most common way in which blunt impact injuries occur. Trauma resulting from assaults is much less common, although of no less importance. Iatrogenic blunt injuries are also occasionally encountered and are dealt with in Chapter 13.

# EXTERNAL INJURIES

External manifestations of severe internal blunt impact trauma may be comparatively scanty, and therefore may give little indication of the underlying injury and its extent. When one is dealing with multiple injuries, in particular, neck trauma may be easily overlooked in the live patient. With single blows to the neck, if death occurs rapidly, there are frequently very few, if any, external signs.

In assessing external injuries, one must bear in mind the curvilinear nature and elasticity of this area. Patterned injuries need to be examined with care, taking into account the contour and the presence and character of injuries that may have been inflicted on other regions of the body. For example, stamping or kicking injuries of the neck are commonly accompanied by similarly produced lesions to the head and/or trunk (Figures 10.1 and 10.2).

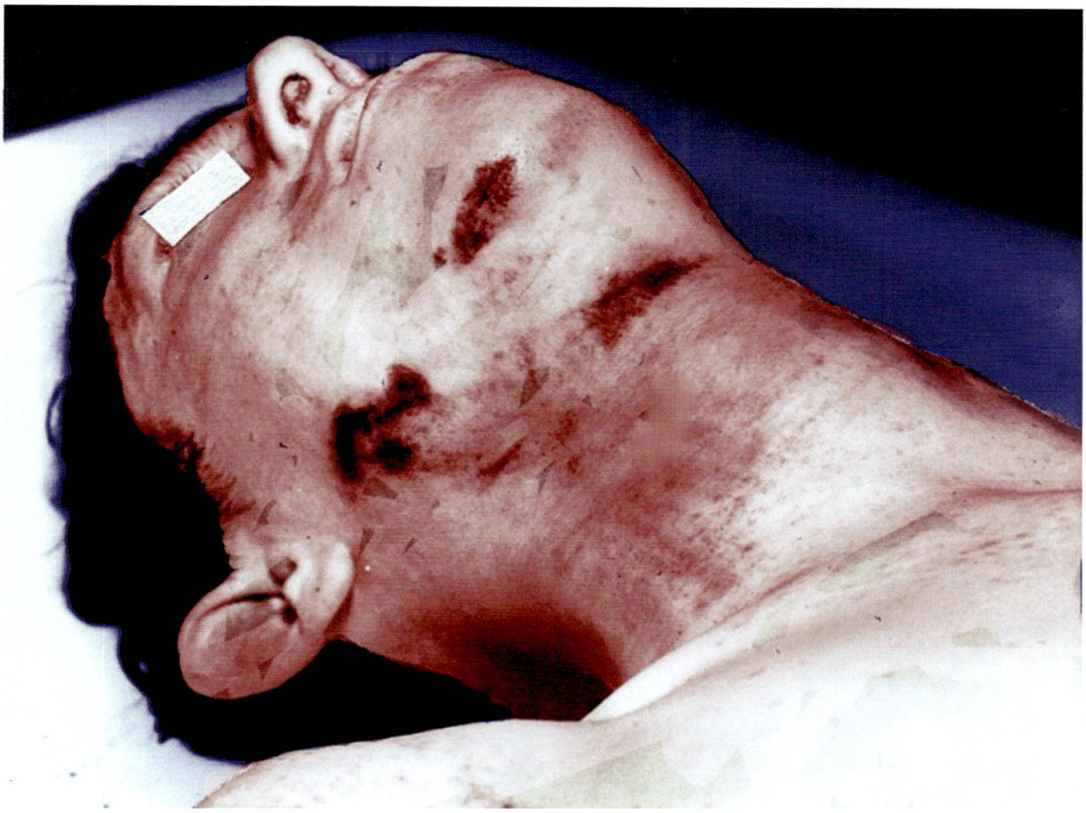

**Figure 10.1** The victim has been kicked about the head and neck, resulting in severe bruising and grazing to the neck, chin, and angle of the right mandible. There was severe underlying soft tissue injury to the neck structures.

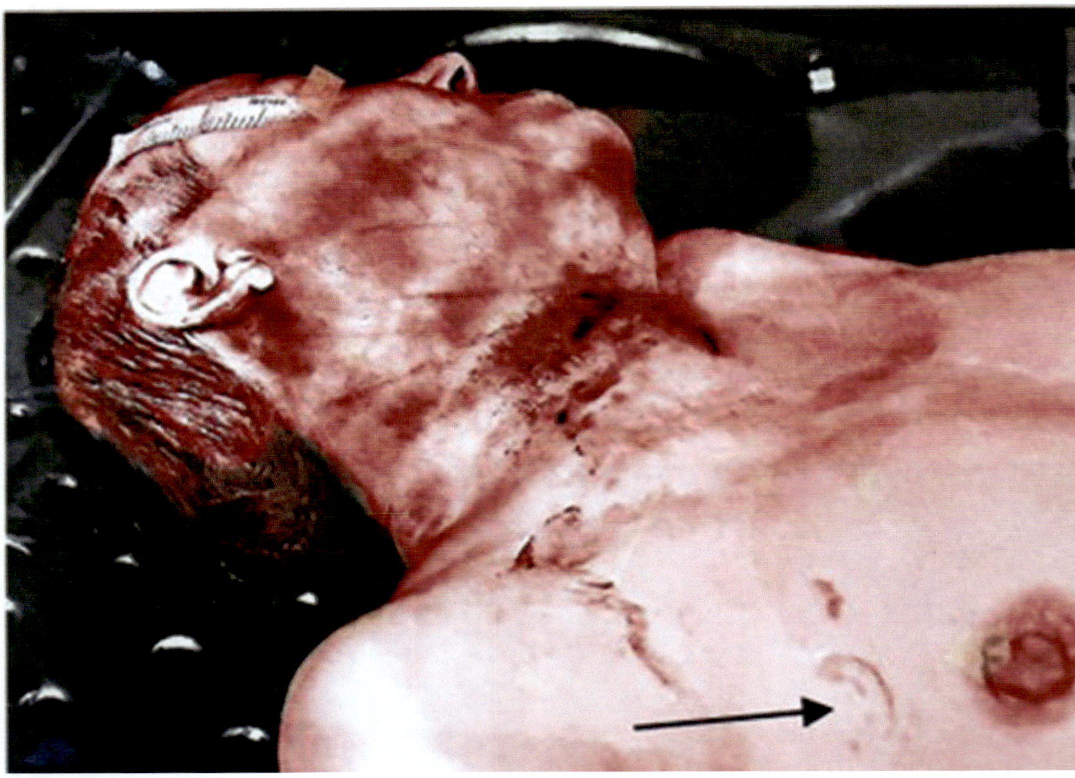

**Figure 10.2** Severe facial and neck bruises and abrasions, resulting from multiple kicks and blows with a rounded metal bar. An impression of the sawn-off part of the bar has been left above the right nipple (arrow).

# INTERNAL INJURIES

The distribution and extent of injury to the various structures of the anterior compartment are of assistance in evaluating the mechanism and force of trauma. The most commonly injured structures are the larynx, hyoid bone, and carotid arteries. Injuries to the pharynx and oesophagus are diagnosed less often but are of equal importance.

## Isolated Hyoid Bone Injuries

Isolated hyoid bone fractures that are not related to strangulation or hanging deaths are extremely rare and much more commonly seen with injury to other nearby structures. Their infrequent injury is due to their protected anatomical location, anteriorly and laterally by the mandible and posteriorly by the cervical spine. Dalati (2005) reported two such cases. One case concerned a 19-year-old man who had fallen on the right side of his neck directly on the hyoid bone while sleeping, but he could not exactly remember how it happened. The other case involved a 26-year-old man who, whilst playing basketball, was struck on his hyperextended neck by another player. Accidental blows to the neck causing isolated hyoid fractures were also seen in two collegiate footballers reported by Cutuk et al. (2012). An isolated hyoid fracture in a two-year-old child who fell down three steps is reported by Chainchel Singh et al. (2020). According to the babysitter, the child fell down, hitting his head first. However, there were no external injuries noted except for a swelling in front of the neck. The child had been under the care of the same babysitter for the nine months prior to the injury, was well taken care of and had no injuries suspicious of child abuse.

In road traffic collisions, isolated hyoid bone fractures are extremely rare. Chebil et al. (2024) reported two cases that occurred following traffic accidents in two male patients. They emphasised that their presentation is subtle and may be missed. Their patients presented with dysphagia and neck pain.

## Laryngeal Injuries (Including Related Trauma to the Hyoid Bone and Cervical Trachea)

### Type of resulting injuries

Depending on severity, six types of internal injury may occur from external trauma:

1. Cartilaginous fracture. This may range from simple minor displacement of a vertical thyroid fracture to severely comminuted fragments of both thyroid and cricoid cartilages. Fragments may overlap, with consequent decrease in the laryngeal aperture.
2. Mucosal laceration and haematoma. These may cause exposure of cartilage and severe distortion of laryngeal anatomy. Tears may occur, particularly in the area of the glottic folds. Furthermore, haematomas in the supraglottic compartment are quite common. Submucosal emphysema may occur if mucosal tears extend to the subglottic region. The mucosa may become oedematous and necrotic, with granulation tissue formation and raw edges on the glottis and ventricular mucosal surfaces.
3. Thyro-tracheal or laryngo-tracheal separation. This results in marked subcutaneous emphysema and possible airway obstruction.
4. Ligamentous tears. These specifically affect the thyroarytenoid ligament, leading to marked blunting of the anterior commissure, hoarseness, and possible airway compromise.
5. Nerve injury. Damage to one or both laryngeal nerves may infrequently occur, producing bilateral abductor paralysis.
6. Cricoarytenoid joint rupture. Injury to this joint may lead to ankylosis.

## Causes of Injury

### Overview

The most common cause of blunt injury to the laryngeal skeleton is during a road traffic collision (Nganzeu et al., 2023). Nevertheless, compared to all types of trauma sustained in such incidents, the incidence of laryngeal injuries as a whole is surprisingly low. The 'clothesline' injury mechanism is a specific subset of blunt trauma. It occurs when a person riding a motorcycle, bicycle, or snowmobile collides with a cable or wire, causing direct injury to the upper airway (Angood et al., 1986). Less frequently, injuries result from physical assaults, falls, or blunt trauma occurring during sporting activities.

### Injuries From Road Traffic Collisions

Most neck injuries in road traffic collisions are in rear-end collisions, in which the occupant's neck is forced into sudden hyperextension. No injury to the larynx or trachea, however, is produced in this fashion. In other collisions (e.g., frontal collisions), the driver, unrestrained by a seat belt, moves forward until his upper abdomen and lower chest strike the lower rim of the steering wheel or the dashboard. At this moment, the head begins to flex forwards. The larynx and trachea, which are protected by the sternum below and the mandible above, are not usually injured. The rare blow to the laryngotracheal area occurs either when the steering wheel is forced forward and upwards into the neck, or when the occupant strikes his head and allows the opposed neck to slide downwards onto the steering wheel rim. In addition, when the head is extended, the larynx is more fixed and immobile, and less able to deflect a direct blow. The risk of this injury may be greater in motorists who are tall or who have long necks. In small cars, the windscreen is closer to the occupant, and the risk is even greater.

Airbags may rarely cause laryngeal and other associated neck injuries. Perdikis et al. (2000) reported a 41-year-old male who was a restrained driver involved in a motor vehicle crash. He crashed into the side of another motor vehicle while travelling at approximately 35 mph, and his airbag deployed. On arrival at the emergency department, he was noted to have extreme stridor. His neck was swollen, and he needed to have a tracheostomy. A computed tomographic scan of his neck revealed a fracture of the thyroid cartilage and a severely comminuted fracture of the cricoid cartilage.

Shoulder harnesses are also known to cause laryngeal and soft tissue neck injury. Guertler (1988) reports a case of blunt laryngeal trauma secondary to use of a shoulder harness in a 26-year-old woman. The patient had been restrained with a lap and shoulder belt and was the occupant of an automobile involved in a rear-end collision.

### Sports Injuries

In relation to sports injuries, Paluska and Lansford (2008) commented that with forceful impact there may be damage to the intrinsic laryngeal muscles, the vocal folds, or the nerve supply to the larynx from the superior and recurrent laryngeal nerves. The hyoid bone, thyroid cartilage, arytenoid cartilage, and cricoid cartilage are also susceptible to direct injury during participation in various sports, including hockey, American football, basketball, and soccer. Dangerous tackles in rugby may cause severe head and neck injuries, and as a result, the rules in relation to dangerous play have taken this into account. Rugby union rules (Laws of the Game Rugby Union, 2024) describe dangerous tackles as follows.

> A player must not tackle an opponent early, late, or dangerously. Dangerous tackling includes, but is not limited to, tackling, or attempting to tackle an opponent above the line of the shoulders even if the tackle starts below the line of the shoulders.

Kitamura and Otani (2023) reported the case of a 22-year-old man playing rugby football at college, who was tackled around the neck by the opponent's shoulder and developed subcutaneous emphysema in the anterior neck and pneumomediastinum, as well as fractures of the cricoid cartilage and thyroid cartilage.

### *Falls*

Eş et al. (2017), in their autopsy study, found 170 cases of non-homicidal falls, and 16 (9.4%) had sustained laryngohyoid fractures. In a systematic review of laryngohyoid fractures in fatal falls, Amir et al. (2024) analysed the characteristics of laryngohyoid fractures in the context of falls to aid in a more accurate interpretation of autopsy findings, particularly with a view to distinguishing such injuries from those caused by ligature or manual strangulation. They included 38 cases in their analysis. The cumulative male-to-female ratio was 1.6:1 with a mean age of 48 years. The fall height ranged from standing height to 60 m. Forty-three fractures to the laryngohyoid complex were identified, with the thyroid cartilage most commonly affected, followed by fracture of the hyoid bone, and finally the cricoid cartilage. Although the fall cases showed laryngohyoid findings that are typical of strangulation, there were also injuries such as fractures of the clavicle and a reduced incidence of conjunctival petechiae.

### *Assaults*

In the retrospective study by Dunsby and Davison (2011), there were 78 cases with laryngohyoid fractures, four of which (5.1%) were due to assaults. The assault victims were all men, all were subject to blunt force head trauma, which in three cases may have involved kicking. One case apparently involved a solitary punch to the face and a fall with impact to the back of the head.

### *Injuries in Children*

In children less than 18 months old, iatrogenic injuries or caustic ingestions account for nearly all laryngeal trauma. With increasing age, the incidence of external trauma rises, whereas iatrogenic injuries decrease. Ford et al. (1995), from a total of 4,491 paediatric patients, found blunt impact neck injuries in 9 cases (0.2% of admissions). There was no significant difference in age or gender distribution between the two groups. The age range was 1 month to 16 years, and 80% were male. Bicycle-related accidents accounted for the majority of injuries seen.

## Level of Injury

The laryngotracheal airway is susceptible to injury at three levels, supraglottic, glottic, and subglottic. In the glottic-supraglottic region, the airway is maintained by a pyramid formed by the thyroid cartilages. The apex is directed anteriorly and is maintained by a fusion of the two cartilages. The base is directed posteriorly but derives its structural strength from the tenuous attachments of each cartilaginous leaf to the hyoid superiorly and the cricoid inferiorly. The application of forces against the pointed apex readily causes fractures and displacement of the thyroid cartilages, producing contracture of the airway with its anteroposterior diameter.

The intact airway in the middle of the glottic region is dependent upon the cricoid, which is the only complete circle of cartilage in the airway. Trauma may cause collapse of the ring, resulting in narrowing of the airway. The oesophagus is most susceptible to injury from compression and tearing of the posterior wall of the cricoid ring.

## Mechanism of Injury

Blunt trauma to the larynx is generally due to one of two mechanisms, or possibly a combination of both, to varying degrees.

One possible type of impact is where the injurious force acts in an anteroposterior direction, causing crushing of the thyroid and cricoid cartilages against the unyielding cervical spine. Such impact generally causes the common vertical fracture within the body of the thyroid cartilage by a 'hammer and anvil' effect (Figures 10.3 and 10.4). In this way, the arytenoids are often displaced and tears in the thyroarytenoid ligaments occur. The anterior cricoid lamina may also be damaged in a similar manner, but the fractures may be located anywhere within the cricoid ring. The musculature, suspended within the rigid laryngeal framework, is thus subject to laceration, oedema, and haematoma formation.

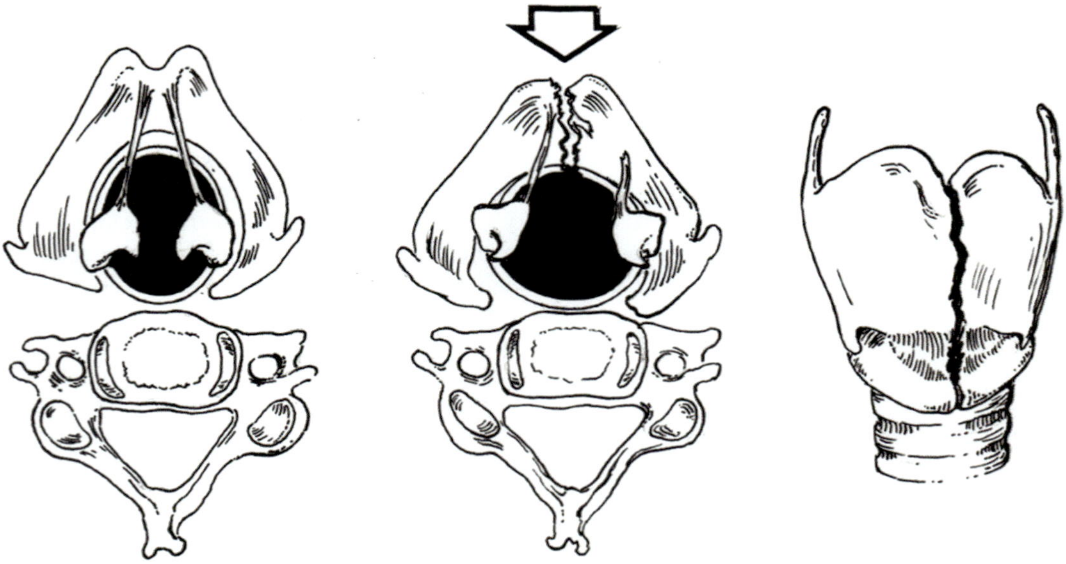

**Figure 10.3** Anterior impact to the larynx, with crushing against the cervical spine, causing vertical fracture to the thyroid and cricoid cartilages.

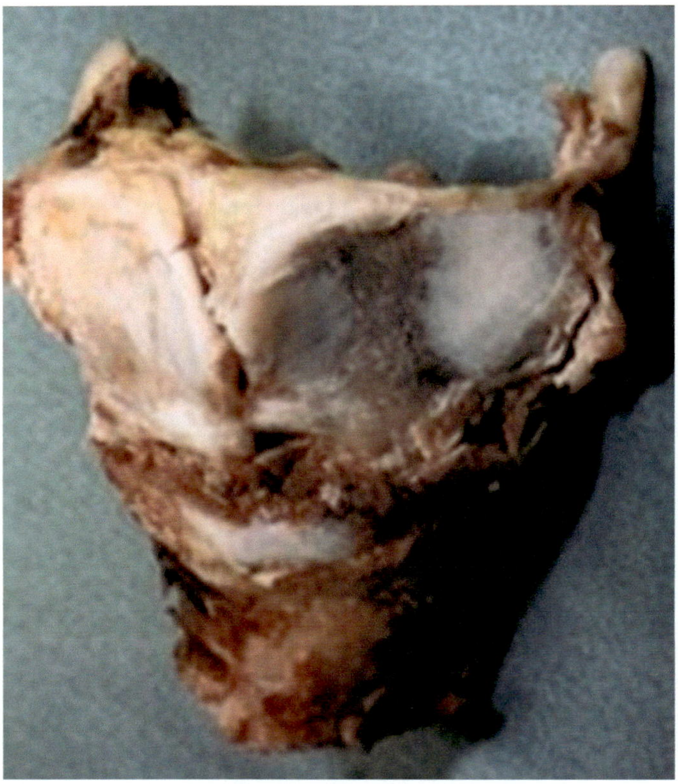

**Figure 10.4** Near-vertical fracture of thyroid lamina, caused by the subject's neck impacting against the dashboard in a road traffic collision.

The second mechanism is the result of a laterally directed force giving rise to a shearing action. Such forces may cause laryngotracheal separation, lacerations in the cricothyroid ligament, rupture of the thyrohyoid ligament, and mucosal tears. Lateral blows can also cause laryngotracheal separation on the side opposite the site of injury, owing to stretching forces that occur in that area. Attention should be directed towards the possibility of cricoarytenoid joint ankylosis, which frequently develops in experimental models. The cricoarytenoid joint is a ball-and-socket joint lined by synovial membrane and surrounded by a capsule. Traumatic disruption of this joint followed by inactivity may result in ankylosis and decreased cord movement on the affected side. Because of their intimate association with the thyroid and cricoid cartilages, the recurrent laryngeal nerves may also be readily damaged by external trauma and cartilaginous fracture. Levine et al. (1994) report the case of a 26-year-old bicyclist who sustained trauma to his neck with fracture of his thyroid cartilage and airway obstruction from vocal cord paralysis due to damage to the recurrent laryngeal nerves.

### Magnitude of Injurious Force

The high kinetic energy, which develops even at low speed in road traffic collisions and must therefore be dissipated, readily explains why serious injuries can be produced. Great forces are distributed over small areas of the body, e.g. the protruding cartilaginous airway, by contact with small surfaces in a vehicle. The pressure developed exceeds the tissue tolerance, and fracture deformation results. The area of the thyroid cartilage receives the majority of injuries to the laryngotracheal-oesophageal area. Travis et al. (1975) examined the response of 24 fresh human larynges to static and dynamic compressive loading. They found that the mean static force values producing thyroid and cricoid cartilage fractures were 15.8 and 20.8 kg, respectively. Dynamic fracture loading at velocities up to 11 mph caused cartilage fractures at forces averaging 30% more when compared with the static data. The interaction of the thyroid and cricoid cartilages with impact force was analysed with reference to airway protection, and they found that at the 50% compressive strain level, structural collapse was imminent and averaged 55 kg.

Earlier studies using intact cadavers revealed that considerably higher loads were required for injury. Nahum et al. (1968), for example, tested cadavers with loads of 91–113kg and produced marginal thyroid cartilage fractures; fractures of the cricoid cartilage occurred at 79–102kg.

### Complications

Complications from complex blunt impact laryngeal injury may be either acute or chronic (Bell et al., 2008; Nganzeu et al., 2023). Acute complications include airway obstruction resulting in asphyxia, recurrent laryngeal nerve injury, infection, or postoperative haematoma. Chronic complications include vocal cord paresis/paralysis, dysphonia, laryngeal or tracheal stenosis, or chronic aspiration. Recurrent granulation tissue formation, as well as stenosis of the supraglottic, glottic, and subglottic regions, may also occur.

## Cervical Tracheal Injury

Cervical tracheal trauma has been included above, to some extent, with injuries to the larynx. Its lumen at the upper cervical level is dependent upon the horseshoe-shaped rings of the trachea, which are open posteriorly. Blunt impact injury to the cervical trachea results from a violent impact to the neck, which pushes the trachea against the rigid cervical spine, causing tracheal cartilage, and soft tissue lacerations but leaving the skin intact. Indeed, the lack of a skin wound in many cases may delay diagnosis (Ye et al., 2013). Compression and fracture will force the centre of the rings inwards to narrow the airway. Damage to the oesophagus is not likely at this level. Permanent compromise of the airway following blunt trauma is unlikely unless there is fracture and dislocation of the major cartilages of the larynx. The rarity of this injury is due largely to the flexibility of the tracheal cartilages and the protection offered by the mandible, manubrium of the sternum, clavicles, and cervical spine.

Associated injuries, particularly in traffic collisions, are commonly seen and may include rib and cervical spine fractures, various soft tissue injuries and occasionally rupture of the oesophagus.

## Pharyngeal and Oesophageal Injury

The most common site of trauma to the cervical oesophagus is at the pharyngo-oesophageal junction. External blunt trauma is an uncommon form of injury and is often associated with other accompanying neck injuries. In such instances, the pharyngo-oesophageal injury may initially be undiagnosed, as in Graf's case (1969), where his patient also suffered a fractured hyoid bone and C2 vertebral pedicle.

Intramural haematoma (Roemmele et al., 2017) or perforation of the oesophageal wall (Uhrenholt et al., 2011) is occasionally seen in whiplash injuries from rear collisions, particularly in the elderly who have more rigid cervical spines. Misiak et al. (2016) discuss the difficulty in early diagnosis of a ruptured oesophagus, particularly when there are multiple associated craniofacial and neck injuries, as seen in their patient. The victim was a 24-year-old male who was a driver involved in a car accident. The car rolled over, and he was projected out of the car through the windscreen. According to the ambulance personnel who transferred him in an unconscious state to hospital, he was not wearing a seat belt.

## Anterior Neck Injuries and Degenerative Disease of the Cervical Spine

Severe laryngeal, tracheal, or oesophageal trauma may occur as a result of relatively mild trauma to the front of the neck, causing crushing of these structures against anterior cervical osteophytes (Vanezis and Tate, 1987). Their series comprised three cases, one of which had an accompanying anterior vertebral body fracture.

One of the cases reported was of a 72-year-old woman who had been in reasonably good health, with no symptoms associated with her cervical spine. She was searching for her front door key when she slipped (it had been raining and her porch was very wet) and fell directly onto a piece of bamboo cane supporting a pot plant. She was found dead by a neighbour very shortly after he had heard her fall. Post-mortem examination revealed bruising on the left side of the neck and an associated 0.5 cm curved laceration. In addition, there was slight grazing on the back of her left wrist. Internal examination revealed severe bruising to the laryngeal musculature, both anteriorly and posteriorly and partial laceration of the thyrohyoid membrane (Figure 10.5). There was also a linear fracture of the main body of the thyroid cartilage and of the cricoid cartilage posteriorly. The laryngeal injuries were at the same level and corresponded with marked osteophyte formation extending from the fourth to the seventh cervical vertebrae (Figure 10.6).

Their second case was of a frail 90-year-old woman who required a walking stick. She had numerous bruises over her body associated with multiple minor falls. She was found dead on the floor of her bedroom. Post-mortem examination did not reveal any recent bruising to her neck structures but internally, she had severe bruising and oedema at the back of the larynx and oesophagus. She also had gross osteophyte formation extending from the second to the fifth cervical vertebrae (Figure 10.7).

A further case was described by Henderson et al. (2007) in a healthy 76-year-old man who sustained closed head and neck trauma after falling down a flight of stairs. Over the following days, he became febrile, his voice changed, and he had difficulty swallowing. Thoracic CT in a local hospital revealed a pneumomediastinum. Because of the mechanism of injury, the cervical oesophagus was explored. Although no substantial injury was found, a prominent cervical spine osteophyte was identified, which was responsible for the micro-perforation of the oesophagus that resulted in mediastinitis. Neck hyperextension was the most likely mechanism of oesophageal injury.

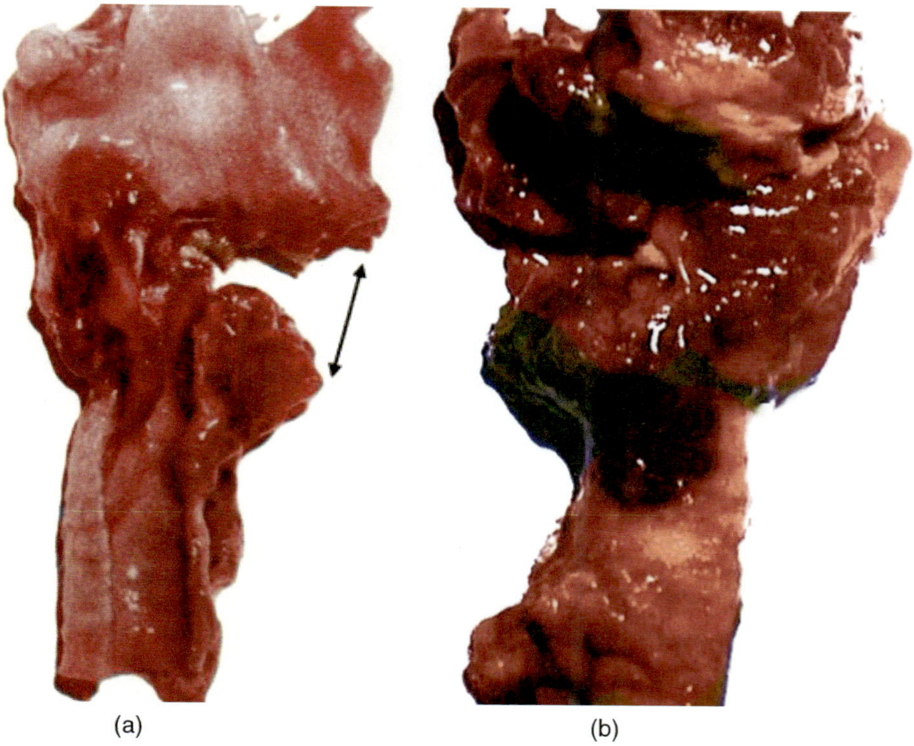


**Figure 10.5** (a) Left lateral view of larynx and trachea, showing severe haematoma of both the anterior and posterior aspects, as well as a gross laceration of the thyro-hyoid membrane (arrow), (b) Anterior aspect of the larynx.

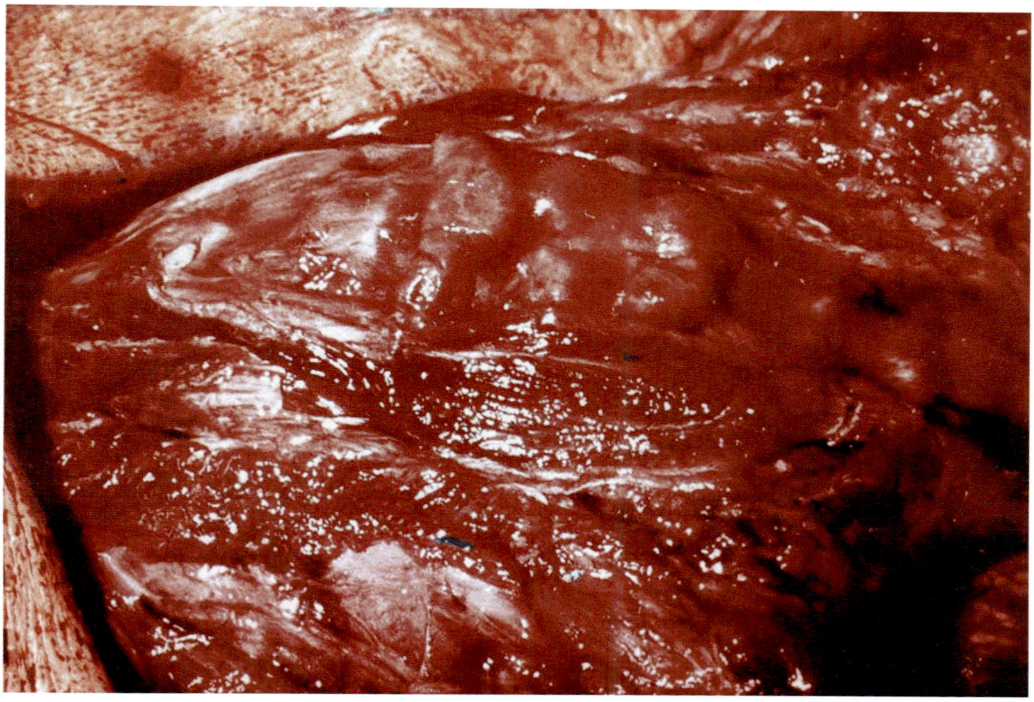

**Figure 10.6** Anterior osteophytes, most prominent from C4 to C7.

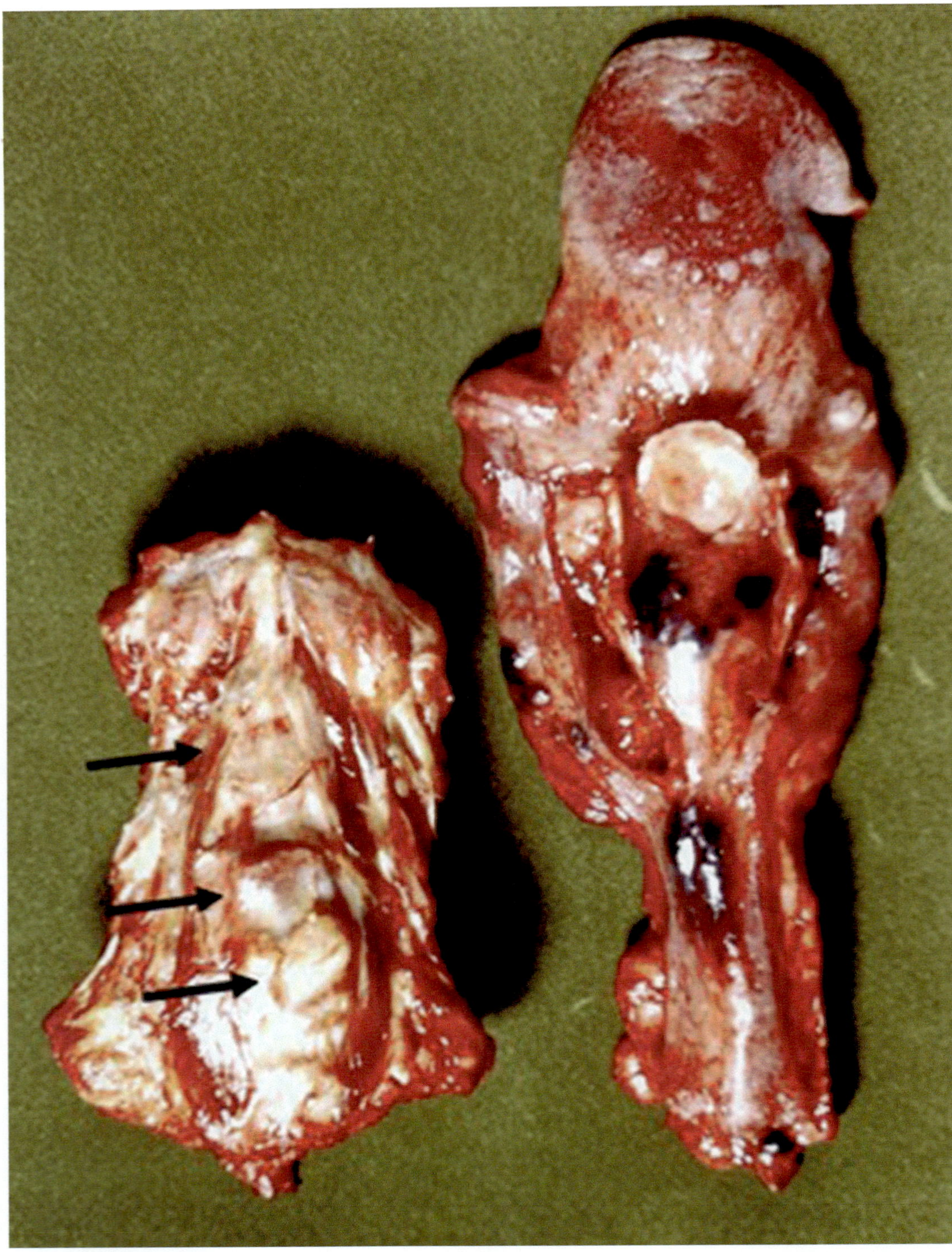

**Figure 10.7** Osteophytes on the anterior surface of the cervical spine extend from C2 to C5 (arrows). There is corresponding bruising of the posterior aspect of the upper larynx and the region of the upper trachea.

## Injuries to the Carotid Arteries

### Causes of Injury and Types of Lesions

Carotid artery injury resulting from blunt impact is seen much less frequently than from penetrating modes of trauma. In most larger series, blunt impact accounts for between 3% and 10% of all reported carotid injuries, with mortality rates for injury reported from 12% to 40% in the larger series (cited by Martin et al., 1991). Sudden blunt trauma usually initiates an intimal dissection and/or a haematoma formation. Thrombosis frequently also occurs and often with delayed neurological deficits. Such low frequencies, as Moar points out (1987), are undoubtedly due to failure to diagnose such lesions, particularly as many do not show external signs of trauma nor evidence of neurological deficit within the first hour (Yamada et al., 1967). The delay in diagnosis is also emphasised by Sanzone et al. (1995). They report two cases of blunt trauma resulting in carotid artery dissection and highlight that initial recognition by clinicians is often difficult because of the diverse clinical manifestations, the delay in presentation, and the associated multi-organ system injuries that accompany carotid artery dissection.

About 60% of blunt carotid artery injuries occur in road traffic collisions, whereas direct blows and falls account for 15% each (Yamada et al., 1967). The vast majority of carotid artery injury cases (24 of 27) reported by Ramadan et al. (1995) were the result of motor vehicle crashes; two were due to falls, and one was due to a crush injury. Moar (1987), from a comprehensive autopsy and histological survey of 200 fatally injured road traffic collision victims, found 57 carotid artery injuries, most of which were tears. A large number of intimal disruptions were encountered (44.7%), which showed extension of the tear to the internal elastic lamina. Compound intimo-medial tears were seen in almost two-thirds of cases, and complete vessel wall transection was seen in more than one-quarter of the arteries.

### Mechanism of Injury

A number of mechanisms, as discussed below, have been implicated in the production of blunt carotid artery trauma. Arthurs and Starnes (2008) describe three basic mechanisms of injury for blunt carotid and vertebral artery injuries that are encountered. They include (1) extreme hyperextension and rotation, (2) a direct blow to the vessel, and (3) vessel laceration by adjacent bone fractures.

#### *Hyperextension*

The most common mechanism is hyperextension of the carotid vessels over the lateral articular processes of the higher cervical vertebrae (C1–C3) and base of the skull. Such injuries are particularly seen in rear-impact collisions (whiplash injuries). Stretching over the bony mass at this level may result in tearing of the intima in one or more places.

#### *Direct Blunt Impact Trauma*

Direct blows to the neck, particularly in older persons, are more likely to damage an atheromatous plaque, which may form an obstructing flap with associated thrombus formation. Vertical tears may be seen with a direct blow. In Emmett-Dunne's victim, who suffered a direct blow from the side of the hand (see Chapter 8), there were tears to both carotid arteries. These may have resulted from displacement of the thyroid laminae impacting in a lateral direction on both vessels (Camps and Hunt, 1959).

A direct impact from a harness on a roller coaster was thought to be the mechanism of carotid artery injury in a thirteen-year-old girl described by Scheer and Carlin (1979). Carotid artery dissection may also result from shearing neck injury associated with roller coaster rides. This was the presumed mechanism of injury in the case reported by Badve and Bhuta (2015). Their patient was a 42-year-old woman with no vascular risk factors who was admitted with neck pain and right-sided Horner syndrome after riding a roller coaster. Magnetic resonance imaging (MRI) of the neck showed a characteristic crescent-shaped intramural haematoma caused by dissection of the artery, which was confirmed by magnetic resonance angiography.

### Lateral Impact to the Head

Such an impact may cause rotation as well as hyperextension of the head and neck thus stretching the carotid artery across the body of C1 and C2 or over the transverse process of C3. The combination of hyperextension and contralateral rotation of the head may be the mechanism involved in unilateral internal carotid artery trauma, although rotation is unlikely to be a significant factor in bilateral injuries. These are much more likely to be due to, predominantly, hyperextension forces.

### Other Mechanisms

A rare mechanism of injury was described by Sakai (1986), in which a dissecting carotid artery aneurysm resulted from a "rubbing" injury caused by a tight head and neck protector worn during practice of the martial art *kendo*. The aneurysm was located in the cervical portion of the internal carotid artery and was thought to have resulted from simple anteroposterior flexion under tight neck fixation.

## Progression of Lesions

Yamada et al. (1967), in reviewing the literature on cases of acute non-penetrating trauma to the carotid artery, identified 52 cases, 75% of which had a history of injury to the head. There was a frequent delay in the onset of symptoms. One postulated mechanism was a gradual build-up of thrombus at the site of the injured intima or at the fractured atheromatous plaque. Another possibility is the subintimal dissection of a haematoma. The intimal tear may act as a nidus for thrombus formation. In most cases, total occlusion of the internal carotid artery was present.

Thrombus may also serve as a source of emboli, leading to subsequent neurological complications. This occurred in the case described by Scheer and Carlin (1979). The tendency for thrombus formation is increased by the tendency of perivascular oedema and haematoma, vasospasm, hypotension, and increased platelet adhesiveness following major trauma. (Figure 10.8).

Palmer et al. (1995) reported that their patient, a 15-year-old boy, was injured whilst playing hooker in a school rugby match. A scrummage collapsed, and his head was forcibly extended on his trunk with the weight of the scrum on top of him. He was removed from the rugby pitch complaining of neck pain and paraesthesia in the right arm and leg. The symptoms initially settled, but the following day he was sent to hospital complaining of dizziness, blurred vision, and persisting paraesthesia. The neurological opinion was that he had suffered an embolic infarct secondary to

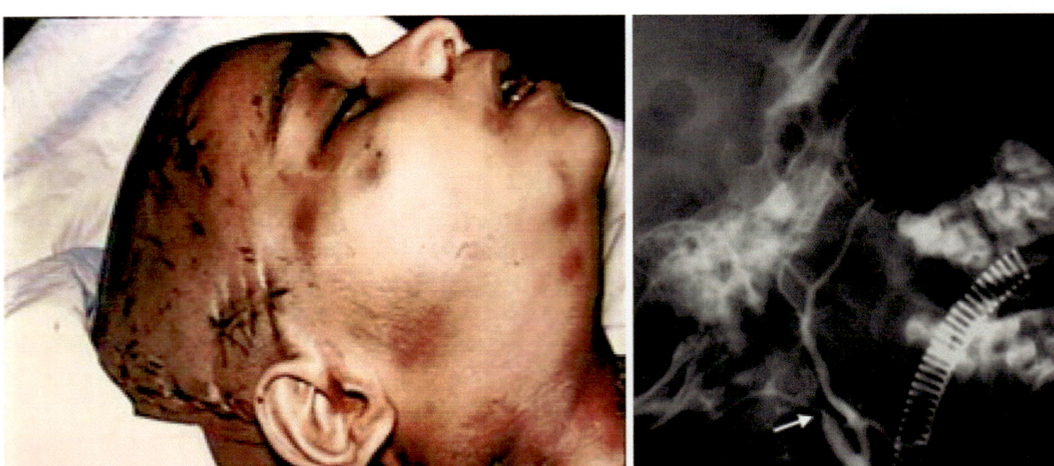

(a) (b)

**Figure 10.8** (a) Extensive bruising seen to the right side of the face and neck, resulting from multiple blunt instrument trauma. A right-sided craniotomy was performed, but no intracranial haematoma was found. The patient deteriorated and died, (b) Carotid angiography prior to death revealed total occlusion by a thrombus (thought to be post-traumatic) of the right internal carotid artery, approximately 1.5 cm distal to the bifurcation (arrow).

damage to the carotid artery, the nature of which was probably a carotid artery dissection. As the patient was essentially well apart from paraesthesia, further investigations (apart from a normal carotid Doppler scan) were not felt to be appropriate. Anticoagulation was considered but rejected due to the risk of haemorrhage into the infarct. The patient improved with some residual numbness in the hand at 4 weeks.

The multicentre study by Cogbill et al. (1995) identified 60 carotid injuries in 49 patients. The authors emphasised the complex nature of such injuries and difficulty in diagnosis, often due to delayed presentation and/or other injuries (particularly in road traffic collisions). They supported those of previous findings in relation to the outcome of such injuries. These included neurological deficits in 14 patients (29%), developed 12 hours after a normal neurological examination. Documented injuries included thrombosis in 20 arteries, arterial dissection in 19, dissection with pseudoaneurysm in six, pseudoaneurysm alone in five, frank arterial disruption in seven and carotid-cavernous fistula in three.

## References


Amir AA, Amir BA, Alghannam AA, Abdeen TH, Alshneiber RM, Alhowaish AA, Menezes R. G Systematic review of laryngohyoid fractures in fatal falls: A potential mimicker of strangulation. *J Forensic Leg Med*. 2024;101:102612. doi:10.1016/j.jflm.2023.102612.

Angood PB, Attia EL, Brown RA, Mulder DS. Extrinsic civilian trauma to the larynx and cervical trachea--important predictors of long-term morbidity. *J Trauma*. 1986;26(10):869–873. doi:10.1097/00005373-198610000-00002.

Arora YR. Closed cervical tracheal rupture. *Br J Clin Pract*. 1963;17:341–342.

Arthurs ZM, Starnes BW. Blunt carotid and vertebral artery injuries. *Injury*. 2008 Nov;39(11):1232–1241. doi: 10.1016/j.injury.2008.02.042. Epub 2008 Sep 3. PMID: 18771765.

Badve MS, Bhuta S. Roller coasters and cervical artery dissection. *Med J Aust*. 2015 Oct 19;203(8):339. doi: 10.5694/mja15.00715. PMID: 26465701.

Bell RB, Verschueren DS, Dierks EJ. Management of laryngeal trauma. *Oral Maxillofac Surg Clin North Am*. 2008 Aug;20(3):415–430. doi: 10.1016/j.coms.2008.03.004. PMID: 18603200.

Camps FE, Hunt AC. Pressure on the neck. *Journal of Forensic Medicine*, 1959;6:116–135.

Chainchel Singh MK, Siew SF, Lai PS. Isolated hyoid bone fracture in a child due to a fall. *Int J Pediatr Otorhinolaryngol*. 2020 Dec;139:110443. doi: 10.1016/j.ijporl.2020.110443. Epub 2020 Oct 12. PMID: 33068949.

Chebil A, Ben Ayed M, Hasnaoui M, Masmoudi M, Jribi A, Jerbi S, Mighri K. Hyoid bone fracture secondary to a blunt neck trauma: A report of 2 cases. *Ear Nose Throat J*. 2024 Feb 8:1455613241230215. doi: 10.1177/01455613241230215. Epub ahead of print. PMID: 38327252.

Cogbill TH, Moore EE, Meissner M, et al. The spectrum of blunt injury to the carotid artery: A multicenter perspective. *J Trauma*. 1994;37(3):473–479. doi:10.1097/00005373-199409000-00024.

Cutuk A, Bissell B, Schmidt P, Miller B. Isolated hyoid bone fractures in collegiate football players: A case series and review of the literature. *Sports Health*. 2012;4(1):51–56. doi:10.1177/1941738111419963.

Dalati T. Isolated hyoid bone fracture. Review of an unusual entity. *Int J Oral Maxillofac Surg*. 2005;34(4):449–452. doi:10.1016/j.ijom.2004.09.004.

Dunsby AM, Davison AM. Causes of laryngeal cartilage and hyoid bone fractures found at postmortem. *Med Sci Law*. 2011;51(2):109–113. doi:10.1258/msl.2010.010209.

Eş H, Şahin MF, Özdemir E. Laryngohyoid fractures in fatal nonhomicidal falls from a height. *Am J Forensic Med Pathol*. 2017;38(4):289–293. doi:10.1097/PAF.0000000000000350.

Ford HR, Gardner MJ, Lynch JM. Laryngotracheal disruption from blunt pediatric neck injuries: Impact of early recognition and intervention on outcome. *J Pediatr Surg*. 1995;30(2):331–335. doi:10.1016/0022-3468(95)90584-7.

Graf C. Laceration of the pharynx with fracture of the hyoid bone: report of a case and discussion. *J Trauma*. 1969 Sep;9(9):812–818. doi: 10.1097/00005373-196909000-00007. PMID: 5808563.

Guertler AT. Blunt laryngeal trauma associated with shoulder harness use. *Ann Emerg Med*. 1988;17(8):838–839. doi:10.1016/s0196-0644(88)80566-3.

Henderson E, Echavé V, Lalancette M, Langlois G. Esophageal perforation in closed neck trauma. *Can J Surg*., 2007;50(5):E5–E6.

Kitamura T, Otani K. Airway obstruction with blunt neck trauma from an accidental high tackle in rugby. *Curr Sports Med Rep*. 2023;22(3):100–104. Published 2023 Mar 1. doi:10.1249/JSR.0000000000001047.

Laws of the Game Rugby Union. (2024) World Rugby, Dublin. Available from: https://www.world.rugby/the-game/laws/home

Levine RJ, Sanders AB, LaMear WR. Bilateral vocal cord paralysis following blunt trauma to the neck. *Ann Emerg Med*. 1995;25(2):253–255. doi:10.1016/s0196-0644(95)70334-9.

Martin RF, Eldrup-Jorgensen J, Clark DE, Bredenberg CE. Blunt trauma to the carotid arteries. *J Vasc Surg*. 1991;14(6):789–795. doi:10.1067/mva.1991.32076.

Misiak P, Jabłoński S, Terlecki A. Cervical esophageal rupture after blunt trauma resulting from a car accident. *Kardiochir Torakochirurgia Pol*. 2016 Sep;13(3):262–264. doi: 10.5114/kitp.2016.62620. Epub 2016 Sep 30. PMID: 27785145; PMCID: PMC5071598.

Moar JJ. Traumatic rupture of the cervical carotid arteries: an autopsy and histopathological study of 200 cases. *Forensic Sci Int*. 1987;34:227–244.

Nahum AM, Gatts JD, Gadd CW, Danforth J. Impact tolerance of the skull and face. *Proceedings of Stapp Car Crash Conference*. 1968;12:302–316.

Nganzeu C, Esce A, Abu-Ghanem S, Meiklejohn DA, Sims HS. Laryngeal trauma. *Otolaryngol Clin North Am*. 2023;56(6):1039–1053. doi:10.1016/j.otc.2023.06.001.

Palmer SH, Emery D, Paterson M. Stroke following neck injury in a rugby player. *Injury*. 1995 Oct;26(8):555–556. doi: 10.1016/0020-1383(95)00114-o. PMID: 8550150.

Paluska SA, Lansford CD. Laryngeal trauma in sport. *Curr Sports Med Rep*. 2008;7(1):16–21. doi:10.1097/01.CSMR.0000308673.53182.72.

Perdikis G, Schmitt T, Chait D, Richards AT. Blunt laryngeal fracture: Another airbag injury. *J Trauma*. 2000;48(3):544–546. doi:10.1097/00005373-200003000-00033.

Ramadan F, Rutledge R, Oller D, Howell P, Baker C, Keagy B. Carotid artery trauma: A review of contemporary trauma center experiences. *J Vasc Surg*. 1995;21(1):46–56. doi:10.1016/s0741-5214(95)70243-1.

Roemmele E, Meighan V, Morrissey B. Intramural oesophageal haematoma following traumatic neck injury. *BMJ Case Rep*. 2017;2017:bcr2017222447.

Sakai H, Kaneko D, Yuki K, Nakamura N. [Carotid dissecting aneurysm due to blunt (rubbing) injury of the Kendo protector]. *No Shinkei Geka*. 1986 Jan;14(1):91–94. Japanese. PMID: 3951667.

Sanzone AG, Torres H, Doundoulakis SH. Blunt trauma to the carotid arteries. *Am J Emerg Med*. 1995;13(3):327–330. doi:10.1016/0735-6757(95)90212-0.

Scheer MS, Carlin DJ. Stroke after roller coaster-induced carotid compression. *JAMA*. 1979 Oct 19;242(16):1769. PMID: 480606.

Travis LW, Olson NR, Melvin JW, Snyder RG. Static and dynamic impact trauma of the human larynx. *Trans Sect Otolaryngol Am Acad Ophthalmol Otolaryngol*. 1975;80(4 Pt 1):382–390.

Uhrenholt L, Freeman MD, Jurik AG, Jensen LL, Gregersen M, Boel LW, Kohles SS, Thomsen AH. Esophageal injury in fatal rear-impact collisions. *Forensic Sci Int*. 2011;206(1-3):e52–e57. doi:10.1016/j.forsciint.2010.08.019.

Vanezis P, Tate GP. Cervical osteophytosis and laryngeal trauma. *Med Sci Law*. 1987;27(2):99–102. doi:10.1177/002580248702700206.

Yamada S, Kindt GW, Youmans JR. Carotid artery occlusion due to nonpenetrating injury. *J Trauma*, 1967;7:333–342.

Ye D, Shen Z, Zhang Y, Qiu S, Kang C. Clinical features and management of closed injury of the cervical trachea due to blunt trauma. *Scand J Trauma Resusc Emerg Med*. 2013;21:60. Published 2013 Aug 7. doi:10.1186/1757-7241-21-60.

# CHAPTER 11

## NON-COMPRESSIVE BLUNT IMPACT INJURIES TO THE POSTERIOR COMPARTMENT

*Peter Vanezis*
*(with contributions from Curtis Offiah and Christopher Paul Johnson)*



The injuries described in this chapter are sustained by the cervical spine, spinal cord, vertebral arteries, and other structures behind the prevertebral fascia. Most injuries to the posterior compartment occur as a result of road traffic collisions. Less frequently, they are due to other forms of impact, either direct or indirect. Although much of the discussion is based on road traffic collision findings, it should be borne in mind that the resulting lesions and mechanisms of trauma are applicable to other circumstances of injury.

DOI: 10.4324/9781003658467-11

# NORMAL MOVEMENTS OF THE CERVICAL SPINE

A great number of injuries occur as a result of a sudden movement of the cervical spine beyond its physiological range. It is therefore appropriate at this stage to summarise the various normal movements prior to the discussion of trauma.

Normal movements of the cervical spine can be divided into those of the upper region between the base of the skull and the axis vertebra (C0–C2) and those of the lower portion, from the axis to the seventh vertebra (C2–C7).

## Upper Cervical Spine

Movements of the upper cervical spine comprise those between the head and neck at the atlanto-occipital (C0–C1) and atlantoaxial (C1–C2) joints.

Movements of the atlanto-occipital joints: The curved surfaces of the joints are well adapted for head flexion and extension (nodding) and allow for a considerable amount of abduction (lateral flexion) of the skull on the atlas. No rotation is possible.

Movements of the atlantoaxial joints: The movements of these joints are simply those of rotation about a vertical axis passing through the odontoid process. The head rotates with the atlas.

## Lower Cervical Spine

While the range of movement between any two cervical vertebrae is not great, the summation of these movements provides for a wide range of movement possible in the intact normal neck. The thick intervertebral discs in the healthy young adult are compressible and deform to accommodate the range made possible by the flat, upward obliquity of the apophyseal joints.

Flexion and extension are free. Extension is stopped by the contact of the superior or inferior facets; flexion is stopped by the apposition of the projecting lower edge of the body above on the sloping upper surface of the body below.

Lateral flexion cannot occur without simultaneous rotation due to the slight medial inclination of the superior facets.

Further movements of the cervical spine as a whole occur when the neck moves either forwards or backwards. In forward movement, there is extension at the atlanto-occipital joint and simultaneous flexion of the rest of the cervical column on the trunk. With backward movement of the neck, the opposite movements occur in the same regions.

## Normal Range of Movements

Neck movements diminish with age. In childhood, the free range of flexion and extension can be such as to allow considerable displacement of one vertebral body upon another. Forward flexion should normally allow the chin to touch the chest. Extension of the neck in children and young adults can, in exceptional circumstances, allow the back of the skull to touch the back. Lateral rotation should encompass a 180-degree arc, and the ear should touch the shoulder.

# GENERAL FEATURES, INCIDENCE AND CLASSIFICATION OF INJURIES

Injuries to the cervical spine (including the cord, vertebral vessels, and other related structures) may be caused by either direct or indirect impact from forces acting directly on the vertebrae, or indirectly on the skull or thorax, or from sudden acceleration or deceleration. All these forces can cause movement of the cervical spine beyond its physiological limits.

A retrospective survey carried out by the author on 804 cases of general trauma autopsied by the Department of Forensic Medicine at the London Hospital Medical College over a period of four years revealed 104 cases (13%) with posterior neck injury due to blunt impact trauma (Vanezis, 1984). In a further, larger clinical prospective survey of 34,069 enrolled patients with blunt trauma who underwent cervical spine x-radiography, 818 (2.4%) individuals were found to have cervical spine injury (Goldberg et al., 2001). Thesleff et al. (2010), using the Fatal Finnish nation-wide register from 1987 to 2010, estimated the overall prevalence of cervical spine injuries among all trauma patients as 3.7%. They agreed, however, as I have found, that a significant proportion of injuries to the cervical spine and related posterior structures may well go unrecorded unless thorough post-mortem examinations are carried out. The value of a comprehensive post-mortem examination, including detailed dissection of the neck region as well as histological examination, was demonstrated in a small prospective study of 24 trauma cases in which posterior neck injuries were not initially suspected. The series revealed seven posterior neck injuries (29%; Vanezis, 1984). It should be emphasised, however, that these injuries were of a minor nature and non-contributory to death, although they may well have played a part in morbidity had there not been a fatal outcome. An approximately comparable proportion of cervical spine injuries was observed in a recent retrospective review of 80 fatalities over a nine-year period from different types of blunt trauma (the vast majority from road traffic collisions). With the aid of Post-Mortem Computed Tomography (PMCT), cervical spine injury was detected in 25% of these cases (Levin et al., 2023).

It is universally appreciated that most blunt posterior neck injuries occur in road traffic collisions. The author, from a study of 49 consecutive cases with suspected neck trauma (34 males, 15 females), found 32 (65%) that had been inflicted in such circumstances. The remainder comprised eight high falls, five low falls, two direct impacts from blows, and two train impacts (Vanezis, 1984).

Classification of cervical spine trauma has generally been based on the mechanism of injury. Although most classifications emphasise resulting injuries to the skeletal and ligamentous elements as applicable to the clinical situation and in conjunction with radiographic appearances, the possible resulting trauma to the cervical cord and vertebral vessels should also be borne in mind, although the range of resulting injuries in these structures is not extensive. Indeed, the type of injury that results in these structures depends more on the magnitude than on the direction of the injurious force.

The classification based on mechanism of injury by Gehweiler et al. (1980), which gives a detailed analysis of the trauma mechanisms involved in cervical spine injury is adopted by the author of this text for descriptive purposes and (from the pathological perspective) assists the reader in gaining a better understanding of the cause of the various injuries encountered (Table 11.1).

Nightingale et al. (1996) carried out an experimental study of the mechanism of injury using an impact model to investigate the relationship between impact to the head and cervical spine injury. The model consisted of the head and neck of a cadaver. They found that, although traditionally, the mechanisms of injury to the cervical spine are associated with flexion and extension motions of the head and neck, these were not always in agreement with the patient's account of the injury or with lacerations and contusions of the scalp, which indicated the site of the impact to the head. They found that in their 11 specimens, observable motion of the head did not correspond to the mechanism of the injury to the cervical spine. Injury occurred 2.2–18.8 milliseconds after impact

**Table 11.1** Classification of cervical injuries according to mechanism (Gehweiler et al., 1980)

| |
|---|
| HYPERFLEXION INJURIES |
| Disruptive hyperflexion |
| Hyperflexion sprain (momentary dislocation) |
| Hypeflexion-dislocation (locked facets); bilateral or unilateral (with associated rotational force) |
| Spinous process fracture |
| Complete hyperflexion |
| Wedge-like compression of vertebral body |
| Comminuted vertebral body fracture |
| Hyperflexion fracture-dislocation ('tear drop' fracture) |
| Hyperflexion or shearing forces |
| Anterior atlanto-occipital dislocation |
| 'Pure' anterior atlantoaxial dislocation (without associated fracture) |
| Anterior fracture-dislocation of the dens |
| HYPEREXTENSION INJURIES |
| Disruptive hyperextension |
| Horizontal fracture of the anterior arch of C1 |
| Hangman's fracture (traumatic spondylolisthesis of C2) |
| Anteroinferior margin of the body of the axis (C2) |
| Hyperextension sprain (momentary dislocation) |
| Spinous process fracture |
| Compressive hyperextension |
| Posterior arch of atlas fracture |
| Vertebral arch fracture (articular pillar, pedicle, lamina) |
| Hyperextension fracture-dislocation |
| Hyperextension or shearing forces |
| 'Pure' posterior atlantoaxial dislocation (without associated fracture) |
| Posterior fracture-dislocation of the dens |
| HYPERROTATION INJURIES |
| Rotary atlantoaxial dislocation |
| Anterior and posterior ligament disruption |
| LATERAL HYPERFLEXION INJURIES |
| Fracture of transverse process |
| Uncinate process fracture |
| Lateral fracture-dislocation of dens |
| Brachial plexus avulsion associated with cervical fractures and/or dislocations |
| Lateral wedge-like compression of vertebral body |
| AXIAL COMPRESSIVE INJURIES |
| Isolated fracture of the lateral mass of the atlas |
| Bursting fracture of Jefferson (C1) |
| Vertical and oblique fractures of the axis body |
| Bursting fracture of a vertebral body |

to the head and before it had moved. However, they agreed that classification of the mechanism of the injuries was descriptive of the local deformations of the cervical spine at the time of the injury.

The recent AOSpine subaxial cervical spine injury classification system, applicable for clinical management, proposed by Vaccaro et al. (2016), describes a morphology-based classification system for subaxial cervical spine injuries. It is based on three injury morphology types: compression injuries, tension band injuries, and translational injuries with additional descriptions for facet injuries, as well as patient-specific modifiers and neurological status (Figure 11.1).

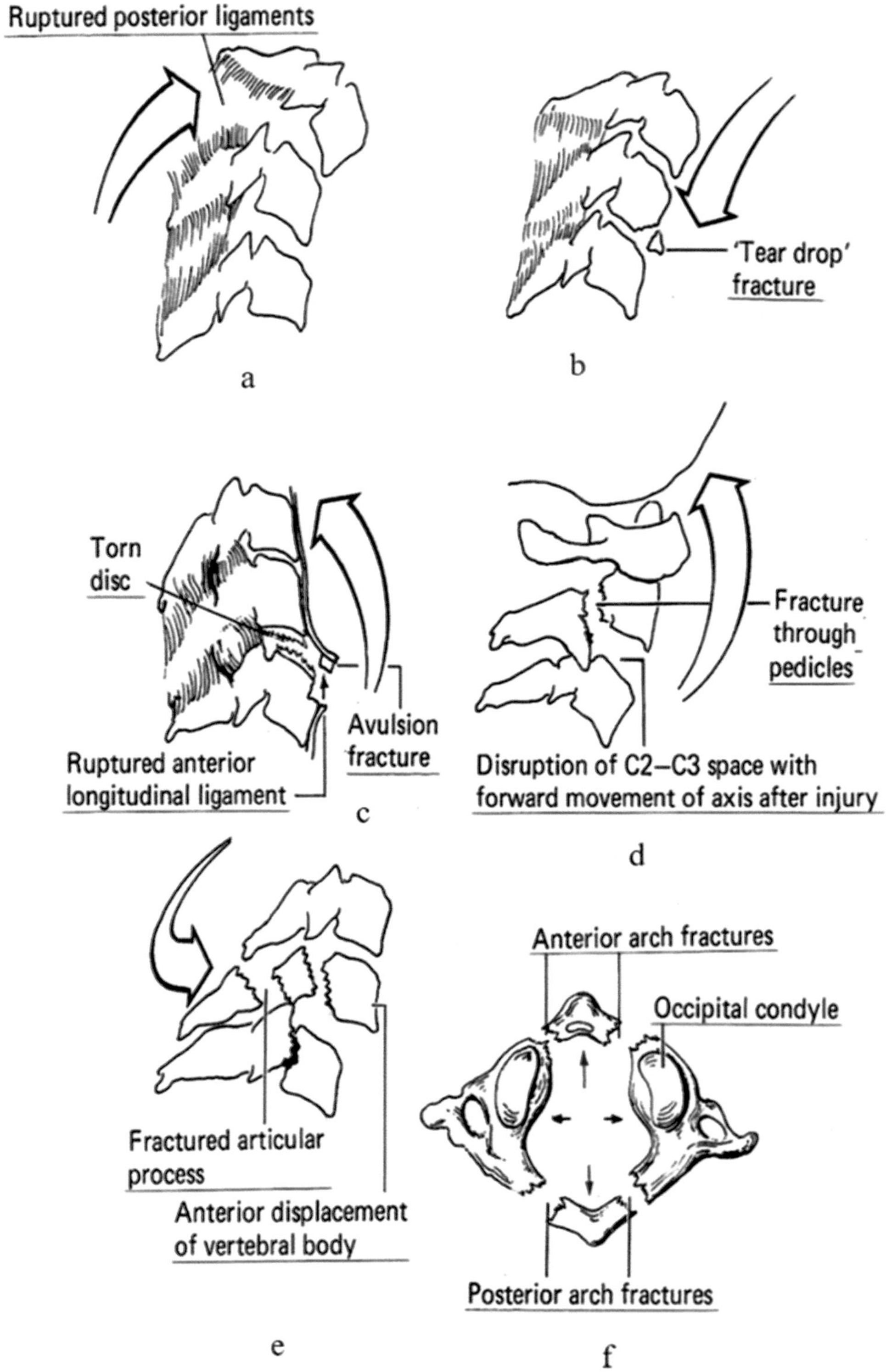


**Figure 11.1** Injuries from exaggerated cervical spine movements, (a) Disruptive hyperflexion; (b) Compressive hyperflexion; (c) Disruptive hyperextension (hyperextension sprain); (d) Disruptive hyperextension (hangman's fracture); (e) Compressive hyperextension; (f) Axial compression (Jefferson's bursting fracture of atlas). (See description of injuries below.)

## Flexion Injuries

### Disruptive Hyperflexion

If the injuring force is directed forward and upward, as with a blow to the occiput from below, a disruptive hyperflexion injury results. At the level of injury, the spinous processes will be distracted, and the posterior ligaments will receive the greatest trauma.

If a more severe force had been applied, the posterior ligaments would be torn, and the articular surfaces of the apophyseal joints would lose all contact and override. After the force is dispelled, the spine springs back toward its normal position, and the articular processes lock. If the trauma occurs in hyperflexion without significant rotation, locking of the articular processes occurs bilaterally (bilateral hyperflexion dislocation). Unilateral hyperflexion dislocation results if a rotary component is added to the force.

### Compressive Hyperflexion

Such injuries are caused by a blow to the top of the head. The force is transmitted downwards along the cervical vertebral column. This results in varying degrees of compression of the vertebral bodies or even in a hyperflexion fracture-dislocation. If the force is mainly compressive, the posterior ligamentous structures may even remain intact. Since the normal intervertebral disc is usually quite resistant to compression, it is the vertebral body that is disrupted by the compressive force. A 'tear drop' hyperflexion fracture-dislocation results from hyperflexion compression (Figure 11.2). The force acting on the spine moves it in an arc. At the level of the injury, the vertebra is displaced posteriorly, causing disruption of the apophyseal joint capsules and the posterior portion of the intervertebral disc below. Either the anterior or the antero-inferior margin of the involved vertebral body is fractured. The fragment, which resembles a tear drop, is displaced anteriorly. After the force passes, the fractured vertebra remains displaced posteriorly on the vertebra below. In a few cases, the vertebral arch is fractured by the pull of the posterior ligaments.

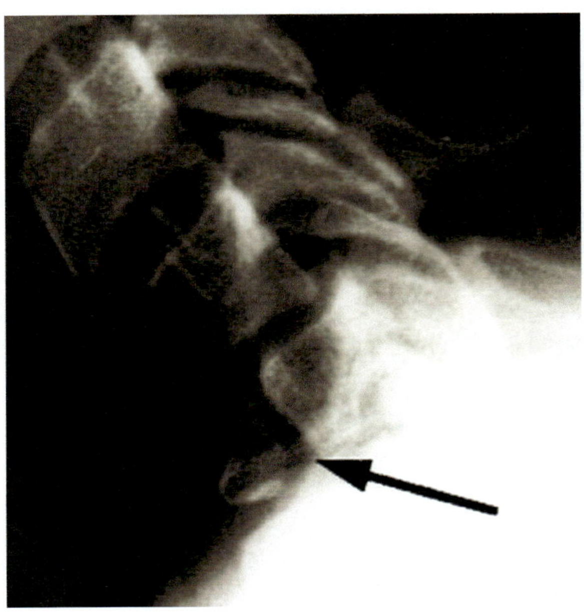

**Figure 11.2** Left lateral radiograph, showing a co ('tear drop') fracture of the fifth cervical vertebral body (arrow), with posterior displacement of the vertebral body resulting from compressive hyperflexion. The sixth and seventh vertebrae are obscured by the shoulders.

## Extension Injuries

### Disruptive Hyperextension

With a blow to the chin, the injuring force is directed backwards and upwards. If the force is sufficient, the anterior longitudinal ligament and the intervertebral disc may be ruptured. The cervical vertebrae above the ligamentous injury are carried posteriorly with the spinal cord. The cord is pinched between the postero-inferior margin of the vertebral body above and the laminae of the vertebra below. As the force is dissipated, the neck may spring back to its position. Since this is primarily a ligamentous injury, it has been termed a 'hyperextension sprain' (rupture). With such a mechanism of injury, there may be normal radiographs with clinical evidence of severe spinal cord injury.

Another quite common type of disruptive hyperextension injury is the 'hangman's fracture' or traumatic spondylolisthesis of the axis. In a recent study by Menon and Taif (2015) of 32 patients injured in road traffic accidents, they found that hangman's fracture is more commonly asymmetrical, with the most frequent pattern being a pedicle fracture on one side and a pars fracture on the other, followed by symmetrical pedicle and symmetric pars[1] fractures. However, variable less frequent patterns were also observed, which involve the vertebral body and lamina in addition to the pedicle and pars.[1] Furthermore, depending on the magnitude of the force applied, fragments from the fractured pedicles may be distracted to yield anterior displacement of the body of the axis with respect to the C3 vertebra below. The remaining portion of the axis remains in place along with the lower cervical spine.

According to Schleicher et al. (2015)., depending on the additional force vector along the longitudinal axis, the injury mechanism can be a hyperextension distraction injury (likely in "judicial hanging") or a hyperextension-compression injury, which is observed, for example, in traffic collisions when passengers' foreheads strike the windscreen. The distraction-type injury may cause a complete disruption of all the ligamentous structures, which will generate severe instability and usually fatal neurological damage to the spinal cord at the C2 level.

At the inquest of the 'Elephant Man' (Joseph Carey Merrick; Figure 11.3), the jury returned a verdict that 'he died as a result of suffocation from the weight of the head pressing on the windpipe'.

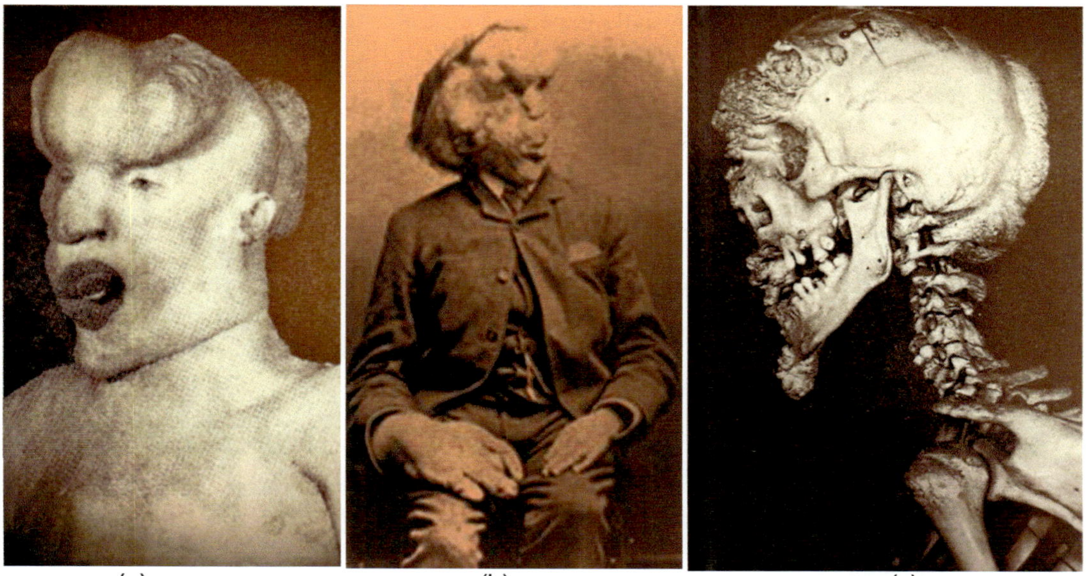

(a) (b) (c)

**Figure 11.3** (a) Cast of the Joseph Merrick's head and upper trunk, (b) Photograph during life, (c) Articulated skeleton, showing his skull and cervical spine (Courtesy of the Royal London Hospital Museum).

It was thought that his heavy head had fallen forward onto his trachea. Nevertheless, Sir Frederick Treves (the surgeon at the London Hospital who housed and cared for him at the hospital) maintained that he had dislocated his neck owing to his head falling backward. An account of the circumstances of his death and subsequent inquest was published in the British Medical Journal of 1890. The Elephant Man's head had apparently grown so heavy that he had difficulty in breathing and holding it up and had to sleep in a sitting and crouching position with his head clasped over his legs and his head on his knees. If he lay down flat, the heavy head tended to fall back and produce a feeling of suffocation. He was found dead by the ward maid lying across his bed. Mr. Treves was of the opinion that the 'ponderous skull had fallen backward and dislocated his neck' (Treves, 1923). The coroner, however, felt that the Elephant Man's windpipe had been compressed by the heavy head causing asphyxia.

Joseph Merrick had an obscure condition that puzzled his contemporaries and fascinates clinicians to this day. Throughout the 1900s, a number of theories were advanced to explain the numerous growths that covered his body. This included neurofibromatosis, Proteus syndrome, and a combination of childhood injury, fibrous dysplasia, and pyarthrosis. There is now a new consensus on the genetic and clinical diagnosis of neurofibromatosis and Proteus syndrome so that it is now possible to conclude that Joseph Merrick was, in all likelihood, suffering from Proteus syndrome (Huntley et al., 2015). Nevertheless, details of his genotype remain unknown, and obtaining intact DNA from his skeleton is challenging; yet it is possible that sequencing Merrick's genome could provide genetic confirmation of his clinical diagnosis.

### Compressive Hyperextension

Several types of fractures may occur with compressive hyperextension. In the upper cervical spine, this injury may fracture the posterior arch of the atlas. Lower in the cervical spine, the force of injury is directed posteriorly and downwards, crushing the vertebral arch components, especially the articular pillars, spinous processes, and laminae.

If the hyperextensive compressive force is of great magnitude, the head may be forced backwards in an arc. Initially, the head moves backwards, then downwards. Assuming the rupture of the anterior longitudinal ligament occurs only late in the course of the trauma, if at all, the force of the injury is initially expended on the articular processes, laminae, and pedicles. Once the articular processes have been fractured, the forces still acting through an arc are now free to displace the vertebral body anteriorly, as it is no longer restrained by an intact vertebral arch.

## Axial Compression

With the cervical spine maintained in the neutral position, an axial compressive force directed caudally through the vertex of the skull may produce a bursting fracture of the atlas (Sherk and Nicholson, 1970). The force of injury is directed to the superior articular facets of the atlas through the occipital condyles. It is opposed by resistance directed upwards through the superior articular facets of the axis. Thus, the triangular lateral masses of C1 are forced laterally, resulting in combined fractures of both the anterior and posterior arches of the atlas – Jefferson's bursting fracture (Jefferson, 1920). Isolated fractures of the lateral masses are rare and are thought to result from asymmetrical compressive forces (see Chapter 3, Figure 3.13). A review by Kakarla et al. (2010) found isolated atlas fractures to be more common, with 40%–44% occurring together with axis fractures. Fractures of isolated anterior or posterior arches were more common and typically seen with other spine fractures. Isolated burst fractures were the second most common type and rarely cause neurological injury. The most common causes were motor vehicle collisions and falls, which account for 80%–85% of all atlas fractures. Other causes included diving into shallow water, motorcycle crashes, and skateboarding.

## Lateral Flexion Injuries

Lateral flexion injuries result from blows to the lateral aspect of the head or the neck. The resultant lateral flexion forces may produce five possible lesions: (i) fracture of the dens with lateral displacement; (ii) lateral wedge compression fracture of the vertebral body; (iii) uncinate process fracture; (iv) fracture of the transverse process; (v) brachial plexus avulsions with associated cervical or upper thoracic spine fractures.

## Rotational Force Injuries

Distinct deformation patterns at the craniocervical junction during dynamic head axial rotation were observed in the study by Zhou et al. (2021). Using a biplane fluoroscopic imaging system, they imaged the skulls and cervical spines of eight asymptomatic female subjects to assess the deformation of the primary ligaments in the craniocervical junction, including the cruciform ligament, alar ligaments, and accessory ligaments.

Rotational forces may be combined with any other mechanism of cervical spine injury. It has been shown that the ligaments of the spine are resistant to tearing or rupture with a pure flexion or extension mechanism of injury. McLain et al. (1994) carried out biomechanical tests on cadaver spines during and after disruptive hyperflexion and hyperextension and observed that in both flexion and extension, the posterior longitudinal ligament and facet capsules provided the greatest resistance to disruption. However, when components of horizontal shear or rotational injury are added, these structures are easily damaged. If the spine is extended and rotated, the anterior longitudinal ligament may be readily torn. With rotation and flexion injuries, the posterior ligaments, apophyseal joint capsules, and the posterior longitudinal ligament may be ruptured in that order. Owing to their normally wide range of rotation, the atlantoaxial joints are not especially subject to hyper-rotational injuries. Locking of the atlas on the axis in rotation is only rarely encountered. The atlas must be rotated beyond 45 degrees on the axis to produce such a locking injury.

# ROAD TRAFFIC COLLISION INJURIES

## Incidence

A retrospective survey of 981 road traffic collisions (Vanezis, 1980) autopsied between 1970 and 1977 inclusive revealed 130 cases with posterior neck injury (13.3%) (cf. the author's general trauma series cited above). Tonge et al.'s survey (1972) revealed an incidence of 15% from 908 cases. In other series, however, the incidence has been found to be 20% or over (Alker et al., 1978; Huelke et al., 1981). The most likely reason for such a discrepancy is that neck injuries were specifically looked for in the latter two series, whereas in the survey carried out by the author (Vanezis, 1980 and, in part, of the 1984 study), original autopsy material was not available for examination. It should be borne in mind that unless the posterior neck region is examined thoroughly, including radiographically, it is very easy to overlook even major injuries. Cain et al. (1989) in a prospective survey using post-mortem radiography of the cervical spine, found almost twice as many cervical injuries that were usually identified in routine post-mortem examinations, confirming, as stated above, that the prevalence of cervical spine injury in road traffic crashes is greatly underestimated.

Bener et al. (2009), in a clinical retrospective survey of injuries in 6,709 persons injured in road traffic collisions and attending Accident and Emergency and Trauma centres, found that the incidence of neck injuries over a six-year period increased from 1.9/10,000 population in 2001 to 3.4/10,000 population in 2006.

## Distribution of Injuries

In fatalities, I have found that the first and fifth cervical vertebrae are the most injured, closely followed by the sixth (Vanezis, 1980). On the other hand, in survivors, the most common areas of injury have been observed in the lower cervical region. Goldberg et al. (2001), in their clinical study of the distribution of cervical spine injury, found from 818 cases that the atlantoaxial region was the most common site of injury, and the sixth and seventh vertebrae were involved in over one-third of all injuries. Other spine levels were much more commonly involved than had previously been appreciated.

## Car Occupants

The type and severity of injuries suffered by car drivers or their passengers will depend on a number of important factors including speed at impact, site of impact (whether frontal, side, rear, or rollover), whether the occupants were ejected out of the vehicle, use of a safety belt (safety harness), and design of the vehicle. Most posterior neck injuries follow indirect trauma to either the head or chest, followed by exaggerated movement of the neck to cause trauma as outlined earlier.

Stein et al. (2011) examined cervical spine trauma using prospectively collected data from eight centres, which were used to identify all vehicle occupants between 1996 and November 2009. The database, known as the Crash Injury Research Engineering Network (CIREN), had been established by the USA Department of Transportation's National Highway Transportation Safety Administration (NHTSA). This is a multi-institutional project that compiles comprehensive crash data, occupant characteristics, and clinical information. Car occupants in the study were older than 14 years, and vehicles of the four most common types were included. Cervical spinal cord and spinal column injuries were identified in 11.5% of cases. They found that car occupants aged 65 years or older and those occupants involved in rollover crashes were more likely to sustain a cervical spine injury. Of all the restraint systems, seat belt use without airbag deployment was found to be the most protective restraint system, whereas airbag-only restraint was associated with the highest risk. The most frequent injury sources in CIREN crashes were the roof of the vehicle and its components (24.8%) and noncontact sources (15.5%).

Sgarlato and Deroux (2010) reviewed all fatalities of vehicular occupants in New York City over a five-year period on whom autopsies were performed (437) to determine the incidence of neck injuries and correlate them with seat belt utilisation. They found 26.5% had neck injuries (mild to severe), and only 10.3% of these occupants were confirmed to be wearing seatbelts. Of those that had documentation of seat belt utilisation, there were twice as many neck injuries in the unbelted group. Two of their cases of submarining (sliding under the belt) with severe neck injuries were related to automatic 2-point shoulder harness restraints without engagement of the lap belt.

## Motorcyclists and Users of Other Two-Wheel Powered Vehicles

Hitosugi et al. (1999) examined 76 forensic autopsies of motorcyclists and bicyclists to assess the severity of injuries and the effects of helmet use. Using the Maximal Abbreviated Injury Scale Score (MAIS), they found that the most commonly injured region was the head or neck (58.0%), followed by the chest (32.9%), abdomen (13.2%), and extremities (7.9%).

Previous studies, including that of Krantz (1985), have also found that head and neck injuries were the most common cause of death among motorcyclists. In Krantz's autopsy study of 132 motorcyclists and moped riders killed between 1977 and 1983 in Southern Sweden, it was shown that 112 victims suffered head or neck injuries. Furthermore, in almost half of the fatal injuries to the head and neck, the site of impact was elsewhere.

The issue of the use of helmets in preventing injuries has, in the past, been subject to mixed opinion, including that of the latter author (Krantz). However, more recent studies have undoubtedly the value of preventing or decreasing the severity of injury to the head and neck region. One of the largest studies, carried out by Crompton et al. (2011), who analysed 40,588 motorcycle collisions from the National Trauma Database (USA), demonstrated that helmeted riders had a lower proportion of cervical spine injury (3.5% vs. 4.4%, $p < 0.001$) compared with unhelmeted riders. Their findings were supported by Croce et al. (2009) and, more recently, by Page et al. (2018). The latter authors also demonstrated that unhelmeted riders in their study sustained a significantly higher number of fractures at spinal levels C-1 and C-5.

The author of this text examined a young adult male who was wearing a helmet (Figure 11.4). He suffered a fatal high cervical spinal injury as a result of his neck hyperextending when he lost control of his motorcycle and struck his head directly onto the trunk of a tree by the side of the road. In such circumstances, a helmet will not prevent a hyperextensive mechanism of injury, as seen in this victim.

## Pedestrians

Pedestrians constitute the largest single group suffering both fatal and non-fatal injuries in road traffic collisions. Frequently, they suffer multiple injuries from both primary and secondary impacts, as well as crush injuries. The patterns of neck injury seen are similar to those seen in other road users.

Vanezis (1980) found the incidence of neck injuries among pedestrians in his series to be 13%, which is comparable to other road users. In a clinical study of 1,672 pedestrians struck by motor vehicles, 47 (3%) sustained cervical spine injuries (Vives et al., 2008). This study takes into consideration the wide spectrum of fatal and non-fatal injuries.

Cain et al. (1989), examining the fatality rate of cervical spine injuries in pedestrians in road traffic collisions in South Australia between 1981 and 1986, found that fatalities in pedestrians were about four times that of vehicle occupants. Part of the reason for this, in their view, was due to the larger proportion of older pedestrians involved (49% were 50 years or older compared with vehicle occupants) and the greater forces of the impacts to which they are exposed.

Yanar et al. (2008), in their study, found that in pedestrians injured in road traffic collisions, the incidence of cervical spine injury was 2.1%, with substantial variation with age, ranging from 0.3% in the paediatric age group to 4.4% in the age group older than 65 years.

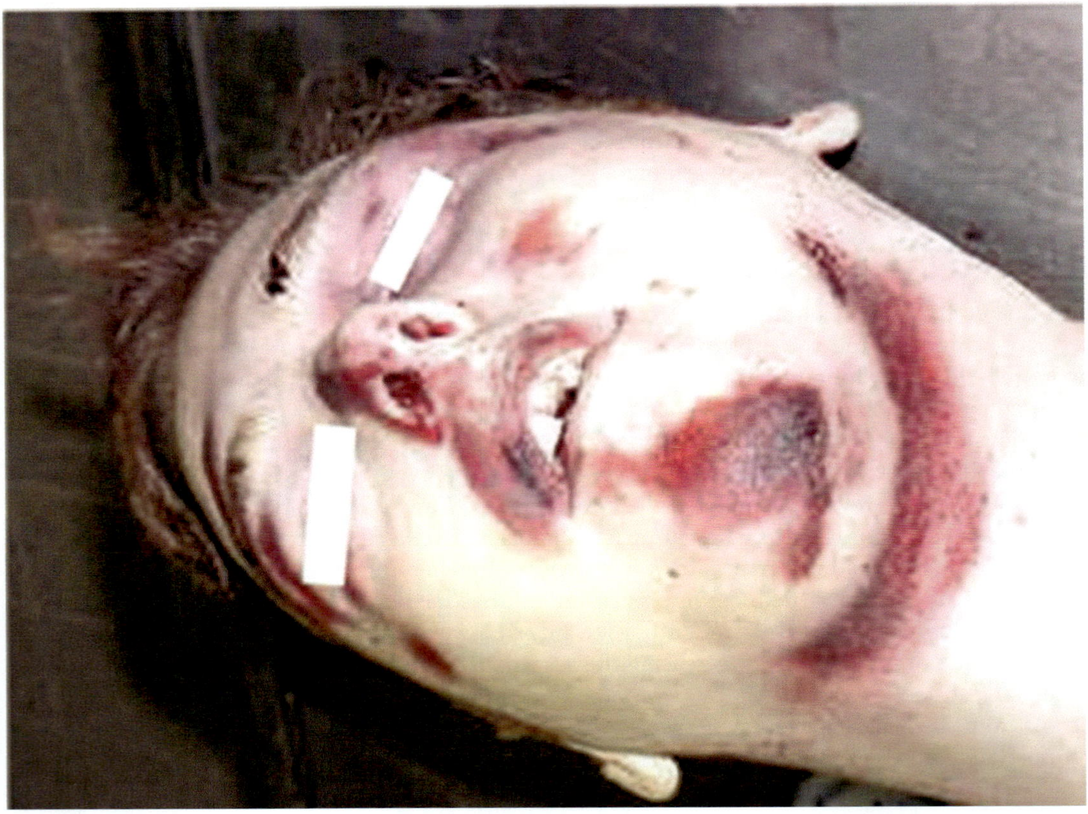

**Figure 11.4** Motorcyclist who was thrown head first onto a tree trunk and died instantly from a hyperextension injury to the cervical spine. Note the abrasions on the face from the impact as well as the curved friction abrasion of his upper neck, caused by the strapping on his helmet.

# WHIPLASH INJURIES

The term "whiplash" was first used by Crowe in 1928 (Crowe, 1964) to describe the effects of sudden acceleration-deceleration forces on the neck and upper trunk due to external forces exerting a lash-like effect. The term 'whiplash injury' was then later adopted by the medical profession and popularised in an article by Gay and Abbot in 1953. However, a number of years later, Crowe himself (Crowe, 1964) described the use of the term whiplash as unfortunate. He explained that the expression was intended to be a description of motion, but it that it had been accepted by physicians, patients, and attorneys as the name of a disease and resulted in its misapplication by many physicians and others over the years.

More recently, the Quebec Task Force on Whiplash-Associated Disorders redefined the term in 1995 (Spitzer et al., 1995) as

> an acceleration-deceleration mechanism of energy transfer to the neck which may result from rear-end or side impact, predominately in motor vehicle accidents, and from other mishaps. The energy transfer may result in bony or soft tissue injuries (whiplash injury), which may in turn lead to a wide variety of clinical manifestations (whiplash associated disorders).

Despite many attempts, however, it has so far not been possible to establish a uniform application for this type of injury complex. In order to obtain a clear, functionally based definition, one must take into account not only clinical signs and symptomatology but also the mechanical aspects and anatomical lesions seen. They are mainly the result of rear impact collisions where the trunk is pushed rapidly forwards.

Saternus (1982) emphasised that whiplash injury should not be confused with hyperextension injury, even though there may be some overlap in the lesions produced. Extension followed by flexion and vice versa can also occur from frontal and side impacts to a significant degree.

The important aetiological factor in such injuries is the dual motion generated by sudden acceleration and deceleration. The biphasic nature of the movements should be appreciated because much of the resulting injury is assumed to occur from the secondary movement. This secondary movement does not, by any means, proceed with low energy but is determined by the mass contraction of muscle groups subjected to primary abrupt hyperextension in relation to their synergists. Injury to only one region of the cervical spine should not be regarded as characteristic of whiplash injury; rather, one should appreciate the frequent occurrence of multiple injuries.

Appreciable forces, therefore, act at different segments of the cervical spine and lead to trauma of soft tissues adjacent to the cervical spine, ligaments, discs, and bony structures. Eck et al. (2001), in their review of whiplash injuries, pointed out that it was important for physicians to understand the biomechanical basis of the injury and to accept that the patient may not have many objective findings. It is also well known that with whiplash-associated disorders, even after treatment, many patients may continue to have localised symptoms for long periods that were not all thought to be psychosomatic.

An interesting study was undertaken by Freeman et al. (2006) of chronic neck pain and whiplash injuries in nine states in the United States to determine whether whiplash injuries contributed significantly to the population of individuals with chronic neck and other spine pain. Four hundred and nineteen patients and 246 controls were randomly enrolled. Patients were defined as individuals with chronic neck pain, and controls as those with chronic back pain. The two groups were surveyed for the cause of chronic pain as well as demographic information. The two groups were compared using an exposure-odds ratio. Forty-five percent of the patients attributed their pain to a motor vehicle accident. From their study, they inferred that a significant proportion of individuals with chronic neck pain in the general population were originally injured in a motor vehicle accident.

In terms of civil litigation, Vanezis, 2016 in addition to Ferrara et al, 2016, pointed out that the assessment of damages for whiplash injuries requires particular care. Allegations of such injuries are easily made and not easily disproved. The medical experts are reliant on the honesty of plaintiffs, and the evidence relating to such a claim requires careful scrutiny. It is for the plaintiff to prove the existence and the nature and extent of the injuries. Exaggerated claims may call into question the very existence of whiplash injury in an individual.

## SPORT INJURIES

Kleeman et al. (2015), in their review of cervical spine injuries in sport, found that they accounted for approximately 10% of all cervical spine injuries in the United States. Such injuries have been reported in football, soccer, wrestling, basketball, trampoline, sledding, baseball, hockey, water sports, diving, and rugby, with the majority occurring in collision sports. Injuries range from transient radiculopathies to permanent, complete spinal cord injury.

Zahir and Ludwig (2010) emphasised the need for a thorough understanding of sport injury patterns to assist in their early recognition and subsequent management. They pointed out that the cervical spine is most stable in the lordotic position, which biomechanically allows for forces to be effectively distributed through the paraspinal neck musculature and ligaments. In the contact sports setting, the cervical spine is at risk when the head is in a flexed forward position at the time of direct impact, eliminating the protective lordosis of the cervical spine; a straightened or slightly kyphotic position places it at increased risk for injury.

Loss of lordosis of the cervical spine places patients at increased risk for permanent neurological injuries because of recurrent axial loading injuries. This is seen in the spear tackler's spine, a condition that often occurs in athletes involved in collision sports in which the head is used as a point of contact. The condition is classically associated with North American football. Characteristics of this condition include cervical spine stenosis with straightening of the cervical spine and loss of normal physiological lordosis, together with a documented history of using spear tackling techniques.

In addition to axial compression, other mechanisms of injury include rotational forces, hyperflexion, hyperextension, and lateral bending. Biomechanical studies have questioned the traditional view of flexion/extension movements causing cervical spine injury. Kuster et al. (2012), from a systematic review of studies which considered rugby union-related cervical spine injury mechanisms, concluded that it was unlikely that hyperflexion was the true mechanism for acute injuries involving the spinal cord. Their view was that the weight of evidence suggested that the primary mechanism for the commonly observed bilateral facet joint dislocation (normally C5–C7) injury was buckling. In opposition, Dennison et al. (2012) stated that it was too early to conclude that buckling was the predominant mechanism of injury. This opposition was partly based on the limitations associated with the ex vivo cadaveric testing on which some of Kuster's evidence was based, and the fact that the same injuries produced via buckling mechanisms in cadavers had not been reproduced in vivo, possibly due to an active involvement of the musculature in protecting from injury. Currently, therefore, the consensus is that the C4–C6 region is the most common area of injury, but the precise mechanisms for acute spinal cord injuries during scrummaging are still not clear.

In relation to martial arts injuries, a recent study was carried out by Stanbouly et al. (2022), which examined and compared 1,707 persons with head and neck injuries admitted to emergency departments following injury whilst practising different types of martial arts. They were able to partially confirm the hypothesis that striking-predominant martial arts are more likely to cause head and neck trauma and hospital admissions than submission-predominant martial arts. This study ultimately determined that karate, taekwondo, and kickboxing accounted for the highest incidences of head and neck injuries, whereas jiu jitsu and judo accounted for the lowest incidences. This can be explained by taking into account whether the martial art at hand is striking-predominant or submission-predominant.

The author of this text has seen two homicides that followed karate blows to the lower face and neck. The assailant was an 18-year-old man who killed his mother and grandmother on successive nights. Both the women were alcoholics, and he had to care for them as well as attend college to better himself. His father had abandoned the family many years before. When he called the coroner's officer the morning after the first death, he was informed that his mother had probably died from alcohol abuse. An autopsy was carried out, which was inconclusive, and toxicology was awaited.

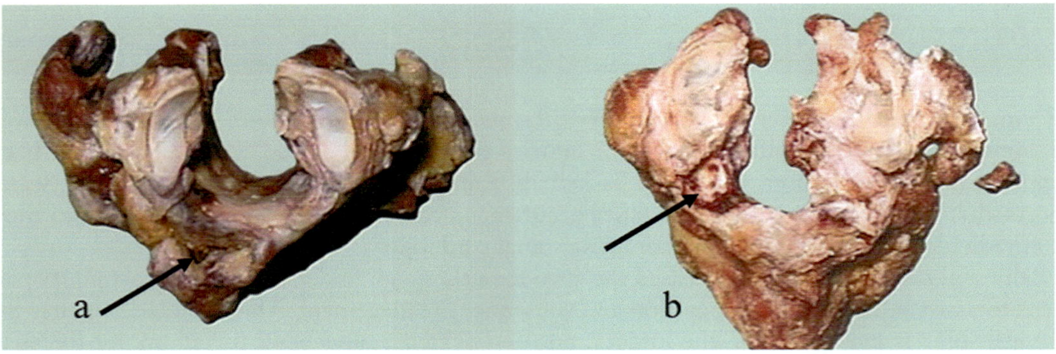

**Figure 11.5** (a) C1 from above, from first victim. Haemorrhage is apparent on the left posterior arch (arrow), (b) C1 from the second victim. Haemorrhage is just posterior to left articular facet (arrow), (c) Cervical cord exposed, showing haemorrhage principally in the epidural space.

He therefore had the impression that they did not think it was a suspicious death, so went ahead and killed his grandmother that evening in the same manner. The police then treated the second post-mortem as suspicious, and the pathologist also re-examined the first autopsy. The findings were found in the upper cervical spine, base of the skull, and spinal cord (Figure 11.5). He had been attending karate classes and had been taught how to deliver potentially "fatal blows". It soon became clear that he had applied such blows to both his mother and grandmother, causing rapidly fatal atlantoaxial dislocation in both cases.

## INJURIES TO THE CERVICAL SPINE AFFECTED BY CHRONIC DEGENERATIVE CONDITIONS

Ankylosing spondylitis involves chronic inflammation, which leads to disorders mainly in the spine and the sacroiliac joints. One of the main findings of the disease in the spine is the ossification of the soft tissues, mainly the ligaments and the disks. This abnormal ossification leads to biomechanical alterations in patients with ankylosing spondylitis, and these patients tend to suffer from spinal fractures even with relatively mild trauma. They are prone to fracture of the rigid and deformed spinal column (Figure 11.6). The most common injury in the spinal column is

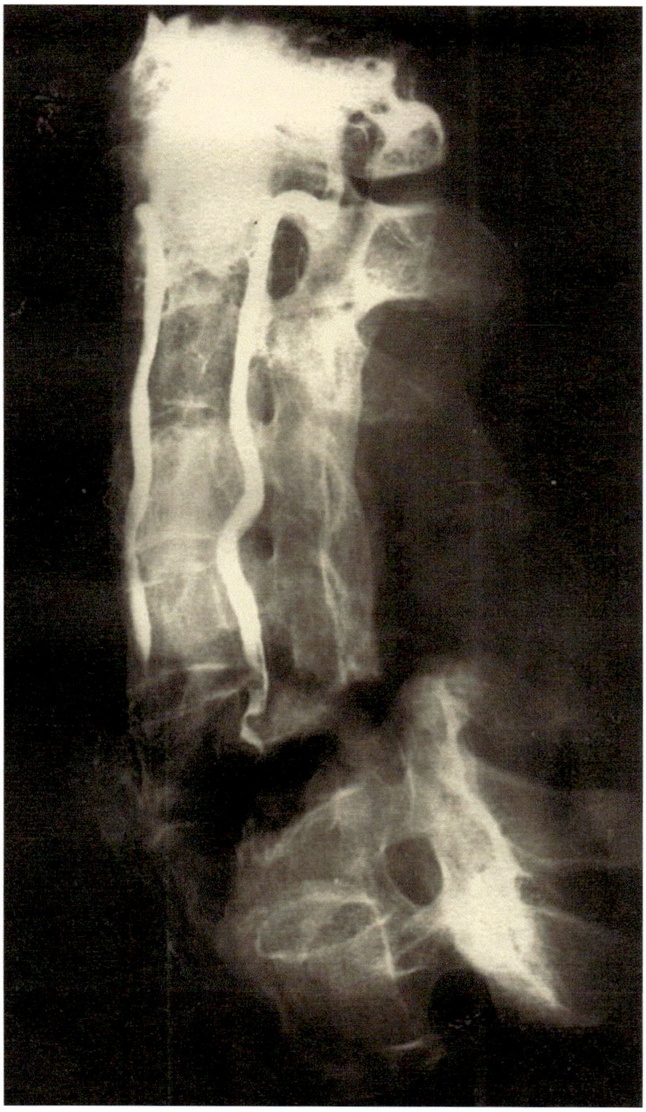

**Figure 11.6** Left lateral radiograph of a 40-year-old male with severe ankylosing spondylitis. There is a complete distractive hyperextension fracture of all bony elements at C5–C6 level with transection of the spinal cord. The deceased had fallen forwards on to his chin. Post-mortem angiography had also been carried out in this case.

observed around the C5 and C7 segments, with neurologic deficits for the patients, although they have been reported occurring rarely in the upper cervical spine. Govender and Charles (1987) report the case of a 52-year-old man who fell onto his forehead and was admitted 6 days later with marked tenderness over the upper part of his cervical spine, with an exaggerated cervical lordosis. His neurological state was normal. Radiographs showed a type II fracture of the dens with marked posterior displacement. The mechanism for this injury was hyperextension and posterior displacement. A further case is reported by Peh and Ho (1995) of a 50-year-old man who sustained fractures of the odontoid peg as well as the body of the second cervical vertebra after a hyperextension injury in a road traffic collision.

Cervical spondylosis, which results from age-related degenerative changes including excess wear and tear, is characterised by degeneration of the disks and joints, associated gross osteophyte formation (Figure 11.7; see also Chapter 10), and narrowing of the anteroposterior diameter of the cervical canal to less than 11 mm, increasing the risk of fracture even with relatively trivial injury.

A crack fracture of a cervical osteophyte nearly caused fatal asphyxia in an elderly man after he incurred a relatively minor hyperextension injury. A tracheostomy with evacuation of a prevertebral haematoma was performed with immediate relief of symptoms (Howcroft and Jenkins,

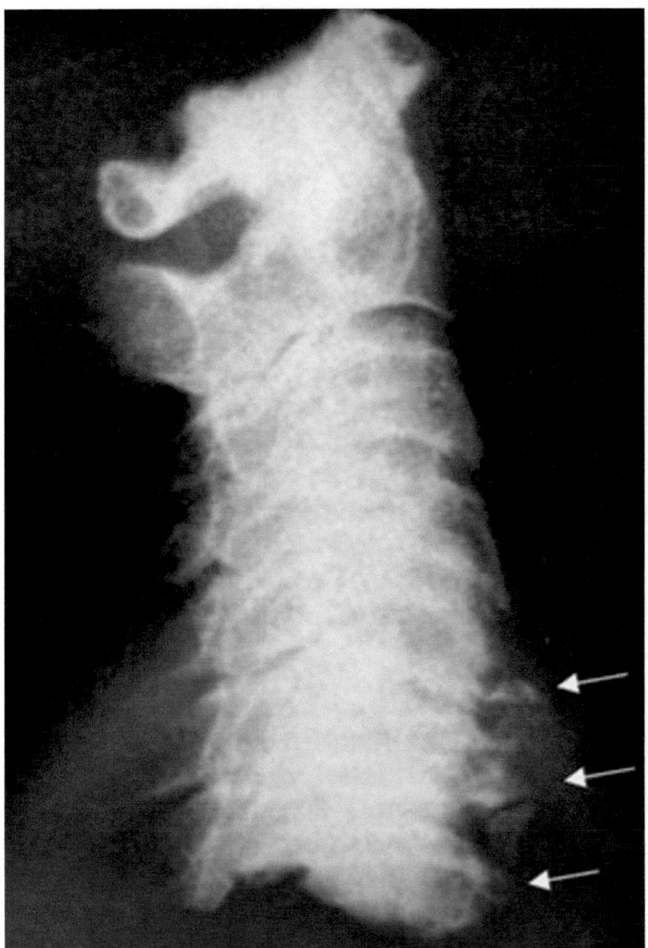

**Figure 11.7** Right lateral radiograph of excised cervical spine, showing gross osteophyte formation at the anterior vertebral bodies of C5, C6, and C7 (arrows).

1977). Spondylotic ridges may press on the cord and impede the blood supply producing cervical myelopathy (Chiles et al., 1999; Lebl et al., 2011). Furthermore, the dura may be adherent to the surrounding bone, and root-sleeve fibrosis may also be present, thus narrowing the cervical canal. With these changes, the cord is firmly anchored in the cervical canal, and the liability to contusion increases. Because of these factors, injury to the cervical cord in patients with cervical spondylosis is common even when there is no fracture or fracture-dislocation. Hyperextension of the cervical spine during anaesthesia or chiropractic manipulation may also damage the cord, especially if muscle relaxants are given.

The pathologist should also be aware of the possibility of a post-mortem fracture of the cervical spine being produced if there is clumsy handling of the deceased's neck prior to the autopsy (Figure 11.8). This is particularly a risk in persons who have degenerative disease of the spine, as discussed above. Although, as a rule, there is very little associated haemorrhage, differentiation from an ante-mortem injury may prove difficult.

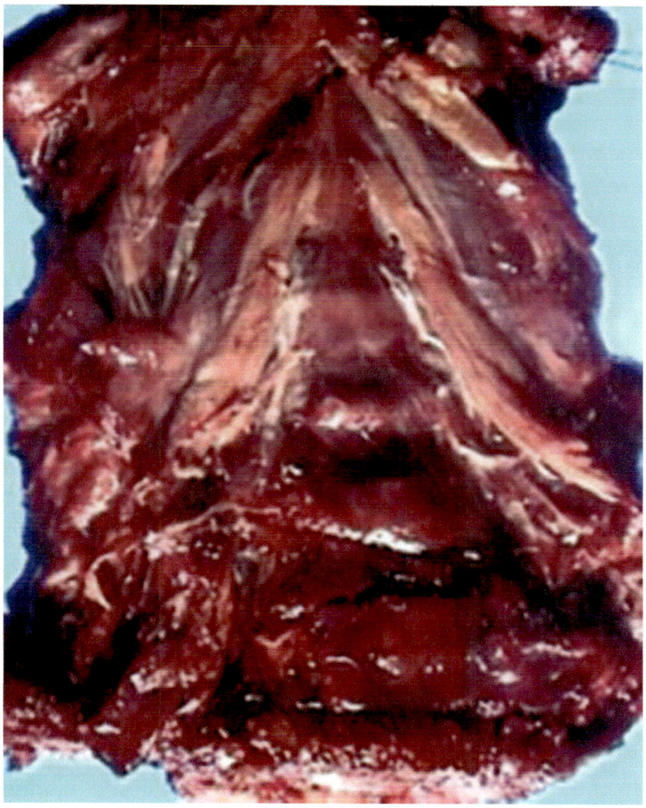

**Figure 11.8** Post-mortem fracture of C6 resulting from clumsy handling of the deceased's neck after death.

# CERVICAL CORD TRAUMA

## Overview

Spinal cord injuries, in general, occur mostly in traffic accidents and falls, as well as from other causes such as assaults or sports. There is a reported male-to-female ratio of 2:1, which is seen more frequently in adults compared to children (WHO, 2013).

Demographically, men are mostly affected during their early and late adulthood (3rd and 8th decades of life), while women are at higher risk during their adolescence (15–19 years) and the 7th decade of their lives. The age distribution is bimodal, with a first peak involving young adults and a second peak involving adults over the age of 60. Injuries in adults older than 60 years of age usually result from falls and age-related degenerative bony changes.

With regard to the cervical spinal cord, 50% of injuries are sustained at this level compared to 35% at the thoracic and 11% in the lumbar region. The most affected level injured in the cervical cord is at the C5 level (Alizadeh et al., 2019). Injuries to the cervical spinal column may be accompanied by cervical cord trauma, depending on whether the force applied is sufficient to exclude elastic deformation. However, Stanners et al. (2024), in a systematic review of the mechanical properties of the spinal cord, concluded that it was not possible to draw conclusions from the published literature as to how the human spinal cord would behave under either mechanical testing or clinical scenarios where forces are applied to the cord, such as degenerative cervical myelopathy.

Neurological involvement occurs when the cord rapidly decelerates by striking a surface, such as the edge of a dislocated vertebra, spondylotic ridge, infolded ligamentum flavum, or fractured bone. A shearing force is produced that displaces the segment above with regard to the segment below the point of force application. This displacement gives rise to shearing stress in the plane of force. Typically, in fracture-dislocations, one vertebral body moves and impacts the cord. Vascular spasm may also occur with tissue displacement and cause ischaemic damage to the cord.

Chen (2008), discusses the most common types of fractures associated with the cervical spine and reviews cervical spinal cord syndromes, pointing out that such syndromes, discovered during the neurological examination, frequently provide the first clue that there is an underlying spinal cord injury. He also informs us that although hyperextension injuries frequently occur without fractures, such injuries often result in a central cord syndrome with profound neurologic deficits. The syndrome is characterised by disproportionately more motor impairment of the upper and lower extremities, bladder dysfunction, usually urinary retention, and varying degrees of sensory loss below the level of the lesion. It may be caused either by direct contusion to the cervical cord with permanent or transient damage to the posterior columns and lateral spinothalamic tract with some degree of sensory loss or by vascular insufficiency. Thompson et al. (2015) noted that it was the most commonly encountered type of incomplete spinal cord injury, typically occurring in patients over the age of 50 with a narrow spinal canal, and follows an acute hyperextension injury of the cervical spine in the setting of low-impact/low-velocity trauma in adults without fracture/dislocation with preexisting cervical spondylosis. This syndrome is characterised by weakness that is greater distally than proximally. Patients frequently have weakness and numbness in the hands and fingers. The upper extremities are affected more than the lower extremities. This is believed to occur because of the topographic distribution of the nerve tracts in the cervical spine such that the representation of the hands and fingers is placed medially or centrally. The hyperextension leads to anterior compression of the blood vessels that supply the central spinal cord.

Avila and Hurlbert (2021) stated that spinal cord injury encompassed a broad spectrum of neurologic deficiencies, with several syndromes showing the unique neurological conditions arising from injury to specific tracts within the spinal cord.

Anterior cord syndrome is associated with occlusion of the anterior spinal artery and typically involves a dense motor deficit, absent light touch and pain appreciation, but preservation of dorsal column deep pressure and position sensation. By contrast, posterior cord syndrome can result from occlusion of the posterior spinal arteries and is characterised by dorsal column deficits (ataxia) but preserved motor, light touch, and pain function.

Brown-Séquard syndrome can occur from a fall or from penetrating injury (see also Chapter 4) and denotes lateral spinal cord injury resulting in ipsilateral motor and dorsal column deficits and contralateral light touch and pain deficits.

## Neuropathology of the Spinal Cord and Roots

Injuries to the cord occur mainly at the time of the inflicted trauma (Figure 11.9). Neural injury may also develop subsequently if there is dislocation with pressure on the cord, or if it is continuously stretched over a bony or cartilaginous protrusion; the resulting ischaemia produces additional

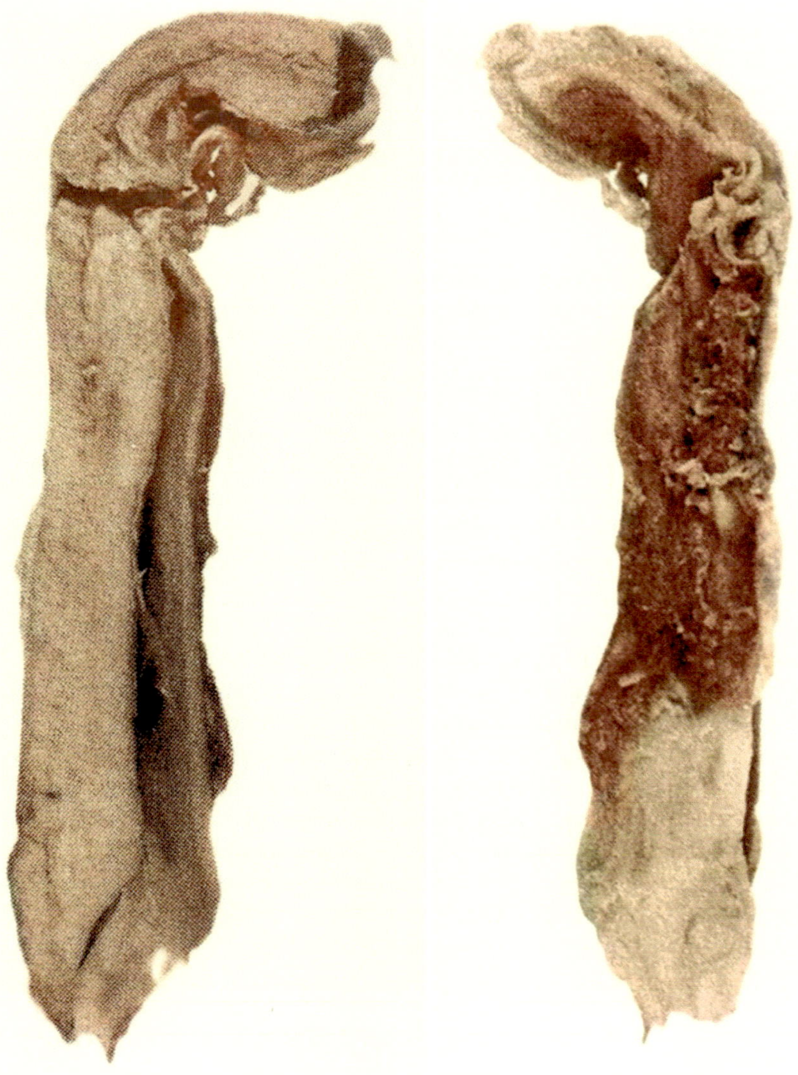

(a) (b)

**Figure 11.9** (a) Sagittal section of excised cervical cord, showing complete transection at the level of C2. Injury followed a fall down from a flight of stairs, causing severe hyperextension fracture-dislocation to the cervical spine, (b) Epidural haemorrhage from the same person.

lesions, or at least hinders recovery. Kakulas (1999) noted that despite its delicate consistency, the human spinal cord was relatively resistant to the initial injury. Of 354 cases in the database with vertebral injuries who were dead at the scene of the accident, the spinal cord was found to be intact at the level of the lesion in 139 (39%).

As noted elsewhere, the most common region of fracture-dislocation is at C5 and C6. With an accompanying fracture, apart from pressure ischaemia and mechanical trauma, spicules of bone may occasionally pierce the cord. The dural sheath, however, affords good protection in most cases against this form of penetrating injury. In addition, nerve roots may be compressed by the dislocation and may contribute to the amyotrophy caused by the destruction of motor cells in the cord.

In some cases, herniation and protrusion of the nucleus pulposus, causing secondary compression of the spinal cord, result immediately from an injury to the cervical spine, but in most cases injuries to the cervical intervertebral discs produce symptoms of more chronic and progressive character which differ little from those seen in cases of cervical spondylosis in which there is no history of trauma. There is no doubt, however, that in patients with existing degeneration of cervical discs, injury may occur from comparatively minor trauma or even from sudden voluntary movement of the neck. In these cases, the cord is subjected to abnormal stresses by being stretched over a cartilaginous or bony protrusion at the level of the degenerated disc. The effects of immediate mechanical stress and compression are often combined, irrespective of whether or not a fracture is present.

## Gross Appearances

In many cases in which paraplegia results immediately from an incident causing sudden movement of the neck, post-mortem examination may show no gross abnormality of the spinal column or canal, or there may be some haemorrhage and softening. On the other hand, one quite commonly observes significant accompanying bony, cartilaginous, and ligamentous injuries as previously described.

In the early stages of injury, the cord is usually swollen and has a bluish-red appearance over one or two segments at the level at which the greatest degree of spinal movement occurred. The pia-arachnoid and subdural space frequently show patches of haemorrhage. The injury typically extends over several segments and is usually associated with central haemorrhagic necrosis, which may involve the surrounding white matter tracts to a variable degree.

On section, the damaged area may be grossly softened but more often shows diffuse swelling with small haemorrhagic points in the grey columns, although the white matter may also be involved to varying degrees. The demarcation of grey from white matter is often blurred, and the tissue may appear abnormally pale. Occasionally, cylindrical cores of softened tissue may also pass upwards and downwards from most of the softened area. They are usually found at the base of the dorsal horns or in the ventral part of the dorsal columns. These consist of myelin and axon debris, sometimes contained in phagocytic cells, along with serous fluid. Cores of this kind are most commonly found when there is gross softening of the cord at one level without tearing of the pia-arachnoid. The swelling of the tissues and the outpouring of serum associated with softening are restrained by the firm pia mater, and thus the softened tissue tends to track in an upward and downward direction along the grey columns or in the line of the nerve fibres. Some of these cores may be artefactual, produced by clumsy removal of the spinal cord at autopsy.

## Microscopical Findings (Figures 11.10–11.12)

In mild cases, there may only be swelling of axons and myelin sheaths at the level of the damaged segment. This may be diffuse and slight, but is usually more severe in a small area. Microscopically, there is hyperaemia with many free red cells within the disrupted tissues. A variable number of polymorphs, appearing at first, are followed by macrophages over several days. These mononuclear cells gradually remove the dead tissue. Axonal damage can be detected within hours of injury by immunocytochemical methods, using antibodies prepared against the βA4 moiety of the amyloid precursor protein (APP).

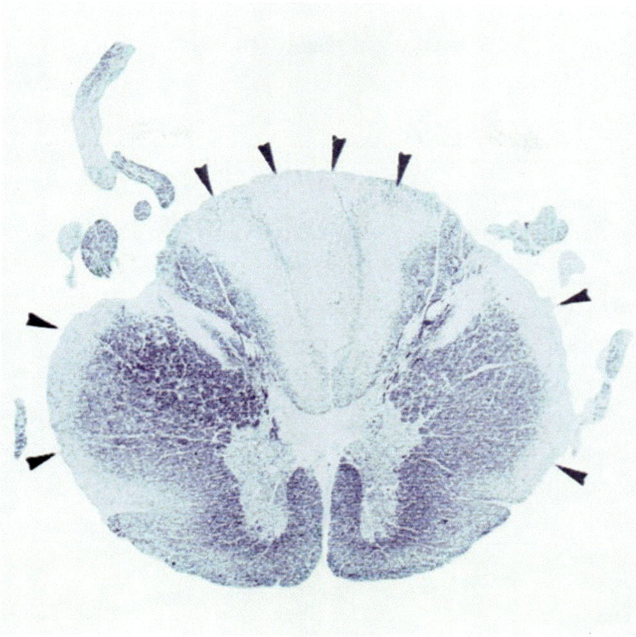

**Figure 11.10** Transverse section of cervical cord, showing destruction of the posterior columns, as well as bilateral anterior and posterior spinocerebellar tracts (arrows) (Luxol Fast Blue × 8). The deceased suffered a relatively minor hyperextension injury without a fracture. The spine showed extensive cervical spondylosis.

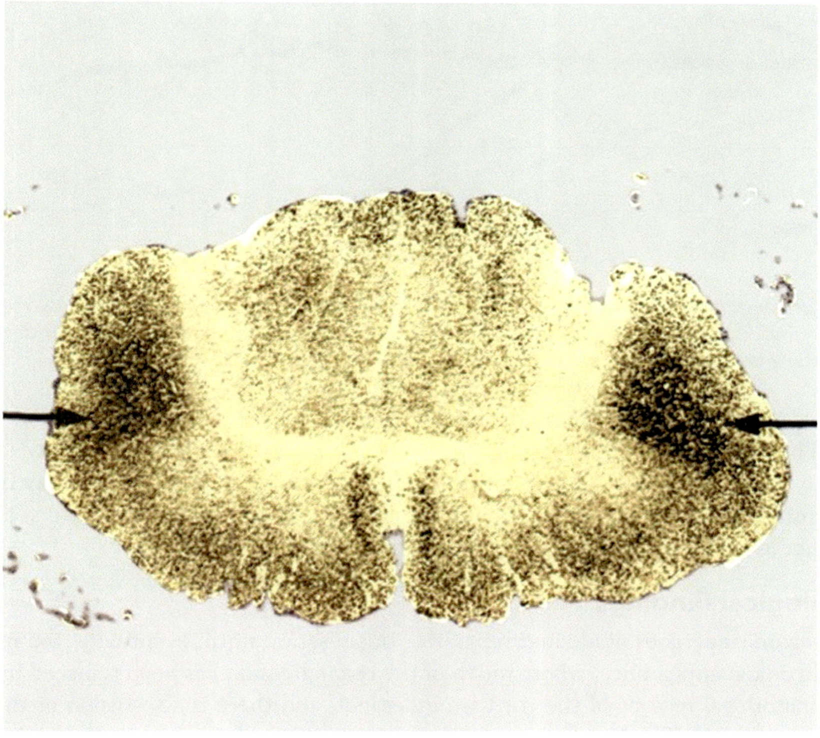

**Figure 11.11** Transverse section of cervical cord, showing degeneration of both lateral corticospinal tracts (arrows) following complete transection (Marchi × 8).

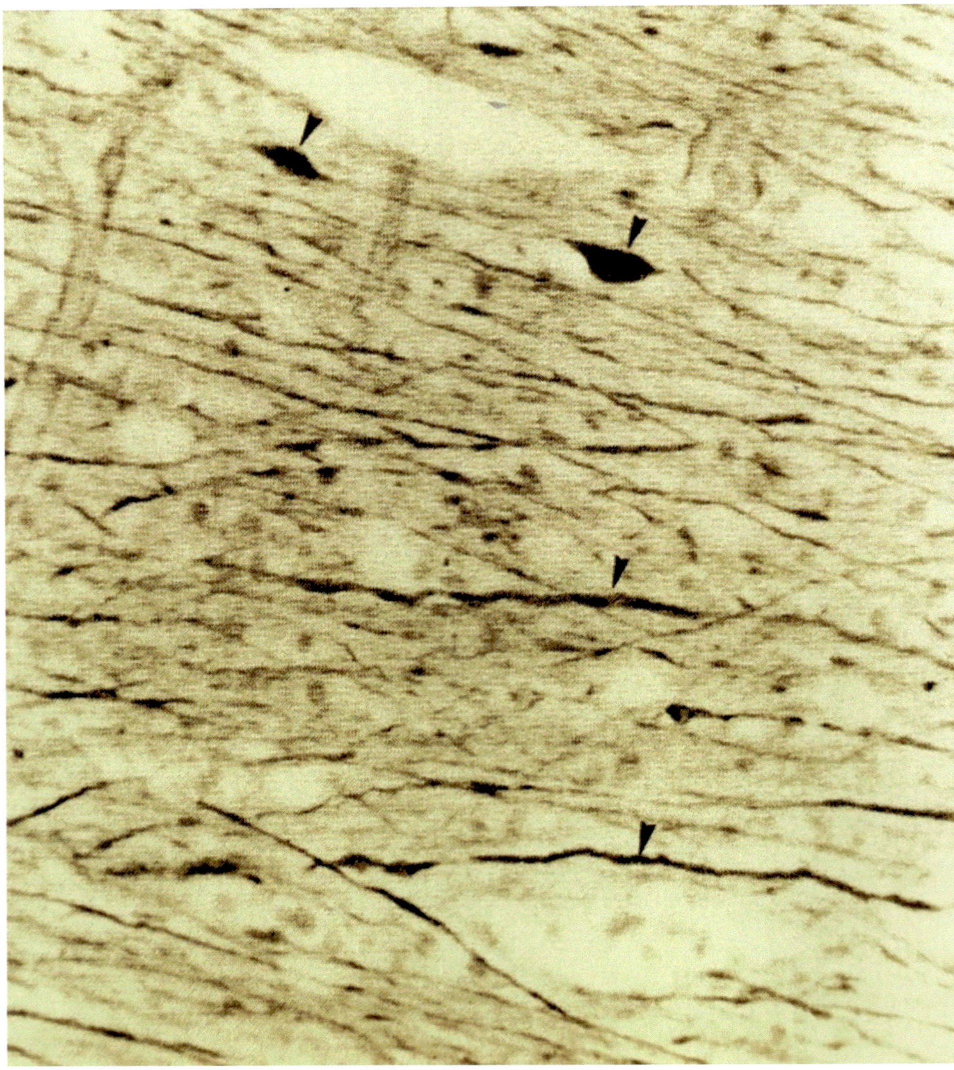

**Figure 11.12** Longitudinal section of cervical cord, showing diffuse axonal injury. There are two retraction balls (arrows) and a number of sinusoidally enlarged axons (arrows). The deceased survived for four days, following a severe hyperextension injury (Palmgren × 60).

Longitudinal sections stained for axons may show beaded swellings or end bulbs where they are torn across. These appearances may persist for weeks. The myelin sheaths are distended in areas corresponding to the injured axons. Nerve cell changes occur in most cases but may be slight and limited to a minor degree of central chromatolysis. Occasionally, ghost cells are seen, and later some loss of nerve cells may be found by comparative counts.

## Late Pathological Findings

The injured region undergoes graduated reparative organisation until, eventually, the initial area of injury has a shrunken appearance, where much of the original lesion has been replaced by scar tissue. The various anatomical regions of the cord are indistinct, and there is also fusion of the meningeal coats to the spinal canal. The less damaged parts of the cord, and, invariably, the region above and immediately below the main site of injury, now present as a region of intense astrocytic fibrous gliosis. The area of partial cord damage is filled with spongy glia, and sometimes a syrinx has formed.

Wallerian degeneration is present in the long tracts of the white columns of the spinal cord. It occurs distal to the level of injury in the descending spinal pathways and proximally in the ascending systems following injury. After injury, the axonal skeleton disintegrates, and the axonal membrane breaks apart. Axonal degeneration is followed by degradation of the myelin sheath and infiltration by macrophages. The macrophages, accompanied by Schwann cells, serve to clear the debris from the degeneration.

A constant feature of spinal cord injury after about five years is the presence of regenerating nerve fibres growing within the connective tissue scar situated in the damaged region of the spinal cord. These fibres have a Schwann cell sheath and grow within the connective tissue but not within the glial areas.

Post-traumatic syringomyelia refers to the development of a cerebrospinal fluid-filled cavity within the substance of the spinal cord (Goetz et al., 2023). As the name suggests, this particular type of syringomyelia occurs after previous trauma with or without clinical spinal cord injury. At autopsy, it is seen as a longitudinal cavity in the spinal cord, which replaces part or all of the spindle-shaped zone of haemorrhagic necrosis present in the acute stage of the injury. The lining of the cavity is of glia and connective tissue, which may form a thick wall. The exact mechanism of these post-traumatic syringes is uncertain, although it is suspected that a communication exists between the syrinx and the subarachnoid space laterally, near the posterior root entry zone.

# SHAKING TRAUMA IN INFANTS AND THE CERVICAL SPINE

With regard to shaken baby syndrome (SBS), Bandak (2005) conducted an injury biomechanics analysis of the reported levels of rotational velocity and acceleration of the head in experimental animal and human neonate cadaver models to assess the effects on the infant head and neck. It was determined that an infant head subjected to the levels of rotational velocity and acceleration described in the SBS literature would experience forces on the infant neck far exceeding the limits for structural failure of the cervical spine. It was also found that cervical spine injury from shaking can occur at much lower levels of head velocity and acceleration than those reported for SBS. The author was also of the view that shaking-induced head accelerations can potentially cause severe, if not lethal, cervical spinal cord or brainstem injury in the infant at levels well below those reported for SBS. Given, therefore, that cervical spine injury is reported to be a rare clinical finding in SBS cases, the results of the study indicated an SBS diagnosis in an infant with intracerebral injury but without cervical spine or brainstem injury, should be regarded as questionable, and that other causes of the intracerebral injury should be explored. The author also felt that cervical spine and/or brainstem injury should be included amongst the factors considered in cases where infant shaking is suspected.

Oehmichen et al. (2008) carried out an autopsy study of 18 selected infant deaths under one year of age that were highly suspicious for SBS, exhibiting the classical SBS triad of acute subdural haemorrhage (SDH), retinal bleeding, and encephalopathy. Gross autopsy and microscopic findings from these infants were compared with those of 19 victims of sudden infant death syndrome (SIDS; control group 1) and of 14 infants who died of disease or injuries/violence not involving the head, neck, or eyes (control group 2). Symptoms of mechanical impact to the head were evident in seven of the SBS infants, but in none of the control infants. Diffuse axonal injury was not detected in either the SBS or control cases. Localised axonal injury was regularly present in the brains of the SBS infants surviving longer than 1.5–3.0 hours, but only occasionally in the craniocervical junction and within the nerve roots of the upper cervical cord; in nearly half of their cases, an epidural haemorrhage of the cervical spine was found, and the authors suggested that it should be regarded as an additional diagnostic criterion of shaking as a traumatic event.

Vinchon et al. (2022) reported wedge fractures and cervical spinal cord lesions caused by shaking. They emphasised that shaking represents a specific mechanism of spinal trauma, with its greatest effect at the most mobile levels of the spine, causing minor wedge fractures, extramedullary bleeding, and potentially fatal contusions of the upper cervical spinal cord. The presence of these lesions corroborates the diagnosis of abuse, and in particular, violent shaking or beating. They emphasised as did the other authors above, that spinal cord studies should be a systematic part of the examination in the evaluation of young children suspected of abuse.

# VERTEBRAL ARTERY TRAUMA

As with cervical spine injuries in general, the forces leading to vertebral artery injury may be directed either at the site of the resulting lesion or at an adjacent site on the neck, head, or thorax. With direct force, the vascular lesion is produced as a result of compression or contusion, with the vessel being pressed against the transverse process. If the latter is fractured then damaged bone edges may pierce the artery, either in addition to or together with compressive trauma. Indirect forces cause injuries by stretching the vessel either in a region where extreme movement is combined with vulnerability, namely, in its curved upper portion between C2 and its intracranial course or over osteophytic spurs. The vessel itself may be diseased from atherosclerotic involvement which may cause great tortuosity and stenosis. An artery in such a condition would be more liable to tear during sudden stretching.

The role of head movement in affecting blood flow and the physical integrity of the vertebral arteries has been widely studied. A recent systematic review by Kranenburg et al. (2019), investigating the effects of head and neck positions on blood flow in the vertebral, internal carotid, and intracranial arteries, found that across 31 studies, craniocervical positions and movements in most people had no effect on blood flow. In a small proportion of the groups "healthy subjects", "vascular patients", and "other patients", blood flow did decrease during some movements, specifically maximum rotation and/or maximum extension. A clinical implication from this review was that the relationship between craniocervical movement and alterations in blood flow does not seem to be as obvious as previously suggested. With regard to movement of the vertebral artery when associated with compression against degenerative changes such as osteophytes, although reported rarely, it is a well-known cause of vertebrobasilar insufficiency, or Bow Hunter's syndrome. The latter eponym was first coined by Sorensen (1978) who reported a case of vertebrobasilar insufficiency, causing a stroke in a hunter who suddenly rotated his neck when using a bow, and pointed out the vulnerability of individuals taking part in this popular activity. Other cases resulting in strokes have been reported by Nishikawa et al. (2017) and Denis et al. (2014). It should also be appreciated that, although vertebral artery compression by spondylosis during neck movements can trigger vertebrobasilar insufficiency symptoms, other factors, such as a narrow, and/or incompetent contralateral artery, may predispose the posterior circulation of some individuals to transient ischaemic attack and stroke.

## Acute Manifestations of Injury

Lacerations and minor tears to the vertebral artery, although much more commonly associated with penetrating injuries, when they result from blunt trauma, present a more challenging diagnostic problem. Most traumatic lesions of the vertebral arteries are incomplete tears, particularly involving the adventitia (Figure 11.13). There are also appreciable accompanying injuries to nearby structures, including tears of the vertebral venous plexus. It should also be appreciated that venous plexus injuries may also be found without accompanying arterial trauma.

In many cases, associated skeletal injury is also found. The initial presentation may range from a rapidly fatal basal subarachnoid haemorrhage to a local haematoma with no apparent morbidity in the acute stage.

Arterial trauma from blunt forces may also cause occlusion, principally as a result of thrombosis or spasm, although both are difficult to detect in the acute stage. In many instances it is the complications (early or late) from such injuries that are diagnosed. The site of arterial injury in the vast majority of cases is at the same or at adjacent levels to other accompanying cervical spine injuries.

As described in an earlier section in this chapter, with regard to degenerative arthritic changes of the cervical spine, in addition to the cervical vertebrae, the subject may be more vulnerable to vertebral artery trauma, particularly where the vessel is stretched over an osteophytic spur. The vessels in many cases, when examined angiographically, usually display a markedly tortuous pattern (Vanezis, 1984).

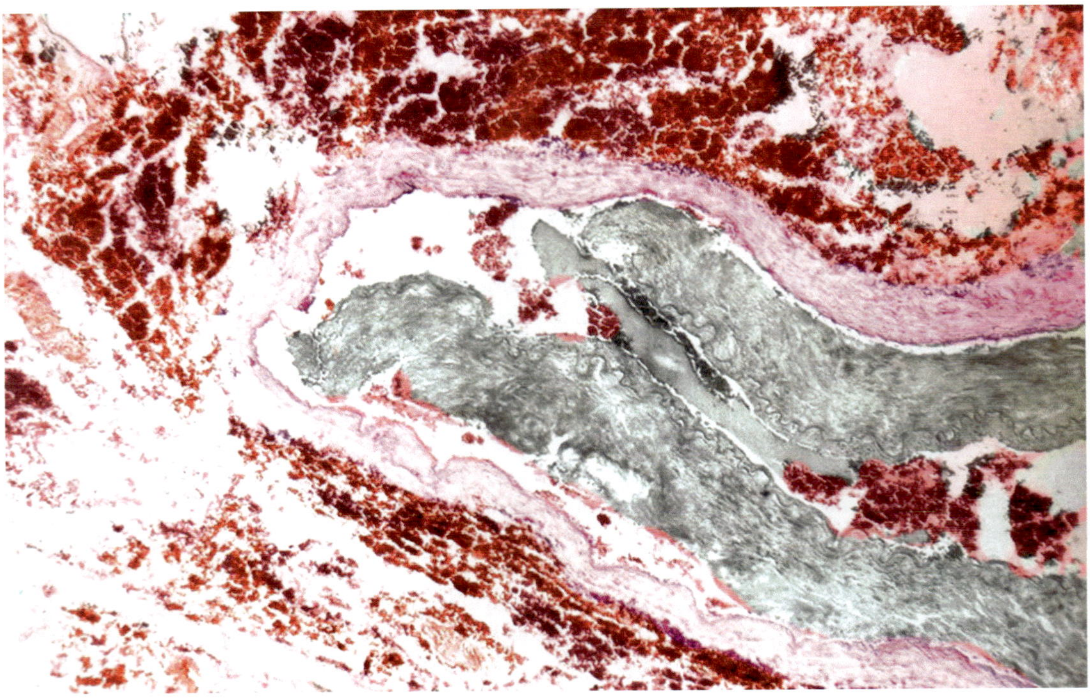

**Figure 11.13** Transverse section of the right vertebral artery at C5, showing substantial perivascular haemorrhage from a tear of the adventitia, which has become partially detached from the media. The tunica intima is also torn and seen in the lumen within the contrast medium (from post-mortem angiography) (Haematoxylin and eosin × 70).

## Later Presentation of Vascular Trauma

Blunt injury to the vertebral artery may present at a later stage as an arteriovenous fistula or aneurysm. In both conditions, it is essential to elucidate a history of trauma to the head or neck and to exclude any non-traumatic structural abnormality.

Vertebral arteriovenous fistulae are extremely rare, and are much more commonly associated with penetrating injuries. Several mechanisms may play a role in the production of such injuries from blunt forces. These include severe hyperextension injuries of the cervical spine or osteophytes in severe osteoarthrosis, possibly causing tearing of the vertebral artery and surrounding venous plexus. Direct blunt trauma to the neck may also give rise to injuries of arteries and adjacent veins by direct compression or contusion.

True traumatic aneurysms, which are thought to follow partial arterial rupture, are very rare, in contrast to false aneurysms, which may occur following complete arterial wall laceration. With true aneurysms, particularly if they are situated intracranially, distinction from a congenital saccular aneurysm, may be extremely difficult. Although a history of head injury is essential for the diagnosis of a traumatic aneurysm, it is insufficient grounds alone for ruling out a congenital lesion. The age of the patient may be of some help in making the distinction, because congenital aneurysms are much less common in young children. Histological findings at the site of an arterial injury and from a congenital saccular aneurysm can be identical. However, in trauma cases, one should also encounter arterial sites where there is some injury dating back to the trauma incident.

In relation to the effects of vertebral artery injury in acute and chronic spinal trauma, a significant study carried out by Schneider and Schemm (1961) examined the role of the resulting insufficiency caused by trauma, in producing acute central cervical cord injury syndrome. They found that vascular insufficiency could occur as a result of indirect damage, secondary to compression of the vertebral artery. This, in turn, would result in relative hypoxia to the central motor pathways of the spinal cord with little or no sensory impairment. Furthermore, such hypoxia, resulting from an occlusion which may be partial or transient, may not be demonstrable grossly, in life or at autopsy. The main sites of compression of the vertebral artery in such cases are thought to be: (i) the intervertebral section of the transverse foramina when cervical dislocation occurs above the C5-C6 interspace; (ii) at the atlantoaxial joint at the C1 intervertebral foramina; or (iii) at the occipital-atlantal junction, at the point where the occipital condyle slides forward over the groove in the laminae of the first vertebra.

## Vertebral Artery Injuries Sustained During Birth

The effects of birth trauma on the vertebral arteries have been studied by Yates (1959). He examined the necks of 60 neonates who had died around the time of birth and found evidence of vertebral artery trauma in 24 of them. He thought it probable that arterial injury might be the cause of cerebral lesions in many cases of cerebral palsy. His explanation for the adventitial haemorrhages surrounding these vessels is based on the pressure differences to which the neonate is subjected, during passage through the birth canal. The presenting parts may be at or near atmospheric pressure, whilst the rest of the body is subject to the additional pressure of the contracting uterus, which may be 200 mmHg. The blood pressure is therefore raised from the normal 90/50 to 290/250 mmHg. The pulse pressure remains the same. With the tissues of the head and neck at normal atmospheric pressure, and the intravascular pressures very considerably raised, any slight tear of a vein or artery will produce a haematoma. If the haemorrhage has occurred within the tough adventitia of the vertebral artery, the haematoma will be unable to disperse rapidly. On completion of delivery, the intravascular arterial pressure returns to normal levels, which may be inadequate to maintain the lumen of the artery past a tense intramural haematoma formed at a pressure of 290 mmHg. By such a mechanism vertebral blood flow may be seriously embarrassed for a period of minutes or hours, which is sufficient for permanent cerebral ischaemia to occur.

## Vertebral Artery Injuries in Road Traffic Collisions

In a personal series, the author of this text has found vertebral artery injuries in 10 of 32 victims (31%) who were fatally injured in road traffic collisions and suspected of having some form of posterior neck trauma (Vanezis, 1986) (see also the earlier section on *Road traffic collision injuries*). This high incidence is not surprising in view of the suspicion that certain symptoms experienced in whiplash injuries may be related to occult vertebral artery trauma. Pötsch and Bohl (1994) examined the autopsy findings of 21 persons with trauma to the head and neck where normal autopsy procedures did not succeed in revealing an obvious cause of death. They observed various types of traumatic extracranial vertebral artery injuries in 15 of them (71%); 10 of these (48%) were from road traffic collisions. Sudden death due to acute brainstem ischaemia was thought to be an explanation in some of their cases.

The vascular lesions are distributed by level in a similar fashion to cervical spine injuries, the highest frequency being seen at the upper cervical spine, particularly at C1 level, then at C6 (Figure 11.14). Indeed, one should always be mindful of the possibility of vertebral artery trauma in suspected high cervical spine injuries, even though there is no evidence of injury on radiographic examination. The combination of extreme movement of the neck, particularly in its upper cervical portion, and the fact that the vertebral arteries are more exposed and vulnerable to stretching in this region should alert the clinician to the possibility of arterial injury.

## Subarachnoid Haemorrhage Following Vertebral Artery Trauma

Blunt force impact to the upper neck or head (particularly the upper part of the mandible and behind the ear) may cause injury to the upper cervical or intracranial portion of the vertebral artery, with resulting basal subarachnoid haemorrhage (Figures 11.15 and 11.16).

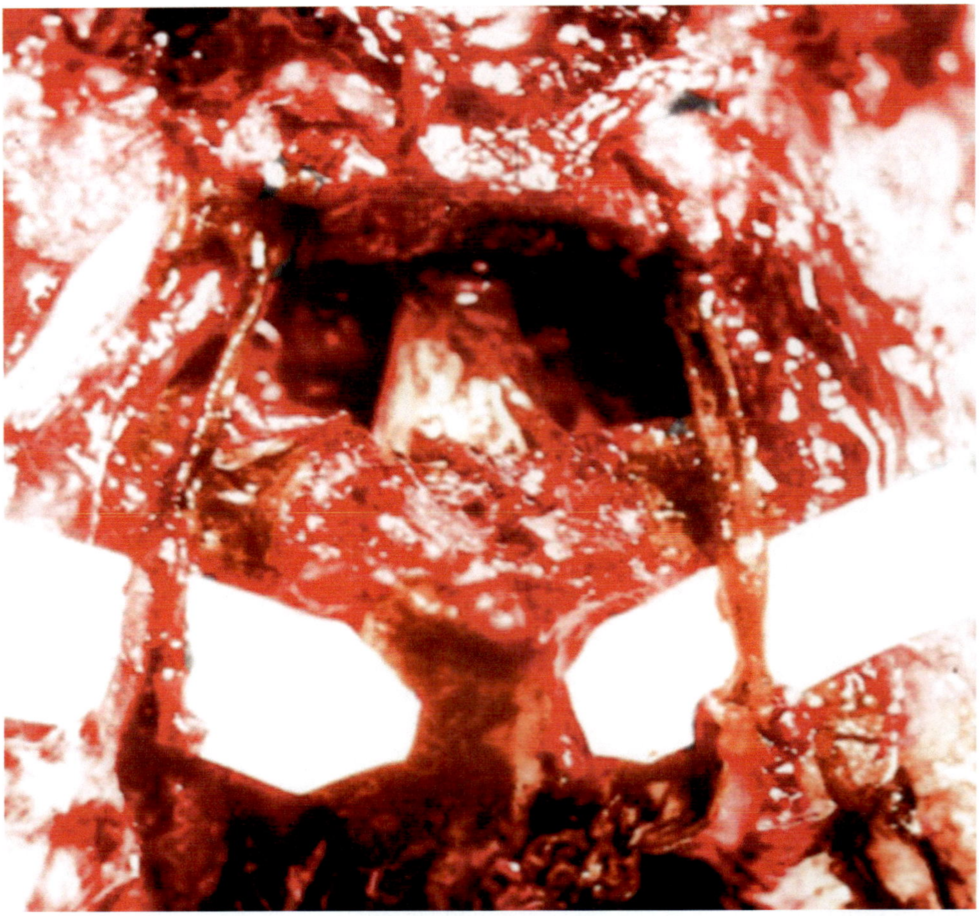

**Figure 11.14** Hyperextension fracture-dislocation of the cervical spine at C6/C7. The anterior longitudinal ligament and the sixth disc have been ruptured. The cervical cord is clearly visible between the adjacent vertebral bodies. In addition, the vertebral arteries have been stretched near their origins (above white markers) and closer examination of their adventitia reveals tearing and a moderate degree of perivascular haemorrhage.

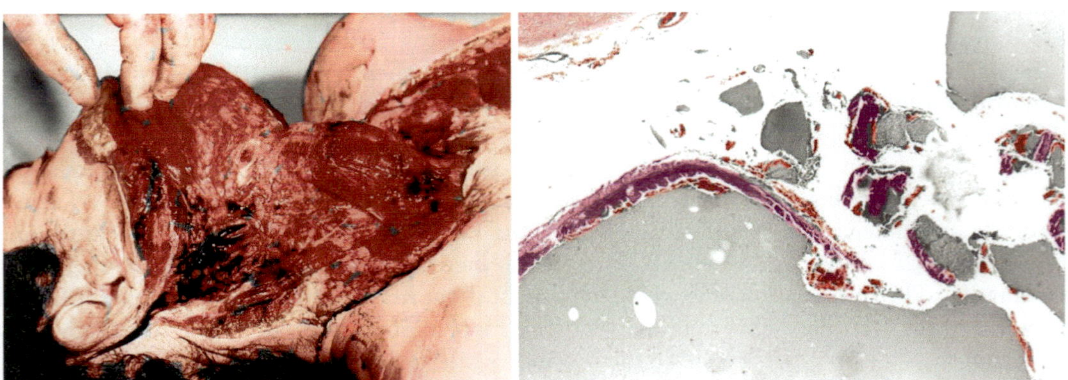

(a) (b)

**Figure 11.15** (a) Right side of neck showing deep haemorrhage into soft tissues, principally behind the ear and angle of the mandible. The deceased collapsed after receiving a kick to this region and was found to be dead on arrival at hospital, (b) Longitudinal section of right vertebral artery just within the foramen magnum. All layers of the vessel have been torn and the contrast medium following post-mortem angiography has leaked into the basal subarachnoid space.

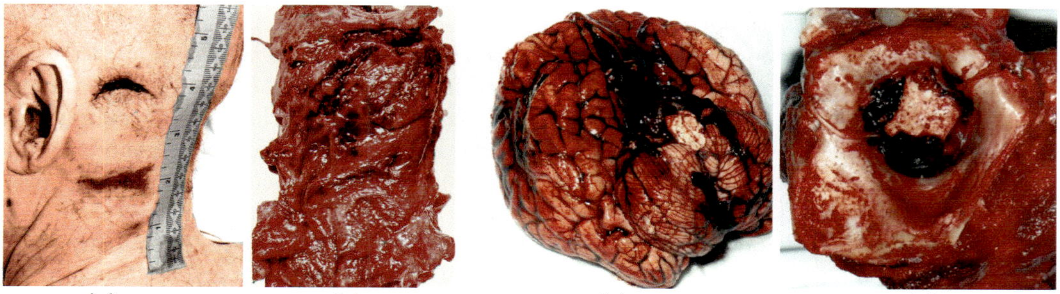

(a) (b) (c) (d)

**Figure 11.16** (a) Left posterior neck region, showing a laceration and abrasion produced by a hammer, (b) Excised cervical spine from the left aspect, showing extensive haemorrhage into soft tissue in the upper cervical spine musculature and close to the left vertebral artery, (c) Base of brain showing subarachnoid haemorrhage. The vertebral artery had ruptured at its entry into the foramen magnum, (d) Excised spine from above, showing extension of haemorrhage into spinal subarachnoid space.

Undoubtedly, in the past, a number of cases of basal subarachnoid haemorrhage which were ascribed to trauma, although no source of bleeding could be found, may in fact have been due to traumatic rupture of a vertebral artery, either intracranially or in its upper cervical course. One reason for the assumed rarity of such injuries was disbelief that such haemorrhages could be primarily traumatic, coupled with a lack of awareness that vertebral artery rupture could be responsible. Such a lesion may easily be overlooked or destroyed on removal of the brain at autopsy. Fortunately, pathologists over the past few years have become much more aware of such injuries following several early publications on the subject (Simonsen, 1967, 1976; Contostavlos, 1971; Cameron and Mant, 1972).

The vascular lesions are mostly incomplete tears, either associated with intramural dissection involving one or two adjacent cervical segments, or confined to the area of injury. Perivascular haematomas resulting from tears are invariably found and may cause secondary compression of the vessel from without (Figure 11.17).

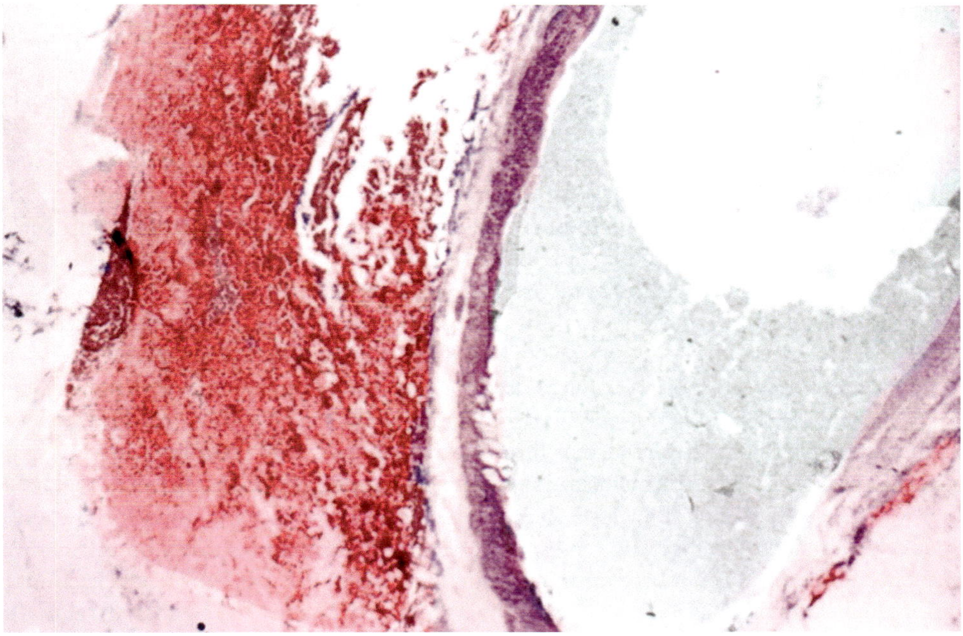

**Figure 11.17** Transverse section of right vertebral artery at C2, showing haemorrhage from the torn advential layer (Haematoxylin and eosin × 30).

The intracranial portion of the vertebral artery is, in most cases, the site of injury, and much less commonly the extracranial portion at C1–C2. In the upper cervical spine and intracranially, the vessels are more vulnerable to injury, being more liable to undergo extremes of movement, especially rotation. Indeed, in the vast majority of subarachnoid haemorrhage cases resulting from vertebral artery trauma seen by the author, the vascular lesion was located very close to the foramen magnum. Furthermore, as previously stated, such lesions thus situated may be quite easily missed or masked by artefactual damage when the brain is removed during an autopsy.

Koszyca et al. (2003) demonstrated from their case, by careful histological examination, that traumatic subarachnoid haemorrhage may result solely from extracranial rupture of the vertebral artery. In their case, the rupture was located 9 mm below the point at which the artery penetrated the dura. This view is supported by the fact that a number of other authors have not observed lesions below the level of C2, and indeed, most injuries have been found very close to the dural perforation (Cameron and Mant, 1972; Bergquist and Rammer, 1974; Gee, 1982; Harland et al., 1983; Simonsen, 1984; Vanezis, 1984).

The mechanism of production of basal subarachnoid haemorrhage from vertebral artery injury at the upper cervical region is thought to be from dissection of the blood upwards into the subarachnoid space from damaged arterial coats. The injury to the vessels needs to be near its perforation through the dura and arachnoid membranes for this to occur.

In order to appreciate the vulnerability of the vertebral arteries in the upper cervical and intracranial portions, one should not only understand that they might be subjected to severe rotational forces when a blow is directed to the head or upper part of the neck, but also realise that there is a significant change in the anatomy of the artery between its extradural and intradural segments. Johnson et al. (1993) carried out a morphometric assessment of the structural changes along the length of the vertebral artery, including those which occur with ageing, and found that the tunica media was much thinner within the intracranial portion (see also Chapter 2).

Structural changes may also occur following trauma, as reported by Pollanen (1996), who described the histological findings in seven cases of traumatic basal subarachnoid haemorrhage following vertebral artery rupture. In all cases, the vessel sustained a longitudinal transmural tear on the same side as the inflicted blow to the head or neck. In addition, the arterial wall proximal and distal to the site of rupture showed evidence of stretching of the tunica media. The distorted lesions appeared as patchy anuclear regions of the media with distinctive pallor of smooth muscle staining. The authors proposed that the forces which cause vertebral artery rupture stretch the artery along its long axis, thereby distorting the artery leading to this characteristic morphological change. Johnson et al. (2000) in biomechanical experiments showed that the vertebral artery was susceptible to longitudinal stretching, with a number of strip samples breaking when extended by as little as 16-20%.

The role of alcohol as an important factor in the commission of violent and other anti-social acts is well known. One must therefore exercise extreme caution in attempting to associate specialised types of traumatic events, such as vertebral artery trauma, with increasing alcohol intake. One can summarise the physiological effects of acute alcohol consumption by stating that it can cause peripheral vascular dilatation and decrease the tone of voluntary muscle. The latter thereby affects general posture. Thus, in response to an impending assault, it is not difficult to appreciate that an appropriate muscular response would be slow because of decreased muscular contractility, rendering the subject more liable to serious injury. It is a fact of life that in countries where alcohol consumption is an integral part of most activities, the majority of violent acts are perpetrated whilst the assailant and/or victim are intoxicated to a greater or lesser degree, and it is not surprising that in Gee's series (1983) of traumatic subarachnoid haemorrhage cases, most occurred within or outside a hostelry (tavern).

A rapid fatal outcome is the most common occurrence. Indeed, most eyewitness accounts of an incident in which someone has been struck on the head or neck and suffered a fatal traumatic subarachnoid haemorrhage from vertebral artery injury, report that the victim rapidly collapses and is then deeply unconscious. This is in keeping with the rapid fatal outcome which is frequently seen. Indeed, most cases are dead by the time they arrive at the nearest hospital. The author found that

13 of 15 victims in his series had died by the time they reached hospital (Vanezis, 1984). This is especially the case where the injury occurs intracranially, with direct severe damage to the brain stem, as in the case reported by Asai et al. (1996).

Delayed rupture of a lacerated vertebral artery resulting in basal subarachnoid haemorrhage may occasionally occur. Smyk and Herath (2018) reported the case of a 47-year-old male who collapsed and died suddenly following recent complaints of a headache and seizure. He had a reported history of potential head trauma that had occurred several days before collapse. Opeskin and Burke (1998) in their study of non-penetrating vertebral artery rupture with associated subarachnoid haemorrhage, found that in 5 of 19 cases there was a delay in death occurring from 10 hours to 3 days (4 were unconscious from the time of injury and in one case, the deceased's vertebral artery ruptured two to three days after neck manipulation).

## Associated Skeletal Injuries

A further important consideration in such injuries is the frequency of accompanying skeletal injury. Fracture of the transverse process, particularly at C1, is a common finding (Figure 11.18). Sheppard et al. (2020) found fracture patterns that were associated with an increased risk of vertebral artery injury. The fractures involved the upper cervical spine, fractures with associated subluxation, and fractures of the transverse process extending into the transverse foramen. Of 68 patients with a confirmed cervical spine fracture using computerised tomography, five (7.35%) were diagnosed with vertebral artery injury. All involved fractures of the upper cervical spine. Two involved fractures extending into the transverse foramen, two involved subluxation of the vertebrae, and one involved both. In all five cases, these fractures resulted from high-energy injuries.

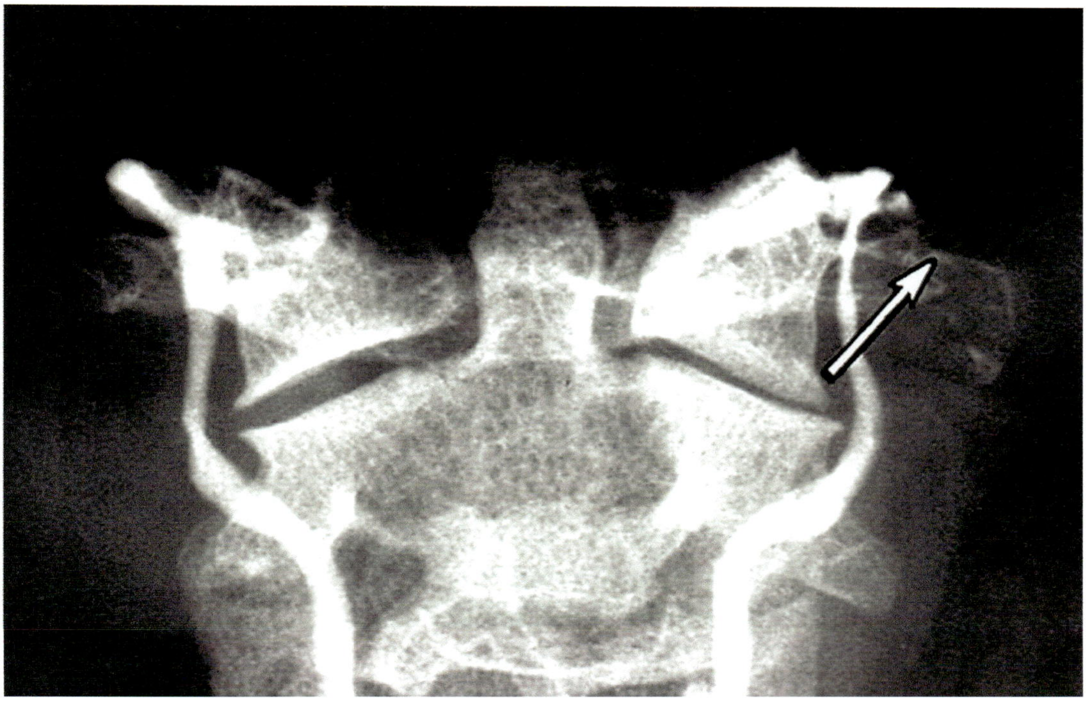

**Figure 11.18** Anteroposterior radiograph of upper section of excised cervical spine. The vertebral arteries have been injected with contrast medium. There is a fracture of the left transverse process of the atlas (arrow). The deceased had suffered a kick to the left side of the neck, which resulted in the rupture of the left vertebral artery, leading to fatal basal subarachnoid haemorrhage.

Despite the common occurrence of transverse process fractures, the majority of vertebral artery injuries, which occur in the upper cervical spine and accompanied by fatal subarachnoid haemorrhage, do not have associated skeletal injuries. Indeed, this finding is in keeping with the view that the inflicted trauma may be relatively trivial. One of Gee's cases (1983) sustained such an injury by violently jerking his head to avoid a blow without any actual bodily contact having been made. Furthermore, there may be little or no external signs of injury to the head or neck that could be related to vertebral artery trauma.

# NOTE

1 The pars interarticularis, or pars, is the part of the vertebra between the inferior and superior articular processes of the facet joint (in the transverse plane it lies between the lamina and the pedicle).

## References


Alizadeh A, Dyck SM, Karimi-Abdolrezaee S. Traumatic spinal cord injury: An overview of pathophysiology, models and acute injury mechanisms. *Front Neurol*. 2019;10:282. doi:10.3389/fneur.2019.00282

Alker GJ Jr, Oh YS, Leslie EV. High cervical spine and craniocervical junction injuries in fatal traffic accidents: A radiological study. *Orthop Clin North Am*. 1978;9(4):1003–1010.

Asai T, Kataoka K, Uejima T, Sakata I, Taneda M. Traumatic laceration of the intracranial vertebral artery causing fatal subarachnoid hemorrhage: Case report. *Surg Neurol*. 1996 June;45(6):566–568; discussion 568-569. doi: 10.1016/0090-3019(95)00354-1. PMID: 8638243.

Avila MJ, Hurlbert RJ. Central cord syndrome redefined. *Neurosurg Clin N Am*. 2021;32(3):353–363. doi: 10.1016/j.nec.2021.03.007.

Bandak FA. Shaken baby syndrome: A biomechanics analysis of injury mechanisms. *Forensic Sci Int*. 2005 June 30;151(1):71–79. doi: 10.1016/j.forsciint.2005.02.033. PMID: 15885948.

Bener A, Rahman YS, Mitra B. Incidence and severity of head and neck injuries in victims of road traffic crashes: In an economically developed country. *Int Emerg Nurs*. 2009;17(1):52–59. doi:10.1016/j.ienj.2008.07.007.

Bergquist E, Rammer L. Postmortem vertebral angiography in cases of traumatic subarachnoid hemorrhage. *Radiology*. 1974 Mar;110(3):709–10. doi: 10.1148/110.3.709. PMID: 4811694.

Cain CM, Ryan GA, Fraser R, Potter G, McLean AJ, McCaul K, Simpson DA. Cervical spine injuries in road traffic crashes in South Australia, 1981–86. *Aust N Z J Surg*. 1989 Jan;59(1):15–19. doi: 10.1111/j.1445-2197.1989.tb01458.x. PMID: 2913989.

Cameron JM, Mant AK. Fatal subarachnoid haemorrhage associated with cervical trauma. *Med Sci Law*. 1972 Jan;12(1):66–70. doi: 10.1177/002580247201200108. PMID: 5024112.

Chen JW. Cervical spine injuries. *Oral Maxillofac Surg Clin North Am*. 2008;20(3):381–391. doi: 10.1016/j.coms.2008.03.006.

Chiles III BW, Leonard MA, Choudhri HF, Cooper PR. Cervical spondylotic myelopathy: patterns of neurological deficit and recovery after anterior cervical decompression. *Neurosurgery*. 1999;44(4):762–770. doi: 10.1097/00006123-199904000-00041.

Contostavlos DL. Massive subarachnoid hemorrhage due to laceration of the vertebral artery associated with fracture of the transverse process of the atlas. *J Forensic Sci*. 1971 Jan;16(1):40–56. PMID: 5555585.

Croce MA, Zarzaur BL, Magnotti LJ, Fabian TC. Impact of motorcycle helmets and state laws on society's burden: A national study. *Ann Surg*. 2009;250(3):390–394. doi:10.1097/SLA.0b013e3181b365a2.

Crompton JG, Bone C, Oyetunji T, Pollack KM, Bolorunduro O, Villegas C, Stevens K, Cornwell III EE, Efron DT, Haut ER, Haider AH. Motorcycle helmets associated with lower risk of cervical spine injury: debunking the myth. *J Am Coll Surg*. 2011;212(3):295–300. doi:10.1016/j.jamcollsurg.2010.09.032.

Crowe H. A new diagnostic sign in neck injuries. *Calif Med*. 1964;100(1):12–13.

Death of the "Elephant Man". *Br Med J*, 1890 Apr, 19;1(1529):916–917.

Denis DJ, Shedid D, Shehadeh M, Weil AG, Lanthier S. Cervical spondylosis: A rare and curable cause of vertebrobasilar insufficiency. *Eur Spine J*. 2014 May;23 Suppl 2:206–213. doi: 10.1007/s00586-013-2983-2. Epub 2013 Sep 3. PMID: 24000075.

Dennison CR, Macri EM, Cripton PA. Mechanisms of cervical spine injury in rugby union: Is it premature to abandon hyperflexion as the main mechanism underpinning injury? *Br J Sports Med*. 2012;46(8):545–549. doi: 10.1136/bjsports-2012-091257.

Eck JC, Hodges SD, Humphreys SC. Whiplash: A review of a commonly misunderstood injury. *Am J Med*. 2001 June 1;110(8):651–656. doi: 10.1016/s0002-9343(01)00680-5. PMID: 11382374.

Ferrara SD, Ananian V, Baccino E, Banczerowski P, Bordignon D, Boscolo-Berto R, Domenici R, Gorriz Quevedo J, Graw M, Hell W, Hernandez Cueto C, Knudsen PJ, Masiero S, Montisci M, Norelli GA, Pinchi V, Raudys R, Raul JS, Sterzik V, Tessitore E, Tuusov J, Vanezis P, Vermylen Y, Vieira DN,

Viel G, Viero A, Villanueva E, Zoia R. Whiplash-Associated Disorders : Clinical and medico-legal guidelines on the methods of ascertainment. *Int J Legal Med.* 2016 Jan;130(1):13–22. doi: 10.1007/s00414-015-1243-x. Epub 2015 Sep 5. PMID: 26342284

Freeman MD, Croft AC, Rossignol AM, Centeno CJ, Elkins WL. Chronic neck pain and whiplash: a case-control study of the relationship between acute whiplash injuries and chronic neck pain. *Pain Res Manag.* 2006 Summer;11(2):79–83. doi: 10.1155/2006/304673. PMID: 16770448; PMCID: PMC2585479.

Gay JR, Abbott KH. Common whiplash injuries of the neck. *J Am Med Assoc.* 1953 Aug 29;152(18):1698–1704. doi: 10.1001/jama.1953.03690180020006. PMID: 13069244.

Gee DJ. Traumatic sub-arachnoid haemorrhage. *Acta Med Leg Soc.* 1983;3:495–498.

Gehweiler JA Jnr, Osborne RI Jnr, Becker RF. *The Radiology of Vertebral Trauma*. Saunders, Philadelphia, 1980.

Goetz LL, De Jesus O, McAvoy SM. Posttraumatic Syringomyelia. [Updated 2023 Aug 23]. In: StatPearls [Internet]. Treasure Island (FL): StatPearls Publishing; 2024 Jan-. Available from: https://www.ncbi.nlm.nih.gov/books/NBK470405/

Goldberg W, Mueller C, Panacek E, Tigges S, Hoffman JR, Mower WR, Nexus Group. Distribution and patterns of blunt traumatic cervical spine injury. *Ann Emerg Med.* 2001;38(1):17–21. doi:10.1067/mem.2001.116150.

Govender S, Charles RW. Fracture of the dens in ankylosing spondylitis. *Injury*. 1987 May;18(3):213–214. doi: 10.1016/0020-1383(87)90141-0. PMID: 3508854.

Harland WA, Pitts JF, Watson AA. Subarachnoid haemorrhage due to upper cervical trauma. *J Clin Pathol.* 1983 Dec;36(12):1335–1341. doi: 10.1136/jcp.36.12.1335. PMID: 6655067; PMCID: PMC498564.

Hitosugi M, Takatsu A, Shigeta A. Injuries of motorcyclists and bicyclists examined at autopsy. *Am J Forensic Med Pathol.* 1999;20(3):251–255. doi:10.1097/00000433-199909000-00007.

Howcroft AJ, Jenkins DH. Potentially fatal asphyxia following a minor injury of the cervical spine. *J Bone Joint Surg Br.* 1977;59(1):93–94. doi: 10.1302/0301-620X.59B1.845237.

Huelke DF, O'Day J, Mendelsohn RA. Cervical injuries suffered in automobile crashes. *J Neurosurg.* 1981;54(3):316–322. doi:10.3171/jns.1981.54.3.0316.

Huntley C, Hodder A, Ramachandran M. Clinical and historical aspects of the Elephant Man: exploring the facts and the myths. *Gene*. 2015;555(1):63–65. doi:10.1016/j.gene.2014.09.056.

Jefferson G. Fracture of the atlas vertebra. *Br J Surg.* 1920;7:407–422.

Johnson CP, How T, Scraggs M, West CR, Burns J. A biomechanical study of the human vertebral artery with implications for fatal arterial injury. *Forensic Sci Int.* 2000 Apr 10;109(3):169–182. doi: 10.1016/s0379-0738(99)00198-x. PMID: 10725653

Johnson CP, Lawler W, Burns J. Use of histomorphometry in the assessment of fatal vertebral artery dissection. *J Clin Pathol.* 1993;46(11):1000–1003. doi:10.1136/jcp.46.11.1000.

Kakarla UK, Chang SW, Theodore N, Sonntag VK. Atlas fractures. *Neurosurgery*. 2010 Mar;66(3 Suppl):60–67. doi: 10.1227/01.NEU.0000366108.02499.8F. PMID: 20173529.

Kakulas BA. The applied neuropathology of human spinal cord injury. *Spinal Cord.* 1999 Feb;37(2):79–88. doi: 10.1038/sj.sc.3100807. PMID: 10065745.

Kleeman LT, Gallizzi MA, Blizzard DJ, Erickson MM. Cervical Spine injuries in sports. *The Duke Orthop J.* 2015;5(1):58–62.

Koszyca B, Gilbert JD, Blumbergs PC. Traumatic subarachnoid hemorrhage and extracranial vertebral artery injury: A case report and review of the literature. *Am J Forensic Med Pathol.* 2003 June;24(2):114–118. doi: 10.1097/01.PAF.0000065165.81345.7f. PMID: 12773844.

Kranenburg HAR, Tyer R, Schmitt M, Luijckx GJ, van der Schans C, Hutting N, Kerry R. Effects of head and neck positions on blood flow in the vertebral, internal carotid, and intracranial arteries: A systematic review. *J Orthop Sports Phys Ther.* 2019;49(10), 688–697. doi: 10.2519/jospt.2019.8578.

Krantz KP. Head and neck injuries to motorcycle and moped riders--with special regard to the effect of protective helmets. *Injury*. 1985;16(4):253–258. doi:10.1016/s0020-1383(85)80014-0.

Kuster D, Gibson A, Abboud R, Drew T. Mechanisms of cervical spine injury in rugby union: a systematic review of the literature. *Br J Sports Med.* 2012;46(8):550–554. doi: 10.1136/bjsports-2011-090360.

Lebl DR, Hughes A, Cammisa FP, Jr, O'Leary PF. Cervical spondylotic myelopathy: Pathophysiology, clinical presentation, and treatment. *HSS J.* 2011;7(2):170–178. doi:10.1007/s11420-011-9208-1.

Levin JH, Pecoraro A, Ochs V, Meagher A, Steenburg SD, Hammer PM. Characterization of fatal blunt injuries using postmortem computed tomography. *J Trauma Acute Care Surg.* 2023;95(2):186–190. doi:10.1097/TA.0000000000004012.

McLain RF, Aretakis A, Moseley TA, Ser P, Benson DR. Sub-axial cervical dissociation. Anatomic and biomechanical principles of stabilization. *Spine (Phila Pa 1976)*. 1994 Mar 15;19(6):653–659. doi: 10.1097/00007632-199403001-00003. PMID: 8009329.

Menon KV, Taif S. Detailed description of anatomy of the fracture line in hangman's injury: A retrospective observational study on motor vehicle accident victims. *Br J Radiol*. 2016;89(1058):20150847. doi: 10.1259/bjr.20150847. Epub 2015 Nov 26. PMID: 26607649; PMCID: PMC4985222.

Nightingale RW, McElhaney JH, Richardson WJ, Best TM, Myers BS. Experimental impact injury to the cervical spine: Relating motion of the head and the mechanism of injury. *J Bone Joint Surg Am*. 1996;78(3):412–421. doi:10.2106/00004623-199603000-00013.

Nishikawa H, Miya F, Kitano Y, Mori G, Shimizu S, Suzuki H. Positional occlusion of vertebral artery due to cervical spondylosis as rare cause of wake-up stroke: Report of two cases. *World Neurosurg*. 2017 Feb;98:877.e13–877.e21. doi: 10.1016/j.wneu.2016.11.071. Epub 2016 Nov 25. PMID: 27890763.

Oehmichen M, Schleiss D, Pedal I, Saternus KS, Gerling I, Meissner C. Shaken baby syndrome: Re-examination of diffuse axonal injury as cause of death. *Acta Neuropathol*. 2008 Sep;116(3):317–329. doi: 10.1007/s00401-008-0356-4. Epub 2008 Mar 26. PMID: 18365221.

Opeskin K, Burke MP. Vertebral artery trauma. *Am J Forensic Med Pathol*. 1998 Sep;19(3):206–217. doi: 10.1097/00000433-199809000-00002. PMID: 9760083.

Page PS, Wei Z, Brooks NP. Motorcycle helmets and cervical spine injuries: A 5-year experience at a Level 1 trauma center. *J Neurosurg Spine*. 2018 June;28(6):607–611. doi: 10.3171/2017.7.SPINE17540. Epub 2018 Mar 6. PMID: 29506463.

Peh WC, Ho EK. Fracture of the odontoid peg in ankylosing spondylitis: Case report. *J Trauma*. 1995 Mar;38(3):361–363. doi: 10.1097/00005373-199503000-00009. PMID: 7897715.

Pollanen MS, Deck JH, Blenkinsop B. Injury of the tunica media in fatal rupture of the vertebral artery. *Am J Forensic Med Pathol*. 1996 Sep;17(3):197–201. doi: 10.1097/00000433-199609000-00004. PMID: 8870868.

Pötsch L, Bohl J. Traumatic lesion of the extracranial vertebral artery--a note-worthy potentially lethal injury. *Int J Legal Med*. 1994;107(2):99–107. doi: 10.1007/BF01225496. PMID: 7819125.

Saternus KS. Zur Mechanik des Schleudertraumas der Halswirbelsäule [The mechanics of whiplash injury of the cervical spine (author's transl)]. *Z Rechtsmed*. 1982;88(1-2):1–11. German. doi: 10.1007/BF00200729. PMID: 7080672.

Schleicher P, Scholz M, Pingel A, Kandziora F. Traumatic spondylolisthesis of the axis vertebra in adults. *Global Spine J*. 2015 Aug;5(4):346–358. doi: 10.1055/s-0035-1550343. Epub 2015 Apr 29. PMID: 26225285; PMCID: PMC4516758.

Schneider RC, Schemm GW. Vertebral artery insufficiency in acute and chronic spinal trauma, with special reference to the syndrome of acute central cervical spinal cord injury. *J Neurosurg*. 1961 May;18:348–60. doi: 10.3171/jns.1961.18.3.0348. PMID: 13748252.

Sgarlato A, Deroux SJ. Motor vehicle occupants, neck injuries, and seat belt utilization: A 5-year study of fatalities in New York City. *J Forensic Sci*. 2010;55(2):527–530. doi:10.1111/j.1556-4029.2009.01270.x

Sherk HH, Nicholson JT. Fractures of the atlas. *J Bone Joint Surg Am*. 1970 July;52(5):1017–1024. PMID: 5479472.

Sheppard R, Kennedy G, Nelson A, Abdel Meguid E, Darwish N. Vertebral artery injury in cervical spine fractures: A cohort study and review of the literature. *Ulst Med J*. 2020;89(2):89–94.

Simonsen J. Fatal subarachnoid haemorrhage in relation to minor head injuries. *J Forensic Med*. 1967 Oct-Dec;14(4):146–155. PMID: 6082135.

Simonsen J. Massive subarachnoid haemorrhage and fracture of the transverse process of the atlas. *Med Sci Law*. 1976 Jan;16(1):13–6. doi: 10.1177/002580247601600105. PMID: 1250096.

Simonsen J. Fatal subarachnoid haemorrhages in relation to minor injuries in Denmark from 1967 to 1981. *Forensic Sci Int*. 1984 Jan;24(1):57–63. doi: 10.1016/0379-0738(84)90152-x. PMID: 6698453.

Smyk DS, Herath JC. Delayed rupture of a vertebral artery laceration: a case report and challenges for the forensic pathologist. *Forensic Sci Med Pathol*. 2018 Dec;14(4):536–540. doi: 10.1007/s12024-018-9999-1. Epub 2018 June 20. PMID: 29926436.

Sorensen BF. Bow hunter's stroke. *Neurosurgery*. 1978 May-June;2(3):259–261. doi: 10.1227/00006123-197805000-00013. PMID: 732978.

Spitzer WO, Skovron ML, Salmi LR, Cassidy JD, Duranceau J, Suissa S, Zeiss E. Scientific monograph of the Quebec task force on whiplash-associated disorders: Redefining "whiplash" and its management. *Spine (Phila Pa 1976)*. 1995 Apr 15;20(8 Suppl):1S–73S. Erratum in: *Spine*. 1995 Nov 1;20(21):2372. PMID: 7604354.

Stanbouly D, Richardson J, Lee KC, Zeng Q, Perrino MA, Chuang SK. A comparison of 2,845 head and neck injuries in various martial arts. *J Oral Maxillofac Surg*. 2022 Apr;80(4):682–690. doi: 10.1016/j.joms.2021.12.001. Epub 2021 Dec 9. PMID: 34973164.

Stanners M, O'Riordan M, Theodosiou E, Souppez JRG, Gardner A. The mechanical properties of the spinal cord: A systematic review. *Spine J*. 2024 July;24(7):1302–1312. doi: 10.1016/j.spinee.2024.02.022. Epub 2024 Mar 1. PMID: 38432298.

Stein DM, Kufera JA, Ho SM, Ryb GE, Dischinger PC, O'Connor JV, Scalea TM. Occupant and crash characteristics for case occupants with cervical spine injuries sustained in motor vehicle collisions. *J Trauma*. 2011;70(2):299–309. doi:10.1097/TA.0b013e3181f8aa91.

Thesleff T, Niskakangas T, Luoto TM, Öhman J, Ronkainen A. Fatal cervical spine injuries: A Finnish nationwide register-based epidemiologic study on data from 1987 to 2010. *Spine J*. 2016;16(8):918–926. doi:10.1016/j.spinee.2015.11.054.

Thompson C, Gonsalves JF, Welsh D. Hyperextension injury of the cervical spine with central cord syndrome. *Eur Spine J*. 2015;24(1):195–202. doi: 10.1007/s00586-014-3432-6.

Tonge JI, O'Reilly MJ, Davison A, Johnston NG, Wilkey IS. Traffic-crash fatalities (1968–73): Injury patterns and other factors. *Med Sci Law*. 1977;17(1):9–24. doi:10.1177/002580247701700104.

Treves, Sir Frederick. *The Elephant Man and Other Reminiscences*. Cassell and Company, Ltd. London, New York, Toronto and Melbourne, 1923.

Vaccaro AR, Koerner JD, Radcliff KE, Oner FC, Reinhold M, Schnake KJ, Kandziora F, Fehlings MG, Dvorak MF, Aarabi B, Rajasekaran S, Schroeder GD, Kepler CK, Vialle LR. AOSpine subaxial cervical spine injury classification system. *Eur Spine J*. 2016 July;25(7):2173–2184. doi: 10.1007/s00586-015-3831-3. Epub 2015 Feb 26. PMID: 25716661.

Vanezis P. Neck injury patterns observed in fatally injured road traffic accident victims – Retrospective study. *J Drug Res*. 1980;5:743–746.

Vanezis P. *Vertebral Artery Trauma. A Postmortem Study*. MD Theses University of Bristol, 1984.

Vanezis P. Vertebral artery injuries in road traffic accidents: A post-mortem study. *J Forensic Sci Soc*. 1986;26:281–291.

Vanezis P. Methods of ascertainment of personal damage in the United Kingdom. In: Ferrara, S., Boscolo-Berto, R., Viel, G. (eds) Personal Injury and Damage Ascertainment under Civil Law. Springer, Cham, 2016. doi: 10.1007/978-3-319-29812-2_11.

Vinchon M, Noulé N, Toubol A, Karnoub MA. Spinal lesions caused by abusive trauma in young children. *Childs Nerv Syst*. 2022 Dec;38(12):2349–2355. doi: 10.1007/s00381-022-05778-z. Epub 2022 Dec 13. PMID: 36512049.

Vives MJ, Kishan S, Asghar J, Peng B, Reiter MF, Milo S, Livingston D. Spinal injuries in pedestrians struck by motor vehicles. *J Spinal Disord Tech*. 2008;21(4):281–287. doi:10.1097/BSD.0b013e3181370703.

WHO| Spinal Cord Injury. WHO, Fact sheet No384 (2013). Available online at: https://www.who.int/news-room/fact-sheets/detail/spinal-cordinjury

Yanar H, Demetriades D, Hadjizacharia P, Nomoto S, Salim A, Inaba K, Rhee P, Chan LS. Pedestrians injured by automobiles: risk factors for cervical spine injuries. *J Am Coll Surg*. 2007;205(6):794–799. doi:10.1016/j.jamcollsurg.2007.06.280.

Yates PO. Birth trauma to the vertebral arteries. *Arch Dis Child*. 1959 Oct;34(177):436–441. doi: 10.1136/adc.34.177.436. PMID: 13846489; PMCID: PMC2012402.

Zahir U, Ludwig SC. Sports-related cervical spine injuries: On-field assessment and management. *Semin Spine Surg*. 2010;22:173–180.

Zhou C, Guo R, Wang C, Tsai TY, Yu Y, Wang W, Li G, Cha T.. Ligament deformation patterns of the craniocervical junction during head axial rotation tracked by biplane fluoroscopes. *Clin Biomech (Bristol*, Avon). 2021;88:105442. doi:10.1016/j.clinbiomech.2021.105442.

# CHAPTER 12

## TOXIC, ENVIRONMENTAL, AND MISCELLANEOUS CAUSES OF NECK INJURY

*Peter Vanezis*



DOI: 10.4324/9781003658467-12

# THERMAL BURNS

In the acute phase, burns affecting the external neck region may produce severe local tissue oedema. Subsequently, neck contractures from healing burn scars may not only distort the way the head is held and its anatomical relationship to the shoulders, but such scars may also affect facial expressions.

The larynx, in particular, is strategically positioned for direct exposure to thermal injury, and as such, laryngeal burn injury is common (Figure 12.1). There is an approximately 50% chance of abnormal laryngeal findings in patients with mild to severe burns. An initial diagnosis of an abnormal larynx following a burn injury raises patients' odds of experiencing significant morbidity in terms of airway, voice, and swallow. The burn injury is often associated with other injuries and complications, and as such, laryngeal injury is often a secondary consideration (Reid and Ha, 2019).

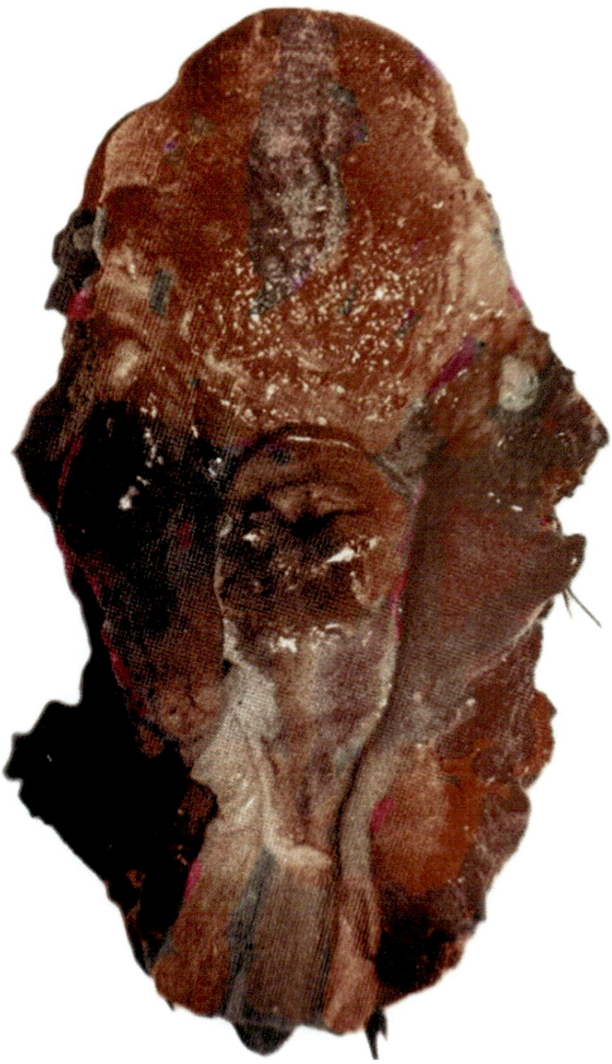

**Figure 12.1** Excised larynx from a two-year-old child, showing laryngeal oedema, sloughing of the surface of the epithelium from the tongue and carbon deposits in the upper part of the larynx.

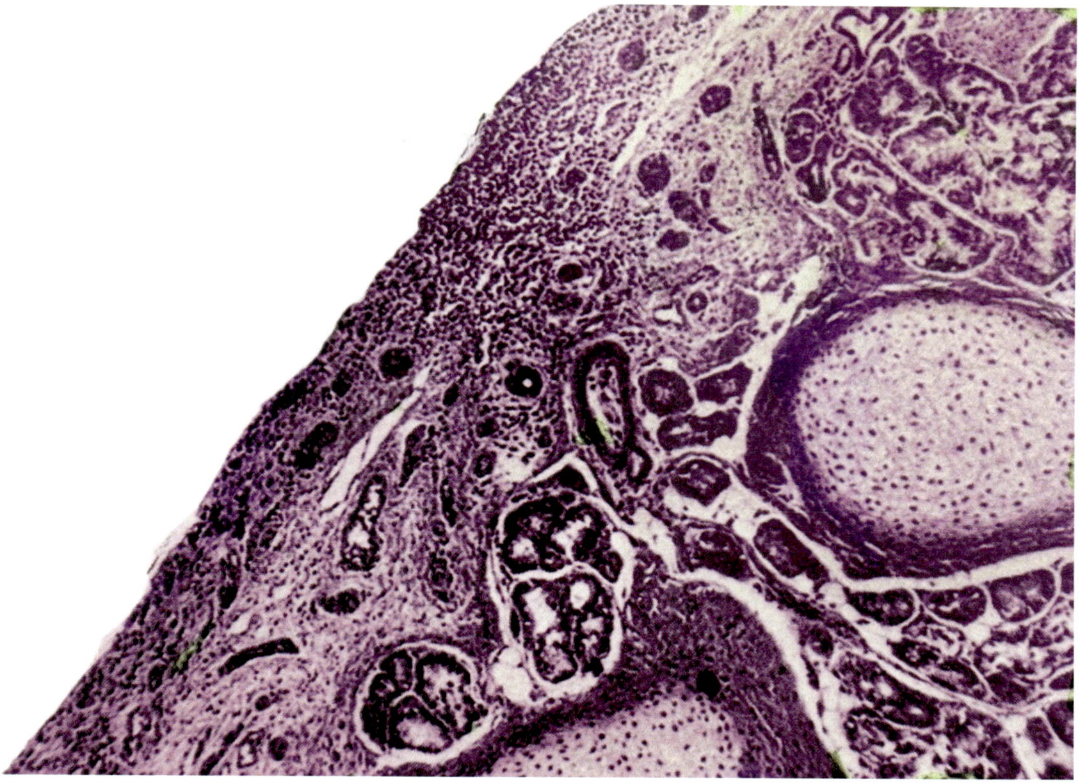

**Figure 12.2** Longitudinal section of the epiglottis in a two-month-old infant who died following steam inhalation. The section shows sloughing of the epithelial surface. There is a dense neutrophil infiltrate in the submucosa (Haematoxylin and eosin × 50).

Inhalation of fire fumes or steam can cause severe acute laryngeal oedema followed by haemorrhage and gross inflammatory changes. An autopsy was carried out by the author on a two-month-old infant who died following steam inhalation. The child had been suffering from a mild upper respiratory tract infection, and the mother had been instructed to boil some water in a kettle to moisten the atmosphere near the child. However, she placed the child in a small room and saturated the atmosphere with steam by continuously boiling and refilling the kettle. The child was found dead, and at autopsy, gross supraglottic swelling was found together with severe pulmonary oedema (Figures 12.2 and 12.3).

In fire victims who have survived a few days, it is not unusual to observe sloughing of the laryngeal mucosa, ulceration, and secondary infection (Figure 12.4).

With prolonged exposure to heat inhalation, as may occur in certain occupations if protection is not adequate, e.g., blast furnace workers and firefighters, laryngitis sicca may develop (due to excessive drying of the mucous membranes), chronic ulcerative laryngitis, or keratosis (Holinger et al., 1968).

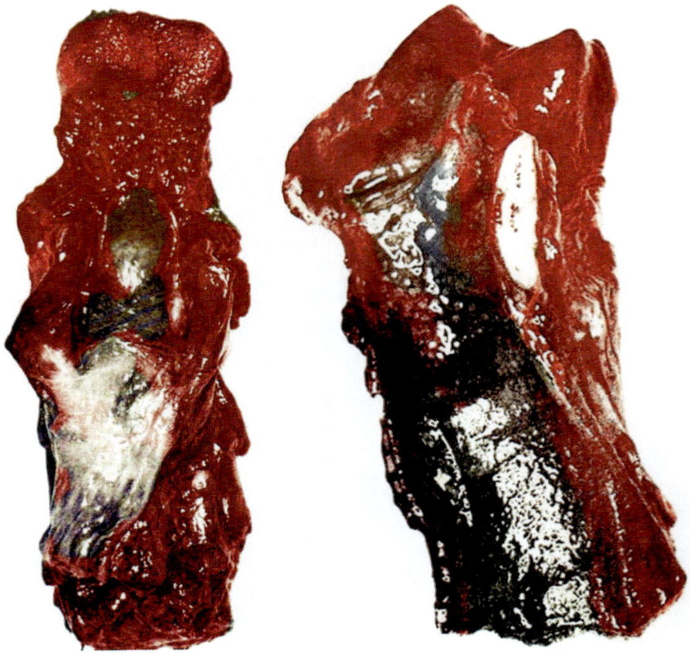

(a) (b)

**Figure 12.3** (a) Acute inflamed larynx and associated structures following inhalation of smoke. Note the blackened tongue and laryngeal inlet. (b) View of interior of the larynx from the same case after bisection, showing a black film of carbon particles.

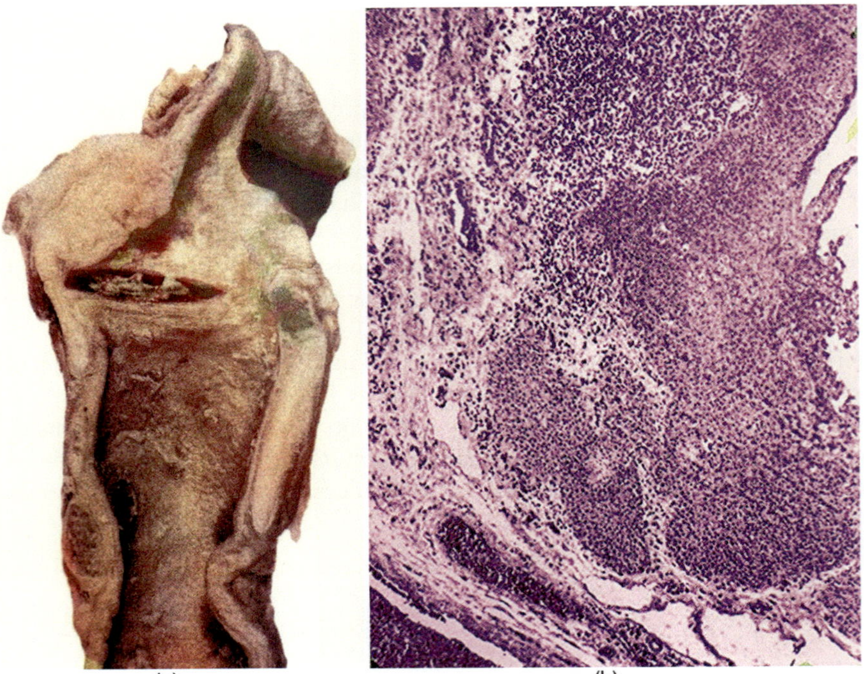

(a) (b)

**Figure 12.4** (a) Bisected larynx in deceased who had inhaled fire fumes and survived for about five days. Sloughing of the mucosa is present as well as fibrinous exudate, particularly in the glottic and subglottic areas. (b) Longitudinal section from the base of the epiglottis, showing dense mixed cellular infiltrate (Haematoxylin and eosin × 640).

# CHEMICAL BURNS

Corrosive substances comprise mineral and organic acids (e.g., hydrochloric, sulphuric, nitric, acetic, and oxalic), strong alkalis (e.g., lye, caustic soda, caustic potash, and ammonia), phenols and cresols (present in household disinfectants). In infants and toddlers, the manner of ingestion is predominantly accidental. Accidental ingestion can also occur in adults. However, suicide is a more likely reason for such an exposure. Their use in such a way is nowadays only occasionally encountered. Such substances were more commonly reported in the early part of the twentieth century, particularly in south-eastern European countries, especially Hungary and the Balkans (Stumboff, 1950). In Bulgaria between 1928 and 1947, 1,221 cases were reported, 979 of which were due to lye ingestion.

Caustic injury to the aerodigestive tract, particularly in young children, remains a significant medical and social concern despite various efforts to minimise the hazards of caustic household products (Riffat and Cheng (2009). Agents with a pH less than two or greater than 12 are extremely corrosive, causing damage that can range from mild to extensive, including oesophageal perforation leading to mediastinitis and death at the extreme scale. The above authors carried out a retrospective study of all admissions to the otolaryngology unit with caustic injury that underwent oesophagoscopy at the Children's Hospital Westmead between 1990 and 2007. Fifty admissions were identified (28 males and 22 females), with a median age of 22 months. Forty-nine cases (98%) were accidental. Thirty-eight cases (76%) occurred within the interiors of the family home, with the kitchen being the common location. Another seven (14%) occurred within the external environment of the home, usually in the garage or pool shed. The causative agents were varied, with 37 (74%) being alkali, three cases (6%) being acidic, and other agents, such as chlorine bleach, being the remainder. The most frequently ingested alkalis were dishwashing powder and disinfectants, closely followed by degreasers. Twenty-five children (50%) drank directly from a container, with the remainder ingesting granules or powder directly.

When such chemicals are ingested, injury to mucosal surfaces occurs within seconds after contact (Figure 12.5).

The nature of the injury caused by acidic and alkaline substances differs considerably (Millar and Cox, 2015). Acid ingestion leads to coagulation necrosis of the mucosa, hard eschar formation, and usually limits acid penetration through the mucosa. By contrast, alkali ingestion leads to tissue penetration with liquefactive necrosis, followed by the destruction of the epithelium and submucosa and frequently extension into and sometimes through all muscle layers. Ischaemia and thrombosis are dominant early processes. Haemorrhage, thrombosis, and marked inflammation with oedema may be seen in the first 24 hours after injury. Depending on the extent of burns, inflammation may extend through the muscle layer until perforation occurs.

A friable discoloured eschar develops, under which tissue destruction continues until the alkali is neutralised. The oesophagus is damaged principally at the cricopharyngeal area, the mid-oesophagus where it is crossed by the aortic arch and left main bronchus, and immediately above the oesophago-gastric junction.

After 48 hours, there is evidence of thrombosis of sub-mucosal vessels, which gives rise to local necrosis and gangrene. Bacterial contamination leads to the development of small intramural abscesses, which may extend to the mediastinum with full-thickness injury.

After several days, necrotic tissue sloughs, oedema decreases, and neovascularisation begins. This early reparative or sub-acute phase is evident from the end of the first week through the second week after injury. Scar formation begins in the third week, when fibroblast proliferation replaces the submucosa and muscularis, and stricture formation commences. Mucosal re-epithelialisation then commences and is usually complete by the sixth week. It is during this period that adhesions may form, narrowing or obliterating the oesophageal lumen. The result may be a fibrotic stricture

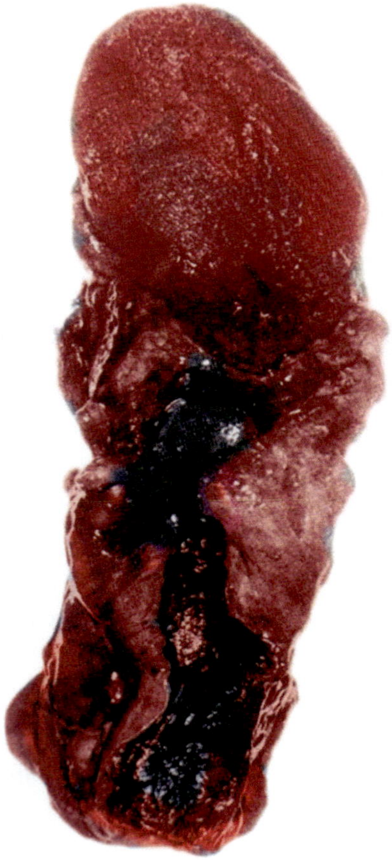

(a)

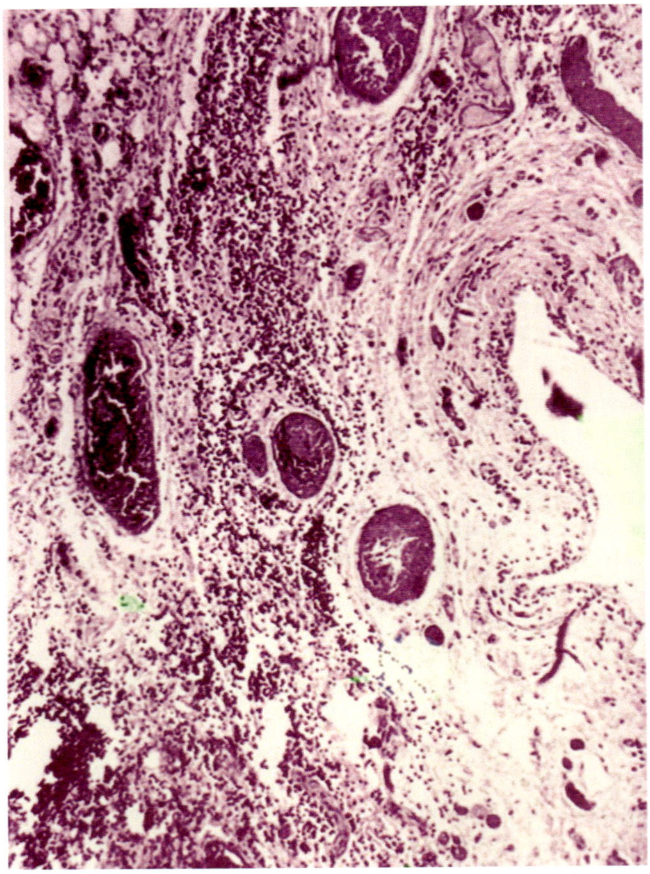

(b)

**Figure 12.5** (a) Excised specimen showing tongue, pharynx, and oesophagus coated black because of formic acid burns. The deceased ingested descaling fluid. (b) Longitudinal section from cervical oesophagus, showing loss of epithelial layer, submucous oedema, congestion, and marked cellular infiltrate (Haematoxylin and eosin × 64).

and a shortened oesophagus. If the injury is transmural, necrosis may extend to the surrounding mediastinum, leading to mediastinitis, or if in an anterior direction, may result in tracheaoesophageal or even aortooesophageal fistulae.

Squamous cell carcinoma of the oesophagus may follow chemical burns to this structure after an interval of years (Appelqvist and Salmo, 1980; Hopkins and Postlethwait, 1981). Appleqvist and Salmo reported 63 cases of squamous oesophageal carcinoma following lye corrosion. The mean age of ingestion of the lye was 6.2 years, and the latent time for the development of the malignancy was 41 years. Five cases were in the cervical region (four females and one male), although 84% of cases were at the bronchial bifurcation level. Zhang et al. (2012) presented the case of a 61-year-old man who ingested sulphuric acid at the age of three years and then developed dysphagia at late follow-up. In 2010, he presented to the outpatient clinic with weight loss and worsening dysphagia to both solids and liquids. A barium swallow radiograph and endoscopy demonstrated a long stricture in the middle third of the oesophagus. Oesophagectomy was carried out, and the resection specimen confirmed a well-differentiated oesophageal squamous cell carcinoma. It is unclear why caustic burns predispose to carcinoma. Nevertheless, severe injury requiring prolonged bougienage is accompanied by recurrent ulceration and epithelial healing. Most patients are asymptomatic for many years after initial treatment, and no apparent sensitising factors are discernible.

Akhavan et al. (2009) described late laryngeal findings resulting from sulphur mustard poisoning (mustard gas), which has historically been widely used as a chemical warfare agent against both military and civilian populations by Iraqi forces during the Iran–Iraq war (1983–1988). They identified functional abnormalities in 50 victims examined nearly 20 years after exposure. Reviewing laryngoscopic recordings, inflammation (oedema and erythema) was observed in varying degrees in 9 (18%) patients in the supraglottic region and 3 (6%) patients in the subglottic region. Inflammation of the true vocal cords and false vocal cords (FVCs) was seen in 7 (14%) and 22 (44%) patients, respectively. Overall, 41 (82%) patients had chronic laryngitis. Six patients (12%) had true vocal cord nodules measuring 1–2 mm in dimension at the junction of the anterior and middle thirds of the vocal folds, and tissue adhesions were observed in 6 patients (12%), ranging from 2 to 4 mm near the anterior commissure. Alongside the objective findings, a considerable number of patients reported of intermittent or continuous dysphonia, compatible with chronic laryngitis. They considered that paralysis of the vocal cords might have been the long-term result of the neurotoxic effect of the gas. Other findings, including adhesions and laryngeal nodules, may have been caused by infections or chronic laryngobronchitis.

# ELECTRICAL INJURIES

Electrical injuries confined solely to the neck are unusual and usually occur together with other electrical injuries at adjacent regions, such as the head or chest. It should be appreciated, as pointed out by Xiao et al. (2022), that scars caused by electrical burns are different from those caused by flame burns. Flame burn scars always involve only skin, which is easy to release. However, the electric current inflicts great damage to subcutaneous blood vessels and tissues, especially the muscles. Given that deep tissues are severely damaged, scars on the neck are always closely adhered to the full thickness of the skin, forming a "frozen neck". Fully releasing the scars and protecting important structures, such as major blood vessels and trachea, are the most important yet difficult aspects of treatment to manage.

Electrical injury causing laryngeal injury was reported by Furnas and Shumrick (1968) in a 68-year-old farmer. Their patient received injuries after colliding with a 7,200-volt power line. He was helping his neighbour push a corn elevator (a 50-foot-long, wheeled device with a conveyor belt projecting upwards on an extension 30 feet above the ground) to a storage shed. The metal extension arm collided with a 7,200-volt overhead power line. At the moment of contact, only the patient was pushing the machine. The neighbour saw a burst of flame and a cloud of smoke on the patient's side of the corn elevator and found him unconscious on the ground. The patient revived spontaneously and was taken to a local hospital. Despite the burns, he had viable true vocal cords and regained normal speech and swallowing following reconstructive surgery.

Kitulwatte and Pollanen (2009) reported a fatality in an industrial worker who sustained a deep electrical injury in the neck complicated by fatal air embolism. He was found dead in an upright position, while his chest and head were resting on top of a live transformer. Among other electrical injuries, there was a deep electrical burn associated with haemorrhage in the neck involving the skin, underlying subcutaneous tissue, strap muscles, and the thyroid gland. Examination of his heart revealed bubbles causing bulging of the right atrium. Their case illustrated that acute complications of electrical burns, rather than electrocution-related cardiac arrhythmia, can be the mechanism of death in rare electricity-related deaths.

# UPPER AIRWAY OBSTRUCTION DUE TO ANAPHYLAXIS

Acute pharyngeal and laryngeal oedema may result from an anaphylactic reaction leading to asphyxia caused by upper airway obstruction. Pumphrey and Roberts (2000) examined 56 deaths due to anaphylaxis. They included 19 reactions to bee or wasp venom, 16 to foods, and 21 to drugs or contrast media. Death occurred within one hour of anaphylaxis in 39 cases. Macroscopic findings included pharyngeal/laryngeal oedema (23 of 56), petechial haemorrhages (10 of 56), signs of asthma (mucous plugging and/or hyperinflated lungs) (15 of 56), but for 23 of 56, there was nothing indicative of an allergic death. The most frequent autopsy findings were angioedema of the upper airways. Mast cell tryptase was raised in 14 of the 16 cases tested; three of the three tested had detectable IgE specific to the suspected allergen.

Martínez-Fernandez et al. (2019), in their cases where histopathology data were available for 40 individuals, observed that the most frequent autopsy findings were angioedema of the upper airways (50%).

In relation to the involvement of the internal neck structures, in Pumphrey and Roberts' series, upper airway oedema was more common in deaths related to food allergens (77% of immediate deaths) than in those after reactions to venom or drugs (40% and 30% of immediate deaths, respectively). The presence of petechial haemorrhages, also suggesting an asphyxial component to the death, was found in ten cases, eight of which were immediate deaths. They also found that in many cases of fatal anaphylaxis, no specific macroscopic findings were present at postmortem examination, which is in keeping with the rapidity and mode of death, which is often the result of shock rather than asphyxia.

# VOICE MISUSE

Excessive and incorrect use of the voice is common, particularly in occupations such as singing, public speaking, for whatever reason, or working in a noisy environment occasioning shouting. This subjects the vocal cords to several forms of mechanical stress. Vocal fold vibration during phonation leads to impact stress during the collision between the left and right vocal fold surfaces. The maximal impact stress occurs in the mid-membranous vocal fold (Johns, 2003). The largest mechanical stresses in vocal fold vibration are the tensile stresses required for pitch increase. Estimates are that they may reach values on the order of 1 MPa of pressure. This would be excessive for epithelial or muscular tissue but appears to be normal for ligamentous tissue. Furthermore, the frequent slapping of the cords against each other results in the exudation of inflammatory blood products into Reinke's space.[1] The vocal ligament limits elongation and assumes most of the tensile stress at high pitches. However, the ligament cannot protect against vocal fold collision, where the stress is transverse to the fibres. Here, the softer tissues of the lamina propria[2] are exposed and absorb most of the impact stress. This is supported by the fact that vocal fold nodules occur bilaterally at the point of maximum impact stress. (Titze,1994).

Such vocal overuse results in wound formation, which, in turn, leads to remodelling of the superficial layer of the lamina propria and, to a lesser extent, the vocal fold epithelium. It is this tissue remodelling that results in the formation of vocal fold nodules, polyps, and cysts. Fibrin is the main blood product that exudes into Reinke's space and is often present directly surrounding blood vessels. Frank haemorrhage is also frequently encountered. Variable and often extensive degrees of connective tissue proliferation contribute to the subepithelial swelling of the polyp or related lesion (Figure 12.6). Abundant fibroblasts and blood vessels are prominent features, and cyst formation sometimes occurs among connective tissue cells. Only a small number of lesions show squamous epithelial changes, consisting of hyaline thickening of the epithelial basement membrane, epithelial dysplasia, or keratosis.

Although the mechanism of formation of a particular type of lesion (nodule, polyp, or cyst) remains incompletely understood, Marcotullio et al. (2002) have attempted to correlate the clinical diagnosis of vocal fold polyps, nodules, and Reinke's oedema with histologic findings following excision. They classified changes in the lamina propria into five stages of maturation: oedematous (least mature), oedematous-angiomatous, angiomatous, angiomatous-hyaline, and hyaline (most mature). They also reported that vocal nodules tend to show earlier changes, whereas vocal polyps show later changes. They suggest that vocal nodules may represent more recent pathologic manifestations of vocal trauma than vocal polyps.

## SELF-INJECTION INTO NECK VEINS

Hope et al. (2017), in their survey, investigated the records of 5,261 injecting drug users between 2011 and 2014 and found that 339 (6%) had injected into a central vein in the previous 28 days. For 52 respondents (1%), the neck was the only injection site they had used in the preceding 28 days. It is well-known that in injecting drug users, there is an increased risk to the heart from infective endocarditis and myocarditis, as well as an increased risk of thromboembolism and bacterial emboli to the heart, lungs, or other major organs, leading to disseminated infection and multi-organ failure.

Duhart Clarke et al. (2022), in their study from samples taken from 239 people who inject drugs in San Francisco between June 2019 and June 2020, found that about a third of the sample reported injecting in their neck within 30 days, the most common reason being lack of available veins. They discussed the increased risk of adverse health outcomes in neck injection, particularly because of the exterior jugular vein's direct path to the heart and lungs.

In relation to first-episode infective endocarditis, Rodger et al. (2018) found that the majority of injecting drug users had right-sided infection (124 from 202 patients [61.4%]); 118 of these cases exclusively involved the tricuspid valve. Staphylococcus aureus infection was the causative organism in 77.2% of cases, followed by 6.4% with a polymicrobial infection and 5.4% caused by enterococci.

Furthermore, with injection into neck veins, the introduction of bacteria into soft tissues may also lead to abscess formation and further serious infections, which could be life-threatening, such as cellulitis involving the mouth (Ludwig's angina) and thrombophlebitis of the internal jugular vein with the risk of the production of septic emboli.

Other complications have also been reported, including unilateral Horner's syndrome following injection into the ipsilateral side of the neck (Hawkins et al., 1977). In addition, Raz and Ramanathan (1984), found unilateral vocal cord paralysis in two chronic drug abusers who had been injecting their jugular veins because they could no longer use their peripheral veins. Both were found to have diffuse fibrosis involving the recurrent laryngeal nerve.

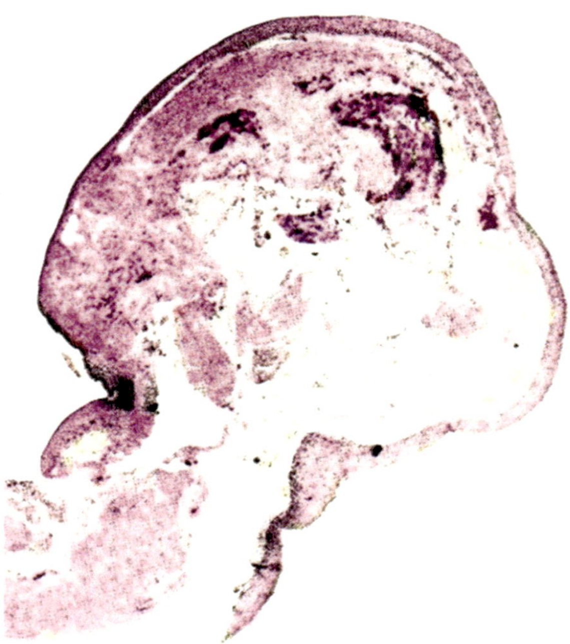

**Figure 12.6** Vocal cord polyp (Haematoxylin and eosin × 32).

# NOTES

1 Reinke's space is a potential space of the true vocal cord, bounded above and below by the junctions of the squamous with respiratory epithelium, anteriorly by the anterior commissure, and posteriorly by the tip of the vocal process of the arytenoid. The squamous epithelium of the vocal cord and the elastic tissue of the vocal ligament represent its superficial and deep boundaries.

2 The lamina propria is a thin layer of connective tissue that forms part of the mucous membrane or mucosa. In the vocal fold, there are three layers (superficial, intermediate, and deep), and they lie between the epithelium and basement membrane.

## References


Akhavan A, Ajalloueyan M, Ghanei M, Moharamzad Y. Late laryngeal findings in sulfur mustard poisoning. *Clin Toxicol (Phila)*. 2009 Feb;47(2):142–144. doi: 10.1080/15563650701613753. PMID: 19280427.

Appelqvist P, Salmo M. Lye corrosion carcinoma of the esophagus: A review of 63 cases. *Cancer*. 1980 May 15;45(10):2655–2658. doi: 10.1002/1097-0142(19800515)45:10<2655::aid-cncr2820451028>3.0.co;2–p. PMID: 7378999.

Duhart Clarke SE, Megerian CE, Suen LW, Wenger LD, Lambdin BH, Davidson PJ, Kral AH. Prevalence and factors associated with neck injection among people who inject drugs in San Francisco, California. *Drug Alcohol Depend*. 2022 Dec 1;241:109686. doi: 10.1016/j.drugalcdep.2022.109686. Epub 2022 Nov 2. PMID: 36402050.

Furnas DW, Shumrick DA. Electrical injury to the larynx. *Arch Surg*. 1968 June;96(6):975–978. doi: 10.1001/archsurg.1968.01330240121029. PMID: 5647584.

Hawkins KA, Bruckstein AH, Guthrie TC. Percutaneous heroin injection causing Horner syndrome. *JAMA*. 1977 May 2;237(18):1963–1964. doi: 10.1001/jama.1977.03270450053022. PMID: 576711.

Holinger PH, Schild JA, Maurizi DG. Internal and external trauma to the larynx. *Laryngoscope*. 1968;78, 944–954.

Hope VD, Iversen J, Cullen KJ, Parry JV, Maher L, Nucbe F. Injection into the jugular vein among people who inject drugs in the United Kingdom: Prevalence, associated factors and harms. *Int J Drug Policy*. 2017 Aug;46:28–33. doi: 10.1016/j.drugpo.2017.05.005. Epub 2017 Jun 3. PMID: 28586700.

Hopkins RA, Postlethwait RW. Caustic burns and carcinoma of the esophagus. *Ann Surg*. 1981 Aug;194(2):146–148. doi: 10.1097/00000658-198108000-00005. PMID: 7259340; PMCID: PMC1345231.

Johns MM. Update on the etiology, diagnosis, and treatment of vocal fold nodules, polyps, and cysts. *Curr Opin Otolaryngol Head Neck Surg*. 2003 Dec;11(6):456–461. doi: 10.1097/00020840-200312000-00009. PMID: 14631179.

Kitulwatte I, Pollanen MS. Electrical injury of the neck and cardiac air embolism: A novel mechanism of death. *Forensic Sci Med Pathol*. 2009;5(1):32–35. doi: 10.1007/s12024-008-9060-x. Epub 2008 Sep 20. PMID: 19291433.

Marcotullio D, Magliulo G, Pietrunti S, Suriano M. Exudative laryngeal diseases of Reinke's space: a clinicohistopathological framing. *J Otolaryngol*. 2002 Dec;31(6):376–380. doi: 10.2310/7070.2002.34517. PMID: 12593551.

Martínez-Fernandez P, Vallejo-de-Torres G, Sánchez-de-León-Robles MS, Navarro-Escayola E, Moro-Moro M, Alberti-Masgrau N, Tejedor-Alonso MA. Medical and pathologic characteristics of fatal anaphylaxis: A Spanish nationwide 17-year series. *Forensic Sci Med Pathol*. 2019 Sep;15(3):369–381. doi: 10.1007/s12024-019-00134-1. Epub 2019 Jul 11. PMID: 31292823.

Millar AJ, Cox SG. Caustic injury of the oesophagus. *Pediatr Surg Int*. 2015 Feb;31(2):111–121. doi: 10.1007/s00383-014-3642-3. Epub 2014 Nov 29. PMID: 25432099.

Pumphrey RS, Roberts IS. Postmortem findings after fatal anaphylactic reactions. *J Clin Pathol*. 2000 Apr;53(4):273–276. doi: 10.1136/jcp.53.4.273. PMID: 10823122; PMCID: PMC1731177.

Raz S, Ramanathan V. Injection injuries of the recurrent laryngeal nerve. *Laryngoscope*. 1984 Feb;94(2 Pt 1):197–200. doi: 10.1288/00005537-198402000-00009. PMID: 6694490.

Reid A, Ha JF. Inhalational injury and the larynx: A review. *Burns*. 2019 Sep;45(6):1266–1274. doi: 10.1016/j.burns.2018.10.025. Epub 2018 Dec 8. PMID: 30529118.

Riffat F, Cheng A. Pediatric caustic ingestion: 50 consecutive cases and a review of the literature. *Dis Esophagus*. 2009;22(1):89–94. doi: 10.1111/j.1442-2050.2008.00867.x. Epub 2008 Oct 1. PMID: 18847446.

Rodger L, Glockler-Lauf SD, Shojaei E, Sherazi A, Hallam B, Koivu S, Gupta K, Hosseini-Moghaddam SM, Silverman M. Clinical characteristics and factors associated with mortality in first-episode infective endocarditis among persons who inject drugs. *JAMA Netw Open*. 2018 Nov 2;1(7):e185220. doi: 10.1001/jamanetworkopen.2018.5220. PMID: 30646383; PMCID: PMC6324402.

Stumboff AV. Chemical burns of the oral cavity and esophagus. *Arch Otolaryngol*. 1950 Sep;52(3):419–426. doi: 10.1001/archotol.1950.00700030441009. PMID: 14770689.

Titze IR. Mechanical stress in phonation. *J Voice*. 1994 June;8(2):99–105. doi: 10.1016/s0892-1997(05)80302-9. PMID: 8061776.

Xiao H, Liu R, Liu X, Wang H, Cen Y, Xu X. Reconstruction of severe neck scar contracture after electrical injury. *J Craniofac Surg*. 2022 Jan-Feb 01;33(1):203–205. doi: 10.1097/SCS.0000000000007852. PMID: 34267134.

Zhang X, Wang M, Han H, Xu Y, Shi Z, Ma G. Corrosive induced carcinoma of esophagus after 58 years. *Ann Thorac Surg*. 2012 Dec;94(6):2103–2105. doi: 10.1016/j.athoracsur.2012.03.110. PMID: 23176921.

# CHAPTER 13

## INJURIES RESULTING FROM THERAPEUTIC, INVESTIGATIVE, AND OTHER RELATED ACTIONS

*Peter Vanezis*
*(with contributions from Andrew Peter Vanezis)*



Iatrogenic and other related injuries to the neck may result from a variety of therapeutic or investigative techniques. The region is particularly vulnerable, as it is frequently subjected to a number of procedures, including airway and oesophageal instrumentation, invasive vascular procedures such as angiography and intravenous cannulation, long-term tracheostomy maintenance, and chiropractic manipulation.

DOI: 10.4324/9781003658467-13

# INJURIES FROM TRACHEOSTOMY

A tracheostomy is indicated in a number of clinical situations, including relieving upper airway obstruction or to provide mechanical ventilation for a prolonged period. Traditionally, a surgical tracheostomy is the procedure performed. The percutaneous dilatational tracheostomy, since its introduction in 1985 (Ciaglia et al., 1985), has become the gold-standard procedure used by intensive care physicians worldwide. This technique consists of inserting a tracheostomy tube using a Seldinger wire inserted through a cannula into the tracheal lumen. Tapered dilators are then passed over the guide wire and dilate the opening in the tracheal wall. A tracheostomy tube snugly fitted over a dilator is then passed into the trachea between the cricoid cartilage and the first tracheal ring.

Tracheostomy, whether performed via the traditional surgical technique or percutaneously, can cause local tissue trauma and may be complicated by granuloma formation, tracheal stenosis, and even perforation. There are also a few reported cases of squamous cell carcinoma of the trachea, developing years after tracheostomy, arising within the stoma (Weissman and Konrad, 1979). Tracheo-oesophageal fistula at the level of the tracheal stoma may also be caused by operative accidents during the creation of a tracheostomy (Green et al., 1983). In addition, cervical soft tissue emphysema may occasionally occur, although it is not usually clinically significant and is self-limiting.

Arola et al. (1980), from their observations on 48 patients who had tracheostomies with varying degrees of cuff-induced tracheal injury, concluded that tracheostomy tubes with large, low-pressure cuffs should be used because they cause less damage. de Kleijn et al. (2019), in a retrospective study of 305 patients, compared the incidence of short- and long-term complications

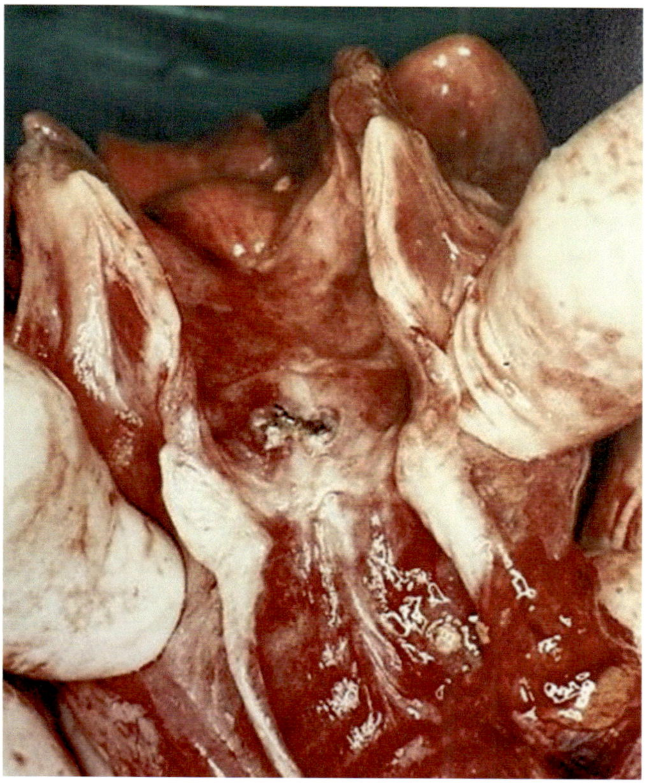

**Figure 13.1** Internal view of the larynx and trachea opened posteriorly, showing suture from previously closed tracheostomy site and accompanying severe fibrous stricture.

in the traditional surgical tracheostomy and percutaneous dilatational tracheostomy. They found that the incidence of complications, including tracheal stenosis, was similar in both groups.

In a case observed by the author of this text, the deceased, a woman aged 38 years, had a closed tracheostomy site that had developed a fibrous stricture. The lumen was further compromised by a nylon suture protruding into it. Whilst eating, she suddenly choked on some food and died. It appeared that she was unable to effectively clear her airway because of the partial obstruction (Figure 13.1).

# INJURIES RESULTING FROM INTUBATION AND OTHER INSTRUMENTATION

## Laryngeal and Tracheal Injuries

There are three areas of contact between an endotracheal tube and the laryngotracheal region that are most susceptible to severe injury. These areas are the cuff and tube tip in the trachea; the shaft of the tube as it presses against the arytenoids; and the subglottis, where the shaft, or more rarely, the cuff, comes into contact (Figure 13.2).

Benjamin (2018) reported on the various injuries resulting from prolonged endotracheal intubation and their classification. He noted that injuries to the trachea caused by pressure from the cuff of the tube are now seldom seen due to the use of high-volume, low-pressure cuffs, but that there has been no corresponding decrease in the incidence of laryngeal damage. Changes due to tube pressure, which affects capillary perfusion, are the important consideration in causing mucosal injury. When pressure from the firm walls of the endotracheal tube exceeds mucosal

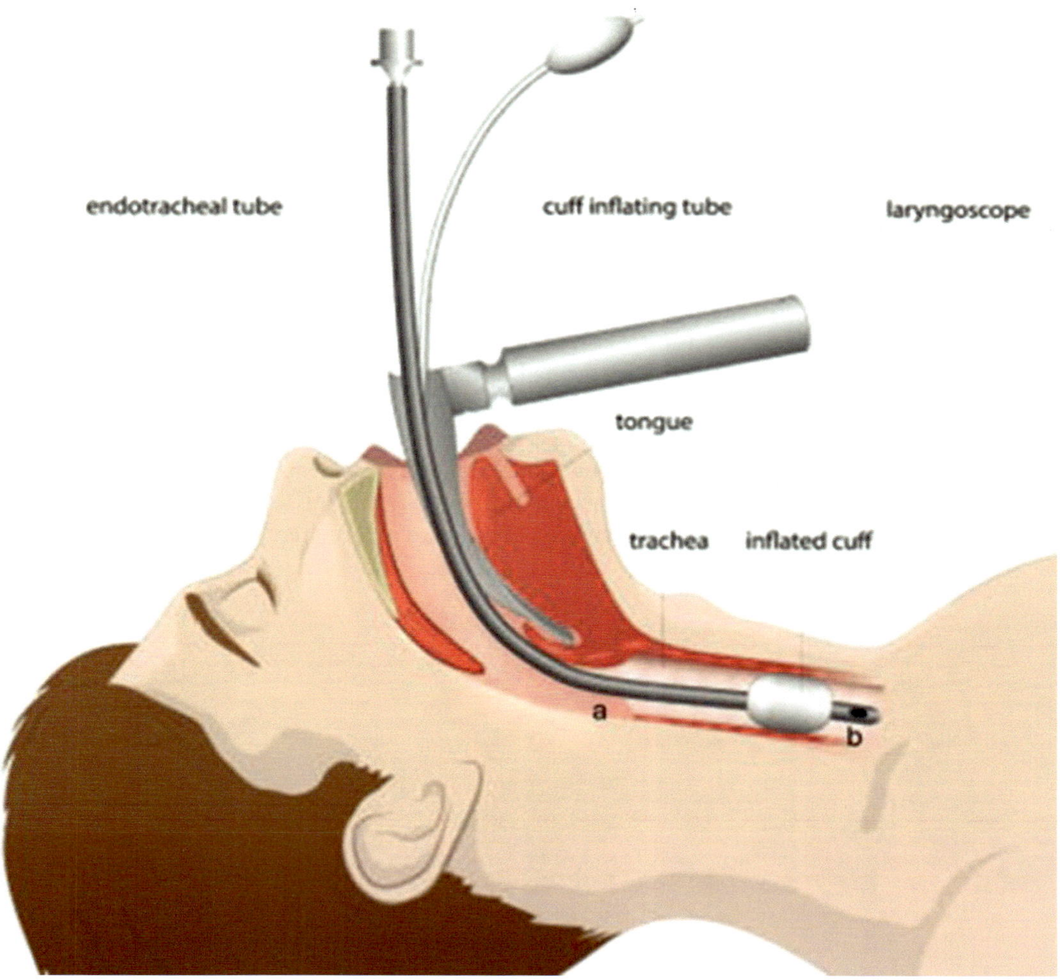


**Figure 13.2** Schematic section of upper airway, showing contact areas most susceptible to severe injury from endotracheal intubation: (a) shaft of tube opposite the arytenoids and (b) cuff and tip in trachea.

capillary pressure, ischaemia occurs, beginning with irritation, followed by congestion, oedema, and eventually ulceration. This may progress to perichondritis and finally necrosis involving the cricoarytenoid joints and the cricoid cartilage. Extensive or deep changes promote the formation of new collagen, which matures into fibrous, firm scar tissue that may result in subglottic stenosis.

In a prospective study of a long-term intubated population, Whited (1985) showed a reduced incidence of isolated tube injury through the addition of a cushion to the shaft where contact occurs glottically or subglottically. An additional benefit of this modification is the centring effect that the cushion has on shaft movement within the trachea. Subsequent tube tip injury is minimised by this centring effect on the tube shaft at the laryngeal level. However, the same study found that the arytenoid and cricoarytenoid interface was becoming more significant as a major and frequent site of trauma. Arytenoid dislocation, however, remains an uncommon complication (Dudley et al., 1984).

One group of chronically ill patients who require endotracheal intubation are those suffering from closed head injuries. Nowak et al. (1987) found that 23 of their 72 patients who required either long-term endotracheal intubation, tracheostomy, or both, had significant laryngeal or tracheal lesions. The main abnormalities noted were vocal cord paralysis, tracheal stenosis, subglottic stenosis, glottic stenosis, and tracheomalacia.

With regard to tracheal perforation from endotracheal intubation, Minambres et al. (2009) reported it to be more common in women, people over the age of 50 and those of short stature and can lead to surgical emphysema, respiratory distress, and haemoptysis, although the overall pooled mortality rates are low at around 0.005% (Borasio et al., 1997). Perforation from endotracheal intubation can occur directly as a result of blunt tip trauma, overinflation of the balloon cuff or by vigorous movement of an already placed tube whilst in situ (Jougon et al., 2000). In addition, adjuncts used to aid in airway intubation such as introducers, gum-elastic bougies, and stylets can also directly cause perforation (Evans et al., 2015).

Histological studies by Bergström et al. (1962) on the larynx of adults intubated for up to 96 hours showed glottic and subglottic mucosal ulceration and necrosis. Hedden et al. (1969) and Donnelly (1969) found similar lesions and described perichondritis of the arytenoid cartilage (Figure 13.3).

In infants, Bozic (1969) found mucosal erosions and perichondritis in 13 of 15 larynges intubated for less than 78 hours, and focal arytenoid cartilage necrosis in two infants intubated for more than 13 days. Joshi et al. (1972) described in detail the mucosal changes in neonates with respiratory distress syndrome who were intubated for up to one week. Hawkins (1978), as part of a wider discussion on the problems of prolonged intubation, briefly comments on mucosal ulceration, perichondritis, and submucosal fibrosis in 30 infant larynges removed at autopsy. In neonates the most common complication of endotracheal intubation is subglottic stenosis with an incidence of between 1% (Strong and Passy, 1977) and 8% (Papsidero and Pashley, 1980).

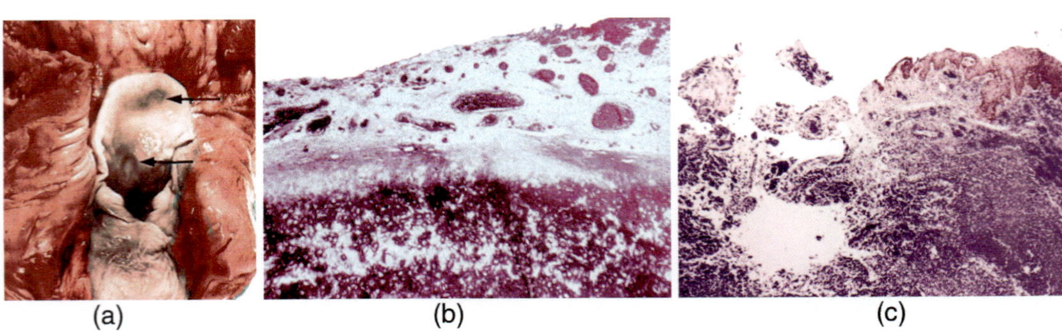


**Figure 13.3** (a) Posterior view of larynx, showing two contact ulcers (arrows) on the epiglottis caused by intubation for about 14 days in a patient with a severe head injury. (b) Longitudinal section of the upper ulcer, showing loss of the mucosal surface and submucosal vascular congestion (Haematoxylin and eosin × 32). (c) Longitudinal section of the lower ulcer. There is dense cellular infiltrate and vascular congestion (Haematoxylin and eosin × 32).

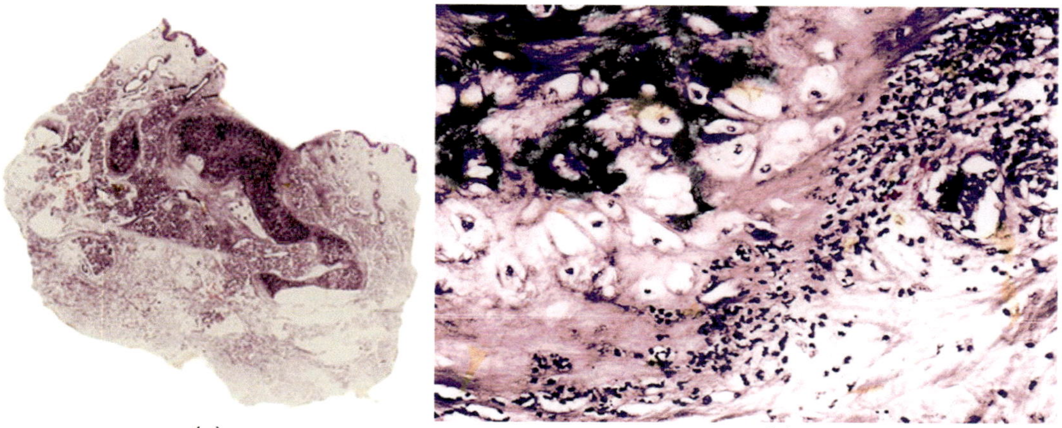

(a) (b)

**Figure 13.4** (a) Ulcer of the laryngeal pharynx region where a nasogastric tube has pressed against the cricoid cartilage anteriorly and the cervical spine posteriorly. The cricoid cartilage forms the ulcer bed (Haematoxylin and eosin × 8). (b) Longitudinal section of cricoid cartilage displaying perichondritis. There is peripheral infiltration and erosion of the cartilage with predominantly polymorphonuclear leucocytes (Haematoxylin and eosin × 160).

A histopathological study on the larynges of neonates who had been intubated was carried out by Gould and Howard (1985). They divided their 58 cases into three groups according to the duration of intubation. Group 1 comprised 26 cases in which intubation lasted less than 3 days. There were nine cases in group 2, with intubation lasting from 3 to 14 days. Focal ulceration was identified in the supraglottis and the anterior glottis. Similar injuries were seen in the posterior glottis and subglottis, but with more pronounced intubation, there was full-thickness mucosal necrosis, perichondritis and partial destruction of the arytenoid and cricoid cartilages. Although the severity of injury progressed with time and many of the most severe injuries occurred early, in the second and third weeks of intubation, the larynx usually healed despite the continued presence of the endotracheal tube.

Laryngeal mucous cyst formation has also been reported following fibreoptic intubation in a 16-year-old youth with juvenile chronic arthritis (Smith, 1986).

Nasogastric tubes may cause serious laryngeal stenosis. Trophic ulcers may develop if the tube lies in the midline and becomes trapped between the cervical spine and the cricoid plate (Figure 13.4). Such ulcers lead to perichondritis and eventual destructive chondritis, cricoid collapse, and chronic laryngeal stenosis. This may not occur until two or three months after the tube has been discontinued.

Laryngeal complications resulting from intubation and tracheostomy have had a significant impact on the management of critical illness during the COVID-19 pandemic (Wallace and McGrath, 2021). Prolonged periods of intubation, widespread use of placing the patient in a prone position and prolonged cuff inflation attributable to aerosol generation, have exacerbated laryngeal complications. This is compounded by the apparent potential of SARS-CoV-2 to directly cause airway oedema and laryngitis and the potential for later laryngeal stenosis. Post-extubation dysphonia and dysphagia are common, can be severe and may persist after hospital discharge (Allgood et al., 2024; Neevel et al., 2021).

## Oesophageal Injuries

Oesophageal lesions such as haematoma, partial-thickness laceration, or perforation may occur with any form of instrumentation. The latter, and most severe, form of injury is seen particularly with difficult endotracheal intubation and the passage of nasogastric tubes. Although most commercially available nasogastric tubes are constructed from pliable synthetic materials and are therefore considered to safeguard against trauma to the upper gastrointestinal tract, the incidence of oesophageal perforation is nearly as great as that caused by difficult tracheal intubation. In one review of all causes of oesophageal perforation (Norman and Sosis, 1986), 72% occurred from various iatrogenic causes, of which 60% were located primarily in the cervical oesophagus, followed by 30% in the mid-thoracic portion and 10% in the distal oesophagus.

Cervical oesophageal perforation, secondary to instrumentation of any kind, is located primarily over the cricopharyngeus muscle on the posterior wall. Here, the oesophagus is thin-walled owing to the absence of longitudinal muscle fibres and marked narrowing of the lumen at the introitus. The posterior muscle band extends over C6 and C7. Hyperextension of the neck, kyphosis, or cervical osteophytes, may exaggerate the pressure of the oesophagus against the cervical vertebrae and predispose the patient to injury at this level. Hypertonicity of the cricopharyngeus and/or thin mucosa, as is often found in the elderly, is an additional hazard during oesophagoscopy. Other factors that increase the risk of perforation include inadequate anaesthesia, failure to deflate the endotracheal cuff, presence of pharyngeal diverticulae, an inexperienced endoscopist, and a biopsy performed beyond the area of direct vision.

Jougon and colleagues (2001) reported five cases over a 20-year period, all of which were associated with elective but difficult intubations. They pointed out that the signs and symptoms of oesophageal perforation are often insidious and difficult to diagnose, especially in patients who remain intubated and sedated. Additionally, these patients have an extremely high mortality rate if left untreated.

Oesophageal perforation may also be seen in the neonates following difficult delivery, usually preterm and requiring aggressive resuscitation, including vigorous suction, difficult intubation or the passage of a nasogastric tube (Mollitt et al., 1981). In a recent multicentre retrospective study (Sorensen et al., 2023), eight neonates were identified as having oesophageal perforation. All but one patient was born at term (>37 weeks), and 75% were extremely low birth weight. There were no significant underlying comorbidities, other than prematurity. The perforation occurred on day 2 of life. Seven patients were intubated and ventilated at the time of diagnosis, of whom five were on conventional ventilation and two undergoing high frequency oscillation. One patient was self-ventilating in air. In all eight patients, an enterogastric tube (orogastric or nasogastric tube) had been placed immediately after birth.

Perforation during oesophagoscopy for removal of a bolus of food has been described by Behnke et al. (1980). In their patient, the weld-on light carrier broke, and a ribbon of mucosa and muscularis had become impinged at the defect.

The consequences of these perforations are due to the contamination of the perioesophageal space with corrosive digestive fluids, food, and bacteria, leading to diffuse cellulitis and localised extensive infection. Suppuration first appears in the perioesophageal space. This space extends from the cranial vault to the diaphragm. Since mediastinal pressure is below the atmospheric pressure during normal breathing, a tear of the oesophagus or upper pharynx can cause suctioning of luminal contents directly into the mediastinal space. The tissue here is poorly vascularised and highly susceptible to infection, especially with anaerobic bacteria. Oral and nasal suction catheters to clear laryngo-oesophageal secretions may also cause pharyngeal trauma. Lesions consist of submucosal ecchymoses or mucosal lacerations (Wolff and Kessler, 1973).

Mortality from oesophageal perforation depends greatly on the site of the lesion as well as the promptness of diagnosis. An autopsy study of the hypopharynx and cervical oesophagus of 103 patients who were subjected to intubation and/or endoscopy during their final period of hospitalisation showed that such injuries are commonly missed (Wolff and Kessler, 1973). Of the patients studied, 60% demonstrated evidence of mucosal ulceration, haemorrhage, and perforation, but only 20% of these iatrogenic injuries were recognised clinically. Nasogastric tubes were inserted in 34 of the 103 patients (33%) and resulted in mucosal damage and post-cricoid ulcers in nine patients (26%) in whom the tubes were retained for an average of five days.

Hamilton et al. (2024) reported the case of a 71-year-old female who underwent oesophageal dilatation for a benign oesophageal stricture. With air inflation following endoscopy, she demonstrated decorticate posturing and a left-sided gaze with dilated pupils. She was found to have an oesophageal rupture. A post-procedure CT without contrast showed pneumomediastinum adjacent to the lower/mid-cervical oesophagus, consistent with rupture of the oesophagus (confirmed at autopsy). CT imaging also revealed the presence of gas bubbles within the brain parenchyma, which were consistent with air emboli resulting in infarction. A commentary on the above article by Bothma and Hussain (2024) discusses the mechanism of air accessing the cerebral circulation when there is no obvious intracardiac or intrapulmonary shunt to facilitate air entering the left side of the heart and the cerebral arterial system. They stressed that the pulmonary capillary filtration system can be overwhelmed when a large amount of air enters the pulmonary capillary system. Bypass channels can then open and allow air to pass into the pulmonary venules, then pulmonary veins, into the left heart. However, it should be appreciated that 25% of the population have a patent foramen ovale; therefore, a Valsava manouevre may easily give rise to a paradoxical embolism involving the cerebral circulation (Nakanishi et al., 2017).

## Cervical Spine Injuries

Cervical spine injury, as described by Feller-Kopman (2003), is a potentially devastating complication of endotracheal intubation. Indeed, all the different methods of establishing an airway can create significant movement within the cervical spine, thus rendering pre-existing pathology in this region (see Chapter 11) an important consideration for proper airway management. Risk factors include head and neck trauma, cervical osteoporosis, atlanto-axial instability as seen in patients with rheumatoid arthritis and Down's syndrome, as well as lytic bone lesions. In one of the largest reviews of cervical spinal injury as a complication of endotracheal intubation, Crosby and Lui (1990) suggest that immobilisation of the head and neck will prevent most spine injuries regardless of the route or method of intubation.

Oppenlander et al. (2015) describe two patients with known cervical pathology who required emergency intubation in the intensive care unit, which resulted in quadriplegia. Their first case was a 68-year-old man with a known history of ankylosing spondylitis who sustained a ground-level fall on ice and experienced severe back pain. On admission, he had full strength without neurological deficit. Imaging revealed a T9–10 fracture-dislocation with shearing through the disc space and the posterior elements. No cervical fractures, subluxation, or other acute findings were identified on his initial cervical CT. Given the unstable thoracic fracture, the patient underwent an uncomplicated posterior decompression and fusion, including T9–10 laminectomy and T8–11 pedicle screw fixation. There was no difficulty with the patient's first intubation in the operating room. Postoperatively, he required further intubation, which proved to be difficult, and he developed quadriplegia. Imaging revealed a C6–7 fracture-dislocation associated with severe central canal stenosis.

The second case was that of a 73-year-old man who fell down a flight of stairs while on a cruise ship in the Baltic Sea. One week after the injury, he was transferred to hospital and, on admission, he displayed central cord syndrome. Imaging revealed diffuse idiopathic skeletal hyperostosis with an acute C6–7 fracture associated with significant spinal cord compression. Posterior decompression and C6–T1 fixation were carried out. On post-operative day 12, the patient developed respiratory distress due to pneumonia and required intubation. This proved to be prolonged and difficult, resulting in the patient developing quadriplegia; imaging revealed spondyloptosis at C6–7.

# INJURIES RESULTING FROM INVASIVE VASCULAR TECHNIQUES

## Lesions Following Angiography

The feasibility of vertebral angiography was first demonstrated by Moniz (1931). However, this was achieved only through operative exposure of the vessel. Soon afterwards, Lohr (1936) first advocated angiography as a safe method for evaluation of head and neck trauma, and it has since been used as a safe investigative procedure for this purpose. The technique has varied over the years; at first, direct needle puncture was used, but this method has now largely been replaced by catheter techniques.

Transient cortical blindness is a rare but well-known complication of cerebral angiography (Lo et al., 2015). Patients complain of cortical blindness within minutes of contrast injection, which usually resolves within a few days. This complication is reported to have a higher incidence in vertebral angiography. Its exact mechanism is unknown, although there are two hypotheses. The first is that it results from the neurotoxic effect of contrast agent, causing osmotic disruption of the blood-brain barrier (Alsarraf et al., 1999). The second hypothesis is that transient cortical blindness is the result of posterior reversible leukoencephalopathy syndrome, which is due to the failure of cerebrovascular autoregulation, leading to perivascular oedema (Saigal et al., 2004).

Failures in technique have also resulted in extravasation of contrast medium, haematoma, occlusion of the vertebral artery, and brachial plexus injury.

Arteriovenous fistulae are rare complications of angiography but have been reported extensively in the earlier literature. Jefferson et al. (1956) pointed out that the high route for angiography by the mastoid tip in which the vertebral artery was punctured as it wound around the back of the lateral mass of the atlas, had resulted in two or three cases where a vertebral artery fistula was suspected. In these cases (which were not published in detail), a bruise developed in the neck and the presumption was that the puncture had produced a leak into the vertebral venous plexus. In no case had this complication been more than a minor inconvenience.

More recently, Aljobeh et al. (2019) reviewed 280 patients with vertebro-vertebral fistulae. These occur when a direct shunt forms between the vertebral artery and the veins forming the vertebral plexus. They categorised them into three subgroups (iatrogenic, spontaneous, and traumatic), based on the mechanism of formation, iatrogenic vertebro-vertebral fistulae, which were more commonly seen in elderly people were found in 68 cases (24%).

Spinal cord infarction is a rare neurological complication when intravascularly injected iodinated contrast is used during cerebral angiography. Numerous cases have been reported since the 1960s. Ederli et al. (1962) reported a case of necrosis of the cervical spinal cord produced by vertebral angiography via the subclavian artery. The injection through the subclavian artery was with a highly concentrated (55%) contrast medium. The authors stated that a large quantity of this had probably been carried into the arterial network of the cord due to a particular pattern of the arterial branches in the neck or because of the direction of the injected stream. Pathak et al., (1999) reported a case of cervical spinal cord injury during vertebral angiography which was initially not suspected. An autopsy nine years later showed evidence of central cervical spinal cord necrosis. Zhuo et al. (2023) recognised that there has been a decrease in spinal cord necrosis since the adoption of non-ionic contrast agents in recent times. There is a greater likelihood of ionic monomer contrast media, due to its hyperosmolality and direct neurotoxicity, to cause contrast-induced encephalopathy and contrast-induced spinal cord injury. Despite the rarity of this complication, the above authors reported a case of spinal cord necrosis after cerebral angiography.

They surmised that the underlying cause might be vertebral artery vasospasm. Other potential risk factors included cervical spondylosis with canal stenosis and unintended injection into the left thyrocervical trunk.

## Internal Jugular Vein Catheterisation

Central venous catheterisation can be a potentially hazardous process. Complications occur either before the catheter is fixed in position (early), or after fixation (late). The early complications include venous laceration, haematoma, arterial puncture, brachial plexus injury, and air and catheter embolism. Late complications include thrombophlebitis, infection, late air embolism, compression by haematoma and arteriovenous fistula. Yamamoto et al. (2023) report a case of vertebral arteriovenous fistula caused by iatrogenic trauma from central venous catheterisation involving the brachiocephalic vein in a 79-year-old female who had been referred for assessment of a vertebral artery aneurysm at V1 (pre-foraminal segment). The patient had no signs other than a vascular murmur on the right side of the neck and was diagnosed 20 years after undergoing central venous catheterisation. Right vertebral angiography revealed a high-flow shunt from the V1 segment of the right vertebral artery and draining into the right brachiocephalic vein. The fistula had a single communication between a pseudoaneurysm and large varix. Previously, Gamulin et al. (1986) reported the case of a 13-year-old girl with multiple complications, including pleural misplacement of the catheter, massive haemorrhage and cardiovascular collapse following catheter removal, and development of an arteriovenous fistula between the right subclavian artery and the right brachiocephalic vein.

A rare complication of internal jugular vein catheterisation is Horner's syndrome (Zou and Yao, 2020). This is a neurological condition characterised by ipsilateral miosis, ptosis, and anhidrosis due to sympathetic nerve block or injury. The incidence of the syndrome caused by internal jugular vein catheterisation is reported to be less than 5%, according to various sources.

When venous puncture is necessary in an infant for diagnostic blood sampling or for the administration of intravenous therapy, large-calibre vessels are employed, one of the most popular being the internal jugular vein. This vessel lies close to the trachea, and it is for this reason that tracheal perforation may readily occur. Goldstein (1949) reported two such cases. His patients were seven and nine days old. Blood was taken in each case for Wassermann reaction. In both cases, severe subcutaneous cervical and mediastinal emphysema occurred, and both infants died. Following tracheal perforation, there is escape and extension of air from the airway into alveolar tissue between the superficial and deep layers of the cervical fascia, with extension into the mediastinum and, by rupture of the mediastinal pleurae, into the pleural cavity, producing a pneumothorax.

# MISHAPS ASSOCIATED WITH SURGERY TO NECK VESSELS

## Latrogenic Vertebral Artery Injury

Many of the early attempts at surgical repair of a wounded vertebral artery ended in failure. One reason for this was incorrect diagnosis of the source of the haemorrhage. In many cases, the carotid artery, rather than the vertebral artery, was mistakenly diagnosed as the injured vessel. Consequently, the carotid artery was frequently ligated in error. Holmes, in his address to the Royal College of Surgeons in 1873, stressed this common error and cited 11 cases in which carotid artery ligation had been carried out with disastrous consequences. It appears from the cases quoted by Holmes that most would have had a fatal outcome in any event despite ligation of the carotid artery, although the latter course of action certainly played a major part in causing death in a few instances.

The high frequency with which inadvertent ligation of the common carotid artery occurred is accounted for by the topographical relationship between the two arteries and the fact that the pressure on the common carotid artery at the root of the neck will control the circulation of the vertebral artery.

Lee et al. (2024) emphasised that it is of paramount importance for surgeons to be aware of not only of normal vertebral artery anatomy but also of anatomic variations that may pose risk of potential injury. They pointed out that iatrogenic injury from cervical spine surgery is rare but may result in potentially catastrophic neurological complications. They highlighted the need for surgeons to recognise the risk of vertebral artery injury during cervical spine surgery. In any event, certain blunt injury patterns in the cervical spine, including fractures at C1–C3, two-level fractures, cervical subluxations/dislocations, facet fractures, and transverse foramen fractures, should raise suspicion of coexisting vertebral artery injury.

## Latrogenic Carotid Artery Injury

A number of authors have identified significant injuries to distal cranial and cervical nerves occurring during carotid artery surgery. Two of the larger series are those of Theodotou and Mahaley (1985), who surveyed the incidence of injuries during 192 carotid endarterectomies, and Weiss et al. (1987), who reported on 536 carotid artery operations. In the latter series, there were 14.4% transient and 6% permanent cranial and cervical nerve injuries. The highest injury rate was observed in the hypoglossal nerve (8.6%), followed by the marginal mandibular branch of the facial nerve (6.2%), and the vagus nerve with its superior and recurrent laryngeal branches (3.7%). Injury to the glossopharyngeal and greater auricular nerves occurred very rarely.

Occasionally, when epistaxis is severe and recurrent, ligation of the external carotid artery may be indicated. The author of this text has seen a case in which the common carotid artery of a young pregnant woman was ligated in error, causing massive fatal cerebral infarction (Figure 13.5). The left common carotid artery was ligated in error just above the superior thyroid artery. This artery, which normally arises from the external carotid, had originated from the common carotid artery, and the surgeon did not take this possibility into account and ligated the artery.

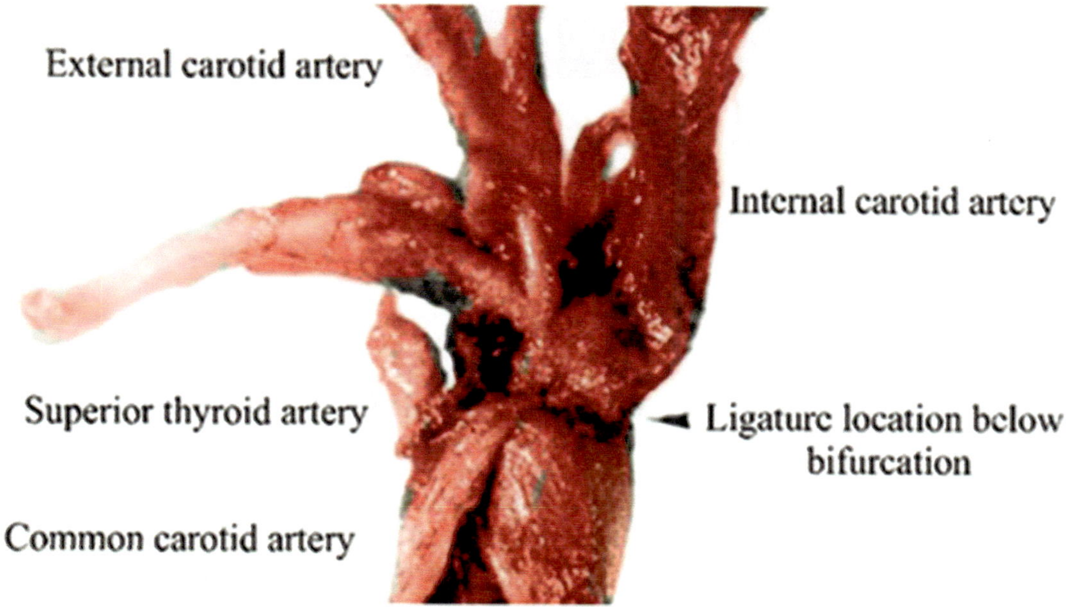


**Figure 13.5** Excised specimen of left carotid artery showing constriction just below the bifurcation, where the ligature was placed (black arrow), and above the superior thyroid artery, which has its origin at the common carotid artery. (Courtesy Dr M.R. Crompton).

## CHIROPRACTIC MANIPULATION OF THE NECK

Complications of chiropractic manipulation of the neck have been reported very infrequently since the inception of the chiropractic profession in 1895. Varying degrees of stroke severity may follow such manipulations. The most frequently reported complication is posterior circulation stroke, usually related to vertebral dissection, occurring during or shortly after cervical manipulation. Anterior circulation stroke appears to be much less common. It should also be appreciated that minor transitory defects may frequently go unreported.

In 1947, Pratt-Thomas and Berger reported two patients with cerebellar injury who became unconscious during chiropractic manipulation and died within 24 hours. In one of their cases, the basilar and right vertebral arteries were found at autopsy to be thrombosed. These vessels showed no other abnormality that may have contributed. The cervical spinal cord was normal, but the cerebellum had been severely disrupted, with obvious infarction. A third fatal case of theirs involved injury to the upper thoracic cord. Since this publication, the risk factors and complications of chiropractic manipulation have been widely recognised and discussed.

In a survey carried out by Lee et al. (1995), 177 neurologists who responded found that, among their patients, 55 suffered strokes, 16 myelopathies, and 30 radiculopathies. Patients were between the ages of 21 and 60, and the majority experienced complications following cervical manipulation. Most of the patients continued to have persistent neurological deficits three months after the onset, and about one-half had marked or severe deficits. Nearly all of the strokes involved the posterior circulation and almost one-half were angiographically proven.

It is well established that stroke may follow dissection of the main cervical vessels (vertebral and carotid arteries). The biologically plausible explanation that suggests a causal connection between chiropractic manipulation and dissection comes from the known stretching of the vertebral and carotid arteries that occurs during neck manipulation. Dandamudi et al. (2012) describe a case of cerebral embolism immediately following cervical spinal manipulation, originating from an extensively calcified internal carotid artery in the absence of dissection. Such a complication had not previously been reported in the literature.

Peters et al. (1995) reported a case of a 29-year-old woman who suffered a fatal right hemispheric infarction due to a dissection of the internal carotid artery after chiropractic manipulation of the cervical spine. Pathological study of several arteries of muscular and elastic type revealed a mediolytic arteriopathy with widespread mucoid degeneration and cystic transformation of the vessel wall, caused by segmental degeneration of smooth muscle cells of the tunica media. They were of the view that mediolytic arteriopathy is a predisposing factor for the dissection of the internal carotid artery after chiropractic manipulation.

Carotid artery aneurysms from chiropractic manipulation are rare. A case of internal carotid artery aneurysm at its origin following neck manipulation is reported by Murthy and Naidu (1988). Their patient, a 40-year-old male was admitted with a swelling on the left side of the neck, hoarseness, and mild drooping of the left eyelid with loss of sweating on the left side of face of one month's duration. He developed these symptoms within one to two hours of neck manipulation by a barber for the relief of pain in the neck. The neck manipulation included sudden jerky rotary movements to either side as well as extension and flexion. In India (from where the case was reported) at that time it was common practice among the rural population to have manipulation of the neck with oil massage by a barber for relief of neck pain. The manipulation consisted of sudden, jerky, and forcible flexion, extensions and rotatory movements with subsequent stretching or compression of the artery against bony prominences of the cervical vertebrae. They concluded that this mechanism was probably responsible for aneurysm formation in their case.

Yelverton et al. (2020) in 25 healthy participants, both male and female between the ages of 20 and 30 years, investigated the haemodynamics of blood flow through the V3 region of the vertebral artery (level of C1–C2), contralateral to the side manipulated during different rotatory head positions and the posterior cervical spinal manipulation. They found no clinical or statistically significant results for any of the haemodynamic parameters in any of the head positions examined. They concluded that haemodynamic measurements of the V3 region of the vertebral artery do not show significant blood flow changes in the measured head positions or following manipulation of the upper cervical spine in patients without pre-existing risk factors.

Fracture of an already diseased cervical vertebra may occur. Cervical spondylosis, which is extremely common in varying degrees of severity, may make the cervical spine extremely vulnerable to injury (see Chapter 11), particularly if manipulative manoeuvres are carried out. Schmitz et al. (2005) reported the case of a 37-year-old, 15-week pregnant patient who presented with acute neck pain and a diffuse paravertebral swelling following cervical manipulation performed by her general medical practitioner five days earlier. Due to the pregnancy, a cervical spine radiographic series was not obtained before treatment. Magnetic resonance imaging revealed a displaced odontoid fracture associated with a tumour in the vertebral body of C2 and a paravertebral haematoma on the left side from C2 to C4. Histological examination identified an aneurysmal bone cyst.

# INJURIES FROM RESUSCITATION

During cardiopulmonary resuscitation (CPR), bruising and grazes (abrasions) in the face and neck can sometimes occur. When such injuries are found during an autopsy examination, it is essential that a pathologist be aware of their possible causes, whether by resuscitation or by an assault, even though they are generally minor in nature.

A study by Härm and Rajs (1983) examined 21 people who died from causes other than mechanical asphyxia, all of whom had undergone resuscitation. The injuries found were predominantly fingernail impression marks (85%), which showed a regular symmetrical distribution tending to form circles around the nostrils and the mouth. Injuries inflicted during mouth-to-mouth ventilation were localised to the nose and lower jaw. The latter were easy to differentiate from strangulation injuries. Injuries inflicted to the cheeks in order to clear the airway were similar to those observed after forceful oral occlusion.

The author of this text conducted the autopsy of a woman of 70 years who, on external examination, was found to have fingernail marks and extensive bruising on her neck. Internal examination revealed haemorrhage from a ruptured thoracic aortic aneurysm, which had tracked upwards into the soft tissues of her neck. Resuscitation was carried out, which was responsible for the fingernail marks to her neck. Initially, the case was treated as a possible homicide (Figure 13.6).

Hlavaty and Sung (2015) investigated 344 infant deaths under one year of age and identified 38 infants (11%) who displayed abrasions and/or contusions, independent of the cause of death. Of those, 27 infants (71%) had been administered resuscitation, whereas 11 infants (29%) had not. In

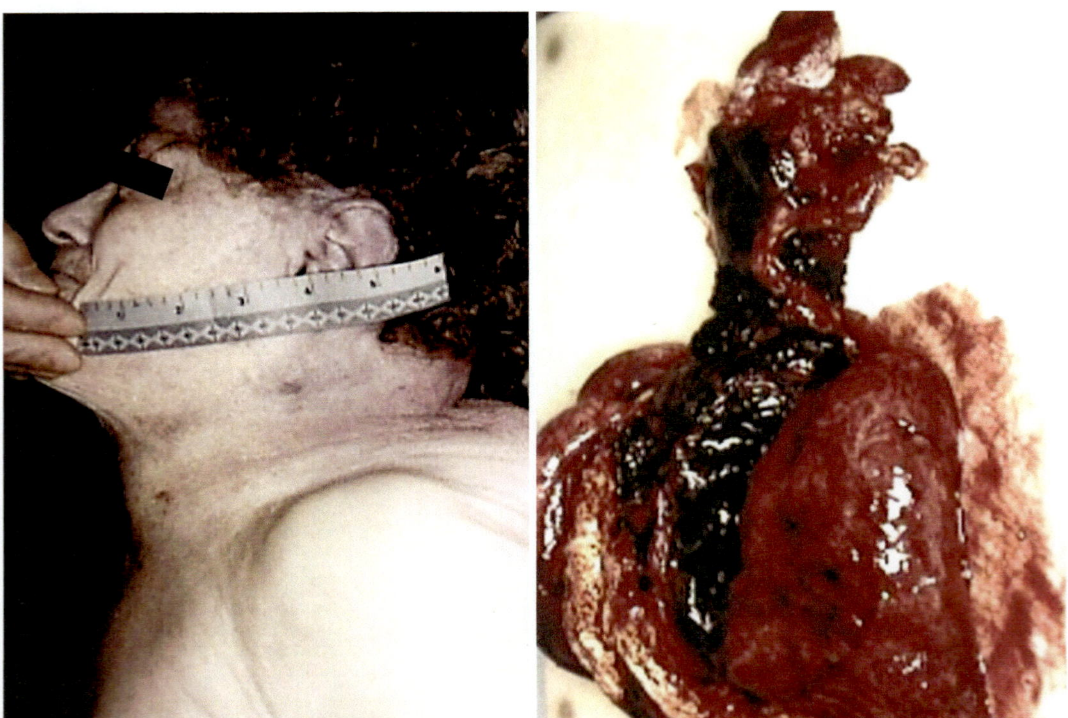

(a) (b)

**Figure 13.6** (a) Bruising and fingernail marks on the neck (arrows). (b) Haemorrhage from ruptured thoracic aorta tracking into the cervical soft tissues.

both groups, contusions were more common in homicide cases and abrasions in non-homicides. In addition, abrasions were frequently seen in infants who had not received resuscitation.

In a more recent study, Wells et al. (2019) investigated the role of CPR in the production of neck contusions in infants. They examined 260 consecutive paediatric autopsies in which resuscitation was attempted. No neck contusions were identified in cases where the manner of death was classified as natural, undetermined, or suicide. Contusions were present in two of 80 deaths classified as accidents and had obvious accidental causes. They concluded that neck contusions in deceased children with no apparent explanation should be regarded as suspicious for abuse and investigated accordingly.

Intubation injuries to the larynx occurring during resuscitation are described in an earlier section of this chapter. While intubation can injure soft and bone tissues of the larynx and pharynx, fractures of the hyoid bone and thyroid cartilage are rarely seen.

Raven et al. (1999), in a series of 50 deaths due to natural and unnatural causes in which there had been endotracheal intubation and chest compression during resuscitation, found that 37 of 50 cases (74%) displayed airway injuries directly resulting from intubation. These injuries, ranging from petechiae to contusions, included oral injury (28%), posterior pharyngeal injury (16%), epiglottic injury (22%), piriform recess injury (12%), laryngeal and tracheal mucosa injury (64%), strap muscle haemorrhage (14%), and cutaneous injury of the neck (4%). In addition, they recorded facial (6%) and conjunctival petechiae (21%) and attributed these changes to resuscitative chest compression. No cases had associated fractures of the hyoid or thyroid cartilage. The authors concluded that resuscitative intubation can cause artefactual injury that may mimic inflicted injuries caused by neck compression, including strangulation and neck holds.

Unlike the experience of the above authors, fractures to the larynx and hyoid bone have been reported by other authors. Gregersen and Vesterby (1981) describe a case in which there was a fracture of the hyoid bone and thyroid cartilage caused by grasping the upper part of the neck during resuscitation. Fractures of the hyoid bone and thyroid cartilages, with associated bleeding into soft tissues, were also observed in several forensic autopsy cases by Hashimoto et al. (2007). They emphasised the importance of distinguishing laryngeal and hyoid bone fractures caused by acts of violence from those resulting from resuscitation attempts. In addition, they pointed out that fractures of the inferior cornu of the thyroid cartilage tend to be seen more frequently after resuscitation than from violence.

In relation to petechial haemorrhages being caused as a result of resuscitation, Maxeiner and Jekat (2010), from their interpretation of reports in the literature, as well as from their own experiences, were able to confirm the absence of actual proof of petechiae being generated by CPR. Furthermore, they state that resuscitation should not simply be accepted as the decisive cause of petechiae when investigating victims with suspicious neck findings who had undergone cardiopulmonary resuscitation.

# INJURIES FROM RADIATION THERAPY

Radiation therapy to the neck may cause tissue damage to a variable and severe extent. Glastonbury et al. (2010) reviewed the imaging findings of expected changes and complications after radiation to this region. They pointed out that damage and death to tissue result from destruction of endothelial cells lining small blood vessels. This leads to ischaemia, oedema, and inflammation, followed by delayed fibrosis and atrophy. Interstitial oedema develops throughout the neck soft tissues during radiation therapy and in the subsequent months after cessation of therapy. There is thickening of the skin and platysma muscle, reticulation of subcutaneous and deep fat, and oedema in deep neck spaces such as the carotid sheath and retropharyngeal space. In the pharynx and larynx, mucositis and submucosal oedema result in thickening of the epiglottis and aryepiglottic folds. Pharyngeal and laryngeal necrosis peaks in the first 12 months after treatment but has been reported to occur more than ten years after therapy.

## Larynx

The main complications of radiation therapy for squamous carcinoma of the larynx are laryngeal oedema, skin damage, perichondritis, and cartilage necrosis. Chondroradionecrosis of the larynx is one of the most serious complications of radiation therapy. The condition may occur from months to years after radiotherapy has stopped and represents the most severe consequence of late radiation injury to laryngeal tissue. The condition has the potential to be fatal because of airway collapse or aspiration. Essentially, the condition is a radiation-induced inflammatory response that produces extensive arteritis and thrombosis in small vessels surrounding the laryngeal cartilage, progressing to tissue death.

The medical records of 294 patients who underwent primary, adjuvant, or salvage radiation for laryngeal cancer from 1991 to 2015 at the University of Wisconsin were reviewed by Gessert et al. (2017) to identify and characterise patients with a diagnosis of chondroradionecrosis. From this cohort of patients, 7 (2.4%) were identified with the condition. Their findings reflect a decrease in incidence of chondroradionecrosis. In the 1970s, it had been estimated to be as high as 12% (Chandler, 1979), compared to more recent estimates ranging between 1% and 5% (Zbären et al., 2006; Oppenheimer et al., 1989). As Gessert et al. (2017) stated in their paper, the reduction in incidence is likely to be due, in part, to improved radiotherapy delivery techniques.

## Thyroid

In humans, there are two major unwanted consequences of radiation: hypothyroidism and an increased risk of developing both benign and malignant thyroid tumours. Radiation to the thyroid leads to impairment of function and growth, with a major effect on the proliferative ability of the follicular cell (Doniach and Williams, 1986). Radiation-induced thyroid damage is related to the inhibition of follicular epithelial function and subsequent progressive alteration of the endothelium, from cell degeneration and necrosis with follicular disruption to vascular degeneration and thrombosis, to acute and chronic inflammation, fibrous organisation, and partial epithelial regeneration.

Hypothyroidism is a common complication that can occur after radiation therapy for head and neck cancers. The thyroid gland is particularly vulnerable to the damaging effects of radiation, which can result in a decrease in thyroid hormone production and the development of hypothyroidism. A recent systematic review by Rooney et al. (2023) found radiotherapy-induced hypothyroidism to be extremely common, with estimates of 40–50%, utilising high-quality thyroid function evaluation and long-term follow-up. Hypothyroidism is also a major consequence of the treatment of thyrotoxicosis with radioiodine and indicates that the doses used are sufficient to sterilise a considerable proportion of the follicular cells.

Radiation-induced tumours including carcinoma have been studied and reviewed, particularly in children and young adults, in a retrospective and prospective study by Massimino et al. (2009). There were 468 patients in their study, of whom 128 (27%) had one or more thyroid nodules, and 73 (57%) of these 128 had concomitant or previously untreated hypothyroidism, while 22 (17%) of the 128 had a differentiated carcinoma.

## Parathyroids

Parathyroid adenomas may occur following treatment with ionising radiation for thyroid carcinoma or other malignancies affecting the neck, such as Hodgkin's disease during childhood and adulthood. The time interval from exposure to diagnosis of parathyroid adenomas can be very variable, due to the frequently slight symptoms of the disease. Karstrup et al. (1984) reported a latent period for benign parathyroid lesions of between 5 and 61 years after irradiation. On the other hand, the median latency period in the study by Rasmuson et al. (2002) was shorter, at 26 years.

Primary hyperparathyroidism occurs more frequently in persons who have been exposed to low-dose therapeutic radiation. Tezelman et al. (1995) examined records from 438 unselected patients with primary hyperparathyroidism and found 49 patients with a history of radiation exposure. There was no difference in gender in their study, although the prevalence of primary hyperparathyroidism is generally known to be higher in women than in men, with a ratio of more than two to one (Heath et al., 1980).

Parathyroid carcinoma is rare, and its aetiology is largely unknown. A potential role for prior neck irradiation is less clear than in the development of benign parathyroid disease (Marcocci et al., 2008). Rarely, it has been reported in patients with longstanding secondary hyperparathyroidism. Ireland et al. (1985) reported a case that was also chronically stimulated because of renal failure, and the authors felt that ionising radiation might have been responsible for the parathyroid malignancy found in their patient. In one of a series of parathyroid carcinomas described by Smith and Coombs (1984), there was a history of radiation to the neck for exophthalmic goitre 53 years previously, followed by 20 years of radiation treatment. There was also chief cell hyperplasia associated with the parathyroid carcinoma in this case.

## References

Allgood S, Peters J, Benson A, Maragos C, McIltrot K, Slater T, Akst L, Best SR, Galiatsatos P, Brodsky MB, Brenner MJ, Pandian V. Acquired laryngeal and subglottic stenosis following COVID-19-Preparing for the coming deluge. *J Clin Nurs*. 2024 Jan;33(1):6–10. doi: 10.1111/jocn.15992. Epub 2021 Aug 8. PMID: 34369020; PMCID: PMC8446981.

Aljobeh A, Sorenson TJ, Bortolotti C, Cloft H, Lanzino G. Vertebral arteriovenous fistula: A review article. *World Neurosurg*. 2019 Feb;122:e1388–e1397. doi: 10.1016/j.wneu.2018.11.063. Epub 2018 Nov 17. Erratum in: *World Neurosurg*. 2020 May;137:505. doi: 10.1016/j.wneu.2020.02.011. PMID: 30458324.

Alsarraf R, Carey J, Sires BS, Pinczower E. Angiography contrast-induced transient cortical blindness. *Am J Otolaryngol*. 1999 Mar-Apr;20(2):130–132. doi: 10.1016/s0196-0709(99)90021-2. PMID: 10203162.

Arola MK, Puhakka H, Mäkelä P. Healing of lesions caused by cuffed tracheostomy tubes and their late sequelae; a follow-up study. *Acta Anaesthesiol Scand*. 1980 June;24(3):169–177. doi: 10.1111/j.1399-6576.1980.tb01528.x. PMID: 7445932.

Behnke EE, Gadlage R, Turner JS Jr. Instrumental perforation of the esophagus. *Laryngoscope*. 1980 May;90(5 Pt 1):842–846. PMID: 7374315.

Benjamin B. Prolonged intubation injuries of the larynx: Endoscopic diagnosis, classification, and treatment. *Ann Otol Rhinol Laryngol*. 2018 Aug;127(8):492–507. doi: 10.1177/0003489418790348. PMID: 30012012.

Bergström J, Moberg A, Orell SR. On the pathogenesis of laryngeal injuries following prolonged intubation. *Acta Oto-Laryngologica*. 1962;55(1–6):342–346. doi:10.3109/00016486209127370.

Borasio P, Ardissone F, Chiampo G. Post-intubation tracheal rupture. A report on ten cases. *Eur J Cardiothorac Surg*. 1997;12(1):98–100. doi: 10.1016/s1010-7940(97)00111-5.

Bothma P, Hussain MA. Fatal cerebral air embolism post esophageal endoscopy with dilatation: A case report. *Med Sci Law*. 2024 July;64(3):250–251. doi: 10.1177/00258024241227712. Epub 2024 Jan 18. PMID: 38238964.

Bozic C. Lésions dues à l'intubation endotrachéale des nouveau-nés [Lesions due to endotracheal intubation in newborn infants]. *Helv Paediatr Acta*. 1969 Oct;24(5):458–462. French. PMID: 5385822.

Chandler JR. Radiation fibrosis and necrosis of the larynx. *Ann Otol Rhinol Laryngol*. 1979 July-Aug;88(4 Pt 1):509–514. doi: 10.1177/000348947908800410. PMID: 475247.

Ciaglia P, Firsching R, Syniec C. Elective percutaneous dilatational tracheostomy. A new simple bedside procedure; preliminary report. *Chest*. 1985 June;87(6):715–719. doi: 10.1378/chest.87.6.715. PMID: 3996056.

Crosby ET, Lui A. The adult cervical spine: Implications for airway management. *Can J Anaesth*. 1990 Jan;37(1):77–93. doi: 10.1007/BF03007488. PMID: 2136808.

Dandamudi VS, Thaler DE, Malek AM. Cereus following chiropractic manipulation in a patient with a calcified carotid artery. *J Neuroimaging*. 2013 July;23(3):429–430. doi: 10.1111/j.1552-6569.2012.00706.x. Epub 2012 Jul 20. PMID: 22818061.

Doniach I, Williams ED. *Biological Effects of Radiation on the Thyroid* ( ED. SH Ingbar and LE Braverman), 5th edn, Lippincott, Philadelphia, chap 17, 1986.

Donnelly WH. Histopathology of endotracheal intubation. An autopsy study of 99 cases. *Arch Pathol*. 1969 Nov;88(5):511–520. PMID: 5347141.

Dudley JP, Mancuso AA, Fonkalsrud EW. Arytenoid dislocation and computed tomography. *Arch Otolaryngol*. 1984 July;110(7):483–484. doi: 10.1001/archotol.1984.00800330065015. PMID: 6732593.

Ederli A, Sassaroli S, Spaccarelli G. Vertebral angiography as a cause of necrosis of the cervical spinal cord. *Br J Radiol*. 1962 Apr;35:261–264. doi: 10.1259/0007-1285-35-412-261. PMID: 13889179.

Evans D, McGlashan J, Norris A. Iatrogenic airway injury. *BJA Education*. 15(4):184–189. doi: 10.1093/bjaceaccp/mku026.

Feller-Kopman D. Acute complications of artificial airways. *Clin Chest Med*. 2003 Sep;24(3):445–455. doi: 10.1016/s0272-5231(03)00047-9. PMID: 14535219.

Gamulin Z, Brückner JC, Forster A, Simonet F, Rouge JC. Multiple complications after internal jugular vein catheterisation. *Anaesthesia*. 1986 Apr;41(4):408–412. doi: 10.1111/j.1365-2044.1986.tb13229.x. PMID: 3518533.

Gessert TG, Britt CJ, Maas AMW, Wieland AM, Harari PM, Hartig GK. Chondroradionecrosis of the larynx: 24-year University of Wisconsin experience. *Head Neck*. 2017 June;39(6):1189–1194. doi: 10.1002/hed.24749. Epub 2017 Mar 11. PMID: 28295829.

Glastonbury CM, Parker EE, Hoang JK. The postradiation neck: Evaluating response to treatment and recognizing complications. *AJR Am J Roentgenol*. 2010 Aug;195(2):W164–W171. doi: 10.2214/AJR.09.4122. PMID: 20651177.

Goldstein P. Fatal interstitial and mediastinal emphysema following accidental needle perforations of the trachea during jugular venipuncture. *Am J Dis Child* (1911). 1949 Sep;78(3):375–383. doi: 10.1001/archpedi.1949.02030050388009. PMID: 18138932.

Gould SJ, Howard S. The histopathology of the larynx in the neonate following endotracheal intubation. *J Pathol*. 1985 Aug;146(4):301–311. doi: 10.1002/path.1711460403. PMID: 4032125.

Green RP, Biller HF, Sicular A, Wright M. Cervical tracheoesophageal fistula. *Laryngoscope*. 1983 Mar;93(3):364–369. doi: 10.1288/00005537-198303000-00023. PMID: 6834962.

Gregersen M, Vesterby A. Iatrogenic fractures of the hyoid bone and the thyroid cartilage. A case report. *Forensic Sci Int*. 1981 Jan-Feb;17(1):41–43. doi: 10.1016/0379-0738(81)90187-0. PMID: 7216081.

Hamilton K, Orde M, Finlayson G. Fatal cerebral air embolism post esophageal endoscopy with dilatation: A case report. *Med Sci Law*. 2024 July;64(3):245–247. doi: 10.1177/00258024231212878. Epub 2023 Nov 13. PMID: 37960837; PMCID: PMC11168012.

Härm T, Rajs J. Face and neck injuries due to resuscitation versus throttling. *Forensic Sci Int*. 1983 Nov-Dec;23(2-3):109–116. doi: 10.1016/0379-0738(83)90139-1. PMID: 6662437.

Hashimoto Y, Moriya F, Furumiya J. Forensic aspects of complications resulting from cardiopulmonary resuscitation. *Leg Med (Tokyo)*. 2007 Mar;9(2):94–99. doi: 10.1016/j.legalmed.2006.11.008. Epub 2007 Feb 2. PMID: 17276125.

Hawkins DB. Hyaline membrane disease of the neonate prolonged intubation in management: effects on the larynx. *Laryngoscope*. 1978 Feb;88(2 Pt 1):201–224. doi: 10.1288/00005537-197802000-00001. PMID: 621987.

Heath H 3rd, Hodgson SF, Kennedy MA. Primary hyperparathyroidism. Incidence, morbidity, and potential economic impact in a community. *N Engl J Med*. 1980 Jan 24;302(4):189–193. doi: 10.1056/NEJM198001243020402. PMID: 7350459.

Hedden M, Ersoz CJ, Donnelly WH, Safar P. Laryngotracheal damage after prolonged use of orotracheal tubes in adults. *JAMA*. 1969 Jan 27;207(4):703–708. PMID: 5818186.

Hlavaty L, Sung L. Resuscitation and prevalence of external facial, neck, and chest injuries in infants. *Am J Forensic Med Pathol*. 2015 Dec;36(4):301–304. doi: 10.1097/PAF.0000000000000187. PMID: 26244594.

Holmes T. The surgical management of aneurism in its various forms. Lecture III. Vertebral aneurism. *Lancet*. 1873;2:105–108.

Ireland JP, Fleming SJ, Levison DA, Cattell WR, Baker LR. Parathyroid carcinoma associated with chronic renal failure and previous radiotherapy to the neck. *J Clin Pathol*. 1985 Oct;38(10):1114–1118. doi: 10.1136/jcp.38.10.1114. PMID: 4056066; PMCID: PMC499451.

Jefferson G, Bailey RA, Kerr AS. Suboccipital arteriovenous aneurysms of the vertebral artery. *J Bone Joint Surg Br*. 1956 Feb;38-B(1):114–127. doi: 10.1302/0301-620X.38B1.114. PMID: 13295324.

Joshi VV, Mandavia SG, Stern L, Wiglesworth FW. Acute lesions induced by endotracheal intubation. Occurrence in the upper respiratory tract of newborn infants with respiratory distress syndrome. *Am J Dis Child*. 1972 Nov;124(5):646–649. doi: 10.1001/archpedi.1972.02110170024003. PMID: 5085478.

Jougon J, Ballester M, Choukroun E, Dubrez J, Reboul G, Velly JF. Conservative treatment for postintubation tracheobronchial rupture. *Ann Thorac Surg*. 2000;69(1):216–220. doi: 10.1016/s0003-4975(99)01129-7.

Jougon J, Cantini O, Delcambre F, Minniti A, Velly JF. Esophageal perforation: Life threatening complication of endotracheal intubation. *Eur J Cardiothorac Surg*. 2001 July;20(1):7–10; discussion 10–11. doi: 10.1016/s1010-7940(01)00766-7. PMID: 11423266.

Karstrup S, Hegedüs L, Sehested M. Hyperparathyroidism after neck irradiation for Hodgkin's disease. *Acta Med Scand*. 1984;215(3):287–288. doi: 10.1111/j.0954-6820.1984.tb05008.x. PMID: 6428167.

de Kleijn BJ, Wedman J, Zijlstra JG, Dikkers FG, van der Laan BFAM. Short- and long-term complications of surgical and percutaneous dilatation tracheotomies: a large single-centre retrospective cohort study. *Eur Arch Otorhinolaryngol*. 2019 June;276(6):1823–1828. doi: 10.1007/s00405-019-05394-9. Epub 2019 Apr 2. PMID: 30941491; PMCID: PMC6529380.

Lee KP, Carlini WG, McCormick GF, Albers GW. Neurologic complications following chiropractic manipulation: A survey of California neurologists. *Neurology*. 1995 June;45(6):1213–1215. doi: 10.1212/wnl.45.6.1213. PMID: 7783892.

Lee MJ, Weaver DJ, El Dafrawy MH. Extracranial vertebral artery injuries. *J Am Acad Orthop Surg*. 2024 May 28. doi: 10.5435/JAAOS-D-24-00244. Epub ahead of print. PMID: 38810231.

Lo LW, Chan HF, Ma KF, Cheng LF, Chan TK. Transient cortical blindness following vertebral angiography: A case report. *Neurointervention*. 2015 Feb;10(1):39–42. doi: 10.5469/neuroint.2015.10.1.39. Epub 2015 Feb 28. PMID: 25763297; PMCID: PMC4355645.

Lohr W. Hirngefassverletzungen in arteriographischer darrstellung: I. Die arteriographie bei compressio cerebri. *Zentrablatt fur Chirurgie* 1936;63:2466–2482.

Marcocci C, Cetani F, Rubin MR, Silverberg SJ, Pinchera A, Bilezikian JP. Parathyroid carcinoma. *J Bone Miner Res*. 2008 Dec;23(12):1869–1880. doi: 10.1359/jbmr.081018. PMID: 19016595; PMCID: PMC3276344.

Massimino M, Gandola L, Mattavelli F, Pizzi N, Seregni E, Pallotti F, Spreafico F, Marchianò A, Terenziani M, Cefalo G, Biassoni V, Meazza C, Trecate G, Collini P. Radiation-induced thyroid changes: A retrospective and a prospective view. *Eur J Cancer*. 2009 Sep;45(14):2546–2551. doi: 10.1016/j.ejca.2009.06.009. Epub 2009 July 14. PMID: 19608408.

Maxeiner H, Jekat R. Resuscitation and conjunctival petechial hemorrhages. *J Forensic Leg Med*. 2010 Feb;17(2):87–91. doi: 10.1016/j.jflm.2009.09.010. Epub 2009 Oct 6. PMID: 20129428.

Minambres E, Buron J, Ballesteros MA, Llorca J, Munoz P, Gonzalez-Castro A. Tracheal rupture after endotracheal intubation: A literature systematic review. *Eur J Cardiothorac Surg*. 35(6):1056–1062. doi: 10.1016/j.ejcts.2009.01.053.

Mollitt DL, Schullinger JN, Santulli TV. Selective management of iatrogenic esophageal perforation in the newborn. *J Pediatr Surg*. 1981 Dec;16(6):989–993. doi: 10.1016/s0022-3468(81)80861-5. PMID: 6802958.

Moniz E. *L'angiographie Cerebrale*. Masson, Paris, 1931.

Murthy JM, Naidu KV. Aneurysm of the cervical internal carotid artery following chiropractic manipulation. *J Neurol Neurosurg Psychiatry*. 1988 Sep;51(9):1237–1238. doi: 10.1136/jnnp.51.9.1237. PMID: 3225611; PMCID: PMC1033038.

Nakanishi K, Yoshiyama M, Homma S. Patent foramen ovale and cryptogenic stroke. *Trends Cardiovasc Med*. 2017 Nov;27(8):575–581. doi: 10.1016/j.tcm.2017.06.016. Epub 2017 Jul 4. PMID: 28709812.

Neevel AJ, Smith JD, Morrison RJ, Hogikyan ND, Kupfer RA, Stein AP. Postacute COVID-19 laryngeal injury and dysfunction. *OTO Open*. 2021 Aug 24;5(3):2473974X211041040. doi: 10.1177/2473974X211041040. PMID: 34458661; PMCID: PMC8392819.

Norman EA, Sosis M. Iatrogenic oesophageal perforation due to tracheal or nasogastric intubation. *Can Anaesth Soc J*. 1986 Mar;33(2):222–226. doi: 10.1007/BF03010835. PMID: 3697818.

Nowak P, Cohn AM, Guidice MA. Airway complications in patients with closed-head injuries. *Am J Otolaryngol*. 1987 Mar-Apr;8(2):91–96. doi: 10.1016/s0196-0709(87)80030-3. PMID: 3592081.

Oppenheimer RW, Krespi YP, Einhorn RK. Management of laryngeal radionecrosis: Animal and clinical experience. *Head Neck*. 1989 May-June;11(3):252–256. doi: 10.1002/hed.2880110311. PMID: 2722502.

Oppenlander ME, Hsu FD, Bolton P, Theodore N. Catastrophic neurological complications of emergent endotracheal intubation: Report of 2 cases. *J Neurosurg Spine*. 2015 May;22(5):454–458. doi: 10.3171/2014.10.SPINE14652. Epub 2015 Feb 27. PMID: 25723119.

Papsidero MJ, Pashley NR. Acquired stenosis of the upper airway in neonates. An increasing problem. *Ann Otol Rhinol Laryngol*. 1980 Nov-Dec;89(6 Pt 1):512–514. doi: 10.1177/000348948008900605. PMID: 7458137.

Pathak M, Kim RC, Pribram H. Spinal cord infarction following vertebral angiography: Clinical and pathological findings. *J Spinal Cord Med*. 2000 Summer;23(2):92–95. doi: 10.1080/10790268.2000.11753514. PMID: 10914348.

Peters M, Bohl J, Thömke F, Kallen KJ, Mahlzahn K, Wandel E, Meyer zum Büschenfelde KH. Dissection of the internal carotid artery after chiropractic manipulation of the neck. *Neurology*. 1995 Dec;45(12):2284–2286. doi: 10.1212/wnl.45.12.2284. PMID: 8848211.

Pratt-Thomas HR, Berger KE. Cerebellar and spinal injuries after chiropractic manipulation. *J Am Med Assoc*. 1947 Mar 1;133(9):600–603. doi: 10.1001/jama.1947.02880090022005. PMID: 20283970.

Rasmuson T, Damber L, Johansson L, Johansson R, Larsson LG. Increased incidence of parathyroid adenomas following X-ray treatment of benign diseases in the cervical spine in adult patients. *Clin Endocrinol (Oxf)*. 2002 Dec;57(6):731–734. doi: 10.1046/j.1365-2265.2002.01616.x. PMID: 12460322.

Raven KP, Reay DT, Harruff RC. Artifactual injuries of the larynx produced by resuscitative intubation. *Am J Forensic Med Pathol*. 1999 Mar;20(1):31–36. doi: 10.1097/00000433-199903000-00008. PMID: 10208333.

Rooney MK, Andring LM, Corrigan KL, Bernard V, Williamson TD, Fuller CD, Garden AS, Gunn B, Lee A, Moreno AC, Morrison WH, Phan J, Rosenthal DI, Spiotto M, Frank SJ. Hypothyroidism following radiotherapy for head and neck cancer: A systematic review of the literature and opportunities to improve the therapeutic ratio. *Cancers (Basel)*. 2023 Aug 29;15(17):4321. doi: 10.3390/cancers15174321. PMID: 37686597; PMCID: PMC10486996.

Saigal G, Bhatia R, Bhatia S, Wakhloo AK. MR findings of cortical blindness following cerebral angiography: Is this entity related to posterior reversible leukoencephalopathy? *AJNR Am J Neuroradiol*. 2004 Feb;25(2):252–256. PMID: 14970026; PMCID: PMC7974594.

Schmitz A, Lutterbey G, von Engelhardt L, von Falkenhausen M, Stoffel M. Pathological cervical fracture after spinal manipulation in a pregnant patient. *J Manipulative Physiol Ther*. 2005 Oct;28(8):633–636. doi: 10.1016/j.jmpt.2005.08.017. PMID: 16226634.

Smith BL. Laryngeal cyst following fibreoptic intubation. *Anaesthesia*. 1986 Apr;41(4):430–431. doi: 10.1111/j.1365-2044.1986.tb13238.x. PMID: 3706693.

Smith JF, Coombs RR. Histological diagnosis of carcinoma of the parathyroid gland. *J Clin Pathol*. 1984 Dec;37(12):1370–1378. doi: 10.1136/jcp.37.12.1370. PMID: 6511982; PMCID: PMC499033.

Sorensen E, Yu C, Chuang SL, Midrio P, Martinez L, Nash M, Jester I, Saxena AK. Iatrogenic neonatal esophageal perforation: A European multicentre review on management and outcomes. *Children (Basel)*. 2023 Jan 26;10(2):217. doi: 10.3390/children10020217. PMID: 36832348; PMCID: PMC9955351.

Strong RM, Passy V. Endotracheal intubation. Complications in neonates. *Arch Otolaryngol.* 1977 June;103(6):329–335. doi: 10.1001/archotol.1977.00780230051006. PMID: 869765.

Tezelman S, Rodriguez JM, Shen W, Siperstein AE, Duh QY, Clark OH. Primary hyperparathyroidism in patients who have received radiation therapy and in patients who have not received radiation therapy. *J Am Coll Surg*. 1995 Jan;180(1):81–87. PMID: 8000660.

Theodotou B, Mahaley MS Jr. Injury of the peripheral cranial nerves during carotid endarterectomy. *Stroke*. 1985 Sep-Oct;16(5):894–895. doi: 10.1161/01.str.16.5.894. PMID: 4049454.

Wallace S, McGrath BA. Laryngeal complications after tracheal intubation and tracheostomy. *BJA Educ*. 2021 July;21(7):250–257. doi: 10.1016/j.bjae.2021.02.005. Epub 2021 Apr 21. PMID: 34178381; PMCID: PMC8212164.

Weiss K, Kramár R, Firt P. Cranial and cervical nerve injuries: Local complications of carotid artery surgery. *J Cardiovasc Surg (Torino)*. 1987 Mar-Apr;28(2):171–175. PMID: 3558466.

Weissman RA, Konrad HR. Tracheal carcinoma after tracheostomy. *Arch Otolaryngol*. 1979 June;105(6):364–366. doi: 10.1001/archotol.1979.00790180062016. PMID: 454293.

Wells K, Castellani RJ, deJong JL. Can neck contusions in unexplained pediatric deaths be explained by cardiopulmonary resuscitation? *J Forensic Sci*. 2019 May;64(3):770–772. doi: 10.1111/1556-4029.13919. Epub 2018 Oct 12. PMID: 30312473.

Whited RE. A study of endotracheal tube injury to the subglottis. *Laryngoscope*. 1985 Oct;95(10):1216–1219. doi: 10.1288/00005537-198510000-00014. PMID: 4046708.

Wolff AP, Kessler S. Iatrogenic injury to the hypopharynx and cervical esophagus: an autopsy study. *Ann Otol Rhinol Laryngol*. 1973 Nov-Dec;82(6):778–783. doi: 10.1177/000348947308200605. PMID: 4761038.

Yamamoto H, Nanto M, Kishida K, Goto Y, Hashimoto N. Iatrogenic vertebral arteriovenous fistula involving brachiocephalic vein due to central venous catheterization: a case report. *J Endovasc Ther*. 2023 Oct;30(5):779–783. doi: 10.1177/15266028221105181. Epub 2022 Jun 23. PMID: 35735198.

Yelverton C, Wood JJ, Petersen DL, Peterson C. Changes in vertebral artery blood flow in different head positions and post-cervical manipulative therapy. *J Manipulative Physiol Ther*. 2020 Feb;43(2):144–151. doi: 10.1016/j.jmpt.2019.09.001. Epub 2020 May 30. PMID: 32482436.

Zbären P, Caversaccio M, Thoeny HC, Nuyens M, Curschmann J, Stauffer E. Radionecrosis or tumor recurrence after radiation of laryngeal and hypopharyngeal carcinomas. *Otolaryngol Head Neck Surg*. 2006 Dec;135(6):838–843. doi: 10.1016/j.otohns.2006.06.1264. PMID: 17141070.

Zhuo S, Cao L, Yang M, Chen J, Yu Z. Contrast-medium injury of spinal cord after cerebral angiography using nonionic contrast agents: A case report and literature review. *Medicine (Baltimore)*. 2023 Dec 15;102(50):e36630. doi: 10.1097/MD.0000000000036630. PMID: 38115328; PMCID: PMC10727595.

Zou ZY, Yao YT. Horner syndrome caused by internal jugular vein catheterization. *J Cardiothorac Vasc Anesth*. 2020 June;34(6):1636–1640. doi: 10.1053/j.jvca.2019.06.031. Epub 2019 Jun 28. PMID: 31350153.

# INDEX

Note: **Bold** page numbers refer to tables and *italic* page numbers refer to figures.